Published by:

John Wiley & Sons, Inc.

111 River St.
Hoboken, NJ 07030-5774

ISBN 978-1-118-04600-5 (paper); 978-1-118-16031-2 (ebk); 978-1-118-15981-1 (ebk); 978-1-118-16032-9 (ebk)

Editor: Jennifer Reilly
Production Editor: Michael Brumitt
Photo Editors: Alden Gewirtz, Ashley Skibicki, and Jennifer Reilly; Richard Fox (cover)
Interior book design: Melissa Auciello-Brogan
Production by Wiley Indianapolis Composition Services

Front cover photo: Emperor penguin on Antarctica © Fritz Poelking AGE Fotostock, Inc.
Back cover photo: A panda cub in China © Heather Angel / Natural Visions / Alamy Images; Angkor Wat © Darryl Villaret / Alamy Images; Venice © David Askham / Alamy Images; Elephant Car Wash © Eric James / Alamy Images

For information on our other products and services or to obtain technical support, please contact our Customer Care Department within the U.S. at 877/762-2974, outside the U.S. at 317/572-3993 or fax 317/572-4002.

Wiley also publishes its books in a variety of electronic formats. Some content that appears in print may not be available in electronic formats.

Manufactured in the United States of America

5 4 3 2 1

About the Authors

Julie Duchaine has been a freelance writer for the past 25 years. Most recently, she contributed to *Frommer's 500 Extraordinary Islands*, *Frommer's 500 Places for Food & Wine Lovers*, and *Frommer's 500 Places to Take Your Kids Before They Grow Up*. She lives in Milwaukee.

Holly Hughes has traveled the globe as an editor and a writer—she's the former executive editor of Fodor's Travel Publications, the series editor of Frommer's Irreverent Guides, and author of *Frommer's New York City with Kids*. She's also written fiction for middle graders and edits the annual *Best Food Writing* anthology. New York City makes a convenient jumping-off place for her travels with her three children and husband.

About the Consultant

Larry West is a professional writer who covers environmental issues for About.com (http://environment.about.com), which is part of The New York Times Company and one of the world's leading online sources of news and consumer information. During his previous career as a newspaper journalist, he was part of an investigative team whose work was nominated for a Pulitzer Prize and received the Edward J. Meeman Award for environmental reporting from the Scripps Howard Foundation. An avid and experienced traveler, he currently divides his time between Oregon and Panama.

An Invitation to the Reader

In researching this book, we discovered many wonderful places. We're sure you'll find others. Please tell us about them, so we can share the information with your fellow travelers in upcoming editions. If you were disappointed with a recommendation, we'd love to know that, too. Please write to:

Frommer's 500 Places to See Before They Disappear, 2nd Edition
John Wiley & Sons, Inc. • 111 River St. • Hoboken, NJ 07030-5774

Advisory & Disclaimer

Travel information can change quickly and unexpectedly, and we strongly advise you to confirm important details locally before traveling, including information on visas, health and safety, traffic and transport, accommodations, shopping, and eating out. We also encourage you to stay alert while traveling and to remain aware of your surroundings. Avoid civil disturbances, and keep a close eye on cameras, purses, wallets, and other valuables.

While we have endeavored to ensure that the information contained within this guide is accurate and up-to-date at the time of publication, we make no representations or warranties with respect to the accuracy or completeness of the contents of this work and specifically disclaim all warranties, including without limitation warranties of fitness for a particular purpose. We accept no responsibility or liability for any inaccuracy or errors or omissions, or for any inconvenience, loss, damage, costs, or expenses of any nature whatsoever incurred or suffered by anyone as a result of any advice or information contained in this guide.

The inclusion of a company, organization, or website in this guide as a service provider and/or potential source of further information does not mean that we endorse them or the information they provide. Be aware that information provided through some websites may be unreliable and can change without notice. Neither the publisher nor author shall be liable for any damages arising herefrom.

Frommer's Icons

We use four feature icons to help you quickly find the information you're looking for. At the end of each review, look for:

 Where to get more information

✈ Nearest airport

 Nearest train station

 Nearest boat service/port

🛏 Recommended hotels

Travel Resources at Frommers.com

Frommer's travel resources don't end with this guide. Frommer's website, **www.frommers. com**, has travel information on more than 4,000 destinations. We update features regularly, giving you access to the most current trip-planning information and the best airfare, lodging, and car-rental bargains. You can also listen to podcasts, connect with other Frommers.com members through our active-reader forums, share your travel photos, read blogs from guidebook editors and fellow travelers, and much more.

Why These 500 Places?

Let's be honest—you can't call a book *500 Places to See Before They Disappear* without assuming that your subjects are on the brink of extinction. Over the months we spent researching this book, we became afraid to open the newspaper in the morning, afraid of more dire headlines. Some were natural disasters, beyond anybody's control—earthquakes in Haiti, New Zealand, and Chile; Mississippi River floods; tornadoes ripping across America's heartland. Then of course there were the man-made disasters, like the BP oil spill that ravaged the Gulf of Mexico. In Japan we witnessed a triple-whammy of both natural and man-made disasters: earthquake, tsunami, and nuclear meltdown. The fate of our planet seems perilous indeed these days.

The litany of environmental concerns is familiar to all of us by now—global warming, pollution, deforestation, desertification, melting ice caps and glaciers, rising oceans, acid rain, invasive species, loss of biodiversity. Some ecosystem changes are inevitable, part of the rhythm of life—glaciers do melt, beaches do erode, rivers do change their course, without any human involvement. But even so-called "natural disasters," scientists now warn us, could be increasing because of the rapid pace of climate change, accelerated by human impact on the environment.

It soon became clear, as well, that we couldn't separate natural and man-made attractions. After all, the damage of an entire city—Venice, say, or New Orleans—can be just as much due to natural causes as the damage of a biosphere, like the Amazonian rainforest. Pollution threatens the Acropolis just as it does the giant redwoods. If changes in the natural environment endanger the piping plover, the Tasmanian devil, and the mountain gorilla, so too have changes in our cultural environment stricken classic amusement parks, ballparks, and movie palaces. Our planet is the poorer every time we allow something beautiful to die.

As we faced the challenge of updating *500 Places to See Before They Disappear*, we worried that we'd need to write a whole new book—that destinations included in the first edition would have since . . . well, DISAPPEARED, or at least become damaged beyond repair. Unfortunately, for many destinations, we found that little or nothing had changed, or conditions had even grown worse. (The economic downturn that began in 2008 put some damaging development projects on hold, but it also eviscerated budgets for maintaining parks and historic buildings, leading to further deterioration.) Nevertheless, several of our sites were still holding on, some even on the road to recovery—usually thanks to preservationists with a will to make a difference. Nearly 20% of the previous edition no longer qualified as "disappearing," and that's good news. Sad to say, we had absolutely no trouble finding newly threatened destinations to include in their place.

When we say these places may "disappear," of course, there are many scenarios. A few are stark and simple: A building may be razed, an entire forest hacked down, a low-lying island chain covered by rising oceans. But not all of our case studies are that clear-cut. The Amazon River basin will still exist, even if its amazingly rich rainforest is slashed and cleared; the Alps will still rise above Europe, even if their glaciers melt away. What has disappeared, though, is some feature that made that place special. We'll show you neighborhoods that may lose their distinctive character, mountain wildernesses where signature species are dwindling, dammed rivers where salmon no longer spawn, historic vistas spoiled by a modern highway, cell tower, or shopping mall.

Depressing as all that may sound, we are neither one of us gloom-and-doom types—we'd always prefer to see the glass as half full. We hope that the overall message of this book is one of hope, of a call to action. That's why a sizable number of the sights we cover are not themselves threatened, but are thriving last-chance havens where now-rare species *are* surviving, where special landscapes *are* still intact, where unique cultural artifacts *have* been preserved. This book is, after all, a travel guide, and we want to offer a carefully chosen list of destinations for eco-conscious travelers to enjoy. That verb "enjoy" is crucial—for in the process of cherishing these natural and cultural wonders, we renew our commitment to preserving them. As you visit them, we hope you'll do so with sustainable travel habits—choosing nonpolluting, fuel-efficient transportation, supporting local suppliers, and leaving as few traces as possible on the land.

Five hundred disappearing destinations—that's a lot. If reading about any of these sights inspires you to experience them for yourself, don't put it off—start booking your trip *now*.

A Note on Hotels & Tours

You'll also find at the end of every write-up useful information about visitors bureaus, transportation options, tour operators, and hotel recommendations. While we didn't have space for full reviews, these choices are solid values with an eco-friendly dimension. The three **price ranges** noted—$$$ (expensive), $$ (moderate), and $ (inexpensive)—are all relative to the local market. A $125-per-night motel room in rural Kentucky would seem expensive, but if you can find something clean and safe at that price in Venice, snap it up! Similarly, in some destinations with less tourist infrastructure, we list tour specialists who can package your visit for you, whenever possible choosing operators with a sustainable travel focus. For fuller descriptions (and other useful travel info), please consult the corresponding Frommer's guides for these destinations. Note that any **phone numbers** listed are what you'd dial from the United States or North America—for local dialing, skip the country code and add a 0 before the first number.

Acknowledgments

We'd like to thank our families and friends who put up with us for months of environmental obsessions—we hope we didn't sermonize too much. Above all, thanks to the devoted corps of Frommer's writers who alerted us to looming crises on their various turfs and answered last-minute questions about the status of various endangered destinations. You're the real experts in your various parts of the world, and we're beholden to you.

Julie Duchaine would like to thank her co-writer, Holly Hughes, who provided invaluable editorial help; Jennifer Reilly, who stayed flexible while keeping this very complicated project on track; and other Frommer's authors who helped with questions great and small. She'd also like to thank friends and family who understood when she said, "Sorry, I'm under deadline."

1 One-of-a-Kind Landscapes

The Burren, Ireland.

The Everglades
Choking the River of Grass
Southern Florida

ENCROACHING DEVELOPMENT, DWINDLING WATER LEVELS, AND POLLUTION ARE ALREADY strangling this peerless ecosystem; what climate change may do to its intricate freshwater-saltwater mosaic is even scarier.

There's nothing else like it on the planet: a vast marshy river that's 40 miles (64km) wide but rarely more than knee-deep. Endangered species such as manatees, hawksbill turtles, panthers, American crocodiles, roseate spoonbills, great egrets, wood storks, snail kites, the Cape Sable seaside sparrow, the Everglades mink, and the white-crowned pigeon thrive in its murky backwaters. It's the only place in the world where alligators and crocodiles live side by side.

An estimated half of the Everglades has already disappeared over the past century, as land is filled in for farms and residential developments for booming south Florida. The national park, which was established in 1947, protects only about one-fifth of this critical ecosystem. Over the years, as Florida's population has grown to six million, the natural flow of water into the wetlands has been diverted for drinking water, sewers, and irrigation; what water does flow in is often contaminated. A comprehensive plan introduced in 2000 to restore the Everglades' natural hydrology is a step in the right direction, but even if Congress approves funding, it will take over 20 years to build new reservoirs, filter marshes, and dismantle canals.

Meanwhile, the looming specter of climate change puts this low-lying coastal area at particular risk. Even slight changes in water level radically alter the hydrology of this marshy plain, affecting nesting areas and food supply. In recent years the

The Everglades.

number of bird species has fallen by 93%, and migratory patterns may be shifting as temperatures rise. Cattails aggressively root in the marshlands, clogging waterways; the balance between salt water and fresh water in the park's southern estuaries gets out of whack, killing the seagrass that shelters so many marine species. With global warming also comes increased storm activity, as well as algae blooms and bleached coral reefs.

You can explore this delicate ecosystem in a variety of ways. Hikers and bird-watchers strike out on boardwalk trails from the Flamingo visitor center, which lead through mangrove swamps, across coastal prairies shaded by buttonwood trees, and around freshwater ponds. Tram tours and cycling paths through the sawgrass prairie lead out from the Shark Valley visitor center in Miami. But to my mind, the best way to experience the Everglades is on the water—and no, not on one of those noisy powered airboats you'll see advertised outside park limits. Eco-friendly boat tours depart from the Everglades City and Flamingo visitor centers; better yet, rent canoes to explore the park's intricate system of canoe "trails," where you can really feel the gentle surging of the park's waters, or contact park-approved operators for guided canoe tours (try **Chokoloskee Enterprises,** www.evergladesareatours. com; or **North American Canoe Trips,** www.evergladesadventures.com). With a guide in the prow of your canoe, you'll know just where to look to uncover the secrets of this amazing terrain.

(i) **Everglades National Park** (📞 **305/ 242-7700;** www.nps.gov/ever). Park entrances in Homestead (40001 State Rd. 9336), Flamingo (Palm Dr./State Rd. 9336), Everglades City (State Rd. 29), or Miami (36000 SW 8th St.).

✈ Miami International Airport

🛏 $$ **Best Western Gateway to the Keys,** 411 S. Krome Ave. (US 1), Florida City (📞 **305/246-5100;** www.best western.com). $$ **Ivey House B&B,** 107 Camellia St., Everglades City (📞 **877/ 567-0679** or 239/695-3299; www.ivey house.com).

---

2 Ecosystems in Peril

The Gulf Coast
Bubbling Crude
Florida/Alabama/Mississippi/Louisiana/Texas

APRIL 2010'S MASSIVE DEEPWATER HORIZON OIL SPILL FOCUSED WORLD ATTENTION ON America's Gulf Coast, throwing its preexisting environmental problems into sharper relief.

President Barack Obama called it "the worst environmental disaster America has ever faced"—the 2010 explosion of the Deepwater Horizon oil rig in the Gulf of Mexico, which killed 11 workers and dumped an estimated 4.9 million barrels of crude oil into the Gulf's warm waters. While the rig spewed oil for months, the media barraged us with images of oil-choked marshes, dead fish washed up on spun-sugar beaches, and tar-feathered water birds. Despite heroic cleanup efforts, the spill's long-term impact on the Gulf's food chain won't be known for years. One thing we do know: The Louisiana fishing industry, which supplies 40% of the nation's seafood, was hit hard; its famous oyster beds may be permanently ruined by fresh water that was pumped in to flush out oily coastal waters.

Even without tar balls washing up on its sands, the Gulf region already had issues, most of them man-made. A dominant feature of the Gulf is the Mississippi River

Delta, a shifting landmass built of rich silt washed downriver—that is, until 20th-century flood-control levees disrupted the natural cycle, leaving the delta steadily eroding without replenishment. (Even levees couldn't control the record floods of spring 2011; see Vicksburg, **147**.) Transportation canals hacked through coastal wetlands have leaked salt water into freshwater marshes, destroying fish nurseries and wintering grounds for migratory water birds. Even worse, agricultural run-off flowing downriver from Midwestern farmlands has created a low-oxygen "dead zone" the size of New Jersey, stretching from Louisiana to Texas. This dead zone, first noted in 1972, reappears annually, from summer to late fall—and it's getting bigger every year, doubling in size between 1985 and 2008. Add to that the hurricanes that pummel this coast, bred in the Gulf's warm shallow waters, and you've got a lot of damaged habitats, ill-equipped to fight off an environmental disaster.

The oil spill had a dramatic impact on the **Gulf Islands National Seashore,** a string of barrier islands in the heart of the Gulf Coast, from Fort Walton Beach, Florida, to Gulfport, Mississippi. (Alabama's Gulf State Park fills in the gap between the seashore's two sections.) With facilities already battered by Hurricane Katrina in 2005 and Hurricane Ike in 2008, the seashore scrambled to recover. Absorbent booms laid along its shoreline held off oil slicks, while volunteers hand-swept the white-sand beaches and roped off nesting areas for sea turtles and seabirds. Behind those dazzling swimming beaches, the barrier islands protect other coastal ecosystems, from live-oak forests to salt marshes (hike the nature trails at **Fort Barrancas** and **Perdido Key** in Florida, or **Davis Bayou** in Mississippi). For a window onto the Gulf Coast's war-torn history, take a ferry from Gulfport to visit flat, scrubby **Ship Island** with its hauntingly half-built brick fort.

As you read on in this book, you'll discover other facets of the Gulf Coast's challenges: On Florida's inlet-fringed west coast, the Everglades **1** and Crystal River **30**; along the marshy shoreline of Alabama, the Grand Bay Savanna **248**; and at the Texas end of the Gulf, the barrier islands Padre Island **29** and Galveston Island **349**.

ⓘ **Gulf Islands National Seashore** (✆ **850/934-2600** or 228/875-9057; www.nps.gov/guis)

✈ Gulfport-Biloxi or Pensacola

🛏 $$ **Holiday Inn Gulfport/Airport,** 9515 Hwy. 49, Gulfport (✆ **877/424-2449** or 228/679-1700; www.ichotelsgroup.com)

Ecosystems in Peril   3

The Great Lakes
By the Shining Big Sea Water
Midwestern U.S. & Canada

GREAT LAKES SHIPPING IS ESSENTIAL TO MIDWESTERN CITIES—BUT RIDING IN WITH THOSE ships, invasive species can wipe out native fish. In the 1960s, it was silvery little alewives; today, it's massive Asian carp.

HOMES—as your grade-school geography teacher may have taught you—is a handy mnemonic for Huron, Ontario, Michigan, Erie, and Superior, collectively known as the Great Lakes, the largest group of freshwater lakes on Earth. On the map they look as if they are reaching down from Canada like a giant claw, grasping the United States by the nape of its neck. This vast watershed drains the heart of North America, sending its waters via the St. Lawrence River to the Atlantic Ocean. They contain 21% of the world's fresh water; spread across the 48 contiguous United States, they'd form a pool 9 feet (2.7m) deep.

Touching seven states—New York, Pennsylvania, Ohio, Indiana, Illinois, Wisconsin, and Minnesota—and dividing Canada and the U.S., the Great Lakes ecosystem is a challenge to regulate. One useful index to its health is the size of its fish population, a matter of concern since the mid–19th century. River dams, it was discovered (too late), prevented salmon and sturgeon from spawning; whitefish and freshwater mussels were overfished nearly to extinction; parasitic lamprey wriggled into the lake from the Erie Canal (437) and decimated lake trout populations. The 20th century brought new concerns, mainly toxic industrial runoff from the many major cities founded on its shores; images of Cleveland's oily brown Cuyahoga River burning in the late 1960s inspired the first Earth Day in 1970 and the Clean Water Act in 1972. For years, raw sewage was also dumped in the lakes, on the mistaken theory that the lake's bacteria could "digest" it.

Environmental activists have had the Great Lakes on their agenda for a long time, however, and with concerted interstate and international cooperation, their waters are cleaner now than they have been in years. The biggest problem lately is invasive species—it's estimated that a new species enters the Great Lakes biosystem every 8 months, often carried in via ship ballast. Electric fences have been set up in Chicago to keep out the latest threat, fast-growing Asian carp, which are already an issue in the Mississippi and Illinois rivers.

What's at stake is some of North America's most iconic scenery. We cover several sites in this book—islands such as Lake Huron's Manitoulin Island ⑯ and Lake Superior's Isle Royale (95), shoreline preserves like Wisconsin's Mink River Estuary (148) and Michigan's Saugatuck Dunes (107) and Sleeping Bear Dunes (161) and lighthouses such as Raspberry Island in Wisconsin's Apostle Islands (450) and Ontario's Nottawasaga Island on Lake Huron (451) It's impossible not to be awed by the panorama of **Niagara Falls,** where Lake Erie spills down into Lake Ontario; cascading torrents rumble the cliffs under your feet and mist spritzes your face. Or cross the soaring 5-mile-long (8km) suspension bridge over the Straits of Mackinac, linking Lakes Michigan and Huron; a ferryboat will then take you to **Mackinac Island,** where you can find relics of early Huron settlements, French fur trappers, an American Revolution fort, and a Victorian-era resort—all the layers of Great Lakes history.

ⓘ http://greatlakesecho.org

✈ Chicago/Toronto/Detroit/Milwaukee/Buffalo/Cleveland

🛏 $$ **Red Coach Inn,** 2 Buffalo Ave., Niagara Falls, NY (✆ **866/719-2070** or 716/282-1459; www.redcoach.com). $$ **Mission Point Resort,** 6633 Main St., Mackinac Island, MI (✆ **800/833-7711** or 906/847-3312; www.missionpoint.com)

4 **Ecosystems in Peril**

The Colorado River Basin

The Great Water Grab

Western U.S./Mexico

More than 20 dams ride the Colorado and its tributaries, watering farmland and slaking cities' thirst all over the Southwest. As its flow slows to a trickle, can engineers reverse centuries of water greed?

Lake Mead.

It's a beautiful river, no question about it. It's beautiful up in Colorado, as passengers on the California Zephyr admire its cascades through Rocky Mountain canyons and valleys. It's beautiful in the stark desert plateau of Utah, thundering along the border of Arches and Canyonlands national parks. It's especially beautiful in Arizona, slashing a narrow gorge through the violently colored striped rock of the Grand Canyon.

But over the past century, Americans have taken the Colorado River for granted. Some 20 dams have blossomed along the Colorado and its many tributaries, creating popular recreational lakes such as Utah's **Lake Powell,** Nevada's **Lake Mead,** and Arizona's **Lake Havasu.** Ninety percent of the water they harness goes to agricultural irrigation, but they also supply hydroelectric power and drinking water to such major cities as Los Angeles, Las Vegas, Phoenix, and San Diego. South of Yuma, Arizona, the world's largest irrigation canal—the All-American Canal—has turned desert land into the agricultural powerhouse Imperial Valley. Meanwhile, a new desert has appeared below the U.S./Mexican border, where this once-great river has been bled into a mere trickle.

Seven U.S. states, as well as two countries, share this mighty river. In 1922, Colorado, Wyoming, Utah, Arizona, Nevada, California, and New Mexico signed a compact to share the water equally between its upper and lower basins. But given the Southwest's population boom in the second half of the 20th century, those allocations are no longer enough, and state water managers constantly negotiate supply and demand. Scientists warn that the original compact's river flow estimates were based on an era of abnormally high rainfall—and the persistent shrunken levels of both Lake Mead and Lake Powell in recent seasons suggest that this isn't a short-term "drought" but normal desert climate. Bad as this may be for weekend boaters and fishermen, it's even worse for the watershed's native fish, especially endangered species like the Colorado pikeminnow, razorback sucker, bonytail, and humpback chub, which may not survive in warmer, shallower waters.

The Colorado is a long river, showing many different personalities along its 1,450-mile (2,330km) course. Perhaps you'll investigate its headwaters atop the Continental Divide in Rocky Mountain National Park **210**; perhaps you'll raft the crashing whitewaters of Cataract Canyon in Canyonlands National Park **224**. Perhaps you'll hike 7 to 9 miles (11–14km) of switchback trails to find the river running along the mile-deep floor of the **Grand Canyon** (the full descent requires an overnight stay, at either the Bright Angel Campground or the rustic, bare-bones Phantom Ranch). Or just drive along Lake Mead's Northshore Drive, stopping to hike on short marked nature trails. Threading around red sandstone monoliths, watch for ground squirrels, lizards, scorpions, and other desert denizens—just one more reminder that nature never intended Lake Mead to be here.

ⓘ **Grand Canyon National Park,** Grand Canyon, AZ (ⓒ **800/638-7888** or 928/638-7888; www.nps.gov/grca). **Lake Mead National Recreation Area** (ⓒ **702/293-8906;** www.nps.gov/lame).

✈ Las Vegas

🛏 $$ **Maswik Lodge,** South Rim, AZ (ⓒ **888/297-2757** or 928/638-2631; www.grandcanyonlodges.com). $$ **Boulder Dam Hotel,** 1305 Arizona St., Boulder City, NV (ⓒ **702/293-3510;** www.boulderdamhotel.com).

The Amazon Rainforest
Paradise Lost?
Manaus, Brazil

DECADES OF CONSERVATION CAMPAIGNS HAD FINALLY BEGUN TO REVERSE AMAZONIAN Brazil's deforestation—and then came record-breaking droughts in 2005 and 2010, sending vegetation die-off into overdrive.

"Save the rainforest!" became a rallying cry in the early 1980s, a cliché for environmental awareness. You'd think by now we would have saved it.

But the crisis is by no means past. The Amazon—the world's largest river—courses through the world's biggest tropical rainforest on its way to the Atlantic Ocean. This dense green jungle shelters myriad endangered and endemic species, including many plants that may be unique sources for lifesaving medicines; it is also, as one catchphrase puts it, the "lungs of the earth," producing more than 20% of the world's fresh oxygen. But recent figures estimate that 18% of the rainforest's biomass has already been lost to deforestation, mostly through clear-cut logging and cattle ranching; the 2005 and 2010 droughts—the worst ever recorded in the region—have accelerated that loss. Scientists warn that if more rainforest cover converts to savanna, the Amazon Basin could eventually *add* to global warming, by releasing gigatons of carbon into the atmosphere. Despite all of this, in May 2011 Brazilian agribusiness interests pressured the government to amend its protective Forest Code, opening more of the Amazon Basin to development.

For the traveler, this fertile wilderness is a textbook definition of paradise: a spellbinding scene of draping vines, waxy blossoms, and leafy canopies, with a soundtrack of chattering monkeys and twittering parakeets. Gaze upward and you'll find comical toucans and iridescent parrots in the trees; peer into the river's mysterious depths and you'll spot furtive anacondas and flitting tetra fish. A fledgling eco-tourism industry offers new economic hope for locals who formerly depended on destructive logging (see the Anavilhanas Ecological Station, **76**, and the tourism infrastructure improves every year.

The region's gateway and largest city is **Manaus,** on the banks of the Rio Negro. Just downstream from Manaus lies the momentous **Meeting of the Waters** (Encontra das Aguas), where the dark, slow waters of the Rio Negro meet the fast, muddy brown waters of the Rio Solimões, officially becoming the capital-A "Amazon." Differences in velocity, temperature, and salinity actually keep the two rivers from blending for miles—you can see the distinct colors of their currents running side by side, a stunning natural phenomenon.

While some visitors are content with a sightseeing flight over the Meeting of the Waters, the Amazon rewards deeper exploration. Various operators offer multiday boat tours out of Manaus, where you can either sleep onboard or stay overnight at jungle lodges; onboard guides take passengers canoeing up side rivers, hiking under the rainforest canopy, piranha fishing, or nighttime caiman spotting. More adventurous tours kayak or hike deeper into the rainforest, camping out overnight. You may even find yourself bird-watching or orchid hunting from a perch in the rainforest canopy. Vote with your eco-tourism dollars and give Brazil an incentive to save the rainforest.

Canoeing on the Amazon.

 Manaus

$$$ **Hotel Tropical de Manaus,** Av. Coronel Texeira 1320, Ponta Negra, Manaus (*C* **55/92/2123-5000;** www.tropicalhotel. com.br). $ **Mango Guest House,** Rua Flávio Espirito Santo, Kissia II, Manaus (*C* **55/ 92/3656-6033;** www.naturesafaris.com.br).

TOUR Viverde (*C* **55/92/3248-9988;** www.viverde.com.br). **Swallows and Amazons** (*C* **55/92/3622-1246;** www. swallowsandamazonstours.com). **Amazon Mystery Tours** (*C* **55/92/3633-7844;** www.amazon-outdoor.com).

Ecosystems in Peril

The Pantanal
Off Road & Under Water
Southwestern Brazil

ALREADY POLLUTED BY PESTICIDE RUNOFF AND MERCURY FROM GOLD MINING, THIS ONE-OF-A-kind flood plain is now threatened by a multinational proposal to build a major shipping channel and hydroelectric dams through its heart.

The Amazon rainforest may grab all the headlines, but here's a little-known secret: The best place in South America to see wildlife is right here, on this treeless savanna. The world's largest freshwater flood plain (equal to the size of France), the Pantanal may not have as many species as the rainforest does, but its densely packed flora and fauna live much less hidden lives, affording constant sightings.

"Flood" is the operative word here. In the rainy season, December through March, the Pantanal's waters may rise as much as 5m (16 ft.), covering up to 80% of this flat region—and leaving an incredibly fecund landscape in its wake. In the rainy season, you'll find mammals clustered on the few remaining humps of dry land while fish and aquatic birds slosh happily through the water. In dry season, the reverse happens: The plain dries up, and animals can be found around the few freshwater pools. Capybaras, caimans, jaguars, maned wolves, Brazilian tapirs, giant otters, Hyacinth macaws—the Pantanal offers endangered critters everywhere you look.

Most of the Pantanal is privately owned by cattle ranches, with less than 3% set aside for conservation—only one small national park (Parque Nacional do Patanal Mato-Grossense, near Poconé in the north Pantanal) and a handful of private preserves. There are few roads here—even the Transpantaeira, a gravel road meant to traverse the entire region, was abandoned after the northern 143km (89 miles). But the proposed Hidrovia project would change all that, dredging and connecting the Paraguay and Parana rivers into a massive shipping channel. Environmentalists and social activists blocked the first Hidrovia proposal, but its backers have revived it recently, claiming that the value of eco-tourism to

this region may not outweigh the canal's commercial benefits.

In the meantime, many cattle ranches *(fazendas)* have gone into business as the Brazilian version of dude ranches; entire tour packages are based on exploring the flood plain by horse. That unfinished Transpantaeira functions as a splendid nature trail, taking visitors into the heart of north Pantanal. Its roadside ditches are favorite feeding grounds for kingfishers, egrets, jabiru storks, and more than four varieties of hawks and three kinds of kites. Beneath the many rickety bridges are small rivers or pools where caimans lurk by the hundreds. On horseback, you can ramble far from settled areas, where the wildlife wanders otherwise undisturbed; rein in your mount and observe a flock of herons fishing in the rich floodwaters, then take off with a splash at a full gallop, startling alligators and snakes underfoot. Unspoiled corners can still be found all over the Pantanal . . . but the clock is ticking.

✈ Cuiabá (North Pantanal)/Campo Grande (South Pantanal)

🛏 $$$ **Araras Eco Lodge,** Transpantaeira Hwy., near Cuiabá (✆ **55/65/ 3682-2800;** www.araraslodge.com.br). $$ **Pousada Xaraés Ecoturismo,** Estrada Parque, Abobral, near Corumbá (✆ **55/ 67/9906-9272;** www.xaraes.com.br).

TOUR Pantanal Tours (✆ **55/67/3042- 4659;** www.pantanaltours.com). **Brazil Nuts** (✆ **800/553-9959;** www.brazil nuts.com).

---

7   **Ecosystems in Peril**

Serengeti National Park
Migration Station
North Tanzania

SIX MILLION HOOFS POUND THE SERENGETI PLAIN AS THE WORLD'S LARGEST MAMMAL migration flows from Tanzania to Kenya. In June 2011, environmental protests finally stopped a projected highway that would have cut it off.

To the native Masai, these vast grassy plains are Siringitu—"the place where the land moves on forever." Standing on this sunburned African savanna, gazing upon a sea of golden grasses that stretches to the horizon, you know exactly what they mean.

It's a continuous corridor of protected plain, as Serengeti National Park flows into the Ngorongoro Conservation Area 55 and Kenya's Masai Mara Game Reserve 53 And that's crucial—because the wildlife here doesn't just stay in one spot, it migrates, following a circular route covering nearly 2,000km (1,200 miles). Nearly a million wildebeest, along with some 200,000 zebra and 300,000 gazelle, head south in October, crossing the crocodile-infested Mara River to find greener pastures. In April, after the rains, they return north along a more western route. It's a punishing journey—many of the wildebeest die of starvation or exhaustion—and one of nature's most compelling dramas.

The rest of the year, safari visitors still can content themselves with viewing great herds of Cape buffalo, clusters of elephant and giraffe, and masses of antelopes—eland, topi, kongoni, impala, and Grant's gazelle. Prides of lions and cheetahs prowl the plains, or survey their prey from the granite outcrops known as *kopjes* (think *The Lion King*), while stealthy leopards hunt the acacia woodlands along the Seronera River. Spotted hyenas and all three African jackal species (*The Lion King* again) scavenge here and there, while black eagles soar above the Lobo Hills, and ostrich and secretary birds strut around open grassland.

With tourism now Tanzania's second-largest industry, protecting the Serengeti is a matter of national importance. First on the agenda: Eliminate the rampant poaching that in the 1970s reduced the elephant population to less than 500 and the black rhinos to two lone individuals. (There are now nearly 20 black rhinos, protected in Moru Kopjes and nearby Ngorongoro Crater.) Impoverished villagers living just outside the park still poach wildlife for meat, however, and Serengeti park managers have had to balance the needs of wildlife and humans, creating a buffer zone of Community Wildlife Management Areas. In days past, periodic fires kept these plains open pastureland for Masai cattle; nowadays, with the grass cropped short by buffalo and wildebeest, there's less fire, allowing patches of acacia woodlands and fig trees to rebound, improved habitat for the 500-plus bird species of the Serengeti.

But in 2010, something new fluttered from the branches of the Serengeti's trees: red plastic ribbons, marking survey points for the new highway. Slashing across a sensitive wilderness section of the park, this highway—following the route of an existing gravel park drive—would create access for poachers, introduce invasive species on car tires, and turn wild animals into roadkill; worst of all, it would stop the migrating wildebeest in their tracks. Unable to reach the watering holes of Kenya, the herd would dwindle to a fraction of its current size, and the entire ecology of the Serengeti would change. Luckily, a storm of environmental protests convinced the Tanzanian government to leave the gravel road and reroute the high-speed highway just south of the park. The construction project may still have an impact on the wildlife, but for now the migration flow can continue as it has for centuries.

ⓘ **Seronera visitor center,** central Serengeti (www.serengeti.org). Also see www.savetheserengeti.org.

✈ Arusha

🛏 $$$ **Bilila Lodge,** Central Serengeti (✆ 255/768/981 890; www.kempinski. com). $$$ **Serena Lodge,** Seronera (✆255/272/545 555; www.serenahotels. com).

TOUR **Tauck World Discovery** (✆ **800/ 788-7885;** www.tauck.com). **Micato Safaris** (✆ **800/642-2861** or 212/545-7111; www.micato.com).

The Maldives
The First to Go
Indian Ocean

VALIANTLY REBOUNDING FROM 1998's EL NIÑO CORAL BLEACHING AND THE 2004 INDONESIAN tsunami, the world's lowest-lying nation may face a death sentence if—make that when—global warming raises sea levels.

In 2008, the new president of the Maldives, Mohamed Nasheed, made a startling announcement: His government planned to buy land in other countries for Maldivian citizens, so that they'd have somewhere else to live when the earth's rising oceans erase their homeland from the face of the earth.

Presidential showmanship aside (Nasheed also held a 2009 cabinet meeting underwater to mimic the islands' possible future), he does have a point. The widely scattered 1,190 coral islands that constitute the Maldives—the peaks of an underwater mountain chain—lie on average only 1.5m (5 ft.) above the current level of the Indian Ocean. If, as climatologists predict, sea levels rise .9m (3 ft.) by the end of the century, much of the Maldives could *simply disappear.*

The Maldives are all about coral reefs, which hold off the sea—for now—around these South Asian islands. With its favorable equatorial climate, tourism is the nation's primary industry; thousands of visitors per year come year-round to dive in its technicolored reefs or lounge on the palm-fringed islands' milk-white sands. Only 200 of these islands are inhabited, but at least half of those have been developed as resorts. From the gateway island, **Malé,** nowhere is farther than a 45-minute flight; most visitors go directly from here to an island resort or live-aboard boat, aka "safari yachts."

The Maldives.

Since the government won't let you make unauthorized visits to uninhabited islands, sanctioned live-aboards are your best option for island hopping. Some specialize in dive expeditions—try **Maldives Scuba Tours** (℡ **44/1284/748010;** www.scubascuba.com) or **Maldives Live-aboards** (www.maldivesliveaboards.com). Renowned dive sites include the HP Reef, with its spectacular coral outcrops; Kandooma Thila, a challenging pinnacle site with beautiful caves; and the breathtaking underwater ridge at Rasdhoo Madivaru. The Maldives boast some amazing marine life, with over 2,000 fish species, many of them endangered—like the giant Napoleon wrasse, leopard shark, and some 250 manta rays (most with wingspans of 3m/10 ft.). You'll see more once you get out to isolated atolls, where barracuda, batfish, unicornfish, fusiliers, and harlequin sweetlips patrol the warm, remarkably clear water.

But diving is only part of the Maldives story. Many resorts organize fishing expeditions, including night-fishing trips, during which you can grill your catch on the beach of a desert island. Dolphin- and whale-watching tours are another draw. Or take a boat tour to a typical Maldivian fishing village, where you can observe the life of resident islanders. It's good to get to know these folks—who knows, someday they may have to pack up and move next door to you.

ⓘ www.maldives.com or www.visit maldives.com

✈ Malé

🛏 $$$ **Angsana Ihiru,** North Malé Atoll (℡ **800/591-0439** in North America or 960/664-3502; www.angsana.com). $$$ **Cocoa Island,** South Malé Atoll (℡ **960/ 664-1818;** www.cocoaisland.como.bz).

Fragile Treasures 9

Great Sand Dunes National Park
The Colorado Dune Buggy
Southern Colorado

A RAGING FOREST FIRE, TOUCHED OFF BY A LIGHTNING STRIKE IN MEDANO CANYON, BURNED 6,000 acres (2,400 hectares) of this Colorado park in June 2010, underscoring the impact of ongoing drought in the American West.

It's right there on the map—Colorado, a landlocked state. So how can it have a park full of sand dunes?

These towering light brown dunes—the tallest in North America—were formed by southwesterly winds blowing across the San Luis Valley, where eroded glacial rock and silt were deposited by mountain streams onto a sandy valley floor. Reversing winds from the mountains piled the sand steeply, eventually reaching up to 750 feet (229m) high.

Such a bizarre isolated habitat is bound to attract unusual species, animals unsuited to Rocky Mountain ecosystems and yet unable to reach ocean dunes. There's the

Great Sand Dunes National Park.

Ord's kangaroo rat, for instance, a long-tailed gerbil-sized rodent that never drinks water, getting its moisture instead from grasses and seeds that it stores in the moist sand below the dune surface. Usually found only in low deserts, this rat has adapted to tolerate the huge range of temperatures up here, from summer highs of 140°F (60°C) to 20 below zero (−29°C) on a winter night. Its long back feet enable it to leap like a kangaroo 5 feet (1.5m) in the air to escape predators.

The kangaroo rat is the dunes' only resident mammal, but several insects found nowhere else on earth also thrive here—like the predatory Great Sand Dunes tiger beetle, a half-inch-long scavenger with a sharply marked brown-and-tan carapace, and the giant sand treader camel cricket, a brown-striped cricket an inch-and-a-half long with special horny scoops on its hind legs to push out of loose sliding sand. They are most active on the face of the sand dunes at night, illuminated by brilliant desert moonlight. There are no designated trails on the dunes, so you can simply wander at will; you can even camp out in the dunes, outside of the day-use area (ask rangers for directions). Be prepared for windy conditions, though—the winds that formed these sand dunes are still at work.

A unique combination of high-elevation habitats surrounds the dunes. Bird-watchers head for the forested **Montville** or **Mosca Pass trails** to look for black-headed grosbeaks, white-throated swifts, yellow-rumped warblers, and broad-tailed hummingbirds; up in the alpine tundra of the park's peaks, both bald and golden eagles can be sighted. Bison and elk graze on sand sheet grasslands; surprisingly, water birds find seasonal wetlands in spring and summer along **Medano Creek**, marked by dazzling white alkali deposits amid salt grass. Sadly, repeated drought seasons have made this unique eco-mosaic vulnerable—a foretaste of what global warming could do.

ⓘ **Great Sand Dunes National Park,** State Hwy. 150, outside Alamosa, CO (✆**719/378-6399;** www.nps.gov/grsa)

✈ Alamosa San Luis Valley

🛏 $$ **Cottonwood Inn,** 123 San Juan Ave., Alamosa (✆**719/589-3882**). $$ **Best Western Alamosa Inn,** 2005 Main St. (✆**800/459-5123** or 719/589-2567; www.bestwestern.com).

10 **Fragile Treasures**

The Burren
Ireland's Stony Wilderness
County Clare, Ireland

THE UNIQUE BOTANICAL MIX OF THIS LIMESTONE KARST PLAIN ATTRACTS RARE BUTTERFLIES, BIRDS, and naturalists. The naturalists' mission: to protect it from the sightseers who crowd County Clare's tourist routes.

The very name Ireland evokes a postcard image of soft, intensely green countryside—so what is this harsh limestone scree doing there? It's as weird as if you had just stepped onto the moon. The name "Burren" comes from the Irish word

boirreann, which means "a rocky place"—what an understatement.

The coach tours that overrun the Cliffs of Moher trundle through here too, but most day-trippers merely stare out the windows at the Burren and move on. It's one thing to

10 Places for Dark Sky

"Dark sky" is like a Holy Grail for stargazers, but on this increasingly populated planet, areas with no light pollution from nearby human settlements are increasingly rare. Forget sky events like the Northern Lights or Perseid meteor showers—even a normal night's constellations look dazzling in a truly dark sky. The following sites not only offer dark skies, but also have stargazing programs with local night-sky experts.

Mauna Kea.

11 Mauna Kea, Hawaii To many native Hawaiians, this cluster of 11 powerful telescopes on the summit of Mauna Kea, the world's tallest mountain (measured from the sea floor), violates its spiritual significance to their culture. But an international group of astronomers prevailed, determined to capitalize on this unique unpolluted site so close to the equator. You can visit the summit's telescopes (one of which is the world's largest) by 4WD vehicles or on a guided tour. ✆ **808/961-5180.** www.ifa.hawaii.edu/info/vis.

12 Natural Bridges National Monument, Lake Powell, Utah Set on a sandstone mesa in the middle of Utah's high-desert plateau, Natural Bridges not only is beautiful by day but also offers some of the darkest, clearest night skies in the nation. The International Dark-Sky Association named it the world's first International Dark Sky Park in 2006. ✆ **435/692-1234.** www.nps.gov/nabr.

13 Great Basin National Park, Twin Falls, Idaho The low humidity, clean air, and high elevation of this remote national park all contribute to its supremely dark night skies. Unless the sky is cloudy, or the moon is too full, head for prime stargazing spots at the Wheeler Peak/Bristlecone Trail parking lot, Mather Overlook, and the Baker Archeological Site. ✆ **775/234-7331.** www.nps.gov/grba.

14 Cherry Springs State Park, Coudersport, Pennsylvania Surrounded by farmland and state forest, with a mountain range blocking the nearest large city, and far inland from the cloud effect that sometimes gathers over the Great Lakes, this 48-acre (19-hectare) park is renowned for its dark skies (and local anti-light-pollution ordinances). An official Pennsylvania State dark sky preserve, the park holds regular public stargazing nights. ✆ **814/435-5010.** www.dcnr.state.pa.us/stateparks/parks/cherrysprings.aspx.

15 Torrance Barrens, Bala, Ontario Set on a flat shelf of bedrock, where the only trees are too stunted to block the horizons, Torrance Barrens is surrounded by other parklands and conservation areas. It's only an hour's drive north of Toronto, but it has remarkably little sky glow and 360-degree views. *www.muskokaheritage.org/natural/torrancebarrens.asp.*

⑯ Gordon's Park, Manitoulin Island, Ontario Set on Manitoulin Island in northern Lake Huron, this eco-campground takes advantage of its remote location by setting aside a portion of the resort, with both tent sites and cabins, as a dark-sky preserve. The skies here are the darkest in Ontario. *☎705/859-2470. www.gordons park.com.*

⑰ McDonald Park Dark Sky Preserve, Abbotsford, British Columbia Named a dark-sky preserve in 2000, this western-Canada park near the U.S. border is shielded by a mountain from the light pollution of the only nearby towns; its views are limited to the southern and western skies, but they are extraordinarily dark, despite the park's proximity to Vancouver. *www.fvas.net/dsp.html.*

⑱ Cypress Hills Dark-Sky Preserve, Alberta/Saskatchewan This 40,000-hectare (98,800-acre) expanse of forest-fringed prairie is Canada's largest designated dark-sky preserve. Stargazers gather in the Centre Block section, on the Saskatchewan side; the Meadows campground has unobstructed sky views. *☎403/893-3833. www.cypresshills.com.*

Cypress Hills Dark-Sky Preserve.

⑲ Galloway Forest Park, Dumfries & Galloway, Scotland Two hours away from the light pollution of either Glasgow or Edinburgh, the U.K.'s largest forest park (300 sq. miles/777 sq. km) is also its first designated Dark Sky Park, where some 7,000 stars are visible with the naked eye on a clear night. Set up your telescopes near any of its three visitor centers or in the Red Deer Range car park. *☎44/1671/402420. www.forestry.gov.uk/gallowayforestpark.*

⑳ Warrumbungle National Park, New South Wales, Australia The night sky looks completely different in the Southern Hemisphere—don't miss it if you're down here. While rock climbers love this park for its volcanic rock spires, flat areas near Camp Blackman offer the most panoramic skies. The country's largest observatory, **Siding Springs** (www.aao.gov.au) sits just outside the park. *☎61/2/6825 4364. www.environment.nsw.gov.au/nationalparks.*

drive along corkscrewing R480 between Corofin and Ballyvaughan through the heart of the landscape, and another thing entirely to get out of your car and hike along portions of the 123km (76-mile) Burren Way footpath signposted from Lahinch to Ballyvaughan, then branching eastward to Corofin and Carran. As you explore more closely, massive sheets of rock and jagged boulders quickly reveal caves, deep hidden potholes, and even tiny lakes and rushing streams. It even has its own terminology—the chunks of rock are known as "clints," the deep cracks riven in them "grikes."

Like a patchwork quilt, the limestone pavements alternate with seasonal ponds ("turloughs"), low hazel scrub woodlands, and a thin layer of grasslands that are a botanical freak—one of the few places on earth where alpine, arctic, and Mediterranean plants thrive side by side, clinging stubbornly to whatever soil they find. There is always something blooming here, even in winter, from fern and moss to orchids, rock roses, milkwort, wild thyme, geraniums, violets, and fuchsia. The blue spring gentian—normally an alpine species—is so common, it's the region's unofficial mascot. Some species are relics of the warmer climate this region knew before the last ice age; others are descendants of seeds dropped by glaciers as they grooved and striated the karst eons ago.

Close as it is to western Ireland's most popular tourist sites, the Burren could easily be overrun by tourists, and locals have had to fight off proposals for car parks and attractions. It seems hypocritical to keep out visitors altogether, though, for the Burren is hardly untouched by man. It's been inhabited since megalithic times, as numerous dolmens, wedge tombs, and ring forts attest. Cattle and sheep grazed for centuries on the stubborn tufts of grass between the rocks, until farms were abandoned during the famine.

Now the region depends more on tourism than agriculture—but so far, the Burren has been managed sensitively. A southeastern corner, near Corofin and Kilnaboy, is designated **The Burren National Park,** but don't expect an official entrance or acres of parking lot. The Burren is already paved by nature—why add to that?

(i) **The Burren Centre,** R476, Kilfenora (✆ **353/65/708-8030;** www.theburren centre.ie). Also visit www.burrenbeo.ie.

✈ Shannon International Airport

🚆 Ennis or Galway

🛏 $$ **The Burren Walking Lodge,** Ballyvaughan (✆ **353/65/707-7037;** www. burrenwalkinglodge.com). $ **Sleepzone @ The Burren Hostel,** Lisdoonvarna (✆ **353/65/707-4036;** www.sleepzone.ie).

Fragile Treasures   **21**

The Camargue
Allez, Allez, Little Dogies
Southern France

AS RISING SEA LEVELS AGGRESSIVELY ERODE THE COASTAL DUNES OF THIS MARSHY DELTA IN southern France, invasive species like the water primrose and the blue lobster creep in.

France's cattle country doesn't look at all like the American West—instead of rolling scrub-covered plains, it's a marshy delta where two arms of the Rhone River empty into the Mediterranean. It's exotic even for

France, with whitewashed houses, plaited-straw roofs, roaming Gypsies, and pink flamingos.

But watching over the Camargue's native black bulls—prized beasts raised for bullfights in nearby Arles and Nimes—you'll find colorful French cowboys, or *gardians,* who wear large felt hats and prod the cattle with a long three-pronged stick. The resemblance isn't coincidence: The first American cowboys are thought to have been *gardians* who emigrated to New Orleans, then hired themselves out to herd cattle in East Texas. They ride distinctive small white horses, descendants of Arabians brought here centuries ago by Saracen soldiers; wild cousins of those horses still roam through the salt marshlands that cover so much of the Camargue. Over the centuries, these sturdy, sure-footed little steeds evolved unusually long manes and bushy tails to slap the pesky mosquitoes that thrive in the wetlands. Spend much time here and you may wish you had a tail, too.

Two to three dozen stables (depending on the time of year) along the highway from Arles to Stes-Maries offer expeditions on horseback into the park, where you can ford the waters to penetrate deep into the interior where black bulls graze, wild ponies gallop, and water birds nest. The Camargue is a watery place indeed, approximately a third of it either reed-covered marshland or large brine lagoons—*étangs*—divided from the sea by shallow sandbars. The most fragile ecosystem in France, it has been a national park since 1970. Rising sea levels pose a

very real threat for this low-lying alluvial plain; its coastal dunes, popular with vacationers, are already eroding. Park managers actively promote reforestation to combat erosion—not an easy campaign in a cattle-breeding region where open pastureland is valued.

In the marshes, however, exotic flora and fauna abound. The bird life here is the most luxuriant in Europe—not only colonies of pink flamingos but some 400 other bird species, including ibises, egrets, kingfishers, owls, wild ducks, swans, and ferocious birds of prey. The best place to see flamingo colonies is the area around **Ginès,** a hamlet on N570, 5km (3 miles) north of Camargue's capital, Stes-Maries-de-la-Mer—a perfectly preserved medieval walled town set amid swamps and lagoons, long ago an embarkation point for the crusades and well worth a visit.

ⓘ **Camargue National Park,** D570 near Stes-Maries-de-la-Mer, France (ⓒ **33/4/9097 1040;** www.parc-camargue.fr)

🚆 Arles

🛏 $$$ **Hotel Les Templiers,** 23 rue de la République, Aigues-Mortes (ⓒ **33/4/6653-6656;** www.hotellestempliers.fr). $$ **Hotel d'Arlatan,** 26 rue du Sauvage, Arles (ⓒ **33/4/9093-5666;** www.hotel-arlatan.fr).

Matsushima
Calm in the Eye of the Storm
Northern Honshu, Japan

TWO NATURAL DISASTERS—A 9.0 EARTHQUAKE AND THE TSUNAMI IT UNLEASHED—WERE tragedy enough for Japan in March 2011. Humans were responsible for the third event: the Fukushima nuclear reactor meltdown.

Gazing across the sweep of deep blue Matsushima Bay is like looking at a gigantic version of a pond in a Japanese bonsai garden: gnarled pine trees writhe upward

from 260 tiny islands of volcanic tuff and white sandstone, fantastically carved by waves. Centuries ago, Matsushima was declared one of Japan's three iconic scenic

Matsushima.

areas (the others are Miyajima in Hiroshima Bay and Amanohashidate on the north Honshu coast). The 17th-century haiku poet Basho was so overwhelmed by its beauty, he could only write, "Matsushima, Ah! Matsushima! Matsushima!"

At the shocking news of 2011's catastrophic tsunami, Japanophiles feared for Matsushima, only half-an-hour's train ride from storm-ravaged Sendai. But by a stroke of fortune, those pine-clad islands actually saved Matsushima, providing a buffer when the tsunami waters hit. Nearby areas saw waves 10m (33 ft.) or higher; in protected Matsushima Bay they were 1 to 2m (3¼–6½ ft.). A few shorefront modern buildings had minor damage, but Matsushima's major sights were intact. In a region desperate to restore tourism, Matsushima's reprieve offers a ray of hope.

Taking a sightseeing boat ride around the bay is essential, of course; you can also walk over red arched bridges to explore a few islands close to shore. The

oft-photographed long red bridge to **Fukuura Island,** with its botanical garden, was wrecked by the storm but should be repaired quickly. Tranquil wooded **Ojima** bears relics of young Buddhist monks' spiritual retreats; the monks' other island, **Godaido,** is barely big enough for one small wooden pagoda, sheltering five holy statues that are displayed to the public only every 33 years (next outing: 2039).

Although the famous Zen temple of Zuiganji is under restoration until 2016 (for reasons unrelated to the tsunami), the temple district is still a must-see. You approach via a serene cedar-shaded pathway, past several shallow meditation caves built by monks. The **Zuiganji Art Museum** displays many of the temple's treasures, including exquisite gold sliding doors and artifacts of powerful lord Date Masamune, the temple's patron (everything in town seems to involve Date Masamune—there's even a wax museum depicting his life and times). You can also visit the half-timbered Zuri, or Zen kitchen, where monks prepared meals. Surrounding the smaller Entsuin temple, a fine set of traditional gardens inspire contemplation.

To cap your Matsushima experience, walk down to **Kanrantei,** the Date family's large but simple wooden teahouse sitting at water's edge. Here you can drink ceremonial green tea while sitting on a tatami mat, gazing at the bay, its islands, and the boats carving ribbons through the water. Ponder Japan's traditional harmony with nature, and hope that this country can quickly heal.

ⓘ **Tourist office,** Kaigan station (✆ 81/22/354-2263) or Kaigan Pier (✆ 81/22/354-2618)

🚃 Matsushima-Kaigan

🚢 Matsushima-Kaigan pier

🛏 $$ **Matsushima Century Hotel,** 8 Senzui, Matsushima (✆ 81/22/354-4111; www.centuryhotel.co.jp). $$ **Taikanso,** 10-76 Inuta, Matsushima (✆ 81/22/354-5214 or 81/22/354-2161; www.taikanso.co.jp).

Antarctica
The Frozen Continent
Southern Ocean

GLOBAL WARMING'S IMPACT MAY BE FELT FIRST IN ANTARCTICA, WHERE RISING TEMPERATURES are already melting sea ice—destroying habitat for marine life, disrupting the food chain, and swelling oceans all over the planet.

Here at the literal bottom of the earth, be prepared for ice like you've never seen it. Monumental peacock-blue icebergs tower in surreal formations; craggy glaciers drop crashing chunks into the sea. Narrow canals knife between sheer ice-encrusted walls, and jagged peaks jut out of icy fields.

Antarctica has long exerted a magnetic pull on those who crave adventure. The first explorers reached the South Pole a century ago, in 1911, when Norwegian Roald Amundsen reached the pole a scant 33 days ahead of rival British captain Robert Scott—whose party tragically died

returning to their ship. Irish explorer Ernest Shackleton tried (and failed) to cross the continent 4 years later.

Unless you're a scientist posted to a research station, you'll most likely come to Antarctica these days on an expedition cruise. Starting in the 1990s, when Russian research ships were retrofitted to bring the first leisure travelers here, travel to Antarctica has grown exponentially, turning what used to be a rugged adventure trip into a luxury cruise. While the first tour ships were svelte icebreakers, ever larger cruise ships now shoulder through the region's

Gentoo penguins in Antarctica.

unpredictable ice floes. Nearly 46,000 travelers visited the region in the 2007–08 season. After the sinking of the Canadian vessel MS *Explorer* in November 2007, however, the 47 nations of the Antarctic Treaty coalition agreed to limit Antarctic travel to ships carrying less than 500 passengers. Meanwhile, the International Maritime Organization now requires Antarctic cruise ships to use lighter fuels, to prevent polluting spillage in polar waters. Because these "greener" fuels are less efficient, some cruise companies may now pull out of this market, leaving it to dedicated specialists.

Ice covers more than 98% of the continent year-round, but it can be visited only in summer (Nov–Mar) when the surrounding sea ice melts enough to let ships reach the landmass. Itineraries vary in length, depending on which sub-Antarctic islands are included en route to the Antarctic Peninsula (all tours include the wildlife-rich South Shetland Islands). Longer tours may venture inside the polar circle or circle around to the iceberg alleys of the continent's west side. Passengers are diverted

with natural-history lectures and shore excursions: One day you may scuba dive, scale a frozen peak, or kayak through calving ice, the next you may observe penguins, seals, or whales, or soak in thermal springs. Bird-watchers spend hours training their binoculars on a variety of unique seabirds, including petrels and albatrosses.

It's an ethical dilemma: Join the swelling ranks of cruisers, or pass up the chance to experience this icebound Eden. By choosing a responsible tour operator, and then supporting measures to regulate Antarctic routes more tightly, you just may be able to have your ice cream and eat it too.

ⓘ www.antarcticconnection.com

✈ Ushuaia, Argentina

TOUR Polar Cruises (☏ **888/484-2244**; www.polarcruises.com). **Lindblad Expeditions** (☏ **800/397-3348**; www.expeditions. com). **Quark Expeditions** (☏ **888/ 892-0334**; www.quarkexpeditions.com). **Adventure Network International** (☏ **801/266-4876**; www.adventure-network.com).

Man-Made Damage **24**

The Galápagos Islands
Nature's Laboratory
Offshore Ecuador

TWO CENTURIES AFTER CHARLES DARWIN WAS BORN, INCREASING TOURISM THREATENS THIS isolated Pacific archipelago he made famous. Expansion of air service in 2010 may bring even more crowds.

Everybody knows the Galápagos, thanks to Charles Darwin. Ever since that upstart English scientist visited in 1835—or at least ever since he described its incredible wildlife in his 1859 book *On the Origin of Species*—this Pacific archipelago has been famous for its natural wonders. If it hadn't been for their extreme location, 966km (600 miles) off the west coast of Ecuador, mass tourism would have spoiled the islands years ago.

Well, don't speak too soon. The pristine Galápagos wildlife experience may already be a thing of the past. Tourism has become Ecuador's fourth-largest industry and the Galápagos its most popular tourist draw by far. The once-sleepy main city of **Puerto Ayora** now bustles with trendy hotels and restaurants. All this traffic inevitably admits new species to the islands, irrevocably altering those once-isolated ecosystems. Immigrant workers have smuggled in

Wildlife on the Galápagos.

goats and pigs that compete with native species for food; exotic fire ants kill baby tortoises; invader rats slip ashore from cruise ships and prey on smaller animals; blackberry and guava plantations run wild. The list goes on and on.

In 2007, Ecuador's president Rafael Correa declared the islands at risk, and several measures were implemented—expulsion of illegal immigrant workers, new waste-management plans, enforcement of a ban on sport fishing, programs to eradicate invasive species, and a moratorium on cruise ships over 500 passengers; in 2012, new regulations banning vessels from revisiting the same site in a 14-day period will go into effect. In 2010, the Galápagos were removed from UNESCO's list of World Heritage Sites in Danger. Some observers fear it was delisted too soon.

There's no question that it's a treasure worth saving. An astounding number of endemic species thrive on these 19 small volcanic islands (plus about 40 islets); boat travel is essential to view them all. Galápagos cruises, which depart from Guayaquil, send passengers out on small dinghies to various islands each day, joining park-approved guides for nature-spotting hikes, climbs, kayak trips, or snorkel outings. **Santiago**'s rocky tide pools are home to rare fur sea lions and many beautiful heron species; **Española** has albatrosses and blue-footed boobies; in **Fernandina** there are vivid marine iguanas and flightless cormorants; **Isabela** is home to Galápagos's penguins (the world's only tropical penguins); **Genovesa** has frigate birds and red-footed boobies; and **San Cristobal** is where California sea lions, red crabs, and lava gulls reside. What's most remarkable about the Galápagos's wildlife is how little they fear humans (some scientists worry that these wild animals have become *too* habituated to human presence).Young sea lions will show off their best moves as you snorkel among them; mockingbirds will peck at your shoelaces; the blue-footed boobie will perform its famous two-stepped mating dance right under your nose.

The 2011 Pacific tsunami swept over the Galápagos but left little damage, except for flooding the Darwin Research

Station in Puerto Ayora. But never fear: The research station's most famous inhabitant, Lonesome George—the last of the giant Galápagos tortoises—was moved inland before the tsunami hit. A true islander like George deserves rescue.

(i) **Galápagos Islands National Park** (© **593/5/252-6189**; www.galapagos park.org)

✈ Baltra (near Santa Cruz Island)

🛏 $$$ **Royal Palm Hotel,** Via Baltra Km 18, Isla Santa Cruz (© **593/5/252-7408;** www.royalpalmhotel.net). $$ **Finch Bay Eco Hotel,** Barrio Punta Estrada, Isla Santa Cruz (© **888/572-0166** from the U.S., or 593/2/298-8200; www.finchbay hotel.com).

TOUR Ecoventura, 6404 Blue Lagoon Dr., Miami (© **800/633-7972;** www.eco ventura.com). **Klein Tours** (© **888/810-6909** in the U.S., or 44/800/097-5537 in the U.K.; www.kleintours.com).

Man-Made Damage — **25**

Lake Baikal
The Blue Eye of Siberia
Southwestern Siberia

ENVIRONMENTALISTS CHEERED IN SEPTEMBER 2008 WHEN A HIGH-POLLUTING PAPER PULP mill closed on the shores of the world's oldest and deepest lake. In January 2010, President Putin allowed it to reopen.

On the surface, it's only the world's seventh-largest lake, but when it comes to deepest? Nothing else even comes close. Plunging 1,500m (5,000 ft.) or more, Lake Baikal contains a full 20% of all the world's unfrozen fresh water—as much water as in all the Great Lakes put together. Scientists believe it's also the world's oldest lake, almost 25 million years old. Located on a widening continental rift, it's even growing a tiny bit every year.

Cupped in a bowl of thickly wooded mountains, Lake Baikal is aptly nicknamed "the Blue Eye of Siberia." Far from any ocean, it's fed by more than 330 rivers and streams; only one, the Angara River, runs out, flowing 2,414km (1,500 miles) to the Arctic Ocean. The waters are so clear you can see down hundreds of feet (it's said that some boaters get vertigo from looking over the side). Almost 1,800 species of flora and fauna live here, two-thirds of them indigenous. Many of those are microscopic invertebrates, including zillions of tiny crustaceans that filter and

oxygenate the water, giving it its astonishing clarity.

Viewed from the lake, the shoreline today is nearly all parkland and preserves. Russian vacationers come in droves to relax on lake cruisers, kayak around sheltered **Chivirkuisky Bay,** or hike through shoreline woods, home to Siberian brown bears, elks, moose, and deer. You can also visit the **Ushkaniye Islands,** a preserve for the adorable plump Baikal seal (the world's only entirely freshwater seal), or ride the lakeside **Circum-Baikal Railway,** a former section of the Trans-Siberian Railway. Experienced hikers can attempt the 100km (62-mile) **Frolikha Adventure Coastline Track** built in 2009 around the lake's northern end.

The 20th century did not treat this Siberian treasure well, however. In the early 1900s, lumber companies began to clear vast tracts of the trees that anchored lakeside slopes. In 1966, a pulp factory opened on the lakeshore at Baikalsk, where chlorine runoff eventually created a dead zone.

While most of the lakeshore was eventually turned into parkland, air pollution still drifted in from Irkutsk and Ulan Ulde and from nearby coal-burning power plants.

After perestroika, in 1987, environmental activists hoped for change. First, they won a long-hoped-for logging ban; then, in 2006, President Putin vetoed a proposed oil pipeline (though plans are still being considered for a nuclear power plant in the area). New antipollution measures were passed that forced that Soviet-era pulp mill to close in 2008, rather than upgrade its operations. In January 2010, however, the mill was allowed to reopen,

a typical Putin-era case of economy trumping environment. International protests have still not reversed the decision. Lake Baikal holds a lot of water—the more of it that's contaminated, the sooner this rare ecosystem will break down.

ⓘ www.irkutsk.org/baikal

✈ Irkutsk

🛏 $$ **Hotel Europa,** 69 Baikalskaya St., Irkutsk (✆ **7/395/220 9696;** www.europe hotel.ru). $$ **Mayak Hotel,** 85A Gorkiy St., Listvyanka (✆ **7/3952/496 911;** http:// mayakhotel.ru).

26 Man-Made Damage

The Dead Sea
Reviving the Dead Sea
Israel

WITH THE JORDAN RIVER HEAVILY TAPPED FOR IRRIGATION, THE DEAD SEA NO LONGER RECEIVES enough water to offset evaporation. Plans to pipe in water from the Red Sea could save it—or damage its unique ecosystem.

Lying at the lowest point on the earth—a remarkable 423m (1,388 ft.) below sea level—the Dead Sea is anything but dead. Granted, no fish live in this salt-saturated inland lake, an hour's drive from Jerusalem, but certain green algae do just fine, plus lots of red archaebacteria. The water looks slightly greenish, and also milky from all its rich minerals—magnesium, calcium, bromine, and potassium. For centuries Dead Sea mud has been touted for its healing powers.

The Dead Sea is mostly fed by the Jordan River, but water doesn't flow out, it just evaporates. And with Jordan River waters increasingly diverted to irrigation projects upstream, there isn't enough water flowing in these days to offset the rapid evaporation caused by this dry climate. Rocky coves all along the shore are edged with snowy encrustations of salt. Lately the water level has dropped as

much as a meter per year. Within 25 years, the Dead Sea could be completely dry.

And with it would go an incredible experience. The sensation of floating in the Dead Sea is genuinely freaky—releasing your body into that incredibly saline water, you'll pop immediately up to the surface, as buoyant as if you were weightless. You'll also feel relaxed and energized by the Dead Sea air, which contains 10% more oxygen than normal. It's definitely hot—up to 107°F (42°C) in summer—but evaporation adds an extra layer of atmosphere that filters the sun's UV rays, making sunbathing fairly safe.

In contrast to the sand-scoured desert ridges around the sea, along the lakeside highway you'll find a few lush oases, many of them with sulfur hot springs. Two main beach areas thrive along the Israeli shore. **Ein Gedi** offers a rather crowded public beach, a kibbutz with a good hotel and

23

The Dead Sea.

spa, and a botanic garden planted with rare trees and shrubs from all over the world. Farther down the coast, past the ancient fortress of Masada, you'll reach **Ein Bokek,** where there are several hotels and free public beaches. Tour operators from either resort offer jeep safaris, desert rappelling excursions, or Bedouin feasts in a tent.

If all goes well, the region's three countries—Jordan, Israel, and Palestine—may put aside political differences to cooperate on refilling the Dead Sea. The proposed plan would utilize salty wastewater left over from a desalination plant in Jordan, where Red Sea water is converted to fresh drinking water. Scientists still worry about how the waters would mix, and how that would impact Dead Sea microorganisms. But as the Sea inexorably shrinks, it may be worth the risk.

ⓘ **The Living Dead Sea center,** Ein Bokek (ⓒ **972/8/997-5010;** www.dead sea.co.il)

✈ Jerusalem/Tel Aviv

🛏 $$$ **Le Meridien Dead Sea,** Ein Bokek (ⓒ **972/8/659-1234;** www.star woodhotels.com). $ **Masada Guesthouse and Youth Hostel,** Masada National Park, Rte. 90 (ⓒ **972/8/995-3222;** www. iyha.org.il).

2 The Last of Their Kind

A green turtle in Tortuguero, Costa Rica.

Tortuguero National Park
The Sea Turtles' Secret Getaway
Tortuguero, Costa Rica

SECLUDED TORTUGUERO IN COSTA RICA PROVIDES IDEAL NESTING CONDITIONS FOR FOUR ENDAN-gered turtle species. These turtles are in constant danger from fishing nets and disruption to reproduction cycles due to the light and sound that accompany development projects.

Tortuguero—the very name refers to sea turtles, or *tortugas* in Spanish, so it's an apt name indeed for this park, the top turtle-nesting site on Costa Rica's Caribbean coast. Luckily for the turtles, it's not easy for humans to get there; there are no roads, only a labyrinthine series of rivers and canals linking it to the port city of Limón, 80km (50 miles) away. Gliding on a boat through this dense green rainforest populated by howler and spider monkeys, three-toed sloths, tou-cans, and great green macaws is almost like a minicruise up the Amazon.

This undeveloped region's greatest resource is its wildlife, as nature lovers visit in ever greater numbers, putting a new stress on the fragile coastal ecosys-tem. A number of lodges perch on the hills around the tiny village of Tortuguero, all catering to the eco-tourist trade. Generally visitors book a package from one of those lodges that includes a bus from San José to Limón, the boat trip from Limón, rooms, and meals. Local guides are available to take you by dugout canoe up murky waterways into the rainforest, where you may see crocodiles, caimans, monkeys, herons, pygmy kingfishers, or river otters (jaguars and ocelots rarely come into view). Unfortunately, the native manatee population is nearly extinct, due to hunt-ing and to chemical runoff from nearby banana plantations.

Packages also include the starring attraction: a guided 2-to-4-hour nighttime visit to the beach to watch sea turtles wade onto the volcanic black sand to lay their eggs. In fact, the only beach access at night is with an approved nature guide.

Darkness and quiet are essential—if a female turtle detects any lights or move-ments, she will return to the sea without laying her eggs. (And given the increasing development of the Caribbean, there are fewer and fewer sufficiently dark, quiet coasts.) The mother crawls onto the beach, digs a huge pit, and then lays her eggs, as many as 100 at a time. Then she covers the pit in sand and crawls back into the ocean, never to see these offspring again.

Protected from local poachers, four species of turtles nest on this 35km-long (22-mile) stretch of black sand—the green turtle, the hawksbill, the loggerhead, and the world's largest turtle, the giant leath-erback. Considering its great size (up to 2m/6½ ft. long and weighing as much as 1,000 lb.), the giant leatherback is truly a spectacular turtle to see if you get the chance (Mar–May). From July to mid-Octo-ber, it's more likely that you will spot green turtles. They are an endangered species all right, but that's hard to believe when you see them massing by the thousands on Tortuguero beach.

ⓘ **Tortuguero National Park,** Tortu-guero, Costa Rica (✆**506/709-8091**)

✈San José

🛏 $$$ **Tortuga Lodge,** Tortuguero (✆ **506/257-0766** in San José, 506/710-8016 in Tortuguero; www.costarica expeditions.com). $$ **Pachira Lodge,** Tortuguero (✆ **506/256-7080;** www. pachiralodge.com).

TOURTours can be arranged at the lodges listed above.

Malpelo Fauna and Floral Sanctuary
Get a Piece of the Rock
Malpelo, Colombia

POLLUTION THREATENS TERRESTRIAL WILDLIFE ON THE ISLAND, AND ILLEGAL POACHING—ESPECIALLY by hunters seeking shark fins—threatens sharks and other marine life in this sanctuary for many rare and endangered species.

By itself, Malpelo Island is nothing—three naked stubs of gray volcanic rock sticking out of the Pacific Ocean. There isn't a single hotel or restaurant or even a beach shack, nothing but a crowd of masked boobies huddling on the lichened rocks and a half-deserted army base, roughly 500km (310 miles) from the nearest mainland. If it weren't for the waters around the island, nobody would come here. Nobody would even have heard of it.

But those waters have been declared a 10km (6-mile) wide no-fishing zone, a strictly patrolled sanctuary where all sorts of fish prosper. Here they can revert to natural patterns of behavior that have grown increasingly rare in Earth's over-fished oceans. There are more than 500 scalloped hammerheads swimming around Malpelo, as well as silky sharks, bull sharks, white-tip sharks, manta rays, barracuda, and an astounding number of moray eels. It's also one of few places in the world where the rare small-tooth sand tiger shark is commonly seen, off a rock wall known as "Monster Face." More friendly-faced creatures in the vicinity include dolphins, sea turtles, and the occasional humpback whale on migratory routes. The prehistoric hammerheads, which measure up to 4.2m (14 ft.) in length and swim in formidable synchronized matrices—a dazzling sight for divers—may look monstrous, but neither they nor any of the other species off Malpelo are aggressive toward humans.

Malpelo is so far out in the ocean, so far from all development, that the waters are breathtakingly clear, and sunlight can penetrate much deeper than usual. Divers also love the steep underwater walls and beautiful caves around the island. One favorite site, an outcropping of three rocks called Three Musketeers, leads to an underwater labyrinth of caverns and tunnels fittingly named The Cathedral, where huge schools of fish dart about. The waters are warm, though often turbulent; because the currents are so tricky, every dive here is a drift dive. It's not for inexperienced divers.

Divers need government permission to visit the sanctuary, which tour organizers will arrange for you. You'll need to travel on a boat with sleeping accommodations, anyway, since no tourists are permitted on the island itself. The island is way too far from shore for a day trip; expeditions last at least a week, and some are done in conjunction with Cocos Island, Costa Rica 98. But hey, it seems only fair to put in some effort, if you want to have the diving trip of a lifetime.

ⓘ www.fundacionmalpelo.org

✈ San José International, Costa Rica.

TOUR Undersea Hunter, Puntarenas, Costa Rica (✆ **800/203-2120** in North America or 506/2228-6613; www.underseahunter.com).

Padre Island National Seashore
The Journey of the Turtles
Corpus Christi, Texas

THE KEMP'S RIDLEY IS THE WORLD'S MOST ENDANGERED SEA TURTLE, EXPERIENCING A SIGNIFICANT loss of population in the 1990s, mostly due to commercial fishing. The best place to see the Kemp's Ridley is Padre Island National Seashore, the largest unspoiled barrier island in the world.

No, I'm not talking about South Padre Island, which might conjure up images (unpleasant or otherwise) of cheap hotels and raucous bar crawls—a scene best left to college spring breakers. Just to the north lies Padre Island National Seashore, a 70-mile (113km) stretch of sand, low dunes, and prairie grasses where south Texans come for fun in the sun and surf. Padre Island became part of turtle conservation efforts in 1978, when the U.S. joined forces with Mexico to establish nesting beaches. In 1992, the first turtles arrived, and now they are over 10,000 strong along the coast of Texas. Each summer,

Padre Island National Seashore.

visitors can view the amazing sight of hatchlings being released to the beach here, finding their way to their home in the Gulf. Fifteen to 25 releases happen each year, the result of eggs cared for at a separate incubation facility.

Everything's bigger in the Lone Star State, including the wildlife: The smallest of five species of sea turtles nesting in the Gulf of Mexico, the Kemp's Ridley is still pretty big—it averages about 23 to 27½ inches (58 to 70cm) and weighs in at about 100 pounds. These striking creatures sport an almost circular shell (either dark grey or olive green, depending on age) and feed on crabs found in the Gulf. The turtles reach adulthood at about 10 to 15 years. Grown males will spend their entire lives at sea when hatched, but females find their way back to the beach to lay eggs about every 2 years.

While current population figures are heartening, much work must still be done to restore the turtles to a healthy number. Ironically, drilling is allowed within the park, near the entrance and northern boundary. Although this seems counterintuitive, limitations are in place to protect the beach. When hurricane Ike hit on September 2008, it dropped vast amounts of debris onto the preserve's beaches. The cleanup took about a month to complete and cost over $100,000. Future hurricanes are a concern because debris can make it difficult for turtles to nest. At press time, the beach was also being checked regularly for any signs of tar balls being swept in from the 2010 Gulf Coast oil spill. So far, the area seems to be free of damage, but that could change.

Along with giving you a chance to get up close and personal with turtles, Padre Island offers other ways to commune with nature. The beaches are some of the best on the Gulf—the sand is fine and white, and the water is warm and shallow, perfect for beachcombing, swimming, and fishing. A trip to the island also wouldn't be complete without a stop at **The Laguna Madre,** one of only six hypersalient lagoons in the world. This is a go-to spot for windsurfers, and hosts a dazzling array of bird life. In fact, the entire island is considered the best place to bird-watch in the entire U.S. Guided tours are available from January to April and can be arranged at the Malaquite Visitor Center (see below).

Most of the island is accessible only by four-wheel vehicle, and campgrounds are available on a first-come, first-served basis—book ahead from early June to mid-August, the best months to see Kemp's Ridley turtle hatchlings released back to the Gulf.

ⓘ **Malaquite Visitor Center** (✆ 361/949-8068; www.nps.gov/pais/index.htm)

✈ Corpus Christi Airport

🛏 $$ **Hampton Inn Corpus Christi–Padre Island,** 14430 South Padre Island Dr. (✆ **361/949-9777;** www.hampton inn.com). $$ **Best Western Marina Grand Hotel,** N. Shoreline Blvd., Corpus Christi (✆ **361/883-5111 300;** www.best western.com).

30 By Sea

Crystal River National Wildlife Refuge
Warm Winter Waters for Manatees
Crystal River, Florida

MANATEES, WHICH BREED INFREQUENTLY AND ARE OFTEN INJURED OR KILLED IN BOATING accidents, could be headed for extinction. Crystal River National Wildlife Refuge provides critical warm-water habitat for 15% to 20% of the entire U.S. manatee population.

It's an image out of *Miami Vice:* a cigarette boat slicing cleanly through Florida's warm coastal shallows. But the TV show never dealt with what happens when a speedboat collides with a nearsighted, 10-foot-long (3m), 1,200-pound manatee. One thing is certain: It's a duel that the manatee never wins.

Between speedboat injuries and dwindling habitat, America's West Indian manatee population has shrunk to about 1,200 individuals, nearly a fourth of which winter in the same prime spot: the protected natural springs of King Bay in the Crystal River National Wildlife Refuge. Created specifically for manatees, the refuge features ideal manatee conditions: clear, warm, coastal shallows and spring-fed rivers where the temperature generally stays a steady 72°F (22°C); in warmer weather, manatees migrate north as far as Virginia or North Carolina). The refuge is reachable only by boat, usually on a guided excursion. Several approved local operators (see below) lead daily boat tours out into the manatees' favorite waters to let human swimmers and snorkelers interact with the manatees.

A manatee at Crystal River National Wildlife Refuge.

There are also manatee tours 7 miles (11km) south of Crystal River in the **Homosassa Springs Wildlife State Park,** where the waters are even shallower—only 4 feet (1.2m) deep. Manatees may even come close enough for you to pet their sleek gray-brown skin and feel the whiskers on their droopy snouts. Tours begin as early as 7:30am, when the manatees are around in greatest numbers; you'll be back at the dock by late morning.

After your face-to-face manatee encounter, you can go underwater in a floating observatory in Homosassa Springs Wildlife State Park to watch manatees in action, with thousands of fresh- and salt-water fish darting around them. As you'll notice through the observation glass, this is a rehabilitation facility that nurses manatees that have been injured by boat propellers. The sight of their scarred bodies,

missing fins, and truncated tails is a sad reminder of the threat of their extinction.

ⓘ **Crystal River National Wildlife Refuge** (𝄐 **352/563-2088;** www.fws.gov/crystalriver). **Homosassa Springs Wildlife State Park,** 4150 S. Suncoast Blvd., Homosassa Springs, FL (𝄐 **352/628-5343;** www.floridastateparks.org/homosassa springs).

✈ Tampa International

🛏 $$$ **Plantation Inn,** 9301 W. Fort Island Trail (𝄐 **352/795-4211;** www.plantationinn.com). $$ **Best Western Crystal River Resort,** 614 NW US 19 (𝄐 **800/435-4409** or 352/795-3171; www.crystalriverresort.com).

TOUR American Pro Dive, 821 SE US 19, Crystal River (𝄐 **800/291-3483** or 352/563-0041; www.americanprodive.com). **Sunshine River Tours** (𝄐 **800/645-5727** or 352/628-3450; www.sunshineriver tours.com).

National Chambal Sanctuary
Bloody River in the Land of Taj Mahal
Uttar Pradesh, India

GHARIAL CROCODILES ARE FACING EXTINCTION DUE TO DESTROYED HABITATS AND ILLEGAL NET fishing, and are also believed to be dying from lead and chromium in the water. These crocodiles, called the monarchs of Indian rivers, can be spotted at the National Chambal Sanctuary, along with endangered Ganges River dolphins.

Ancient Indian myth gives the Chambal River some pretty bloody origins—created supposedly by the gushing blood of thousands of holy cows, cruelly slaughtered by the Aryan King Rantideva. But this unholy reputation turned out to be lucky for the Chambal River. Unlike the Ganges and other nearby rivers, it was left alone—and therefore unspoiled. Nowadays it's one of India's most pristine rivers, a crystal-clear waterway winding through Rajasthan, Mayar Pradesh, and Uttar Pradesh.

This long, narrow nature preserve lies only a couple hours' drive from the fabled Taj Mahal, but it seems a world unto itself. It's a tossup as to which rare wildlife sightings are the most exciting along this calm, wide, shallow river. Is it the sight of enormous, narrow-snouted brown gharial crocodiles (the sanctuary plays host to about 800), basking on rocky islands? Or is it a flashing glimpse of Ganges River dolphins (practically vanished from the Ganges), arcing playfully from the shimmering blue-gray surface? Bird-watchers might claim it's the chance to see flocks of beautiful Indian skimmers hunting for fish, dipping their long curved orange bills into the water. Or maybe it's a brown hawk owl, roosting in the fig tree over your head, the marsh crocodiles lazing on the mud banks, or smooth-coated otters sliding into the water's edge.

The dry season (Oct–Apr) is the best time to visit, when the raging monsoon waters recede to leave dazzling white-sand beaches and grassy spits along the river, and migratory birds settle in the shallows and marshes for the mild winter. Nature hikes, jeep tours, and even camel safaris are available, but the best way to explore the sanctuary is via motorboat, cruising through a mazy series of eroded sandy ravines thickly planted with acacias and other thorny tropical scrub thickets. Those forests are full of sambars, nilgiris, blackbucks, wolves, wild boars, and the dreaded dacoits (go with an armed guide for safety). You can also visit a nearby wetlands area that's an important breeding ground for the stately, elegant gray Sarus cranes. You won't see the blood of Rantideva's slaughtered cows, but you won't see pollution or overdevelopment, either.

ⓘ National Chambal Sanctuary, access points near Bah or Nandagaon, Uttar Pradesh

✈ Agra

🛏 $$ **Chambal Safari Lodge,** Jarar (Oct–Apr only; ✆**91/94126 51921;** www.chambalsafari.com)

Turtle Islands Park
From Egg to Hatchling in the South China Sea
Sabah, Malaysia (Borneo)

MANY ADULT GREEN TURTLES ARE ACCIDENTALLY CAUGHT BY FISHING BOATS AND DROWNED; and the survival rate of turtle hatchlings at most nesting sites is very low. Here, visitors can help park rangers gather eggs for incubation and release baby turtles into the sea.

Like a marine version of Cirque Du Soleil, the sea turtles seem to have taken this extraordinary egg-laying act of theirs on the road. Halfway round the globe, the very same drama in Tortuguero ㉗ is enacted every night on a tiny tropical island, off the coast of exotic Borneo.

Pulau Selligan is one of three islands in this state-run nature sanctuary in the Malaysian part of Borneo, that big island in the South China Sea. (Borneo itself is divvied up between Brunei, Malaysia, and Indonesia). Lying 40km (25 miles) offshore from the town of Sandakan, the sanctuary accepts only 50 tourists per night (book with a local tour company). Accommodations are extremely basic, and you have to stay overnight—because this spectacular show plays only nighttime performances.

After arriving by speedboat from Sandakan, you're free to laze around on the beach all afternoon, lulled by the tropical sun and the beautiful blue waters of the Sulu Sea. Here's the extent of your daytime entertainment options: Study turtle exhibits in the park headquarters (two species nest here, green turtles and hawksbills), visit turtle hatchlings being raised in an outdoor nursery, or snorkel on the shallow coral reef that surrounds the island, busy with tropical fish. (Borneo in general is a fantastic scuba destination, though its most renowned site, Sipadan, has recently had resorts removed to prevent further degradation.) On the soft white-sand beaches, you may notice some curious tracks, evidence of last night's turtle invasion—deep round flipper scoops on either side of a wide, shallow groove where the shell drags along.

As darkness falls, all visitors are confined to the park headquarters, waiting for a signal from a ranger. Curtain time could be anywhere from dusk until dawn, and you can't wait on the beach—if the turtles detect humans when they crawl ashore, they turn right around and swim away. Once the signal comes, guests go with a guide down to the beach to watch the female turtles deposit their ping-pong-ball–shaped eggs into a hole they've scooped in the sand. They lay anywhere from 50 to 200 eggs at a time, trying to overcome with sheer numbers the vast odds against any one egg's surviving.

The next act is even more memorable—the audience-participation part of the show. Rangers move the new-laid eggs to a nursery to incubate for the next 60 days—a measure that has dramatically increased the survival of these endangered creatures—and then a number of already-hatched baby turtles are brought down from the nursery for guests to release back into the sea. You actually get to hold a sturdy little hatchling, set it down on the beach, and watch it hustle back into the sea. It's completing the cycle of life—and you helped!

ⓘ www.malaysiasite.nl/turtle.htm

✈ Sandakan

TOUR Discovery Tours, Wisma Sabah, Lot G22, Jalan Haji Saman (© **60/88/221-244;** www.discoverytours.com.my)

33 By Sea

The Cape Town Colony
March of the African Penguins
Cape Town, South Africa

FROM A POPULATION OF TWO MILLION AT THE START OF THE 20TH CENTURY, THE NUMBER OF African penguins has declined more than 90%, and the species continues to slide toward extinction. Oil pollution, overfishing of their food supply, and poaching are ongoing threats.

It was the world's worst coastal bird disaster—an oil spill off the shores of South Africa in 2000 that coated the feathers of some 20,000 African penguins, 40% of the world's population, living on Robben and Dassen islands. Thanks to hundreds of devoted volunteers, the birds were rescued, hand-cleaned, and transferred to a sanctuary, from which they were eventually rereleased into the wild.

Despite that heroic effort, though, the African penguin is still endangered, and in 2010 it was listed on the International Union for the Conservation of Nature's Red list. Its numbers have been depleted by egg and guano poaching (the African penguin prefers to lay its eggs in guano deposits). Overfishing has robbed the ocean of the anchovies, sardines, and squid that they feed on. Fur seals and feral cats prey upon them. With commercial shipping on the rise, oil spills have become more and more frequent. Even conservation efforts may be harming them, as controversy still swirls around the practice of clipping metal tags on their flippers for scientific monitoring purposes.

All the more reason, then, for the penguin reserve at **Boulder Coastal Park.** Surprisingly close to Cape Town, near popular Foxy Beach, a thriving population of some 2,500 African penguins nests among large granite boulders, where they can dig a protected burrow in the sand and lay their eggs. With commercial fishing banned from False Bay, the nearby waters have plentiful fish for the penguins to feed on. Unfazed by the presence of humans, the penguins often waddle right onto Foxy Beach.

African penguins return year after year to this haven, where they breed and nest from fall through winter (that's Mar–Aug in South Africa). You can view them from a raised boardwalk overlooking Foxy Beach—look for eggs in nests, tucked beneath beach vegetation or buried in the sand, or newly hatched chicks covered with fluffy gray down. Older penguin babies have blue-gray backs and white stomachs, in contrast to the adults' black and white with a black stripe across their chests. Even the tallest adults are only about 50cm (20 in.) tall. The

Penguins at Cape Town Colony.

species is also called blackfoot penguins because of their webbed black feet, or jackass penguins because of their braying calls.

Come in the late afternoon, when the seabirds have finished their day of ocean-fish catching and return home to disgorge partially digested fish into the mouths of their chicks. If you're out in the water, you can feel them whiz right past you, swimming at speeds up to 24kmph (15 mph). Technically, they're flightless birds—but underwater, they fly just fine.

ⓘ **Boulder Coastal Park,** in Table Mountain National Park, Cape Town, South Africa (✆ **021/701-8692;** www.cpnp.co.za)

✈ Cape Town International

🛏 $$ **De Waterkant Village,** 1 Loader St., De Waterkant (✆ **021/409-2500;** www.dewaterkant.com). $$ **Best Western Cape Suites Hotel,** Corner of De Villiers and Constitution (✆ **21/461-0727**).

By Land **34**

Hudson Bay
Where Polar Bears Play
Manitoba, Canada

CLASSIFIED AS A THREATENED SPECIES, THE POLAR BEAR FACES ITS GREATEST DANGER FROM global warming. Their habitat is literally melting, and that is making it hard for these striking bears, which previously have thrived at Hudson Bay, to find food.

The Hudson Bay area of Churchill, Manitoba, has a reputation as being the polar bear capital of the world, hosting 13 bear populations. But even this bear stronghold is in danger: The population has decreased 22% in 17 years. There are now fewer than 1,000 polar bears and their condition has deteriorated to the point where the declining weight of the females raises concerns that they will not be able to bear cubs in the future.

For now, at least, you can view these beautiful giants in their Hudson Bay home. While their coats help them blend in, their size makes them easy to spot: They are the world's largest land predators. Adult males can weigh from 775 to more than 1,500 pounds, while females weigh in at about 330 to 500 pounds. Females normally give birth to two cubs, which stay with their mothers for about 2 years. Males lead solitary lives, unless they want to mate, but they take no part in raising the young. Their primary prey is seal, and they hunt for them in open areas of water between ice.

Unlike most bears, polar bears do not hibernate, and most remain active throughout the year. The exception is pregnant

Polar bears at Hudson Bay.

females, which will stay in dens with their young until they are able to hunt for themselves. Both genders can reduce their metabolic rate according to the availability of food. Surviving without food is known as "walking hibernation." In the winter the bears sleep in shallow pits dug in the snow, but in spring and summer, they just curl up on the tundra.

While most adult polar bears keep to themselves, they have been known on occasion to play for hours, and those cute, cuddly-looking cubs are extremely playful. Young males participate in mock fights, to prepare themselves for future bouts with other males. Witnessing this play often makes polar bear fanatics out of bystanders, inspiring many visitors to make return trips.

Despite their size, polar bears are not usually that aggressive or territorial, like grizzlies. A well-fed polar bear will rarely attack a human, but if one gets hungry enough, all bets are off. Because of this possibility, it is imperative to view the bears as part of a guided group. The best time to view the bears depends on ice formation, a period ranging from October to December. October and November are normally peak months for bear spotting. Natural Habitat Adventures (see below) offers tours that allow close-up views of the bears from the comfort of Polar Rovers, so you don't even have to get cold.

ⓘ http://everythingchurchill.com

✈ Churchill Airport, Churchill, Manitoba

TOUR Natural Habitat Adventures (ⓒ **800/543-8917;** www.nathab.com/polar-bear-tours)

---

35 By Land

Newborough Forest
The Squirrel's Tale
Isle of Anglesey, Wales

NEWBOROUGH FOREST IS A CRITICAL HABITAT AND REFUGE FOR RED SQUIRRELS, A NATIVE BRITISH species forced to the brink of extinction by non-native gray squirrels. Community and conservation groups are fighting against plans to clear-cut half of the forest.

The gray squirrel is like a bad downstairs neighbor: He seems like a friendly guy when he moves in, but soon he's intruding on your space, borrowing your food, raising a pack of bratty kids, carrying in nasty germs, and playing loud music all night.

Okay, maybe they don't play music. But the North American gray squirrel—first introduced to England in 1876 as a novelty species, now numbering some 2.5 million throughout the U.K.—is running the native red squirrel off its home turf. Red squirrels are now almost extinct in Wales and England, though they're hanging on in parts of Cumbria, Northumberland, and Scotland. It's not that grays are attacking the smaller, tufted-ear red squirrels—they simply evolved in a more competitive eco-niche. Reds spend up to 70% of their time up in trees, preferably conifers, and hate to cross open ground; grays spend 85% of their time foraging on the ground, like either deciduous or conifer woods, and will travel up to 2km (1½ miles) without tree cover. As Britain's old-growth spruce and pine forests were increasingly replaced with oak trees (grays love acorns; reds can't digest them), the red squirrel was doomed. Fences replaced the protective foliage of hedgerows, so reds no longer had corridors to move from one woods to another. Opportunistic grays, which survive the winter by beefing up in autumn, raided the precious food caches red squirrels needed to get through winter. And the final blow: Grays carry a squirrelpox virus, which they're immune to, but which will kill a red squirrel in 2 weeks.

Red squirrels are still common throughout continental Europe (though grays released in Italy are beginning to repeat the U.K. scenario). But they're a woodland species particularly dear to Britons, and their plight has been watched anxiously. It's been illegal to import gray squirrels since 1930, but the damage was already done. It's been illegal to kill red squirrels since 1981, but that's not enough. They need more conifer forest havens, which is what they've found in the Newborough Forest, in Wales's Isle of Anglesey.

Isolated from the mainland by the Menai Strait, Anglesey began with an aggressive gray squirrel extirpation program, and in 2004 reintroduced red squirrels—brought from Yorkshire, Cumbria, and Scotland, for a healthy genetic mix—to this 750-hectare (1,853-acre) forest park, where they'd been extinct since 1996. Newborough is mostly thick stands of Corsican pines, planted in the 1940s and 1950s to protect the wide beaches and coastal dunes of adjacent Llanddwyn Island. A number of walking trails lead into the dusky woods; as you stroll around, listen for the rustle of squirrels in the branches and look for nest boxes, built to enhance breeding rates, and feeders put out to supplement winter food caches.

At present Anglesey's red squirrel population has boomed to more than 300—nearly half of all the red squirrels in Wales may now be on this one small island. New deadly viruses continue to threaten the squirrels, however. Animal lovers are holding their breaths—will this Cinderella story end in tragedy?

ⓘ **Newborough Forest Reserve,** Newborough, Anglesey, Wales. Save Our Squirrels (www.saveoursquirrels.org.uk). **The Friends of the Anglesey Red Squirrels** (www.redsquirrels.info).

✈ Liverpool

🛏 $$ **Gazelle,** Glyn Garth, Menai Bridge (℅ **44/1248/713364**). $$$ **Tre-Ysgawen Hall,** off B5111, Rhosmeirch (℅ **44/1248 750750;** www.treysgawen-hall.co.uk).

By Land **36**

Red Deer Range
The Great Stags of Scotland
Galloway, Scotland

ONCE NEARLY EXTINCT, THE RED DEER OF SCOTLAND HAVE ADAPTED SO WELL THAT THEY ARE now considered a nuisance. With no natural predators except for hunters, red deer are being blamed for devouring vegetation that supports other animals.

Raising its majestic antlers to the Highlands sky, the red deer is a rugged Scottish icon, as much a fixture of the national image as kilts and whiskey. It's hard to believe that at one time these great beasts were nearly extinct in Scotland.

Looking uncannily like North American elk (though scientists declare they're two different species), the red deer is the U.K.'s largest wild mammal. Once common throughout England, Wales, and Scotland, its traditional stronghold was Scotland's great Caledonian Forest. But as forests across the British Isles—including the Caledonian Forest—were cut down in the 18th century, the red deer began to vanish as well. By the mid–19th century, they seemed well on their way to extinction in the wild.

And yet somehow the red deer have survived, by adapting to different landscapes—pushed north to the cooler, more thinly vegetated mountains and moors of the Highlands, where they browse on heather and blaeberry, rowan, aspen, and willows. The modern red deer is considerably smaller than its ancestors, though, and this may not just be a function of altered diets. Today's red deer are descended not from wild deer but from game herds that British aristocrats traditionally kept on their estates in Scotland, which were eventually released into the wild. Over the years these sportsmen tended to kill the largest and most magnificent stags, thus weakening the genetic pool, whereas natural predators like the wolf, the lynx, and the brown bear (all now extirpated from Britain) helped strengthen the genetic stock by culling the old and the weak. Another size factor may be hybridization with the smaller sika deer, imported as game animals from Japan.

Whatever they've done to survive, as many as 350,000 red deer now roam in Scotland—quite a comeback. In fact, some farmers are beginning to complain about too many red deer, overgrazing sparse pastureland. One proposal to control deer numbers is to reintroduce the wolf to the Highlands. It's as if nature has come full circle.

A reliable place to observe red deer in the wild is not in the Highlands, but down in the Lowlands, in **Galloway Forest Park.** From A712, halfway between New Galloway and Newton Stewart, a .8km (.5-mile) trail leads to a viewing area where a number of red deer are protected in their own woodland range. (Nearby is a similar range for wild goats.) This area is ancient farmland that's been allowed to go back to forest, and the deer have happily returned—you can even observe their rutting rituals in the autumn, with stags proudly clashing antlers. One can only imagine how bonny they were once, in their Caledonian prime.

ⓘ **Galloway Forest Park,** Clatteringshaws, A712 (✆ **44/1671/402420;** www.forestry.gov.uk/gallowayforestpark)

✈Prestwick

🚃Dumfries

🛏$$ **Longacre Manor,** Ernespie Rd., Castle Douglas (✆ **44/1556/503-576;** www.kayukay.co.uk/dumfrieshotels/longacrecastledouglas.html). $$$ **Fernhill Hotel,** Portpatrick, Dumfries and Galloway (✆ **44/1776-810-220;** www.mcmillanhotels.co.uk/fernhill-hotel/index.html).

---

37 By Land

Regional Nature Park of Corsica
Welcome Home, Deer
Corsica

PEOPLE ARE THE BIGGEST THREAT TO CORSICA'S REGIONAL NATURE PARK. TOURISM HAS SPARKED plans to build new parking lots and allow more motorized vehicles in the park. Additionally, professional arsonists have been setting fire to large sections of the park.

It may be called the Corsican red deer, but since 1970 there weren't any more left on Corsica. There were 300 Corsican red deer, however, in a sanctuary on neighboring Sardinia. And so in 1985, two breeding pairs were shipped across the strait between the two islands, launching a great experiment: to restore the Corsican red deer to Corsica.

Nowadays as many as 150 Corsican red deer live on this large Mediterranean island off the coast of Italy (though officially it has been part of France since 1768). Carefully bred in special reserves in the Parc Naturel Regional du Corse, which covers almost 40% of the island's rugged interior, they are then released into the wild in increasing numbers. Smaller than most types of European red deer, the Corsican deer has shorter legs—the better to scramble up mountains, perhaps—as well as shorter antlers and a longer tail. If you want to get technical, they are an introduced species, having been brought to the island 8,000 years ago from North Africa by seafaring Phoenicians. But having evolved as a separate species from North African red deer (which are practically extinct themselves), they qualify as natives by now—all the more reason to make sure they live here.

In Corsica's Mediterranean climate—hot, dry summers and mild, rainy winters—the characteristic local terrain is maquis, a low shrubby growth of juniper, gorse, myrtle, and oleander mixed with a dizzying profusion of scented herbs: rosemary, thyme, lavender, and marjoram. It's an aroma that native Corsicans (like Napoleon Bonaparte) never forget. But Corsica's mountainous interior also has forests more typical of northern Europe, especially old-growth evergreen oak forest (mostly holm oak and cork oak), the Corsican deer's preferred habitat, where they browse on fresh buds and branch tips.

Corsica's coastal lowlands were cleared long ago, however, and more recently grazing and logging have eaten into the mountain forests. Tourism is an important industry here, but most holidaymakers head for the Riviera-like beaches, or take scenic drives around the spectacular rugged coast; the idea of protecting those inland forests for eco-tourism has only recently taken hold. But with a well-developed system of long-distance hiking trails crisscrossing the island, Corsica's interior makes a great hiking area. Hiking is the prime way to spot the island's many endemic species—a rare mountain sheep known as the mouflon, the little Corsican nuthatch, a rare woodland salamander, and several small orchids and ferns. And, of course, the red deer—if you see one when you're out walking, welcome him home.

(i) **Parc Naturel Regional du Corse,** information office in Corte (✆ **33/4-95-46-26-70;** www.parc-naturel-corse.com)

✈ Ajaccio

🛏 $$–$$$ **Les Roches Rouges,** Piana (✆ **33/4-95-27-81-81;** www.lesroches rouges.com). $ **Colombo Porto,** Route de Calvi (✆ **33/4-95-26-10-14**).

By Land 38

Okapi Wildlife Reserve
Held Hostage in the Congo
Northeastern Democratic Republic of the Congo

WAR IS AN ONGOING THREAT TO BOTH PEOPLE AND ANIMALS IN THE CONGO, CAUSING SERIOUS damage to conservation efforts. In 2011, President Laurent Kabila was assassinated, hinting at continued conflict in the Congo's never-ending civil war. Coltan mining also threatens this fragile ecosystem.

In July 2002, war crashed into the Ituri Forest. This pristine stand of evergreen rainforest—traditional home to the Mbuti pygmies and a refuge for thousands of elephants, primates, and the endangered okapi—was invaded by two opposing insurgent groups in the Democratic Republic of the Congo's ongoing civil wars. They looted and plundered local villages, driving out the deeply traditional Mbutis for the first time in history. They set up camp in the forest, ruthlessly dining on chimpanzee.

The soldiers have left now, and thankfully not one okapi was lost. But it was a major setback to all the progress made by conservation officials since 1992, when one-fifth of the Ituri was set aside as the Okapi Wildlife Reserve. Nearly a third of the world's okapi population lives here, along with forest elephants, leopards, forest buffalo, pangolin, water chevrotain, and at least 13 different primates. Major threats to this forest habitat have been poaching for bush meat, deforestation, and small-scale gold mining. All of those illegal activities sprang back quickly when the staff was forced to leave in 2002, and since their return, it's been an uphill battle. Although relative peace has returned to the reserve after the recent assassination of President Kabila, care must be taken when visiting the Congo; it is estimated that unrest has claimed as many as five million lives here, and hostilities continue. If you visit, it's best to go as part of a group and check travel advisories before planning your trip.

Also keep in mind that if you venture into the war-torn DRC to visit the Ituri Forest, you might not be able to see any okapis—they are notoriously elusive, their striped legs providing ideal camouflage for moving silently through these dense green forestlands. (Even the pygmies rarely spot any.) The only known relative of the giraffe, these tall creatures live nowhere else but the Congo basin; though it's hard to pin down their numbers, it's estimated that as many as 6,000 may live here in the Ituri Forest. You may be able to see some at the reserve's research center, which tends to injured okapis (often rescued from traps) and breeds some in captivity, sending a few of their offspring to zoos to keep the genetic pool varied (unlike the early days of this breeding center, established in 1952 to capture wild okapis and ship them off to American and European zoos). Several Mbuti earn a living at the center by gathering leaves for the fussy okapi to eat, since these forest experts know exactly which trees these beautiful, shy creatures favor.

It's not a place for the casual tourist—at least, not yet. But conservation efforts include converting local people from a dependence on poaching and destructive farming practices into sustainable agriculture and eco-tourism skills—convincing them to regard the rainforest's rich flora and fauna as a precious resource worth protecting. In 2010, a few committees fortunately were established to address these problems. Eco-tourism could be the saving of the Ituri Forest—and of the okapis.

✈ Goma

TOUR Go Congo Tours (✆ **243/811-837010;** www.gocongo.com)

By Land

39

Bwindi Impenetrable Mountain Forest
The Last of the Great Apes
Virunga Mountains, Uganda

ONLY A FEW HUNDRED MOUNTAIN GORILLAS STILL EXIST AND ALL ARE INCREASINGLY AT RISK FROM a variety of threats, including poaching, habitat destruction, and diseases transmitted by humans and war. Bwindi's lush forest isn't easy to get to, but it is well worth it if you want to see these great apes.

Impenetrable as this mountain forest may be, there's one compelling reason to venture here: mountain gorillas. Gorilla safaris are an important tourist draw for Uganda, since nearly half the mountain gorillas in the world are found in one 330-sq.-km

(127-sq.-mile) preserve, in the southwestern corner's Virunga Mountains, where Rwanda, the Congo, and Uganda meet.

Considering only 790 or so of these magnificent primates are left (the other, smaller groups are nearby in Rwanda's Volcanoes National Park and the Congo's Virunga National Park), it's impressive that Bwindi has so many. Bwindi now has four groups of gorillas to visit, each clan gathered around at least one silverback (adult male). You may not see all of them while you're here, though—the process involves tracking them through the densely verdant park. Slopes can be slippery, and the forest floor is matted with tangled vines, mouldering leaves, broken ferns, and fallen branches. But along the way you may also see chimpanzees, blue monkeys, or black-and-white colobus monkeys, with their flowing white tails and wizened faces. You might even surprise elephants, giant forest hogs, or small shy antelopes.

Once located, mountain gorillas provide spectacular viewing, because they are most active during the day, and spend more time on the ground than other primates, browsing and grooming and lolling about. Darker and larger than other gorillas, with longer hair (suitable for their cool high-altitude home), these apes have such humanlike feet and such intelligent dark brown eyes that it's easy to feel a spontaneous connection. They're endangered for the usual sad reasons—poaching, habitat destruction, diseases contracted from humans, war (it's still unknown whether the Congo gorillas survived a September 2007 outbreak of violence), and human interference (oil companies want to drill on the preserve).

You'll need a special government permit, obtainable either through your tour operator or by directly contacting the **Uganda Wildlife Authority,** Plot 7 Kira Rd., Kamwokya, P.O. Box 3530, Kampala, Uganda (© **256/414-346 287** or 256/414-355 000, fax 256/414-346 291; www.uwa. or.ug). Permits are strictly controlled and in great demand, so plan up to a year in advance. Only 12 tourists a day are allowed into Bwindi to track gorillas, though you may see some researchers as well, since it is a major international base for primate research. The dry seasons (Jan–Feb and June–Sept) are best for trekking through this damp, lush woodland.

They could just as well have called it the Bwindi Inaccessible Forest, because it's so hard to reach. Getting to Bwindi from Kampala requires a long drive on dusty roads across most of Uganda. But if it hadn't been so inaccessible, the ancient rainforest wouldn't have been left undisturbed—and the gorillas wouldn't still be here.

✈ Kampala

TOUR Abacus Vacations Ltd., Kampala (© **256/312-261 930,** 256/752-827 492, or 256/772-331 332; www.abacusvacations. com). **Jewel Safaris,** Kampala (© **256/772-867 943;** www.jewelsafaris.com).

By Land **40**

Dja Faunal Reserve
Gorillas Going, Going, Gone . . .
South-Central Cameroon

POACHING IS A SERIOUS PROBLEM IN THE DJA FAUNAL RESERVE. WHEN TIMES ARE HARD, MANY low-income people in the region supplement their diets or their incomes with bush meat. In 2010, construction also began on a Trans-African highway, which will run along the reserve's southern boundary, and could make access easier for poachers.

Not so long ago, the mountain gorillas were the ones in real danger. These days, things look even grimmer for their lowland cousins.

It was bad enough that widespread logging and cocoa and coffee plantations were eliminating their rainforest habitat. Then falling prices for African coffee and cocoa drove more of the local population to poaching (an adult gorilla yields an awful lot of bush meat). Now an epidemic of Ebola virus has swept like wildfire through central Africa, killing more than half of the lowland gorilla population, especially in the Congo and contiguous areas like Lobeke National Park.

The gorillas at Dja are still hanging in there, though. Ever since 1932, when Cameroon was still a French colony, this peaceful patch of jungle nestled into a great loop of the Dja River enjoyed protected status; 90% of it is still untouched evergreen rainforest, with a dense tree canopy nearly 60m (200 ft.) high. Though extensive logging and agriculture line its borders, there's never been any inside the reserve. All local residents were moved out in 1946—vines and creepers invade the shells of their abandoned villages. The only hunters permitted are local pygmies, using traditional methods, although the reserve has such limited staff (don't expect rangers or a visitor center), enforcement of the hunting ban is haphazard.

Dja is an unbelievable hot spot for primates—not only gorillas, but chimpanzees, black-and-white colobus, pottos, mangabeys, guenons, talapoin monkeys, and mandrill baboons with their colorful red-and-blue face masks also thrive. Between the jungle and the river, it's also a great birding area, with several species of finches, sunbirds, flycatchers, woodpeckers, turacos, barbets, and hornbills; unusual birds here include Bates's weavers, Dja River warblers, and rare breeding colonies of gray-necked picathartes (rock-fowl). A few elephants wander through, scaly anteaters and wild boars root around, and leopards silently stalk smaller creatures like buffaloes, warthogs, striped bongos, and the odd marsh-dwelling antelopes called sitatungas.

No animals stalk the lowlands gorilla, though. The biggest and most powerful of all primates—males can be 1.8m (6 ft.) tall, females 1.5m (5 ft.)—they seem laid-back and sociable, plucking leaves and berries as they roam the jungle. Generally they're more slender and agile than the mountain species, colored gray or brown rather than black, with tufts of reddish hair on top of their skulls. But poachers have made them wary of humans—it's most likely you won't see one on a casual hike through the reserve. You'll have to become a gorilla detective, looking for their droppings, mats of flattened grass where they've rested, perhaps remnants of the sleeping platforms they build in trees every night as they migrate around the park.

Dja's future is uncertain. With increased tourism, Dja Faunal Reserve would inevitably add much-needed facilities, but floods of day-trippers might damage virgin habitat.

ⓘ **Dja Faunal Reserve,** east of Sangmélima (✆ **237/23-92-32**)

✈ Yaounde

🛏 $$$ **Hilton Yaounde,** Blvd. du 20 Mai, Yaounde (✆ **237/2-223-36 46;** www1. hilton.com). $$ **Mercure Yaounde Centre,** Av. El Hadj Ahmadou Ahidjo (✆ **237/2-222-21 31**).

The Bifengxia Panda Base
The Chinese Giant After the Quake
Ya'an City, China

ONLY ABOUT 1,600 GIANT PANDAS STILL LIVE IN THE WILD, AND THAT NUMBER IS DECREASING steadily. Roughly 10% of the world's population lived at Wolong Nature Reserve in Sichuan until a 2008 earthquake forced them to relocate—now the best place to view pandas in the area is the Bifengxia Panda Base.

In 2003, in an effort to help the giant panda (one of the planet's most endangered species and a symbol of goodwill for the Chinese nation), the Bifengxia Panda Base opened as part of the world's largest giant panda migration. In 2008, a devastating 7.9 earthquake struck the Sichuan Province of China. Almost 70,000 people were killed, and extensive damage was done to a sister panda base in Wolong, about 4 hours from Chengdu. Amazingly, only one panda was lost, one injured, and another missing from the Wolong Nature Reserve. But in the chaos that followed the disaster, the Wolong pandas were temporarily moved to the Bifengxia Panda Base in Ya'an, Sichuan, making Bifengxia China's most important panda protection program.

Of course, it would be the thrill of a lifetime to glimpse a giant panda in the wild—sighting one of these shy, highly endangered black-and-white bears in its native bamboo jungle would be an incredible coup. But until the Wolong Nature Reserve reopens, you can be sure of seeing giant pandas, and lots of them, at Bifengxia—and you'll be supporting panda preservation in the process.

Bifengxia's natural landscape is beautiful, with waterfalls, forest, rolling rivers, and expansive grounds covering almost 15,000 acres (6070ha). Whenever possible, after training in this wild but protected zone, feral pandas are returned to free-range environments. Six kinds of bamboo grow here, and more than 80% of the habitat is covered in vegetation, so it is panda paradise. More than 20 spots in the broad-leaf-shaded grounds have been set aside for panda-related activities—including dedicated grazing grounds, "kindergartens" for young pandas, and a panda hospital/nursery/research institute.

The panda base's most important contribution lies in research on panda procreation. Pandas reproduce very slowly—often a female will bear only one child in her entire lifetime—and their young often die in infancy. These issues are the biggest factors in the shrinking panda population, more even than poaching or habitat destruction.

Various volunteer options are available at the base so that you can help out. During your time volunteering at this mountain getaway, you will be trained in the care of pandas and might be asked to do a range of tasks, from cleaning enclosures, preparing their vegetarian diet, gathering and recording behavioral data, and the part you'll talk about most when you get home--interacting with the adult and baby pandas.

ⓘwww.cnto.org
✈Ya'an

Sepilok Orang Utan Rehabilitation Center
The Art of Being an Orangutan
Sandakan, Malaysia

ORANGUTANS ARE ONE OF THE MOST ENDANGERED SPECIES IN MALAYSIA. FOUND ONLY IN Borneo and Sumatra, the orangutans' survival is constantly threatened by loss of habitat—due to logging, burning, or agriculture—and illegal hunting.

It isn't easy being an orangutan.

First of all, their home territory is the rainforests of Borneo and Sumatra—where rainforest has been disappearing at an alarming rate over the past 50 years, hacked down for timber or cleared for palm oil plantations. Solitary, territorial creatures, orangutans don't thrive when they are crammed into increasingly small patches of habitat. These large vegetarians (males can be 1.5m/5 ft. tall and weigh 200 lb., though females are half that) need massive amounts of fruit to eat—but in the less fertile higher elevations they're being forced into, there are fewer fruit trees than in the lowlands. Ten years ago, there were perhaps 27,000 orangutans in these forests. Today, there may be less than 10,000, and fewer every day.

Exclusively tree dwellers—the world's largest arboreal mammals, which even find their drinking waters in the treetops—orangutans don't have a tail to swing from tree to tree like their neighbors, the proboscis monkeys. They use their arms instead to move around the rainforest canopy, which is probably why their arm span is up to 2.4m (8 ft.) wide. Baby orangutans are undeniably cute, but that's a problem too, since poachers supplying

A baby orangutan at Sepilok.

the illegal pet market kill adults to steal their babies. Even their intelligence works against them—mothers need at least 6 years to pass on their complicated survival techniques to their young. When they lose their mothers as babies, they are deeply, deeply at risk.

That's where the Sepilok orangutan sanctuary comes in. Founded in 1964, this 43-sq.-km (17-sq.-mile) facility abutting the **Kabili Sepilok Forest Reserve** takes in orphaned young orangutans (many of them confiscated from poachers), feeds and nurses them—and teaches them all the skills their mothers would have taught. Today about 25 youngsters live at the sanctuary; another 60 to 80 have already been released into the reserve. Contact with humans is minimized to keep them from getting too dependent on humans, but from a walkway visitors can watch them being fed daily at 10am and 2:30pm. After that, you can hike through the reserve where you may spot more, swinging through the trees as nature intended. (*Hint:* Look for nests up in the canopy—an orangutan makes a fresh nest in a new spot every night.) A half-day walk on the Mangrove Forest Trail will take you past

water holes through transitional forest, lowland rainforest, and on into the mangrove forest. In the forest, look for mouse deer, wild boars, gibbons, macaques, and fleshy-nosed proboscis monkeys; the mangrove swamp is home to dugongs and dolphins.

The sanctuary also houses a couple of endangered Sumatran rhinos, and occasionally other animals such as Malaysian sun bears, gibbons, or elephants. Sandakan is on the northwestern coast of Borneo, which is part of Malaysia; with dazzling beaches, preserved rainforest, and offshore coral reefs, it's a popular destination for those who love outdoor sports—and orangutans.

ⓘ **Sepilok Orang Utan Rehabilitation Centre**, 25km (16 miles) west of Sandakan (✆ **60/89/531180**). **Orangutan Appeal UK** (www.orangutan-appeal.org.uk).

✈ Kota Kinabalu

🛏 $$ **Sepilok Nature Resort** (✆ **60/ 89/765200**; http://sepilok.com). $ **Sepilok Jungle Resort**, Labuk Rd., Sandakan (✆ **60/89/533031**; www.sepilokjungle resort.com).

By Land **43**

Corbett National Park
Tiger, Tiger, Burning Bright
Northern India

INVASIVE SPECIES AND WEED INFESTATION CONTINUOUSLY THREATEN CORBETT NATIONAL PARK. Partly to blame is the Ramganga River Project, which changed the character of the park by replacing large tracts of grassland habitat with wetlands.

Of course you want to see a tiger. You're in India; you can't go home without seeing a Bengal tiger.

In 1973, the Indian government's Project Tiger was launched right here, at India's oldest national park, to protect the country's drastically dwindling tiger population. Tiger poaching is still a widespread underground industry, so Project Tiger has had

to step up its efforts, adding roughly 40 other sites. At press time, however, the Indian government was questioning its policy of promoting "tiger tourism" after concerns were raised that increasing tourists contribute to the decline of the species.

For now, sprawling Corbett, spread along the banks of the Ramganga River in the foothills of the Himalayas, remains a huge draw, not least because it's a lot more accessible than the other Project Tiger sites. Streams feeding into the Ramganga furrow Corbett's terrain into wooded ridges and ravines, with sal and bamboo forests providing excellent cover for predators such as Bengal tigers (there are reportedly 150 in the park), leopards, and black bears. Wild boar snuffle around the trees, while a host of rhesus monkeys chatter overhead, warning of loitering pythons. Meanwhile herds of wild elephants, delicate spotted deer, sambars, and four-horned antelopes (chausingha) roam the park's grassland savannas (chaur). Flocks of cormorants, marsh mugger crocodiles, and enormous golden mahseer carp share the river, and endangered gharial crocodiles lazily poke their long snouts up out of the Ramganga Reservoir. (A no-swimming sign on its shore warns that survivors will be prosecuted.)

Perhaps the best way to go looking for tigers is to take a 2-hour elephant ride from either Dhikala or Bijrani, tracking through the forests and across the plains, at either sunup or sunset when the tigers are most active. Book your place a day in advance if possible. If you do see a tiger, it's customary to give your elephant handler (mahout) an extra tip. Night safaris are

another good option for spotting tigers and leopards, but you must book these with a tour operator—you're not allowed to drive your own car through the park at night.

Excursions of all kinds, from nature walks to bird-watching to jeep safaris to elephant rides, are usually booked through your hotel. Permits are required for entering the park—Corbett is divided into five tourist zones, and you're allowed to visit only one at a time (schedule a few days here if you want to see a range of habitats). March through June is the best season for wildlife viewing; the park is closed during the monsoon season, mid-June through mid-November, when the Ramganga floods its banks and park roads become impassable.

ⓘ **Corbett National Park,** Ramnagar (✆**91/5947/25-1376**)

✈ Delhi

🚆 Ramnagar

🛏 $$ **Claridges Corbett Hideaway,** Zero Garjia, Dhikuli (✆**91/5947/28-4133**; www.corbetthideaway.com). $$$ **Infinity Resorts,** Dhikuli (✆ **91/5947/25-1279**; www.infinityresorts.com).

44 By Land

Wild Ass Wildlife Sanctuary
Salty Tales in the Indian Desert
Gujarat, India

SALT-MINING OPERATIONS NEARBY DESTROY NATIVE HABITAT AND CREATE AIR AND NOISE pollution that threaten Gujarat's endangered wild asses. It is also home to most of India's highly polluting textile, pesticide, and chemical plants.

In the Little Rann of Kutch, the animals don't need a calendar to know what the season is. When the monsoons sweep through this low-lying desert land (*rann* means desert in Gujarati), only a few humps of land rise above the flood. Some 2,000 animals cluster on the islands, or

bets, waiting out the rains. Once the waters recede, though, the lower land becomes a vast salt flat, and the animals spread out to browse on the dry thorny scrub. Up the slopes from the flats, animals can also graze on less salty intermediate areas known as *kala-lana*. Toward the end of the dry season, they drift back toward those bets, where the last thick stands of grass still grow.

This is the largest wildlife sanctuary in India, nearly 5,000 sq. km (1,930 sq. miles), originally founded in 1972 to protect India's rare wild asses, one of the last three species of wild ass in the world (the other two are in Central Asia and Tibet). About 2,000 of these Indian wild asses survive today, all here in the Rann of Kutch. The blazing heat of summer and long weeks of drought conditions are nothing to these hardy little creatures. With their tawny backs and white underbellies, they blend perfectly into the desert salt-flat landscape. They're just about impossible to catch, because they can reach a speed of 70km (43 mph), and can sustain a 24kmph (15 mph) pace for a good 2 hours at a time; tracking them on an open jeep safari is your only hope of getting a sustained up-close sighting.

Along with the asses, the sanctuary harbors blackbuck, chinkara, hedgehog, wolf, jackal, fox, striped hyena, caracal, jungle cat, and desert cat. There are birds here, too—cranes, flamingoes, larks, pelicans, falcons, even the rare Houbara bustard—although they tend to settle in during the monsoons, where the land is one vast marsh, and migrate elsewhere when things get dry. Watchtowers have been set up for panoramic wildlife observation; sunrise or sunset are prime viewing times.

Looking at this bleak desert landscape, you'd think there would be no competition to threaten the wild asses, but there is. Since this is a saline desert, salt mining is a major local industry, yielding 25% of India's salt supply, and illegal operations steal into the park continually. There's also an Indian army firing range within the sanctuary. Still, it takes a lot to shake the Indian wild ass from its native ground. So far, nobody has.

ⓘ **Wild Ass Sanctuary,** Zainabad, India

✈ Ahmedabad or Bhuj

🚆 Viramgam

🛏 $$ **Rann Resorts,** near Dasad Village (www.india-safaris.com/resorts-in-dasada.html). $ **Desert Coursers,** east of Hwy. 10 (✆ **91-22-240-4-2211;** www.nivalink.com/desertcoursers/contact.html).

By Land 45

Komodo National Park
Here Be Dragons
Indonesia

KOMODO NATIONAL PARK IS HOME TO THOUSANDS OF KOMODO DRAGONS—A TYPE OF MONITOR lizard whose large size and aggressive nature earned it a scary name. Although the Komodo population has stabilized, there are threats to the environmental integrity of their home.

It takes a tough species to survive on a place like Komodo Island. This rugged volcanic island off the northwest tip of Flores, Indonesia, is wickedly hot and dry 8 months of the year—and then the monsoons drench it. Much of the island is rocky and barren, with patches of hardy savanna, bits of mossy bamboo cloud forest on higher ridges, and a tropical deciduous forest in the valleys, full of trees that are water-retention specialists.

Not many species can make it here, but the king of the island looks perfect for the job: the Komodo dragon, world's biggest lizard, a scaly monster 2.4 to 3m (8–10 ft.) long that hasn't evolved much in 4 million years. This hefty reptile weighs anywhere from 100 to 330 pounds, depending on

A Komodo dragon.

how recently it has gorged on carrion. But it's no mere scavenger: The Komodo lies in wait in the grass, springs out and slashes its victim (Timor deers, wild pigs, buffaloes) with powerful serrated teeth, and then lets them struggle off into the bush to die, poisoned by bacteria in the Komodo's saliva. Flicking its forked yellow tongue, the lizard "tastes the air" to detect the scent of rotting flesh, then ambles over to the corpse and feasts. Komodos are not only carnivores, but cannibals; they'll even eat their young, which are forced to spend their first few months of life in the rainforest canopy to escape being eaten. (Luckily, they hatch just after the Jan–Feb rainy season, when there's plenty to eat up there.)

There are nearly 6,000 of these "dragons" (really a giant monitor lizard) on Komodo and a few neighboring islands, and most park visitors come here in hopes of sighting one. A Komodo station at Loho Liang is baited twice a week to draw Komodos for tourist viewing. You may also catch them basking in the sun in the early morning, raising their body temperatures (they are, after all, cold-blooded) before slinking off to hunt.

The park was initially established in 1980 to conserve the Komodo dragon, but as their population has stabilized, the real issue has become what's happening offshore, in the seagrass beds, mangrove forests, and coral reefs that make this a superb scuba diving destination. Tidal currents make these interisland waters particularly rich, with more than 1,000 species of fish as well as dugong, sharks, manta rays, whales, dolphins, and sea turtles. But several fishing villages remain within the park, all established before 1980, and their population has boomed to some 4,000 villagers. Intensive fishing is damaging the reefs and exhausting the waters—but can conservation officials deny the resident population their traditional livelihood, just to satisfy international environmental ideals? It's a hot issue, with no easy answer in sight.

ⓘ **Komodo National Park,** Loho Liang, Indonesia (www.komodo-gateway.org). **Komodo Foundation** (www.komodo foundation.org).

✈ Bima

🛳 From Sape (Sumbawa Island) or Labuan Bajo (Flores Island)

TOUR Flores Exotic Tours, Labuan Bajo, Flores (✆ 62/385-270-5022; www.komodo island-tours.com). **Floressa Bali Tours** (✆ 62/361-467625; www.floressatours.com).

By Land
46

Ujung Kulon National Park
Java Hideaway
Java, Indonesia

UJUNG KULON NATIONAL PARK IS ONE OF THE LAST EXTENSIVE AREAS OF LOWLAND RAINFOREST in Java and the final refuge of the Java rhinoceros. Rhino poaching is still a serious threat to the small population of Java rhinos that inhabit the park.

The Indian rhinoceros has it easy, compared to Asia's other one-horned rhino, the Java rhinoceros. Fewer than 60 individuals remain, scrounging around this once-remote peninsula of earthquake-prone Java, in the shadow of the feared volcano Krakatoa. (Another half-dozen cousins have been reported in Vietnam.) Slightly smaller than their Indian cousins, with different folds in their thick-skinned "armor," these Javans also have a long upper lip—and why not, since they're really pachyderms. Hiding out in the dense lowland forests of this protected park, they're safe at last from the widespread poaching that whittled their numbers so drastically; they're also far from the agricultural crops they used to raid, which gave them an unfair local reputation as pests.

This part of Java used to be farmland too—until August 1883, when the offshore volcano Krakatoa erupted, killing more than 36,000 people. Farmers fled and, with continued eruptions over the years—in 1952, 1972, 1992, 1994, 2011—they never moved back. The jungle reclaimed the land swiftly, especially fast-growing figs and palms. Protected by the sea on three sides and mountains on the other, the peninsula's like a Hollywood version of tropical beauty, with loads of orchids clambering over the trees—luminous white moon orchids, deep red pipit orchids, mauve dove orchids, and tiny white squirrel-tail orchids, which open for only 1 day—and large soft-petaled blossoms scattered over the beach every dawn.

The rhinos roam widely over these densely forested lowlands, which are especially active at night; they leave the tree cover to wallow in mud pools and venture onto beaches, but few park visitors actually spot one. Still, as you hike around Ujung Kulong trails, look for telltale rhino hoof prints and droppings on the trails. Be careful: Javan rhinos can run as fast as humans, and they're likely to charge fiercely if they see you.

The Javan tiger was driven out over 40 years ago, but leopards, wild dogs, fishing cats, civets, and the Javan mongoose still thrive. Ujung Kulon also has five rare species of primates: the glossy black Javan silverleaf monkey and its slightly heavier gray relative the grizzled leaf monkey in the mountains; black-faced gray Java gibbons and nocturnal slow lorises in the forest; and long-tailed crab-eating macaques, which scamper around beaches and reefs at low tide. More than 250 species of birds live here, mostly hidden in the dense tree canopy (you'll hear their songs, all right), as well as a number of herons and storks and other water birds in the freshwater swamp and mangrove forest along the north coast.

The best way to get here is by boat from Labuan (5–6 hr.), where you can get entrance permits and make lodging reservations at the PHPA parks office; hire required local guides at Tamanjaya.

ⓘ **Ujung Kolon National Park,** visitor center at Tamanjaya. International Rhino Foundation (www.rhinos-irf.org)

✈ Jakarta

🛏 Several guesthouses in Tamanjaya and Peucang Island

TOUR **Wanawisata Alamhayati PT,** Jakarta (© **62/21-571-0392** or 21/570-1141). **Arthamara Wisata** (© **62/21-** **887-2924;** www.thousandisland.co.id). **Travelindo, Yogyakarta** (© **62/27-454-1409;** www.travelindo.com).

47 By Air

Michoacán Monarch Biosphere Reserve
Butterflies Are Free—and Homeless?
Near Morelia, Mexico

MONARCH BUTTERFLIES FACE A VARIETY OF RISKS ALL ALONG THEIR 2,000-MILE (3,220KM) migration route between Canada and Mexico, including pesticides and inclement weather. Meanwhile, deforestation of their winter habitat could be the fatal blow to their survival.

If anyone gave a prize for long-distance migration, monarch butterflies would clearly win. Their yearly autumn trek is over 2,000 miles (3,220km)—pretty amazing considering that not a single individual in the immense swarm has ever flown the route before. (After all, they were hatched only a few weeks earlier.) And yet, without a GPS system, they head unerringly for the same nesting grounds high in the mountains of northeast Michoacán, Mexico, where their ancestors have overwintered since time immemorial.

Monarchs at Michoacán.

But the fate of the species hangs on the fate of those nesting grounds—and right now, things are looking dismal. Relentless logging of the surrounding pine and oyamel (fir) forests is gobbling up the monarchs' habitat at a fearsome rate. Living close to the poverty line, the local loggers—*los ejidatarios*—use cheap methods that completely strip the mountainsides. With denuded mountain slopes surrounding the Michoacán Monarch Biosphere Reserve, 45% of the nearby forest canopy has degraded over the past 30 years. Without the protection of a healthy microclimate, a severe winter storm in January 2002 killed 75% to 80% of the monarch butterfly population. In 2001, the first steps were taken when Mexican President Vicente Fox established the Monarch Trust to protect the monarchs' winter home, but much still needs to be done. Without a long-term reforestation program, these glorious black-and-orange wonders could cease to exist forever.

The ancient Aztecs revered these poisonous butterflies, which they believed were the reborn spirits of fallen warriors, dressed in battle colors. (Note that the first butterflies tend to arrive on Nov 1, Los Dias de Los Muertos—the Day of the Dead.) Stepping into a grove of monarch-laden fir trees is like stepping into a kaleidoscope, with fragments of obsidian and gold flitting randomly around you. The branches on all sides sway under the weight of the butterflies, their gossamer wings whispering softly as the wind blows through the forest.

There are actually seven monarch nesting grounds in Michoacán (nesting season lasts from mid-Nov to Mar). Only two, however, are open to the public: **El Rosario** and **Chincua,** both reachable by day trip from the colonial-era city of Morelia, about halfway between Mexico City and Guadalajara. It is possible to visit the sanctuaries on your own, but a licensed English-speaking guide is a worthwhile investment—guides can answer scientific questions, transport you reliably over the back roads to the sanctuary, and steer you right to the nucleus of the butterfly colony, which constantly shifts around the mountain throughout the season.

ⓘ **Michoacán Monarch Biosphere Reserve,** near Angangueo and Ocampo, Mexico

✈Morelia

🛏$$$ **Villa Montaña Patzimba 201,** col. Vista Bella, Morelia (✆**800/223-6510** or 52/443-314-0231; www.villamontana. com.mx). $$ **Best Western Hotel Casino,** Portal Hidalgo 229, Morelia (✆ **52/443-313-1328;** www.hotelcasino.com.mx).

TOUR Natural Habitat Adventures (✆**800/543-8917;** www.nathab.com)

By Air **48**

Veracruz River of Raptors
Raptor Rapture
Veracruz, Mexico

EVERY YEAR, MILLIONS OF NORTH AMERICAN RAPTORS COME TO VERACRUZ, STOPPING TO REST en route to their winter habitats in Latin America. Threats include habitat loss due to agriculture, ranching, and development.

It's not a real river at all, not in the watery sense—but when you see the stream of huge birds soaring overhead, you'll know why this migration route is traditionally referred to as the River of Raptors.

It's a bird-watching miracle you'll never forget. Each fall, large predatory birds funnel into the state of Veracruz, Mexico, soaring in from every major North American flyway en route to their winter grounds in Central and South America. Some five to six million cruise through, including just about all the broad-tailed hawks, Swainson's hawks, and Mississippi kites in existence. There are a million-and-a-half turkey vultures, not to mention sharp-shinned hawks, American kestrels, merlins, northern harriers—just about any swooping avian predator you can think of.

It's a sort of geographic fluke, a bottleneck created where Mexico's eastern Sierra Madre converges with the east end of the central volcanic belt, pouring into a narrow lowland passage in east-central Mexico. Add to that the effect of abundant thermal updrafts in this warm coastal plain, and you've got ideal flying conditions for big birds like these raptors, which are already tired from their long migrational flights.

And so they arrive, between late September and mid-October. One great base for viewing them is Cardel, a coastal town surrounded by lowland thorn forest and lagoons that provide prey for those hungry raptors. Set up in the afternoons with your binoculars and telephoto camera lenses (find a spot in the shade—it can be very warm here) and you'll be astonished at the number and variety of raptors you may identify. Note how they converge toward a useful thermal, swirling one after another into an upward spiraling vortex, known as a "kettle." Coming out of the kettle into a long straight glide, they tend to settle into layers according to body weight, with heavier birds like turkey vultures riding at the bottom, streamlined broadwings cruising at the top.

Another prime raptor-viewing site is right where the bottleneck occurs: up in the mountains at Xalapa, a handsome colonial-era city that's the capital of Veracruz. This stunning highland landscape (you may recognize its wooded gorges and tumbling waterfalls from the movie *Romancing the Stone*) has cloud forests, shade-coffee plantations, and pine-oak forests that harbor many other interesting bird species to watch when you get tired of the raptors. As if you could ever get tired of the raptors.

✈ Veracruz

🛏 $$$ **Hotel Mocambo,** Boca del Rio, Veracruz (🕾 **229/932-0205;** www.hotel mocambo.com.mx). $ **Hotel Colonial,** Miguel Lerdo 117 (🕾 **229/932-0193**).

TOUR Pronatura/HawkWatch International (🕾 **800/726-4295** or 801/484-6808; www.hawkwatch.org). **Borderland Tours** (🕾 **800/525-7753** or 520/882-7650; www. borderland-tours.com).

49 By Air

Colca Valley
The Flight of the Condors
Southern Peru

THE ANDEAN CONDORS THAT GLIDE ABOVE PERU'S COLCA VALLEY ARE AN ENDANGERED species—only a few thousand still exist. Programs designed to reintroduce these enormous birds to the wild are working to increase their number, but much work lies ahead.

It's a simply stunning Andes panorama: the Rio Colca gorge, twice as deep as the Grand Canyon, set amid towering volcanic peaks. Now just imagine how it looks from the high-flying perspective of an Andean condor.

A condor in the Colca Valley.

Colca Canyon was largely unexplored until the 1970s, but now it's a popular region for rafting, rock climbing, and mountain biking, organized through tours from the handsome colonial city of Arequipa. En route to the canyon, you'll drive through a string of traditional villages, isolated from modern times until roads were built in the 1980s. Local farmers have dealt with the mountain geography by building elaborate terraces for their crops; some of these terraces are 1,000 years old, surviving centuries of avalanches, landslides, earthquakes, and volcanic eruptions, which have always been a fact of life around here.

The road passes through the Salinas and Aguada Blanca Nature Reserve, where alpacas, guanacos, and vicuñas graze on the thin scrub of the altiplano plateau. While llamas and alpacas are common domestic animals, grazing near every village (llamas are raised as pack animals, alpacas for their wool), guanacos and vicuñas are wild endangered species, quicker and more delicate than their sturdy, shaggy cousins. Their tawny deerlike coats blend perfectly into the dry grasses. As you drive past, identify which is which—guanacos are larger than vicuñas, with black faces, while vicuñas have a slight camel-like hump. Peru still has more than any other country, but poaching is rapidly depleting the numbers of these graceful mountain camels.

The town of Chivay is most tours' overnight base, where you can adjust to the thin mountain air. Tours venture out next morning to the **Cruz del Condor,** an overlook 1,200m (3,940 ft.) high on the rim of the canyon, where you can witness a truly awesome natural spectacle: the world's largest birds in flight. Andean condors are so big (their wingspans average around 3.5m/11½ ft.), they can't just take off from the ground like other birds—every morning they jump from a cliff and gradually ride upward on thermal air currents rising from the canyon. From Cruz del Condor, you'll see these giant beauties circling the gorge below, rising higher with each circle, until eventually they are flying right above your heads.

An up-close view of these majestic birds is an unforgettable experience, and you'll wish it went on all day—but it doesn't. Once in the air, the condors go off in various directions searching for carrion, and the camera-clicking tourists leave. The birds return in the late afternoon—the homeward leg of their commute—but it's not as spectacular. June through September is the best time to witness large numbers of condors, but their numbers are dwindling every year. Don't put this one off.

✈Arequipa

TOUR Giardino Tours (☎ **51/54/221-345;** www.giardinotours.com). **Southern Exploration Tours** (☎ **877/784-5400;** www.southernexplorations.com/peru-travel).

Bracken Bat Cave &
Eckert James River Bat Cave
Sunset at the Bat Cave
Texas

FOR YEARS, BATS HAVE BEEN GIVEN A BAD RAP, WHEN, IN REALITY, THEY PLAY IMPORTANT ROLES in pest control, pollination, and producing guano used as fertilizer. Threats to this species include human interference and a slow reproduction rate.

It makes for a dramatic sight: at dusk, millions of bats rise from their cave and darken the sky as they rise upward, looking for prey. The swarm keeps growing, swirling like a tornado, the high-pitched chirps and screeches rising to deafening levels. Their prey, of course, is not human blood, but insects—each of these little brown bats has to eat nearly its own weight in insects each night, including thousands of mosquitoes, moths, and cutworms. It's nature's pest control, and it's a whole lot better than DDT.

The Bracken Bat Cave is the world's largest bat colony, hosting more than 20 million Mexican free-tailed bats during the summer months and offering visitors the chance to view a spectacle they'll never forget. The cave is located on 697 acres (292 hectares) of Texas Hill country in Schertz and is protected by Bat Conservation International. Without their efforts, this pristine area would have been swallowed by subdivisions. Instead, each summer, pregnant bats give birth to a single pup in June or July, and put on an awe-inspiring aerial show every evening at dusk.

It's one of the few places on earth where you can still observe this fragile species. Because Mexican free-tails live in such huge colonies, human interference with just one roosting site can wipe out a significant percentage of the species, and they reproduce so slowly that they can't catch up; their numbers keep declining dramatically every year.

Visitors can visit the preserve March through October, but they must buy a membership to **Bat Conservation International** (© **512/327-9721**). Each member is allowed to bring three guests, and the preserve provides an email with directions after a visit has been booked. The maximum number of visitors allowed is 60, so everyone gets a good view of the bats.

Another great spot to see Mexican free-tails is just a 2-hour drive away—the Eckert James River Bat Preserve, which is one of the largest bat nurseries in the country. The 8-acre (3.2-hecatare) preserve's immense cave provides a habitat for some four million pregnant bats between May and September. Besides protecting this specific site, the refuge also aims to educate the public about bats in general.

A century ago, ranch owner W. Phillip Eckert saw this cave as a productive source of bat guano, which he mined and sold as crop fertilizer. In 1990, his grandson saw the cave in an entirely different light: He and his wife donated it to the Nature Conservancy as a bat refuge. The conservancy now runs interpretive tours of the site from mid-May to early October, Thursday to Sunday from 6 to 9pm. (Some sunrise tours where you can watch bats returning to the cave are also available.) It's important to call ahead to check on the status of the James River, since it is prone to flash floods.

(i) **Bracken Bat Cave,** Schertz, TX (✆ **512/327-9721;** www.batcon.org). **Eckert James River Bat Cave Reserve,** James River Rd., Mason, TX (✆ **352/347-5970;** www.nature.org)

✈ San Antonio

🛏 In San Antonio and Schertz: $$$ **Hyatt Regency San Antonio,** 123 Losoya (✆ **220/222-1234**). $$ **Fredericksburg Inn & Suites,** 201 S. Washington, Fredericksburg (✆ **800/466-0202** or 830/997-0202; www.fredericksburg-inn.com).

By Air **51**

Aransas National Wildlife Refuge
The Story of the Gulf Survivors
Austwell, Texas

RISING SEA LEVELS AT THE ARANSAS NATIONAL WILDLIFE REFUGE THREATEN TO DROWN OUT beaches that provide critical habitat for many bird species, including the whooping crane, once nearly extinct.

It's a story environmentalists like to tell over and over again, to lift their hearts when they get discouraged: how North America's largest bird, the whooping crane, was brought back from the brink of extinction. By 1941, there were only 15 of these beautiful giants left—an entire species, reduced to just 15 birds. Yet today, thanks to a dedicated team of conservationists, their numbers are back up to roughly 250 individuals in the wild, and still growing.

To look at a whooping crane, you wouldn't call it fragile or vulnerable—an adult male stands a full 5 feet (1.5m) high, with a commanding 7-foot (2m) wingspan. But cranes are not rapid reproducers. Females don't begin to lay eggs until they are 4 years old, and when they do, they lay two eggs but hatch only one chick. To save the species, wildlife biologists decided to steal the second egg (the mother's going to abandon it anyway) and hatch it elsewhere. Using those extra hatched chicks, the scientists have been able to establish a few new flocks elsewhere and get the whooping cranes back on the road to survival.

The descendants of those 1941 survivors still winter down on Texas's gulf shore in the Aransas National Wildlife Refuge;

technically, they are the only natural population in the world. Though these cranes migrate some 2,400 miles (3,900km) up to the Northwest Territories of Canada in summer, they faithfully return here every year from November through April, where they feed on blue crabs, crayfish, frogs, and wolfberries. Beginning in late winter, you can observe them from a 16-mile (26km) paved road that loops through several habitats; the best views are from the 40-foot (12m) observation tower or on a boardwalk trail through a salt marsh to the coast. To be certain of seeing whooping cranes, however, you can book a half-day guided tour along the shoreline in a shallow-draft boat past the birds' most popular waters.

With the luxurious long legs and throat typical of shorebirds, whooping cranes have an especially elegant plumage—solid white, with just a touch of black on the wing tips and around the eyes, like an artful touch of mascara, and a dashing red cap on the top of the head. If you're lucky, you may see their distinctive courtship ritual, a dance that includes wing flapping, head bowing, acrobatic leaps into the air, and—yes, you guessed it—loud whooping.

(i) **Aransas National Wildlife Refuge,** FM 2040, Austwell, TX ((C) **361/286-3559;** http://southwest.fws.gov/refuges)

✈ Corpus Christi

🛏 $$–$$$ **The Lighthouse Inn,** 200 S. Fulton Beach Rd., Rockport ((C) **866/790-8439** or 361/790-8439; www.lighthouse

texas.com). $$ **Village Inn Motel,** 503 N. Austin St., Rockport ((C) **800/338-7539** or 361/729-6370).

TOURRockport Chamber of Commerce ((C) **800/826-6441** or 361/729-6445; www.rockport-fulton.org)

---

52 By Air

The Eagles of Skagit River
Baldy Bed & Breakfast
North Cascades Mountains, Washington

RISING AIR AND WATER TEMPERATURES COULD HAVE A PROFOUND EFFECT ON BIRD AND OTHER animal species and the intricate ecosystem that supports them. For now, hundreds of bald eagles have found refuge at Skagit River.

Bald eagles know a good thing when they find one. Escaping the frigid Canadian winter, they cruise down to the North Cascades of Washington State, to a cozy little spot on the Skagit River. They know what happens here every December through February: Millions of exhausted chum salmon, coming to the tail end of their spawning runs, are going to wash up dead on the gravel bars of the Skagit. As far as the eagles are concerned, it's an all-you-can-eat buffet.

The accommodations can't be beat, either: old-growth forests of hemlock, cottonwood, and Pacific silver fir, perfect roosting trees for bald eagles. No wonder this is one of the best bald-eagle wintering grounds in North America—by mid-January, as many as 300 baldies may be hanging out here. The premium suites are Barnaby Slough's thick stands of mature cottonwood, alder, and bigleaf maple, set right by the shallows where those tasty dead salmon pile up, ripe for the plucking—it's nature's version of room service. If that hotel's sold out, there are plenty of other trees elsewhere, thanks to a cooperative effort by various state, federal, and private entities, which have combined

parcels of land along this Skagit corridor to protect the eagles.

Humans can't go into the eagle refuges, but with so many birds around, it's easy viewing right from the roadside. Stop in first at the Skagit River Interpretive Center to get maps and other information. Three special eagle observation sites have been set up, all along State Road 20: at **Howard Miller Steelhead Park,** at the **Mile Post 100 rest area,** and at the **Marblemount Fish Hatchery,** where you may also enjoy a weekend tour of their salmon spawning operations. Trained eagle guides are on hand to help you get the best sightings. The best times of day are dawn until about 11am, at which point the eagles are satiated and head back to their roosts to nap and digest. Cloudy days are actually better for viewing, because on sunny days the eagles tend to soar farther afield after their meal, joy-riding on the updrafts rising from the Skagit River Valley.

For a really exciting up-close view, take a guided 10-mile (16km) raft trip down the Skagit from Marblemount to Rockport. You're not allowed to enter the river until after 11am, so the eagles' brunch won't be disturbed, but there's still plenty to see

10 Places to Sight Big Game

African hunters called them the Big Five: the lion, leopard, rhinoceros, elephant, and Cape buffalo—the five trophy animals that were hardest to find, most dangerous to stalk, and toughest to kill. Today, safari tours offer a different kind of shooting—with cameras, not guns—but the rare and elusive Big Five are still a thrill to spot. Except for Cape buffaloes, these species are all threatened or endangered in the wild. If you're heading for Asia instead, focus on the even more endangered Bengal tiger, Asiatic lion, Asiatic elephant, and Indian rhinoceros.

A zebra in Masai Mara.

53 Masai Mara, Kenya   The Masai Mara is the northern end of the Greater Serengeti migration corridor, a land of lush grasses where Kenya's richest concentration of wildlife gathers. More than a million wildebeest pass through here, along with zebras and gazelles, and predators like lions, cheetahs, and hyenas lurk in the acacia trees. *Abercrombie & Kent:* ✆ **800/554-7016** or 630/954-2944. www.abercrombiekent.com. *Micato Safaris:* ✆ **800/642-2861** or 212/545-7111. www.micato.com.

54 Samburu National Reserve, Kenya   This is one of Kenya's lesser known big-game parks, but it definitely deserves a visit. Its location along the Ewaso Nyrio River attracts such stars as lions, leopards, and cheetahs and it's home to more than 900 elephants. Adding to this embarrassment of riches are rare species like the reticulated giraffe, gerenuk, ostrich, and beisa oryx. You can stay on-site and the park offers game drives, as well as bird-watching and nature walks. *Edge East African Safaris:* ✆ **27/021-762-2180.** www.east-africa-safari.com. *Africa Geographic Travel:* ✆ **254/020-218-9909.** www.africageographic.com.

55 Ngorongoro Crater, Tanzania   This ancient collapsed volcanic caldera in Tanzania is like a great fertile 19km-deep (12-mile) bowl, a self-contained 264-sq.-km (102-sq.-mile) wilderness that's home to some 30,000 animals. Lions, black rhinos, and elephants can be easily spotted in the relatively short grass. *Micato Safaris:* ✆ **800/642-2861** or 212/545-7111. www.micato.com. *Overseas Adventure Travel:* ✆ **800/493-6824.** www.oattravel.com. *Abercrombie & Kent:* ✆ **800/554-7016** or 630/954-2944. www.abercrombiekent.com.

56 Lower Zambezi National Park, Zambia   Elephants are the chief draw in this relatively undeveloped park across from Zimbabwe's Mana Pools. Canoeing along the Zambezi through a flood plain rich in acacia, winterthorn, and baobab trees, you'll see large herds of elephants, as well as buffaloes, waterbucks, kudus, zebras, lions, and leopards. Swarms of hippos populate the river pools, and more than 300 bird species roost along its banks. *Wilderness Safaris:* www.wilderness-safaris.com. *Geographic Explorations:* ✆ **800/777-8183** or 415/922-0448. www.geoex.com. *Abercrombie & Kent:* ✆ **800/554-7016** or 630/954-2944. www.abercrombiekent.com.

57 Palmwag Concession, Namibia   Camel-back expeditions into this private conservation area in the remote and rocky red hills of Damaraland focus on the last remaining free-ranging black rhinos, as well as desert-adapted Namibian elephants. Along the way you'll also view Hartman's mountain zebra, giraffe, oryx, springbok, kudu, and possibly lions, hyenas, and leopards. *Wilderness Safaris: www.wilderness-safaris. com. Geographic Explorations:* © **800/777-8183** *or 415/922-0448. www.geoex.com.*

58 Chobe National Park, Botswana   Botswana's oldest national park specializes in elephants—some 120,000 are drawn by Chobe's baobab trees, a vital water source in this semi-arid Kalahari Desert region. During the dry season the river is a vital watering spot for thousands of animals, including spectacular zebra migrations, large groups of giraffes, and plentiful wildebeest. *Odysseys Unlimited:* © **888/370-6765** *or 617/454-9100. www. odysseys-unlimited.com. Overseas Adventure Travel:* © **800/493-6824.** *www.oattravel.com.*

59 Hwange National Park, Zimbabwe   Near Victoria Falls and along the edge of the Kalahari Desert, Hwange offers a mix of teak forests and arid savanna, where man-made water holes have been placed to attract the grazing hordes: giraffes, sable antelope, buffaloes, and so many elephants that there's been talk of culling the herd, especially after recent droughts. Hwange has rare brown hyenas and one of the last populations of African wild dogs. *Overseas Adventure Travel.* © **800/493-6824.** *www.oattravel.com.*

60 Kruger National Park, South Africa   Huge Kruger National Park has more mammal species than any other African game park, 147 in all. The large Sabi Sands Game Reserve, which includes the well-known bush camp Mala Mala, is one of the best places to view leopards in the wild. *Backroads:* © **800/462-2848** *or 510/527-1555. www.backroads.com. Abercrombie & Kent:* © **800/554-7016** *or 630/954-2944. www.abercrombiekent.com. Wilderness Safaris: www. wilderness-safaris.com.*

A lion in Kruger National Park.

61 Gir Wildlife Sanctuary, India   The African lion has it easy compared to his Asiatic cousin. Somewhere around 300 Asiatic lions are left, and all live in this verdant region of Gujarat, part of Gir National Park. Other species in the park include king vultures, hyenas, leopards, nilgai, chinkara gazelles, and chousinghas. *Taj Gir Lodge.* © **866/969-1825** *in North America, or 800/4-588-1-825. www.tajhotels.com.*

62 India's Project Tiger Parks   If you don't sight a Bengal tiger at Corbett **43**, Panna **197**, or Sundarbans **115** National Parks, you will at Ranthambore National Park or Bandhavgarh National Park, where the tiger population is even denser. Elephants and one-horned rhinos are the main attraction at Kaziranga National Park. *Big Five Tours & Expeditions.* © **800/244-3483** *or 772/287-7995. www.bigfive.com.*

along the river, including the beavers, river otters, and black bears that work this river, too—that is, once the eagles have finished bellying up to the buffet.

ⓘ **Skagit River Interpretive Area,** Howard Miller Steelhead Country Park, 52809 Rockport Park Rd., Rockport (ⓒ**360/ 853-7626;** www.skagiteagle.org; Fri–Mon)

✈️ Seattle/Tacoma

🛏️$ **Buffalo Run Inn,** 60117 State Rd. 20, Marblemount (ⓒ **877/828-6652** or 360/873-2103; www.buffaloruninn.com). $$ **Grace Haven,** 9303 Dandy Place, Rockport (ⓒ **360/873-4106**; www.word ofgraceministries.homestead.com/grace haven.html).

TOUR Blue Sky Outfitters (ⓒ **206/938-4030;** www.blueskyoutfitters.com). **Wild-water River Tours** (ⓒ **800/522-9453** or 253/939-2151; www.wildwater-river.com).

By Air **63**

Hakalau Forest Refuge
Under the Volcano
Upcountry Hawaii

SEVENTY-FIVE PERCENT OF ALL U.S. SPECIES THAT HAVE BECOME EXTINCT ARE HAWAIIAN, including half of the islands' native bird species, and many more are threatened or endangered. Some members of these endangered species have found safe haven in Hakalau.

You need to call ahead to get the combination to unlock the refuge gates—that's how carefully this sanctuary for forest birds is guarded. Even so, you can visit only on weekends. But the Big Island of Hawaii has a right to be protective of its native birds; there aren't many, and they're disappearing fast.

Driving on the Saddle Road across Hawaii's rugged interior, you'd hardly expect to find a rainforest—not on the volcanic slopes of Mauna Kea, the world's tallest mountain (if you count the fact that it starts thousands of feet under the ocean surface). But the eastern slopes of Mauna Kea get a lot of rain—250 inches (635cm) annually at the lower elevations—and lush tropical greenery will flourish here, given half a chance. While the upper reaches of this 33,000-acre (13,400-hectare) refuge are still rebounding from years as a cattle ranch (ongoing work is replacing over-grazed pastures of alien grasses back to native vegetation), the lower elevations feature beautiful stands of tall koa trees

and red-blossomed ohia. There are even two lobelia trees, many species of which are endangered.

The name *hakalau* means "many perches," and there couldn't be a better description of this bird-rich habitat. Flitting through the closed-canopy forest, these endemic birds are bright with tropical color; with patience and a good pair of binoculars, you should spot several. Three kinds of honeycreepers live here: the yellow amakihi and the tiny scarlet iwi and apapanes, with their sharply curved beaks to dig deep for nectar in ohia blossoms. (**Note:** The iwi's the one with the red beak; the apapane's is black.) Then there's the dusky yellow chickadee-like Hawaii creeper; the plump little blue elepaio, a flycatcher that snags its prey in midair; the yellow aki-apolaau, with its bright black eye and a curved beak to dig caterpillars out of trees; the finchlike orange honeycreeper known as the akepa; and the omao, which looks like a robin but with a soft blue breast.

Soaring above the canopy, you may even spot the endangered Io, the buff-and-brown Hawaiian hawk that many traditional Hawaiians claim as their aumakua, or guardian spirit. The hawks do what they can to get rid of the feral cats, rats, and mongooses that prey on small forest birds, but the refuge's rangers still need to be vigilant as well.

You'll need a four-wheel-drive vehicle to get up here, what with bumpy Saddle Road (Hwy. 200), a 2-mile (3.2km) climb north up steep Mauna Kea Summit Road, and then 17 miles (27km) east on gravel-surfaced Keanakolu Road to that locked gate. But to see birds like this, it's worth it.

(i) **Hakalau Forest Refuge,** Keanakolu Rd., Hawaii (© **808/443-2300;** www.fws. gov/hakalauforest)

✈ Hilo

🛏 $$–$$$ **The Palms Cliff House Inn,** Honomu (© **866/963-6076;** www.palms cliffhouse.com). $ **Dolphin Bay Hotel,** 333 Iliahi St., Hilo (© **808/935-1466;** www. dolphinbayhilo.com).

TOUR Hawaii Forest & Trail (© **800/ 464-1993** or 808/331-8505; www.hawaii-forest.com)

---

64 By Air

Booby Pond Nature Reserve
Safety in Numbers
Little Cayman Island

COMMERCIAL FISHING IS DEPLETING THE RED-FOOTED BOOBIES' FOOD SUPPLY WHILE COASTAL development is eliminating many of the trees and shrubs where the birds nest. Another threat is hurricanes predicted for the coming years. A good place to observe these improbable-looking birds is Little Cayman Island, which has the largest colony in the Western Hemisphere.

If this scene had a soundtrack, you'd hear ominous drum rolls and deep bassoons: Cue up a massed horde of red-footed boobies, thousands of them, hovering tensely at twilight above the Caribbean Sea. Now enter, stage left, a circling crew of magnificent frigate birds, marauders famous for stealing other birds' food, stretching their 2.4m-wide (8-ft.) pointed black wings. The boobies draw a breath; then suddenly they spiral upward in a column, wheel swiftly, and dive like torpedoes toward shore. The magnificent frigate birds dart in to attack. Who will win this battle for survival?

This drama is played out every evening in nesting season on Little Cayman Island, an isolated, sparsely inhabited scrap of coral and sand in the Caribbean Sea, due south of Cuba. About 5,000 nesting pairs of red-footed boobies—the largest colony of this species in the Western Hemisphere, a third of all the red-footed boobies in the entire Caribbean—hatch their chicks each February in the landlocked saltwater lagoon of Little Cayman's 82-hectare (203-acre) Booby Pond Nature Reserve. By day, the red-footed boobies roam long distances from Little Cayman, flying as far as Cuba or Jamaica, to fill their crops with squid and small fish to take back to their chicks. Back at the lagoon, they disgorge that food into the chicks' waiting beaks—that is, if they can get past the frigate birds first.

The smallest species of booby, the red-footed boobies are still good-size birds, with a wingspan of nearly 5 feet (1.5m). Adults are either buff-colored or white with dark wingtips, blue bills, and, of course, unmistakably bright red feet. Their wetland nesting grounds are strictly off-limits to visitors, but lookout platforms have been built around the edges of the pond so you can witness this twilight battle; there are also telescopes on the veranda of the visitor center, a traditional Caymanian gingerbread bungalow.

During the day, other rare water birds visit the pond as well, including the shy West Indian whistling duck and a lot of snowy egrets, pure-white long-necked birds with a distinctive shaggy plume at the back of their heads. Instead of red feet like the boobies, they have yellow feet at the end of long black legs—they almost look as if they have stepped in paint.

While the boobies' daily struggle with the frigate birds is dramatic, a more serious drama here is Cayman's susceptibility to hurricanes. When 2004's Hurricane Ivan devastated Little Cayman, ornithologists waited nervously for news of the boobies' nesting grounds. Luckily, the mangroves survived, and the colony's numbers have held steady. In 2008, Hurricane Paloma pounded the island with high winds and rains, but the hearty little boobies survived yet again. Will they be so lucky next time?

(i) **Booby Pond Nature Reserve,** near Blossom Village, Little Cayman (www.nationaltrust.org.ky/info/rfboobies.html)

✈ Grand Cayman

⊨ $$ **Paradise Villas Resort,** Paradise Villas Lane (✆ **345/648-0001** or 877/322-9626; www.paradisevillas.com). $$ **The Anchorage,** Seven Mile Beach, Grand Cayman (✆ **813/333-6532** or 345/945-4088; www.theanchoragecayman.com).

By Air 65

Kapiti Island

A Haven for Kiwis

New Zealand

THE LITTLE SPOTTED KIWI CAME TO THE ATTENTION OF THE ENGLISH ORNITHOLOGIST JOHN GOULD in 1847. Unfortunately, that discovery came at a big cost to the birds, already besieged by predators. Isolated Kapiti Island is a haven for these intriguing national icons.

New Zealanders love their national bird, the kiwi; they even proudly refer to themselves as "Kiwis" from time to time. But these days it's well-nigh impossible to see these funny, flightless birds in the wild, unless you visit their main sanctuary: Kapiti Island. There, you'll find the largest population of this bird in the world. The island's wildlife preserve also hosts other varieties of rare birds (gannets, penguins, terns, and shearwaters, to name just a few) and an abundance of sea life.

Kapiti was forged after being lifted by an earthquake and eroded by an ocean, and today this temperate sanctuary rises to 521m (1,709 ft.) above sea level. The New Zealand government has managed the island for over a hundred years in an effort to protect the native animals and plants that call the unique landscape home. Through their efforts, the island is entirely free of predators. Along with a wealth of wildlife, visitors can observe evidence of tribal groups that once inhabited the island—including Maori chief Te Rauparaha, who commanded his empire from here during the 1800s—through historical sites and artifacts.

But the island's main event, of course, is spying the endangered little spotted kiwi—distinguished from other types of kiwis by its distinctive spots. Adults are about the size of a bantam, and all have sharp talons and a long beak, perfect for digging into the ground to find insects and grubs; these kiwis are also known to eat fruit. Overnight kiwi-spotting walks are available and are the best way to view the birds. Along the way, you may spot some of the other unusual native birds on the island, including the weka, saddleback, stitch bird, North Island robin, and the royal spoonbill.

Visitors to Kapiti can also enjoy a stop at a seal colony with a guided cruise, and the island's coast is a great place to spot whales and seals. The **Kapiti Marine Reserve** is popular among divers and snorkelers, and, as luck would have it, it is near the **Kapiti Nature Lodge,** which offers rustic cabin accommodations with stunning views. Meals and bathroom facilities are located by the main building; meals at the lodge are communal, making it easy for you to swap stories of animal sightings with other travelers.

Day trips are also available. A ferry departs from the Kapiti Boating club at Paraparaumu Beach, located 50km (31 miles) north of the capital city of Wellington. Whether you come for the day or stay overnight, a permit is needed to visit. One can easily be obtained through the lodge,

Kapiti Island.

or through **Wellington Bookings** (✆ **64/4/ 384-7770**).

ⓘ www.kapitiislandalive.co.nz

✈ Paraparaumu Airport

🛏 **Kapiti Nature Lodge** (✆ **64/6/362- 6606;** see website above).

66 By Air

Mission Beach
Make Way for Cassowaries
Queensland, Australia

CASSOWARIES HAVE LOST ABOUT **50%** OF THEIR CRITICAL HABITAT IN THE PAST DECADE, AND living close to humans puts them in danger. In February 2011, they were dealt an even greater blow when the Yasi cyclone wiped out many of their food sources and devastated the Mission Beach area.

The people of Mission Beach are rightfully proud of their cassowaries and are making great efforts to ensure the survival of this endangered bird in the wake of a cyclone that claimed 11 birds and damaged vital rainforest where the birds feed. When Yasi touched down, it caused significant damage to buildings and many people were left homeless. It's a testament to the local love of cassowaries—Australia's largest land creatures—that a major post-storm priority was to ensure their survival; at press time, volunteers and government agencies were working together to implement conservation plans, including setting up feeding sites in the area.

Although complete reconstruction will take a while, tour operators are hopeful that Mission Beach will soon rebound and even flourish as a tourist destination. Before the cyclone, the area had managed to fly under the tourist radar—quite a feat, considering that Mission Beach is only an hour's boat ride from the Great Barrier Reef. When you take the Mission Beach turnoff from the Bruce Highway, at first you seem to be in the middle of nowhere. Dense tangled vine forests almost hide the town from view until you round the corner to Mission Beach proper, an appealing cluster of shops, restaurants, and hotels. You know you're finally here when you see the sign: danger—cassowary crossing.

If Mission Beach weren't so laid-back, the cassowaries wouldn't have stayed here. After all, these highly endangered 1.8m-tall (6-ft.) birds abandoned areas like the Mabi Forest inland—a significant loss for those forests, since roaming cassowaries disperse an extraordinary number of seeds in their excrement. Scientists reckon only about 900 southern cassowaries remain in the Wet Tropics, but about 100 of these ostrichlike black birds live in the last patches of rainforest around Mission Beach, which is actually a cluster of four small towns strung along an 18km-long

(11-mile) beach. Before the 2011 storm, the area was known as a surprisingly diverse habitat, with half of the world's remaining licuala fan palms, six ancient flowering plant families, and 60% of all Australia's butterflies. (As the rainforest recovers, the flora and fauna are expected to rebound as well.)

Though they mostly keep to the forest, cassowaries have been known to stroll right through town, cruising for the fallen fruit and low-hanging fruit that's the staple of their diet. (Being flightless, they can't forage any higher than that.) They're certainly spectacular to look at, with a peacock blue neck, long red wattles, and a stiff blue casque like an Aztec headdress. Despite their stately walk, however, they're aggressive creatures, with enormous claws that can swiftly disembowel an enemy. Never approach one, and if you do accidentally disturb one, back off slowly and hide behind a tree.

Even in conservation-minded Mission Beach, cassowaries have lost about 50% of their critical habitat in the past decade. And living around humans really isn't healthy for them, between dog attacks, car accidents, and the temptations of unsuitable snacks stolen from humans. (Never hand-feed a cassowary.) Still, Mission Beach promotes itself as the cassowary capital of the world, and officials are hopeful that all the recent media attention will encourage more people to want to preserve these astonishing birds.

(i) **C4 Environment Centre,** Porters Promenade, Mission Beach (© **61/7/4068 7197;** www.cassowaryconservation.asn.au)

✈ Cairns

🛏 $$$ **The Elandra,** Mission Beach (© **61/7/4068 8154;** www.elandraresorts. com). $ **Mackays,** 7 Porter Promenade, Mission Beach (© **61/7/4068 7212**).

3 Islands

A Cozumel reef.

Madagascar
Land of the Lemurs
Off the Coast of Eastern Africa

FOR GENERATIONS, THE PRACTICE OF SLASHING AND BURNING FORESTLAND HAS BEEN AN ACCEPTED way for impoverished locals to create farmland. But this practice has decimated Madagascar's interior forests. Political unrest makes the future of the island even more uncertain.

Fourth-largest island in the world? That's impressive to start with. But now consider that a hefty 5% of the world's species live on this Indian Ocean island, off Africa's east coast—and nearly 75% of those species live nowhere else. That's why Madagascar is such a vital destination for any nature lover.

You'll see the glorious yellow comet moth with its 20cm (8-in.) tail, the sticky-pawed tomato frog, neon-green day geckoes, petite chameleons less than an inch long, spiny insect-gobbling tenrecs, and leathery-winged flying foxes. Though Madagascar has only 258 bird species, nearly half of them are also unique to the island, including the pheasantlike ground birds known as couias. The only amphibians here are frogs—but there are 300 species of them, nearly all endemic.

Madagascar has cornered the market on lemurs; no other country has any lemurs whatsoever. In Madagascar, though, lemurs seem to drip from the trees, in both the rainforest and the western dry forest. They come in all shapes and colors and sizes, resembling pandas, raccoons, monkeys, rats, bats, whatever you can imagine. It's truly mind-boggling.

A village in Madagascar.

But like many other undeveloped countries, Madagascar has seen wide deforestation and the ravages of slash-and-burn agriculture (coffee, sugar cane, and vanilla are its main exports). The interior's dense woods have mostly been leveled, and the tropical rainforest areas are rapidly following suit. With their habitats reduced, those one-of-kind species are increasingly endangered. Several species have already been lost due to human depredation—pygmy hippos, the stately elephant bird, giant tortoises, and lemurs. Former President Marc Ravalomanana had backed aggressive conservation programs, but current President Andrew Rajoelina overthrew him with the help of rebel soldiers in 2009. Attempts have been made on Rajoelina's life and further political turmoil makes the future of conservation on the island uncertain.

Andasibe-Mantadia National Park, a 3-hour drive from the country's capital Antananarivo, is the most accessible wildlife preserve, known especially for the black-and-white lemur called the indri, whose cry sounds uncannily like a whale song. Farther south along Route 7 lies the country's most developed rainforest park, Ranomafana (60km/37 miles from Fianarantosa), a romantic terrain of rocky slopes, waterfalls, and moss-draped trees. Continue south for L'Isalo National Park, where you can hike around tapia forests, narrow canyons, and sheer sandstone crags. On the east coast near Morondava you can gape at the Avenue of the Baobabs, a remarkable collection of those upside-down tropical trees, another of Madagascar's specialties.

Even if you're normally a go-it-alone traveler, it's advisable to take an organized tour to Madagascar, especially if you want to move around the countryside. Local roads are spotty at best, and booking hotels can be a gamble. You'll need local guides, anyway—how else will you tell all the different lemurs apart?

 Antananarivo

TOUR **Madagascar Travel** (℆ **44/20 7226 1004** in the U.K.; www.madagascar-travel.net). **Ilay Tours** (℆ **33/1-4253-7161** in France, or 261/2022-390 36; http://madagascarilaytours.com).

68 Islands at Risk

Bali
Trouble in Shangri-La
Indonesia

ONLY ABOUT 38% OF INDONESIA'S PRISTINE FORESTS REMAIN, AND MUCH OF THE DESTRUCTION has taken place in the past few years due to wholesale burning by businesses and locals to create farmland and make charcoal.

What a canny choice of location for the December 2007 U.N.-sponsored conference on global warming. White-sand beaches, sparkling blue seas, lush gardens, and a wide assortment of luxury resorts—a perfect setting for those environmental delegates, for if they began to get depressed about the fate of the planet, all they had to do was look out the window and they'd feel just fine.

Bali seems to have it all—exotic Southeast Asian culture, tropical Pacific natural beauty, and a tourism infrastructure that can coddle even the most finicky Western travelers. But on closer inspection, Bali also has degraded offshore coral reefs, a deforested interior, waterways polluted and clogged by plastic waste, and a location right in prime tsunami territory, at the mercy of rising oceans. The December 2004 tsunami that laid waste to Sumatra and southern Thailand could just have easily swept over Bali, which lies close to the same fault line. And just about 12 hours before the massive Tohoku earthquake hit Japan in March 2011, Bali was clobbered by a 6.2-magnitude quake that struck the island's northeast coast. Luckily, no damage or injuries were reported, but the threat was serious enough to inspire change. The government is finally addressing its internal issues, with aggressive measures to promote recycling and to reclaim damaged mangrove stands and upland forests. But when it comes to global warming, the problems require international action—it's more than one little Indonesian Shangri-La can solve on its own. Unfortunately, if action isn't taken soon, destinations like Bali will pay the price first.

It's not as if the resort developers haven't discovered Bali. You can stay at a five-star property in the manicured beach resort enclave of Nusa Dua and have no idea that you're in a foreign country at all. But stay inland instead in the town of Ubud and you'll have more contact with the Balinese people, as well as a better sense of the island's volcanic topography. River rafting on the Ayung River, through phosphorescent rice paddies and deep-cut jungle gorges, is one tempting option; day hikes to neighboring villages and into the hills are also popular. Animal lovers may want to visit **Elephant Safari Park,** Jalan Bypass Ngurah Rai, Pesanggaran (✆**361/721480**), or **Monkey Forest** (at the end of Monkey Forest Rd., naturally), although both attractions are a bit zoolike and hokey; even better, try a bird-watching walk with **naturalist Victor Mason** (✆**62/361-975009** or 62/812-3913801) to study some of Bali's 100 tropical species.

A water palace on Bali.

Day trips to the active volcanoes of Gunung Agung and/or Gunung Batur give a fascinating insight into this region's geothermal instability. Ubud's also within handy distance of resortlike activities such as surfing at Kuta or lolling on the wide beach at Jimbaran Bay. After all, what's the point of visiting Shangri-La without at least a little hedonism?

ⓘ www.bali-paradise.com. www.indo.com. www.baliguide.com.

✈ Ngurah Rai

🛏 $$$ **Maya Ubud,** Gulung Sari Peliatan, Ubud (✆**62/361/977888;** www.mayaubud.com). $$ **Alam Sari,** Keliki, Tromoi Pos 03, Kantor Pos Tegallalang, Ubud (✆**62/361/981420;** www.alamsari.com).

TOUR Bali Adventure Tours (✆**62/361/721480;** www.baliadventuretours.com)

Papua New Guinea
The Natives vs. Exxon
Southwestern Pacific Ocean

EXXON MOBILE'S PLAN TO EXTRACT AND SHIP GAS FROM AROUND THE WORLD IS PUTTING AN island known for its primitive peoples and unfettered nature in serious danger.

Papua New Guinea, occupying half of the world's largest island (it shares the island of New Guinea with the Indonesian provinces of Papua and West Papua), is an ecologically lush area with a population of more than six million people. If you've ever seen the Travel Channel's *Living with the Kombai Tribe*, about Papua New Guinea's primitive tree people, you already have some idea that this is truly another world. It's home to more than 800 indigenous peoples and discrete languages. Rigid tribal rules, masks, and body paint are not just cultural archives trotted out for visitors' benefit, but represent the only life that many people of these tribes know. It's

not a show for the tourists; it's a way of life untouched by time—but perhaps not for much longer.

Tensions are currently simmering between Exxon Mobile and Papua New Guinea's inhabitants. The oil giant has butted heads with landowners who have forced the company to suspend work at construction sites. This comes as no surprise, considering that more than 60,000 people own 97% of the land targeted by Exxon. Much of this anger is also prompted by a lack of government presence. Residents have to put up with unpaved roads, and no electricity or running water. The oil project will bring $30 million into this

A wreck near Papua New Guinea.

impoverished area, but leaders fear that Exxon's promises will fall short, fueling further anger by locals. Leaders also worry that the money will spark social problems, like binge drinking and polygamy—with more money the men will be able to afford more dowries.

At the moment, though, Papua New Guinea is still one of the wildest places in the world, culturally. From an ecological perspective, Papua New Guinea is also among the richest habitats in Oceania, with a diversity of flora and fauna—both on land and undersea—that rivals that of Australia and other, more well-known Micronesian destinations. Throughout the country, dozens of dive operators offer land-based day trips or multiday excursions to phenomenal reefs, coral walls and gardens, and an incredible number of sunken World War II wrecks. **Rabaul, Kavieng, Madang,** and **Milne Bay** are the top spots for immersing yourself among Papua New Guinea's vivid marine life and fascinating relics. Australian operator **Diversion OZ** (✆**61/7/4039 0200;** www.diversionoz.com) is a reputable outfitter with a variety of trip options.

ⓘ www.pngtourism.org.pg

✈ Port Moresby International

🛏 $$ **Madang Resort Hotel,** book though Melanesian Tourist Services (✆**675/854-1300;** www.mtspng.com)

Islands at Risk 70

Phu Quoc
Wild & Pungent, for Now
Vietnam

THERE ARE PLENTY OF ISLAND PARADISES IN SOUTHEAST ASIA THAT HAVE BEEN DISCOVERED BY tourists, but Phu Quoc is still in its natural state. Plans to turn the island into a tourist mecca could ruin what makes it great.

Located just west of the Vietnam mainland, Phu Quoc has some of the best and least crowded beaches in the world. All of this could change very quickly, however, since Prime Minister Nguyen Tan Dung would like to make Phu Quoc a world-class tourist center. A new international airport, which will be ready in 2012, will allow for many more tourists to visit at a given time. Although construction is on hold for the moment, the island has also been divided into lots to accommodate marinas and thousands of new villas to shelter an increasing number of visitors.

Modern infrastructure may make getting around a little easier—for now the only way to get to many of the island's beaches is by scooter or rides with a local fisherman or motorist—but instead of finding a quiet beach, you may find the kind of crowds that throng Bali 🔟 For now, though, Phu Quoc is an unspoiled getaway, where luxury hotels are still affordable and touring is done by moped. The north and northeast part of the island has wonderfully sleepy beaches. **Ganh Dau Beach** even offers a view of Cambodia, 18km (11 miles) away. If you decide to explore on your own, always pack a lunch and bring water, in case you find yourself in a place without a restaurant.

Duong Dong, the island's main town, is on the west coast, where the airport, seaport, and most hotels are located. **An Thoi,** on the southern coast, is the next largest town, but it is a bit out of the way. In its favor, however, is its proximity to the white-sand beaches of **Bai Sou** and **Bai Kem.**

The coasts of Phu Quoc are home to smaller villages where visitors can get a nontouristy view of island life. For example, Cua Can is known for its old wooden bridges. Tours up the Cua Can River can be arranged with local fishermen. If you are looking for a water-based adventure, **Famous Tony** organizes tours for individual groups (© **84/913/197-334;** http://discoverphuquoc.com).

Because of its limited transportation connections, Phu Quoc is usually visited as part of a longer trip to Vietnam and Cambodia. You can fly from Ho Chi Minh City or catch the ferry from Rach Gia or Ha Tien. Once there, an adjustment every visitor must make is tolerating the island's smell; it's one of the largest manufacturers of fish sauce in Vietnam, and the scent permeates the entire island. It's a small price to pay to get away from the crowds while you still can.

ⓘ www.discoverphuquoc.com

✈ Duong Dong airport (50 min. from Ho Chi Minh City)

🚢 Duong Dong Express from Rach Gia, 2½ hr. (© **84/77-3981648;** www.duongdongexpress.com.vn)

🛏 $$ **Cassia Cottage,** Cassia Cottage Rd., Ba Keo Beach (© **84/439-284973;** www.cassiacottage.com). **Grand Mecure La Veranda,** Tran Hung Dao St. (© **84/77-3982988;** www.mgallery.com).

---

71 Islands at Risk

Wrangel Island
Arctic Circle Refuge
Chukchi Sea, Russia

BEFORE WRANGEL ISLAND BECAME A NATURE RESERVE, SNOW GEESE AND POLAR BEARS LIVING on the land were being hunted to death. Global warming also threatens this delicate ecosystem.

Northwest of the Bering Strait, the arctic winters are long, and I mean loooooong. For 2 months, from November 22 to January 22, the sun never rises at all. A lonely landmass in the Chukchi Sea, Wrangel Island lies shrouded in snow until June, an icy wind moaning overhead.

And yet the sun does return every spring, and when it does, it's miraculous. Tens of thousands of migratory birds—black-legged kittiwakes, pelagic cormorants, glaucous gulls—arrive to nest on the jagged cliffs. Ringed seals and bearded seals dip their snouts through holes in the ice, hungry for fish. Walruses lumber out onto narrow spits to give birth. Female polar bears emerge drowsily from their winter dens, newborn cubs snuffling in their wake. Arctic foxes scavenge the rocky beaches, where snowy owls swoop down on unsuspecting lemmings.

A few months later, in the summer, the tundra teems with life. Rivers, swelled with snowmelt, gush through the narrow valleys, and the last remaining Russian population of snow geese paddles around glacial lakes in the island's interior. Brilliantly colored arctic wildflowers mantle the slopes in shades of pink and yellow. Shaggy musk oxen browse sedges and grasses of the ancient tundra, a relic of the Ice Age. The walruses bask on ice floes and rocky spits, going through their annual breeding rituals. It's a sight to see—but very few travelers ever get the chance.

Located 193km (120 miles) off the coast of Siberia, right on the 180-degree line that divides the Western and Eastern hemispheres, Wrangel Island became a nature reserve (or *zapovednik*) in 1976 to protect the delicate arctic ecosystem, in particular the snow geese and polar bear, which were being hunted to death. Today, the snow geese are making a recovery, and the area has the largest density of polar bear dens in the world—but poachers still pose a very real threat, especially to the bears.

There are no lodgings on the island—a small research island is the only habitation—so the only way to visit is on a ship (and an icebreaker at that), with smaller craft for shore visits. On your way through the Bering Strait, you'll also have a good chance of sighting minke, gray, and even beluga whales. These are long, expensive, summer-only expeditions, and few companies run them. Try **Heritage Expeditions** or **Polar Cruises** (see below) to plan a once-in-a lifetime adventure.

TOUR Heritage Expeditions (http://ewen bell.com/itenerary-wrangel.php) or **Polar Cruises** (© **888/484-2244** or 541/330-2454; www.polarcruises.com).

Islands at Risk 72

Sylt
The Shape-Shifting Island
Germany

SYLT HAS LONG BEEN A PLAYGROUND FOR THE RICH, BUT THE ISLAND IS IN GRAVE DANGER. IT'S practically nothing but beach, and that beach is disappearing every day due to erosion.

When we think of endangered places, images of vanishing species and erosion come to mind, but the island of Sylt is a unique case. The winds make the sand shift so that this island, which is only about 550m (1,800 ft.) wide at its narrowest point, literally changes shape each day, and there are genuine fears that the sea may reclaim it.

Sylt (pronounced *Zoolt*) has existed only since 1362, when the Great Mandrenke flood deposited sediment in the sea that built up into a long T-shaped sand spit running parallel to the coast of Denmark. Reminders of the island's exposure lie everywhere—in the iodine tang of the air, the constant whipping winds, and the rain-soaked climate that Germans call *Reizklima;* even the most fashion-conscious visitors regularly go about in yellow slickers, nicknamed Sylt "mink."

Despite issues of erosion, glamorous visitors—many from Germany—come to Sylt to enjoy nude beaches, spas, shops, and restaurants. If things don't change, these may be fleeting pleasures. This remarkably fragile island bears the brunt of the North Sea's volatility on the west. In contrast, quiet Wadden Sea on the east is so shallow that migratory birds flock to its mud flats at low tide. The area is so popular with avian visitors that it has been deemed a bird sanctuary.

The island's sand dunes shift by as much as 3 to 4m (10–13 ft.) a year; efforts to stabilize the sands by planting marram grass and wild Siberian roses and letting sheep graze on the man-made dikes in hopes that their hooves will pack down the soil have not fully succeeded. Some residents have even gone so far as to build homes on the dikes. And, when municipal funds are available, barges are moored offshore, pumping sand from deepwater sites back onto the beaches. Despite all of this, storm surges continue to erode the land; on some mornings after violent storms, vast areas of beach simply disappear, sucked out into the North Sea.

For now, at least, Sylt still beckons with its soft white beaches and its traditional Frisian culture. The eastern peninsula, known as **Sylter Friesendörfer,** is dotted with villages full of reed-thatched cottages and locals who speak Söl'ring, the native dialect. Every year on February 21, the islanders celebrate **Biikebrennen,** an ancient pagan rite in which towering stacks of wood on the beaches are set ablaze, lighting the night sky. Afterward, everyone adjourns to local restaurants for a traditional dinner featuring savory kale (distinctly seaweedy in appearance), while those bonfires flicker on through the long northern night, driving away winter, appeasing the ravenous gods of the sea.

(i) **Tourist office,** Strandstrasse 35, Westerland (📞 **49/4651/82020;** http://en.sylt.de or www.westerland.de)

✈ Sylt

🚂 Westerland (around 3 hr. from Hamburg, via railroad causeway from Niebüll)

🚢 **Rømø-Sylt Line** (📞 **49/180/3103-030;** www.syltfaehre.de). List (from Havneby, Denmark), 40 min.

🛏 $$ **Hotel Wünschmann,** Andreas-Dirks-Strasse 4 (📞 **49/4651/5025;** www.hotel-wuenschmann.de). $$$ **Stadt Hamburg,** Strandstrasse 2 (📞 **49/4651/8580;** www.hotelstadthamburg.com).

---

73 Islands at Risk

Herschel Island
Whaling Ghost Town
Yukon Coast, Canada

IT'S DESERTED TODAY, BUT THIS 117-SQ.-KM (45-SQ.-MILE) ISLAND WAS, FOR A BRIEF PERIOD, a vibrant place shared by whalers and their families as well as native tribes. Rising sea levels threaten to claim what is left.

When Herschel Island was inhabited, native Inuvialuits, Inuits descended from the Thule people, called it Qikiqtaruk ("island"). The island is now designated as Herschel Island–Qikiqtaruk Territorial Park, administered by the Government of Yukon. At the edge of the Beaufort Sea off the north coast of Canada's Yukon Territory, Herschel Island was first inhabited a millennium ago by the Thule—ancestors of the present-day Inuit. Following the discovery in the late 19th century that the Beaufort Sea was home to a large population of bowhead whales—prized for their oil—whalers came. In its heyday, hundreds of American men—some with families—would pass the cold months when their whaling ships were trapped by ice with balls, ballgames, even theater. When the bottom dropped out of the market,

they left, and the natives soon followed. Today, their presence is a mere echo, and vestiges of their cultures are in danger of being claimed by the sea.

Even though Herschel Island is protected as a national park, the surrounding ocean has slowly been rising and climate change is speeding up the process. At risk are the island's shorelines, including what remains of its whaling buildings, and the European-American settlement of **Pauline Cove,** along with Inuvialuit structures and graves. All of this will disappear under water unless it's moved. The World Monuments Fund placed Herschel on its 100 Most Endangered Sites list in 2008; in the meantime, the island is a likely candidate to become a UNESCO World Heritage Site.

Getting to Herschel Island can be a bit of a challenge but is worth it; although it's only 6.4km (4 miles) from the mainland of Yukon and 72km (45 miles) from the north coast of Alaska, there are no regularly scheduled flights or boats. However, charters can be arranged and kayakers traveling the Firth River can make a stop. The trip from the mainland is an attraction in its own right. Beluga and bowhead whales still swim in the Beaufort Sea offshore, unharried by the whalers' harpoons. Onshore, a near-encyclopedic sampling of Arctic mammals can be seen at various times of the year. Porcupine caribou are commonly sighted, and moose and musk oxen are also present. Black bears, polar bears, and grizzlies are all known to have dens on this fragile island, too.

ⓘ www.environmentyukon.gov.yk.ca

✈ Charters from Inuvik (250km/155 miles away)

🚢 Boat charters only

🛏 $ Camping; see the Environment Yukon website above for details.

TOUR Uncommon Journeys, Whitehorse (✆ **867/668-2255;** www.uncommon yukon.com)

Islands at Risk 74

The Channel Islands
Channel-Surfing
California

OFF THE COAST OF SANTA BARBARA IS AN ARCHIPELAGO THAT OFFERS A CHANCE TO SEE CALIfornian habitats in their natural state. Unfortunately, it is threatened by human activities and climate change.

Santa Cruz Island.

The Channel Islands archipelago boasts rugged beauty and ecological diversity that prove that the natural treasures of California don't end with the Golden State's sun-kissed coastline. Channel Islands National Park consists of five islands—Anacapa, Santa Cruz, Santa Rosa, San Miguel, and Santa Barbara—a Pacific habitat where visitors can still enjoy species of flora and fauna found nowhere else. The islands are home to some 150 species of endemic plants and animals, including island foxes, skunks, Channel Island lizards, and the Torrey pine. Isolation has played a big part in the continued success of these species; the islands are about 20 to 80 miles (32km to 129km) from the mainland. Many of the animals and plants here exist on only one of the five islands in the national park. For instance, there's a bird—the island scrub jay—on Santa Cruz Island that you won't find on Anacapa, Santa Rosa, San Miguel, or Santa Barbara islands, even though only a few miles of ocean separate them.

The largest island at 96 square miles (249 sq. km) is **Santa Cruz,** an impressive sight with its coast of jagged cliffs and a 2,450-foot-tall (747m) peak called Mount Diablo. Painted Cave, along the northwest coast, features one of the largest sea caves in the world. The island is also the most biologically diverse in the archipelago. Tour boats take visitors to see natural attractions by sea, but boats also dock here, affording visitors a chance to explore the island through a series of hiking trails.

Positioned in the heart of coastal California's rich biosphere, the Channel Islands' waters are teeming with marine life. One-third of the world's species of cetaceans are regularly spotted in the **Santa Barbara Channel,** including gray, blue, humpback, sperm, orca, and pilot whales and dozens of dolphins and porpoises. Visitors can whale-watch from the shore or from boat charters from Santa Barbara or Ventura year-round. It's also inevitable that you'll see California sea lions or harbor seals any time of year, as the Channel Islands provide well-established colonies for these pinnipeds.

While all of this may sound idyllic, fires, farming, and livestock grazing, as well as home and road construction, have altered the islands in recent years. The island fox was threatened by golden eagle predation and canine distemper and was placed on the endangered list in 2004. Removing golden eagles and placing a ban on pets helped the foxes rebound. Other wildlife are vulnerable to invasive species like black rats and the European rabbit.

Preservation of the Channel Islands' natural resources is strictly supervised to prevent further habitat destruction, so there are no services on the islands apart from a few basic facilities. You can enjoy either a day trip or an overnight stay at one of the campgrounds, the largest being the Scorpion Ranch Campground on eastern Santa Cruz Island, open year-round.

ⓘ **Visitor center,** 1901 Spinnaker Dr., Ventura (✆ **805/658-5730;** www.nps.gov/chis)

✈ Santa Barbara Airport (25 miles/40km)

⛴ Transport available through tour operators (see below).

🛏 $ **Scorpion Ranch Campground** (✆ **877/444-6777;** www.nps.gov). $$$ **Inn of the Spanish Garden,** 915 Garden St., Santa Barbara (✆ **805/564-4700;** www.spanishgardeninn.com).

TOUR Island Packers, 1691 Spinnaker Dr., Ventura (✆ **805/642-1393;** www.islandpackers.com). **Truth Aquatics,** 301 W. Cabrillo Blvd., Santa Barbara (✆ **805/963-3564;** www.truthaquatics.com).

Iceland
World of Fire & Ice
North Atlantic Ocean

EUROPEAN AIR TRAFFIC WAS DISRUPTED FOR WEEKS IN APRIL 2010 WHEN ICELAND'S EYJAFJAL-lajokull volcano erupted, spewing a gigantic ash cloud right into the jet stream. In May 2011, Grímsvötn's eruption halted air travel again on a smaller scale.

The name "Iceland" is totally misleading—this North Atlantic island nation is a land of fire far more than ice. Those active volcanoes that messed up air travel in 2010 and 2011 are just two of some 200 conical black volcanoes dotted around this seismic hot spot; on average, there's an eruption every 3 years. Icelandic farmers know to keep their sturdy, shaggy ponies indoors when there's an ash cloud, and not to let their sheep drink from the temporarily contaminated streams in agricultural areas near an eruption. The sturdy, brightly colored buildings of Reykjavik are built to withstand constant tremors.

It's not just the volcanoes, either—active geysers bubble everywhere, constantly shifting and reshaping the nation's stony terrain. The area's otherworldly landscape is evident the moment you get off the plane in **Keflavik.** Steam rises out of cracks in the treeless basalt plain and the air smells of sulfur. It's a landscape so lunar that NASA astronauts trained here in preparation for landing on the moon.

So-called "volcano tourism" spiked during the Eyjafjallajokull eruption, with tourists clamoring to be driven close enough to the crater to view its lava flows. The eruption officially ended in October 2010,

Gullfoss Waterfall, Iceland.

but **Volcano Tours** (www.volcanotours.is) still runs luxury jeep tours to **Eyjafjalla-jokull** to view its cindery black slopes. Better yet, take their full-day tour, which explores all the dramatic contrasts of Iceland's terrain—the black lava-sand beaches of the south coast, sparkling waterfalls like **Gullfoss** and **Skógafoss,** the glittering ice of the **Sólheimajökull glacier,** the spurting hot springs of **Geysir** (after which all geysers are named).

To fully engage with Iceland's unearthly interior, however, visit the hot springs of **Landmannalaugar,** just 48km (30 miles) south of Eyjafjallajokull. After a soak in the bathtub-warm thermal pools, take an overnight hike into the nearby mountains, which undulate like folds of silk, tinted with rare mineral colors—blues, yellows, bright reds, even shocking pink. Marked trails lead through the surrounding Fjallabak Nature Reserve, where hikers can sleep overnight at mountain huts run by the Iceland Touring Association (www.fi.is/en). In July and August they book up far in advance, so plan accordingly. Or hike all the way from Landmannalaugar to the nature reserve of Þórsmörk, a challenging 3- to 4-day walk that's Iceland's premier hike. After traversing a stark terrain of snow, ice, and rock, it's a relief to wind up in Þórsmörk's gentle woods and meadows, with a backdrop of glacial peaks. Iceland's not just about the volcanoes, after all.

ⓘ **Reykjavik Tourist Office,** Aðalstræti 2 (② **354/590-1550;** www.visit reykjavik.is). Also www.visiticeland.com.

✈ Reykjavik

🛏 $$ **Hotel Bjork** (② **354/511-3777;** www.bjorkhotelreykjavik.com). $$ **Arctic Comfort Hotel,** Aðalstræti 19,108 Reykjavik (②**354/588-5588;** www.arcticcomfort hotel.is).

76 Singular & Separate

Anavilhanas Ecological Station
Hiding Place of the Jungle Manatee
Novo Airão, Brazil

THE AMAZONIAN MANATEE, ENDEMIC TO THIS REGION, FACES A HIGH RATE OF EXTINCTION IN THE wild. While this area is protected by government decree, hunting and pollution from ships traveling the Rio Negro put the area at risk.

All manatees are not created equal. Take the Amazonian manatee, for example. It's the only freshwater manatee, and it's smaller than the other two species, on average only 3m (10 ft.) long and 450kg (granted, that's still big). A timid creature, it minds its own business in the backwaters of Amazon basin rivers. Since it has only molar teeth, its diet is limited to soft aquatic plants. Mothers have only one calf at a time, which they nurse for up to 2 years. So when the natives hunt them for meat and leather, invade their waterways with motorboats, and destroy their specialized habitat—well, it's hard for the manatees to hold their own.

The Amazonian manatee is just one species being studied and protected at the Anavilhanas Ecological Station, a Brazilian government nature reserve just northwest of Manaus (access is through the lodge of the same name); river dolphins are also under threat here—it's common for fishermen to kill and sell them as bait to unsuspecting customers. Set in the Rio Negro, a major Amazon tributary, the reserve encompasses some 400 islands and hundreds of lakes, rivers, swamps, and sandbanks, the world's largest archipelago in a river. Since the reserve was created in 1981, it has relocated nearly all the inhabitants of the archipelago. And still, residents of Novo Airão and Manaus visit the islands to fish, hunt, and cut wood; Manaus building companies take sand and stones from the riverside, though rangers are monitoring this activity closely. Ships cruising the Rio Negro add pollution to the equation. And, of course, politics snarl up everything, with many locals increasingly resistant to international "interference" by conservation groups.

Though the islands of Anavilhanas are covered with forests, these are special forests, adapted to the fact that the islands are largely submerged during the high-water period, April to June. Notice, for example, the tree's aerial roots as you navigate around the islands in small boats—those come in handy when a tree is flooded for months at a time. You'll see a lot of palm trees, orchids, lichens, and, on some islands,

straggly shrub lands; a lot of trees have curved, thin trunks and leathery leaves that can store water for the dry months. Animals are driven to higher ground, too, until the waters recede, revealing beaches and deeper channels. September and October may be your best months if you want to see wildlife.

Given the changing conditions of the river, the landscape is constantly shapeshifting, with islands relocating and channels altering their courses. A local guide, however, can help you keep your bearings, as well as identify the flora and fauna, most of which are unique to this one-of-a-kind environment. As you maneuver around its labyrinth of channels and lakes, keep an eye peeled for those elusive manatees—or at least the playful river dolphins.

✈ Manaus

🛏 **$$$ Anavilhanas Jungle Lodge** (📞 **55/92/3622-8996;** www.anavilhanas lodge.com)

Singular & Separate **77**

The Falkland Islands
Penguin Paradise
Off the Coast of Argentina

SEWAGE AND GARBAGE DUMPED BY LOCAL SANITATION COMPANIES, THE SHIPPING INDUSTRY, and fishing boats threaten marine life in the Falkland Islands. But its biggest woe is offshore drilling for oil.

Say "Falkland Islands" and most folks will recall late-night comedians joking over Argentina's quixotic 1982 invasion of this virtually unknown British possession. But say "Falkland Islands" to an ornithologist and he'll see something way different: a sunny vision of penguins, seals, and albatrosses, frolicking on unspoiled rocky islands.

Sketch in an image of offshore oil rigs, though, and it's a darker picture indeed. One of the reasons Britain fought to retain this offshore territory was the promise of

oil here, 482km (300 miles) off Argentina's Atlantic coast. Drilling began in 2011, despite a strong public outcry.

Often lumped into an Antarctic cruise itinerary, the Falklands—also known as the Malvinas—deserve a visit on their own merits. Individual tourists (and there aren't many) can fly in from Santiago, Chile, though there is also a weekly RAF charter from the U.K. Instead of daredevil glacier climbing, Falklands visitors enjoy more contemplative pursuits, such as photography, birding, cross-country tramping, and trout fishing. Penguins are the stars of the show, with no fewer than five varieties colonizing the islands' white sandy beaches: gentoo, Magellanic, macaroni, rockhopper, and king penguins. Sea lions, fur seals, and elephant seals hide in the tall tussock grass, alongside tiny spiky tussock birds; rare seabirds such as the black-browed albatross, the giant petrel, and the striated caracara (known here as the Johnny rook) roost on tiny rocky sanctuaries scattered around the two main islands. Local tour companies will help you organize the 4WD vehicles or small planes you may need to reach the more remote wildlife spots.

The Falklands have their own defiantly unglitzy charm, the no-nonsense air of a distant outpost where the settlers simply soldier on. Residents cling to a sense of empire, with the Union Jack proudly on display; the port town of Stanley has a Victorian air, though most houses sport gaily colored tin roofs that look more like Reykjavik than Dover. Southerly as they are, the Falklands are still in the temperate zone, with temperatures similar to London's; even in the depths of winter the sun shines at least 6 hours a day. The landscape is a scrubby, hardy terrain of eroded peat and rocky scree, where dwarf shrubs stand in for trees. But those penguins, they think the island is paradise—and naturalists would like to keep it that way.

ⓘ **Falkland Islands Tourist Board** (✆**500/22215;** www.visitorfalklands.com)

✈Mount Pleasant

🛏$$ **Malvina House Hotel,** 3 Ross Rd., Stanley (✆**500/21355**). $$ **Upland Goose Hotel,** 22 Ross Rd., Stanley (✆**500/21455**).

TOUR **Falkland Islands Holidays** (✆**500/ 22622;** www.falklandislandsholidays.com). **International Tours and Travel** (✆**500/ 22041;** www.falklandstravel.com). **Polar Cruises** (✆ **888/484-2244;** www.polar cruises.com).

Christmas Island
The Indian Ocean's Galapagos
Australia

CHRISTMAS ISLAND'S ISOLATION HAS BEEN A BOON FOR ITS ENDEMIC FLORA AND FAUNA, WHICH is comparable to what Darwin found in the Galapagos Islands. But years of phosphate mining have destroyed some of its rainforest.

This tiny paradise about 135 sq. km (52 sq. miles) from its mother country of Australia was named in 1643 when Captain William Mynors of the British East India Company landed here on December 25. The first scientific explorations of the island were not carried out until the latter part of the 19th century, however, when researchers collected specimens of the island's unique flora and fauna. In 1888, a severe blow to the ecosystem was dealt when large quantities of pure phosphate were discovered—the island was annexed by the British Crown and mining soon began. This destroyed precious rainforest, leading to a habitat less hospitable to its local species; some of the fauna identified by those early scientists, like two endemic species of rat and some birds and bats, are now extinct because of mining.

More than a century of mining later, Christmas Island's phosphate stores are running low, and in 2010, Environment Minister Peter Garret rejected a proposal that would have removed forest to expand mining operations. In more good news, many conservation measures are present on the island, which has been an Australian territory since 1958, and 63% of the island has been protected as **Christmas Island National Park** (www.environment.gov.au/parks/christmas) since the 1980s.

Christmas Island boasts an outstanding variety of wildlife that should be protected—some of the unusual wildlife that can be viewed here includes boobies and the Christmas Island frigate bird at **Margaret Knoll,** and rare sea turtles at **Dolly Beach.** But the island's biggest stars, known for their spectacular breeding ritual, are red crabs. Every year, at the start of the wet season, more than 100 million of them travel from the mountain rainforests to the sea, where they release their eggs. During the migration, which can last up to 18 days, many roads are closed to protect them from being crushed. Visitors can view this fascinating spectacle from approximately October 2 to the end of December.

The obvious home base here is the Settlement on the northeast tip of the island and the only inhabited part of the island.

The harbor is known as **Flying Fish Cove,** where you'll find accommodations, restaurants, and great beaches for snorkeling and shore diving among tropical fish and the occasional whale shark. Christmas Island is also known for its immigrant detention center, only one of two such facilities in the entire nation where illegal refugees are held by border patrol. It made the news in 2010 when more than 20 asylum seekers were killed in a shipwreck. The island's legendary isolation makes it hard to escape, and in this case, that had tragic results.

ⓘ ✆ **61/8/9164 8362;** www.christmas.net.au

✈ Christmas Island, connections to Perth, Australia, and to Kuala Lumpur, Malaysia

⊨ $$$ **The Sanctuary,** The Settlement ✆ **61/8/9164 8382;** www.christmas.net.au/accom_sanctuary.html)

TOUR Christmas Island Expeditions ✆ **61/8/9164-7168;** www.christmasislandexpeditions.com/index.html)

Singular & Separate 79

Tasmania
God Save the Tasmanian Devil
Australia

MANY UNIQUE SPECIES THRIVE IN TASMANIA, BUT INCREASING DEVELOPMENT IS THREATENING its emblematic Tasmanian devil, along with many of the island's most beautiful places.

What does a country do when its mascot is dying? Granted, there's nothing cuddly about the Tasmanian devil—these stocky, sharp-snouted little black beasts are vicious scavengers, not nearly as funny as Bugs Bunny's jabbering cartoon pal. But Tasmanians are perversely fond of those cranky doglike critters, and there's a passionate campaign afoot to save them from extinction. They may be the victims of their own bad habits—an appetite for roadkill on busy highways, and their habit of biting each other's faces while quarreling over carrion, thus spreading a rare facial cancer—but the loss of any species is a tragedy.

Dingoes wiped out the Tasmanian devils from Australia long ago, but dingoes never crossed Bass Strait to reach Tasmania, the big island that punctuates the Australian continent like the dot under an exclamation point. Island isolation gave Australia a menagerie of unique species, but Tasmania kicks it up another notch. While Australia's climate is mostly tropical, Tasmania lies in the temperate zone, which puts an entirely different spin on its ecosystem. Tasmania's got wallabies, bandicoots, wombats, and possums, but it's got different wallabies, bandicoots, wombats, and possums. It's also a land of unique tree frogs and parrots, a place of such ecological rarity that its wilderness has won World Heritage status.

Only a couple hours' drive from Hobart, Tasmania's capital, you'll find yourself in a rugged terrain of incredible beauty. Running through it like a spine is the 85km (53-mile) **Overland Track,** the best-known hiking trail in all of Australia. At one end the trail is anchored by Cradle Mountain, a spectacular jagged gray ridge face with four craggy peaks; at the other lies the long, narrow glacier-carved **Lake St. Clair,** Australia's deepest freshwater lake. The trek between them traverses high alpine plateaus, marshy plains of rare button grass, springy heath land, fragrant eucalypt forest, dusky woods of myrtle beech (one of the few Australian native trees that isn't an evergreen), and one of the planet's last temperate rainforests. The path is well marked and improved, including stretches of boardwalk and a series of public sleeping huts. Tour companies run 5-to-10-day guided treks along its length; plenty of shorter hikes are available as well.

Along the way, you'll run into red-bellied pademelons (the kangaroo's Tasmanian cousins) and hordes of other scampering marsupials. As for the Tasmanian devils—well, they're shy little guys, despite that hideous screech they make. You may not see them in the wild, not if

A Tasmanian devil.

they can help it, unless there's a tasty dead possum to feed on.

ⓘ**Tasmania Parks & Wildlife Service** (www.overlandtrack.com.au). **Save the Tasmanian Devil** (www.tassiedevil.com.au).

✈Hobart

🛏$$$ **Cradle Mountain Lodge,** Cradle Mountain Park (☎**800/225-9849** in North America, 44/20/7805-3875 in the U.K., 61/3/6492 1303 in Australia: www.cradle mountainlodge.com.au). $ **Waldheim Cabins,** Cradle Mountain Park (☎**61/03-6491-2271;** www.parks.tas.gov.au/index. aspx?base=7560).

TOURTasmanian Expeditions (☎**61/03-6331-9000;** www.tas-ex.com)

10 Places to See Coral Reefs

Scuba divers will testify—there's no more jaw-dropping sight than a healthy coral reef, with its vivid colors, mazy shapes, quicksilver fish, and dreamy anemones. But a quarter of the world's coral reefs are now dead, and marine biologists estimate that 70% could be gone by 2020. We wouldn't just lose those coral palaces; the species they shelter would have no other home (one-quarter of all fish species dwell only in coral reefs). Sure, some reefs are more imperiled than others, but make no mistake—they are all at risk.

These 10 extraordinary reefs illustrate how important coral reef preservation is throughout the world:

80 Biscayne National Park   Pulsing with parrotfish and angelfish, gently rocking sea fans, sea turtles, and dolphins, Biscayne Bay's reef shelters some 512 species, all told. Daily snorkel/dive tours and glass-bottom boat tours are offered by **Biscayne National Underwater Park, Inc.** (✆ **305/230-1100**). *Biscayne National Park.*✆ ***305/230-7275. www.nps.gov/bisc.***

81 Bonaire   Thanks to the pioneering Bonaire Marine Park—which includes 80-plus dive sites along with permanent boat moorings and attentive rangers—this Caribbean island's reefs remain in prime condition. It's a haven for more than 355 species, from beautiful parrotfish and damselfish to huge groupers and tough moray eels. Operators include **Dive II** (✆ **599/717-8285**) and **Bonaire Dive and Adventures** (✆ **599/717-2229**). *InfoBonaire.*✆ ***800/BONAIRE** [266-2473]. www.infobonaire.com.*

82 Saba   Saba may look tiny and rocky above the water, but undersea it's got a wealth of dive sites, especially around a number of spiky offshore pinnacles, richly encrusted with coral and sponges. The protected **Saba Marine Park,** Ford Bay (✆ **599/416-3295**), circles the entire island, including four seamounts (underwater mountains), more than two dozen marked and buoyed dive sites, and a snorkeling trail. Operators include **Sea Saba Dive Center** in Windwardside (✆ **599/416-2246**) and **Saba Deep Dive Center** in Fort Bay (✆ **599/416-3347**). *www.sabatourism.com.*

83 Cozumel   Off the Yucatan coast, Cozumel is often rated the top dive site in the Western Hemisphere, with spectacular reefs built up by a strong (and somewhat tricky) coastal current. Known for its dramatic underwater topography of steep drop-offs and underground caverns, it's best navigated with seasoned dive operators like **Aqua Safari** (✆ **52/987/872-0101;** www.aquasafari.com) or **Liquid Blue Divers** (✆ **52/987-869-7794;** www.liquidbluedivers.com). *www.islacozumel.com.mx.*

84 Great Barrier Reef   Australia's Great Barrier Reef is so immense, it's visible from the moon. Snorkelers can view the reef's profuse marine life in the shallow waters around the coral cay of Green Island or sandy Beaver Cay, an hour's boat ride from Mission Beach, south of Cairns. Scuba divers may prefer the dazzling reef architecture out on the rainforested islands of the Outer Reef: Base yourself in the Whitsunday

Islands, where operators such as **Reef Dive** (✆ **61/7/4946 6508**) and **Kelly Dive** (✆ **61/7/4946 6122**) explore the Great Barrier Reef Marine Park. *Great Barrier Reef Visitors Bureau.* ✆ **07/3876 4644.** *www.great-barrier-reef.com.*

85 Tumbalen   Perhaps the most diverse coastal environment in the world lies on the east end of Bali **68**, where divers spot many small, fugitive species that exist nowhere else on earth. The most spectacular reefs are offshore from Amuk Bay and the Lombok Strait harbor. Base yourself in the small resort town of Candi Dasa, where storefront dive operators abound, or the nearby fishing village Padangbai, the base of **Geko Divers** (✆ **62/363/41516**). *www.bali-paradise.com.*

86 Wakatobi National Marine Park   Set up in the mid-1990s in southeast Sulawesi, Indonesia, this remote four-island marine preserve is reachable only from the Wakatobi Dive Resort. It's a spectacular reef with astonishing diversity and some truly beautiful coral formations, both hard and soft. More than 40 dive sites are available, many of them quite shallow. ✆ **62/868/121 22355.**

87 Cape Verde Islands   Tourism hasn't yet overwhelmed this Portuguese colonial outpost in the Atlantic, west of Africa. Its lava shoal reefs—many of which formed around shipwrecks—are rich in marine life, including manta rays, sharks, tuna, dolphins, and turtles, not to mention underwater flora and surprising caves. Humpback and gray whale migrations in March and April are an added attraction. *www.caboverde.com.*

88 Belize's Barrier Reef   This UNESCO World Heritage site is the second-largest barrier reef next to Australia's Great Barrier Reef. It offers visitors the chance to snorkel, fish, and engage in watersports along its 288km (179-mile) span. Here you'll find clear waters and a wide variety of reef formations, including the Blue Hole, which is visible from space; despite its seemingly pristine nature, it's estimated that 40% of this reef has been damaged since 1998. *Natural Habitat Adventures.* ✆ **800/543-8917.** *www.nathab.com/index.aspx.*

89 Buck Island, USVI   Buck Island is considered one of the finest marine gardens in the Caribbean. This protected island and its reef teem with life, including the hawksbill turtle and the brown pelican. It's most famous with snorkelers who explore its passages through its underwater trail. Half-day and full-day trips are available. *Big Beard's Adventure Tours:* ✆ **340/773-4482** *or 866/773-4482. http://bigbeards.com. Caribbean Sea Adventures:* ✆ **340/773-2628.** *www.caribbeansea adventures.com.*

Buck Island.

Shiretoko National Park
Japan's Last Frontier
Hokkaido, Japan

HARSH WEATHER CONDITIONS PROTECT THIS REGION FROM THE RAVAGES OF HUMAN DEVELOPMENT, but the fragile balance between terrestrial and marine ecosystems is dependent upon the stability of sea ice, which climate change may affect.

The ancient Ainu people called it Shiretoko, "End of the Earth," and that's what this peninsula still feels like—remote, rugged, uninhabited, set at the farthest tip of Japan's farthest north island. Its virgin forests are home to Yezo sika deer and one of the last large populations of Hokkaido brown bears (watch out for them in spring, when they grumpily emerge from hibernation); its extensive wetlands attract droves of migratory birds. Cormorants, white-tailed sea eagles, and the Blackiston's fish owl hover watchfully over its waters, while seals and sea lions flop around its rocky coves.

Though most visitors come here in summer, what makes Shiretoko unique is the sea ice drifting offshore in winter in the Sea of Orkhost—it's the farthest south that ice floes are found in the Northern Hemisphere. The combination of sea ice and relatively temperate latitude makes it a virtual resort destination for marine mammals like fur seals and Steller sea lions; whales frequently circle around the headlands.

There are no roads at all in the northern quarter of the peninsula—to explore its beauty, you need to hike and camp, or else take a boat tour around the western coast, leaving from the gateway town of Utoro. While the western coast's dramatic waterfalls can be viewed on any of the various tours, the longer cruises—3 to 4 hours—go all the way to the tip of the peninsula, where your wildlife-spotting opportunities are best.

It would be a shame, though, to come here and not walk through the picturesque woodlands, even if you don't attempt a strenuous wilderness trek. Easy walking trails circle the peaceful forested **Five Lakes,** only 15km (9⅓ miles) from Utoro. An even more special experience is wading up a warm mountain stream to **Kamui-kukka Falls,** where you can bask in the hot springs basin at its base. Even if you don't reach the main falls—stretches of the river may be closed due to falling rocks—slipping around the algae-coated rocks and plunging into warm pools along the way is exhilarating.

Rugged volcanic ridges kept out human settlers for centuries, protecting the wildlife; nowadays it's up to park management to protect this rare marine/alpine ecosystem. And sometimes politics intrude— UNESCO has informed Japan and Russia that they're jointly responsible for one hotly disputed section, the offshore Kurile Islands, which the former Soviet Union invaded 2 weeks after V-J Day ended World War II. Territorial disputes or not, this wildlife haven must be kept pristine. It's one of those frontier spots that nobody paid attention to for years—which is just what makes it so worth saving.

ⓘ www.shiretoko.or.jp

✈ Metambetsu

🛏 $$$ **Hotel Shiretoko,** 37 Utorokagawa, Shari Cho (✆ **81/152/24-2131**). $ **Shiretoko-Iwaobetsu Youth Hostel,** at Iwaobetsu bus stop (✆ **81/152/24-2311**).

Socotra
Frankincense & Myrrh
Yemen

SOCOTRA HAS LONG BEEN DESCRIBED AS A FORGOTTEN EDEN. BUT WHILE ISOLATION HAS KEPT ITS natural features distinctive, that same isolation has led to poverty; the island lacks the economic resources to remain sustainable.

At 250km (155 miles) long, Socotra is the largest island in the Middle East, and the most isolated—this main island in a rocky archipelago of the same name lies way out in the northwestern Indian Ocean off the Horn of Africa. It's that very isolation that has made it such a gem—native species have changed little from the ancient flora and fauna of the Mesozoic period, earning it the nickname "the Galapagos of the Indian Ocean." Its ecological importance cannot be overstated: 37% of Socotra's 825 plant species, 90% of its reptile species, and 95% of its land snail species occur *only on the island*. All this has prompted scientists to declare that the island is one of the most endangered in the world.

Socotra is also home to birds you won't see anywhere else, including the Socotra Warbler, the Socotra Sunbird, and the Socotra Grosbeak, as well as its national bird, the Golden-winged Grosbeak. (And it's host to about a dozen additional avian subspecies that are native to the island.) Introduced species like goats and donkeys have thrived in its tough and varied terrain, composed of tropical desert to limestone plateau and mountain ranges. Divers seek out the waters surrounding the archipelago, which boasts 253 species of reef-building corals, 730 species of coastal fish, and 300 species of crab, lobster, and shrimp.

Socotra, whose population of 44,000 is of mixed Arab, Somali, and South Asian origins, has one foot in the Arab world and another in Africa. Its rural areas are populated by fishermen descended from ancient South African tribes and seminomadic farmers raising goats, sheep, cattle, or camels and cultivating date palms. The island was given World Heritage Site status in 2008 by UNESCO, and currently three-quarters of it is protected. There are hopes to make this a thriving eco-tourist destination, since outside dollars could help sustain the impoverished island and take some of the pressure off the current government. As quiet as it is now, Socotra once bustled, attracting ships seeking frankincense, myrrh, dragon's blood, and aloe; even Marco Polo thought it worth a mention in his *Travels*. With luck, eco-tourism will allow Socotra's future to live up to its romantic past.

ⓘ www.socotraisland.org; consult your embassy about travel conditions before your visit.

✈ Yemenia Airlines flies between Sana'a-Mukkala and Socotra (3 hr.).

🛏 To arrange lodging in a guesthouse, overnight camping, and tours, contact the **Socotra Ecotourism Society** (✆ **05/660-132;** www.socotraisland.org).

TOUR Socotra Adventure Tours (✆ **00/967/5-660136;** www.socotraisland adventure.com)

Mount Desert Island
The Falcons Are Back, Baby
Acadia National Park, Maine

ENDANGERED PEREGRINE FALCONS HAVE FOUND A HOME AT ACADIA NATIONAL PARK, BUT THE species still faces grave threats outside the sanctuary. Nest robbing, hunting, and pesticides are all taking their toll on the falcon population.

There's a bunch of hackers loose in Acadia National Park. But among ornithologists, hackers are the good guys—the ones who hand-rear chicks and reintroduce them into the wild. At Acadia National Park, those hackers are proud to say that they got peregrine falcons nesting in the wild again for the first time in almost 40 years.

Acadia is a glacier-chiseled mound of rugged cliffs, picturesque coves, and quiet woods connected by causeway to the coast of Maine—a perfect habitat for these beautiful soaring raptors. But peregrines are endangered these days, due to nest robbing, hunting, and toxic pesticides; even though these are banned in the U.S., peregrines may eat migrant songbirds from countries where the use of DDT is still common. By the mid-1960s, researchers said peregrines were no longer breeding anywhere in the eastern United States.

In response, in 1984 specialists at Acadia started breeding peregrines in captivity in a strictly controlled program to prepare them for the wild. The first 22 chicks were hacked into a cliff face overlooking Jordan Pond each spring from 1984 to 1986. In 1991, the first hacked birds finally bred, nested, and hatched their own chicks, raising them in the cliffs of Champlain Mountain.

Park resource managers monitor peregrines' comings and goings carefully, so don't be surprised if trails are temporarily closed to protect mating and nesting spots. Even if the trails are closed, the Precipice Trail parking area offers prime viewing of their nesting cliff on Champlain Mountain (daily from mid-May to mid-Aug, rangers lead a program describing peregrine activity). During mating, the birds feed each other in midair and show off with elaborate swoops, tumbles, and dives. In April and May they take turns nest sitting; in June you may spot the tiny white balls of fluff that are baby falcons. In July and August watch fledgling falcons try out their wings with ever-longer forays from the cliffs.

Your best introduction to Acadia is a circuit on the 20-mile (32km) **Park Loop Road,** a spectacular drive that follows the island's rocky shore past picturesque coves, looping back inland along Jordan Pond and Eagle Lake with a detour up **Cadillac Mountain,** the highest point on the East Coast north of Rio de Janeiro. But don't stop there. Go kayaking around **Frenchman's Bay,** populated by seals and osprey; bike around the forested interior on crushed-rock carriageways laid out for Gilded Age tycoons; visit a series of geological formations using a GPS system to track down EarthCache clues; or take a catamaran cruise to the offshore feeding grounds of humpback, finback, minke, and (occasionally) right whales. And never forget to look up in the sky—the peregrines could be there, watching you.

ⓘ **Acadia National Park visitor center,** Rte. 3 north of Bar Harbor (✆ **207/288-3338;** www.nps.gov/acad)

✈ Trenton

🛏 $ **Bar Harbor Campground,** Rte. 3, Salisbury Cove (✆ **207/288-5185**). $$ **Harborside Hotel & Marina,** 55 West St., Bar Harbor (✆ **800/328-5033** or 207/288-5033; www.theharborsidehotel.com).

Assateague Island
Do the Pony on the Eastern Shore
Eastern Shore, Maryland & Virginia

ITS PROXIMITY TO POPULATED AREAS HAS CAUSED PROBLEMS FOR ASSATEAGUE ISLAND. BOATING and clam fishing cause pollution, and every year erosion causes the island to move closer to the mainland.

Legend has it that the ponies swam ashore from a shipwrecked Spanish galleon centuries ago, washing up on this barrier island off Virginia's Eastern Shore. The truth may be a little more prosaic; more likely they were put there in the late 1600s by English settlers who found the island a natural corral, but at this point it hardly matters. They're shaggy, sturdy little wild horses, running free on this one narrow barrier island. How cool is that?

Misty of Chincoteague was one of my favorite books as a child—it's practically required reading for any girl in her "horse phase"—and as every Misty-lover knows, they may be called Chincoteague ponies but they are really from Assateague Island. Neighboring Chincoteague Island comes into the picture because every July, Chincoteague townsfolk row over to uninhabited Assateague, round up the tough feral ponies, make them swim across the narrow channel separating the two islands, and sell the foals to raise money for the local fire department.

But 37-mile-long (60km) Assateague is also a prime Atlantic flyway habitat where peregrine falcons, snow geese, great blue herons, and snowy egrets have been sighted. Dolphins swim offshore; bald eagles soar overhead. Like most of the Eastern Shore, it's a tranquil, wind-ruffled shoreland with a lot of wildlife refuges and weather-beaten charm. Lying close to heavily populated areas, however, its delicate coastal environment is threatened by recreational boating, commercial clam fishery, and agricultural runoff pollution. Every year the island moves closer to the mainland, as its oceanward beaches erode and sediment fills in the landward shore.

A causeway connects Chincoteague to the mainland, and another causeway leads to Assateague, though a strict quota system controls the number of cars on Assateague at any one time. Since the island lies partly

Wild ponies on Assateague Island.

in Maryland and partly in Virginia, half of the horses live in a state park on the Maryland side, while the other half live in Virginia's national wildlife refuge. It's the herd from this refuge that supplies ponies for the annual Chincoteague roundup, which sustains the herd at a manageable size; the Maryland herd, unculled, exerts constant pressure on its marshy grazing lands.

Wildlife cruises operate from either Chincoteague or nearby Ocean City, Maryland, taking visitors to explore the coasts of the island. Narrated bus tours also run along a paved 4½-mile (7.2km) **Wildlife Drive** through the marshes of the Chincoteague refuge (you can also walk or cycle along the road, or drive your own car after 3pm). At the end of the main road,

you come to the **Assateague National Seashore,** a pristine beach with bathhouses, lifeguards, and a visitor center. It's a great place to settle on the sand, feel the wind in your face, and imagine the ghost of a wrecked Spanish galleon.

ⓘ **Chincoteague National Wildlife Refuge,** Assateague Island, VA (✆ **757/336-3696;** www.nps.gov/asis)

✈ Norfolk

🛏 $$$ **Island Motor Inn Resort,** 4391 N. Main St., Chincoteague (✆ **757/336-3141;** www.islandmotorinn.com). $$ **Refuge Inn,** 7058 Maddox Blvd., Chincoteague (✆ **888/868-6400** or 757/336-5511; www.refugeinn.com).

Wildlife Sanctuaries **94**

Cumberland Island National Seashore
Tern to the Left, Plover to the Right
Southeastern Georgia

MORE THAN 335 SPECIES OF BIRDS (MANY OF WHICH ARE ENDANGERED) SHOW UP HERE AT SOME point during the year, drawn by empty dunes, whispering marshes, and—yes—the blessed absence of pesky humans.

It takes 45 minutes by ferry to chug over to Cumberland Island, an undeveloped barrier isle at the southern end of the Georgia coast, practically into Florida. Considering that it's a National Seashore, its gleaming sands are often surprisingly deserted— that is, from a human perspective. Only 300 people are allowed on the island at any given time. But from a bird's point of view, it's a veritable Las Vegas, a major destination on the Atlantic flyway.

"Undeveloped" isn't quite accurate: Cumberland Island was once a sea cotton plantation and then a summer retreat for the Carnegies, and a handful of buildings are still scattered around the island, one of them being the island's only lodging, the Greyfield Inn (see lodging info below). But Cumberland's been basically uninhabited

for a long time, and the wilderness has closed in. The island's roadways seem mere tunnels through a vine-draped canopy of live oaks, cabbage palms, magnolia, holly, red cedar, and pine, a maritime forest that covers 15,000 acres (6,000 hectares). An even larger portion of the island on the western side is fertile salt marsh. The abundant wildlife includes alligators, armadillos, raccoons, deer, and wild turkeys, as well as a herd of about 170 wild horses, which graze (some ecologists say overgraze) on the marsh grasses. Loggerhead turtles nest on its sands, as do several birds—please respect cordoned-off beach areas in season.

Cumberland's 16-mile-long (26km) beach isn't just a bland strip of powdery sand, like some manufactured oceanfront resort: Little meadows nestle between the dunes, creeks cut their way to the sea from freshwater ponds, and tidal mud flats glisten. All of this makes it inviting for birds. Hike or bike down to Pelican Banks, the southernmost point of the island, and you'll be able to view black skimmers, numerous ducks, and the endangered American oystercatcher, a sleek black-and-white bird with a bright-red bill that lives here year-round. Another threatened species, the least tern, arrives on the tidal flats in late April, where it courts, breeds, and nests, hatching chicks by mid-June. Farther north, along the main beach, the Roller Coaster Trail leads past dunes where gray-and-white Wilson's plovers—endangered gray shorebirds with black-banded necks and thick black bills—build their nests. Freshwater ponds behind the dunes provide perfect nesting terrain for white ibis, herons, egrets, and the endangered wood stork, a magnificent white wader with a dark head and black-tipped wings.

In late spring and summer, birds far outnumber humans on Cumberland Island. It's their resort—trespass with care.

Hiking on Cumberland Island.

ⓘ **Cumberland Island National Seashore,** St. Mary's, GA (ℂ **912/882-4336,** ext. 254; www.nps.gov/cuis)

✈ Jacksonville, FL

🚢 45 min. from St. Mary's, reservations (ℂ **912/882-4335** or 877/860-6787)

🛏 $$$ **Greyfield Inn,** Cumberland Island (ℂ **904/261-6408;** www.greyfield inn.com). $$ **Emma's Bed & Breakfast,** 300 W. Conyers St., St. Mary's (ℂ **877/749-5974** or 912/882-4199; www.emmas bedandbreakfast.com).

---

95 Wildlife Sanctuaries

Isle Royale National Park
Lake Woods Wilderness by Design
Michigan

CLIMATE CHANGE HAS PUT ISLE ROYALE'S MOOSE AND WOLF POPULATIONS AT RISK. AIR pollution, rising mercury levels in fish, and reduced government funding have also contributed to a decline in this national landmark.

In most other national parks, you have to worry about whether the parking lot is full. At Isle Royale, you worry about low lake levels. If boats can't maneuver past Lake Superior's treacherous rocks, you just can't get here.

Inaccessibility is part of the deal at Isle Royale—that's why it's so unspoiled. This

45-mile-long (72km) island gets fewer visitors in an entire season than Yosemite may get in just 1 day. Since 1976 it's been a designated wilderness area, which specifies that 99% of the island must remain undeveloped, roadless backcountry; in 1980, it was designated an International Biosphere Reserve. There's an oasis of creature comforts at Rock Harbor, with its rustic resort hotel and limited services at a couple other ports around the island; only a few steps from those areas you plunge deep into Northwoods solitude.

Thick forests cover the island today, but that's deceptive; it's anything but virgin wilderness. Native Americans mined copper here since time immemorial; French fur trappers exploited its wealth of beaver; a 19th-century copper boom sank numerous pits into its bedrock. Yet nature has a way of reclaiming its territory, and Isle Royale stands as a pristine example of how wilderness can be resurrected. These may be second-growth forests, but they're so dense and rich with wildlife, it doesn't matter. The predominant species used to be lynx and caribou, which are now extinct, but in their place Isle Royale has moose and wolves, introduced from the mainland—the only place in the world where these two populations coexist in such balance. Bears and raccoons, common on the nearest mainland, never arrived here, but mink, ermines, and otters, as well as the native red squirrel, thrive. Grebes and loons breed in its wetlands, while great horned owls, pileated woodpeckers, and yellow-bellied sapsuckers nest in the forest tops.

Glaciers left this outcropping of land—the largest island in the world's largest freshwater lake—pocked with lakes and bogs, carving ancient volcanic rock into one long jagged ridge along its spine. Canoes and kayaks can be rented at Rock Harbor or Windigo to explore the shoreline or penetrate the wilderness. Anglers fish in its teeming inland lakes; scuba divers scout out numerous wrecks offshore, testament to Lake Superior's dangerous shoals. Park rangers lead daily walks ranging from bird-watching to visiting the many lighthouses that protect Isle Royale's shores.

Ferries run from Copper Harbor (the *Isle Royale*, © **906/289-4437**) and Houghton, Michigan (the *Ranger III* icebreaker, © **906/482-0984,** which can carry smaller boats), and from Grand Portage, Minnesota (the *Voyageur II* and *Wenonah*, © **888/746-2305** or 715/392-2100). Seaplanes can be booked out of Houghton, Michigan (Royale Air Service, © **877/359-4753** or 218/721-0405; www.royaleairservice.com). These services, however, run only from late spring to early fall. The rest of the year, Isle Royale is left to the wolves and the moose—as it should be.

ⓘ **Isle Royale National Park,** 800 E. Lakeshore Dr., Houghton, MI (© **906/482-0984;** www.nps.gov/isro)

🛏 $$$ **Rock Harbor Lodge,** Isle Royale National Park (© **906/337-4993** in summer, 866/644-2003 in winter; www.rockharborlodge.com)

Wildlife Sanctuaries   96

The San Juan Islands
Nature's Patchwork Marvel in Puget Sound
Offshore Washington

POPULATION GROWTH IN THE SAN JUAN ISLANDS HAS INCREASED GROUND AND WATER POLLUTION, while legions of commercial and private whale-watchers disturb whales and other marine creatures.

Standing on the deck of a Puget Sound ferryboat, gazing at the snowcapped peaks of the Olympic Peninsula, it seems odd to imagine the thickly strewn San Juan Islands surrounding your boat as mountain peaks themselves. But today this ancient range, submerged at the end of the last ice age, is simply dwarfed by those towering youngsters across the way.

Now here's the twist: The Olympic range casts what's called a "rainshadow" over the sound, blocking the rainfall that soaks most of the Northwest. As a result, the San Juan Islands are a rare mosaic of microclimates, some rainforest, some desert, often on the same islands. Here you'll find rare and endangered plants, such as the brittle cactus, the naked broomrape, and the golden paintbrush, alongside patches of ferns, mosses, and lichens, and old-growth forests of cedar, hemlock, yew, and alder. These tiny specialized habitats are often unrecognized, tucked away in crevices of coastal cliffs, in a patch of grassland or small stand of trees. They're not big enough to be marked as nature preserves—but they need to be preserved all the same.

San Juan Island.

The San Juan archipelago has 175 islands big enough to be given names; another 500 or so smaller outcroppings punctuate the waters in between, accessible only by boat. Ferries visit only four islands (San Juan, Orcas, Lopez, and Shaw), and only those first three have tourist accommodations. For years, the San Juans preserved unspoiled habitats, with approximately 83 islands designated wildlife refuges. The San Juans have the largest breeding population of bald eagles in the United States, and they're a magnet for migrating wildlife—not only orcas and minke whales (whale-watching expeditions set out from all the main harbors June–Sept), but also trumpeter swans, snow geese, and salmon. You're likely to spot Dall's porpoises, Steller sea lions, harbor seals, and brown river otters too, especially if you venture around in a kayak.

Unfortunately, all this natural beauty may be the islands' undoing. The word is out, and San Juan County has attracted so many new residents, its population has almost tripled since 1990. As more and more homes are crowded onto the islands, less land is open to shelter those fragile microclimates. Alien species such as red foxes and rabbits overrun some islands, crowding out native species. An upsurge in tourism is also a problem, as more hikers tramp through its parks and venture too close to seabird-nesting areas or the rocky coves where harbor seals bask. The popularity of boating around these islands has begun to wreak havoc with its offshore eelgrass and kelp beds, so vital for sustaining marine life.

Visit the San Juan Islands if at all possible—but be the best sort of visitor you can. Stay on walking paths, observe beach closures, moor your boat only at designated sites, and deal with eco-conscious tour groups. It's the least a nature lover can do.

ⓘ **San Juan Islands Visitors Bureau** (ⓒ **888/468-3701** or 360/468-3663; www.travelsanjuans.com)

✈ San Juan, Orcas, and Lopez islands

🛏 $$$ **Lakedale Resort,** 4313 Roche Harbor Rd., Friday Harbor (☏**800/617-2267** or 360/378-2350; www.lakedale.com). $$ **Lopez Islander Resort,** Fisherman Bay Rd., Lopez Island (☏**800/736-3434** or 360/468-2233; www.lopezfun.com).

TOUR San Juan Safaris (☏ **800/450-6858** or 360/378-1323; www.sanjuan safaris.com). **Deer Harbor Charters** (☏**800/544-5758** or 360/376-5989; www. deerharborcharters.com).

Wildlife Sanctuaries 97

Coiba Island
Take a Walk on the Wild Side
Panama

HOME TO 147 SPECIES OF BIRDS AND 36 SPECIES OF MAMMALS, COIBA ISLAND IS AN EXOTIC habitat. However, logging and tourism disrupts the native species, and illegal fishing remains a threat to its abundant marine life.

You're walking through an uninhabited tropical island. Overhead, a flock of scarlet macaws takes flight, their distinctive squawks and screams filling the air. But don't spend too much time taking in the spectacle—you might miss the howler monkeys on the tree next to you.

After hiking for hours, you've seen more exotic birds and animals than you could ever imagine, and you are falling under the breathtaking spell of Coiba Island, an untamed mosaic of forests, beaches, mangroves, and the second-largest coral reef in the eastern Pacific, far off the coast of Central America.

Coiba stayed in this wild state almost by accident: Ever since 1912 it had been a penal colony, and a very effective one, too. Far from the mainland, covered with wild jungle, surrounded by shark-infested waters, who would even try to escape from such a place? As a result, settlers who might have harvested Coiba's magnificent hardwood forests or cleared the land for housing never moved here. The prison closed in 2004, but Panama's National Authority of the Environment still has a strong presence on the island, protecting this natural treasure, which draws visitors from all over the globe. The entire 495-sq.-km (191-sq.-mile) island is open to hikers,

with trails that even amateurs can walk with ease, as well as so-called "machete" trails which require—well, you get the picture.

Along with the scarlet macaw, Coiba is a haven for the crested eagle, which can be seen soaring overhead looking for prey. Easily identified by the frill of upstanding feathers on top of its black head, the crested eagle loves to fish, but it also has a special fondness for snakes—and Coiba has many snakes, some of them extremely poisonous. (Another deterrent to prison escapes.) There's plenty of prey on Coiba for the crested eagle, and it plays an important role in the habitat, keeping down the numbers of certain species that might overrun this little slice of Eden. With 147 species of birds, along with 36 species of mammals, it's incredibly biodiverse. Four whale and dolphin species can also be spotted in offshore waters, including killer whales (orcas), humpback whales, and the rare pantropical spotted dolphin. The flora is so lush and abundant, botanists have yet to finish categorizing it.

Coiba Island also contains remnants of pre-Columbian settlements, which disappeared when the Spanish arrived in the 15th century. Except for the penal colony, it has remained uninhabited since then. Only an hour's flight from Panama City, it can be visited as a day trip, an escape from civilization you won't soon forget. A trip to this lush wonderland also affords a chance to see the Panama Canal, which is equally under threat. It's soon doubling its capacity, so if you want to sail through the original canal, you'll have to do so before 2014.

✈ Marcos A. Gelbart Airport

🛏 $$ **Avalon Grand Panama,** Panama City (✆ **800/507-1239** in the U.S. and Canada, 00/800-845-6506 in Europe, 52/1-504-1157 in Mexico; www.hotelavalongrandpanama.com). $$ **Country Inn & Suites by Carlson,** Panama City (✆ **888/201-1746;** www.countryinns.com/panamacitypan).

---

98 Wildlife Sanctuaries

Cocos Island Marine Park
Cuckoo for Cocos Island
Costa Rica

WHILE ITS REMOTE LOCATION HAS PROTECTED COCOS ISLAND FROM HUMAN DEVELOPMENT, many rare and endemic plant species are endangered by feral pigs, deer, and rats. Pollution and climate change affect both land and marine habitats.

After a day-and-a-half boat ride, any spot of land would look good—but when Cocos Island rises out of the Pacific, a lush green tropical Eden with waterfalls spilling from its jungle cliffs, it's easy to think you've come to paradise.

Well, don't get carried away. This mountainous former pirate hideout, 482km (300 miles) southwest of the Costa Rican coast, has defeated settlers for centuries. (Though there are no native mammals on the isolated island, feral pigs, goats, rats, cats, and deer roam the wild interior, abandoned by residents who gave up years ago.) The rainfall is prodigious (600cm/240 in. a year); the high-altitude cloud forest is impenetrable; landslides carry off chunks of the coast when you least expect it. Today the only sign of civilization is a tin-roofed ranger station with a handful of rangers. The government forbids any land-based tourism at all, but that's okay—most people who come here are more interested in strapping on a tank and mask and heading under water.

To limit environmental damage, at present only three tour companies are regularly allowed to bring dive boats to Cocos Island,

anchoring in one of its two large beach-fringed bays (Chatham and Wafer Bay) before heading for the offshore dive sites. Rather than exquisite coral reefs, the underwater terrain here is on an epic scale—huge jagged basaltic ridges, violent chasms, abrupt cliffs, boulders as big as a brontosaurus. The marine life is on an equally large scale: giant moray eels, whitetip reef sharks, droves of hammerhead sharks, dolphins, sailfish, hefty tuna and marlin, and occasionally the world's largest fish, the whale shark. A manta ray gliding overhead casts an immense shadow, momentarily blocking out the sun. Round a corner and you'll run into an octopus, lazily extending its fleshy tentacles.

With so many species crowding these fertile waters, it should come as no surprise that Cocos Island would also have a pack of its own homegrown endemic fish species, 27 at last count. Very few creatures in the sea look as weird as the red-lipped batfish, for example, with its pale triangular forehead, bulbous eyes, and scarlet kisser.

While you're anchored off Cocos Island, you may take a shore excursion to hike into the jungle, swim in a crystalline waterfall, or observe rare exotic birds like the Cocos Island cuckoo, the Cocos Island flycatcher, or the Cocos Island finch—a relative of Darwin's finch, from the nearby Galapagos Islands ㉔. Sure, the Galapagos are a few hundred miles away, but for Cocos Island, that qualifies as a next-door neighbor.

✈ San José

TOUR Undersea Hunter (✆ **800/203-2120;** www.underseahunter.com). **Okeanos Aggressor** (✆ **800/348-2628** or 985/385-2628; www.aggressor.com). **Dive Discovery** (✆ **800/86-7321** or 415/444-5100; www.divediscovery.com).

Palau

The Ace of Aquatic Life

Micronesia

PALAU HAS BEEN DUBBED ONE OF "THE SEVEN WONDERS OF THE WORLD" BY VISITORS WHO come to nose around its hundreds of coral species and fish and spot numerous endangered and vulnerable land animals. Unfortunately, this magnet for divers is threatened due to overfishing and climate change.

Known for its diverse natural beauty, which was featured prominently on a season of *Survivor,* Palau is one of the most spectacular diving destinations in the world. Its waters are home to saltwater crocodiles, sea turtles, giant sea turtles, giant clams, and the dugong, a creature similar to the manatee. Palau, an archipelago located about halfway between the Philippines and Guam, also supports 1,200 plant species and hundreds of birds and bats, including the Palauan fruit bat, found only here.

For generations, natives have depended on the archipelago's reefs and forests, but these are under threat from overfishing and nonsustainable forest practices. In 1998, El Niño dealt this paradise another blow: coral bleaching. If left unchecked or worsened by future climate change (the whitening of corals has been blamed on shifts in temperature), the archipelago's coral reefs could decline at an alarming rate. Luckily, The Nature Conservancy is working with Palau to protect its reefs, beaches, and jungles. The government also instituted an initiative in 2005 that

will protect 30% of nearby shore marine resources and 20% of the land by 2020.

Most divers visiting Palau head for the **Rock Islands,** which can be visited on day trips from Koror, Palau's former capital and commercial center. Thanks to a roughly decade-old ban on commercial fishery, threatened shark, barracuda, and wrasse species thrive off the deep drop-offs of this Pacific chain of limestone islands. Of its 76 dive sites, 20 also feature shipwrecks. Two other islands are part of the state of Koror, including Malakal, which has a harbor serving as the starting point for excursions, and Arakebesang, home to the five-star Palau Pacific Resort. Koror Island itself boasts two waterfalls, and it's possible to book day hikes to the Ngardmau waterfall on Palau's tallest peak, Mount Ngerchelechuus, and to the Ngatpang waterfall on the Tabecheding River.

Not to be missed is **Babeldaob,** the largest island in the archipelago. Here, you can see stone monoliths, walk ancient footpaths, and visit *bai,* men's meeting houses, with traditional stories carved in their wooden beams and gables. Completing the archipelago to the south are the islands of Peleliu and Angaur. Peleliu saw its share of battle in WWII. More than 15,000 men were killed here in 1944 and war relics still can be found. On Angaur, monkeys outnumber people by a huge margin, earning it the fitting nickname Monkey Island.

ⓘ www.visit-palau.com

✈ Palau International, Airai (30 min. to Koror)

🛏 $$$ **Palau Pacific Resort,** Arakebesang (✆ **680/488-2600;** www.palauppr.com)

Cousin Island Special Reserve
Where the Birds Watch You Back
The Seychelles

SINCE IT WAS ESTABLISHED IN 1968, THE WORLD'S FIRST INTERNATIONALLY OWNED BIRD RESERVE has preserved habitats that support many rare species, from forest wetlands to seashores. However, beach erosion threatens nesting areas of the endangered hawksbill turtle.

Such a cheeky bird, the magpie robin. With bold black-and-white plumage similar to the European magpie, and a friendly, curious personality like the tame European robin, it's fearless toward humans—especially when the humans in question have food. They'll follow you as you walk down the beach, and even seek out dinner on your kitchen table, if you've been careless enough to leave an open window or door.

One of the few places in the world to see this big-personality bird is Cousin Island, a tiny granite speck of an island in the Indian Ocean. Small as it is, this former coconut plantation has been restored to its original cover of lush tropical forest, and it's become known as an amazing haven for birds. Cousin Island—the world's first internationally owned bird reserve—was established in 1968 to protect the endangered Seychelles warbler, a melodious bird whose call is similar to the human whistle. Today this island sanctuary supports many rare species. In addition to the magpie robin and Seychelles warbler, it hosts the Seychelles fody, a small yellowish bird that was once hunted to the verge of extinction because it competed with humans for the eggs of seabirds.

There's the Seychelles blue pigeon with its bright red cap, the Seychelles sunbird with its curved black beak, and a host of terns, noddies, and shearwaters hanging out along the shore.

It's not all birds, though: Cousin Island is also the area's most important nesting site for hawksbill turtles. Up to 100 turtles come ashore to bask in the daylight, where you can easily observe them. On other beaches on the island, they nest and lay their eggs under cover of dark. Cousin Island has its own giant tortoises, which at one time were nearly eradicated from the Seychelles; a plethora of geckos, skinks, and other lizards also call it home.

Though the Royal Society for Nature Conservation owns the island, it is administered by the International Council for Bird Preservation, now known as BirdLife International. Thanks to the efforts of the ICBP, magpie robins were brought here from Fregate Island, and fodies were transferred from Cousin to Aride Island, establishing new populations to ensure species viability.

More than 10,000 nature lovers visit Cousin Island each year, binoculars in tow, and many educational groups also make the trek. There is no lodging on the island—apart from bird nests, of course—but the Cousin boat takes only about 90 minutes from Praslin, an island well stocked with hotels, fabulous beaches, and breathtaking mountain views. Plan your trip to coordinate with the sanctuary's hours, Monday to Friday between 10am and midafternoon.

ⓘ **Cousin Island Special Reserve** (𝒞 **248/60-1100;** www.natureseychelles.org)

✈ Seychelles Airport

🛏 $$ **Indian Ocean Lodge,** Grand Anse Beach (𝒞 **248/233-324**). $$$ **Berjaya Praslin Beach Resort** (𝒞 **248/286-286;** www.berjayaresorts.com).

Wildlife Sanctuaries **101**

Kangaroo Island
The Purity of Island Living
South Australia

NATIVE ANIMAL SPECIES PROLIFERATE IN KANGAROO ISLAND'S UNIQUE, SELF-CONTAINED ENVIronment with its lack of natural predators. But koalas, not native to the island, were introduced in the 1920s and the population is thriving, threatening native gum trees and destroying the habitats of endangered birds.

To understand the virtues of island isolation, look no further than Kangaroo Island. Lying just across the strait from metropolitan Adelaide, this Southern Hemisphere ecosystem flourishes in a miraculously unspoiled state. No foxes or rabbits were

Wildlife on Kangaroo Island.

ever introduced to prey on the island's inhabitants—the koalas, kangaroos, and wallabies that are Australia's iconic wildlife. (The kangaroos here, however, are a distinct species from the mainland's.) The island was also never colonized by the dingo, Australia's "native" dog that's really a feral scavenger introduced from Asia some 4,000 years ago. Even along the roadsides, the underbrush is mostly native eucalyptus scrub.

To preserve all this, strict regulations monitor what visitors bring on and off the island. Tourists are asked to wash the soil off their shoes and car tires to prevent the spread of fungus. Bushwalkers are required to stay on marked paths and not to feed the wildlife; drivers are encouraged to drive slowly, especially at dusk, when koalas, echidnas, bandicoots, and kangaroos may wander onto the roads.

Of the many preserves on the island (about one-third of the island is conservation area), you'll score the most wildlife sightings at **Flinders Chase National Park** on the western end of the island. Birders have recorded at least 243 species here, including the endangered glossy black cockatoo; koalas are so common they're almost falling out of the trees (the government has in fact had to take steps to reduce the koala population). Kangaroos, wallabies, and brush-tailed possums are so tame that a barrier was erected around the Rocky River Campground to stop them from carrying away picnickers' sandwiches. Platypuses have been sighted, too, but they're elusive—you might need to wait next to a stream in the dark for a few hours.

At Cape du Couedic, the southern tip of the park, the hollowed-out limestone promontory called Admiral's Arch is home to a colony of some 4,000 New Zealand fur seals (despite the name, a legitimately native species). Rangers at the southern coast's **Seal Bay Conservation Park** (✆ 61/8/8559 4207) lead guided tours along boardwalks through the dunes to a beach where you can hobnob with Australian sea lions.

Up on the north coast, Lathami Conservation Park, just east of Stokes Bay, is a superb place to spot wallabies in the low canopy of casuarina pines. If you want to see little penguins—tiny animals that stand about a foot high—the **National Parks & Wildlife South Australia** (✆ 61/8/8553 2381) conducts tours of their colonies around Nepean Bay at both Kingscote and Penneshaw. Last but not least, **Clifford's Honey Farm** (✆ 61/8/8553 8295) is the home of the protected Ligurian honeybee, found nowhere else on earth but on this seemingly magical island.

ⓘ **Tourism Kangaroo Island,** Howard Dr., Penneshaw (✆**61/8/8553 1185;** www.tourkangarooisland.com.au)

✈Kangaroo Island

🛏$$$ **Aurora Ozone Hotel,** The Foreshore, Kingscote (✆ **61/8/8553 2011;** www.auroraresorts.com.au). $$ **Kangaroo Island Lodge,** Scenic Rd., American River (✆ **61/8/8553 7053;** www.kilodge.com.au).

Wildlife Sanctuaries

Lord Howe Island
The Lords of Lord Howe Island
Australia

SINCE LORD HOWE ISLAND BECAME PROTECTED AND MANAGED BY THE LORD HOWE ISLAND Board in 1953, the most serious threats to this island are oil and chemical water pollution, as well as groundwater pollution from sewage management.

There are a lot of outdoor things to do on a Lord Howe Island holiday—swim in a crystal-clear lagoon, marvel at tropical fish in a coral reef, hike trails through palm and banyan forests—but sooner or later the place turns every visitor into a birdwatcher. Not only does it have a lot of birds, but it has rare birds—and, best of all, they aren't shy of people.

Possibly Australia's best birding site, Lord Howe Island is a carefully preserved nature sanctuary, where only 400 tourists are allowed at a time. Seventy-five percent of the island, including much of the southern mountains and northern hills, is a permanent protected nature reserve. Many of its 350 residents are ancestors of the island's first 18th-century settlers. Life here is slow paced; people get around on bikes instead of cars and just about everybody diligently recycles.

Lord Howe Island is home to more than 130 bird species, between residents and migratory visitors. There are 14 species of seabirds alone, which roost and nest here in huge numbers. Walking trails along the island's ragged east coast provide great views of seabirds such as terns, boobies, noddies, and shearwaters. Star among them is one of the world's rarest birds, the Providence petrel, which nests near the summit of **Mount Gower.** This sturdy-looking seabird is so trustful of humans that it can be called out of the air—and might even decide to rest in your lap.

The rarest resident of all is the Lord Howe Island woodhen, found nowhere else but Lord Howe Island. This flightless brown bird, about the size of a bantam rooster, is listed as an endangered species, but the combined efforts of Australia's national wildlife service, the Lord Howe Island Board, and the Foundation for National Parks and Wildlife have resulted in a successful breeding program, and they now populate many parts of the island—some have even nested in residents' backyards. The best place to see them is on the 3km (2-mile) **Little Island trail,** where you can also see some beautiful emerald ground doves.

For impressive aerial feats, look to the skies, especially over the tropical forests of the northern hills, and you'll see the beautiful red-tailed tropic bird, with its elegant red tail streamers. When courting, it will fly backward, in circles, and, for good measure, throw in some vertical displays. It's a splendid sight, and one few birders ever get to see.

A speck off of Australia's east coast, equidistant from Sydney or Brisbane, Lord Howe Island is only a 2-hour plane ride from the mainland. Conveniently, there are just enough hotels on the island to handle all 400 visitors.

ⓘ **Lord Howe Island visitor center** (✆ **1800/240 937** or 61/2/6563 2114; www.lordhoweisland.info)

✈ Lord Howe Island

🛏 $$$ **Blue Lagoon Lodge** (✆ **61/2/6563 2006**). $$$ **Pinetrees Resort Hotel** (✆ **61/2/6563 2177;** www.pinetrees.com.au).

TOUR Lord Howe Nature Tours (✆ **61/2/6563 2447;** www.lordhoweisland.info/services/nature.htm)

Wildlife Sanctuaries **103**

Balranald
The Corncrake in the Crofts
North Uist, the Hebrides, Scotland

RISING SEA LEVELS DUE TO GLOBAL WARMING ARE THE LEADING THREAT TO MACHAIR, A RARE TYPE of habitat that occurs mostly in Scotland and Ireland. Balranald is also home to a large population of the endangered corncrake.

The Western Isles aren't exactly the most far-flung of Scotland's islands—that honor goes to the Shetlands—but stand on the rocky headlands of Balranald, looking west onto the cold, gray North Atlantic, and you feel like you're hanging onto the rim of the continent. This windswept landscape is the last stop before Newfoundland, which is why so many birds end their westward flights here.

It's an extraordinary refuge for waders and seabirds, its marshes and sandy bays hosting dunlins, sanderlings, terns, sandpipers, and lapwings aplenty. If that were all North Uist had to offer, birders would still have a reason to come here. But a few steps inland, you'll find what makes this island really special: the machair.

With its rich tapestry of summer flowers—wild pansies, poppies, marigolds, marsh orchids, eyebrights, silverweed, daisies, purple clover—the machair is a unique sort of grassland, a sort of peaty low-lying pasture that takes over a beach after a drop in sea level creates a new beach. Because its soil is mostly crushed seashells, it's tremendously fertile.

The machair's bird life is amazing: Being so close to the sea, it attracts both meadow species—twites, skylarks, meadow pipets, and corn buntings—and shorebirds like ringed plovers, redshanks, oystercatchers, greylag geese, and barnacle geese. But the real star attraction here is one of Europe's most endangered species, the corncrake. On the U.K. mainland, the corncrake has been driven out of its natural habitat by industry and intensive farming practices; the Outer Hebrides now have two-thirds of the U.K. corncrake population. Yet here it's quite common from mid-April to early August. You can hear its spooky rasping call everywhere, especially at night, but sighting one of these secretive birds is a different matter. Once the machair grows tall in mid-June, the bird is much harder to spot, with its barred brown-and-white back for camouflage. Looking like a slimmer sort of partridge, it steps deftly through the grasses, but the bright chestnut of its wings and legs make it instantly recognizable when it rises in flight.

A 4.8km (3-mile) nature trail winds through the croft land, traversing the machair and leading to the headlands. There's a visitor center open in summer, at Goulat, near Hougharry, and guided tours are led twice a week.

(i) **Balranald Nature Reserve,** Hougharry, 4.8km (3 miles) northwest of Bayhead, North Uist (✆ **44/1463 715000**)

✈ Benbecula

🚢 Lochboisdale (from Oban), Lochmaddy (from Skye);

🛏 $$ **Langass Lodge,** Locheport (✆ **01876/580-385;** www.langasslodge.co.uk). $ **Lochmaddy Hotel,** Lochmaddy (✆ **01876/500-331;** www.lochmaddyhotel.co.uk).

4 Where Sea Meets Shore

A harbor in Crete.

Cape Cod National Seashore
Turtle Time on the Outer Cape
Chatham to Provincetown, Massachusetts

CAPE COD'S DELICATE HYDROLOGY BALANCES INTERIOR FRESHWATER PONDS, OCEAN AND BAY seawater, and the salt marshes in between. Will rising sea levels and pollution from residential housing growth tip that precarious balance?

In the old children's tale, "slow and steady wins the race"—but slow and steady hasn't worked so well for turtles lately. Complex factors—habitat loss, pollution, disease, global climate change—have reduced their numbers, both in the U.S. and around the world. Although several marine turtles swim offshore (loggerheads, leatherbacks, ridleys, hawksbills, green turtles), Cape Cod naturalists are more concerned about the turtles that live on the edge of the Atlantic, where beach meets estuary meets creek, hibernating in tidal mud flats in winter, mating in the salt marshes in spring, nesting in the sand dunes come summer (that is, if raccoons don't steal their eggs). On this narrow, low-lying barrier strip, bisected by busy Route 6, just imagine how hard it is for a little spotted turtle to cross from ocean to bay without becoming roadkill.

Running for 30 miles (48km) along the Atlantic coast of Cape Cod, the Cape Cod National Seashore was set aside in 1961 to preserve the towering dunes and magnificent white sands of the Outer Cape. Drive along Route 6, or cycle up the Cape Cod Rail Trail, and you'll see signs directing you to its various stunning beaches: Coast Guard and Nauset Light beaches in Eastham, Marconi Beach in Wellfleet, Head of the Meadow Beach in Truro, and Provincetown's Race Point and Herring Cove beaches. Those dunes are one of the country's most significant sites for the endangered piping plover, while huge communities of gray seals and harbor

seals cluster on rocks and sandbars closer to water's edge.

Yet just yards away from white sand and surf lies a whole other natural world, with its own meditative rhythms: a rich wilderness of marsh and wetlands tucked away behind the beach. Here, rare eastern spadefoot toads burrow out of the sand on warm rainy spring nights to croak and breed in shallow vernal ponds, and seashore rangers carefully monitor not only the threatened northern diamondback terrapin and eastern box turtle, but even common freshwater species like painted turtles and snapping turtles, and the less

The Cape Cod National Seashore.

99

common pond-dwelling musk turtle and spotted turtle.

At the Salt Pond Visitor Center (Nauset Rd., Eastham), you can pick up a brochure identifying the turtles, then walk the splendid **Nauset Marsh Trail,** where you're likely to spot painted turtles basking on logs. The **Massachusetts Audubon Society's Wellfleet Bay Wildlife Sanctuary** in South Wellfleet (www.wellfleetbay.org) has no fewer than 5 miles (8km) of trails through pine forests, moors, and salt marsh, a favored habitat for diamondback terrapins. And for box turtles, which prefer fields and forest, Wellfleet's conservation trust (http://wellfleetconservationtrust.org) protects a

6½-acre (2.6-hectare) parcel in the middle of the intertidal marsh, designated—what else?—Box Turtle Woods.

ⓘ**Cape Cod National Seashore** (✆**508/771-2144;** www.nps.gov/caco)

✈Hyannis

⊨ $$ **Viking Shores Motor Lodge,** 5200 State Hwy. (Rte. 6), Eastham (✆**800/242-2131** or 508/255-3200; www.viking shores.com). $$ **Even'tide,** 650 State Hwy. (Rte. 6), South Wellfleet (✆**800/368-0007** or 508/349-3410; www.eventide motel.com).

Shorelines in Trouble 105

Cape Hatteras National Seashore
A Battered Barrier Island
Outer Banks, North Carolina

DISSENSION STILL SIMMERS OVER A 2007 LAWSUIT BY DEFENDERS OF WILDLIFE, DEMANDING that the National Seashore protect nesting shorebird habitat against recreational beach use, particularly by off-road vehicles.

Stand on the barrier islands of North America's Atlantic coast and you can feel in the soles of your feet how fragile they are, mere strips of sand slammed by the pounding surf. With rising ocean levels and more frequent storms, those frail islands are more at risk than ever. Covering 70 miles (113km) of North Carolina coastline, the Outer Banks are also known as "the Graveyard of the Atlantic" for their treacherous waters and shifting shoals. With no offshore coral reefs to protect them, the Outer Banks' beaches are particularly vulnerable to erosion; the riptides and currents are so strong, dabbling in the surf is preferable to swimming.

Still, repeat visitors are hooked on the Outer Banks' edgy wind-scoured beauty, and every summer brings a steady stream of beachgoers. Cape Hatteras Seashore is an informal, barefoot hangout—you can easily beach hop, pulling into beach-access parking lots, crossing a small boardwalk over dunes of sea oats, and plopping down in the tawny sand. North Carolina Highway 12 runs along the national seashore, linking its long, narrow islands—from north to south, Bodie Island, Hatteras Island, and Ocracoke Island (a car ferry links Hatteras to Ocracoke). But look up and you'll notice it's paralleled by another highway: the Atlantic Flyway, the East Coast route of choice for migrating birds. As a designated Globally Important Bird Area, among the endangered shorebirds that nest here are piping plovers, least terns, and black skimmers. A 2007 lawsuit has

Cape Hatteras National Seashore.

made the Seashore's rangers vigilant about posting beach closures during nesting season, and banning off-road vehicles at night when endangered loggerhead turtles are nesting. On Bodie Island, guided ranger walks explore the delicate ecosystem of Coquina Beach, home to blue crabs and sea turtles. Across the bridge on Hatteras Island, you can birdwatch on a nature trail at the **Pea Island Wildlife Refuge.**

Each island has its own lighthouse, but the tallest is the black-and-white diagonally striped **Cape Hatteras Lighthouse,** built in 1870 where easternmost Cape Point juts bravely out into the Atlantic. At 208 feet (63m), it's the tallest brick lighthouse in the United States; visitors can climb 268 steps to the top for an awesome view. In 1999, however, the beach had eroded to within 100 feet (30m) of the lighthouse. To protect it, engineers moved the lighthouse inland 2,900 feet (884m)—only to lose half of that buffer of sand in 2003's Hurricane Isabel. The lighthouse now stands 1,500 feet (457m) from the water. But for how long?

(i) **Hatteras Island Visitor Center,** Buxton ((C) **252/473-2111;** www.nps.gov/caha)

✈ Norfolk International

🛏 $$ **Cape Hatteras Bed & Breakfast,** 4223 Old Lighthouse Rd., Buxton ((C) **800/ 252-3316** or 252/995-6004; http://cape hatterasbandb.com). $$ **Ocracoke Harbor Inn,** 144 Silver Lake Rd., Ocracoke ((C) **888/456-1998** or 252/928-5731; www. ocracokeharborinn.com).

Blowing Rocks Preserve
Spouting Off
Hobe Sound, Florida

ERODING DUNES, MARAUDING PREDATORS FROM DOGS TO SEAGULLS, AND A BLAZE OF BEACH-front lighting make nesting a risky business for endangered sea turtles along Florida's resort-packed east coast.

Up at the north end of the Miami sprawl, nature finally gets room to breathe again—and that's good news for endangered sea turtles. On the beaches of North Palm Beach County, turtles swim ashore to lay clutches of eggs from May to August, burying them in the warm sand. It's hard to believe that this all happens only 20 miles (32km) away from glitzy Palm Beach, but it does—and preservationists are determined to keep those nesting beaches safe from high-rise developers.

Start your visit at the **Loggerhead Marinelife Center,** 14200 US 1, Juno Beach (www.marinelife.org), which will quickly get you up to speed with its hands-on exhibits about Florida's tropical ecosystems. In June and July, the peak of turtle-breeding season, guided nighttime walks visit a nearby beach where the nests are laid. These walks are so popular, they often book up as soon as reservations are taken, so call early (© **561/627-8280**).

Then head north to the south end of Jupiter Island, a barrier island between the Atlantic and Indian River Lagoon. Here, a rubbly limestone ridge along the shore creates a curious phenomenon: At high tide in rough weather, waves forced through erosion holes in the rock are sent whistling sky-high—hence the beach's name, Blowing Rocks. Despite this coastal wall, some 600 loggerhead turtles crawl onto the small beach in summer to lay their eggs; nesting areas are roped off and must be strictly observed.

Entering through a tunnel of thick ever-green sea grapes, you can take a mile-long (1.6km) hike along the oceanfront dunes. Coastal hammocks are planted with local sabal palms, and the distinctive gumbo-limbo tree (nicknamed the "tourist tree" because its peeling red bark looks like a sunburned tourist) is gradually replacing the invasive Australian pines that once overran the beach before it was donated to the Nature Conservancy in 1969. Across the highway, the preserve backs onto the Indian River Lagoon, a threatened estuary 156 miles (251km) long that is slowly being coaxed back to health after decades of pollution and overdevelopment. Here a boardwalk trail passes mangrove wetlands, tidal flats, and oak hammock, which shelter hordes of fiddler crabs and, occasionally, manatees. It's like a minicourse in Florida habitats; there's even a butterfly garden featuring native plants. Stand atop the dunes and appreciate one of the few Florida beaches that escaped being turned into a white-sand cliché. No wonder the turtles come back year after year.

ⓘ **Blowing Rocks Preserve,** 574 S. Beach Rd., State Rd. A1A (© **561/744-6668**)

✈ Palm Beach

🛏 $$$ **Jupiter Beach Resort,** 5 N. A1A, Jupiter (© **866/943-0950** or 561/746-2511; www.jupiterbeachresort.com). $ **Baron's Landing Motel,** 18125 Ocean Blvd., Jupiter (© **561/746-8757**)

The Saugatuck Dunes
The Fight for Shore Acres
Saugatuck, Michigan

TRYING TO EXPAND PROTECTION FOR LAKE MICHIGAN'S PRISTINE DUNE LANDS, THE MICHIGAN Dune Alliance in 2009 acquired the Saugatuck Harbor Natural Area—but between that and the state park lies a developer's resort project.

You think you'll never get there—trudging through oak hickory forest, climbing up towering sand dunes, some over 200 feet (61m) tall. Then you reach the top, and there it is: Lake Michigan in all its sparkling blue glory, tiny whitecaps cresting the waves as they lap the shore. The kid in you longs to run down the dune's sandy face, feet pumping so fast you'll kick yourself from behind.

Best of all, you'll have the beach practically to yourself. Though this is an official state park, there's no lifeguard, no jetty, no boardwalk, no snack bar blaring pop music. Parking was intentionally sited far from the beach to protect the fragile dunes from excess traffic and to discourage short-term visitors (a bike trail from the town of Saugatuck offers an even more eco-friendly option). Thanks to persistent local conservationists, the Saugatuck Dunes have been left undeveloped, an unspoiled stretch of rare freshwater dunes, their sugary white sands anchored by marram grass and wildflowers—beach pea, sand cress, smooth rose, bearberry. The interdunal ponds and ponds between them support even rarer species like the Blanchard's Cricket Frog, Houghton's goldenrod, and the Zigzag Bladderwort wildflower. Bird-watchers and hikers outnumber beachgoers some days; the park has 13 miles (21km) of sandy hiking trails, the most challenging being the 5.5-mile (8.9km) South Trail, which loops through a designated natural area.

Originally, this stretch of premium lakefront was Shore Acres, the 1920s summer estate of office-machine inventor Dorr Felt. Augustinian monks then turned the peaceful property into a seminary and retreat. But when the state of Michigan acquired the property in the 1970s, the mansion was converted for offices, and a medium-security prison was built nearby. (The prison still occupies 44 inland acres of the park.) With 2.5 miles (4km) of shoreline, the site seemed natural for a state beach, a major summer recreation zone for the Saugatuck-Douglas area. But concerned citizens countered with a plan for low-impact recreation—and for once, they prevailed. Today, the only off-road vehicles permitted here are Saugatuck Dune Rides' schooners, offering nature tours of the dunes (www.saugatuck duneride.com).

Even with that battle won, the war isn't over. In 2003, advocates defeated two proposals to build water-treatment plants within the park; though the Michigan Dune Alliance acquired the Saugatuck Harbor Natural Area to the south in 2009, a real estate developer with plans for housing, hotels, and a marina still owns the land in between. Expensive legal wrangling continues.

ⓘ **Concerned Citizens for Saugatuck Dunes State Park,** 6575 138th Ave., Saugatuck (✆ **269/637-2788**; www.saugatuck dunes.org)

✈ Grand Rapids

⊨ $$ **BeachWay Resort,** 106 Perryman St., Saugatuck (✆ **269/857-3331**; www.beachwayresort.com). $$$ **Lake Shore Resort,** 2885 Lakeshore Dr., Saugatuck (✆ **269/857-7121**; www.lakeshore resortsaugatuck.com).

Point Reyes National Seashore
The White Cliffs of Marin
Point Reyes Station, California

IN 2005, THE U.S. GEOLOGICAL SURVEY IDENTIFIED POINT REYES NATIONAL SEASHORE, WITH its low coastal slopes, as one of America's most at-risk shorelines for rising sea levels.

When Sir Francis Drake and his globe-circling crew hauled the *Golden Hinde* onto this sweeping beach in 1579, one look at its bleached limestone bluffs made them homesick for the white cliffs of Dover. What Drake didn't know was that this peninsula was a long-distance traveler, too, a chunk of continent transported some 300 miles (483km) by the San Andreas Fault. The fault line runs right under Tomales Bay, nudging Point Reyes northwestward roughly 2 inches (5cm) a year—except for 1906, when it heaved almost 20 feet (6m), lying at the epicenter of the earthquake that devastated San Francisco, 30 miles (48km) to the south.

Today you can learn about the San Andreas Fault Zone by walking the Earthquake Trail, which begins at the Seashore's Bear Valley Visitor Center. But earthquakes, destructive as they can be, are the least of Point Reyes' concerns these days. If global temperatures continue to rise, the park's moss-cloaked Douglas firs and California redwoods, which thickly cover Inverness Ridge, could sicken and die off. Even more threatening is another facet of climate change—sea levels predicted to rise along the California coast by at least 3.3 feet (1m) by the year 2100. With some 80 miles (129km) of spectacular rugged shoreline, Point Reyes has several wide sand beaches, both along the sheltered curve of Drake's Bay and on the surf-pounded Pacific Ocean front (swimmers beware: you'll need a wet suit in these cold waters), while a sweeping plain of low-lying coastal scrub is threaded with estuaries, creeks, and lagoons. All of it could be washed away.

Point Reyes' unique geology has created a rich mosaic of habitats. It's renowned as a birding hot spot, with 490 bird species recorded—nearly half of all North American birds—the highest avian diversity of any national park. Four species of pinnipeds live on these rock-edged beaches: harbor seals, California sea lions, Steller sea lions, and a booming winter population of the once-rare Northern elephant seal. From January to April, mother gray whales cruise with their calves along the shoreline. Take some time to explore the seashore's special places—like **Abbot's Lagoon** (off Pierce Point Rd.), a serene habitat for migrating shorebirds in the fall and ducks in winter, where snowy plovers nest in the dunes every summer. (A 2011 project to hand-remove invasive European beach grass and ice plant will restore this beach for rare native dune plants.) Or walk south from popular **Limantour Beach** to **Sculptured Rock Beach,** where the secret life of tide pools is revealed among the namesake rocks at low tide. Life at the edge of the sea is fragile—you don't need an earthquake to knock it out of whack.

ⓘ **Point Reyes National Seashore,** 1 Bear Valley Rd., Point Reyes Station (✆ **415/464-5100;** www.nps.gov/pore)

✈ San Francisco/Oakland

🛏 $ **Point Reyes Hostel,** Point Reyes National Seashore (✆ **415/663-8811;** http://norcalhostels.org/reyes). $$ **Abalone Inn,** 12355 Sir Francis Drake Blvd., Inverness Park (✆ **877/416-0458** or 415/663-9149; www.abaloneinn.com).

Lyme Bay

Protecting Wildlife on the Jurassic Coast

East Devon/Dorset, England

A 2007 OIL SPILL FROM A WRECKED CONTAINER SHIP DEVASTATED THE MARINE ECOSYSTEMS of Lyme Bay, whose famed coral reefs were already being ravaged by scallop-dredging operations.

Talk about environmental horror stories— imagine the wreck of a huge commercial container ship carrying 3,500 tons of oil, right off the pebbled coast of Dorset and East Devon, England's foremost World Heritage Site.

After its hull split in an English Channel storm, the foundering *Napoli* began to leak so badly, it was deliberately run aground on Branscome Beach in Lyme Bay—a baffling decision, considering Lyme Bay's importance as a wildlife habitat, with offshore reefs full of unusual species like the Devon cup coral and the rare pink sea fan. An 8km (5-mile) oil slick spread, and hundreds of guillemots, gulls, and razorbills washed ashore, their feathers covered in tarry oil. Five dolphins were found dead; mounds of rotting fish piled up on beaches.

While the oil spill was eventually cleaned up, its long-term effects on the local wildlife are still being reckoned. Luckily, in 2008 the Devon Wildlife Trust finally won its campaign against destructive scallop-dredging operations around the coral reefs, when a 60-square-mile (155-sq.-km) zone was declared off-limits for dredging and trawling—giving the reefs more of a chance to recover. The Trust also operates the **Fine Foundation Marine Centre** in Kimmeridge Bay (southeast of Plymouth), where you can explore the Purbeck Marine Wildlife Reserve's rock pools, marine tanks, and snorkel trail.

This stretch of English coastline is often called the Jurassic Coast because of the wealth of fossils in its rocky shingle beaches and colorful cliffs—cliffs that are seriously at risk for erosion, due to poorly designed breakwaters and seawalls and too many tourists collecting fossils (since 2007 a Fossil Warden has patrolled the area to promote "responsible collecting"). But with its mix of cliffs, estuaries, and beaches, it's also a natural haven for seabirds. Across the river from Exmouth, the **Dawlish Warren Nature Reserve's** enormous mud flats are vital feeding grounds for shorebirds; ringed plovers and Sandwich terns breed on the shore, and larks and linnets nest in the dunes. At the eastern end of Lyme Bay, between Portland and Weymouth, **Chesil Beach** is a long sweep of barrier beach sheltering a brackish lagoon (the Fleet) that's one of Europe's most important—and most fragile—tidal habitats. Peer through a telescope at the Chesil Beach Centre to watch the little terns, ringed plovers, Brent geese, and other birds that breed in the Fleet. Just east of Chesil Bank, gulls, guillemots, and kittiwakes nest on the spectacular sea cliffs of the **Isle of Portland;** it's such an ornithological hot spot, the old lighthouse here has been converted to a bird-watching center.

ⓘ **The Jurassic Coast World Heritage Site** (www.jurassiccoast.com)

🚂 Dorchester or Axminster

🛏 $$ **The Royal Lion Hotel,** Broad St., Lyme Regis (✆ **44/1297/445622;** www. royallionhotel.com). $ **Portland Bird Observatory,** the Old Lower Light, Portland Bill (✆ **44/1305/820553;** www.port landbirdobs.org.uk).

The Algarve
Miami on the Mediterranean
Southwest Portugal

URBANIZATION, ROAD CONSTRUCTION, AND DEFORESTATION THREATEN PORTUGAL'S GOLDEN coast. Western stretches still offer some undeveloped beaches and nature reserves, but for how long?

In the mid-1960s, as the rise of air travel fueled a boom in vacation travel, Portugal's tourism officials focused on their yet-undeveloped jewel: the long southern coast, the wild west of the Mediterranean, with its dramatic cliffs, coves, and clean sandy beaches. Named the Algarve—a corruption of its Moorish name Al-Gharb—this balmy southwestern corner of Portugal seems more like North Africa than Europe, full of lemon and fig trees, almond and olive orchards. Officials vowed that they'd never repeat Spain's overdevelopment of its Costa del Sol. Oops.

Driving west from the Faro airport today, you'll pass resort town after resort town, every inch of their golden beaches occupied. There's Quarteria, swallowed by a sea of boxy high-rise hotels and timeshares, and Vilamoura, with its 1,000-boat marina and mass of anonymous "holiday villages." The once-charming fishing village of Albufeira has become a mini–St. Tropez, its Moorish fretwork chimneys disappearing

The Algarve.

amid bland modern developments. There are still sardine canneries in bustling Portimão, but even that hasn't spared it from encroaching resorts.

It's not just a question of tasteless architecture; all this development has very real environmental impact. According to a 2010 European Commission report, the Algarve's coastal resorts have seriously begun to damage sensitive dune ecosystems. In 2009, hundreds of dead fish washed up along Albufiera's Lagos de Salgados lagoon after a sewage-plant leak. A boom in golf course construction has converted "useless" coastal marshes to fairways by planting exotic ground-drying eucalyptus trees; with the wild grasses dried up, the rabbit population has declined, meaning less food for the near-extinct Iberian lynx. As farming dwindles, drastically fewer butterflies remain; dredging and boating may be killing off seahorses, too.

You'll have to go farther west, past the historic Moorish port of Lagos, to find unspoiled areas. Just west of Lagos, the **Ponta da Piedade** (Point of Piety) is a beautiful rocky headland with red and yellow sandstone cliffs, wave-hollowed hidden grottoes, and quiet cove beaches. Continue on to the extreme southwestern tip of Europe, where the rocky escarpment of Sagres juts into the Atlantic Ocean. Here at **Cap St. Vincent,** Henry the Navigator founded a school of navigation that launched Portugal and the rest of Europe into the Age of Exploration (Magellan and Vasco da Gama apprenticed here). Today, a huge stone compass dial marks the reconstructed site of Henry's wind-swept fortress—on Europe's Land's End.

✈ Faro International, Faro

🛏 $$$ **Romantik Hotel Vivenda Miranda,** Porto de Mós, Lagos (© **351/ 282/763-222**; www.vivendamiranda.com). $$ **Pousada do Infante,** Ponta da Atalaia, Sagres (© **351/282/620-240**; www. pousadas.pt).

111 Shorelines in Trouble

The Beaches of Crete
Where Zorba the Greek Danced
Crete

AS RAMPANT URBANIZATION DISRUPTS SAND DUNES AND OFFSHORE SEAGRASS BEDS, ENDANGERED species like the Mediterranean monk seal and loggerhead turtles are deserting Crete's north coast.

You'd swear developers were trying to replicate the labyrinth of ancient King Minos. In the beach resorts of north Crete, massive concrete hotel complexes shoulder each other along water's edge, eradicating sand dunes. Greece's largest island attracts a crush of package-tour visitors from mid-July to August, pouring in via cruise ship and ferry and charter jet to the gritty modern seaport of Iraklion, home to half of Crete's population. From there they spread out east and west, to nightlife-busy towns like Malia and Hersonisos and Agio Nikolais. Tour buses line up outside the great archaeological sites—Minos's palace at Knossos, his brother Radamanthis's palace at Phaestos—as holidaygoers shuffle wearily through the sun-baked ruins.

It's only natural that developers would target the north coast, with its broad sandy beaches and Mediterranean climate. Crete's main harbors are all on the Sea of Crete side, facing the Grecian mainland; for centuries (1212–1669) Iraklion, Chania, and Rethymno were wealthy Venetian trading centers, as their historic centers still attest. But these days, to find a more authentic Crete, you'll have to head south across the rugged mountainous interior to the Sea of Libya.

About 90 minutes south from Chania or Iraklion via Highway 97, the former fishing village of **Agia Galini** (the name means "serenity") tumbles down steep scrubby hillsides to a modest harbor. (Legend claims that this is where Daedalus's son Icarus jumped off a cliff trying to fly.) Agia Galini is hardly undiscovered—it has plenty of tidy little hotels and tavernas, and sunbathers line its sand-and-pebble beaches—but its narrow streets and low-rise white buildings are still refreshingly human-scale. Hire a boat to take you up the coast to secluded beach coves tucked among the cliffs, such as Agio Georgios, Agio Pavlo, or stunning palm-lined Phoenix Beach beneath the monastery at Preveli. Dolphin-watching tours are also popular (there's a reason dolphin icons fill ancient Minoan art).

Building a highway along this mountainous coast was too challenging, so a string of south coast towns from Paleohora to Hora Sfaklion found a typically Cretan solution: ferry service. The village of **Loutro,** for example, has no road access whatsoever; it's reachable only by boat or by the E4 walking trail, which traces old goat paths along the shoreline's cliffs. Set around a tiny sheltered bay, peaceful Loutro is a low-key base for outdoor activities. Within an hour you can walk to beautiful beaches at Sweetwater or Marmara, or take a day hike up into the dramatic **Imbros Gorge,** where wild thyme perfumes the grassy slopes. All the day-trippers will be herding through the famous Samaria Gorge to the west—you'll have Imbros gloriously to yourself.

✈ Iraklion or Chania

🚢 6–10 hr. from Athens (www.ferries.gr)

🛏 $$$ **Hotel Irini Mare,** Agia Galini (© **30/28320/91488;** www.irinimare.com). $$ **Hotel Minos,** Agia Galini (© **30/28320/91292;** www.minos.agiagalini.com). $$ **Hotel Porto Loutro,** Loutro (© **30/28250/91433;** http://hotelportoloutro.com).

Mangroves **112**

The Shores of Biscayne Bay
Last Stand of the Mangroves
Homestead, Florida

MANGROVE STANDS USED TO LINE FLORIDA'S COAST, UNTIL HOTEL DEVELOPERS STARTED RIPPING them out to gain access for beachfront high-rises. Today, it's illegal to cut down mangroves, but the damage is already done.

Snorkelers and scuba divers are so eager to get down to Biscayne Bay's enormous coral reef (80), they often miss the park's most spectacular secret: its shoreline. In these surprisingly shallow waters—Biscayne Bay is actually an estuary, a gradual transition zone from fresh water to saline sea—an overwhelming variety of life thrives in pillowy seagrass beds and tangled mangrove stands.

The best way to explore this fascinating transition zone is with a canoe or kayak (rent from **Biscayne National Underwater Park, Inc.,** © **305/230-1100,** at the Convoy Point visitor center, or check the park schedule for ranger-led canoe tours).

Paddle along the western shore of Biscayne Bay and you'll see three species of mangroves—red, black, and white—all with distinctive arching prop roots, cigar-shaped seedpods, and thick-bladed leaves. Mangroves are uniquely adapted to handle salt water, with their salt-blocking root systems and leaves that secrete excess salt. Those dense above-water roots trap the waters flowing into the bay and let sediment settle out; they also shelter the smallest marine organisms, which feed on disintegrated leaves (and then provide food themselves for fish, pink shrimp, crabs, and the Florida spiny lobster). The treetops create a canopy where many birds, including the endangered brown pelican, breed and nest.

Farther out in the bay, sediments settling onto the bay's shallow floor make an ideal base for flowering seagrasses, which depend on the oozy shallows' plentiful sunlight. Seagrass beds feed and shelter myriad sea creatures, especially juveniles that aren't ready for open water. Look down through the amazingly clear water and identify the three major types of seagrasses: shoal grass in the shallowest

waters; wide-leaved turtlegrass, the most common; and cylindrical-leaved manatee grass.

Unlike land-based parks, which can erect barriers to keep out invaders and pollutants, an underwater park like Biscayne has to deal with whatever flows in. The mangroves and seagrass can only do so much to clean south Florida's water. As it is, imagine what would have happened if developers had been allowed to dredge the bay and build resorts in the early 1960s. Instead, conservationists fought to preserve the bay and its 44 tiny islands as a national park. Their victory was a win for all of us.

(i) **Biscayne National Park,** 9700 SW 328th St., Homestead, FL (© **305/230-7275;** www.nps.gov/bisc)

✈ Miami International

🛏 $$ **Silver Sands Beach Resort,** 301 Ocean Dr., Key Biscayne (© **305/361-5441;** http://silversandsbeachresort.net). $$ **Indian Creek Hotel,** 2727 Indian Creek Dr., Miami Beach (©**800/491-2772** or 305/531-2727; www.indiancreekhotel.com).

Searching for marine life in Biscayne Bay.

Salt River Bay
Columbus's American Landing
St. Croix, U.S. Virgin Islands

CARELESS LOCALS HAVE DAMAGED ARCHAEOLOGICAL SITES AND SPOILED THE SENSITIVE NATURAL environment of this coastal area on Salt River Bay, including one of the last stands of mature hardwood trees left on St. Croix.

It must have looked inviting—the lush north coast of this 28-mile-long (45km) Antilles Caribbean island, the largest of its neighbors. Christopher Columbus promptly christened it Santa Cruz (Holy Cross), anchored his fleet of 17 ships, and sent some men ashore to the village to find fresh water. Naturally, along the way the crewmen decided to pick up a couple of the native Tainos for slaves. But they didn't expect the Carib Indians—themselves aggressive invaders who'd only recently taken over the island—to come at them with spears and arrows. By the time the Europeans sailed away, one Carib and one Spaniard lay dead. And so began the history of European settlement in the United States.

The site of Columbus's first landing on what is now U.S. soil was recorded as November 14, 1493, in the logbook from his second New World expedition; on the 500th anniversary of that landing, this coastal area was declared a national park. For many St. Croix locals, however, the Salt River Bay refuge remained just a handy place to camp out and dump loads of trash (including burned-out cars).

The park's historical features are still sadly undeveloped, although recently a hilltop white estate house was converted into a visitor center (open Nov–June) to direct visitors to several remarkable archaeological sites—including vestiges of a prehistoric settlement, the remains of a ceremonial Taino ball court, and the ruins of a 17th-century Dutch colonial fort.

Most visitors, however, focus on the park's ecological features, which are outstanding. Even among St. Croix's world-class diving locations, Salt River Bay's submarine coral canyon is a draw, plunging 350 feet (107m) deep and furnished with ledges, grottoes, and caverns to explore. Closer to shore, the bay's mix of fresh and salt water nourishes the largest remaining mangrove forest in the Virgin Islands, a stand that features all four species of mangroves—red, white, black, and buttonwood. Baby sea turtles, oysters, and crustaceans hide out among their spreading root systems, while snowy egrets patrol the shallows and ospreys glide overhead, looking for young fish to snatch. **Caribbean Adventure Tours** (✆ **340/778-1522;** www.stcroixkayak.com) runs naturalist-guided kayaking trips out of Salt River Marina; the nighttime ones are particularly intriguing, where you can explore the bioluminescent waters of the bay glowing at night.

ⓘ **Salt River Bay National Historical Park and Ecological Preserve,** Rte. 75 to Rte. 80, Christiansted (✆ **340/773-1460;** www.nps.gov/sari)

✈ Henry E. Rohlsen Airport, St. Croix

🛏 $$$ **The Buccaneer,** Gallows Bay, North Shore (✆ **800/255-3881** or 340/712-2100; www.thebuccaneer.com). $$ **Arawak Bay: The Inn at Salt River,** Kingshill (✆ **877/261-5385** or 340/772-1684; www.arawakbaysaltriver.co.vi).

Placencia Lagoon
Catching the Breeze in Belize
Belize

WHEN BELIZE'S PRIME MINISTER ANNOUNCED IN 2010 THAT CRUISE TOURISM WOULD BE COMING to low-key Placencia, villagers and local tourism operators rose in opposition.

For eons, Placencia Lagoon has quietly done its job—cleaning the fresh water flowing from a marshy savanna, mixing it with Caribbean salt water, absorbing carbon dioxide, releasing oxygen, and nourishing rare marine creatures like the West Indian manatee, Morelet's crocodile, and Atlantic spotted dolphin. Shellfish, sponges, and algae cling to the mangroves' arched roots, while orchids bloom in their canopy; juvenile fish shelter underneath. More than half of the shallow lagoon floor is a pillow of rare seagrasses, protected from the open sea by the Placencia Peninsula, a beautiful 11-mile-long (18km) strip of dazzling white sand and susurrating palms.

But all that was before Placencia became Belize's hottest new tourism destination. In the space of just a few years, hotels have sprouted along the peninsula's white sand beaches; though Belize requires a permit for developers to remove mangroves, permits were freely granted in the interests of developing beachfront. Although most visitors focus on the gentle Caribbean surf and the outlying coral reef, inevitably the population increase has resulted in sewage leaked into the lagoon.

Meanwhile, on the lagoon's mainland side, a booming shrimp aquaculture industry has added its own pollution, flushing effluents into the lagoon and dumping silt into the creek mouths. Shrimp farmers have simply assumed that the mangroves can process those extra nutrients—after all, that's what mangroves always have done. But several farms now line that shore, and the mangroves may soon reach their capacity. Local conservationists have been working with shrimp farmers to

develop more sustainable practices, and are lobbying to make the lagoon a Marine Protected Area while the ecosystem is still relatively healthy.

Belize is clearly banking on Placencia's growth as a tourist destination. A new paved highway speeds the 2-hour drive from Belmopan, Belize's capital; a modern airport has opened on the southern end of the peninsula. But even the local tourism community protested when the government and Royal Caribbean Cruises announced plans in 2010 to make Placencia a second Belizean cruise port. (Belize City is currently the country's only cruise stop.) Royal Caribbean's bid was rejected, but the cruise industry is still eyeing Placencia.

There's more to do here than just laze on the sand or dive along the reef. The sorts of tourists who seek out Placencia also go bird-watching in kayaks along the lagoon or up the mangrove-lined Monkey River, explore Mayan ruins at Lubaantun and Nim Li Punit, experience the African-flavored Garifuna village culture at Seine Bight, or take tours of the Cockscomb Basin Wildlife Sanctuary (also known as Jaguar Jungle). The people of Placencia understand the attraction of their relaxed, low-key beach town, and know that increased mass tourism would ruin it. Now if only the government would finally get the point.

✈ Placencia

🛏 $$ **Nautical Inn,** Seine Bight Village (✆**800/688-0377** or 501/523-3595; www.nauticalinnbelize.com). $$ **Singing Sands Inn,** Maya Beach (✆**888/201-6425** or 501/520-8022; www.singingsands.com).

10 Disappearing Beaches

When seas rise, it's inevitable—beaches disappear. Even setting climate change aside, scientists predict a 10- to 12-inch (25–30cm) rise in ocean levels by the end of this century, and for each inch the ocean rises, a beach gets on average 3¼ feet (1m) narrower. Add human interference with natural beach topography—channel dredging, sand replacement, seawalls, jetties—and it's a recipe for disaster.

Here are 10 notable beaches in need of saving:

115 Montauk, New York   Jetties built 20 years ago to protect the beaches of posh East Hampton have prevented natural sand migration along this Atlantic coast summer resort—leaving beachfront homes in neighboring Montauk virtually beachless, and vulnerable to the crashing waves of winter storms. Dwindling dunes from Sagaponack to Westhampton suggest the problem is widespread. *www.hamptonsweb.com/beaches.*

Miami Beach.

116 Miami Beach, Florida   Really a barrier island, Miami Beach has been pumping up its high-profile beach since 1976, spending millions of dollars to preserve the 10-mile-long (16km) strand lined with high-rise hotels. Years of building seawalls and "borrowing" sand from the sea floor have accelerated erosion, while frequent tropical storms make it impossible to keep sand in place. As the local sand supply runs out, Miami now must import sand from other countries. *www.ecomb.org.*

117 Santa Barbara, California   The "American Riviera," Santa Barbara is known for its Spanish-Mediterranean architecture and well-groomed, palm-lined, white beaches. But battered by periodic El Niño events, armored with seawalls that only intensify wave action, and robbed of replenishing sediments by several upriver dams, Santa Barbara's beaches are in trouble. Goleta Beach Park has been severely reduced, and in a domino effect, Arroyo Burro Beach is following suit. *www.santabarbaraca.gov.*

118 Waikiki Beach, Oahu, Hawaii   With seas rising all around Hawaii, beach erosion presents a challenge, especially along Honolulu's densely built-up Waikiki beach. A sensitive $2.5-million project in 2010 aimed to replenish the eroding sands of borrowed sand from offshore shoals, leaving the local sand volume unchanged and matching new sand to old. It remains to be seen whether this scheme will succeed where 2006's beach nourishment failed. *www.gohawaii.com/oahu.*

119 Cancun, Mexico   Repeatedly hit by Category 4 and 5 hurricanes over the past decade, this heavily developed resort coast has spent millions to pump sand from the sea bottom to re-create its white-sand beaches. Damage to underwater life and coral reefs aside, this fine sand has proven to erode even more quickly, as tall beachfront hotels funnel winds that used to dissipate over sand dunes. *http://cancun.travel.*

120 Negril, Jamaica   Starting in the 1970s, a wave of resort building along Negril's beautiful Seven-Mile Beach capitalized on its glorious sand. But degraded offshore coral reefs, dredged seagrass beds, and drained wetlands left the existing sand vulnerable to wave erosion. Tropical storms periodically pummel this flat, low-lying area, and every year, natural processes have a harder time replenishing the steadily eroding beach. *www.negril.com.*

Cancun.

121 The Holderness Coast, Northeast England
The fastest-eroding coastline in Europe is this 62km (39-mile) stretch north of the Humber Estuary, where soft clay cliffs are battered by powerful North Sea waves. Beaches at the foot of those low crumbling cliffs lose nearly 2m (6½ ft.) per year. Groynes and other man-made revetments protect the holiday sands at resort towns like Hornsea and Mappleton, but steal sand from other areas. *www.yorkshire.com.*

122 Kololi Beach, The Gambia   Mainland Africa's smallest country has only 50 miles (80km) of Atlantic shoreline, but with its economy dependent on beach resort tourism, severe coastal erosion is a grave concern. A $20-million sand replacement widened popular Kololi Beach to 100m (328 ft.), but in 2 years it had already shrunk back to 26m (85 ft.). Rising sea levels could flood the nearby capital, Banjul. *www.visitthegambia.gm.*

123 Pattaya Beach, Thailand   In 1952, quiet Pattaya Beach was 36m (118 ft.) wide; after a resort boom since the mid-1990s, it may be down to its last 4 or 5m (13–16 ft.). Changing wave patterns in the Gulf of Thailand no longer deposit enough sand to replenish normal tidal erosion, but the problem is exacerbated by crowds of sunbathers and jet-skiers. Beachfront businesses, crowded onto an ever-narrowing strip of sand, pile sandbags to protect their property. *www.pattayatourism.com.*

124 Portsea Beach, Australia   In just a few months, as much as 15m (49 feet) was swept away from this iconic Mornington Peninsula beach, popular with scuba divers and affluent Melbourne weekenders. Locals blame the 2009 dredging of the channel into Port Phillip Bay, designed to improve shipping for the Port of Melbourne. Sandbags and piled boulders occupy the last narrow strip of beach, waiting for sands that may never return. *www.visitmorningtonpeninsula.org.*

Sundarbans National Park
Man-Eaters in the Mangroves
Ganges Delta, Bangladesh/India

CAUGHT BETWEEN THE POLLUTED OUTFLOW OF THE RIVER GANGES AND THE RISING SEA LEVELS of global warming, the immense Sundarbans delta persists, providing a haven for threatened species.

Sundarbans is used to dancing on the edge—on the edge between India and Bangladesh, on the edge between the saline Bay of Bengal and the three freshwater rivers that feed it, on the edge between monsoon floods and a dry season that's not all that dry. And now, tectonic shifts are actually tilting the Bangladesh half of this vast delta, further disrupting the balance between fresh and salt waters that bred this unique ecosystem in the first place.

Traditionally, Sundarbans—despite a name that means "beautiful forest"—was considered a dangerous wasteland. Now it's recognized as a World Heritage Biosphere, home to threatened species like water monitor lizards, olive ridley turtles, Gangretic dolphins, spotted chital deer, and macaques, as well as such amazing birds as brown-winged kingfishers, gray-headed lapwings, Pallas's fish eagles, and mangrove whistlers. And what other place in the world has a fish like the mudskipper, which actually climbs trees?

And then there are the native Bengal tigers. It's unclear why they're so much more aggressive than other Bengal tigers; it could be the salt water they drink while swimming between the scattered mangrove islands, or the fact that shifting tides obliterate the scents that help them mark their territory, or inherited behavior from generations of scavenging on drowned humans during monsoon floods. Whatever it is, they're renowned man-eaters, and Sundarbans visitors must always be on their guard—cruising intricate tidal waterways by boat, observing wildlife from enclosed watchtowers, or wearing face masks on the back of their head to confuse the tigers, which prefer to attack humans from behind. Although the tigers can be dangerous, they're also an endangered species, and in June 2011 the Bangladesh government established a special tiger protection patrol to guard the tigers from poachers.

The Sundarbans is not necessarily unspoiled wilderness; you'll see local residents harvesting the sundri trees for timber or charcoal, using trained otters to fish for the shrimp that shelter within the mangrove roots, and hunting for beehives in honey season (Apr–May). There are only a few basic accommodations within the park; many visitors come on a government-organized 2- to 3-day tour (the best season is Nov–Mar), which ferries guests around on boats to sites such as the Sajnakhali Bird Sanctuary, the Bhagatpur Crocodile Project, or the ridley turtles' nesting site at Kanak.

Yes, there could be a crocodile basking on that next muddy bank, or a tiger lurking in the tangled understory of a mangrove island. But just as easily you could be delighted by a rhesus monkey chattering in the thick green treetop canopy, or a stately heron promenading through the shallows. Hold your breath, stay alert, and you're sure to be surprised.

✈ Kolkata

🛏 $$ **Sunderban Tiger Camp,** Dayapur, India (☏ **91/33/3293 5749** or 91/933/1092632; www.sunderbantigercamp.com).

TOUR **Bangladesh Ecotours** (✆ 880/ 189/318345 or 880/171/264827; www. bangladeshecotours.com). **Oriental Tours and Travel** (✆ 91/987/118 8779; www.

wildlifeindiatour.com). **Vivada Inland Waterways** (✆ 91/33/2463 1990; www. vivada.com).

126 Coastal Marshes

Big Cypress National Preserve
Panther Party
South Florida

BALANCING RECREATIONAL USE AGAINST THE INTERESTS OF WILDLIFE, THE MANAGERS OF THIS sensitive wetlands have from time to time closed trails, banned airboats and off-road vehicles, and managed controlled wildfires.

Don't let the name deceive you. You won't see giant cypresses here—most are mere upstarts, descendants of trees felled for timber in the 1950s. Still, it deserves to be called Big Cypress Forest because the tract itself is so big. Together with neighboring Everglades National Park, it covers 2.7 million acres (1.1 million hectares)— that's a lot of south Florida.

The Everglades ❶ gets all the press, but without the Big Cypress swamp, there would be no Everglades. Its cypress sloughs and marshes pour fresh water into the Everglades, feeding the marine estuaries along Florida's southwest coast. Cypress trees love water, and they anchor this swamp with tough roots and stout buttressed trunks that can withstand strong winds, a good thing in hurricane-prone Florida.

Big Cypress allows more recreation than the Everglades does, though off-road vehicles have caused concern lately; they damage this sensitive drainage ecosystem, already impaired by misguided canal building and highway construction in years past. Backcountry camping and hiking can lead you deep into the wilderness, through dwarf cypress forest, slash pine forests (home to the endangered red-cockaded woodpecker), and saw grass prairie. (Examine a blade of saw grass and you'll see the jagged edges that earn it its name.) Perhaps you'll even go deep enough to surprise a Florida panther chasing down a deer— there are 30 to 35 of these elusive, endangered cats living here. More likely you'll see a bobcat or a black bear; this is one of the last places in Florida with significant numbers of black bears.

If the trails look too wet, you can still spot wildlife by driving the 27-mile (43km) **Loop Road,** or, while it's closed for reconstruction, the 17-mile (27km) **Turner River/ Wagonwheel/Birdon Roads Loop,** which follows two canals that attract wading birds. Graceful coastal plain willows trail their leaves into the canals, where you'll see herons stalking along the banks, an anhinga fishing with its long spearlike beak, or the double-crested cormorant (aka "snake bird") gliding surreptitiously with just its head above water. The dazzling white of egrets—cattle, snowy, and great egrets—makes them easy to spot from above, but for gullible fish looking upward, they appear like clouds in the sky. You're bound to notice dark alligators basking on the canal rims, too. Unlike crocodiles, alligators only live in fresh water—but that's what Big Cypress has. And if it wasn't here to keep the water fresh, who knows what would happen to the rest of south Florida?

Big Cypress National Preserve.

ⓘ **Big Cypress National Preserve,** Oasis Visitors Center, 33100 Tamiami Trail, Ochopee (ⓒ **239/695-1201;** www.nps.gov/bicy)

✈ Miami International

🛏 $$ **Ivey House B&B,** 107 Camellia St., Everglades City (ⓒ **877/567-0679** or 239/695-3299; www.iveyhouse.com). $$ **Rod & Gun Lodge,** 200 Riverside Dr., Everglades City (ⓒ **239/695-2101;** www.evergladesrodandgun.com).

Coastal Marshes 127

Kawainui Marsh
Marsh Madness
Oahu, Hawaii

THE LARGEST REMAINING WETLAND IN HAWAII, HOME TO A NUMBER OF RARE AND ENDANGERED species, has been polluted by trash disposal and sewage; invasive species further degrade habitat for native birds and plants.

Viewed from up high, from the Pali walking trail, you wonder how such a broad green meadow escaped the development that has eaten up most of Oahu. Nearly 1,000 acres (400 hectares) of open land, Kawainui is a stone's throw from Kailua. But step on it and it jiggles underfoot, like walking on a waterbed. That's not grass at all; it's a dense mat of floating vegetation.

Early Polynesian settlers used this marsh (an ancient bay that silted in—hence the name, which means "big water" in Hawaiian) as a giant fish farm; later Chinese settlers made it a rice paddy. Ecologists fought to preserve it from development in the 1960s; after years of wrangling, in 2007 government funding was finally allocated to build a visitor center, lay down walking trails, and restore open water habitat for birds. Until that work's finished, the best way to see the marsh is from the paved bike path along the Kawainui Canal.

What you see is actually two different kinds of floating green stuff: bulrushes underlaid with peat, and a seasonally flooded bog meadow of California grass. Slopes above the marsh are anchored with exotic trees and shrubs like koa haole, guava, Chinese banyan, and monkeypod. Spreading across the southern end, water lilies, water hyacinth, and water lettuce float on branching pools of open water that shelter four endangered native birds. (Sadly, Hawaii leads the nation in endangered native bird species.) First there's the black-headed Hawaiian moorhen (gallinule), or *alaeula*, recognized by its red frontal shield and beak (legend says the moorhen scorched its beak bringing fire from the gods to the Hawaiian people). *Alaeulas* build nests of reeds among the vegetation at water's edge. The Hawaiian coot, or *alae keokeo*, looks like a slightly larger moorhen, but with a white frontal shield and beak; it builds its nest right on top of the floating mat of grass. Standing 16 inches (40cm) tall on long pink legs, Hawaiian stilts, or *aeos*, are black on top and white underneath, with a long skinny black bill; they nest on mud flats and feed in nearby marshy shallows. The mottled brown Hawaiian duck, or *koloa maoli*, is an adaptable bird—so adaptable that it breeds freely with common mallards, thus driving itself into extinction. (The *koloa maolis* here are mostly hybrids; the only true Hawaiian ducks left are on Kauai.)

Reconnecting those fragmented pools is the first order of business for Kawainui's guardians, to create a healthy open water habitat for those water birds. If this wetlands dries up, where else could they go?

ⓘ **Kawainui Marsh,** Kapaa Quarry Rd., east of Kailua (www.kawainuimarsh.com)

✈ Honolulu

🛏 $$ **Paradise Bay Resort,** 47-039 Lihikai Dr., Kaneohe (✆ **800/735-5071** or 808/239-5711; http://paradisebayresort hawaii.com). $$ **Pagoda Hotel,** 1525 Rycroft St., Honolulu (✆ **800/472-4632** or 808/923-4511; www.pagodahotel.com).

128 Coastal Marshes

Kakadu National Park
Crocodile Dundee Territory
Northern Territories, Australia

OWNED BY ABORIGINES BUT MANAGED BY THE AUSTRALIAN GOVERNMENT, KAKADU'S VAST parkland surrounds two lucrative uranium mines, with more rich underground deposits lying untapped—so far.

Freshwater crocodiles are mild mannered and relatively harmless; it's the vicious saltwater ones you have to worry about. But despite the name, saltwater crocodiles mainly live in fresh water, and both kinds lurk in the rivers and lagoons of Kakadu National Park. Confused yet?

Australia's largest national park, Kakadu is full of such fascinating contradictions. This is one destination where it really pays to have a guide. Given the radical difference between wet and dry seasons, only experienced guides know where to find wildlife at any given time. The dry season (*Gurrung*, Aug–Oct) is the best time for viewing wildlife, as all animal life clusters around the shrinking water holes. During monsoon season (*Gudejweg*, Dec–Mar), many tour companies simply close down—opt for a scenic flyover instead, where you can see the swollen rivers and waterfalls and see the flood plain turn lush green.

Kakadu's habitats range from bushland and wetlands to stony escarpment and pockets of monsoon forest, from red cliffs and waterfalls to lush lagoons, each with its own array of rare flora and fauna. Those seasonal extremes require tough, specially adapted vegetation; resurrection grasses, sedges, and spear grass, as well as banyans and kapok trees and freshwater mangroves, help stabilize the ground when it's completely underwater. Kakadu is particularly bird rich, with 275 species, one-third of all Australia's bird species. Birders gravitate to the various wetlands, such as the Mamukala wetlands, near Jabiru, where you can observe swarms of magpie geese; or the yellow-water billabong, near Cooinda, where narrated cruises let you watch sea eagles, kites, and kingfishers hunt for fish among the mangrove roots and water lilies. In the eastern section of the park, Jim Jim Falls and Twin Falls spill dramatically from the red stone escarpment, tempting many park visitors to swim in the deep pools at their bases (remember to watch out for those crocs!). Increasingly the park has also highlighted its world-renowned examples of Aborigine rock art at sites like Nourlangie and Ubirr.

Kakadu is technically Aborigine land, which the government converted to parkland in 1981 to give its traditional owners an alternative to raising water buffaloes that overgrazed the land for years. The water buffaloes are mostly gone now, but a new threat hovers: government factions eager to exploit the land's rich uranium deposits, which have generated much wealth for the Aboriginal landowners. Though one study contends that the two existing mines have had no negative environmental impact, another found massive amounts of contaminated water leaking from the Ranger mine. It's a complex debate—yet another of Kakadu's contradictions.

ⓘ **Bowali Visitor Center,** Kakadu Hwy. (✆ **61/8/8938 1120;** www.deh.gov.au/parks/kakadu)

✈ Darwin

🛏 $$$ **Gagudju Crocodile Holiday Inn,** 1 Flinders St., Jabiru (✆ **61/8/8979 9000;** www.gagudju-dreaming.com). $$ **Gagudju Lodge Cooinda,** Kakadu Hwy., Jim Jim (✆ **61/8/8979 0145;** www.gagudju-dreaming.com).

TOUR Gagudju Adventure Tours (✆ 61/8/8979 0145; www.gagudju-dreaming.com). **Kakadu Culture Camp** (✆ 61/428/792 048; http://kakaduculturecamp.com).

iSimangaliso Wetland Park
Zulu Zoo Supreme
Zululand, South Africa

ILLEGAL POACHING OF ENDANGERED BLACK AND WHITE RHINOS, AS WELL AS LOGGERHEAD AND leatherback sea turtles, is an ongoing issue for South Africa's first World Heritage Site, a haven for many endangered species.

iSimangaliso means "miracle" in Zulu—that's how King Shaka's trusted advisor Ujeqe described this stretch of coastland when he first wandered into it (on the run from his enemies, but that's another story). Formerly known as the Greater St. Lucia Wetlands Park, iSimangaliso is a truly miraculous, Noah's Ark sort of place. Tropical Africa merges into subtropical Africa here, yielding five distinct ecosystems; it also sits on several migration routes, adding up to a mind-boggling total of species—over 100 different butterflies and some 530 types of birds alone.

At the park's heart lies Lake St. Lucia, a vast estuary teeming with hippos, Nile crocodiles, and flamingos. Since non-native pine and eucalyptus plantations have been cut down, the once overly saline lake's water quality has rebounded. Even when severe drought hits the rest of Africa, there's water here, so it's a vital bird migration spot. You can take guided tours on the **Santa Lucia lake cruiser** (℃ 27/35/590-1340); at the mouth of the St. Lucia River, visit the **Crocodile Centre** in St. Lucia Village—not just some tourist trap but a significant research center with fine exhibits about Africa's many crocodile species.

From the lake's western shores, drive into savanna and thornveld, where kudu, nyala, impala, duiker, and reedbuck roam. Even more unusual are the wooded hills on the lake's eastern shores—the world's largest vegetated sand dunes. Conservationists in the 1990s fought to prevent mining companies from digging up the rich titanium and zirconium deposits under these rare dunes; follow a trail through their peaceful dusky gloom and marvel at what might have been lost. At the end of that road is Cape Vidal beach, where you can watch migrating whales from an observation tower from July to November. Scuba divers head farther north for warm Sodwana Bay, which has almost as many varieties of fish as the Great Barrier Reef; north of there, the mineral-rich sands of **Kosi Bay Nature Preserve** are Africa's last major nesting site (Nov–Mar) for loggerhead and leatherback sea turtles.

The **uMkhuze Game Reserve** is like a greatest-hits version of the park, with a little of every habitat: mountain slopes, acacia savanna, swamps, riverine forest. In winter (June–Sept) you can settle into game-viewing hides next to the Kubube, Kamasinga, and Kwamalibala watering holes and see black and white rhinoceroses, elephants, giraffes, blue wildebeests, wart hogs, and myriad antelopes. Bird hides at Nsumo Pan afford a spectacular year-round view of pelicans, ducks, and geese on the waterway; from here you can also take a guided walk through the lovely, rare Sycamore Fig Forest. Ujeqe had it right—the whole place is a miracle indeed.

ⓘ **iSimangaliso Wetland Park** (℃ 27/35/590 1633; www.isimangaliso.com)

✈ Richard's Bay

🛏 $$$ **Makakatana Bay Lodge** (℃ 27/35/550-4189; www.makakatana.co.za). $ **Cape Vidal Camp,** Cape Vidal (℃ 27/35/590-9012; www.kznwildlife.com).

TOURKZN **Wildlife** (www.kznwildlife.com)

Delaware Bayshores
Atlantic Flyway Hot Spot
New Jersey/Pennsylvania/Delaware/Virginia

THIS STOPOVER FOR MIGRATING BIRDS BECOMES LESS INVITING EVERY YEAR, AS NESTING HABITAT is eaten away by urban sprawl, invasive reeds, and shoreline erosion, and vital food sources—oysters and horseshoe crabs—dwindle.

It's hard not to love the jaunty little red knot. Though it's only 10 inches (25cm) tall, weighing less than 5 ounces, that's big for a sandpiper. Just watch this robust little shorebird strut along the tidal mud flats of the Delaware Bay, poking its straight beak into the sand. All it wants is to gorge itself on horseshoe crab eggs, double its body weight in 2 weeks, and then fly on north—*way* north. A prodigious long-distance flier, the tiny red knot covers some 10,000 to 15,000 miles (16,000–24,000km) from northern Canada to Tierra del Fuego each season. And along with millions of other Neotropical birds migrating along the Atlantic Flyway, that springtime stop-off on the Delaware Bay is essential for refueling.

But the intricate web of life around Delaware Bay has been disrupted. Lying between the Delmarva Peninsula ("del" for Delaware, "mar" for Maryland, "va" for Virginia) and New Jersey's southern shore, Delaware Bay is the culmination of a vast watershed that runs upstream through Pennsylvania to Hancock, New York. Once the bay held one of the country's greatest oyster beds; ravaged in the 1950s and 1990s by parasites, the oyster population is still in critical condition. Even more vital to birds—not only red knots, but other shorebirds such as sanderlings, dunlins, semipalmated sandpipers, ruddy turnstones, and short-billed dowitchers—is the rapid decline in the once-abundant horseshoe crab population, after drastic overharvesting in the late 1990s. While New Jersey has banned horseshoe harvesting, it is the only state bordering the bay that has done so, and recent invasion

by alien Chinese mitten crabs could finish off the species.

Thanks to coordination by the U.S. Fish and Wildlife Service, the Nature Conservancy, and local Audubon society chapters, a patchwork of local parks preserves as much of this landscape as possible, not an easy task in this thickly settled Northeast corridor. In Pennsylvania, only a mile from Philadelphia International Airport, you can visit the shimmering tidal marsh of the **John Heinz National Wildlife Refuge,** 8601 Lindbergh Blvd., Philadelphia (© **215/365-3118;** http://heinz.fws.gov). In Delaware State, the tidal salt marshes of **Bombay Hook,** 2591 Whitehall Neck Rd., Smyrna (© **302/653-9345;** http://bombayhook.fws. gov) provide prime nesting grounds for wood ducks, bluebirds, purple martins, barn owls, and eastern screech owls.

You'll have to head south of the Bay, to Virginia's Atlantic barrier islands, to find the last redoubt of the red knots, which still descend en masse every May and June upon the wildlife refuge of **Metompkin Island.** Its north end lies in the **Chincoteague National Wildlife Refuge** (© **757/336-6122;** www.nps.gov/asis), its south end in the **Nature Conservancy's Virginia Coast Reserve** (© **757/442-3049;** www.nature.org). Take a boat from Gargathy Neck in Accomac—your reward will be seeing thousands of plucky red knots, feasting greedily on the tiny green crab eggs they've flown so far to find.

(i) **Delaware Bayshore Center,** 2350 Rte. 47, Delmont, NJ (© **609/861-0600;** www.nature.org/newjersey)

✈ Philadelphia, Dover, or Norfolk

🛏 **$$ Refuge Inn,** 7058 Maddox Blvd., Chincoteague (☎ **888/257-0038** or 757/336-5511; www.refugeinn.com).

$ Best Western Smyrna Inn, 190 Stadium St., Smyrna, DE (☎ **302/659-3635;** www.bestwestern.com).

---

131 Wildlife at Water's Edge

Baja California
A Whale of a Time in Mexico
Bahía Magdalena & El Vizcaino, Mexico

THOUGH GRAY WHALES WERE REMOVED FROM THE ENDANGERED LIST IN 1994, SCIENTISTS WORRY how they'll be affected by climate change, as ocean acidification reduces their food stock and shrinking sea ice alters their Arctic feeding grounds.

Seeing a gray whale close up can be a mystical experience. It's not just that they're so big. It's not even their air of regal calm, or the effortless way their long mottled bodies slide through the water, mastering the sea. It's something more, something primordial in their meditative gaze and upcurved baleen smile, as if they possess some ancient secret wisdom.

Once hunted to near extinction, gray whales were given protected status way back in the 1930s. They are now extinct in the Atlantic Ocean and severely depleted in the western Pacific, but the eastern Pacific population rebounded enough to be removed from the endangered list in 1994—a marine conservation victory. Every year an estimated 19,000 gray whales migrate from the Bering Strait, their summer feeding grounds, to their winter home off Mexico's Baja California peninsula, where they'll spend January through March in warm protected bays, mating or giving birth.

Perhaps the best base for whale-watching is funky laid-back **Loreto,** an old colonial town on the Sea of Cortez that's popular with kayakers, sailors, and divers. From here, tour guides will drive you across the desert to the Pacific coast's Bahía Magdalena, where you board a light skiff called a *panga* and spend 2 hours in the coastal lagoon, getting close to the gray whales

and possibly a few humpbacks as well. If you're lucky, you'll encounter "friendlies"— whales that'll swim right up to your tour boat, even letting people pet them.

Farther north from Loreto on the Transpeninsular Highway, straddling the peninsula, lies the vast **El Vizcaino Biosphere Reserve,** which contains two other important gray whale refuges: Laguna San Ignacio and Ojo de Liebre. (You'll need a permit to visit, which tour operators can arrange for you.) Inland, El Vizcaino is an arid, wind-swept desert, damaged by overgrazing, agricultural pollution, and highway construction, but its narrow strip of Pacific coastline is temperate and lovely. Laguna San Ignacio and Ojo de Liebre are also wintering sites for harbor seals, California sea lions, northern elephant seals, and blue whales, as well as osprey, brown pelicans, and terns. Bobbing around the lagoon in a *panga,* you can observe the shorebirds in their wetlands and the seals' rocky islands.

Still up in the air: How will the bays of Baja California be impacted by Mexico's ambitious Escalera Náutica project, which plans a chain of recreational boat harbors along the Pacific and Sea of Cortez coastlines, including three in El Vizcaino? If the gray whales' mating grounds are disturbed, where can they turn next?

121

✈ Loreto

🛏 $$$ **Posada Las Flores,** Av. Salvatierra at Francisco y Madera, Loreto (✆ **619/ 378-0103** in the U.S. and Canada or 52/ 613/135-1162 in Mexico; www.posadade lasflores.com). $ **Desert Inn,** San Ignacio

(✆ **800/800-9632** in the U.S., or 52/613/154-0300; http://desertinns.com/SanIgnacio).
TOUR Arturo's Sport Fishing, Loreto (✆ **52/613/135-0766;** www.arturosport. com). **Ecotourism Kuyimá,** San Ignacio (✆ **52/615/154-0070;** www.kuyima.com).

Wildlife at Water's Edge 132

Shark Bay
Dolphins & Dugongs & Sharks, Oh My!
Northwest Cape, Western Australia

NAMED A WORLD HERITAGE AREA IN 1991, SHARK BAY IS TURNING TO TOURISM TO REPLACE sheep herding, fishing, and salt mining, all of which have damaged this ecological gem. Will excessive recreational boating create new problems for Shark Bay's rare marine life?

Shark Bay—how much more adventurous could a place sound? But the truth is, most visitors come here not to see bloodthirsty sharks but to ooh and aah over the bottlenose dolphins that cruise every morning into the shallow water of a former pearling camp known as Monkey Mia. (And no,

Shark Bay.

there are no monkeys here either.) Rangers instruct visitors to stand still in the knee-deep water while the dolphins glide past; you're not even allowed to pet them, though they playfully nudge the tourists from time to time.

But don't stop with that tame packaged thrill. A 2½-hour cruise on the sailing catamaran **Shotover** (✆ **61/8/99 481 481;** www.monkeymiawildsights.com.au), leaving from the Monkey Mia resort, will show you waters heaving with fish, manta rays, sea turtles, sea snakes, and either migrating humpback whales (June–Oct) or the world's largest population of dugongs, aka manatees (Sept–Apr), attracted by—no coincidence—the world's largest seagrass meadows.

On the harsh Peron Peninsula, which juts out into Shark Bay, a former sheep station has found new life as **Francois Peron National Park**, where the Wanamalu Trail offers sweeping sea views from dunes and dramatic red coastal cliffs. Nature takes some bizarre shapes around here. At Shell Beach, 45km (28 miles) southeast of Denham, what looks like white sand turns out to be billions of tiny white seashells. Continue southeast on the signposted Shark Bay World Heritage Drive to the **Hamelin**

Pool Marine Nature Reserve, where a boardwalk leads past lumpy foot-high rock formations called stromatolites, rare ancient fossils formed in the pool's hypersaline waters.

So where are the sharks? Up on the Northwest Cape, a day's drive north on Highway 1. At **Exmouth,** tour boats take people out to snorkel with gentle whale sharks, the world's largest fish (true whales are bigger, but they're mammals), from late March to June. If you're here November through late February, nighttime turtle-watch tours witness green and loggerhead turtles nesting on the cape's beaches. Any time of year, diving is excellent on the Cape's **Ningaloo Reef,** which offers 250 species of coral and 450 kinds of fish to marvel at—grouper, manta rays, octopuses, morays, potato cod, false killer whales, and large sharks.

The seas teem with life in this unspoiled setting, much less crowded than the Great Barrier Reef. Sure, you seem to drive forever to get anywhere, and it can be insufferably hot between November and March. But plan your trip accordingly, and it may be the best ocean experience of your life.

(i) **Monkey Mia visitor center** (© 61/8/ 9948 1366; www.sharkbay.asn.au)

✈ Shark Bay or Exmouth

🛏 $–$$$ **Monkey Mia Dolphin Resort,** Monkey Mia Rd. (© **61/8/9948 1320;** www. monkeymia.com.au). $$ **Ningaloo Reef Resort,** Robinson St., Coral Bay (© 61/8/ 9942 5934; www.coralbay.org/resort.htm).

TOUR **Exmouth Diving Centre** (© 61/8/ 9949 1201; www.exmouthdiving.com.au). **Ningaloo Reef Diving Centre** (© 61/8/ 9942 5824; www.ningalooreefdive.com).

---

133 Wildlife at Water's Edge

Texel Island
Wadden Sea Eco-Paradise
The Netherlands

ONLY 10% OF SEABIRDS IMMERSED IN OIL SPILLS WASH ASHORE ALIVE. WILDLIFE BIOLOGISTS AT Texel Island's Ecomare research station rehabilitate oil-spill survivors with a special bird-washing machine.

As the tides pull out from Texel Island, they expose broad mud flats, glistening where the North Sea had been lapping only hours earlier. It's a landscape in constant flux, making and remaking itself daily, and as such it's a salutary reminder of the ultimate impermanence of landscapes. That enormous displacement of water stirs up so many vital nutrients that a host of creatures thrive here, from plankton to seals to as many as 300 species of birds. Prowl around the flats at low tide and you never know what you'll find crawling about underfoot.

The largest and most populated of the Frisian Islands archipelago—it's actually two islands that were poldered together centuries ago—Texel (pronounced *Tess*-uhl) divides the Wadden Sea from the North Sea. Running along the entire 24km-long (15-mile) North Sea coast, the Dunes of Texel National Park is a fascinating intertidal ecosystem, from its mud flats to stretches of gently waving marsh grass dotted with sea lavender and sea aster. South of the coastal village of De Koog, the wildlife biologists at the Wadden Islands' research center **Ecomare,** Ruijslaan 92 (© **0222/317-741;** www.ecomare.nl), provide a great resource for understanding this coastal dune system's natural wonders. Their on-site sea aquarium serves as a primer for the local habitats of sea, dune, and rocky coast; outdoors, crowds gather for the ever-popular daily feedings of the rescued seals in their seal sanctuary. From there you can follow a computer-guided walk through their Dune Park, or tag along on one of their guided "mud excursions" at low tide. Ecomare naturalists also lead tours of three nearby nature reserves: **De Schorren, De Bol,** and **Dijkmanshuizen,** where the bird-watching is superb. Expect to see healthy numbers of spoonbills, oystercatchers, Bewick swans, eider ducks, Brent geese, avocets, marsh harriers, snow buntings, ringed plovers, kestrels, short-eared owls, and bar-tailed godwits.

At least one-third of Texel Island is dedicated to nature preserves; it's a sunny, serene place to get close to wildlife, a cinematically picturesque landscape of sea and mud flat, sand dunes and meadows, with nearly as many grazing sheep as human residents. Seven charming villages dot the island, many with historic 16th- and 17th-century Dutch architecture and cobblestone streets (one, Den Hoom, is enveloped in flowering fields of bulbs in the spring).

Extensive bike paths make cycling an ideal way to explore this relatively flat island. The 20-minute trip across the Marsdiep Strait to Texel is an attraction in itself, aboard the largest ferry in Netherlands waters, the *Dokter Wagemaker*. Try to grab a seat on "panorama deck," where you can take in 360-degree views of the Wadden Sea—and great gulps of invigorating North Sea salt air.

ⓘ **Tourist office,** Emmalaan 66, Den Burg (☎ **31/222/314-741;** www.texel.net)

✈ Den Helder (small private planes can land on Texel)

🚆 Den Helder

🚢 **TESO car ferry** (☎ **31/222/369-600;** www.teso.nl) from Den Helder

🛏 $$ **Hotel de Lindeboom,** Groeneplaats 14, Den Burg (☎ **31/222/312-041;** www.hotelgroeptexel.nl). $$$ **Hotel Greenside,** Stappeland 6, De Koog (☎ **31/222/327-222;** www.hotelgroeptexel.nl).

Dramatic Coasts **134**

Golden Gate National Recreation Area
Bay Area Bio-Gem
San Francisco, California

WITH A SURPRISING NUMBER OF THREATENED OR ENDANGERED SPECIES, THIS URBAN SANCTUARY fights to preserve native Northern California habitat, stressed by city pollution, invasive species, and heavy recreational use.

Sometimes a land grab is a good thing. The Golden Gate National Recreation Area, the largest urban park in the United States, was pieced together from narrow strips of coastal naturelands, snapped up before real estate development could ruin them. Sandwiched between some of the country's most expensive real estate, who'd expect to find one of the world's top 25 biological hot spots?

The GGNRA covers a lot of territory, though it's not a continuous corridor. You'll find the Presidio, Land's End, and Ocean Beach in San Francisco itself; Angel Island out in the bay; oceanfront points and ridges down in San Mateo County; and across the Golden Gate Bridge, the Marin headlands, Stinson Beach, and Muir Woods. The "R" in GGNRA stands for recreation, and these sites get constant use—hiking, cycling,

Golden Gate National Recreation Area.

picnicking, sailing, rock climbing, and hang gliding. GGNRA rangers have to be vigilant about keeping visitors on roadways and trails (196 miles/315km of trails!), enforcing dog leash laws, controlling predators like foxes and feral cats, and eradicating invasive species like the tenacious Cape Ivy.

Most of the GGNRA is coastline, so the endangered watch list includes plenty of shorebirds—the western snowy plover, California least tern, bank swallows, peregrine falcons—as well as southern sea otters and Steller sea lions basking on the rocks. Offshore, humpback whales migrate past in spring and fall, and threatened salmon and steelhead have their winter feeding grounds. On any coastal drive, you'll see long-winged, long-billed brown pelicans poking around the water's edge—an environmental success story, they have rebounded from near extinction. The old-growth redwoods of Muir Woods—themselves a dwindling habitat—shelter the threatened northern spotted owl.

But as hikers and cyclists know, the Golden Gate area also includes marshes and grasslands. You may not see elusive creatures like the salt marsh harvest mouse,

the San Francisco garter snake, or the California red-legged frog, but you can't miss the wildflowers that spangle those brown hills just north of the Golden Gate Bridge in spring. Many of these are rare plants, from dune flowers (California seablite, San Francisco lessingia) to desertlike plants (fountain thistle, Tiburon paintbrush) to tiny hillside blossoms (San Mateo woolly sunflower, Marin dwarf-flax, Presidio Clarkia, San Mateo thornmint). And where there are wildflowers, there are butterflies—including such rare species as the delicate Mission blue, the gaudy bay checkerspot, and the dusty-brown San Bruno elfin.

Then there's the Presidio Manzanita, a shrub so rare that only one individual remains in the wild (if you can call this former military base "the wild"). Because it doesn't self-pollinate, it's most likely the last of its species. On the other hand, the 2-foot-tall (.6m) showy Indian clover, once considered extinct, has successfully been reintroduced to Marin County slopes. Anything is possible.

ⓘ ✆ **415/561-4700;** www.nps.gov/goga
✈ San Francisco International

✉ $$ **Hotel des Arts,** 447 Bush St. ✆ **800/956-4322** or 415/956-3232; www. sfhoteldesarts.com). $$$ **The Argonaut,** 495 Jefferson St. ✆ **866/415-0704** or 415/ 563-0800; www.argonauthotel.com).

Dramatic Coasts
135

Kenai Fjords
Where Mountains Slide into the Sea
Seward, Alaska

THOUGH IT HAS RECOVERED FROM 1989'S EXXON VALDEZ OIL SPILL, THE KENAI PENINSULA IS still losing habitat from logging and recreational use, while seismic forces impact the Kenai Mountains' topography.

It's hard to imagine anything more permanent than a mountain—unless you're talking about the Kenai Mountains in south-central Alaska. At this very minute, colliding tectonic plates are pulling the Kenai range into the sea. The deep coastal fjords that make this area a must-see Alaska cruise stop were once alpine valleys, with glaciers nestled inside. In the spring of 1964, an earthquake dropped this dynamic bit of Alaska shoreline 6 feet (1.8m) farther underwater in just 1 day.

The glaciers in the Alps and the Rockies are valley or piedmont glaciers, but Kenai Fjords National Park presents something much rarer: tidewater glaciers, massive cliffs of ice as high as 1,000 feet (305m), dropping abruptly into the icy Gulf of Alaska. Huge chunks of ice sheer off frequently, with puffs of frozen mist mixed with sea spray. As they break off, they resound with a boom that can be heard 20 miles (32km) away. Though Kenai Fjords has inland glaciers too—notably Exit Glacier and the vast Harding Icefield, both of them inexorably receding—the coastal glaciers are the star attraction.

To view this dramatic coast from the water, several companies offer day tours out of nearby **Seward Harbor.** These tours are the best way to see a lot of wildlife in a short time—nesting colonies of black-legged kittiwakes, cormorants, murres, and puffins; frolicking sea lions and sea otters; resident orcas and Dall's porpoises; migrating humpback and gray whales. (Half-day tours stick to **Resurrection Bay,** where you'll see much of the same wildlife but no tidewater glaciers.) Those who want a little more adventure can explore by sea kayak. To kayak around the fjord glaciers, take a water taxi or charter boat from Seward to Aialik Bay or Northwestern Lagoon and then launch your kayak; otherwise, stay in Resurrection Bay, because it's not a good idea to round turbulent Aialik Cape in such a small craft. Along the coastline, there's a sobering sight: "ghost forests" of dead trees, still standing, whose roots were submerged in salt water during the 1964 quake.

The 2½-hour drive from Anchorage to Kenai Fjords is memorable in itself, taking the scenic Seward Highway with its jaw-dropping views of Turnagain Arm, Kenai Lake, glaciers, wetlands, and rugged mountains. May through September, a scenic train ride on the Alaska Railroad takes 4 hours from Anchorage. Kenai Fjords is open year-round, but most services shut down between October and April. The only part of the park accessible by road is Exit Glacier, and that road is open only in summer—the rest of the year you'll need skis, a snowmobile, or a dog sled.

ⓘ **Kenai Fjords National Park,** Seward (✆ **907/224-7500;** www.nps.gov/kefj)

✈ Anchorage

🛏 $$ **Seward Windsong Lodge,** Mile 0.5, Herman Leirer Rd. (✆ **877/777-4079** or 907/224-7116; www.sewardwindsong.

com). $$$ **Holiday Inn Express,** Seward Harbor, 1412 4th Ave., Seward (✆**877/865-6578** or 907/224-2550; www.ichotelsgroup. com).

TOUR **Major Marine Tours** (✆ 800/764-7300; www.majormarine.com). **Kayak Adventures Worldwide** (✆ **907/224-3960;** www.kayakak.com). **Sunny Cove Sea Kayaking Co.** (✆ 800/770-9119 or 907/224-4426; www.sunnycove.com).

---

136 Dramatic Coasts

Glacier Bay
Some Like It Cold
Alaska

As many Alaskan wildlife species face shrinking or degraded habitat and depleted food supplies outside Glacier Bay National Park, increasing numbers seek haven in this protected territory.

You can't blame global warming for what's been happening at Glacier Bay—this glacier's been receding for at least 2 centuries. When Captain George Vancouver visited this southeastern Alaska coast in 1794, he described the bay as a mere 5-mile (8km) notch in a massive 20-mile-wide (32km) glacier that reached more than 100 miles (160km) to the St. Elias Mountains. Fast-forward 85 years and you get naturalist John Muir's 1879 account of a bay more than 30 miles (48km) long. By 1916, it was 60 miles (97km) deep; it's now a 65-mile-long (105km) fjord. At its mouth, mature spruce forests have been long established, but moving deeper into the fjord, you'll see the vegetation gradually become smaller and sparser, according to how many years that terrain has been exposed, until finally you reach a band of mosses, lichen, and loose rocky scree— and then a stark curtain of ice.

Glacier Bay.

Retreating glaciers are good news for some of Glacier Bay's residents, as new ice-free terrain is opened up for brown bears, mountain goats, and wolves, as well as moose and coyotes, relatively new species that have moved into the park. Brown bears and moose are prodigious swimmers, often spotted paddling across the Bay. Arctic terns, jaegers, and puffins nest in the barren cliffs nearest to the glaciers, but as the hillsides become more vegetated, Neotropical songbirds arrive in increasing numbers for their summer pilgrimage.

Lying in one of the world's largest protected biosphere reserves, Glacier Bay provides a haven for many threatened animal species. Humpback whales make it their summer home, while minke whales, orcas, Dall's porpoises, and harbor porpoises feed in the icy waters offshore. You may still see harbor seals on the ice floes of St. John's Inlet, although their population has mysteriously declined recently. On the other hand, frisky little sea otters were reintroduced to the park in the 1960s and are now thriving in the Bay's rocky coves. On the rocky islets at the mouth of the bay, every year there are more huge, tawny Steller sea lions, in contrast to their decline elsewhere in Alaska.

Most visitors view the park from the water, either from the deck of a big cruise ship (park rangers come aboard to point out natural features) or from catamarans that drop passengers off to hike, kayak, or camp. For some serious bird-watching, come May through September—there are any number of great spots to hike to around **Bartlett Cove,** or you can kayak to the **Beardslee Islands** or **Point Gustavus.** The more you put into exploring, the more you'll see.

ⓘ **Glacier Bay National Park,** Bartlett Cove ℰ **907/697-2230;** www.nps.gov/glba)

✈ Juneau

🛏 $$$ **Glacier Bay Lodge,** Bartlett Cove, Glacier Bay National Park ℰ **888/229-8687** or 907/264-4600; www.visit glacierbay.com). $ **Bartlett Cove Campground,** Bartlett Cove (walk-in site, no reservations).

TOUR Glacier Bay Tours ℰ **888/229-8687** or 907/264-4600; www.visitglacier bay.com). **Glacier Bay Sea Kayaks** ℰ **907/697-2257;** www.glacierbaysea kayaks.com).

Dramatic Coasts **137**

Fiordland National Park
Middle-earth Under the Ozone Hole
South Island, New Zealand

THE HOLE IN THE OZONE LAYER THAT HAS THREATENED SOUTH ISLAND FOR DECADES HAS STARTED to close, but it will take many years for the damage to be entirely reversed.

To film those intensely green, mist-shrouded Middle-earth landscapes, the *Lord of the Rings* movies didn't need stage sets or computer animation: Director Peter Jackson simply shot the films in New Zealand. The South Island's Fiordlands are perfect examples of that primeval *Lord of the Rings* look, with plunging waterfalls, pristine

lakes, virgin forest, and steep peaks surrounding deep-gouged fiords. It's spectacularly different from the geothermal spots like Rotorua that travelers used to associate with New Zealand.

In the 1980s, however, New Zealand faced an environmental crisis: A hole in the ozone layer, discovered over Antarctica, was letting in dangerous levels of UV radiation. Not only would this expose humans to high skin-cancer risks, but vegetation also could be damaged and ocean plankton could die off. For the South Island, which lay closest to the ozone hole, it was scary news indeed. But thanks to widespread bans on the refrigerants, solvents, and aerosol sprays that did most of the damage, the hole seems to be growing smaller with each Antarctic summer, though it may take another 50 or 60 years for the ozone layer to be completely restored. Be extra vigilant in applying sunscreen when you visit.

The entrance to the Fiordlands' most dramatic fiord, 23km-long (14-mile) **Milford Sound,** is so narrow, Captain Cook missed it completely when he first sailed around New Zealand some 200 years ago. Plenty of tourists have discovered it since, though—sightseeing planes and helicopters do regular flyovers, tour buses clog up the stunningly scenic Milford Road from Te Anau, and cruises chug around the water. Head instead for the park's largest fiord, **Doubtful Sound,** which is much more peaceful and remote. Real Journeys (see "Tour," below) leads day sails on catamarans or overnight cruises on the Fiordland Navigator; out on the water you're likely to have the bottlenose dolphins, frisky fur seals, and rare crested penguins all to yourselves.

The quintessential Fiordlands experience, though, is reserved for hikers, who can study the striations of its glacially carved rocks, discover delicate alpine wildflowers and mossy hollows, and feel the waterfalls' spray on their skin. New Zealand's Department of Conservation regulates the famous **Milford Track,** a 4-day hike from Laek Te Anau to Milford Sound's Sandfly Point. While you can take day hikes on shorter sections, to do the full route in peak season (Oct–May) you must reserve with the park's **Great Walk Booking Desk,** Box 29, Te Anau (✆ **64/3/ 249-8514;** www.doc.govt.nz). For a guided option, go with Ultimate Hikes or get a 1-day sample with Trips 'n' Tramps (see below for both). Hobbit sightings are few and far between, but there are plenty of other wonders to compensate.

ⓘ www.fiordland.org.nz

✈ Te Anau

🛏 $$ **Milford Sound Lodge,** Hwy. 94, Te Anau (✆ **64/3/249-8071;** www.milford lodge.com)

TOUR Real Journeys (✆ **64/3/249-7416;** www.realjourneys.co.nz). **Ultimate Hikes** (✆ **64/3/450-1940;** www.ultimatehikes. co.nz). **Trips 'n' Tramps** (✆ **64/3/249- 7081;** www.milfordtourswalks.co.nz).

⬤**138** Dramatic Coasts

Peninsula Valdés
A Home Where the Guanacos Roam
Argentina

WATER POLLUTION, OIL-TANKER TRAFFIC, AND INCREASING TOURISM ON ARGENTINA'S ATLANTIC coast are degrading offshore habitat for orcas, penguins, southern elephant seals, and migrating southern right whales.

Virtually an island, connected to the Argentine mainland by the slenderest of isthmuses, barren Peninsula Valdés lies far from either Buenos Aires or Tierra del Fuego. This is not the sort of destination

travelers stumble onto accidentally—to enter, visitors need a paper signed by an Argentinean travel agency. Those who do come have one item on their agenda: viewing wildlife.

A few gravel roads loop around the relatively treeless coastal plateau, where you'll spot guanacos, the llama's small Patagonian cousins, scurrying away from your car. You also may see choiques (ostrichlike birds); the strange-looking mara, a hare that runs on four legs like a dog; armadillos and foxes; and lots of sheep, property of the few remaining family-run ranches in the reserve, grazing on the golden grasses of the arid plain.

But the most spectacular wildlife gathers on the coasts, where rugged cliffs and gravelly beaches meet the calm, mild waters of two sheltered gulfs. What you'll see depends upon the season. From April to December, the park's only village, **Puerto Pirámides,** offers whale-watching tours during the annual breeding visit of endangered southern right whales, a species that was nearly hunted to extinction. June through December, the Atlantic beaches at Caleta Valdés swarm with elephant seals; January to June, hundreds of sea lions congregate at the northeastern tip of the peninsula, Punta Norte. September through March, a huge colony of Magellan penguins breed at Punta Tomba at the **Estancia San Lorenzo Reserve** (✆ **54/2965/458-444**). Whichever breeding colony you observe, look out to the open ocean to see orcas, which lurk offshore year-round, shifting their hunting to wherever vulnerable babies are. And in your hurry to enter the park, don't miss the first stop: an observation platform where high-powered telescopes allow you to watch masses of gulls, great egrets, cormorants, oystercatchers, and penguins on the offshore island of Isla de los Pajáros.

Day tours from Puerto Madryn will cover the highlights, but to explore in depth, it's better to stay overnight. Several ranches now offer lodging, with guided treks and tours included; there are also hostels and small hotels in Puerto Pirámides. All things considered, the ideal time to visit is October or November, when the penguins are guarding their nests, whales and their new calves are swimming in the bays, and the elephant seals mass on the beaches with their pups. But there's always something happening on the beaches of Peninsula Valdés—it just takes a little traveling to get here, that's all.

ⓘ ✆ **54/2965/450489;** www.peninsula valdes.org.ar

✈ Puerto Madryn

🛏 $$ **Faro Punta Delgada Country Hotel,** Punta Delgada (✆**54/2965/458444;** www.puntadelgada.com). $$ **Del Nomade Ecolodge,** Av. de las Ballenas, Puerto Pirámides (✆ **54/2965/495044;** www.ecohosteria.com.ar).

5 Let The River Run

Chesser Prairie in Okefenokee National Wildlife Refuge.

Hells Canyon
The Salmon's Lost Home
Snake River, Idaho/Oregon/Washington

IT TOOK NEARLY A CENTURY TO RESTORE HELLS CANYON FROM FARMLAND TO WILDERNESS. THE challenge now is to restore the full Snake River as a habitat for salmon.

Shoshone Falls used to be the stopping point for the salmon, white sturgeon, and steelhead trout swimming up the Snake River every year to spawn. They could navigate even the whitewater rapids of Hells Canyon—the deepest gorge in North America—but not the thundering heights of Shoshone Falls.

Then the dams came. Above Shoshone Falls, several dams were built in the early 20th century, largely to provide irrigation for agriculture. That didn't affect the fish— until the 1950s and 1960s, when three dams went up in Hells Canyon, tapping those churning rapids for hydroelectric power. Blocked out of Hells Canyon, the big fish resorted to spawning in the Lower Snake—but soon after came another four dams on the Lower Snake River, which not only manufactured electricity but converted this turbulent river into a safe shipping channel.

The four Lower Snake dams were equipped with fish ladders, of course, as well as locks to move barges up and down the river. But the degraded habitat of the watershed became problematic. All that irrigated farmland upstream has overloaded the aquifer with agricultural runoff and sediment (not to mention raising the Snake's temperature—a critical problem for these sensitive fish). What's more, the

Hells Canyon.

Lower Snake dams have transformed the river into a series of placid reservoirs, without strong currents to guide fish upstream.

A proposed bill to remove the Lower Snake dams—the largest dam removal project in American history—could spell the difference for these endangered wild fish. After all, look at Hells Canyon, which since 1975 has been returned to wilderness after centuries of agriculture. Forest once again shrouds the banks, preventing erosion and providing wildlife habitat. Though the salmon may never return, deer and elk populations have rebounded, and even bighorn sheep—which used to contract a deadly parasite from domestic sheep, until flocks were moved elsewhere—once again scramble nimbly around the canyon's rocky heights.

With such dizzying elevation changes, the natives of Hells Canyon range from mountain goats and Ponderosa pine on the heights to prickly pear cactus and rattlesnakes on the desertlike canyon floor. River rafters tend to focus on Hells Canyon's great stretch of Class III–IV whitewater, where a standard 3-day rafting trip covers about 36 miles (58km). It's not rapids all the way, though—there are plenty of placid sections where rafters can relax and enjoy stunning views of the Seven Devils Mountains and the Summit Ridge. When you're not rafting, there's plenty else to do: trout fishing, horseback riding, swimming, and short hikes to view Native American pictographs on canyon walls, or to find the abandoned cabins of early 1900s settlers.

The Lower Snake could still be turned around, too, restoring a healthy river environment for those precious fish. To win this key environmental victory, however, dam-removal advocates must offer viable alternatives for all the power those dams provide, as well as shipping alternatives. It won't be easy.

ⓘ **Hells Canyon National Recreation Area,** 88401 Hwy. 82, Enterprise, OR (✆ **541/426-5546;** www.fs.fed.us/hells canyon)

✈ Lewiston, ID

TOUR Northwest Voyageurs (✆ **800/ 727-9977;** www.voyageurs.com). **O.A.R.S.** (✆ **800/346-6277;** www.oars.com). **Zoller's Outdoor Odysseys** (✆ **800/366-2004** or 509/493-2641; www.snakeraft.com). **Backcountry Outfitters** (✆ **855/645-3593;** www.backcountryoutfittersinc.com).

140 All Dammed Up

Kootenai River
Damming the Sacred River
Idaho/Montana/British Columbia

DUCKS AND GEESE LOST HABITAT WHEN IDAHO'S KOOTENAI WETLANDS WERE DRAINED; A DAM ON Montana's stretch of the Kootenai also has decimated a rare population of white sturgeon.

Looking at Kootenai Falls—a site sacred to the Kootenai Tribe—it makes perfect sense that the Kootenai consider it the center of the world, a vortex for spiritual forces. Its vivid green waters crash violently over boulders, dropping 300 feet (91m) in just a few hundred yards. No wonder the filmmakers of *The River Wild* used this location for the dreaded whitewater called the Gauntlet in the movie (after complex negotiations with the tribe for permission to film this holy place). At Kootenai Falls County Park, you can view the falls from a swinging bridge that spans the rugged gorge, or hike

Kootenai River.

their typical life span is 100 years or more, biologists fear these relics may die off by midcentury.

Humans can't seem to keep from messing around with the Kootenai River—also known as the Flat Bow River, an apt description of the wide arc it cuts from British Columbia, down the Rocky Mountain Trench into Montana, westward into the Idaho panhandle, and back north to British Columbia, where its waters eventually flow into the Columbia River. There are five dams along its course, mostly in Canada; in the 1970s, there was even briefly a scheme to divert the lower Kootenai directly into the Columbia. While logging and mining are the region's chief industries, back in the 1920s wetlands along the river in northern Idaho were drained to create farmland, despite the fact that it's a significant migratory stopover for some 200,000 birds, including about 67,000 ducks and geese.

In the past few years, however, as tourism becomes more important to the region, the Kootenai's whitewater rapids are being viewed as a plus, attracting fly fishermen, whitewater rafters, birders, and photographers. Aggressive restoration has restored some of those Idaho wetlands, and the migrating water birds have flocked back. If a new plan to allow seasonal flood surges from Libby Dam does the same for the sturgeon, the spiritual forces presiding over Kootenai Falls may have cause to rejoice.

a narrow path through the woods down to the river. Admire those incredible falls—and be glad there's no power plant looming over them.

Montana's Kootenai Falls remains the last major waterfall on a northwest river with no hydroelectric plant, although the tribe has fought several dam proposals over the past century. Only 31 miles (50km) upstream, however, Libby Dam was built in 1972, altering river flows and temperatures so significantly that Kootenai white sturgeon—a genetically unique landlocked population—may not survive another 30 years. While the glacier-fed river remains rich in trout, these immense ghost-white fish with their prehistoric sucker mouths are now confined to a sluggish, silty section of river below the falls, where spawning seems to have ceased. Only about 1,000 Kootenai sturgeon remain, and though

ⓘ **Kootenai Falls County Park,** US Hwy. 2, between Libby and Troy, MT

✈ Kalispell, MT

🛏 $$$ **Kootenai River Inn Casino & Spa,** 7169 Plaza St., Bonners Ferry, ID (✆ **800/346-5668** or 208/267-8511; www. kootenairiverinn.com). $ **Caboose Motel,** 714 W. 9th St., Libby, MT (✆ **800/627-0206** or 406/293-6201; www.thecaboose motel.com).

141 All Dammed Up

Klamath Basin Wildlife Refuges
The Western Everglades
Oregon & California

As the wetlands in the Klamath Basin shrink, salmon are dying, crops are thirsting, and the migrating bird population is dwindling. Farmers are pitted against wildlife experts, and water managers against both.

It seemed like a bright idea in 1905: Build dams along the Klamath River and turn its wetlands—approximately 185,000 acres (74,900 hectares) of shallow lakes and freshwater marshes in southern Oregon and northern California—into agricultural land. Trouble was those wetlands sat right on the Pacific Flyway. Dubbed the "Western Everglades," they were a major migration stopover for over six million waterfowl, as well as a year-round home for American white pelicans, double-crested cormorants, and several types of herons.

Today, the Western Everglades fare even worse than their Florida counterpart. Less than a quarter of those original wetlands remain, mostly in six patches of wildlife refuge. President Theodore Roosevelt created the Lower Klamath Refuge—the nation's first waterfowl refuge—in 1908, followed in 1911 by the Clear Lake Refuge; two more were added in the 1920s, Tule Lake Refuge and Upper Klamath Refuge. In 1958, the Klamath Marsh Refuge was acquired from the Klamath Indians. In 1978, the last piece fell into place: Bear Valley Refuge, which despite the name is really all about bald eagles. A sheltered northeast slope covered in towering old-growth ponderosa pine, incense cedar, and white and Douglas firs, Bear Valley is exactly the sort of place where wintering bald eagles want to roost.

Though visitors can't enter the Bear Valley refuge, on early winter mornings birders plant themselves on Highway 97 at the base of the refuge to watch hundreds of eagles fly out to their hunting grounds

in the nearby marshes, culling dead and dying ducks and geese from the winter flock. You can also see them circling overhead from 10-mile (16km) auto-drive routes in the Tule Lake and Lower Klamath refuges, which also offer excellent views of the massive spring and fall waterfowl migrations. (Look for new artificial islands created specifically for nesting Caspian terns.) You'll need a canoe to visit Upper Klamath and Klamath Marsh, summer hot spots for pelicans, egrets, herons, ibises, ducks, and grebes.

Since the 1990s, various interest groups in the Klamath Basin—farmers, fishermen, conservationists, Native American tribes—have fought over how to manage the river's water resources. Conservationists counted a victory in 2010 with the federal government's Klamath Hydroelectric Settlement Agreement, a plan to consider removing the Klamath's four hydroelectric dams, and the Klamath Basin Reclamation Agreement, a water-management plan that would balance the competing needs for water flow.

Implementation may be years away, however. And with drought conditions in 2010, much of the Lower Klamath refuge's marshes and lakes had been turned to one big weed-infested dustbowl. The 2010 fall migration, typically as much as 1.8 million birds, fell to 100,000 birds. If that's not an emergency, what is?

(i) **Klamath Basin National Wildlife Refuges** ((C) **530/667-2231;** www.fws. gov/klamathbasinrefuges). **Bear Valley NWR,** off Hwy. 97, near Worden, OR. Tule

Lake NWR, Hill Rd., Tulelake, CA. **Lower Klamath NWR,** Stateline Hwy. 161, Tulelake, CA. **Upper Klamath NWR,** West Side Rd. (Hwy. 140), south of Fort Klamath, OR. **Klamath Marsh NWR,** Silver Lake Rd., Sand Creek, OR.

✈ Klamath Falls

🛏 $$$ **Shilo Inn,** 2500 Almond St., Klamath Falls ✆ **541/885-7980;** www.shiloinns.com). $$ **Best Western Olympic Inn,** 4061 S. 6th St., Klamath Falls ✆ **541/882-1200;** www.bestwestern.com).

All Dammed Up 142

Mono Lake
Who Stole the Water?
Lee Vining, California

MONO LAKE NEARLY BECAME A DRY SALT BED AFTER MUCH OF ITS WATER SUPPLY WAS DIVERTED to slake Los Angeles's thirst. After a 1994 court decision, the state now manages the water supply and is rebuilding wetlands.

Back in 1941, four of the five rivers that feed Mono Lake—California's largest natural body of water—were diverted to provide water for booming Los Angeles. With evaporation exceeding the flow of water into this desert salt lake, its water level began to drop drastically. Naturally twice as salty as ocean water, it became three times saltier than the ocean. A creepy complex of tufa towers, previously submerged, rose above the surface like the bleached bones of a skeleton.

Mono Lake.

Environmental protests and lawsuits throughout the 1970s and 1980s finally forced the state to take action. More efficient river dams now send regulated amounts of water back into 60-square-mile (155-sq.-km) Mono (pronounced Mow-no) Lake. From their 1982 low point, the waters are slowly rising, though you can still see a band of exposed alkali along its shoreline. Recent saline levels are back to 2.7 ounces per liter, heading for a goal of 2.4 ounces per liter. The willows and cottonwood forests that once lined the lake's freshwater tributaries are on the rebound, now that water flows in those channels again.

With its wetlands restored, Mono Lake is a major bird-watching area, with about 300 species either resident or migrating through; ospreys and rare California gulls nest on those accidental islands. Since no native fish can survive in this alkaline lake, birds don't have to compete for their favorite treat, Mono's endemic brine shrimp. Thick swarms of alkali flies on the lakeshore (the name Mono actually means "flies" in the native Yokut language) may be annoying to humans but they're a feast for birds, especially for the tiny Wilson's phalarope, which gorges on them every August before migrating back to South America.

Ironically, those risen-from-the-dead tufa towers—limestone deposits formed by underground springs—have now become an attraction in themselves. Just north of Lee Vining, Mono Lake County Park has a boardwalk through the restored wetlands; on the south shore of the lake, there's a walking trail through the South Tufa grove of limestone towers. Hike up to **Panum Crater**, a 650-year-old volcano, for a birds-eye view of the lake, or visit a gold-mining ghost town in nearby **Bodie State Historic Park.** On summer weekends, **guided canoe tours (🕿 760/647-6595)** get you out onto the lake. Notice the underground springs, which fed the lake all those years when the streams were sent elsewhere—keeping Mono Lake alive until humans finally did the right thing.

ⓘ **Mono Basin Scenic Area Visitors Center,** US Hwy. 395 at 3rd St., Lee Vining, CA (🕿 **760/647-3044;** www.monolake.org)

✈ Reno-Tahoe or Fresno-Yosemite

🛏 $$ **Fern Creek Lodge,** 4628 US Hwy. 158, June Lake, CA (🕿 **800/621-9146** or 760/648-7722; www.ferncreeklodge.com). $$ **Lake View Lodge,** 51285 US Hwy. 395, Lee Vining, CA (🕿 **800/990-6614** or 760/647-6543; http://lakeviewlodge yosemite.com).

143 **All Dammed Up**

The Aysen Wilderness
Damming Patagonia
Baker & Pascua Rivers, Chile

MASSIVE HYDROELECTRIC DAMS AND POWER LINES ARE PLANNED FOR THIS PRISTINE WILDERNESS in Chile's sparsely populated south—a magnet for adventure tourists and a haven for species.

Starved for energy, the Chilean government thought it had an ideal solution. Why not dam up a couple of rivers down in Patagonia, that southern Chilean region where hardly anybody lives anyway?

Well, hardly anybody lives there except rare endemic species—like the torrent duck, the southern river otter, the culpeo fox, the endangered puma, and the Andean huemul deer, not to mention unique beech, conifer, and cypress forests. And while the Aysen region is mostly wilderness, its glacier panoramas and unspoiled temperate rainforest have increasingly become a top draw for adventure hiking, biking, rock climbing, trout fishing, rafting, and kayaking. Only one road—the Carreterra Austral—strings through Patagonia, its ragged coastline deeply indented by fjords and milky-blue glacial lakes, including Lago General Carrera (South America's second-largest lake) and Lago O'Higgins (Chile's deepest lake). Between Cohaique and Puerto Natales, towns are few and far between; adventure tourists generally fly into the region rather than drive.

The planned locations of the $4-billion project's five dams are along the turbulent Pascua River and the Baker River, Chile's largest. The waters of both are exceptionally pure—mostly meltwater from the Patagonian Icefield, the largest expanse of permanent ice outside Antarctica and Greenland. Once dammed, those rivers would flood nearly 6,000 hectares (14,800 acres) of biodiverse rainforest. On top of that, the plan also requires clear-cutting the world's longest power corridor through that forest, slashing a broad scar punctuated with 5,000 metal towers for 2,317km (1,440 miles) north to Chile's cities and copper mines. Some 14 national parks and protected reserves will be radically affected by the project.

Chile desperately needs energy—the country currently imports up to 70% of its power—and the five hydroelectric plants to be built by the international conglomerate HidroAysén would increase Chile's power supply by 20%. Advocates point out that it would take seven coal-fired plants to produce that same amount, which would generate 16 million tons of greenhouse gases.

After HidroAysén submitted its first environmental impact assessment in August 2008, a storm of protests delayed the review process until June 2010. The review was postponed again after the devastating earthquake of February 2010 and a subsequent change in government. New president Sebastian Piñera threw his support behind the dam, however, recognizing Chile's pressing need for new energy sources; in June 2011, the plan was again blocked by an appeals court. Construction would take years, but that work will inexorably begin to alter the Aysen Wilderness's fragile beauty. The sooner you get here, the better.

ⓘ www.nrdc.org. www.international rivers.org.

✈ Balmaceda/Puerto Natales

TOUR Mountain Travel Sobek (✆ **888/ 831-7526;** www.mtsobek.com). **H2O Patagonia** (✆ **828/333-4615;** www.h2o patagonia.com).

All Dammed Up **144**

Lake Chapala
The Incredible Shrinking Lake
Southwestern Mexico

DRAINED TO SUPPLY WATER TO THE NEARBY CITY OF GUADALAJARA, LAKE CHAPALA AND ITS VITAL wetlands have been damaged by runaway development, upstream pollution, and invasive species.

It seems like the ideal retirement spot—Mexico's largest freshwater lake, a serene alpine lake set amid gently rounded green mountains. Cool breezes, balmy winters, spectacular sunsets, and a cheap cost of living, yet only 45km (28 miles) south of the amenities of Guadalajara—how could you beat that?

The trouble is a lot of people got the same notion. Since 1975, the real estate boom in the Lake Chapala area, led by a flood of retirees from North America, helped swell the Guadalajara area's population fivefold. A string of resort towns along the north shore became known as the Chapala Riviera, an English-speaking haven for expatriate snowbirds. Despite the Anglo invasion, the Chapala Riviera preserved an old-fashioned Mexican quaintness, with cobblestoned streets, hand-carved wooden gates, and brilliant little gardens.

But unbridled growth could spoil any paradise. Guadalajara's mushrooming need for fresh water began to drain the lake, and to make matters worse, faulty city water mains lost nearly half the water pumped out of the lake. Upstream communities built unauthorized dams along the Lerma River, the lake's main feeder, and released sewage and chemical runoff to pollute the remaining water, with high amounts of phosphorous, heavy metal, and bacteria. By 2002, the lake had shrunk to one-quarter of its original volume. Some lakeside villages now barely had water views, and coastal marshes became solid land that farmers promptly took over. Fish and bird populations dwindled, and huge masses of water hyacinth, or *lirio*, coated the shallow lake's surface, feeding eagerly on the heavy metals in the water.

Yet Central Mexico needs Lake Chapala, and not just as a reservoir for drinking water. Many other local lakes and ponds have dried up in the past couple of decades, leaving Chapala a vital wildlife habitat. Some two million migratory birds have been counted here in recent years, including yellow robins, snowy egrets, great egrets, and a significant population of American white pelicans.

Since 2002, thanks to intervention by local activists like Amigos del Lago, Lake Chapala has come back somewhat from the brink. A succession of rainy seasons helped the water levels rise again; the removal of some illegal dams contributed to the rise as well. Water treatment plants installed along the Lerma have improved water quality a bit. Boating is now considered safe, and some people even swim in the lake. Eating fish caught in Lake Chapala, though—well, don't push your luck.

ⓘ **Amigos del Lago** (✆ **33/376/766-4249;** www.amigosdelago.org)

✈ Guadalajara

🛏 $$$ **Quinta Real,** Av. Mexico 2727, Guadalajara (✆ **866/621-9288** in North America, or 52/33/3669-0600; www.quintareal.com). $$ **La Villa del Ensueño,** Florida 305, Tlaquepaque (✆ **52/33/3635-8792;** www.villadelensueno.com).

145 All Dammed Up

The Three Gorges
The Rising River
Central Yangtze River, China

THIS CONTROVERSIAL DAM—BUILT TO GENERATE ENERGY AND CONTROL DOWNSTREAM FLOODING—has altered entire ecosystems, threatened traditional fisheries, and created serious health risks to millions of local residents.

China's massive Three Gorges Dam—the world's largest hydroelectric plant—could be seen as a boon to the environment. Completed in November 2009, this stupendous curtain of concrete across the Yangtze River at Mount Wushan supplies the vast central Yangtze basin with clean electric power, much less polluting than the oil or coal power previously used.

The Three Gorges.

But while this massive dam is without question an engineering marvel, to many Chinese, damming the Three Gorges is a sacrilege, on the scale of filling up the Grand Canyon or turning off Niagara Falls. The area's stunning scenic views of mountain peaks towering over steep chasms have been celebrated in Chinese poetry and paintings since the 5th century A.D.; while sightseeing cruises are still popular, the river above the dam is now a narrow, murky lake, 660km (410 miles) long and 1,100m (3,600 ft.) wide. Since construction began in 1992, 13 cities, 140 towns, and 1,350 villages were flooded over and many archaeological sites submerged; 1.3 million people were relocated, most with only meager compensation. The dam's location on a seismic fault troubles many observers, though it did successfully weather a disastrous May 2008 earthquake. It's still uncertain whether the dam will prevent seasonal floods (like the disasters of 1911, 1931, 1935, 1954, and 1998), since swifter downstream currents now pummel preexisting levees.

The ecological effects have been even worse. Massive deforestation has left the riverbanks vulnerable to erosion and landslides. The reservoir above the dam is now grossly polluted, full of backed-up toxins and effluents from upstream areas, especially industrialized Hubei. Silt from upriver is now deposited in the reservoir instead of downstream in the delta; without sediment, delta wetlands shrink, and seawater migrates farther and farther upstream, creating huge algae blooms and invasions of jellyfish. Fishermen report drastically smaller catches, the drinking-water supply has been compromised, and waterborne diseases are on the rise. The critically endangered Siberian crane has lost its principal winter habitat in wetlands above the dam; the Chinese sturgeon, the river sturgeon, the Chinese paddlefish, and the finless porpoise teeter on the edge of extinction, while the Chinese river dolphin (baiji) appears already extinct.

Chinese top officials have sought to distance themselves from the project, hastily slapping bandages on the ravaged landscape. A new nature reserve in the Tian'ezhou oxbow lake has been stocked with the last few finless porpoises, as well as a herd of 600 Pere David's deer, formerly native to the Yangtze wetlands and long extinct in China. Dykes have been removed, reconnecting lakes to the Yangtze; trees are being replanted on denuded riverbanks; and waste treatment plants are being installed in populous urban areas. At the same time, nearly 100 new dams have been proposed for the Yangtze basin, 12 of them on the main river. How long will China, desperate for energy, ignore the environmental cost of such projects?

(i) **Hubei Tian'ezhou Oxbow Wetland Center** (© **86/27/8274-3845**). **International Rivers** (© **510/848-1155**; www. internationalrivers.org).

$$$ **Xierdun Jiudian** (Hilton), Zhongshan San Lu 139, Chongqing (© **800/820-0600** or 86/23/8903-9999; www.hilton. com). $$ **Qing Chuan Jiari Jiudian** (Riverside Holiday Inn), Xi Ma Chang 88, Wuhan (© **888/465-4329** or 86/27/8471-6688; www.ichotelsgroups.com).

TOUR Viking River Cruises (© **800/304-9616**; www.vikingrivercruises.com). **Yangtze River Cruise** (© **866/926-4893** or 86/717/625-1390; www.china-tourism.org).

146 **All Dammed Up**

The Mekong River
King of the Golden Triangle
Chiang Saen/Chiang Khong, Thailand

AS CHINA, THAILAND, AND VIETNAM SEEK TO BUILD MORE DAMS ON THE MEKONG RIVER, habitat is destroyed for the critically endangered giant catfish, already overfished nearly to extinction.

When it comes to growing huge fish, no waterway even comes close to the Mekong River. And among its monster fish, the prizewinner is the Mekong giant catfish, a sleek but toothless gray-and-white bottom feeder. How big is big? Would you believe nearly 2.7m long (9 ft.) and 646 pounds? That's the size of a female caught near Chiang Khong in May 2005, officially the largest freshwater fish ever caught.

Along the course of the Mekong, people regard it as a sacred fish—this mystical vegetarian that seems to meditate like a Buddhist monk in the deep, stony pools of the river. It even appears in cave paintings in northeast Thailand dating over 3,500 years old. But the number of these proud giants—"the king of fish," according to its Cambodian name—is falling, and falling fast. Scientists estimate that the giant catfish's numbers have declined 80% to 90% in the past 20 years, due to overfishing, destruction of habitat, river dredging, and the construction of dams along the Mekong and its tributaries. A fish this big needs a lot of river to roam, and it was once prevalent

Canoeing on the Mekong River.

from southwest China down to the Mekong Delta in Vietnam and Cambodia. Nowadays, it's confined to the Golden Triangle, a small area where Thailand, Laos, and Myanmar meet. Thailand, Laos, and Cambodia have outlawed catching giant catfish, but this law is weakly enforced. The giant catfish may become the first Mekong species in historic memory to go extinct.

The northern Thai border town of Chiang Khong will give you a good idea of what's happening to the Mekong. Chiang Khong is a frontier town, popular with backpackers en route to Laos, and it's close to several waterfalls and rapids where various Mekong giant fish breed. (Khon Phi Laung are the rapids most linked with giant catfish.) Head upstream 70km (43 miles) from Chiang Khong and you'll reach the sleepy village of Chiang Saen, where you can take a longtail boat tour of the Golden Triangle, at the junction of the Mae Ruak River and the Mekong. (The Golden Triangle was once a hotbed of the international opium trade, which explains the Hall of Opium museum located here.) Stand at the crook of the river and you can see both Laos and Myanmar from the Mekong's Thai shore.

The Mekong laces together many countries—and given the rocky state of regional politics, this only makes conservation efforts harder. Visiting this rural province, you'll understand what a lifeline the Mekong River provides for the local population. What are they willing to sacrifice to save one fish—especially one fish that could feed an entire village?

✈ Chiang Rai

🚃 $ **Chiang Saen River Hill Hotel,** 714 Moo 3, Chiang Saen (✆ **66/53/650 826;** www.chiangsaenriverhillhotel.com). $$$ **Anantara Resort and Spa Golden Triangle,** 229 Moo 1, Chiang Saen (✆ **800/ 225-5843** in North America., or 66/53/784 084; www.anantara.com).

Down on the Delta **147**

Vicksburg
Higher Ground
Vicksburg, Mississippi

SWOLLEN BY A HARSH WINTER'S MELTING SNOWS AND AN UNUSUALLY RAINY SPRING, A TURBULENT Mississippi River surged to record heights in May 2011, flooding millions of acres around blufftop Vicksburg.

Sitting on a bluff high above a curve of the Mississippi River, Vicksburg rode out the 2011 flood as it had the great floods of 1927 and 1937, its historic mansions and battlefield park intact. But as the river swelled to record heights of more than 57 feet (17m; downriver Natchez got closer to 63 ft./19m), low-lying communities outside of town and across the river in Louisiana did not fare so well. Two riverfront casinos temporarily closed, and many residents had to evacuate. Roads were submerged, and harbors up and down the river filled with silt. Millions of acres of rich delta cropland lay under up to 20 feet (6m) of murky brown water after the U.S. Army Corps of Engineers opened spillways to prevent flooding in New Orleans. The region will take a long time to recover.

Vicksburg is sited up on that bluff—the second-highest place on the riverbank between Memphis and New Orleans—for good reason. Hailed as the Gibraltar of the Confederacy, during the Civil War Vicksburg's Fort Hill trained its guns down on the river, protecting this crucial ferry port.

A mansion in Vicskburg.

(No bridge spanned the river until 1930.) The landscape made the fort nearly impossible to assault, but in spring 1863 wily Union commander Ulysses S. Grant instead laid siege to the city itself for 47 brutal days (look for cannonballs still lodged in walls downtown). A 16-mile (26km) driving trail winds through **Vicksburg National Military Park** (3201 Clay St.; www.nps.gov/vick); the **Vicksburg Battlefield Museum** (4139 N. Frontage Rd.) explains the battle in more detail.

These days Vicksburg's historic downtown hardly seems like a war zone. Several gracious antebellum homes survived the siege, many of them now bed-and-breakfasts; postwar rebuilding added a number of red-brick Italianate Victorian mansions. Perhaps the most imposing Civil War survivor is the **Old Court House Museum** (1008 Cherry St.; www.oldcourthouse.org), with its ornate cupola and weighty gray granite pediments; inside are nine rooms full of historical exhibits. The **Biedenharn Museum of Coca-Cola Memorabilia** (1107 Washington St.; www.biedenharn coca-colamuseum.com) preserves the red-brick candy factory where a canny confectioner first bottled the fountain drink Coca-Cola in 1894.

Perhaps the sight that best sums up Vicksburg's complicated relationship with the great river is the flood wall that runs along Levee Street. What could have been left as a forbidding expanse of stained concrete has been turned into a piece of public art, with 30-plus murals by artist Robert Dafford celebrating memorable moments in Vicksburg history. There's a panel for the 1927 flood—will a new one be added for 2011?

ⓘ www.visitvicksburg.com

✈ Jackson, MS

🛏 $$ **Annabelle,** 501 Speed St. (ⓒ**800/ 791-2000;** www.annabellebnb.com). $ **Battlefield Inn,** 4137 N. Frontage Rd. (I-20) (ⓒ **800/359-9363** or 601/638-5811; www. battlefieldinn.org).

The Mink River Estuary
Blending the Great Lakes Shore
Door County, Wisconsin

A MIGRATORY STOPOVER FOR MORE THAN 200 SPECIES OF BIRDS, THIS PRISTINE ESTUARY IS ALSO home to two species on the U.S. Fish & Wildlife Service's threatened and endangered list: the Hine's emerald dragonfly and the dwarf lake iris.

Some estuaries lie between fresh and salt water, but not up in the Great Lakes. Here, they're a vital transition point between freshwater river and freshwater lake. The salinity of the water may not vary, but their ebb and flow still makes them dramatic, dynamic places—and often very fragile. With the Great Lakes ecosystem already edging toward crisis, vacation-home development in popular Door County only adds to the pressure on shoreline habitats. All of which makes the Mink River—one of the last and most pristine estuaries, protected by the Nature Conservancy—more important than ever. Where else can lake fish come to spawn? Where else would migrating birds rest before and after crossing those huge lakes?

The Mink River is only a few miles long, running from alkaline springs in the central Door Peninsula to Rowley's Bay on Lake Michigan. Most of it is estuary, where the lake and river waters surge and flush together. At some seasons it's an expanse of flooded marshes; at others, the marshes are dry, with just a few distinct spring channels running through. Whatever grows here must be adaptable—like the sedges, blue-joint grass, and reed grass at the marshy river's edge, backed by taller water-loving shrubs like willows, red osier dogwood, and alder. Going deeper into the marsh, you'll fight your way through thick stands of bulrushes, wild rice, narrow-leaved cattail, and bur reed. The wettest areas display water lilies and water milfoil. A low-lying white cedar swamp borders the marshes, and a small beach runs along Rowley's Bay, where threatened dune thistle clings to the sand.

Numerous birds nest in these wetlands—bitterns, loons, ducks, great blue herons, marsh hawks, and threatened species like the yellow rail, black duck, black tern, black-crowned night heron, northern harrier, and—rarely—a sandhill crane or two. In late summer and fall, you may even spot double-crested cormorants and red-breasted mergansers on their seasonal visits. And then there are, of course, the sort of mammals that thrive happily at water's edge—beaver, porcupine, and muskrat.

There are few trails through this soggy landscape; the best way to explore it is by canoe (contact **Door County Kayak Tours,** ✆ **920/868-1400;** www.doorcountykayak tours.com). Pause often to let the silence descend around you, to hunt for birds with your binoculars. Let yourself lap and drift with the water, feeling the subtle interchange of waters. That's what an estuary's all about.

ⓘ **Wisconsin's Nature Conservancy** ✆ 608/251-8140)

✈ Green Bay

🛏 $$**Rowley's Bay Resort,** 1041 County Rd. ZZ, Ellison Bay ✆ **800/999-2466** or 920/854-2385; www.rowleysbayresort. com). $ **Edgewater Resort,** Hwy. 42, Ephraim ✆ **800/603-5331** or 920/854-2734; www.edge-waterresort.com).

The Okavango Delta
Mokoro Cruising
Botswana

BOTSWANA'S CONTROVERSIAL PLAN TO EVICT NATIVE BUSHMEN FROM THE KALAHARI DESERT underscores how much this parched African nation still depends on the seasonal floods that annually turn this inland delta into a waterlogged oasis.

Every winter—which in Botswana begins in July—the Okavango River flows south out of the uplands of Angola, its waters swollen to bursting by the rainy season. By the time it gets to this vast basin, an ancient lake bed, it overruns its banks, spreading out throughout the delta. Crystal-clear pools, channels, and lagoons spring up everywhere, creating a rich mosaic of different habitats that host an incredible diversity of wildlife, all flocking here to escape the adjacent Kalahari Desert.

The Okavango is no ordinary river delta. For one thing, it doesn't flow into the sea, but into the Kalahari, where it mostly evaporates. Because the waters do not flush away, minerals and salts are deposited around the roots of plants—you'll notice white crusts at the center of many of those tiny seasonal islands. Safari operators market the Okavango Delta as the "Predator Capital of Africa" for the number of lions and leopards you can sight, but a safari here isn't like your typical grasslands safari. Game lodges in the delta are classified as "wet" or "dry" according to whether they are surrounded by water during flood season, but being surrounded isn't a

The Okavango Delta.

145

problem—it just means you'll do all your traveling around by *mokoro*, a narrow canoelike boat propelled through the water by a human with a long pole. Traditionally carved out of tree trunks, nowadays most are made from fiberglass.

These silent, shallow craft make it possible to get really close to birds and animals for wildlife viewing. As you glide along, the air is filled with the sounds of birds calling, frogs trilling, and the endemic red lechwe antelope rustling in the reeds. Wildebeest, hartebeest, buffalo, and zebra roam the islands before you; saddle-billed storks and wattled cranes stalk through the marshland; elephants wade across channels guarded by hippos and crocs.

Game camps in the Okavango are generally tented affairs—the operators are required to make no permanent marks on the land—but some of these are quite luxurious tents indeed. Most of the camps are set within the Moremi Game Reserve,

in the northeastern segment of the delta, which was created in 1962 by the local BaTawana people. Given the complexities of travel within Botswana, it's best to book your lodgings as part of a package trip through a safari specialist company (see "Tour," below). They're pricey, yes, but the experience is once-in-a-lifetime special.

ⓘ **Moremi Game Reserve,** Botswana (http://moremi.botswana.co.za)

✈ Maun Airport

TOUR Abercrombie & Kent (✆ **800/554-7016** in the U.S., or 27/11/781-0740 in South Africa; www.abercrombiekent.com). **Conservation Corporation Africa** (✆ **27/11/809-4300** in South Africa, or 888/882-3742 in the U.S.; www.ccafrica.com). **Wilderness Safaris** (✆ **27/11/895-0862** in South Africa; www.wilderness-safaris.com).

Down on the Delta **150**

The Peace-Athabasca Delta
Leave It to Beavers
Northeastern Alberta, Canada

INCREASING EXTRACTION OF TAR SANDS OIL FROM NEARBY FORESTLAND REDUCES WATER FLOW into this seasonal wetland, killing fish and disrupting one of the world's most important habitats for migrating waterfowl.

In 2007, satellite imagery turned up an astounding sight in the north Alberta wilderness: the world's largest beaver dam, stretching nearly half a mile (850m/2,790 ft.) through a heavily forested stretch of marshland. More than twice as long as Hoover Dam, it's so big that it can be seen from space. Park staff estimate that generations of beavers have worked on this engineering marvel over some 20 years, in spruce and balsam poplar forests so dense and so remote that no human beings noticed.

The Peace-Athabasca Delta holds a lot of world records. It's the world's largest

boreal delta, a flat inland delta situated where the Athabasca, Peace, and Slave rivers flow into Lake Athabasca. Seasonal ebbs and flows create an ever-shifting network of marsh, mud flats, thickets, woodland, lakes, and channels. An internationally important Ramsar wetlands, it is the one magic spot where all four of North America's major bird migration flyways converge. More than one million birds, including tundra swans, snow geese, and countless ducks, arrive here every autumn, including one very special guest: the critically endangered whooping crane, whose only known nesting grounds are here. Nearby, the world's largest free-ranging herd of wood bison, some 5,000 strong, roams on the grasslands and sedge meadows of the delta's **Wood Buffalo National Park**—which also happens to be North America's largest expanse of protected wilderness, larger than the entire country of Switzerland.

Wood Buffalo National Park has always benefited from its remoteness. A single highway runs along its northeastern edge from the Northern Territories; most visitors come by water or air, flying from Edmonton to either Fort Smith, in the Northern Territories, or Fort Chipewyan, Alberta, where you can get backcountry camping permits from the park offices. Canoes, the ideal vehicles for this park with few roadways, can be rented in Fort Smith.

But in today's world, remoteness is no protection against human interference. For the past 50 years, local First Nations peoples have been suing the government over the building of Bennett Dam on the Athabasca River, claiming that it has lowered water levels throughout the delta.

Now, they've got something new to worry about, as Canada has permitted stepped-up tar-sands oil extraction in forests south of the delta. Whatever long-term effect this has on water levels, the most immediate effect has been the influx of polluted industrial wastewater. In 2008, 1,600 ducks died after landing in a tar-sands waste pond; environmentalists are concerned that toxins are spreading through the entire food web. No beaver dam, however gigantic, can block out dangers like that.

(i) **Wood Buffalo National Park.** Visitor centers in Fort Smith (149 Macdougal Rd., ✆ **867/872-7960**) and Fort Chipewyan (Mackenzie Ave., ✆ **780/697-3662**). www.pc.gc.ca/pn-np/nt/woodbuffalo/index.aspx.

✈ Fort Smith or Fort Chipewyan

🛏 $$$ **Pelican Rapids Inn,** 152 Macdougal Rd., Fort Smith (✆ **867/872-2789**). $ **Pine Lake Campground,** Pine Lake Rd. off Hwy. 58, 60km (37 miles) south of Fort Smith.

---

151 Swamps & Bayous

Nassawango Creek Preserve
The Chocolate Bog
Snow Hill, Maryland

AGRICULTURAL RUNOFF, INCREASED RESIDENTIAL DEVELOPMENT, AND WETLAND ALTERATIONS EXERT pressure on the edges of this protected river system, a rare northern instance of a bald cypress swamp.

Don't worry if Nassawango Creek's waters look chocolate brown—they've looked that way since Pocahontas's friend Captain John Smith first canoed up this stream in 1608. Naturally darkened by tannin from fallen leaves, Nassawango Creek is actually one of the most pristine tributaries of the equally dark Pocomoke River, which starts out in Delaware's Great Cypress Swamp and ends up in Chesapeake Bay. Combined with adjacent private lands, it's Maryland's largest unspoiled wildlife corridor, spooling its tranquil way through

rare bald cypress swamp and forests of Atlantic white cedar, loblolly pines, and seaside elder, where rare orchids bloom and endangered warblers sing.

Captain John Smith had one thing right—canoeing is the best way to explore Nassawango Creek. This 18-mile (29km) stretch of water is part of a network of canoe routes called the Bogiron Water Trail, in honor of the iron-rich bogs around here, which gave rise to a thriving iron-smelting industry in the early 19th century. (The historic village of Furnace Town, center

147

of that industry from 1828–50, lies inside the preserve boundary—information is available at the visitor center.) Rental canoes are available in Snow Hill; check with preserve staff to join a guided tour. From a boat launch on the west side of the creek, just off Red House Road (look for yellow nature sanctuary signs), you can canoe all the way to the Pocomoke River. As you paddle along the creek, keep an eye out for river otters and painted turtles, and for white-tailed deer and gray foxes in the woods around you; listen for the rat-tat-tat of the pileated woodpecker. In fall the marsh blazes red and gold with cardinal flowers and spotted jewelweed. You can also take a short, easy forest hike on the Paul Leifer Trail, where in spring you'll see wildflowers such as pink lady's slipper, mayapple, wild lupine, and jack-in-the-pulpit.

When John Smith steered through here, there was nothing special about Nassawango Creek except its natural dark color.

But these days, bald cypress forests rarely grow this far north. Nassawango Creek shows us what the eastern shore was like, once upon a time. Nature can be hardy: Despite the years of iron smelting, the bog habitat replenished itself, with a little help from the Nature Conservancy, which has done controlled burns, thinned hardwoods in the bogs, and planted new trees—persimmon, pin oaks, and Atlantic white cedars. If this last sliver of the old woods goes, we'll never see its like again.

ⓘ **Nassawango Creek Nature Preserve,** 3816 Old Furnace Rd. (ⓒ **410/632-2032**)

✈ Baltimore/Washington International

🛏 $$$ **River House Inn,** 201 E. Market St., Snow Hill (ⓒ **410/632-2722;** www.riverhouseinn.com). $ **Days Inn,** 1540 Ocean Hwy., Pocomoke City (ⓒ **410/957-3000;** www.daysinn.com).

Swamps & Bayous 152

The Okefenokee Swamp
Land of the Trembling Earth
Georgia

HUMAN ACTIVITIES FROM LOGGING TO UPSTREAM DEVELOPMENT HAVE UNBALANCED THIS immense swamp's delicate ecosystem. As peat fills in the wetlands, the natural habitat of countless plants and animals disappears.

Over the years man has tried to tame the great Okefenokee Swamp—and always the swamp prevailed. Paddling around its inky backwaters, you'll see a few abandoned farmsteads, a half-built drainage canal, and ghostly remains of major logging operations. Stumps of half-century-old cypress trees thrust out of the murk, surrounded by the slim black gum and white-flowered bay trees that defiantly sprang up to replace them.

But human meddling inevitably has thrown the ecosystem out of whack. In 1891, the Suwannee Canal was built, a first vain attempt to drain the swamp. Cypress

logging in the early 20th century left only a few original stands of virgin cypress. In 1960, sinking water levels were raised by the Suwannee River Sill in an attempt to prevent fires, an effort that luckily failed, since current science welcomes periodic fires, which clear out ground vegetation. Without the fires, increased vegetation eventually creates peat buildups, which could turn to solid land, altering the wetlands forever. (In April 2011, severe drought and lightning caused a rare fire that ravaged 300,000 acres of the refuge.)

Meandering over 650 square miles (1,683 sq. km) of southeastern Georgia, cut off by Trail Ridge from the coastal plain, this vast wilderness is a watery mosaic of various habitats—wet prairies, peat marsh, pine uplands, hardwood hammocks, small lakes and "gator holes," and floating mats of peat that have become their own islands. No wonder the Creek Indians called it "Land of the Trembling Earth." To keep the various interconnected habitats in balance, 90% has been set aside as a national wildlife refuge, which shelters endangered and threatened species such as the wood stork, the sandhill crane, the red-cockaded woodpecker, the indigo snake, the carnivorous parrot pitcher plant, and the Florida black bear. Bobcats prowl, marsh rabbits skitter for cover, and possums (the models for the comic strip character Pogo) cling to tree trunks. And yes, venomous snakes and alligators add their notes to the deliciously creepy atmosphere.

No roads invade the wilderness, except for a 9-mile (14km) driving trail from the eastern entrance. The park areas developed around the edges, however, offer interpretive centers, nature trails, and canoe-rental facilities. The best way to explore is on 120 miles (193km) of marked canoe trails, mirrorlike dark waterways where you can glide under low-hanging trees, always keeping an eye out for alligators and an ear tuned for the rat-tat-tat of a woodpecker or the agile slither of an otter. To camp deep in the wilderness, you'll need to make reservations no more than 2 months in advance with the **U.S. Fish and Wildlife Service** (✆ **912/496-3331**). Being lulled to sleep by a chorus of a dozen different kinds of frogs—that's the prime Okefenokee experience.

ⓘ **Okefenokee National Wildlife Refuge:** www.fws.gov/okefenokee. East entrance: **Suwanee Canal Recreation Area,** GA Spur 121, Folkston (✆ **912/496-7156**). West entrance: **Stephen C. Foster State Park,** GA 177, Fargo (✆ **912/637-5274**). North entrance: **Okefenokee Swamp Park,** GA 177, Waycross (✆ **912/283-0583;** www.okeswamp.com).

✈ Jacksonville, FL

🛏 $$ **Holiday Inn Express,** 1725 Memorial Dr., Waycross, GA (✆ **888/465-4329** or 912/548-0720; www.holiday-inn.com). $ **Stephen C. Foster State Park** campground, GA 177, Fargo (✆ **800/864-7275** for reservations).

TOUR Okefenokee Adventures (✆ **866/THESWAMP [843-7926]** or 912/496-7156; www.okefenokeeadventures.com)

153 Swamps & Bayous

Cypress Island Preserve
The Year of the Empty Nests
Lafayette, Louisiana

DREDGING IN NEARBY BAYOUS HAS CHANGED THE NATURAL WATER FLOW INTO THIS LOUISIANA wetland, while recreational boating and fishing disturb a major waterfowl nesting area.

The bird-watchers were there, same as every year. So what happened to the birds?

The south end of Louisiana's Lake Martin is perhaps North America's most renowned rookery for wading birds, named by the Audubon Society as one of the country's top 10 bird-watching sites. As many as 20,000 wading birds—herons, egrets, ibises, roseate spoonbills, and other long-legged beauties—nest in among the cypress trees and buttonwood bushes every spring.

But in the spring of 2006, something ruffled their feathers. Thousands of nesting pairs suddenly flew away, abandoning eggs they had already laid, never to be hatched. Though trespassing is prohibited in the rookery's waters during nesting season, February to July, rangers speculate boat-traffic commotion may have scared off the birds in 2006. The Nature Conservancy installed cameras to monitor the area and cordoned off the rookery during nesting season with thick metal cables.

Ornithologists let out a sigh of relief in 2007 when breeding season proceeded as normal. They were all back again—the white ibis, the American anhingas, the black crowned night herons, the great egrets, the snowy egrets, the cormorants, the little blue and the great blue herons. To enhance the bird-watching experience, on the southern end of Rookery Road a new boardwalk walking trail and 20-foot (6m) viewing tower have been built unobtrusively hidden among the cypress trees, so people can get an even closer glimpse of nesting areas.

That one anomalous year underscores the fragility of this 9,500-acre (3,845-hectare) preserve around Lake Martin, a picturesque cypress-tupelo swamp hung with curtains of trailing Spanish moss. A levee has been built to keep water levels high enough to support wildlife and recreation (it's a very popular fishing lake). The rest is bottomland hardwood forest and live oak forest, where vireos and thrushes fill the air with bird song.

Lake Martin also is the best spot in Louisiana to see big alligators, with nearly 2,000 of the big reptiles, some as long as 10 feet (3m). They're so prevalent, the 2.5-mile (4km) walking trail along the top of the levee is closed during alligator nesting season, June to October. The alligators lurk right around where the birds build their nests, hoping to snap up a drowned chick or two. But they actually improve matters for the birds, scaring off raccoons and beavers and opossums that might otherwise raid the nests. Whatever happened in 2006, you can't blame the gators.

ⓘ **Cypress Island Preserve,** Rookery Rd. at Hwy. 353, Beaux Bridge, LA (© **337/342-2475**).

✈ Lafayette

🛏 $$ **Maison Des Amis,** 111 Washington St., Beaux Bridge (© **337/507-3399; www.maisondesamis.com**). $$ **Bois des Chênes Inn,** 338 N. Sterling, Lafayette (© **337/233-7816;** http://boisdechenes.com).

Swamps & Bayous **154**

Caddo Lake State Park
Down on the Texas Bayou
East Texas

THE ONLY NATURAL LAKE IN TEXAS, CADDO HAS BEEN INVADED BY A NOXIOUS AQUATIC FERN called Salvinia molesta, or giant salvinia, which doubles in size every 2 to 4 days and quickly suffocates life below the water's surface.

Canoeing through this East Texas wildlife haven, following murky moss-hung backwaters between immense bald cypress trees, you get the feeling that anything could happen down here. Persistent sightings of a Bigfoot-type denizen—called (what else?) the Caddo Critter—seem entirely possible. But it's the channel-clogging invasion of an aquatic plant—the giant salvinia, inadvertently carried into the lake by careless boaters—that's the real horror story here these days. Aggressive herbicide sprays keep it at bay, but it's tough to eradicate.

Caddo Lake State Park.

Though Caddo Lake lies in Texas, it's actually the western half of one big bayou that stretches into Louisiana. The South's largest natural freshwater lake, it's also the largest intact cypress forest left in the world. It has endured many threats—dammed in 1911, dotted with oil derricks in the early 20th century, polluted by an ammunition factory until the 1990s—but since 1993, Caddo has been a protected refuge. Instead of open water, Caddo is an intricate maze of overgrown sloughs, ponds, and waterways. Fishermen love its 42 miles (68km) of twisting boat roads, teeming with largemouth bass, catfish, and crappie. But it's equally a hot spot for bird-watchers, with about 240 species to look for, from red-tailed hawks to pileated woodpeckers and more waterfowl than you could shake a stick at.

Local birders recommend hanging out along Big Cypress Bayou and Mill Pond; in the summer sky you may spot anhingas and Mississippi kites sailing overhead. In the nearby town of Uncertain, a shallow slough called Goose Prairie (in front of Crip's Camp) is generally full of wading birds, wood ducks, and the occasional shorebird. In winter you may even see a migrating bald eagle. Half a mile (nearly 1km) west of the park entrance, a hill at the intersection of TX 43 and FM 2198 is handy for observing the fall migration of white ibis, wood stork, osprey, Mississippi kite, bald eagle, chimney swift, and purple martin. A swampy area where Harrison Bayou crosses Plant Road (C.R. 2607) is prime habitat for wood ducks, great egrets, cattle egrets, green herons, little blue herons, and great blue herons. Go south of the park on TX 43, turn east on FM 805, and near Pine Needle Lodge you can often find yellow- and black-crowned night herons, as well as fish crows, brown nuthatches, and a ton of warblers in summer. Keep your eyes open, and who knows? You may even spot the Caddo Critter.

ⓘ **Caddo Lake State Park,** FM 2198, Karnack, TX (🕐 **903/679-3351**)

✈ Shreveport, LA

🛏 $$ **Excelsior House,** 211 W. Austin St., Jefferson (🕐 **903/665-2513;** www.theexcelsiorhouse.com). $ **Shady Glade Resort,** 449 Cypress Dr., Uncertain (🕐 **903/789-3295;** www.shadygladeresort.com).

10 Places to See Piping Plovers Nests

It's not hard to drum up support for the piping plover. Anybody who's encountered these bright-eyed little puffs of sand-colored feathers scurrying along a beach knows how adorable they are. In 1985, their East Coast population had sunk to 722 breeding pairs, but by 2009 they had rebounded to 1,849, thanks to aggressive efforts to protect their traditional nesting areas. However, matters are riskier for the Great Lakes population, which had declined to only 12 to 13 pairs; the count's back up to 63 pairs, but they're still endangered.

These birds like the same kinds of beaches we do—open sands close to the tide line, preferably with some sparse dune vegetation nearby. Check out the following protected beaches, where, with binoculars, in late spring and summer you can observe plovers foraging and raising their downy chicks.

155 Rachel Carson National Wildlife Refuge, Kennebunk, Maine Named for the pioneering environmentalist, author of *Silent Spring*, this refuge protects a dozen parcels of salt marsh, just inland from the famous beaches of Maine's southern coast. More than half of the state's piping plover population nests around here from April to July. Near Ferry Beach, the short Goose Fare Brook Trail leads to an interpreted observation platform with automatic-focus binoculars.© *207/646-9226. www.fws.gov.*

Fire Island National Seashore.

156 Fire Island National Seashore, Long Island, New York Very few summer residents bring cars over to Fire Island, a popular resort barrier island linked by ferry to the south coast of Long Island. Just as well, because starting in March, driving is banned on the seashore's series of Atlantic beaches (kite flying and unleashed dogs are banned as well), as nesting habitat in the silvery high dunes is fenced off for piping plovers.© *631/687-4750. www.nps.gov/fiis.*

157 Goosewing Beach, Little Compton, Rhode Island This narrow Rhode Island Sound beach provides piping plovers with an ideal setup—level sands for nesting, with the muddy flats of a salt pond behind it supplying food. The Nature Conservancy has hired an on-site plover warden to monitor the beach, where piping plovers and least terns nest side by side, mid-April to early September.© *401/331-7110. www.nature.org.*

158 Griswold Point, Old Lyme, Connecticut At the mouth of the Connecticut River, this mile-long sand spit between the river's marshy estuary and Long Island Sound is fenced off from Memorial Day to Labor Day, but you can view nesting piping plovers, osprey, and least terns from adjacent White Sands Beach (where plovers often visit). *www.nature.org.*

159 Mashomack Preserve, Shelter Island, New York   Between the North and South forks of heavily populated Long Island, residential Shelter Island has set aside a third of its land for this 2,039-acre (825-hectare) preserve off of Route 114. Although piping plover nesting areas on the beaches are fenced off in season, several trails allow you to explore the surrounding mosaic of tidal creeks and salt marshes.✆ *631/749-1001. www.nature.org.*

160 Cape May Migratory Bird Refuge, West Cape May, New Jersey   This bird-watching hot spot at New Jersey's southern tip offers an unspoiled beach, dunes, and salt marshes, free from the feral cats and rats and recreational vehicles that plague much of the Jersey shore. Recent restoration created a new raised walking trail and observation tower, as well as a foraging pond and dune "crosswalks" specifically designed for nesting plovers.✆ *609/861-0660. www.nature.org.*

161 Sleeping Bear Dunes National Lakeshore, Empire, Michigan   The dune-lined shore of Lake Michigan is the last stronghold of the Great Lakes piping plover population. They're present from late April to August, with new chicks hatching in June. Prime spots to see them (from afar, of course—you may need to do some wading) are on the mainland near the mouth of the Platte River, in the Sleeping Bear Point area, and on North Manitou Island.✆ *231/326-5134. www.nps.gov/slbe.*

162 John E. Williams Preserve, Turtle Lake, North Dakota   One of the world's largest concentrations of breeding piping plovers settles every spring into this treeless landscape in central North Dakota, on the gravelly, salt-crusted fringes of shallow alkali lakes, which teem with the tiny crustaceans that plovers love. Nesting beaches are closed off in season, so bring your binoculars to view the plovers from other spots on the lake.✆ *701/794-8741. www.nature.org.*

163 Lake McConaughy, Ogallala, Nebraska   As the North Platte River's sandbars disappeared, the piping plovers moved on to the wide white beaches of 12-mile-long (19km) Lake McConaughy, created in the Depression by the construction of Kingsley Dam. Drought years are actually good news for nesting plovers—lower lake levels just mean wider beaches for plover nests.✆ *308/284-8800. www.ngpc. state.ne.us.*

164 Quill Lakes, Wynard, Saskatchewan   This set of three shallow, saline lakes in east-central Saskatchewan are full of mud and gravel, surrounded by freshwater marsh—perfect for piping plovers. At the Wadena Wildlife Wetlands, on the shore of Little Quill Lake, you may be able to spot nesting plovers from the Plover's Path trail, along the lakeshore beside the Jesmer Marsh.✆ *306/338-3454. www.wadena.ca.*

Keoladeo National Park
Jewel in the Crown
Bharatpur, Rajasthan, India

A SERIES OF FAILED MONSOONS HAS LEFT THIS WORLD-FAMOUS BIRD MARSH HALF-DRIED OUT, invaded by thorny scrub and grazed by feral cattle. In 2009, UNESCO threatened to put it on its list of World Heritage Sites in Danger.

Flash back to the days of the Raj, when privileged members of the British ruling class amused themselves at this duck-hunting preserve, not far from the Taj Mahal. Imagine the champagne corks popping as Lord Linlithgow, viceroy of India, strode in from a record-setting day of shooting—an incredible 4,273 birds downed in just 1 day.

Since 1956, however, there's no shooting in Keoladeo, formerly known as the Bharatpur Bird Sanctuary. With over 230 species of birds, it's the number-one bird-watching destination in India. Sure, it started out as a maharaja's hunting ground, when Maharaja Suraj Mal in 1726 flooded a natural depression of land to attract swarms of ducks (some 20 duck species are still found here). But that history of protection kept this compact chunk of wetlands, woods, and grassland a complex mosaic of habitats.

Winter is the best season, when migrants from the north join year-round residents around Keoladeo's shallow, marshy lakes. From perky little shorebirds like the greater painted snipe and the solitary lapwing, to long-legged waders like the black bittern and Sarus crane, there's a rich community at water's edge. Some of the park's most stunning residents are its storks—black-necked, painted, Asian openbills—stepping gracefully through the shallows. In the woods near the water, you may see dusky eagle owls and all sorts of spotted eagles. In the grasslands, one must-see bird is the iconic Indian courser, a speedy little ground bird with beautiful black-and-white

stripes like an eye mask on its russet-colored head.

Paved walkways make it easy to get about the park, on foot, on bicycle (rent them at local lodges and hotels), or, easiest of all, by hiring a rickshaw-wallah, a trained guide who will transport you in his cycle-rickshaw. With a million visitors a year in a relatively small area, however, Keoladeo hardly feels like a wilderness, its main road clogged with traffic. Noisy water pumps and a recently redredged canal feed water into the marshes from the nearby Ajan Dam, but in dry years there's not much water to spare, and ponds have shrunk drastically or been overtaken by algae. A wet 2010 monsoon season helped, but the future is still shaky.

Keoladeo's marquee attraction, a pair of critically endangered Siberian cranes, seems to have stopped migrating into the park. All the more reason to appreciate the rare species that still come here—and remember that they too grow more vulnerable every day.

ⓘ **Bharatpur-Keoladeo Ghana National Park,** National Hwy. 11, Bharatpur (✆ **91/5644/222777**)

✈ Delhi

🚂 Bharatpur

🛏 $$ **Laxmi Vilas Palace,** Kakaji Ki Kothi, Bharatpur (✆ **91/5644/223523;** www.laxmivilas.com). $$$ **The Bagh,** Old Agra-Achnera Rd., Bharatpur (✆ **91/5644/225415;** www.thebagh.com).

Buffalo River
The National River That Started It All
Arkansas

RESIDENTIAL DEVELOPMENT IN THE OZARKS AND NEW WATER RESERVOIR CONSTRUCTION HAVE limited natural cave habitat for the Ozark big-eared bat. When a 2010 fungus outbreak caused white-nose syndrome in bats, human visitors were banned from park caves.

In 1972, the early days of the environmental movement, Congress did a radical thing: It declared this backwoods Ozark waterway America's first national river. That meant that its 150 miles (241km) would never be dammed or dredged, but simply allowed to flow as nature intended. It was a bold experiment—and it worked.

Beginning in the remote and rugged Ponca wilderness, the Buffalo cuts a winding descent through tall limestone bluffs forested with deciduous trees—oaks, locust, sweet gum trees—then meanders into the White River, leading to the Arkansas River, then the Mississippi, and finally the Gulf of Mexico. It's not totally unspoiled wilderness—evidence suggests that the ancient Rock Shelter People dwelt in caves in those bluffs, and 19th-century farmhouses scattered around the park recall an era of hardscrabble homesteading. In the 20th century, first mining and then logging companies set up operations for a time. But since 1972, the preserve has returned to its natural state, with clear water and healthy woodlands.

The prime way to enjoy the Buffalo River is on the water, whether you shoot the swift rapids in the upper river or take an easy float on the peaceful middle stretches, stopping off at sandbars and swimming holes or fishing for plentiful smallmouth bass or catfish. Check out river conditions before you go, since they vary widely from section to section (like rivers are supposed to). But don't overlook what's onshore, with over 100 miles (160km) of hiking trails and several disused roads converted to horse trails. Tucked around those riverside bluffs are natural springs, waterfalls, and rock arches to explore, though several caves have recently been closed as park staff members battle the *Geomyces sp.* fungus, which causes white-nose syndrome in bats.

The American bison for which the river was named are long gone, but black bears still inhabit the woods, and great blue, little green, and white herons stalk along the banks. You'll also have a very good chance of spotting elk, thanks to a diligent restocking program in the early 1980s. The woods are full of songbirds—finches, cardinals, mockingbirds, wrens, and thrushes. In spring, flowering trees—sarvis, redbud, dogwood—blossom in the woods, with wildflowers, ferns, and azalea bushes filling out the understory. And the fall foliage? It's nothing short of spectacular.

ⓘ **Tyler Bend Visitor Center,** Hwy. 65, St. Joe, AR ✆ **870/439-2502;** www.nps. gov/buff)

✈ Harrison, AR

🛏 $$$ **River Wind Lodge & Buffalo River Cabins,** Jct. Ark Hwy. 43 & Hwy. 74, Ponca ✆ **800/221-5514;** www.buffalo river.com). $$ **Buffalo Point Lodge & Cabins,** 2261 Hwy. 268E, Yellville ✆ **870/ 449-6206;** www.buffalopoint.com).

TOUR Buffalo River Outfitters, St. Joe, AR ✆ **800/582-2244** or 870/439-2244; www.buffaloriveroutfitters.com). **Silver Hill Canoe Rental,** St. Joe, AR ✆ **870/ 439-2372;** www.silverhillcanoe.com).

The Walls of Jericho
The Grand Canyon of the East
Alabama/Tennessee

HOME TO THREE GLOBALLY IMPERILED FISH SPECIES AND 45 SPECIES OF MUSSELS, THIS RICH river-gorge habitat supplies the missing link to connect other large Cumberland Plateau forest tracts in Alabama and Tennessee.

Once upon a time, famed woodsman Davy Crockett hunted here. In the late 1800s, an awestruck traveling minister gave its cathedral-like limestone gorge the biblical nickname the Walls of Jericho. When it was owned by a family named Carter, they left the land open to cavers and hikers. But in 1977 a lumber company bought the area, closed it off, and began to hack down the forest that had kept the Paint Rock River headwaters so clean and clear.

Enter the Nature Conservancy and Forever Wild Alabama, two conservation organizations that finally purchased the Walls of Jericho in 2004. Now visitors can see this beautiful rock formation again, explore its intricate cave systems—a vital habitat for rare bats and even rarer salamanders—and hike or ride horses through its leafy upland forest and serene wooded ponds. Canoers know it as a fine wild whitewater run, one of the cleanest in Tennessee, with Category IV cascades and some portaging required to pass chattering waterfalls. Bird-watchers come in spring to hear a host of migratory warblers and other songbirds. Photographers discover a delicate wealth of Appalachian wildflowers—yellow and pink lady's slippers, showy orchids, white fringeless orchids, white nodding trilliums, Cumberland rosinweeds, bloodroots, Dutchman's-breeches, and the rare limerock arrowwood.

The purchase came just in time. The upper Paint Rock River—which is formed by the gorge's Hurricane Creek merging with the Estil Fork—is one of the southeast's last few large watersheds that is still intact and functional. It's home to 100 fish species (including the imperiled snail darter, sawfin shiner, and blotchside logperch) and an impressive 45 species of mussels, including two (pale lilliput and Alabama lampshell) that occur nowhere else.

The trail to the Walls is about 3 miles (4.8km) each way, crossing lots of little streams that quickly swell in rainstorms, leaving the trail muddy for days. You'll hike through a forest of maple, oak, hickory, beech, eastern red cedar, and tulip tree, passing rock outcroppings that may conceal caves, springs, or sinkholes. Farther up the narrow gorge (you'll cross the state line into Tennessee), you reach the Walls: a large, bowl-shaped natural amphitheater, 150 feet (46m) wide with sheer 200-foot-high (61m) walls. As Turkey Creek cascades through the Walls, water spurts out of big holes and cracks in the canyon wall during heavy rains or the big spring flows. You'd almost swear the canyon was spouting for joy, so glad that it and its woods have been saved.

ⓘ **Walls of Jericho,** Hwy. 79 (Rowe Gap Rd.), Hytop, AL (✆ **615/781-6622**)

✈ Huntsville, AL

🛏 $$ **Comfort Inn,** 23518 John T. Reid Pkwy., Scottsboro, AL (✆ **256/259-8700;** www.choicehotels.com). $$ **Jameson Inn Scottsboro,** 208 Micah Way, Scottsboro, AL (✆ **800/JAMESON [526-3766]** or 256/574-6666; www.jamesoninns.com).

Delaware Water Gap
Mind the Gap
Pennsylvania/New York

NATURAL GAS EXTRACTION COULD CREATE UNTREATABLE TOXIC WASTEWATER IN THE UPPER Delaware River—the source of drinking water for 17 million people.

To look at the Delaware River's lazy waters sparkling in the summer sun, you'd never imagine that 17 million people eventually drink its water, including most of New York City and Philadelphia. Despite the dramatic gorge of the Delaware Water Gap, it's a relatively placid, shallow stretch of river with just a few riffles and quiet pools parting for tiny scrubby islands.

The Delaware can take its time, because it's the last undammed big river in the East, though just barely—much of the land upstream from the Gap was once cleared for a planned hydroelectric project, which accounts for the absence of houses along 40 miles (64km) of riverbank. Having already appropriated the land, in 1978 the government instead turned it into a park, designating roughly 73 miles (117km) of the Upper Delaware River between Hancock, New York, and Mill Rift, Pennsylvania, as one of the original National Wild and Scenic Rivers.

If it doesn't exactly look "wild," it's certainly scenic, a welcome getaway from the great metropolitan areas that drink its water. Access points have been created along the river every 4 to 10 miles (6.4 to 16km), which makes it ideal for short canoeing, kayaking, and tubing trips. Local outfitters provide river maps and rent equipment; they'll even drive you to your access point and pick you up afterward— all you have to do is slather on the sunblock and hit the water. As you drift along, you'll have time to gaze at the forested ridges on either side, to see map turtles basking on rocks in the sun, and to eyeball the bald eagles soaring overhead.

Having escaped that hydroelectric dam, however, the Delaware faces a new threat from another energy source: natural gas. The Upper Delaware watershed sits atop a geological formation known as the Marcellus Shale, and that shale is full of natural gas. Multinational energy corporations have recently acquired rights to drill gas wells into nearby land. To extract the gas, they'll need to take millions of gallons

The Delaware Water Gap.

157

of clean river water, add possibly toxic chemicals, and inject it into the wells. Surface water and groundwater may become toxically polluted and soil contaminated and eroded—not to mention the air pollution and habitat fragmentation caused by water tankers shuttling between the river and the wells. Throughout 2009 and 2010, protests and lawsuits have flown thick and fast, pitting citizen's watchdog groups and national park officials against the federal government's Delaware River Basin Commission. That shared border is another problem—New York City environmental leaders may oppose the plans, but Pennsylvania tends to be more friendly to energy industries. A moratorium was placed on exploratory drilling in 2009, but how long it will hold is anybody's guess.

ⓘ **Delaware Gap National Recreation Area: North entrance,** 209 E. Harford St., Milford, PA; south entrance, or River Road, Smithfield Beach, PA (✆ **570/426-2452;** www.nps.gov/dewa)

✈ **Lehigh Valley International,** Allentown, PA, 65 miles (105km). Newark International, Newark, NJ, 70 miles (113km).

🛏 $ **Delaware River Family Campground,** 100 Rte. 46, Delaware, NJ (✆ **800/543-0271** or 908/475-4517; www.njcamping.com/delaware). $$ **Hampton Inn,** 114 S. 8th St., Stroudsburg, PA (✆ **800/426-7866** or 570/424-0400; http://hamptoninn1.hilton.com).

TOUR Pack Shack Adventure, 88 Broad St., Delaware Water Gap (✆ **570/424-8533;** www.packshack.com). **Chamberlain Canoes,** River Road, Minisink Acres Mall, Minisink Hills (✆ **800/422-6631;** www.chamberlaincanoes.com).

Along the Banks 169

The Cedar River
Flood Plain Revival
Northeastern Iowa

TRADITIONAL FLOOD-CONTROL STRUCTURES LIKE DYKES AND LEVEES MAY NO LONGER PROTECT this deluge-prone Iowa watershed, made more vulnerable by the widespread loss of flood plain and wetlands.

When the Cedar River rampaged through northeastern Iowa in 1993, hydrologists called it a "500-year flood"—an event so cataclysmic, it might happen only twice a millennium. Five hundred years? Try 15—because in 2008, an even worse flood hit, taking out bridges and forcing thousands of evacuations. More than 1,000 blocks lay under water in Cedar Rapids, the state's second-largest city, its very name a reminder of the river's power. The city's star cultural attraction—the Cedar Rapids Museum of Art, known for its collection of paintings by native son Grant Wood—remained closed for months.

The Cedar River Watershed Coalition, working with conservation groups like American Rivers and the Nature Conservancy, is now pressing the state to restore nature's original flood-control scheme: wetlands and forested flood plains. Over the years, plowed cornfields and housing developments replaced the old landscape of tallgrass prairie, marsh, and meandering streams, and now spring rains dump way too quickly into the snowmelt-swollen river. Flows in the Cedar River have nearly doubled over the past 50 years—too much for antiquated levees along the Cedar's 300-mile (480km) course.

North of Cedar Rapids, the Cedar Valley Nature Trail reveals how beautiful the restored bottomland could be, a forested flood plain rich in wildflowers and songbirds. Built along an abandoned rail bed, the trail covers 52 miles (84km) from the Cedar Rapids suburb of Hiawatha up nearly to Waterloo. The northern half of the trail is particularly good for bird-watching, although portions may still be closed due to 2008 flood damage. There are several access points to the trail—look for the trail head off Boyson Road in Hiawatha, or start midway at the historic railroad depot in Center Point. As you walk along, notice the "pocket prairies"—patches where invasive vegetation has been cut back (or even burned away) to allow the original tallgrass habitat to revive. Scientists from Northern Iowa State University are studying the prairie vegetation to gauge its possible use as a biofuel, which could add economic punch to the idea of restoring prairies.

Birders may want to head to **George Wyth Memorial State Park,** where over 200 bird species have been recorded, including nesting populations of red-shouldered hawks, pileated woodpeckers,

and osprey. And if you're dying to get onto the water, George Wyth SP offers canoers and kayakers one of the state's first paddling trails, a 10-mile (16km) loop of river and lakes, with occasional short portages. Paddling through woods and wetlands, you'll share the water with various residents of the river's edge—the occasional swimming muskrat, basking softshell turtle, or wading heron. Squint your eyes and you could almost imagine it had all been left this way.

ⓘ www.cedarvalleytrail.com. **George Wyth State Park,** 3659 Wyth Rd., Waterloo (✆ **319/232-5505**; www.exploreiowa parks.com).

✈ Cedar Rapids

🛏 $$ **The Blackhawk Hotel,** 115 Main St., Cedar Falls (✆ **800/488-4295** or 319/277-1161; www.blackhawk-hotel.com). $ **George Wyth State Park campground** (✆ **877/427-2757**; http://iowastateparks. reserveamerica.com).

---

170 Along the Banks

San Miguel River Preserve
The River Nobody Messed With
Telluride, Colorado

THREE PRESERVES ALONG THE SAN MIGUEL RIVER PROTECT AN UNSPOILED RIPARIAN HABITAT, home to a globally rare woodland mix and the endangered birds that dwell therein.

There's been so much tinkering with the Colorado River Basin, it's a relief to find a river like the San Miguel. There are no dams along the San Miguel River; it hasn't been dredged or rerouted. It flows just as nature intended it, 72 miles (116km) from its source above Telluride, in the San Juan Mountains, down into the Dolores River, in

the southwestern Colorado Desert. Preserving rivers like the San Miguel not only protects the water supply system of the West, but also protects the wildlife that lives alongside rivers—which happens to be more than 80% of the wildlife in Rocky Mountain Colorado.

Along the San Miguel, riverside forests reflect the rising levels of the river's natural flood cycles. Each of the river's three nature preserves showcases a different rare mix of trees and shrubs. Walk the boardwalk trail through the **South Fork Preserve,** just northwest of Telluride, and interpretive signs point out Colorado blue spruce, black twinberry, and narrowleaf cottonwood. Upstream in the red sandstone gorge of the San Miguel River Canyon Preserve, northwest of Norwood, the twinberry is replaced with thinleaf alder. And in the flood plain area of the Tabeguache Preserve, Rio Grande cottonwoods grow alongside coyote willow and skunkbrush sumac. Given the unusual composition of these woodlands, preserve managers vigilantly watch out for exotic invaders such as tamarisks, Chinese elms, and Russian olive trees.

Impressive stands of ponderosa pines, aspen groves, and water birches occupy other stretches of the riverbank. These great forests attract so many species of birds—including the endangered peregrine falcon, Swainson's thrush, fox sparrow, and American dipper—that it's been designated as an Important Bird Area by the Audubon Society. You may not see the black bears and mountain lions that still prowl around here, but you'll see signs of beaver activity, and you'll probably spot river otters in the water—a species that had once nearly disappeared from the San Miguel, until conservationists successfully reintroduced them.

It's a rugged landscape, no question about it—look upward from the South Fork Preserve and you'll see 14,000-foot (4,270m) **Wilson Peak** of the western San Juan Mountains. Other nearby landmarks are **Ophir Needles,** a granite pillar topped with jagged outcroppings that's a designated National Natural Landmark, and **Ames Wall,** a shingled rock face composed of stratified rock types (granite, sandstone, and shale). In this untamed mountain wilderness, an untamed river flowing through it may hold the key to restoring the American West's rivers.

ⓘ **South Fork Preserve,** Ilium Valley Rd., Telluride, CO. **San Miguel River Canyon Preserve,** State Rd. 145, Norwood, CO. **Tabeguache Preserve,** Hwy. 141, Uravan, CO.

✈ Telluride

🛏 $$$ **Hotel Telluride,** 199 N. Cornet St., Telluride ✆ **866/468-3501** or 970/369-1188; www.thehoteltelluride.com). $$ **The Victorian Inn,** 401 W. Pacific Ave., Telluride ✆ **800/611-9893** or 970/728-6601; www.tellurideinn.com).

Along the Banks 171

Dunstan Homestead
A Spawning Odyssey
Middle Fork John Day River, Oregon

HIGH SUMMER TEMPERATURES IN 2007 CAUSED DIE-OFFS OF THE CHINOOK SALMON POPULATION in this prime Oregon spawning ground—but conservationists are planting shade trees and deepening river pools to give salmon cooler waters.

First of all, you have to get the right river—there are two John Day rivers in Oregon. And then you have to locate the proper fork, since the big John Day has four major tributaries: the main-stem John Day, the North Fork John Day, the South Fork John Day, and the Middle Fork John Day. They're all named after John Day, an early-19th-century explorer who wandered around this arid part of Oregon between the Blue

Mountains and the Cascade range in the winter of 1811–12. It's kind of a strange choice, naming so many rivers after a guy who got lost.

The John Day is the second-longest dam-free river in the United States, and it's never had fish hatcheries—which means it's a paradise for wild Chinook salmon and steelhead trout. The explorer John Day needed maps, but these magnificent fish don't; they simply wrestle upstream for 484 miles (779km) from the Pacific to get to the gravel shallows of the Middle Fork John Day River, where they spend their summers getting ready to spawn. They have to fight past three major Columbia River dams en route, but they persist, faithful to some age-old instinct.

Along the Middle Fork, the Dunstan refuge—named for the homesteading family that once owned this ranch land—protects 4½ miles (7.2km) of river that's a critical breeding ground for redband trout, bull trout, and Pacific lamprey, as well as the steelhead and salmon. The first challenge is to get the river back to its original meandering course, altered by gold miners in the early 1940s. The straightened river lacked the clear shallows and deep pools in which fish spawn best; the alders, cotton-woods, and willows that kept the river waters shady and cool had been cleared away, and several riverside meadows—essential for seasonal overflow and sediment deposits—were blocked off by piles of loose rock-mining detritus. Refuge managers have also begun to thin the tangled upland forests of ponderosa pines and Douglas firs, making it a better home for Rocky Mountain elk, mule deer, white-tailed deer, grouse, sandhill cranes, Canada geese, and Columbia spotted frogs. As the dark green pine forest becomes more inviting, the elk and deer won't browse so heavily on river's-edge vegetation.

Park your car along County Road 20, which follows the course of the Middle Fork for several miles. Venture on foot into the woods—the preserve lies within the **Malheur National Forest**—or find your way to the river's banks. Peer into the teeming shallows to catch the silvery glint of young salmon come home to spawn.

ⓘ C.R. 20, mileposts 13–17, near Galena, OR

✈ John Day regional airport

🛏 $$ **Dreamer's Lodge,** 144 N. Canyon Blvd., John Day ℂ **800/654-2849** or 541/575-0526; http://dreamerslodge.com). $ **Middle Fork Campground,** Malheur National Forest, C.R. 20, 9 miles (14km) west of Austin Junction ℂ **541/575-3000**).

---

172 Along the Banks

Swan River Oxbow Preserve
Vanishing Flower of the Marshes
Swan Lake, Montana

HABITAT LOSS AT THE SWAN RIVER PRESERVE HAS MANY CAUSES—TIMBER HARVEST DEFOR-estation and runoff, drainage for residential and agricultural development, removal of native vegetation, and the invasion of noxious weeds.

Such a tiny, unassuming little flower, the Howellia aquatilis. A delicate white-blossomed annual, it likes to be submerged in water, like the marshy ponds nestled inside the swan's-neck curve of Montana's Swan River. But there's just one catch: The water howelia's seeds germinate only on dry land. In order to reproduce, it needs a marsh that dries up in summer—like the ones inside the curve of the Swan River. In

California, Oregon, Idaho, and Washington, the water howelia's special wetlands are being drained or flooded; in other locations, it's being choked out by reed canary grass, a hardy intruder that likes exactly the same growing conditions. In order to save the water howelia, we need the Swan River Oxbow Preserve.

So who cares about one little aquatic flower? Well, the water howelia is an indicator of wetlands health; the same marshes that nurture it are ideal for many other flowers—round-leafed pondweeds, small yellow lady-slippers—as well as water birds such as the common loon, ring-necked duck, mallard, cinnamon teal, spotted sandpiper, common goldeneye, and Canada goose. Marsh wrens, song sparrows, and yellow-headed blackbirds dabble at water's edge, and Neotropical migrants like the western tanager, Swainson's thrush, red-eyed vireo, and Lincoln's sparrow have been known to visit. It's not only the wetlands, but the entire mosaic of habitats: It's an important grizzly bear corridor between mountain ranges (you may want to avoid peak grizzly season, mid-Apr to mid-June); elk, moose, and deer graze in adjoining sedge fens and meadows; and bald eagles, red-tailed hawks, and osprey roost in the cottonwood trees to the west. It's a quiet, undeveloped place, with no spectacular sights to see.

Yet the Swan River Oxbow is a paradigm of change—in a good, natural, untampered-with way. In this steep-sided glacial valley, the Swan River gradually shifted course over the years, forced by accumulations of silt to curve westward. The land inside the curve—the "oxbow"—floods in late spring, when the river is swollen with snowmelt, and hidden springs and water seeping up through the limestone till keep the water table high. In effect it's an inland delta, and one with remarkably pure water. As you walk through it on the interpretive nature trail (stay on the path—it passes through some very boggy patches), you may not notice the water howelia at all. But you're bound to see something else subtle and beautiful.

(i) **Swan River Oxbow Preserve,** off Porcupine Creek Rd., 2½ miles (4km) south of Swan Lake, MT (© **406/644-2211**)

✈ Kalispell

🛏 $$$ **Bridge Street Cottages,** 300 Bridge St., Bigfork (© **888/264-4974** or 406/837-2785; www.bridgestreetcottages. com). $$ **La Quinta Inn and Suites Kalispell,** 255 Montclair Dr., Kalispell (© **406/257-5255;** www.lq.com).

6 Forest & Jungle

A redwood forest in California.

The Redwood Forests of California
Earth's Largest Living Things
Crescent City, California

AS CLIMATE CHANGE DISRUPTS THE ECOLOGICAL BALANCE IN THE REDWOOD FOREST, RISING temperatures raise the threat of forest fires even for these fire-resistant giants.

Respect must be paid to the giant redwood trees, and it must be paid now. Perhaps the planet's most ancient living things—some are dated at more than 2,200 years old—these massive conifers grow only in temperate rainforests. And one of the last few temperate rainforests left on the earth is here, on the Pacific Coast of the United States.

It's hard to explain the feeling you get striding between the immense trunks of old-growth coast redwoods—the word "awe" doesn't begin to capture it. Everything is huge, misty, and primeval: Flowering bushes cover the ground, 10-foot-tall (3m) ferns line the creeks, smells are rich and musty, and an ancient unhurried silence reigns. Sheathed in rough reddish bark, the stout straight trunks shoot up 100 feet (30m) or more before a canopy of branches begins, arching overhead like the roof of a Gothic cathedral.

For many years, the redwoods and their cousins, the giant sequoias, thrived in peace on this relatively isolated coast. Miraculously fire-resistant, the trees could withstand most forces that threatened other local timber. But as human development spread, by 1968 the federal government realized the need to create a haven for them in **Redwood National Park** (nowadays combined with three state redwood parks). Reforestation is ongoing, but replacing giants that took centuries to grow is a slow process.

The most developed area is along the Avenue of the Giants, a 33-mile (53km) stretch of US 101 through the **Humboldt Redwoods State Park** (✆ **707/946-2263;** www.humboldtredwoods.org), where you'll still see attractions like the Shrine Drive-Thru Tree, relics of an earlier age of tourism. Short hikes from most parking areas lead you to highlights such as Founders Grove, honoring those who started the Save the Redwoods League in 1918, the fallen Dyersville Giant (once the world's tallest tree), the Stratosphere Giant, and the 950-year-old Immortal Tree.

Some 100 miles (160km) farther north, there are grander views on two roads that parallel 101: the Newton B. Drury Scenic Parkway, passing through redwood groves and meadows where Roosevelt elk graze, and unpaved Coastal Drive, which twists and turns to offer sudden sweeping Pacific views. Pick up a park map to hike to Tall Trees Trail, a 3.3-mile (5.2km) round-trip trail to a 600-year-old tree often touted as the world's tallest (get a permit at the Kuchel visitor center in Orick); the mile-long (1.6km) Lady Bird Johnson Grove Loop; the short, very popular Fern Canyon Trail; or the quarter-mile-long (.4km) Circle Trail, a paved trail leading to—what else?—a Big Tree.

ⓘ **Redwood National and State Park,** 1111 Second St., Crescent City, CA (✆ **707/464-6101,** ext. 5064; www.nps.gov/redw)

✈ Crescent City Airport

🛏 $$$ **Lost Whale Bed & Breakfast,** 3452 Patrick's Point Dr., Trinidad (✆ **800/677-7859** or 707/677-3425; www.lostwhaleinn.com). $ **Curly Redwood Lodge,** 701 Redwood Hwy. S. (US 101), Crescent City (✆ **707/464-2137;** www.curlyredwoodlodge.com).

Great Basin National Park
The Methuselah Trees
Baker, Nevada

DEPLETED GROUNDWATER AND INVASIVE PLANT AND FISH SPECIES ARE BAD ENOUGH, BUT NOW Great Basin faces a critical threat—proposed coal-fired power plants nearby that could pollute park air and deposit chemicals in its lakes and rivers.

We all know what a desert looks like—hot and sandy, right? But Nevada's desert plateau isn't hot, and it isn't sandy: It's downright chilly on these mountain slopes, where special drought-adapted plants like sagebrush, juniper, pinyon pine, manzanita, rabbitbrush, greasebrush, and Mormon tea cling to rocky soils and prevent erosion. Set along the Utah-Nevada border, Great Basin National Park isn't as well known as its Utah neighbors Bryce and Zion, but it offers great panoramas of surrounding desert and mountains—and groves of bristlecone pines, the planet's longest-living trees.

The oldest tree ever recorded was a Great Basin bristlecone pine *(Pinus longaeva)* called Prometheus, removed from the park in 1964 and carbon-dated to 4,900 years old. Though bristlecones are very slow-growing trees, they compete by thriving at high elevations and exposed rocky sites, where other trees just can't grow. As you hike around the park, you'll notice trees that have been bent and twisted by the wind and snow, often losing all branches on their windward sides (a condition called *krumholtz*). Ice crystals have polished their trunks, and the short dark-green needles are fire resistant as well as drought resistant. For bristlecones, slow growth is actually a virtue; it makes their wood so dense, it resists rot, fungi, insects, and even erosion. Take a look at its distinctive cones: The immature cones are purple to absorb heat, and mature brown cones have bristles at the end of their scales to aid with dispersal.

In summer, rangers often lead guided hikes to a bristlecone grove—check for times at the visitor center (where you can also buy tickets to visit the **Lehman Caves,** Great Basin's star attraction). Or you can go on your own, starting at the parking area at the base of Wheeler Peak, a 4.6-mile (7.4km) round-trip hike. Though the trail isn't steep, the high elevation (10,000 feet/3,000m) may make you tire more easily than normal. The bristlecone grove lies 1.4 miles (2.3km) from the trail head, with a self-guided nature loop leading through the pines; note how they cling to glacial

Great Basin National Park.

moraines of quartzite, an unusual feature for limestone-loving bristlecones. Hike another mile to the end of the trail to see an ice field and what is believed to be a rock glacier—a rock-covered permanent mass of ice moving very slowly downhill. A glacier in a desert—who'd have thought?

ⓘ **Great Basin National Park,** off NV 488, Baker, NV (ⓒ **775/234-7331;** www.nps.gov/grba)

✈ Cedar City, UT (142 miles/229km)

🛏 $ **Silver Jack Motel,** downtown Baker (ⓒ **775/234-7323;** www.silverjackinn.com). $ **The Border Inn,** US 50/6 at Nevada-Utah border (ⓒ **775/234-7300;** www.greatbasinpark.com/borderinn.htm).

Trees of Life 175

The Cedars of Lebanon
Grove of the Gods
Bsharre, Lebanon

ALREADY CAUGHT IN THE CROSSFIRE OF ARMED CONFLICTS AND POLITICAL UNREST, THE ANCIENT cedars in this iconic grove are planted so close together, new saplings compete for sunlight and struggle to reproduce.

It takes ages to grow a cedar. But that's how long this grove has stood here, the last vestige of a primeval forest of cedar, cypress, pine, and oak that once covered Mount Lebanon. It was famous already in biblical times, a source of wood for Phoenician ships; Egyptians used cedar resin to embalm mummies, Moses directed Jewish priests to use its bark to cure leprosy, and both King Solomon and King David ordered cedar beams from here to build their famous temples in Jerusalem. In the Epic of Gilgamesh, this was the dwelling of the gods.

From stone markers laid out by the Roman emperor Hadrian, archaeologists have measured the forest's original vastness. But as the Dark Ages and Middle Ages passed, villagers felled trees to fuel their kilns and cleared the land for farming. Nineteenth-century Ottoman troops cleared away forest cover, and the occupying British army in World War II cut cedar railroad ties for a railway to Tripoli. All that's left are a few isolated patches in hard-to-reach mountain areas—and

this ancient grove, the famous **Arz el Rab (Cedars of the Lord)** in Bsharre, above the Qadisha valley on Mount Makmel in northern Lebanon.

About 4km (2½ miles) up a twisting road from the ski resort village of Bsharre—also known as the birthplace of Kahlil Gibran—Arz El Rab still has some 375 aged cedars, enclosed by a protective stone wall built in 1876 by Queen Victoria. At least four of these trees stand nearly 35m (115 ft.) high—huge for a cedar—with great spreading crowns of dark-green evergreen needles. Interspersed among them, several thousand young trees have been planted over the past 35 years, but it takes 40 years before a cedar can produce fertile seed cones. The wall does keep out free-roaming goats, which would nibble on young saplings, but it makes the trees grow so close together, the saplings don't get enough light. A new scheme to create a cedar plantation outside the wall may turn things around, however, expanding this cramped grove into a full-fledged forest.

Since 1985, conservationists have been fertilizing, pruning, spraying pests, and eliminating widespread tree rot. They have laid out new walkways so that visitors don't trample the vegetation under the trees, which not only protects new growth but also attracts birds that kill tree-boring insects. They've even installed lightning rods so that no more trees are lost before those youngsters have time—oh, say, a century or two—to catch up.

ⓘ **Arz el Rab,** Kenata St., Bsharre (✆ **961-6-672 562;** www.cedarfriends.org); check with your embassy about travel conditions before visiting.

✈ Beirut

🛏 $$$ **Cedrus Hotel,** Cedars Main Road (✆ **961/6/678 777;** www.cedrus hotel.com). $$ **Hotel Chbat,** Rue Gibran, Bsharre (✆ **961/6/671 237**).

Cedar trees in Lebanon.

176 **Trees of Life**

Wollemi National Park
The World's Rarest Tree
Blue Mountains, Australia

ONLY AROUND 40 WOLLEMI PINES STILL EXIST IN THE WILD. TO PRESERVE THE SPECIES, private companies are now allowed to grow seedlings and sell them, but the wild originals' location is a closely guarded secret.

Colored a hazy blue by sunlight glancing off of evaporating droplets of oil from the ever-present eucalyptus trees, the **Blue Mountains** are weird enough. But in the middle of it all is the ultimate weirdness: the world's rarest tree, a throwback to the Jurassic age that exists in only one remote gorge in this immense mountain park.

The Wollemi pine has been extinct for 30 million years—at least, that's what scientists thought until 1994, when three small stands were discovered in a hidden pocket of coachwood-sassafras rainforest. Soaring

35m (115 ft.) high, they have pebbly cocoa-brown bark and waxy leaves of an exotic lime-green color. Promptly nicknamed the "dinosaur tree," this species seems identical to trees recorded in Jurassic age fossils, but not in any later fossils. As a casual visitor, you won't be able to see the Wollemi pines—access is strictly controlled, and the location of the canyon is kept secret by park management. Disappointing as this may be for tourists, it's all for the good of the trees. Botanists who are granted access for research purposes may one day be able

Wollemi National Park.

to propagate new Wollemi pines for the rest of the world to enjoy.

Besides, a park with Wollemi pines is bound to have other unusual and rare natives. There's the *banksias conferta subsp. penicillata*, a rare endemic mountain shrub with a brushy cylindrical yellow flower. Along with koalas, wombats, and platypuses, you may spot unusual-even-for-Australia species like the brush-tailed rock wallaby or the glossy black cockatoo. Near an old oil shale mine at Wolgan (the park contains a few such industrial ghost

towns), an abandoned railway tunnel is eerily illuminated even in daytime by a population of glowworms.

Dramatic gorges, cliffs, caves, and steep sandstone escarpments make Wollemi spectacularly rugged, with three rivers—the Wolgan, the Colo, and the Capertee—carving through the wilderness. (Only the Colo is navigable by canoe or kayak, and then only in high water; canoeists can, however, paddle around atmospheric Dunns Swamp.) Most visitors venture only a short way into this huge park, but long-distance hikers and rock climbers can really get into untrammeled wilderness. Almost 90% of the park is eucalyptus forest (no wonder koalas like to hang out here), but it's anything but monotonous, with 70 different eucalyptus species represented. As you tramp around, take time to note the differences in their barks and evergreen leaves and flowers, and to inhale deeply their distinctive fragrance. No wonder the Blue Mountains look so blue!

ⓘ **Wollemi National Park** (℘ **61/2/6372 7199** or 61/2/6573 5555)

✈ Sydney

🛏 $$$ **Hydro Majestic Hotel,** Medlow Bath (℘ **61/2/4788 1002;** www.hydro majestic.com.au). $$ **Jemby-Rinjah Lodge,** 336 Evans Lookout Rd., Blackheath (℘ **61/2/4787 7622;** www.jembyrinjah lodge.com.au).

Into the Woods **177**

The Laurissilva
The Laurel Trees That Got Away
Madeira, Portugal

The largest remaining laurel forest in the world, the Laurissilva is feeling the squeeze from Madeira's population growth and increasing tourism.

Eons ago, the whole Mediterranean basin was covered with forests like these—tall evergreen hardwoods, with a rich tangled understory of ferns and flowering shrubs. The bay laurels that most people know were just one part of it; virtually unheard-of variants such as *Laurus azorica* and *Laurus novocanariensis* grew everywhere. But as the region became more arid, these subtropical species simply vanished, withered up, and died. The only place they remained were here, in the humid climate of Portugal's Atlantic Islands—Madeira, the Canary Islands, and the Azores.

Settled by Portuguese sailors in the 15th century, **Madeira**—the largest island in its own little archipelago—is a resort spot, known for Madeira wine, exotic flowers, and beaches full of holidaymakers. Two-thirds of the island is a conservation area, however, with a thick band of primary laurel forest cutting a swath across the mountainous spine of the island's cloud-wreathed interior. Covering some 150,000 sq. km (58,000 sq. miles)—almost 20% of the total island—it's much larger than the surviving bits on the Canaries or Azores, which have been whittled down by grazing and farming. Some 76 species occur only here, including some beautiful rare brushes and orchids.

Growing on steep slopes and down into deep ravines, these dense silvery forests with their fine-cut leaves are a remarkable sight. Gnarled trunks tip dramatically downhill as if yearning toward the sea.

Cascading waterfalls and tiny lakes punctuate the forests, and frequent fog and rain keep these uplands moist, just as the trees like it. Rare mosses and lichens drape tree trunks and trail from their branches. Among the unusual birds you may see here are buzzards, kestrels, chaffinches, the long-toed Madeiran laurel pigeon, and the firecrest.

Many walking paths into the forest follow *levadas,* hand-built raised stone aqueducts unique to Madeira; it's a good idea to go with a guide so you don't miss the most picturesque spots. Striding through this ancient landscape is like visiting another world, far from the beaches and bars on the coast. Don't miss it.

✈ Funchal

🛏 $$$ **Quinta Jardins do Lago,** Rua Dr. João Lemos Gomes 29, Funchal (ⓒ **351/291/750 100;** www.jardinsdolago.com). $$ **Quintinha São João**, Rua da Levada de São João, Funchal (ⓒ **351/291/740 920;** www.quintinhasaojoao.com).

TOUR Nature Meetings (ⓒ **351/291/524 482;** www.naturemeetings.com). **Madeira Wind Birds** (ⓒ **351/291/09-80-07;** www. madeirawindbirds.com).

---

178 Into the Woods

Bluebell Forests of East Anglia
The Essence of English Spring
Norfolk, England

RECENT LAWS PROTECT ENGLAND'S FAVORITE WILDFLOWER FROM HUMAN DESTRUCTION—BUT the ever-earlier springs of global warming have begun to critically abbreviate the bluebell's seed-setting process.

Like a watercolor by Beatrix Potter, it's the quintessential English countryside—hollyhocks and larkspur by the garden gate and bluebells carpeting the woods. Imagine, then, the public outcry in the United Kingdom in 1981 when conservationists announced that they were putting the English bluebell on the protected list. Hybridization with the invasive alien Spanish bluebell has corrupted this woodland beauty, turning its deep-violet tightly curling bells on a sweetly drooping stem into flaccid, pale blue cones on a stiff stalk. Worst of all, the new hybrids barely have any scent, whereas a true bluebell's perfume is like the essence of spring.

In 1998, when reporters caught vandals stealing 7,000 bluebell bulbs from the ancient Thursford Wood, a nationwide protest erupted. It's now against the law to remove bluebells from your land or to dig up its bulbs. And if anybody tried it, the neighbors probably would be up in arms—that's how strongly the British feel about these iconic wild hyacinths.

English botanists generally judge the health of ancient woodlands by their profusion of old-fashioned bluebells—and by that standard, two oak forests in the Norfolk countryside are still in prime condition. The largest is **Foxley Wood National Nature Reserve,** near Foxley Village (22km/14 miles northwest of Norwich), a 121-hectare (300-acre) woodland that's so old, it was listed in the Domesday Book. Though it's principally oak, field maple, and birch, it also has such rare trees as wild service, small-leaved lime, and midland hawthorn. (Several conifers, introduced years ago as timber sources, are gradually being removed.) Along with the bluebells, you'll find early purple orchid, dog's mercury, and meadowsweet; the lazy flitting of butterflies fills the air in summer.

You'll find even older oaks nearby at **Thursford Wood,** which lies 5km (3 miles) northeast of Fakenham on A148. The River Stiffkey runs through this 10-hectare (25-acre) remnant of original heath, where some trees are 500 years old or more. For centuries the oak trees have been pollarded—their main branches cut back to promote thicker foliage rather than height—and their lumpy trunks are shaggy with moss, lichens, and fungi. Ferns and rhododendrons flourish in the understory, heightening a distinctly Druidic atmosphere. In May the ground here is completely hazed over with drooping violet bells—it would do Beatrix Potter's heart good to see it.

ⓘ **Foxley Wood National Nature Reserve,** Fakenham Rd., Foxley (access off Tremelthorpe Rd.; ✆ **44/1362/688706**). Thursford Wood Nature Reserve, Holt Rd., Little Snoring.

🚆 Norwich

🛏 $$ **The Maid's Head Hotel,** Palace St., Norwich (✆ **44/1603/209955;** www.maidsheadhotel.co.uk). $ **Norwich Nelson City Centre,** Prince of Wales Rd., Norwich (✆ **44/1603/760260;** www.premierinn.com).

Into the Woods **179**

Sherwood Forest
Ye Old Shire Wood
Nottingham, England

THE U.K. IS THE FOURTH-LEAST-WOODED COUNTRY IN EUROPE, AND CLASSIC BROADLEAF FORESTS account for only 6% of its woodlands. Restoring this iconic forest may spark crucial public support for woodlands conservation.

Even back in Robin Hood's day, Sherwood—meaning "shire wood"—Forest wasn't pure forest, but a mixed landscape of heath, pastureland, and wooded glades, with a few scattered hamlets. This royal hunting ground sprawled over 40,500 hectares (100,000 acres). Only the king and

his subjects could hunt here, but peasants could gather acorns, collect firewood, make charcoal, or graze sheep and cattle. It was truly the heart of Nottinghamshire.

Today, Sherwood Forest has shrunk to a shadow of its former self, just a 182-hectare (450-acre) park surrounding the village of

Edwinstowe, squeezed between the urban areas of **Nottingham** and **Sheffield.** Around 600 stout oak trees survive, but they're dying off fast from sheer old age. The most famous, the Major Oak—touted as Robin Hood's tree, though bark analysis suggests it may be younger than the 13th century—requires a lot of props and cables to stay standing.

Half a million tourists come here every year. Kitschy models of Robin Hood and his Merry Men are on display, and Robin Hood souvenirs sell like hot cakes in the gift shop. A weeklong summer Robin Hood festival features costumed jousters and jesters and troubadours aplenty.

But there's more to Sherwood Forest than the Robin Hood legend. The organization English Nature is fighting to keep Sherwood Forest vital, designating it as a National Nature Reserve in 2002. In 2007, the protected area was nearly doubled by adding the **Budby South Forest,** a stretch of gorse-covered heath previously used for military training. In this larger contiguous parcel, already the local populations of nightjars and woodlarks are increasing, not to mention the great-spotted woodpecker, green woodpecker, tawny owl, and redstart, which need old-growth forests to live. Dead trees and fallen branches are deliberately left in place in the bracken ground cover to feed spiders and beetles. Grazing cattle have been brought in to keep the woodlands open, and footpaths and bridleways run through the trees, a peculiarly English mix of oak, silver birch, rowan, holly, and hawthorn.

The tale of Sherwood Forest reads like a minihistory of Britain. Originally cleared by Roman legions, the Nottinghamshire countryside became fragmented in medieval times as great landowners enclosed their estates. During the Industrial Revolution, towns and factories sprang up, destroying more woodland. In the post-war era, woods were replanted for timber, but with quick-growing conifers. As several area coal mines have closed down, there may be a window of opportunity to revert more of this East Midlands region to woodlands, planting new oaks and creating a continuous corridor—but Britain's new fiscal austerity may put an ax to those plans. The next chapter of Sherwood's story? It still remains to be written.

ⓘ **Sherwood Forest Park,** A614, Edwinstowe (ⓒ **01623/823 202**). **Sherwood Forest Trust** (www.sherwoodforest.org. uk). **Sherwood: The Living Legend** (www.robinhood.co.uk).

✈ Nottingham East Midlands

🛏 $$$ **Strathdon Hotel,** 44 Derby Rd., Nottingham (ⓒ **01159/418 501;** www. strathdon-hotel-nottingham.com). $$ **Park Inn Nottingham,** 296 Mansfield Rd., Nottingham (ⓒ **01159/359 988;** www. nottingham.parkinn.co.uk).

180 Into the Woods

Białowieża Forest
The Bison Will Abide
Poland/Belarus

AIR POLLUTION, INVASIVE SPECIES, AND A NEARBY RAILWAY LINE THAT CARRIES TOXIC CHEMICALS threaten this forest. Although logging of old-growth trees was recently halted, only about 8% of the forest lies within a strictly protected national park.

It's all about the bison.

The big-shouldered European bison was a major game animal in this ancient forest, back when it was the royal hunting ground of the kings of Poland. (The name Białowieża, or "White Tower," refers to a hunting manor of 15th-century King Jagiello.) In 1541, the forest was made a hunting reserve to protect bison, although when Russia took over and the tsar divided the forest among his nobles, hunters overran it and cut the bison population to fewer than 200. But Tsar Alexander I declared it a reserve again in 1801, and the number of bison climbed to 700; in 1888, the Romanovs made it a royal retreat, sending bison as gifts to various European capitals while importing deer, elk, and other game animals for their hunting pleasure. Then came 1917 and the Russian Revolution; soon the tsars themselves were extinct. German occupation in World War I ravaged the forest, and the last bison was killed in January 1919, 1 month before the Polish army swept back in.

Undaunted, in 1929 the Polish government bought four European bison from various zoos (the world population was down to about 54 individuals), bred them in captivity, and eventually reintroduced them to the forest, now a national park. Since then the bison have thrived, with more than 300 today in the Polish section alone. The Poland-Belarus border runs through the forest, marked with a security fence that divides Poland's purebred bison from Belarus's hybrid bison and keeps them genetically isolated.

It's difficult for foreign tourists to visit the Belarus section, which requires permission from the ministry of interior in Brest. On the Polish side, the heart of the park is a strictly controlled area of 4,747 hectares (11,730 acres), viewable only by guided tour, though there are walking trails through an adjacent area that's only slightly less pristine. (There's also an adjacent reserve where you can see European bison, Polish tarpan ponies, elk, deer, roe deer, wild boars, and wolves.) Thanks to 6 centuries of protection as a hunting preserve, the core zone contains relict habitats of the primeval forest that once covered Europe—sandy spruce pine woods, peat bogs, lowmoor, oak-hornbeam-linden forest, alder and ash woods along the Hwoźna and Narewka rivers, and hollows of swampy alders. You'll see a number of massive ancient oak trees, each given its own name. Several of them are dead or dying, but that just makes them great hosts for the hermit beetle or the white-backed woodpecker.

No tree in this area has ever been cut down by man; no tree was ever planted by man. It's not a restored forest, it's the original forest—how rare is that?

ⓘ **Białowieża National Park,** 17-230 Białowieża, Park Pałacowy 11 (℗ **085/682-9700;** www.bpn.com.pl)

✈ Warsaw

🚆 Bialystock (62km/39 miles)

🛏 $$$ **Best Western Hotel Zubrowka,** 6 Olgi Gabiec St., Białowieża (℗ **085/681-2303;** www.bestwestern.com). $$ **Hotel Białowieski,** 218B Waszkiewicza, Białowieża (℗ **085/681-2022**).

Into the Woods 181

Nilgiri Biosphere Reserve
Forest upon Forest upon Forest
Kerala/Karnataka/Tamil Nadu, India

AMBITIOUS HIGHWAY-BUILDING SCHEMES HAVE BISECTED THE RICHLY BIODIVERSE FORESTS OF the Nilgiri Hills, fragmenting wildlife habitat and turning rare animals into roadkill.

Stretching like a lazy cat across the intersection of three South Indian states—Karnataka, Kerala, and Tamil Nadu—the Nilgiri Biosphere Reserve blankets the majestic steep slopes of the western Ghats. Altitudes and moisture levels differ so dramatically here, the preserve encompasses a wide array of forest habitats, rainforest giving way to moist evergreens, then thorn forest and scrub, morphing into grassland and the short, dense Shola forest—often referred to as "living fossils"—atop the plateau. With such different ecosystems in close proximity, the 5,520-sq.-km (2,131-sq.-mile) Nilgiri was named an International Biosphere Reserve in 1986. Along with tigers and elephants, it's a protected home for the Nilgiri tahr, the glossy black Nilgiri langar, and the endangered lion-tailed macaque. Of its 3,330 species, 1,232 are endemic.

Just south of Mysore, three superb wildlife sanctuaries—**Bandipur National Park, Nagarhole National Park,** and **Mudumalai National Park**—show off tigers and elephants and leopards to nearly 200,000 visitors a year. Other parks within the reserve are known for their bird-watching or for their rare orchids; there's even a narrow-gauge train climbing to the charming old hill station of Ooty. This humid tropical wilderness is so rich in flora and fauna, cameras and binoculars can barely catch it all.

Yet the Nilgiri Hills also shelter more than a million individuals from various indigenous peoples, hunter-gatherers and forest dwellers who depend on the forests for their survival. What we call poaching and illegal logging are time-honored ways of life

to them, and it is unlikely that tourism jobs created by wildlife viewing can replace their traditional means of subsistence.

And development continues to encroach upon the Biosphere, altering adjacent lands with hydroelectric dams, coffee plantations, and logging operations. Balancing the competing needs of wildlife and human residents is politically sensitive. Only after concerted efforts by conservationists did the government drop plans to build a broad-gauge railway through the Sathyamangalam forests, a corridor of woodlands that's home to some 2,500 elephants. Meanwhile, traffic speeds along the upgraded National Highway 15, which runs right through Bandipur Park, endangering animals trying to cross the road. Park officials fought for permission to close parkland stretches of highway at night, winning the animals a few hours' respite. It's better than nothing.

✈ Bangalore

🛏 $$ **Jungle Retreat,** Masinagudi, Tamil Nadu (✆ **91/423/2526469;** www.jungleretreat.com). $$ **Bandipur Safari Lodge,** Bandipur National Park, Karnataka (✆ **91/80/40554055;** www.junglelodges.com).

TOUR Ecomantra Nature Adventures (✆ **91/22/6128 0100;** www.ecomantra.com)

---

182 Into the Woods

Bandelier National Monument
Juniper Jewel
New Mexico

DROUGHT-RESISTANT PIÑON PINES AND JUNIPER THRIVE IN THIS DESERT MOSAIC—BUT WHEN they choke out the understory, severe soil erosion threatens some of the Southwest's finest Ancestral Puebloan dwellings.

North of Santa Fe, nestled in the varicolored Jemez mountains, the vistas are simply spectacular, from the sweeping Valles

Caldera across the Pajarito Plateau. Technically it's a desert plateau, but deserts can contain woodlands too—in fact, several different kinds of woodlands, as Bandelier National Monument proves. Following the course of Frijoles Creek as it drops from the snowy summit of Cerro Grande to the Rio Grande, Bandelier plunges 5,000 feet (1,500m) in elevation in just 14 miles (23km), a descent that creates a striking mosaic of ecosystems. Hike the park's 70 miles (113km) of trails and you'll see an astonishing range of wildlife. Elk lumber around windswept montane grasslands, browsing on slender aspen, while tiny hummingbirds dart through wildflower-spangled canyons. Tuft-eared squirrels nibble hardy ponderosa pine cones upland, while wild turkeys strut through scrubby piñon-juniper woodlands.

Ancestral Puebloans knew a rich landscape when they saw it. Between A.D. 1100 and 1500, they centered a large and thriving community around Frijoles Canyon, hollowing complex kivas and cliff dwellings out of the canyon walls. Today Bandelier boasts one of the country's highest densities of prehistoric cultural sites, wonderfully accessible along an easy mile-and-half walking trail from the visitor center. (The visitor center has its own quaint appeal, with its 1930s rustic lodge-style architecture.)

While the archaeological sites are Bandelier's main claim to fame, environmental scientists view this conglomeration of habitats differently: as a prime laboratory for studying how mountain ecosystems respond to climate change (the USGS Global Change research program has an active field station here). Far from being a perfect environmental gem, Bandelier is a case study in how to turn around years of careless land management. Heavy livestock grazing finally ceased in the 1930s, but subsequent decades of fire suppression altered the terrain's natural balance. The piñon-juniper woodlands are now too dense for grass cover to put down roots. Knocking matters further out of whack, since the Cochito flood-control dam was built in the 1970s, the winding Rio Grande has become a sluggish brown ghost of its former self. The canyon's parched bare soil, pummeled in summer by frequent thunderstorms, is eroding at a critical rate—putting at risk those famous archaeological sites, built into fragile volcanic tuff.

Working against time, park management has begun to slash down trees, thinning out the woodland. Trunks of felled trees are laid as a sort of erosion blanket across the exposed soil, to give the understory a chance to rebound. In the quiet bird song of early morning, when the rising sun throws the shadows of the canyon into sharp relief, one can almost imagine the spirits of the Ancestral Puebloans watching—and approving.

ⓘ **Bandelier National Monument,** 15 Entrance Rd., Los Alamos, NM (ℂ **505/ 672-3861,** ext. 517; www.nps.gov/band)

✈ Santa Fe/Albuquerque

🛏 $$ **Hampton Inn and Suites Los Alamos,** 124 State Hwy. 4, Los Alamos (ℂ **505/672 3838;** hamptoninn.hilton. com). $ **Juniper Campground,** 2 miles from visitor center (ℂ **505/672-3861,** ext. 517).

A Puebloan dwelling at Bandelier National Monument.

Big Thicket National Preserve
An American Ark
Southeast Texas

A RARE BIOLOGICAL CROSSROADS, RICH IN BIRDS AND FLOWERS, THIS EAST TEXAS PRESERVE IS increasingly hemmed in by development and suburban sprawl.

Frankly, the National Park Service got here too late. While the name Big Thicket promises an intact tangle of woods, this national preserve, founded in 1974, lies scattered in various parcels around a well-settled East Texas area. The logging industry got a foothold here in the 1850s, decimating the great woods that baffled early-19th-century settlers; on many neighboring lands, cheap slash-pine forests replaced the ancient stands of pine and cypress. Then, around 1900, oil was discovered, and you know what that means in Texas. Though logging is now prohibited, oil and gas are still extracted from the preserve, which also allows hunting, trapping, and fishing.

But luckily, early timber baron John Henry Kirby set aside a portion of the old woods as hunting grounds, preserving enough of this unique biological crossroads—often called "an American ark"—to make it well worth visiting. It's like a naturalist's version of Disney's Epcot: An amazing confluence of species, driven south by Ice Age glaciers, coexist in one small area. A mere drive-through visit misses the point; you have to get out of your car and walk a couple of different short trails before you really get the point of Big Thicket. Its bogs and blackwater swamps resemble those of the southeast, rife with ferns, orchids, and insect-eating pitcher plants (follow the **Pitcher Plant Trail** to see four out of five North American species, all in one place). Along the **Kirby Nature Trail,** bluebirds flit around eastern hardwood forests, yet nearby on the Sandhill Loop there are roadrunners roaming arid sandhills that look like they belong in New Mexico. Over at the Hickory

Creek section, the **Sundew Trail** displays a riot of wildflowers on a prairie savanna more typical of the Central Plains. In fact, rangers have tallied nearly 1,000 different types of flowering plants around the preserve. You won't see them all, of course, but bring a field guidebook and it'll be well thumbed by the time you leave.

The American Bird Conservancy has named the preserve a Globally Important Bird Area, with nearly 186 resident or migratory species in one or another of its varied habitats. During migrations (late Mar to early May or Oct–Nov), patient birders can sight brown-headed nuthatch, Bachman's sparrow, and the red-cockaded woodpecker. The best locations are on the Hickory Creek savanna and along the short Kirby Nature Trail or the longer Turkey Creek Trail.

One long parcel added to the preserve follows the Neches River, great for whitewater canoeing; another canoe trail on the Pine Island Bayou, down south close to Beaumont, lets you paddle through haunting stands of ancient bald cypress and tupelo, where you may even see an alligator or two. Sometimes it's hard to remember what state you're in—is this really Texas?

ⓘ **Big Thicket National Preserve,** 6102 FM 420, Kountze, TX (✆ **409/951-6700;** www.nps.gov/bith)

✈ Beaumont or Houston

🛏 $$ **Pelt Farm B&B,** 12487 Pelt Rd., Kountze (✆ **409/287-2279;** www.peltfarm. com). $ **La Quinta Inn Beaumont Midtown,** 220 Interstate 10 N., Beaumont (✆ **409/838-9991;** www.lq.com).

Cache River Wildlife Refuge
Corridor of Hope in the Big Woods
Augusta, Arkansas

ITS WETLANDS POLLUTED BY ADJACENT AGRICULTURE AND INDUSTRY, ITS WOODLANDS FRAGMENTED by development, the Big Woods badly needs preservation. One extinct bird species may turn out to be its savior.

The ivory-billed woodpecker? Extinct, ornithologists said. After all, for 60 years no one had sighted this striking large bird with its red crest, long pale bill, and black-and-white–striped wing feathers. That's why it was headline news in 2004 when birders reported seeing this rare bird—the largest North American woodpecker—in eastern Arkansas's Cache River Wildlife Refuge.

If a rare woodlands bird was going to reappear, it would naturally be in a place like the Cache River refuge, itself a rare survivor. Back in the 1970s, a storm of public outcry saved this river from being dredged and rechanneled for flood control, a move that would surely have destroyed its native mosaic of wetlands and hardwood forest. (Local conservationists are still fighting to save the nearby White River from a similar fate.) A refuge was established in 1986, today following some 70 miles (113km) of the Cache River. This patched-together strip of hardwood forest, cypress-tupelo swamps, shallow sloughs, and oxbow lakes is still far from complete—many refuge areas must be reached by crossing private land—but joined to contiguous wildlife management areas, it provides an ever more continuous corridor for wildlife. While many of its mighty bald cypress trees may be as old as 1,000 years, other parcels of land that were previously agricultural have only recently been reforested with native oaks, cypress, gum, and pecan trees. It's a target destination for birders, an international RAMSAR wetlands with more than 265 bird species, including a mass of migrating Neotropical songbirds in spring and the world's largest population of mallards in winter.

The Cache River refuge is only part of the **Big Woods of Arkansas**—or rather, what's left of the Big Woods, which once stretched across seven states. The Big Woods now stretches roughly 120 miles (193km) long and up to 20 miles (32km) wide, a mix of public and private lands that's home to more than 70 distinct natural plant communities, not to mention diverse aquatic habitats. Besides the ivory-billed woodpecker and the impressive mallard population, the Big Woods boasts rare mussels in extensive mussel shoals, and a unique population of American black bears roaming its murky, mysterious cypress-tupelo swamps.

Which brings us back to the ivory-billed woodpecker. Immediately after its 2004 sighting, the Cache River refuge limited access to the bird's known habitat, to avoid disturbing it. Now the refuge not only welcomes visitors to that area, but has even set up viewing towers and printed handouts of ivory-bill spotting tips. Visitors are urged to report any sightings promptly. After all, if the ivory-billed woodpecker can rise from the dead, so can the great Big Woods.

ⓘ **Cache River National Wildlife Refuge,** 26320 Hwy. 33 S., Augusta, AR (© **870/347-2614;** www.fws.gov/cacheriver)

✈ Little Rock

🛏 $ **Augusta Motor Lodge,** 220 Hwy. 64 E., Augusta (© **870/347-1055**). $$ **Hampton Inn Searcy,** 3204 E. Race, Searcy (© **501/268-0654;** www.hampton inn.hilton.com).

The Cumberland Plateau
In the Spirit of John Muir
Eastern Tennessee/Kentucky

AS PAPER AND TIMBER COMPANIES MOVE OUT, SECOND-HOME DEVELOPMENT AND INCREASED recreational use may fragment and degrade this vast mountain wilderness.

"The Cumberland must be a happy stream," mused naturalist John Muir, tramping across the Cumberland Plateau in 1867, a hike recounted in *A Thousand-Mile Walk to the Gulf.* "I think I could enjoy traveling with it in the midst of such beauty all my life."

It's only fitting that a trail through this spectacular wilderness should be named after John Muir. In fact, there are two trails: The John Muir Recreational Trail, a 21-mile (34km) trail in the **Cherokee National Forest** (trail head near Reliance, TN, off Hwy.

315), and the 44-mile (71km) John Muir Trail in **Big South Fork National River and Recreation Area** (trail head at the O.W. Railroad Bridge, near the Bandy Creek visitor center). The first is a relatively easy trail, known for its wildflowers; the second plunges deep into the landscape that so inspired Muir, the father of America's national parks movement.

The Cumberland is the world's longest hardwood-forested plateau, stretching diagonally for hundreds of miles across

The Cherokee National Forest.

177

eastern Tennessee and into southern Kentucky. Incredibly biodiverse, the Cumberland forest ranges from a mix of beech, sugar maple, tulip, and ash to dusky hemlock forests with a rhododendron understory. Geologically, it's a rugged terrain of rocky ridges, steep gorges, natural stone arches, and the world's highest concentration of caves, full of rare bats and invertebrates like the Cumberland dusky salamander and the lampshade spider.

But it's also the Southeast's largest unprotected forest, much of it still owned by timber companies and mining interests. And as they divest themselves of their holdings, developers are snapping up this scenic wilderness for weekend getaways and retirement homes, polluting streams and laying roads across forest corridors where the black bear roams and peregrine falcons fly. Without protection, felled hardwoods are often replaced with a monoculture of loblolly pines. That's why a unique coalition of conservation groups and state environment departments has formed to woo new buyers who are committed to responsible forestry—putting together a jigsaw puzzle of public and private lands, all with the goal of keeping the forest healthy and intact.

Wild as it looks, the Cumberland Plateau isn't virgin forest—far from it. In the Big South Fork park, the layered history of this wilderness becomes clear. You can wander miles of woodland trails, on foot, mountain bike, or horseback; you can fish or paddle through stretches of pristine whitewater river. But hike the **Blue Heron Trail** and you'll find an abandoned coal mine; the **Rock Creek Loop Trail** (which overlaps part of the John Muir Trail) passes vestiges of an old logging railroad; the **Litton/Slaven Trail** visits an old farmstead. The park's annual spring planting festival and a fall storytelling festival commemorate the Cumberland's human past as well. The human future—well, that's still to be decided.

(i) **Big South Fork National River and Recreation Area** (© 423/286-7275; www.nps.gov/biso). **Bandy Creek visitor center,** off Hwy. 297 between Oneida and Jamestown, TN.

✈ Knoxville

🛏 $$ **Big South Fork Wilderness Resort,** 1511 Wilderness Trail, Oneida (© **423/569-9847;** www.wildernessresorts.com). $ **Pickett State Park campground,** 4605 Pickett Park Hwy., Jamestown (© **877/260-0010;** www.tn.gov/environment/parks/reservations).

Into the Woods   **186**

Bad Branch Preserve
Colonel Boone's Wilderness
Cumberland Mountains, Kentucky

THOUGH IT'S A SMALL PRESERVE, THIS FOREST GORGE HAS AN UNUSUAL NUMBER OF RARE SPECIES. The invasion of just one non-native species, however, could destroy its intricate ecosystem.

Daniel Boone would feel right at home in this Cumberland Mountain wilderness, where a river rages down the side of **Pine Mountain,** taking less than 3 miles (5km) to drop 1,000 feet (300m) in elevation. The sandstone cliffs of Bad Branch Gorge rise out of the dark-green forest with lots of crags and caves; sheer rock faces glisten with seeping water, and big boulders muscle up to the creek bank. One particularly gorgeous 60-foot (18m) cascade is beloved by photographers trying to capture the "perfect" wilderness waterfall. Bad Branch is officially one of Kentucky's Wild Rivers, and clearly deserves the title.

But get past the thunder and majesty of the falls and you'll find a delicate patchwork of habitats. A rare fish called the arrow darter populates highly aerated pools of clear water just below the falls. The endangered long-tailed shrew skitters around the hemlock forest, and snakes (some of them venomous, so beware) slither around the talus caves formed by piled-up boulders. Somewhere up in those magnificent cliffs lives a pair of nesting ravens, Kentucky's last two survivors of this once-common species.

Although this 2,400-acre (971-hectare) tract saw some logging in the 1940s, the diversity of plants growing here—especially the number of flowers—shows that it wasn't extensive. Bring a field guidebook with you when you walk through the forest, because it's anything but a monoculture—the forests feature a rich mix of sweet birch, yellow birch, basswood, tulip poplar, American beech, and buckeye trees (squirrels love the beechnuts and glossy brown buckeye nuts), while smaller trees in the understory include flowering dogwood and umbrella magnolia, perfuming the air in spring along with sweet pepperbush and dense thickets of rosebay rhododendron. Several rare plants here, like matriciary grapefern, Fraser's sedge, and American burnet, are generally found farther north, and only in old-growth forests.

Best of all are the mature stands of shaggy Eastern hemlocks, some of which may have been around long enough to have seen Daniel Boone himself explore these woods. But in Colonel Boone's day, the woolly hemlock adelgid—a visitor from Asia that feeds on delicate hemlock needles—hadn't yet made its appearance. Now the park's managers, fearing for the hemlock's survival, have resorted to a soil injection treatment to get rid of the pests, which were probably brought in by campers in firewood.

If you're an ambitious hiker, there's a steep, strenuous 7.5-mile (12km) trail to the top of Pine Mountain (actually a 21-mile-long/34km ridge), where the massive outcropping of High Rock provides an awesome panorama of the Cumberland Valley; you may be able to see into nearby Virginia or even farther south to Tennessee. Only a hardy handful make it to the top, though; the 2-mile (3.2km) trail to the falls is vigorous enough.

(i) **Bad Branch Nature Preserve,** 2½ miles (4km) east of US 119 on KY 932, Whitesburg, KY

✈ London-Corbin, KY

🏨 $$ **Hampton Inn,** 70 Morton Blvd., Hazard, KY (☎ **606/439-0902;** www.hamptoninn.com). $$ **Guest House Inn & Suites,** 192 Corporate Dr., Hazard (☎ **800/214-8378** or 606/487-0595; www.guesthouseintl.com).

187 Into the Woods

The Adirondacks
Getting Wet & Wild
Upper New York State

SEVERE FLOOD DAMAGE RESULTING FROM AUGUST 2011'S HURRICANE IRENE RIPPED UP roads and knocked out dams throughout this magnificent sprawl of upstate wilderness, protected since 1892 as a "forever wild" area.

The Adirondacks.

The largest protected landscape east of the Mississippi, Adirondack State Park covers 6 million acres (2.4 million hectares), comprising nearly one-sixth of New York State. Despite scattered pockets of settlement—ski resorts, motels, lakefront homes, and nearly a hundred small towns—the heart of this park is a network of some 3,000 lakes and ponds that are deliberately left inaccessible, connected not by highways but by 1,500 miles (2,400km) of rivers, leaving plenty of corridors where wildlife can roam freely.

When Hurricane Irene's torrential rains swept through the Eastern Adirondacks in August 2011, the impact was devastating. Road closures left several already-isolated small towns completely cut off from civilization. Popular backcountry hiking trails were washed out or blocked by landslides. Bridges and dams were shattered, including the photo-op favorite bridge over Marcy Dam. Yet by early September, State Highway 73 had been repaired and reopened, campgrounds were back in business, and hikers were back on the high wilderness trails, gingerly climbing over washouts and using compasses to find detours.

The Adirondack region could not afford to lose that prime hiking season—its resources are already strained by the battle against environmental threats, which often migrate in from far away. There's acid rain, for example, drifting in to deposit industrial pollutants such as mercury in those pristine lakes. Mercury's impact can be measured through the dwindling numbers of what ecologists call a "sentinel" species—the common loon, a striking black-and-white water bird with red eyes whose haunting call is a quintessential sound of the North Woods. Fish-eating loons live high on the food chain, so when their mercury levels are high, it suggests that all the lakes' species are affected. Adirondack residents also battle invasive species that may sneak in on an innocent fishing reel or boat propeller—such as the Eurasian water-milfoil, a scraggly herb that crowds out native species on the lake bottom and can trap swimmers. The watermilfoil has spread to more than 50 of the Adirondacks' lakes, including **Lake Placid** and **Saranac Lake**. With dams knocked out, it will be even harder to control passage between lakes.

To sample a mosaic of healthy Adirondack habitats, walk the nature trails around the Adirondack Park Visitor Center at Paul Smiths (12 miles/19km north of Saranac Lake), crossing bog and marsh to **Barnum Pond** where you can sight loons, ducks, herons, and common goldeneye (another "common" species that has become uncommon). Ultimately, the best way to appreciate this huge park is via canoe: Rivers connect all three of the Saranac lakes, and in the Tupper Lake area, there's a popular route along the Raclette River. The only sounds you may hear are birdcalls and the dip of your paddle as it slices through the glassy water.

(i) **Adirondack Regional Tourism Council** (℗ **518/846-8016;** www.adirondacks.org)

✈ Adirondack Regional Airport, Lake Clear; Plattsburgh International

▭ $$ **Hotel Saranac,** 101 Main St., Saranac Lake (℗ **800/937-0211** or 518/891-2200; www.hotelsaranac.com). $$ **Golden Arrow Lakeside Resort,**

2559 Main St., Lake Placid (℗ **518/523-3353;** www.golden-arrow.com).

TOUR Adirondack Lakes and Trails Outfitters, 541 Lake Flower Ave., Saranac Lake (℗ **800/491-0414;** www.adirondackoutfitters.com). **St. Regis Canoe Outfitters,** 73 Dorsey St., Saranac Lake (℗ **518/891-1838;** www.canoeoutfitters.com).

---

188 Into the Woods

Ossipee Pine Barrens
Pitch Perfect
Ossipee/Madison/Freedom, New Hampshire

ONE OF THE RAREST TYPES OF FOREST IN NORTH AMERICA, THIS SMALL SURVIVING PATCH OF pitch pine barren depends on strategic burning to reproduce the natural cycle of drought, fire, and regeneration.

Forget all that stuff Smokey the Bear told us—sometimes fire is good for forests.

At least it is for some forests—like northern pitch pine/scrub oak pine barrens. There are only about 20 such woodlands left, one of the largest being the Ossipee Pine Barrens, a patch of New Hampshire woods just east of Lake Winnipesaukee and south of the White Mountains. Once upon a time, fires swept through here periodically—say, every 25 or 50 years—but with increased settlement, fire prevention became the rule. Fire, however, turns out to be beneficial to this type of forest, thinning out the common white pines and letting other species get a foothold. Scrub oaks, which have very deep roots, recover quickly, and pitch pine seeds actually germinate better on burned ground, sending up fresh shoots that constitute a whole new food for certain insects. Charred debris adds nutrients to the soil. Wild blueberry bushes—which the Ossipee Pine Barrens are full of—grow noticeably thicker and bushier after a fire. The temporarily leveled woodlands make room for the thickets and patches of meadow that

rabbits and snakes love, types of growth that white pines often push out.

Several endangered moths and butterflies that live here—like the frosted elfin butterfly—specifically feed on pitch pine rather than the red pines or white pines that have taken over many of New England's forests. And as a result, birds that feed on those moths and butterflies, such as whippoorwills, nighthawks, Eastern towhees, prairie warblers, vesper sparrows, and brown thrashers, are drawn to these woods, even as their numbers swiftly decline elsewhere. When was the last time you heard a whippoorwill's song?

Such fires must be handled carefully, of course. The woods are now full of dead branches and dense understory that could blaze out of control; before a fire is set, the woods must be thinned, and buffer belts cleared away. Large white pines, which (unlike pitch pine) burn quickly, are removed and sold for timber, which helps to fund the project. A few parcels of the Ossipee Pine Barrens have already been burned; when you visit, take any of the various short walking trails and look at the differences between these "new" woods and the sections that haven't been burned. Some of the really mature pitch pines, best seen along Hobbs Trail, are 150 years old; others are mere saplings. Smokey the Bear would agree that a healthy forest needs both.

ⓘ **Ossipee Pine Barrens,** Rte. 41, 2 miles (3.2km) north of Rte. 16, Ossipee, NH

✈ Laconia

🛏 $$ **Wolfeboro Inn,** 90 N. Main St., Wolfeboro, NH ⓒ **800/451-2389** or 603/569-3016; www.wolfeboroinn.com). $$ **Stonehurst Manor,** Rte. 16, North Conway, NH ⓒ **800/525-9100** or 603/356-3113; www.stonehurstmanor.com).

Cranesville Swamp Preserve
Frost Pocket
West Virginia & Maryland

LOGGING, FOREIGN INSECTS, AND AN EXCESSIVE DEER POPULATION HAVE DEPLETED THE FORESTS that shelter this rare ecosystem, letting in sun and wind to dry and warm its cold, wet swampland.

Be sure to bring an extra layer when you come to Cranesville Swamp. Even in the height of summer it can be chilly and damp, with traces of snow scattered about. But what else would you expect when you visit a frost pocket?

What biologists call "frost pockets" are rare freaks of nature, a combination of geologic, botanical, and historic factors. Back in the Ice Age, glaciers never got as far south as this neck of the Appalachians, but the coniferous forests they drove ahead of them did. When the glaciers receded, so did the conifers, to be replaced by deciduous forests—everywhere except for this tiny valley. It's as if a tiny fragment of Ice Age climate had been trapped in this crevice of the mountains.

Situated on the border between the western bit of Maryland and West Virginia, the Cranesville Swamp Preserve has two habitats: a wet bog along tannin-dark Muddy Creek that drips with sphagnum moss, speckled alder, skunk cabbage, and rare sedges and grasses; and, where the ground has better drainage, an acidic conifer swamp forest full of northern species like tall eastern hemlock and red spruce,

which you'd never expect around here. Even though this land was cleared from time to time—for logging, for farming, and most recently for power lines—the trees that grew back are still those relict species, which are best suited to this sliver of microclimate. You'll find tamarack (eastern larch) trees here, even though the next closest ones are 200 miles (320km) north.

A boardwalk walking trail allows visitors to explore even the wettest parts of the bog. Dense patches of rhododendron, unusual ferns, and mossy ground cover make it feel as primordial as it is; there's even a species of ground cover called trilobite liverwort. Of course, where you get rare vegetation you get rare fauna as well—like the northern water shrew, the star-nosed mole, dark-eyed junco, Canada warbler, and the saw-whet owl. Unfortunately, other species make their way into the Cranesville Swamp as well—non-native cattails compete with rare bog plants, and local deer browse heavily on its vegetation, requiring constant vigilance by park staff.

Take a look upward and you'll see that Cranesville is snuggled inside a bowl. Not only does the swamp share the cool air and heavy snowfall of the surrounding mountains, but the bowl actually pushes cold air down into the swamp, where it's not warmed by sunlight. Now here's the big question: How far can global warming alter seasonal temperatures before the frost pocket melts—along with the cold-loving species it shelters?

(i)**Cranesville Swamp Preserve,** Cranesville Rd., Cranesville, WV

✈ Morgantown, WV

🛏 $$ **Riverside Hotel,** 639 Water St., Friendsville, MD (📞 **301/746-5253;** www.riversidehotel.us). $$ **Clarion Hotel Morgan,** 127 High St., Morgantown, WV (📞**304/292-8200;** www.clarionhotelmorgan.com).

190 Into the Woods

Walden Pond
Thoroughly Thoreau
Concord, Massachusetts

DEVELOPMENT ENCROACHES ON THOREAU'S FAMOUS RETREAT: NEARBY SEPTIC SYSTEMS POLLUTE its waters, while the shoreline is seriously eroded from recreational overuse.

Even back in 1859, Walden Woods were in danger of being leveled for farmland. "All Walden wood might have been preserved for our park forever," Henry David Thoreau noted sadly in his journal, nostalgic already for the way Walden Pond looked when he lived there in a simple cabin from July 1845 to September 1847.

Today, Thoreau's 1854 book, *Walden; or, Life in the Woods,* is revered as a bible of the conservation movement. But when Thoreau lived beside this deep kettle-hole pond in the Massachusetts farmlands, Concord was a separate village, not yet overtaken by Boston suburban sprawl. Although Walden Pond—now a designated National Historic Landmark—is surrounded by 2,700 acres (1,090 hectares) of woods, development presses right up to its margins. In the mid-1980s, a condo development and an office building were nearly built on two adjoining tracts of land until the Walden Woods Project conservation group was formed to buy those tracts of land. The Project scored another victory when it got an adjacent landfill capped in 2001; the landfill is now being converted to grassland habitat.

Within the park, recreational use has taken its toll. The pond is popular for swimming and boating in summer; folks wandering off the hiking trails trample the vegetation at water's edge, causing the shoreline to erode. To many visitors, these

Walden Pond.

183

woods aren't a literary shrine, they're a state park, and the rangers have had to ban dogs, bicycles, and outdoor grills, and limit visitors to 1,000 a day. The pond's pickerel have died out; it's artificially stocked now. Visitors unwittingly bring in invasive species, and swimming inevitably leads to clouds of algae.

Still, it's better than it was—from 1866 to 1902 there were cafes, swings, a baseball diamond, and a dining pavilion on the shore. Most of the woods had been cleared by 1922 when the state acquired the property (a 1938 hurricane mowed down many more trees, including some white pines Thoreau himself planted). Walden Pond and its woods were restored to a more natural state in the '60s and '70s, however, as the burgeoning environmental movement championed Thoreau's "experiment in simplicity." The woods have grown back, the same native mix of pitch pine, hickory, and oak Thoreau knew. A replica has been built of Thoreau's one-room cabin, but it's across the road, next to a parking lot (a trail leads you to the original site overlooking the pond). Nowadays you'll have to come on a weekday, or in spring or fall, to experience the solitude Thoreau enjoyed.

ⓘ **Walden Pond State Reservation,** Rte. 126, Concord ✆ **978/369-3254;** www.mass.gov/dcr/parks/walden). **Walden Woods Project** ✆ **781/259-4700;** www.walden.org).

✈ Logan International, Boston

🛏 $$ **Doubletree Guest Suites,** 400 Soldiers Field Rd. ✆ **800/222-TREE** [8733] or 617/783-0090; www.doubletree.com). $ **The MidTown Hotel,** 220 Huntington Ave. ✆ **800/343-1177** or 617/262-1000; www.midtownhotel.com).

Rainforests **191**

Kamakou Preserve
Hawaii's Hidden Eden
Molokai, Hawaii

SMALL, ISOLATED KAMAKOU PRESERVE IS A HAVEN FOR RARE ENDEMIC PLANT SPECIES—BUT with so few individual specimens, the next hurricane or disease could wipe out a species.

Tucked away on the highest mountain of Hawaii's least developed island—we're talking remote here—lies a remarkable bit of undiscovered Eden. Draped with mosses, sedges, and lichens, this misty humid habitat feels like a land lost in time.

Though you'd hardly believe it from the rugged, red-dirt appearance of most of Molokai, up in the mountains it rains more than 80 inches (200cm) a year—hence the rainforest, which supplies 60% of the island's water. An amazing 250 plant species thrive here, 219 of them found nowhere else on earth. There's the alani, a citrus-fruit cousin to oranges and lemons; the hapuu, or Hawaiian tree fern; and Hawaii's iconic ohia

lehua, a knee-high tree with brilliant red, yellow, or orange blossoms.

It's not just thrills for botanists, either. Birders can train their binoculars on precious species such as the brilliant green amakihi, the nectar-sipping apahane, and the endangered Hawaiian owl. The last time anybody caught sight of a Molokai thrush, it was here in this lush rainforest. Same goes for the Molokai creeper bird (kakawahie).

Of course, you don't preserve rare species like this by letting just everybody tramp through. The Nature Conservancy carefully protects this nearly 3,000-acre (1,215-hectare) haven, which was ceded to them by the vast Molokai Ranch that dominates Molokai's interior. The conservancy offers once-a-month guided walks along a 3-mile-long (5km) narrow boardwalk (the **Pepeopae Trail**) spanning the rainforest's boggy ground. The hike ends at a breathtaking vista over Molokai's inaccessible north coast, with its plunging emerald-green cliffs—truly a once-in-a-lifetime sight.

If the guided tour is full—reserve way in advance if you don't want to be disappointed—you can still visit on your own, though without a naturalist guide you may miss the rarest species. It's still worth the effort, but getting here isn't easy. Go west from Kaunakakai 3½ miles (5.6km) on Highway 460, turn right onto an unmarked road that eventually turns to dirt, and drive 9 miles (14km) to the Waikolu Lookout, where you sign in. Drive another 2½ miles (4km) through the Molokai Forest, its

stands of sandalwood trees still rebounding after being stripped for the shipbuilding industry. Go left at the fork to reach the trail head. The drive takes 45 minutes, the hike itself another 90 minutes (unless you dawdle—and of course you'll want to dawdle). But hey, if it were easy to get to, it wouldn't be so pristine, would it?

ⓘ **Kamakou Nature Preserve,** Molokai Forest Reserve Rd., Molokai, HI (✆ **808/ 537-4508** or 808/553-5236; for tours, email hike_molokai@tnc.org)

✈ Molokai Hoolehua airport

🛏 $$ **Ke Nani Kai Resort,** Kaluakai Rd., West End (✆ **800/367-2984,** 808/553-8334; www.molokai-vacation-rental.com). $ **Hotel Molokai,** Kamehameha V Hwy., Kaunakakai (✆ **877/553-5347** or 808/553-5347 in Hawaii; www.hotelmolokai.com).

---

192 Rainforests

Monteverde Cloud Forest
Quetzal Quest
Monteverde, Costa Rica

ONE OF COSTA RICA'S PRIME ECO-TOURIST DESTINATIONS, THIS LUSH MOUNTAINTOP JUNGLE IS A haven for many endangered species. Reforesting adjacent land and managing water resources is key to keeping it healthy.

The steep, rutted dirt road passes through mile after mile of dry, brown pasture-lands—a landscape that was once verdant forest, until humans entered the picture. All the more reason to appreciate what you find at the top of the mountain: a lush, tangled swath of greenery, where orchids and ferns trail from the treetops while monkeys chatter, tree frogs croak, and hummingbirds hum. Monteverde means "green mountain," and there couldn't be a better name for it. Walking here in the early-morning mist with the whispering of leaves and disembodied birdcalls all around can be an almost out-of-body experience.

Cloud forests are always on mountain-tops, where moist warm air sweeping up the slopes from a nearby ocean condenses swiftly in the higher elevation, forming clouds around the summit. The clouds, in turn, condense moisture on the forest trees, giving rise to an incredible diversity of life forms—Monteverde boasts more than 2,500 plant species, 400 bird species, and 100 mammal species. It's pretty hard to resist the option of a canopy tour, where you can zip around harnessed to an overhead cable, going from platform to platform high above the forest floor in the treetops, where two-thirds of the species live. Two top operations are **Sky Trek**

185

Monteverde Cloud Forest.

(☏ **506/2645-5238;** www.skytrek.com) and **Selvatura Park** (☏ **506/2645-5929;** www.selvatura.com), both located outside the reserve near the town of Santa Elena.

Monteverde is no secret, and its main trails are often crowded with eco-tourists, all gaping (generally without any luck) to see rare and elusive species like the quetzal with its 2-foot-long (.6m) tail feathers. The density of the cloud forest, however, makes it possible to escape the crowds, once you branch off the central paths. Book a guided tour through your hotel, which will also reserve your admission (only 160 people at a time are allowed inside the reserve); the guide will be able to identify far more of the flora and fauna than you could spot on your own. To take advantage of early-morning and late-night

tours, which often score more sightings, it's a good idea to stay overnight nearby. Slightly less crowded than the Monteverde Reserve but with much the same flora and fauna, the community-based **Santa Elena Cloud Forest Reserve** (☏ **2645-5390;** www.reservasantaelena. org) may be a good alternative.

ⓘ **Monteverde Biological Cloud Forest Preserve** (☏ **506/2645-5122;** www. cct.or.cr)

✈ Juan Santamaria International, San José

🛏 $$$ **Monteverde Lodge** (☏ **506/ 2257-0766** or 506/2521-6099; www. monteverdelodge.com). $ **La Casona,** on the reserve grounds (☏ **506/2645-5122** or 2645-5579; www.cct.or.cr).

Mamirauá Nature Reserve
Birds of the Flood
Upper Amazon Basin, Brazil

DESIGNATED AS LATIN AMERICA'S FIRST "SUSTAINABLE DEVELOPMENT RESERVE," MAMIRAUÁ may offer a model for other Amazon basin areas, which have been destroyed by burning, logging, mining, and poaching.

When the rainy season hits this part of the Amazon Basin, it really hits. Sediment-rich ice melt gushes down from the Andes, and waters can rise as much as 12m (39 ft.), covering many treetops. The forest floor lies mostly submerged for up to 4 months. The only animals that survive are those that live in the trees—monkeys and sloths—and water dwellers, such as the rare Amazon manatee, pink dolphins, and black caimans. But it doesn't bother the birds. Birds never need ground anyway, do they?

An astonishing total of some 400 different bird species have been recorded in the Mamirauá Nature Reserve, a 57,000-sq.-km (22,000-sq.-mile) protected *varzea*, or seasonally flooded forest, at the juncture of the Japurá and Solimões rivers. Follow trails through the lush rainforest—on foot in the dry season, by canoe in flood season—and you'll see (and hear) a host of tropical birds such as parrots, toucans, and scarlet macaws in the treetop canopy. You may even see the harpy eagle, the world's biggest raptor, which dives down into the canopy with talons as big as a grizzly bear's claws to snatch up canopy-dwelling sloths, monkeys, and opossums for his dinner.

Take a boat along the narrow channels that connect the reserve's many lakes, and a host of water birds can be spotted—snowy egrets, herons, cormorants, kites, grullas, tinamous, bitterns, ospreys, curassows. You may even see a couple of very strange creatures, like the hoatzin, a pheasantlike marsh bird with a wild spiky feathered crest, which is quite common around here—mostly because its horrible manurelike smell (it's nicknamed the "stink bird," and rightly so) means that only the most desperate creatures would ever eat it. And talk about showy head crests—there's none showier than the cotinga, otherwise known as the umbrella bird for the elaborate fan of head feathers it spreads during courtship.

A constant flow of botanists and biologists come to Mamirauá to do research, but it's a social experiment as well. Dozens of villages remain within the area, home to some 20,000 people—*ribeirinhos*—who are being taught sustainable farming methods and given eco-tourism jobs. The **Pousada Uakari Lodge,** for example—a hotel built on floating rafts to accommodate the waters' rise and fall—is staffed as much as possible by local people, many of them guiding lodge guests into the rainforest. Now that they've been given a vested interest in keeping the rainforest healthy, they've become proactive in protecting its amazing flora and fauna. It's an important model for saving the rainforest—no doubt the birds would approve.

✈ Tefé

🛏 $$ **Pousada Uakari Lodge** (✆ 55/97/ **3343-4160;** www.uakarilodge.com.br), 564km/350 miles west of Manaus

TOUR Amazon Adventures (✆ 800/ **232-5658** or 512/443-5393; www.amazon adventures.com)

Manu Biosphere Reserve
The Other Amazon
Peru

ONCE KEPT PRISTINE BY ITS INACCESSIBILITY, MANU BIOSPHERE RESERVE HAS BEGUN TO SEE increased eco-tourism traffic. Logging, both legal and illegal, nibbles along park boundaries, and poaching is common.

As any school kid will tell you, the Amazon rainforest ❺—the one ecologists are so desperate to save—is in Brazil. True enough, but it's not all in Brazil. The source of the Amazon lies in Peru, in the Andes mountains; in fact, fully half of Peru is covered with Amazonian rainforest. What's more, despite a period of rubber exploitation in the early 20th century, this large swath of it has been protected as a national park since 1968; it hasn't suffered the same degree of deforestation that the Brazil rainforest has. If virgin rainforest is what you're after, head for Peru's Manu Biosphere Reserve.

Biodiverse? Manu has been documented as the most biodiverse place on earth, with more than 15,000 species of plants, 1,000 types of birds, and 1,200 different butterflies. There are 13 various primates, not to mention tapirs, spectacled bears, ocelots, jaguars, and giant otters. In the thick jungle growth, you may not be able to see all of these elusive creatures, but a good guide will increase your chances. The butterflies, hummingbirds, howler monkeys, tamarins, capuchins, and macaws alone should make your trip satisfying.

Riverboats enable you to view the rainforest from one perspective, where black caimans bask on the sandy verges, agile giant otters fish in shallow oxbow lakes, and thousands of brilliantly colored macaws and parrots gather at the **Blanquillo Macaw Lick** (Colpa de Guacamayos) to feed on a riverbank cliff of mineral salts. Trails have also been laid out to lead away from the river to various types of jungle habitat—bamboo, freshwater swamp, *tierra firme* forest, and flood plain, each with its different vegetation, birds, and animal life. Harpy eagles nest in the tops of Brazil nut trees, wide-branched cacao trees bear their large red fruits, and huge strangler figs grow down from the canopy around other trees until they take root and become trees themselves. Passionflowers blossom on thin trailing vines, and deadly nightshade perfumes the night air, as you're lulled to sleep by a murmurous chorus of frogs and insects.

Named a World Heritage Site in 1987, Manu has remained unspoiled partly because it's so sparsely inhabited, and partly because it's so strictly controlled. There are two sections of reserve: the **Cultural Zone,** inhabited by several nomadic peoples and open to all visitors, and the much smaller **Reserve Zone,** which you can visit only with an authorized guide. Many tours come overland from Cusco, a 2-day journey through mountains and orchid-laden cloud forest before you come down into the lush lowland jungles. Flying to Boca Manu instead is expensive, but it'll get you into the heart of the reserve right away.

✈ Boca Manu

TOUR Tropical Nature Travel (© 877/827-8350; www.tropicalnaturetravel.com). **Manu Expeditions,** Peru (© 51/84/226-671; www.manuexpeditions.com). **Manu Nature Tours,** Peru (© 51/84/252-721; www.manuperu.com).

Daintree Rainforest
Time Warp on the Queensland Coast
Queensland, Australia

THOUGH IT ESCAPED THE DEVASTATING QUEENSLAND FLOODS OF LATE 2010, THIS SPECTACULAR Wet Tropics jungle lies in a flood-prone coastal valley.

It's like someone stopped the clock—135 million years ago. This prehistoric landscape of bizarre plants like giant strangler figs, fan palms, cycads, and epiphytes like the basket fern, staghorn, and elkhorn is unlike anyplace else on earth. It has some of the weirdest plants you'd ever want to see, including poisonous species like the idiot fruit, burrawang palm, and towering wild ginger; be careful while hiking not to snag your skin on the prickly wait-a-while vine or stinging tree. Approximately 430 species of birds live among the trees, including 13 species found nowhere else on earth. And then there's the iridescent blue Ulysses butterfly flickering through the giant ferns—spot one of those and you'll feel like a portal just opened to another world.

Daintree's battle was launched way back in the 1980s, with conservationists seeking to evict a long-established timber industry from the old-growth forest. In 1983, controversy arose over the construction of a road along the coastal fringe from the Daintree River to Cooktown, a rough four-wheel-drive track that would provide access to formerly untouched sections of the rainforest. Several parcels of land along the corridor were sold to private owners. Luckily, conservation-minded politicians were voted into office and successfully pursued World Heritage Site status for the Daintree Rainforest, which has halted logging and mining activities. But those private landowners remain, and some of them press for modern amenities such as power lines, bridges, and fences that would disrupt this rare ecosystem.

Most visitors take a guided day trip into the park out of Port Douglas. Most tours include common features: a 1.1km (.7-mile) hike along the boardwalk of the Marrdja Botanical Trail, a stroll along an isolated beach, a picnic lunch in a secluded rainforest glade (each tour guide has a favorite spot), a 1-hour croc-spotting cruise on the Daintree River, and a stop off to see the churning rapids at Mossman Gorge.

If you want to get a little deeper, try a more specialized naturalist guide. Get into some nitty-gritty bushwalking with **Heritage & Interpretive Tours** (*℀* **07/4098 7897;** www.nqhit.com.au), see crocodiles

Daintree Rainforest.

by night with **Dan Irby's Mangrove Adventures** (ℭ **07/4090 7017;** www.mangroveadventures.com.au), or focus on bird-watching with **Fine Feather Tours** (ℭ **07/4094 1199;** www.finefeathertours.com.au). You may also want to supplement your rainforest excursion with a visit to the **Wildlife Habitat** (Port Douglas Rd.; ℭ **07/4099 3235;** www.rainforesthabitat.com.au), where you're guaranteed a close-up of elusive exotics like bandicoots and musky rat kangaroos and sugar gliders and giant tree frogs; its aviary is a special treat, where some 70 Wet Tropics varieties of birds squawk, flutter, and preen all around you.

ⓘ **Daintree National Park** visitor centers at Cape Tribulation (ℭ **61/7/4098 0052**) and Mossman Gorge (ℭ **61/7/4098 2188**)

✈ Cairns

🛏 $$$ **Daintree Eco Lodge & Spa,** 20 Daintree Rd., Daintree (ℭ **61/7/4098 6100;** www.daintree-ecolodge.com.au). $$ **Port Douglas Retreat,** 31-33 Mowbray St., Port Douglas (ℭ **61/7/4099 5053;** www.portdouglasretreat.com.au).

Rainforests **196**

The Mabi Forest
Hang with the Tree Kangaroos
Yungaburra, Australia

LOGGING AND FARMING HAVE BROKEN THIS UNIQUE RAINFOREST INTO SCATTERED FRAGMENTS. Their high edge-to-area ratio leaves them vulnerable to invasive species and damage by north Queensland's frequent cyclones.

Seen one Australian rainforest and you've seen them all, right? Think again. The Mabi forest is a whole other deal, a sun-filtered forest with a riot of exotic vines and shrubs and giant ferns covering the forest floor. Its fertile red basaltic soil makes the leaves here grow big and nutritious, perfect for tree-hugging mammals like possums and tree kangaroos (*mabi* is the Aboriginal name for the local tree kangaroo). And birds? It has more avian species than any other spot in the Wet Tropics, 114 different honeyeaters and kingfishers and bowerbirds and cuckoos, not to mention the chowchilla and the laughing kookaburra.

But soon—very soon—we may have to speak of the Mabi forest in the past tense. Extensive logging for red cedars has whittled the forest to 4% of its original area, which once blanketed this tableland southeast of Cairn. Roads and clearings have sliced up the habitat and trapped its animals in tiny redoubts, threatened by exotic smothering vines and feral dogs. Two of its most vital residents, cassowary birds and musky rat kangaroos—both prime seed dispersers—have already fled elsewhere; the spectacled flying fox and ring-tailed possum may be next. With government grants, landowners who own isolated patches of Mabi forest have made efforts to reconnect and regenerate the habitat, but there's a long way to go.

The largest extant chunk of Mabi forest—nearly a third of what's left—lies in 270-hectare (667-acre) **Curtain Fig National Park.** From its elevated boardwalk, visitors can look down into the understory, which is much denser than in other rainforests, a riot of shrubs, woody lianas, and trees' buttress roots. Look up and you'll notice that the canopy in a Mabi forest isn't one impenetrable green ceiling but a varied skylight of evergreen and deciduous treetops of different heights. White cedars and red cedars predominate, but there's an astonishing variety of other unusual trees, including incensewood, candlenut, and black bean trees, along with bollywood, satinash, and silky oak. It's only a 10-minute walk along the boardwalk to the star attraction, a 500-year-old fig tree almost 50m (164 ft.) tall, skirted with an immense curtain of aerial roots that drop 15m (50 ft.) to the forest floor. This fig actually began life in the canopy, then grew vertical roots that over centuries strangled its host tree. The host tree rotted away and, *voilà!* a huge free-standing fig tree, its trunk a thick braid of interwoven roots.

Nighttime walks in the park are particularly rewarding. Use a low-beam spotlight with a red or yellow filter, walk quietly, and speak softly. Be alert for telltale rustles in the canopy, or eyes flashing from the understory—eerie wildlife encounters you won't soon forget.

ⓘ**Curtain Fig National Park,** Atherton-Yungaburra Rd., Yungaburra (✆ **61/13/0013 0372;** www.derm.qld.gov.au/parks/curtain-fig)

✈Cairns

🛏 $$ **Chambers Rainforest Lodge,** Lake Eacham, Atherton Tableland (✆**61/7/4095 3754;** http://rainforest-australia.com/accommodation.htm). $ **Atherton Rainforest Motor Inn,** Kennedy Hwy. and Simms Rd., Atherton (✆ **61/7/4095 4141;** www.rainforestmotorinn.com.au).

---

197 Rainforests

Panna National Park
In the Shadow of the Rajahs
Madya Pradesh, India

IN 2009, OFFICIALS DECLARED THAT POACHING HAD WIPED OUT THE TIGER POPULATION IN THIS popular Tiger Reserve park. Although a few tigresses have since been imported, the program's success is still up in the air.

Back in the days of the rajahs, this spread of jungle, forest, and grassland along the Ken River was a royal hunting ground, a *shikargah,* where tigers were protected—only so that they could wind up as a trophy adorning some prince's palace. Then in 1981 Panna became a national park, and part of India's famed Project Tiger chain of preserves, offering true protection to these beautiful endangered wild cats.

Poaching, however, seemed to have eliminated the park's elusive small Bengal tiger population as of 2009. Park officials have reintroduced a few tigresses, but without adult males, it will be difficult to rebuild the population. The program is currently on hold, as the Indian government has begin to reverse its policy of promoting "tiger tourism," realizing that an influx of tourists has only further stressed the habitats of this already-threatened species.

Panna should be an ideal setting for Bengal tigers: an undulating valley full of the sort of prey tigers have a taste for—nilgais, Indian gazelles, chitals, sambars, and four-horned antelopes. Though the park is relatively small, within that compact space the habitats are varied, which allows predators—tigers, leopards, wild dogs, hyenas, and wolves—to venture onto the grasslands for hunting and then slip back into the jungle and deep ravines for safety. The park's relatively small size also meant that tiger sightings were fairly frequent, that is, when the tigers were still there.

Despite the disappearance of the tigers, which visitors may not have spotted anyway, Panna is still a beautiful park full of

191

wildlife, well worth a visit. In this dry, hot region, the jungle you'll venture into (elephant rides are a popular option) looks much different than a rainforest jungle. Deciduous trees such as teak, Indian ebony, and flame-of-the-forest grow thickly here, along with several flowering species. Blossom-headed parakeets and paradise flycatchers dart about, with peacocks—India's national bird—strutting their stuff on the forest floor. Bar-headed geese and white-necked storks dabble in the river, while the king vulture and honey buzzard patrol the tawny grasslands, looking for whatever carrion the hyenas haven't picked clean.

If you can stand the heat—and summers can be scorching here until the monsoons begin in July (the park is closed July–Sept)—early summer is often the best time for wildlife sightings. Even animals who normally live outside the park wander in from the parched countryside, seeking the river's cool water. With fewer tigers to pick them off, Panna is a better refuge for those animals than ever.

ⓘ **Panna National Park,** Madla Village
☏ **91/7732/25-2135;** www.pannatigerre serve.in)

✈ Khajuraho

🛏 $$ **Ken River Lodge,** Madla Village
☏ **91/7732/27-5235;** www.kenriverlodge. com). $$$ **Radisson Jass,** By-Pass Rd., Khajuraho ☏ **800/395-7046** or 91/7686/27-2344; www.radisson.com/khajuraho-hotel-in/indkhaj).

Rainforests **198**

Gunung Leuser National Park
Paradise Lost
North Sumatra, Indonesia

INDONESIA HAS THE WORLD'S WORST RECORD FOR RAINFOREST DESTRUCTION, CUTTING DOWN THE equivalent of 300 soccer fields every hour. Luckily, it still has Gunung Leuser National Park, one of the world's largest remaining tropical rainforests.

It used to be a tropical rainforest paradise—Sumatra, the large Indonesian island across the Strait of Malacca from Singapore. At one time, Sumatra had 16 million hectares (40 million acres) of lowland rainforest. About 5% of that remains, mostly in Gunung Leuser National Park, which spreads like a pair of gasping lungs across the island.

Formed in the mid-1990s out of several smaller reserves and parks, mountainous Gunung Leuser is truly a land of wonders. It's the only place in the world where viable populations of orangutans, tigers, rhinos, elephants, and clouded leopards live in the same region. The iconic rainforest bird, the helmeted hornbill, with its colorful long curved beak, builds its nests in the top of the tallest trees. The planet's largest flower,

the *Rafflesia arnoldi,* a 1m-wide (3¼-ft.) red-brown bloom, as well as the planet's tallest flower, the weirdly phallic 1.9m-high (6¼-ft.) *Amorphophallus titanum,* both grow naturally, both nicknamed "the corpse flower" for their horrible scent.

Trekking through the park, you may not see orangutans, elephants, or rhinos in the wild—and you probably won't meet a Sumatran tiger, though there are more than 100 of these rare cats here, evading poachers. But you'll certainly see lots of noisy gibbons, beautiful birds, chattering waterfalls, and bright tropical blooms amid lush green foliage. Because it's so vast, the park mixes several types of forest—lowland evergreens, montane rainforests, peat swamp forest, subalpine heath land—for increased biodiversity.

The main gateway is the bustling tourist village of **Bukit Lawang,** also home to a thriving orangutan rehabilitation sanctuary. The Bohorek River flooded out this village in 2003, but it was quickly rebuilt; tubing on the river rapids is a popular activity. To trek into the park you must hire a guide, several of which tout in the streets of Bukit Lawang; local lodges also offer tour packages. Hikers with guides may also enter through Ketembe.

Saving this rainforest won't be easy. Logging on the outskirts of the park whittles away habitat, disrupting animals' migratory patterns and forcing them into the core of the park. Though the park itself was spared in the 2004 tsunami, much Gunung Leuser timber was taken to rebuild tsunami-leveled Banda Aceh at the tip of Sumatra. But there is hope: a 2007 change in Indonesian forestry law allowed conservation groups to take over a 100,000-hectare (247,000-acre) swath of damaged rainforest in southern Sumatra, near Jambi, which was on the verge of becoming a palm oil plantation. Renamed the **Harapan Rainforest,** it is rapidly rebounding—proof that Indonesia could still save its rainforest.

✈ Medan

🛏 $$ **Sam's Bungalow,** Bukit Lawang (✆ **62/813/7009-3597;** www.bukitlawang accommodation.com). $$$ **Bukit Lawang Eco Lodge,** Bukit Lawang (✆ **62/812/607 9983;** http://ecolodge.yelweb.org).

199 Rainforests

Khao Yai National Park
March of the Elephants
Thailand

As agriculture expands to the east of Khao Yai National Park, luxury resorts and golf courses spring up to the west, while highways slash across the park's wildlife corridors.

Wild Asian elephants are the marquee attraction at Khao Yai, Thailand's oldest national park, named a UNESCO World Heritage Site in 2005. There are 120 elephants still in the wild here—surely you ought to see some. After all, they are omnivorous vegetarians, eating grass, branches, leaves, and fruit as they ramble through many different vegetation zones. An elephant is an awfully big animal—how could you miss it?

So you hike through mainland Asia's largest swath of monsoon forest, where towering moss-draped trees support a bewildering mass of creepers, climbers, lianas, strangler figs, orchids, and lichens. You spot your first evidence: birds pecking at a ball of elephant dung. In a bamboo forest, you spy gentle guars munching shreds of bamboo stalks left behind by choosy elephants, which like only the middle parts. You take a night safari in a jeep, using spotlights to catch nighttime wildlife activity—civets, sambars, a wild hog . . . but no elephant.

But then you get distracted. You cross the grasslands and hear the barking deer utter their distinctive cry. You hike up to a waterfall and surprise a waddling porcupine. You spend time in the observation towers, bird-watching for magnificent giant hornbills or great flocks of Indian Pieds. A gibbon hoots in the trees above you; comical macaques loiter alongside the roads like furry little hitchhikers. At evening, your guide leads you to the bat cave on the edge of the park, where hundreds of thousands

Khao Yai National Park.

of tiny insect-eating bats swarm out to do their night's hunting.

Hiring a guide is a good idea, for Khao Yai is a big park, even though only 20% is open to visitors. Elusive species like tigers and clouded leopards can escape tourists completely, and large roaming species like elephants have plenty of room to range. Rangers and conservationists are joining forces to end the rampant poaching that endangers so many of Thailand's rare species.

Early next morning, as you head for the salt lick—the jungle equivalent of the village green—you're not expecting elephants anymore. And then, you come around a bend in the trail and see the great gray pachyderm, placidly working at the salt with her pink tongue. You stand stock-still, awed and overcome. She lifts her head, gazes at you, then swings her trunk and trots away.

Now you can go home.

ⓘ **Khao Yai National Park,** Thanarat Rd., Pak Chong (✆ **66/44/249 305**)

✈ Bangkok

🛏 $$ **Eco Valley Lodge,** 199/16 Moo 8, Nongnamdaeng, Pakchong (✆ **66/44/249 661;** www.ecovalleylodge.com). $$ **Baan Saranya Lodge,** Thanarat Rd. (✆ **66/44/ 297 597;** http://baansaranya.com).

TOUR Contact Travel (✆ **66/53/850 160;** www.activethailand.com). **DTC Travel** (✆ **66/22/594 535;** www.dtctravel.com).

Central Suriname Nature Reserve
Stalking the Cock-of-the-Rock
Suriname

WILDLY INACCESSIBLE, THE HUGE CENTRAL SURINAME NATURE RESERVE PROTECTS SEVERAL pristine ecosystems—but outside its boundaries, several large-scale mining and logging concessions are going strong.

The former Dutch colony of Suriname—which has fewer than 500,000 inhabitants—remains one of the most heavily forested nations on earth, with woodlands covering 90% of its land area. In 1998, as several multinational timber and mining companies threatened to move in, conservationists managed to snap up a forested wilderness the size of New Jersey—12% of Suriname's land area—protecting the country's untrammeled interior just in time. Ten years down the road, conservationists point with pride to the fact that they are now sitting on a gold mine in carbon-trading credits.

Uninhabited is one thing; unexplored is something else. The Central Suriname Nature Reserve can't even publish a definitive catalog of its flora and fauna, because they just don't know what's there yet. Resorts? Visitor centers? Try a primitive airstrip with rudimentary guesthouses. If roughing it is right up your alley, this sprawling park could be the adventure of a lifetime.

The northern section of the reserve, **Raleighvallen (Raleigh Falls),** exhibits a particularly rich and dense example of the country's characteristic moist highland forest, featuring some 300 different species of trees. The canopy can be as high as 50m (165 ft.), with buttress roots and stilt roots helping these towering trees maximize the nutrients they can suck from this thin soil. Palms dominate the understory, while ferns and fern mosses carpet the forest floor. Every inch of this complex web of vegetation seems crawling with life—butterflies, birds, snakes, lizards, you name it.

The best infrastructure is in the Raleighvallen area. You can fly in from Paramaribo or take the scenic route: Drive to Bitragon and then take a 4-to-5-hour boat trip up the Coppename River to reserve headquarters on **Foengoe Island.** Several hiking trails have been laid out here, linking Foengoe Island to the airstrip and several natural landmarks—like the 250m-high (820-ft.) **Voltzberg Dome,** a bare granite inselberg rising abruptly high out of the forest. Raleighvallen is famous among ornithologists as a prime place to sight superb jungle birds like red and green macaws and the stunning crested orange-and-black cock-of-the-rock.

Though you may not see the resident jaguars, giant armadillos lumber around, and giant river otters play in the various rivers and streams. Sloths, tapirs, pumas, six kinds of monkeys—howler monkeys, tamarins, capuchins, saki, spider monkeys, squirrel monkeys—everything you'd expect from a South American jungle. It may have disappeared in other countries, but in Suriname, it's still here.

ⓘ **Central Suriname Nature Reserve** (☏ 597/421-305; www.ci-suriname.org)

✈ Paramaribo

🛏 Guesthouses in the park can be booked through **The Foundation for Nature Preservation** in Suriname (STINASU; ☏ 597/476-597; www.stinasu.com).

TOUR Access Suriname Travel (☏ 597/424 533; www.surinametravel.com). **METS Tours & Travel** (☏ 597/477-088; www.surinamevacations.com). **Tropical Gem Tours** (☏ 597/887 8639; www.tropicalgemtours.org).

7 Mountains

Denali National Park.

Qomolangma National Nature Preserve
The Melting of Mount Everest
Tibet

A DEVASTATING 2010 MUDSLIDE IN DRUGCHU UNDERSCORES THE DRASTIC CONSEQUENCES OF global climate change for this tiny Himalayan preserve, where glaciers are melting, forests have been leveled, and grasslands have turned to desert.

Tibet has the world's highest airport, the world's highest town, the world's highest hiking trail—and now, the world's highest rate of glacier melt. That's grave news, especially since tiny Tibet—sometimes called "The Third Pole"—has the world's third-highest number of glaciers, after Antarctica and the Arctic. It's even worse because Tibet's glaciers are the source of seven major Asian rivers—the Ganges, the Indus, the Brahmaputra, the Mekong, the Irrawaddy, and China's Yellow and Yangtze rivers. *Nearly half the world's population* lives in those river systems. If—as predicted by a U.N. panel—the Himalayan glaciers vanish by 2035, the consequences would be staggering.

Sitting at the top of the world, Tibet has been hit hard by conditions that its impoverished citizens did nothing to create. For 3 decades Tibet's Chinese rulers exploited its forests; driving across this mountain-ringed plateau, you'll see how withered the alpine grasslands have become. Without grasses to absorb moisture, Tibet's temperatures are rising at two to three times the world average. That achingly blue mountain sky is often hazed these days with air pollution from Chinese and Indian factories, which traps and intensifies the heat at these extreme elevations.

Decades ago, the Rongbuk glacier on the north slope of Qomolangma (**Mount Everest**) swept majestically through the Himalayan peaks, a glistening white river of ice. But Rongbuk has been receding 20m (66 feet) per year; today you'll see a desiccated track where patches of ice alternate with brown rocky soil. The majestic white face of Everest is still a heart-stopping

sight, and yet its elevation has recently been downsized to 8,846m (29,022 ft.)—whether or not because of a thinning ice cap, experts disagree.

Scaling that formidable peak is one thing, a challenge only for the hardy few. But other visitors can also stay overnight at one of its base camps (your tour agency—required for visiting Tibet—will help you get the necessary permits). Qomolangma sits on the Nepal-Tibet border, so you can approach from either side: the Nepal approach is an 8-day village-to-village hiking trek, while Tibet's North Base Camp can be reached either by car from Pelbar or a traditional 3-to-5-day trek from Old Tingri, through the dramatic La Langma pass to the Rongbuk monastery.

There's another camp nearby where serious climbers set up their expeditions and acclimate to the altitude, but **North Base Camp** definitely has its own frontier buzz. Polyglot groups of adventurers and native Sherpa guides wander around the ramshackle teahouses and clusters of tents, their nylon colors gaudy against the plain's harsh gray rocks. Above the tents, flags of all nations snap in the wind. Jangling donkey carts arrive, loaded with tourists; woolly yaks lumber past, their pack loads swaying. Adventure's in the air.

ⓘ www.trekkingtibet.com or www.visit nepal.com

🛏 **Zhufeng Zonghe Fuwu Zhongxin** (Qomolangma Service Center), Pelbar (✆ **892/826-2833**). **Xuebao Fandian** (Everest Snow Leopard Hotel), Old Tingri (✆ **892/826-2775**).

The Jungfrau
Europe's Dwindling Ice Cap
Bernese Highlands, Switzerland

RECENT HEAT WAVES IN EUROPE HAVE ACCELERATED THE LOSS OF SWITZERLAND'S GLACIAL ICE pack. In the short term, glacial melting will flood major rivers throughout Europe; in the long term, it will rob Europe of its main water supply.

A trio of dramatic Alpine peaks loom atop the Bernese Highlands: the Jungfrau ("Maiden"), the Eiger, and the Mönch ("Monk"), their very names bespeaking purity, aloofness, and icy solitude. This region holds the largest glacier in Europe, or for that matter, in all Eurasia: the **Aletsch Glacier,** which winds through the mountains, a slow-moving river of ancient ice 23km (14 miles) long. But like glaciers all over the world, it's shrinking every day. Photographs reveal that the Aletsch has retreated 1.4km (nearly 1 mile) since 1950, and the pace of retreat lately has increased radically—between 2005 and 2006 alone, receding 100m (330 ft.). By 2050, 75% of Switzerland's glaciers could disappear; by 2100, even the great Aletsch could conceivably be gone.

You'll get an awesome view of the Aletsch from the **Jungfraubahn,** the highest rack railway in Europe. A series of trains start at Interlaken East rail station and climb upward, at some points tunneling right through the rock of the Alpine massif. At the Eismeer stop, get out to peer through windows cut into the rock. You'll be staring right into the heart of the vast Eismeer, or "Sea of Ice." At the top (Jungfraujoch, the highest train station in Europe), go to the Sphinx Terraces observation deck to see the Aletsch Glacier stretched out in its full glory, dark bands of centuries-old glacial debris striping it like ski tracks. The Eispalast ("Ice Palace"), also at the Jungfraubahn terminus, is a kitschy but historic attraction boasting several

rooms hewn out of the ice, 20m (66 ft.) below the glacier's surface.

Another stop on the Jungfraubahn is the resort town of **Grindelwald,** 22km (14 miles) south of Interlaken. You can study the striated ravine at the base of the Lower Grindelwald glacier at an observation deck just outside of town, or hike in summer right out onto the glacier (you may want to take a cable car partway up). A half-day hike will take you to the base of the Upper Grindelwald Glacier, following the Milchbach River (so named because it looks milky from minerals in the melting glacier's ice). At the receding snout of the glacier, you can visit the ice-carved chamber of the Blue Ice Grotto.

Northeast of Interlaken, at **Brienz** (a 20-min. train ride from Interlaken east), you can see the glacier's melting snows plunge downhill at dramatic Geissbach Falls. From there they flow into Lake Brienz, and eventually into the Mediterranean. The glaciers' fate isn't just a Swiss problem, after all.

(i) **Interlaken Tourist Office** (✆ **41/33/ 826-5300;** www.interlaken.ch). **Jungfraubahn railroad** (✆ **41/33/828-7233;** www. jungfraubahn.ch).

✈ Bern

🛏 $$$ **Royal St. Georges,** Höheweg 139, Interlaken (✆ **41/33/822-7575;** www. royal-stgeorges.ch). $$ **Hotel Alphorn,** Rothornstrasse 29A, Interlaken (✆ **41/33/ 822-3051;** www.hotel-alphorn.ch).

Columbia Icefields
End of the Ice Age?
Alberta, Canada

THE WORLD'S LARGEST NONPOLAR ICE MASS IS A VITAL SOURCE OF FRESH WATER FOR NORTH America—but its receding glaciers provide less every year. In the Athabasca River alone, annual runoff has declined 20% since 1960.

The Columbia Icefields straddle the top of the North American continent like a great crystalline mother embracing her children. Massive amounts of pure, century-old ice and snow lie packed in and around these peaks, in some spots 750m (2,460 ft.) thick. Covering some 325 sq. km (125 sq. miles), this vast frozen dome mantles the eastern face of the Canadian Rockies. But the ice mother's arms seem to clutch her children ever closer, as the edges of the ice field recede an ominous 10m (33 ft.) per year. What this means for the North American watershed is anybody's guess.

Whereas the Arctic and Greenland ice caps are made of salt water, the Columbia Icefields are freshwater ice. Melt from its outlying sections creates what's known as a hydrologic apex, a major source of water for North America, eventually flowing into three different oceans (Atlantic, Pacific, and Arctic). It's true that the ice field is so massive, it's not going to vanish completely anytime soon. The hydrologic apex, however, may already be critically compromised. The melt at present is ancient snow, free from modern pollutants, but once the melt reaches polluted 20th-century snows, its water quality may be drastically different.

The most accessible section of the ice field is the Athabasca Glacier in **Jasper National Park,** where the Icefield Visitor Center (open mid-Apr to mid-Oct only) is set in a valley that was long ago buried in the glacier. An outdoor timeline demonstrates where the ice edge lay at various milestone dates in the past. Rocky debris left behind by the melting glacier lies in all-too-evident scraggy piles. From the lodge beside the visitor center you can book a 90-minute ride onto the glacier surface with **Brewster Snocoach Tours** (✆ 877/423-7433; www.columbiaice fields.com), which uses a specially designed bus with balloon tires. Hiking on the glacier's surface is the highlight of these tours, a literally dazzling opportunity to stand on a glittering expanse of solid ice and feel its frosty exhalations.

The drive to get here is spectacular in itself: along the 287km (178-mile) **Icefields Parkway,** a majestic stretch of highway between Banff and Jasper national parks that climbs through deep river valleys; beneath soaring, glacier-notched mountains; and past dozens of hornlike peaks shrouded with permanent snowcaps. Along the way, visit the jewel-like resort town of **Lake Louise,** set on a vivid turquoise lake cupped in a dramatic bowl of glaciers. Don't panic when you see the unearthly greenish color of the lake; it's not caused by pollution, but rather by the way that minerals deposited by glacier melt refract the sunlight. This beautiful land of ice transforms everything.

ⓘ **Icefield Visitor Center,** Sunwapta Pass, Alberta, Canada (✆780/852-7030; www.jaspernationalpark.com)

✈Calgary

🛏 $$$ **Glacier View Inn,** Sunwapta Pass (✆ 866/875-8456; www.national parkreservations.com). $$ **Becker's Chalets,** Hwy. 95, Jasper (✆780/852-3779; www.beckerschalets.com).

Glacier National Park
The Spine of the World
West Glacier, Montana

GLOBAL WARMING IS MELTING THE GLACIERS THAT GIVE GLACIER NATIONAL PARK ITS NAME; BY 2030, they all could be gone. As the ice retreats, new habitats arise that favor predatory hawks, eagles, and grizzly bears.

Blackfoot tribes call the Continental Divide "the spine of the world," that ridge of the Rockies from which—remember Geography 101?—all rivers flow either east or west. When the Ice Age ended millennia ago, retreating ice floes along the Divide revealed a stunning valley gouged out of what is now the state of Montana and lower Alberta, Canada. Majestic mountain crags loom above the valley, their crevices hiding lakes and ponds that are really just melted glacial leftovers. Icy waters spill over the crags in spectacular waterfalls.

Glacier National Park.

The glaciers are still receding—faster than ever, in fact, adding opalescent runoff to those mountain lakes and exposing rocky slopes that haven't seen the sun for eons. In 1850, early European explorers documented some 150 glaciers draping the limestone peaks; by the early 1960s, aerial surveys showed 50 glaciers; today there are 25. Scientists estimate they may be gone entirely by 2030.

With the ice dwindling, the ecosystem is in the grip of radical, rapid change. Along the tree line, stunted conifers, low scrubby foliage, and meadows take over, creating a habitat that's increasingly vulnerable to fire and prone to avalanches. Those meadows are, however, hospitable to bighorn sheep (Glacier has a booming population), nimble snow-white mountain goats, and predatory hawks and golden eagles. Meadow berries make good food for foraging grizzly bears as well, of which Glacier has more than its share.

Between late May and mid-September, you can circle the park on the spectacular 50-mile (80km) **Going-to-the-Sun Road,** running from the West Glacier park entrance (U.S. Hwy. 2 near Columbia Falls, Montana) to the St. Mary visitor center at the eastern edge of the park. You'll trace the shore of **Lake McDonald,** then wind dramatically up 3,400 feet (1,036m) into the mountains (keep an eye out for circling hawks) to the Logan Pass visitor center. The **Jackson Glacier** turnout gives you a good view of the shifting glacial terrain; note that Jackson was once connected to neighboring Blackfoot Glacier, but is now a separate and much smaller entity.

With more than 700 miles (1,127km) of hiking trails, Glacier truly rewards getting out of the car to explore on foot. Visitors do everything from day hikes and rafting on the Flathead River to cross-country skiing in winter and weeklong backcountry camping trips. Climb through alpine meadows spangled with glacier lilies, cool off in new-growth conifer woods, scramble over rock faces striated from glacial grind—and hope you don't encounter grizzlies.

ⓘ **Glacier National Park** (📞 **406/888-7806;** www.nps.gov/glac)

✈ Kalispell

🛏 $$ **Lake McDonald Lodge,** on Lake McDonald (📞 **406/892-2525;** www.glacier parkinc.com). $ **Fish Creek Campground,** Glacier National Park (📞 **406/888-7800;** www.recreation.gov).

TOUR Glacier Guides, Inc. (📞 **800/521-RAFT [7238];** www.glacierguides.com)

205 Shrinking Glaciers

North Cascades National Park
Snowmelt, Whitebark, & Tree Line
Marblemount, Washington

SINCE 1900, GLACIERS IN THE NORTH CASCADES HAVE SHRUNK TO 50% OF THEIR ORIGINAL mass. Old-growth trees are dying off, while new trees invade subalpine meadows, shifting habitats for hundreds of species.

A tree line is just what it sounds like: a line of trees, marking the highest elevation where trees can grow. Twisted and bent by the wind (an effect called *krummholz*), those uppermost trees are hardy pioneers—and season after season, they're inching farther up the Cascade peaks.

With more than 300 glaciers, the North Cascades National Park Complex—which combines North Cascades National Park, Ross Lake, and Lake Chelan National Recreation Areas—is one of the snowiest places on earth. Each winter's snowfall piles onto the glacier; each summer evaporates and melts the ice pack, sending torrents of water down the jagged mountainsides and creating the park's namesake cascades. But climate change and rising temperatures have skewed this cycle, making summer melt exceed winter accumulation. As the glaciers shrink, older snow—increasingly full of pollutants—melts into the mountain lakes, which are also getting warmer (a dangerous change for temperature-sensitive fish). Newly exposed slopes convert to

alpine vegetation, and the subalpine zones below it creep higher.

State Route 20 cuts through the park, a spectacular drive following a series of reservoirs—**Gorge Lake, Diablo Lake, Ross Lake**—formed by dams along the Skagit River. But to see the Cascades only from a car window would be to miss the richness of this mosaic of habitats. No other national park offers so many plant species, distributed across eight different biozones, from the needle-carpeted forest floor to trout-filled lakes to rocky ridges; even its west-facing slopes, which catch weather systems drifting inland from the Pacific, have entirely different habitats from the eastern slopes.

Stop at Newhalem to walk the short, easy **"Trail of the Cedars"** Nature Walk through an old-growth forest's massive trees (which are dying at increased rates throughout the Pacific Northwest, due to climate change). From the Diablo trail head, hike the 3.6-mile (5.8km) **Thunder Knob Trail** through several other forest types, from Douglas fir and Western hemlock to lodgepole pines. Then turn off route 20 onto the Cascade River Road to reach the spectacular **Cascade Pass Trail** (3.7 miles/6km), an upward climb through forests and meadows to Cascade Pass. Along with whitebark pines, in summer you'll see meadows spangled with yellow glacier lilies and pink mountain heather. Look for the Clark's Nutcracker, a bird that lives almost entirely on the whitebark's seeds, or Douglas squirrels, great gatherers of the whitebark's purplish cones. Northern flickers and mountain bluebirds nest in the whitebarks, and elk browse on them in summer.

Pivotal as the whitebark pines are, they themselves are under siege—from blister rust, a fungus that proliferates in warm summers, taking down entire stands of whitebarks. Forest rangers are desperately working to propagate those few whitebarks that are fungus-resistant. It's a race against time—but then, so is everything else in the Cascades.

✈ Seattle/Vancouver

🚃 $$ **Buffalo Run Inn,** 60117 S.R. 20, Marblemount, WA (☏ **877/828-6652** or 360/873-2103; www.buffaloruninn.com). $ **Newhalem Creek Campground,** milepost 120, S.R. 20, North Cascades NP (☏**877/444-6777;** www.recreation.gov).

Shrinking Glaciers 206

Los Glaciares National Park
A Patagonian Balancing Act
Argentina

THE SOUTHERN PATAGONIAN ICEFIELD'S RAPIDLY THINNING GLACIERS CONTRIBUTE HEAVILY TO rising sea levels, as a result of their relatively low elevations, their proximity to the ocean, and their unique "calving" dynamics.

It's ironic that the one South American glacier most adventure tourists see is **Perito Moreno Glacier,** in Patagonia's Los Glaciares National Park. Oh, the White Giant is spectacular all right: A jagged wall of 3,000-year-old ice measuring 5km (3 miles) across and roughly 60m (200 ft.) tall, towering above the channel that connects the two halves of Lago Argentina. But Perito Moreno is a sort of freak among glaciers, for it actually adds around 2m (6½ ft.) of ice every day. As new snow falls on the far-off crest of the Andes, the glacier pushes old compacted ice outward, building up pressure inside the ice. And as the ice face expands, massive chunks "calve," or shear off the face, dropping into turquoise Lago Argentina with a thundering crash. Tourists scampering along walkways built over the glacier face ooh

and aah; cameras click and whir from the decks of excursion boats on the lake.

Perito Moreno is an impressive natural phenomenon, and it is relatively easy to get to, located only 80km (50 miles) from the town of El Calafate, the gateway to this rugged Andean wilderness region. But Los Glaciares has 46 other glaciers—part of the largest ice cap outside of Antarctica and Greenland—and some 200 smaller glaciers. And unlike Perito Moreno, where new ice and broken-off icebergs balance out, those other glaciers are rapidly getting thinner, due to climate change and that same calving process. In fact, these glaciers are shrinking even faster than their Northern Hemisphere counterparts.

To educate visitors about the impact of climate change on the ice cap, the park opened a stunning new **Glaciarium**

Museum (© 54/2902/497912; www. glaciarium.com) in 2011, only 5km (3 miles) from El Calafate. The angular metal facade of the Glaciarium instantly evokes an iceberg, seeming to heave up out of a barren rocky steppe. State-of-the-art multimedia displays inside present the latest information on how climate change affects glaciers around the world.

Armed with information from the Glaciarium, you can take a boat tour on the north half of Lago Argentina, sailing past several other impressive glaciers—including **Uppsala Glacier,** South America's largest (it covers an area three times the size of Buenos Aires), and **Spezzini Glacier,** known for its high sheer face—and hike over to Lago Onelli to view three more glaciers, **Agassiz, Onelli,** and **Bolados.** Or take a guided trek across the surface of the Perito Moreno, scrambling around on the rough surface of ancient ice and peering deep into sapphire-hued crevices. It's an exhilarating experience, to say the least.

ⓘ **Los Glaciares National Park** (© 54/ 2902/491-00; www.losglaciares.com)

✈ El Calafate

🛏 $$$ **Los Notros, Parque Nacional Los Glaciares** (© 54/11/4813-7285 or 54/2902/499510; http://losnotros.com/ tarifas). $$ **Hotel Posada Los Alamos,** Gobernador Moyano at Bustillo, El Calafate (© 54/2902/491144; www.posada losalamos.com).

TOUR Caltur (© 54/2902/491368; www. caltur.com.ar). **Hielo & Aventura** (© 54/ 2902/492205; www.hieloyaventura.com).

Torres del Paine National Park
A Second Act in the Andes Highlands
Chile

FIFTY YEARS AGO, THE CHILEAN GOVERNMENT TRANSFORMED TORRES DEL PAINE INTO A STUNNING wilderness area. Now Patagonia's retreating glaciers could radically alter the ecosystem again.

Not so very long ago, the Torres del Paine was just ranchland—and worn-out ranchland at that. Rare beech forests were burned down to expand pastureland, and vast herds of sheep had grazed the steppes down to the soil.

Since the Chilean government took over the land in 1959, nature's done a remarkable turnaround. Nowadays hikers tramp through leafy forests, across golden pampas, and along the shores of startling blue lakes, their waters turned milky by glacial melt. Native populations of guanacos, flamingos, pumas, and ostrichlike rhea birds have rebounded from near extinction; Andean condors roost on its breathtakingly jagged peaks.

Down here on the Chilean side of Patagonia, fierce winds whip down from the crest of the Andes, and even in summer (Jan–Feb) the weather can be chilly. The "Torres" in the name means towers, as in the three namesake salmon-colored granite peaks, wind-eroded giants that soar from sea level to upward of 2,800m (9,186 ft.). Paine is the Tehuelche Indian word for "blue," referring to the startling blue lakes of the surrounding glaciers, the park's other most striking feature. And those glaciers are rapidly receding, as much as 19m (62 ft.) a year, leaving behind a visible band of rocky scree on the newly exposed slopes.

Torres del Paine National Park.

Its Argentine neighbor Los Glaciares ⓞⓞ⑥ may be easier to reach, but there's more to do in Torres del Paine, starting with the obvious choice, hiking. The classic day hike leads from the Hotel Las Torres to the Torres formations, but another popular route follows the shores of Lago Grey for spectacular up-close views of the gigantic blue iceberg feeding the lake; day hikes across the surface of **Glacier Grey,** prowling through its frosty caverns, are also available. Serious backpackers can do overnight treks from 4 to 11 days, depending on your route, staying along the way in tents or cabinlike refugios (Oct–Apr is the best season). Horseback treks are another popular option. If glaciers are your thing, you can also book a cruise on an open Zodiac boat past the glaciers Tyndall and Geike to the Torres del Paine entrance and up the Rio Serrano to the knifelike **Serrano Glacier,** where you can hike around the surface before sailing back to Puerto Natales.

Although a new highway from Puerto Natales opened in 2010, Torres del Paine is still hard enough to get to. Most of your fellow visitors will be serious outdoor types, determined to snag these wilderness experiences while they last.

ⓘ**Parques Nacional Torres Del Paine** (🕾 **56/61/247845;** www.torresdelpaine. com)

✈Punta Arenas

🛏 $$ **Aquaterra Lodge,** Bulnes 299, Puerto Natales (🕾 **56/61/412239;** www. aquaterrapatagonia.com). $$$ **Hotel Las Torres** (🕾**56/61/617450;** www.lastorres. com).

TOUR Aventour (🕾**56/61/241197;** http:// aventourpatagonia.cl). **Onas** (🕾 **56/61/ 411539;** www.onaspatagonia.com). **Andes Mountain** (www.andesmountain.cl).

The Greenbrier Valley
The Ache in Appalachia
Southeastern West Virginia

MOUNTAINTOP-REMOVAL COAL MINING THREATENS ECOSYSTEMS THROUGHOUT THE CENTRAL Appalachian Highlands, degrading alpine peaks, shale barrens, and underground caves, as well as whitewater rivers and scenic gorges.

There's a reason why West Virginia is nick-named the Mountain State. You'll understand it when you walk the short nature trail circling the summit of Spruce Knob, the state's highest mountain: the dense boreal spruce forest, tumbled boulders, and wind-twisted trees could as easily be in Canada. Nearby, the massive Seneca Rocks thrust upward from the forest, attracting rock climbers from all over the country. A couple hours farther south, whitewater rafters navigate the stunning gorges of the Gauley River (www.nps.gov/gari) and New River (www.nps.gov/neri), on plunging Class IV and V rapids fed by hundreds of mountain streams. At the **Canyon Rim Visitors Center** (© 304/574-2115), you can walk over the 1,000-foot-deep (300m) New River gorge on the world's longest single-arch steel bridge.

But West Virginia is also a coal-mining state, and even these protected scenic areas feel its effects. Since the 1960s, underground mining has been super-seded by the cheaper mountaintop removal method (MTR), in which surface rock and soil are blasted away to reveal the coal seam. (Jonathan Franzen depicted MTR's effects in his 2010 best-selling novel *Freedom.*) The surface debris is later replaced, either on that mountain or in nearby valleys—but often mixed with toxic byproducts. Forests that were cleared for MTR take years to grow back as well. And lo and behold, every time there's an oil crisis in America, coal mining ramps up again.

Besides deforestation and pollution, surface mining wreaks havoc on what's underground—which in West Virginia is something special. The Greenbrier Limestone—that same layer of ancient rock that heaved aboveground to form the Seneca Rocks—is honeycombed with caves, some 500 of them in this valley alone. Those caves harbor many vulnerable plant and animal species: bats, beetles, spiders, millipedes, shrimplike crustaceans, cray-fish, and salamanders. Entire caverns have been gobbled up by quarries, and highway and building construction leads to cave-ins, causing contaminated groundwater to seep in. You can see unspoiled cave habitat at **Lost World Caverns** on Fairview Road in Lewisburg (© 304/645-6677; www.lostworldcaverns.com), and **Organ Cave** on Route 63 in Ronceverte (between Routes 293 and 60; © 304/645-7600; www.organcave.com).

Mining also affects one of the state's rarest ecosystems: shale barrens, mountainside habitats with flaky surface rock and few trees. Most West Virginians see these crumbling steep slopes as worth-less; roads and utility lines bisect them, and adjacent pastures often introduce aggressive invasive weeds. Yet these rare and fragile ecosystems harbor a number of sun-loving endemic flora, much more like desert plants from Arizona or New Mexico than their Appalachian cousins. **Kate's Mountain,** in the Greenbrier State Forest, has some spectacular shale bar-rens; you'll find them near the high point of the 2.1-mile (3.4km) **Rocky Ridge Trail.** It's a refuge for several rare plants—like the fine-leaved Kate's Mountain clover and box huckleberry, a low glossy-leaved shrub that's a relic of the Ice Age, perhaps the oldest plant species on earth. If that's not worth preserving, what is?

ⓘ **Spruce Knob/Seneca Rocks National Recreation Area,** Monongahela National Forest, Elkins, WV (ⓒ **304/636-1800;**

www.fs.usda.gov). **Greenbrier State Forest** (ⓒ **304/536-1944;** www.greenbriersf.com).

✈ Greenbrier Valley, Lewisburg

🛏 $$$ **The Greenbrier,** 300 W. Main St., White Sulphur Springs (ⓒ **800/453-4858** or 304/536-1110; www.greenbrier.com). $$ **Smoke Hole Resort,** Seneca Rocks (ⓒ **800/828-8478** or 304/257-4442; www.smokehole.com).

High Wilderness **209**

Shenandoah National Park
The Bear Necessities
Skyline Drive, Virginia

AIR POLLUTION FROM MID-ATLANTIC AND MIDWESTERN CITIES AND FACTORIES HANGS OVER THE Blue Ridge Mountains, adding an ugly white haze to their natural blue mist. Its sidekick, acid rain, falls on already acidic soil and kills pH-sensitive fish in the streams.

What's a North American forest without black bears? They're part of our national mythology, as iconic as Davy Crockett and Teddy Roosevelt. Before the Europeans came, some two million black bears padded around North America; by the early 1900s, they'd vanished completely from the eastern Blue Ridge Mountains. But set aside a big enough chunk of land and even large mammals that need plenty of roaming territory will return. The American bison hasn't returned to Shenandoah National Park, but bobcats, black bears, and cougars have, along with the beaver, the river otter, and the white-tailed deer, happy to range again in a vast expanse of mixed forestland.

The oldest national park in the East, Shenandoah is a long strip of wilderness along the **Skyline Drive,** so called because it traces the spine of the Blue Ridge for 105 miles (169km). Most visitors simply drive through, pausing to admire mountain panoramas at one of 75 roadside overlooks—and adding car exhaust to the ever-increasing air pollution from

outside the park. Yet several short, easy walking trails lead away from the drive, like the 1.8-mile (2.9km) **Story of the Forest Trail** (a great hands-on seminar in forest succession), the 1.3-mile (2km) **Limberlost Trail,** with its profusion of mountain laurels in spring, or the 1.3-mile (2km) **Frazier Discovery Trail.** And that's just for starters—Shenandoah has 500 miles (805km) of hiking trails, including a section of the Appalachian Trail.

Even if you don't meet an actual bear in the woods, you may spot signs of one—droppings, tracks, or claw-slashed tree trunks. Black bear returnees were sighted in 1937, soon after Shenandoah was created as a New Deal project. Once the Civilian Conservation Corps had restored the hardwood forests, and trees began to produce acorns, the bears' numbers zoomed into the hundreds. Bears are good for the environment: Though they eat smaller animals, they also like berries, acorns, and fruits, thereby dispersing seeds in their droppings. Tearing apart decayed logs in search of insects, they

Shenandoah National Park.

speed the decomposition process that makes forest soil rich.

Some Shenandoah visitors, unfortunately, aren't so good for the environment—such as the large-leaved ailanthus tree (aka stinking sumac) or the kudzu vine, both of which aggressively drive out native species. Gypsy moths, which killed millions of trees between 1986 and 1995, threaten to recur every season. The newest pest is the woolly hemlock agelid, a tiny European insect that can ravage riverside hemlock forests. Even the bears don't want to see *that* many dead trees.

ⓘ **Shenandoah National Park** (☎ **540/999-3500;** www.nps.gov/shen)

✈ Washington Dulles or Charlottesville

🛏 $$ **Big Meadow Lodge,** Mile 51.2, Skyline Dr. $$ **Lewis Mountain Cabins,** Mile 57.5, Skyline Dr. (for both ☎ **888/896-3833;** www.visitshenandoah.com).

210 High Wilderness

Rocky Mountain National Park
The Wonder of the Tundra
Estes Park, Colorado

As global warming creates warmer and drier conditions, the Lower 48's largest expanse of alpine tundra is steadily degrading, putting cold-weather plants and animals at risk.

A tree in Rocky Mountain National Park.

Drive along Rocky Mountain National Park's spectacular Trail Ridge Road and you'll feel like you're at the top of the world. Bisecting the park east to west, this 48-mile (77km) route rolls through gnarled alpine tundra, bare granite, and heathery slopes, straddling the Continental Divide at altitudes of 8,000 feet (2,430m) and up.

It's a harsh environment, but certain species like it that way—like the North American elk (also called wapiti, to distinguish it from the European elk, which is actually a moose—go figure). Though intensive hunting once decimated their population, over the past century the U.S. Forest Service carefully restored the herd, importing new specimens from Yellowstone and eliminating predators such as grizzly bears and gray wolves. Nowadays, the park is home to anywhere from 1,000 to 3,000 elk, drifting in and out of the park seasonally in search of grazing land. In late spring you'll see elk cows with their spotted calves, foraging along mountain creeks; a prime vantage point in summer

is the viewing platform at the Alpine Visitor Center, up at Fall River Pass. In the fall mating season, head for the montane meadows of **Kawuneeche Valley, Horseshoe Park, Moraine Park,** and **Upper Beaver Meadows** at dawn or dusk to watch the spectacle of bull elks bugling and displaying their powerful antlers to attract females.

Reintroductions have also built the Rocky Mountain park's bighorn sheep population to as many as 600. A prime place to see them in late spring and early summer is the **"Bighorn Crossing Zone"** across Highway 34 at Horseshoe Park, where the sheep migrate to the meadows around Sheep Lakes for summer grazing. Or visit their alpine range: Take the short but strenuous trail near **Milner Pass** to the edge of the Crater (closed May to mid-July for lambing season).

But alongside the bighorns and the mighty elk, there's another species whose numbers are up—and that's problematic. It's a tiny pest called the pine beetle, which feeds on evergreen trees, turning their foliage to rusty red and destroying broad swaths of pine forest. In the traditional balance of nature, the pine beetle population would be kept in check by the minus-30-degree temperatures of Rocky Mountain winter nights. But with the warmer seasons of recent years, pine beetle infestations have ravaged forests throughout the Colorado range, leaving scars slashed across this prime section of otherwise protected wilderness. That's one species the Rockies could do without.

ⓘ **Rocky Mountain National Park,** US 36, Estes Park, CO (ⓒ **970/586-1206;** www.nps.gov/romo)

✈ Denver

🛏 $$$ **Glacier Lodge,** 2166 Tunnel Rd., Estes Park (ⓒ **800/523-3920;** www. glacierlodge.com). $ **Moraine Park Campground,** Rocky Mountain National Park (ⓒ **877/444-6777** or 888/448-1474; www. recreation.gov).

Yosemite National Park
The Dawn Chorus
Yosemite National Park, California

BETWEEN AUTO EMISSIONS ON CROWDED PARK ROADS AND ACID DEPOSITS IN THE SNOW AND rain, air pollution is Yosemite's gravest environmental threat, followed by invasive species such as wild turkeys and the Himalayan blackberry.

Every American should visit Yosemite National Park at least once. But some summer weekends, it seems they've all decided to come at the same time. The park is only 3½ hours from San Francisco and 6 hours from Los Angeles, and that accessibility, coupled with the park's justly famous natural beauty, spells tourist crowds. Most of those visitors crowd onto the Yosemite Valley Loop Road, which visits several iconic vistas—**Bridalveil Fall,** the Glacier Point overlook, the rounded summit of Half Dome, and the awesome 7,549-foot-high (2,300m) sheer rock face called **El Capitan,** the world's tallest granite monolith. Upper **Yosemite Fall** is the tallest waterfall in North America, closely followed by Ribbon Fall and Sentinel Fall. Then there's the classic Yosemite photo op of **Mirror Lake,** offering up a near-perfect reflection of the surrounding mountain scenery—though with tons of glacial debris from snowmelt washing into the lake every spring, Mirror Lake is swiftly shrinking and may soon revert to forestland.

At midday, it's a zoo, with crowds of cars and RVs inching along the Yosemite Valley road, passengers gaping at 3,000-foot-high (900m) glacier-carved granite walls and the waterfalls that drop down them. But show up at dawn and you'll find another zoo, the kind with real animals.

Those towering cliffs? A perfect place for peregrine falcons to nest. Recently removed from the endangered list, peregrines returned to Yosemite a few years ago, and there are now at least four nesting pairs, dark-hooded raptors soaring around the central valley near the massive granite outcrops of El Capitan or Glacier Point. Those signature waterfalls? Where else would a black swift build its nest? Even famous Bridalveil Fall, off the Yosemite Valley loop, may attract this rare high flier, though you'll have to get there at dawn to see one.

Those great old-growth forests? A welcome refuge for forest birds like the pileated woodpecker, hermit thrush, Williamson's sapsucker, Nashville warbler, golden-crowned kinglet, dusky flycatcher, mountain chickadee, spotted owl, or, high overhead, the endangered northern goshawk. Drive down Glacier Point Road, south of the Yosemite Valley loop, and stroll along the road to the Bridalveil campground. Better yet, hike up to a meadow—McGurk or Peregoy, also along Glacier Point Road, are good ones—to find mountain quail, mountain bluebirds, and calliope or rufus hummingbirds. The red-breasted sapsucker may be working an aspen tree at meadow's edge, and if you're really lucky you may even see a great gray owl perched watchfully, waiting for meadow prey.

ⓘ **Yosemite National Park,** entrances on CA 41, CA 120, and CA 140 (☏ **209/372-0200;** www.nps.gov/yose)

✈ Fresno-Yosemite International

🛏 $$$ **The Ahwanee,** Yosemite Valley (☏ **801/559-4884** or 559/252-4848; www.yosemitepark.com). $ **Tuolumne Meadows Campground** (☏ **877/444-6777;** www.recreation.gov).

Mirror Lake in Yosemite National Park.

High Wilderness 212

Yellowstone National Park
A Grizzly Scene
Northwest Wyoming

ON THE YELLOWSTONE RANGERS' WORRY LIST: DAMAGE FROM SNOWMOBILES, LAKE TROUT STEALing habitat from cutthroat trout, elk herds decimated by predators—and now pine beetle infestation, of vital concern to a park that is 80% forest.

Let's get one thing straight: This is not Jellystone Park, and those bears are not lovable Yogi and Boo-Boo. Bring a telephoto lens, or at least a pair of binoculars, because you don't want to get too close to Yellowstone's signature species—bald eagles, gray wolves, and grizzly bears. And don't even *think* of feeding them.

This isn't an issue for most Yellowstone tourists, who stick to the Lower Loop

Road—where **Old Faithful** geyser spouts every 90 minutes—or drive up to see the spectacularly colored rocks of **Mammoth Hot Springs** just inside the north entrance. Of course, there is wildlife to be spotted here too. Just near the Madison junction, for example, you can hike the easy .6-mile (1km) Harlequin Lake Trail to a small lake populated with all sorts of waterfowl; at the Riverside turnout, watch rare trumpeter swans dabble in the shallows of the Madison River; from the lookout at Gibbon Falls, see hungry bald eagles circling overhead, ready to snatch trout out of the Madison. Deeper into the park but still along the Grand Loop Road, at Dunraven Pass there are often traffic jams in summer as a band of Rocky Mountain bighorns—often including lambs—browse alongside the road.

But for prime wildlife encounters, take the less traveled road east from Mammoth across the top of the park—the Blacktail Plateau Drive loop, for example, or the road through the deep Lamar Valley. Put on your hiking boots and strike out away from the roads; trails are well marked, and the hiking terrain tends to be moderate. This northern range is full of hoofed grazing animals—elk, moose, bison, pronghorn antelopes, deer, and Rocky Mountain bighorn sheep—as well as bears, eagles, and wolves. **Yellowstone Lake** is one of the bald eagles' favorite summer fishing spots; off the Mammoth-Norris road near Liberty Cap, the 5-mile (8km) Beaver Ponds Loop offers views of moose as well as beavers. The 6-mile (9.6km) round-trip hike up **Mount Washburn** rewards you with a 10,243-foot-high (3,122m) view over much of Yellowstone, a panorama of forested slopes that was continuously green before the pine beetles chomped their way through stands of white-bark pine. (Those patches of rusty foliage? Pine beetle infestations.) And in season (mid-June to Aug) with a backcountry permit, you can venture even farther, like around **Shoshone Lake** (prime moose viewing) or along the 14-mile (23km) **Sportsman Lake Trail,** a daylong hike through sagebrush plateaus full of elk and a meadow popular with moose. Early morning and dusk are the best times for spotting wildlife—a very good reason to camp in the park or stay at an in-park lodge, so you can snag those precious sightings.

ⓘ **Yellowstone National Park** (☏ 307/344-7381; www.nps.gov/yell)

✈ West Yellowstone Airport or Yellowstone Regional Airport, Cody, WY

🛏 $$ **Mammoth Hot Springs Hotel** (☏ **866/439-7375** or 307/344-7311; www.yellowstonenationalparklodges.com). $ **Madison Hotel,** 139 Yellowstone Ave., West Yellowstone (☏ **406/646-7745;** http://madisonhotelmotel.com).

213 | High Wilderness

Denali National Park
Alaska's Big Five
Alaska

ISOLATION HAS BLESSED THIS SUBARCTIC WILDERNESS WITH EXCEPTIONALLY PURE AIR AND relatively few invasive species. However, its intricate mosaic of winter-adapted habitats could be thrown into disarray by global warming.

Africa has its Big Five, a checklist of important game animals to see on a safari. Well, Alaska has its own Big Five. Visitors to Denali National Park can check them off: Here's a shaggy moose, browsing in a stand of willow; there's a stately caribou, its branching antlers outlined against the sky; there's a curly-horned Dall sheep clinging to a rocky hillside; there's a massive grizzly bear, raking open a salmon with its long claws; and finally, there's a gray wolf, restlessly surveying the tundra from a heathery knoll.

Private cars can drive only to Mile 15 of the park's 92-mile (148km) road, so most visitors use the bus service to explore the park—either shuttle buses or interpretive bus tours narrated by naturalists. The wildlife in Denali is so abundant, you actually do get major wildlife sightings from the bus. Mile 9 is the best place to see moose, which prefer forests close to lakes and marshes. At Mile 34, the rocky crags of **Igloo Mountain** are major Dall sheep habitat. Miles 38 to 43 mark **Sable Pass,** where grizzlies amble about. At Mile 46, the **Polychrome Pass** overlook reveals caribou herds on the valley below. Mile 53 is a good place to hike around (you can reboard a later shuttle bus) in the rich bottomlands of the glacier-fed **Toklat River,** where bears, caribou, and wolves roam.

All Big Five mammals have thriving populations here, although the caribou herd fluctuates—one harsh winter, like the winter of 1990–91, can cut their numbers as much as a third. Denali's are just about the only Dall sheep population with such healthy numbers despite the close proximity of major predators. Wolves may be endangered elsewhere, but not in Alaska—although Denali's wolf population dropped to around 65 wolves in 2009, a number finely calibrated to the amount of available prey. Grizzly bears, of course, aren't limited to eating meat—they'll eat anything from berries to caribou. In late July, they go into a feeding frenzy called hyperphagia, eating so ravenously that they don't notice that bus full of camera-snapping tourists parked nearby.

All of Denali's animals are well adapted to life in the subarctic. But what will happen if global climate change warms the temperature, an effect even more pronounced in high latitudes? Everything from the food they eat to the way their coats grow has evolved for harsh Alaskan winters. In a few years, could the Big Five become the Big Four . . . or the Big Three . . . or. . . .

ⓘ **Denali National Park,** Denali Park Rd., AK (✆ **907/683-2294;** www.nps.gov/dena)

✈ Fairbanks or Anchorage

🛏 $$ **Earthsong Lodge** (✆ **907/683-2863;** www.earthsonglodge.com). $$$ **Denali Bluffs Hotel,** Mile 238.4 Park Hwy. (✆**866/683-8500** or 907/683-7000; www.denalialaska.com).

TOUR Bus reservations (essential): **Denali Park Resorts** (✆ **800/276-7234;** www.denaliparkresorts.com)

High Wilderness

214

Purnululu National Park
The Kimberley's Striped Secret
The Kimberley, Western Australia

THE STARK BEAUTY OF THE BUNGLE BUNGLE MOUNTAINS ATTRACTS MORE VISITORS EVERY YEAR to this pristine but fragile wilderness area, strictly protected by a coalition of white and Aboriginal stewards.

Rising out of the vast and lonely landscape of the Kimberley, the Bungle Bungle Mountains are so stunning, it's a wonder that they aren't on everybody's must-see list. Yet their very existence wasn't even known until the early 1980s—that's how rarely people travel to this sparsely inhabited, forgotten corner of Western Australia.

But perhaps that's why these fragile sandstone marvels have held up so well. Soon after they were discovered, this national park was created to protect them.

It's promptly closed every year during the January to March rainy season, known here simply as the Wet, and in the dry season, the only access is by four-wheel-drive vehicles. The park has a rich repository of Aboriginal art and burial sites, but they're kept off-limits to casual visitors. Purnululu's park management—a joint effort by white Australians and the local Aboriginal people—has evidently benefited from the mistakes other, older parks have made in managing their natural wonders. Let's hope they got it right this time.

Geologists get excited talking about this unique range of sandstone domes (*purnululu* means "sandstone" in the local language). They're rare examples of cone karst formations made of sandstone rather than limestone, heaved up from the floor of an ancient sea. Etched by erosion into filigreed beehives, they're also vividly striped in contrasting orange and gray bands by ancient algae trapped inside the permeable stone. (Layers of sandstone containing more clay attracted bacteria that colored that stone orange.) The domes rise 200 to 300m (660–980 ft.) high, and cover an area of 45,000 hectares (111,200 acres), punctuated by knifelike gorges and palm-draped pools.

The domes look spectacular from the air—that's the way most people see them, on 2-hour sightseeing flights from Kununurra. During the Wet, in fact, a plane is your only option. Once the waters subside, however, hikers take over the park, heading for spectacular **Cathedral Gorge,** the rock pool at **Frog Hole Gorge,** and palm-filled **Echidna Chasm.** Stark as the landscape looks from the air, on foot you'll find it's full of wildlife, particularly birds (rainbow bee-eaters, budgerigars), the rare nail-tailed wallaby, and a kangaroo cousin known as the euro. For all the effort it takes to get here, the rewards are spectacular.

ⓘ **Purnululu National Park,** Duncan Hwy., Kununurra (✆ **61/8/9168 1177;** www.environment.gov.au/heritage)

✈ Kununurra

🛏 $$$ **Bungle Bungle Wilderness Lodge,** Purnululu National Park (✆ **61/1800/889 389** or 61/3/9277 8555; www.kimberleywilderness.com.au). $$ **Country Club Hotel,** 47 Coolibah Dr., Kununurra (✆ **61/1800/808 999** or 61/8/9168 1024; www.countryclubhotel.com.au).

TOUR East Kimberley Tours (✆ **61/8/9168 2213;** www.eastkimberleytours.com.au). **Slingair Heliwork** (✆ **61/8/9169 1300;** www.slingair.com.au). **Alligator Airways** (✆ **61/8/9168 1333;** www.alligatorairways.com.au).

215 High Wilderness

Simien Mountains National Park
Trekking over the Roof of Africa
Ethiopia

CRISSCROSSED BY ROADS, DOTTED WITH HUMAN SETTLEMENTS, THIS SPECTACULAR SWATH OF Ethiopian highlands is home to several rare plant and animal species—but with all that human activity, their populations continue to decline.

"The Roof of Africa"—what a perfect nickname for Ethiopia's Simien Mountains. Situated north of Lake Tana and the Tississat Falls, source of the Blue Nile, it rests high on a volcanic ridge, a majestic massif rising abruptly out of the hazy lowland plain. Standing on its rim, you can see for miles and miles and miles.

This isn't a place for a simple drive-through, although roads do cut across the park (road construction is controversial here, as it disturbs wildlife). By far the best way to see it is on foot. For many visitors, this includes climbing **Ras Dejen,** Ethiopia's highest mountain, but even if you don't scale the summit, shorter hikes are spellbinding.

Ascending through the sere highland meadows, you'll see Ice Age relics such as the pineapple-like lobelia tree, which looks like a cactus but is really an evergreen, or the red-hot poker plant with its spiky flowers. Troops of gelada baboons crouch on gravelly hillsides, their long reddish hair visible against the dry scree. Once common throughout Africa, these shaggy baboons—nicknamed "lion monkeys" because of the males' flowing manes—now live only in Ethiopia. In fact, this is the largest intact population of them anywhere, for in many regions they have been exterminated as crop-raiding pests. You can get quite close without upsetting them, perhaps even close enough to see the bare red patches on their chests that earn them their other nickname, "bleeding heart baboons."

Hike a little farther north and you'll find bare crags of dramatic purplish rock, interspersed with eroded gullies and narrow waterfalls wreathed in mist. Hawks, kites, and eagles ride the updrafts above the cliffs, and the resident mountain goats—a very rare ibex called the walia—hide out in the crevices, nibbling on lichens, herb grass, and heather. With their chestnut-brown backs, white underbellies, and long back-curved horns, they are beautiful indeed. There are nearly 500 of them in the park, the last population in the world, so you have a good chance of spotting some, if only in the distance. Rare Simien foxes live up here too, but they rarely reveal themselves to visitors.

At the gateway town of **Debarq,** outside the park entrance, you can hire a guide (required for park entrance), and perhaps rent a mule for your trek into the park. Several campgrounds are located throughout the park, as well as a few villages and their grazing herds of livestock. Park officials have urged human residents to relocate—only then will the geladas and walias truly be protected.

✈ Gondar

🛏 $$ **Simien Eco-Lodge,** Buit Ras, Simien Mountain National Park ((℃ **251/582/ 310 741;** http://simiens.com)

TOUR Wild Frontiers (℃ **44/20/7736 3968;** www.wildfrontiers.co.uk). **Dragoman Overland Adventure Travel** (℃ **44/ 1728/861-133;** www.dragoman.com).

Alpine Flowers **216**

The Valley of Flowers
The Fairies' Flowerpatch
Uttaranchal, India

HUNDREDS OF SPECIES OF RARE SUBALPINE FLOWERS BLOOM IN THIS REMOTE HIMALAYAN VALley, many of them so endemic, they don't even grow on Nanda Devi, the rugged peak 25km (16 miles) to the southeast.

Ever since 1939, when British mountaineer Frank Smith sang its praises in his book *Valley of Flowers*, botanists have yearned to visit this remote Himalayan valley, a once-before-I-die sort of destination just across the border from Tibet. Local villagers refused to live here, though, convinced it was inhabited by fairies who would kidnap them (though they did graze sheep and goats here—no point in wasting good pastureland). Gazing upon its flower-filled meadows, you tend to agree with them—who else but fairies could be responsible for a place this beautiful?

Since it became a national park in 1982, grazing has been forbidden in The Valley of Flowers, leaving flowers to run riot. This narrow east-west ravine hangs at the head of the Bhyundar Ganga valley, fed by the Pushpawati River flowing off Tipra Glacier. Gentle slopes climb from forests of white birch, Himalayan maple, fir, and yew to rich alpine meadows dominated by dwarf shrubs, cushion herbs, grasses, and sedges. Here you'll find exquisite blue primulas, calendulas, trilliums, lady-slippers, angelica, snow-white anemones, saxifrages, the rare blue Himalayan poppy, and the aptly named cobra lily, with its hooded bloom swaying on a tall stalk. Above that lies a rocky moraine where stunted herbaceous shrubs like juniper cling to the rocks, with mosses, lichens, and delicate flowers tucked into crevices.

Unless you're a botanist specializing in Himalayan species, you won't be able to identify every flower you see. Starting in June, you'll find meadows carpeted with color, the display changing daily over the next 3 months—the rosy June glow of pinks and reds gradually giving way to warm yellows in July. The place simply hums with wild bees and butterflies, and the fragrance is intoxicating (surely the work of fairies!).

Note that the park is closed for snow season (Nov–May), and the best months for blooms are also monsoon-and-landslide season. Getting here requires some effort—the last stage from Govindghat is a steep 13km (8-mile) bridle path, which you can negotiate on foot, on muleback, or in a litter carried by porters (roughly a 5-hr. journey). There are marked paths through the valley, but you'll be accompanied by local guides, to make sure you don't trample or pick any flowers.

While Westerners are familiar with the nearby spiritual retreat of Rishikesh (where the Beatles communed with the Maharishi in 1968), Govindghat has important Sikh and Hindu shrines too; many pilgrims visit this valley in conjunction with a temple visit. Whatever deities—or fairies—dwell in this hidden paradise, you'll feel like you're communing with something supernatural up here.

ⓘ **Valley of Flowers National Park,** Ghangria

✈ Dehradun

🚆 Rishikesh

🛏 Various small guesthouses are clustered at both **Ghangria** and **Govindghat.**

TOUR Garhwal Himalayan Explorations (✆ **91/135/244-2267;** www.thegarhwal himalayas.com). **Himalayan Eco Adventure** (✆ **91/988/210-0093** or 91/1902/251-812; www.himalayaneco adventures.com). **GMVN Tours** (✆ **91/135/243-1793;** www. gmvnl.com).

---

217 **Alpine Flowers**

Ben Lawers
Where the Wild Mountain Thyme Grows
Perthshire, Scotland

YEARS OF SHEEP GRAZING AND HUMAN HABITATION NEARLY DESTROYED THIS SCOTTISH MOUNTAIN'S RARE HABITAT FOR ALPINE FLORA. AS THE NATIVE RED DEER RETURN, THEIR NUMBERS MUST BE KEPT IN CHECK.

Ben Lawers isn't the tallest mountain in Scotland—in fact, it's not quite 1,220m (4,000 ft.), though some cunning locals in the 19th century built a cairn on top to boost it over that mark. Its lake, Loch Tay, isn't the Highland's most romantic (that would be Loch Lomond), or most beautiful (Loch Rannoch, its northern neighbor). It doesn't even have a monster, like Loch Ness does.

But this rugged Perthshire peak has a lock on one claim to fame: Botanists say it has the U.K.'s richest display of alpine wildflowers, with 130 species identified so far. By a geologic fluke, Ben Lawers—the tallest peak in the seven-peak Munro range—has schist rocks at just the right altitude to support arctic and alpine flora. From June to August, on the trail to the summit you may see pale blue alpine forget-me-not, frilly golden roseroot, snow pearlwort, blue alpine gentian, the daisylike alpine mouse-ear, and the five-petaled cups of various colored saxifrage, including the almost extinct Highland saxifrage. Fragrant flowering herbs like Alpine lady's mantle, blaeberry, moss campion, and wild mountain thyme perfume the air; peer closer to discover rare lichens, mosses, and liverworts clinging to the rocks. Keep your eye out as well for Ben Lawers's rich bird life—ravens, ring ouzels, curlews, ptarmigans, dippers, and red grouse.

Even if you don't do the full 5-hour climb to the peak (scaling neighboring Beinn Ghlas en route), you can see much of the Alpine vegetation from a sign-posted nature trail near the reserve entrance. You'll begin on a boardwalk over a sample of a rare alkaline bog habitat, then climb a stile and follow Edramucky Burn (that's Scottish for stream); it should take at least an hour to do the full circuit. In July and August rangers lead weekly guided wildflower hikes; call in advance to book a place.

Extensive woodlands restoration has been slowly resuscitating this preserve, after years of being grazed and trampled by flocks of Highland sheep. Native red deer have rebounded so well that the park now must cull the deer herd annually, to keep it at a sustainable level. Yet park ecologists believe that a certain amount of grazing is good for Ben Lawers, since this controls grasses that compete with fragile alpine wildflowers or that could overwhelm the sedges anchoring those rich pockets of fen. Keeping nature in balance—that's the challenge.

ⓘ **Ben Lawers Nature Reserve,** off the A827, 10km (6¼ miles) east from Killin (ⓒ **44/1567/820 397;** www.nts.org.uk/Property/94)

🚂 Crianlarich or Stirling

🛏 $$$ **Kinnaird Estate Cottages,** Dunkeld (ⓒ **44/1796/482-831;** www.kinnaird estate.com). $$ **Ben Lawers Hotel,** A827, Lawers (ⓒ **44/1567/820436;** www.ben lawershotel.co.uk).

Mount Cook National Park
The Buttercup Brigade
South Island, New Zealand

Though it lies well inland, the glaciers that blanket New Zealand's highest mountain shivered and calved icebergs in response to the 2011 earthquake that devastated Christchurch.

In the shadow of New Zealand's highest mountain—the awesome peak where Sir

Edmund Hillary trained before tackling Mount Everest—who has time for a modest

Mount Cook National Park.

little white flower? Most visitors to Mount Cook National Park are in search of much bigger thrills—flight-seeing, downhill skiing, mountaineering, kayaking around glaciers, that sort of thing.

For naturalists, though, spotting a Mount Cook lily is a definite thrill. This rare white flower doesn't grow anywhere else but the Southern Alps of New Zealand's South Island. Yet here, on the sheltered slopes of Mount Cook (or Aoraki, to give it its Maori name), Mount Cook lilies grow by the thousands throughout the New Zealand summer, November through January. Actually, the Mount Cook lily isn't a lily at all but a buttercup—and a giant buttercup at that, growing up to 1m (3¼ ft.) tall with flowers 5 to 8cm (2–3 in.) across, flaunting a double layer of dazzling white petals and conspicuous bright yellow stamens.

It's definitely a moisture-loving plant, which is good, because an awful lot of mist and rain rolls through these mountains, frustrating many a traveler who drove all the way here just to view a famous mountain peak and then move on. At this elevation, more than a third of the park lies under permanent snow cover and glacier

ice—**Tasman Glacier,** New Zealand's longest, lies just east of the summit. (Although this park is nearly 200km/124 miles from the epicenter of the 2011 Christchurch earthquake, the glacier still trembled and sheared off ice chunks in response to that massive quake.) The remaining two-thirds is still mostly above the tree line, making it perfect terrain for alpine flowers. There are 550 species of flora in the park, an overwhelming number of them endemic. Alongside that giant buttercup you'll see mountain daisies, snow gentians, mountain flax, fierce spikes of golden Spaniard, loose clusters of the petite alpine avens, and tiny-flowered South Island edelweiss. Unfortunately, a number of animals introduced long ago for trophy hunting—red stag, fallow deer, Alpine chamois, wapiti—threaten to overrun the park, despite efforts by park rangers to keep them from overbrowsing the alpine meadows.

From the park entrance at Mount Cook Village, a half-day ramble on the **Hooker Valley trail** offers plenty of flower viewing. Along the way, you'll cross two swinging bridges over gorges, pass two pristine lakes, traverse a boardwalk over boggy tussocks, and wind up right at the frosty face of a glacier—probably encountering along the way at least a couple of keas, those nervy olive-green mountain parrots that are Mount Cook's unofficial mascots. Is that enough adventure for you?

(i) **Mount Cook National Park,** Bowen Dr., Mount Cook Village ((C) **64/3/435-1186;** www.doc.govt.nz)

✈ Mount Cook

🛏 $$–$$$ **Hermitage Hotel,** Terrace Rd., Mount Cook Village ((C) **64/3/435-1809;** www.mount-cook.com). $ **Mount Cook YHA Hostel,** Kitchener and Bowen Dr., Mount Cook Village ((C) **64/3/435-1820;** www.yha.org.nz).

Alpine Flowers **219**

Grandfather Mountain
Heavenly Flowers
Blue Ridge Mountains, North Carolina

IN FEBRUARY 2011, THIS POPULAR NORTH CAROLINA PARK WAS CLOSED WHILE INVESTIGATORS searched bat caves for the deadly white-nose fungus; the woolly hemlock adelgid is another invader, a tiny insect that ravages old-growth forests.

Grandfather Mountain.

"The face of all Heaven come to earth"—that's how naturalist John Muir described Grandfather Mountain when he first encountered it in 1898. Granted, Muir tended to rhapsodize about nature, but in the case of Grandfather Mountain, he was right on the mark. One of the world's oldest peaks—geologists estimate its glittering quartzite rock is more than a billion years old—at 5,964 feet (1,818m), Grandfather towers above its neighbors, the patriarch of the Blue Ridge range.

Grandfather Mountain looks rugged and forbidding indeed—winters can be harsh and snowy, and even in summer wind buffets the mountainside and thick fog rolls in regularly. Upland trees and shrubs are stunted and hardy, a surprising subalpine environment for this far south. Fierce birds of prey soar on its updrafts, even rare species like the Cooper's hawk, shark-shinned hawk, and peregrine falcon. Large flocks of bats swoop in and out of its caves—although like most Eastern parks, Grandfather Mountain has detected traces of the white-nose fungus, which could rapidly decimate the bat population, throwing off the entire food chain.

But get closer and you'll find Grandpa has a softer side as well. Those jumbled rocks and crevices shelter more globally rare species than any other mountain east of the Rockies. Many are liverworts, lichens, and mosses, which love its cool, damp mountain climate and acidic soil. Several others are delicate mountain flowers, like the spreading avens, bent avens, mountain bittercress, the roan mountain bluet, Gray's lily, Heller's blazing star, and late summer's dainty Blue Ridge goldenrod.

Despite the rugged landscape, this has been developed as a tourist attraction since the 1950s, with a restaurant, an old-school nature museum, and plenty of picnic areas. The park's most popular site—the **Mile High Swinging Bridge,** the highest suspension footbridge in America—is reachable by elevator, as well as an easy half-mile trail that's gaudy with rare azaleas in late spring. Bird-watchers may prefer the **Black Rock Nature Trail,** rambling through a hardwood forest full of songbirds—red-breasted nuthatches, winter wrens, hermit thrushes, magnolia warblers, and chestnut-sided warblers, not to mention the sharp rat-a-tat-tat of the yellow-bellied sapsucker. Yet some of the park's trails are very strenuous—in a couple of places, ladders have been built to scale steep spots—and the ever-changing landscape rewards hikers for their efforts. The full spectrum of habitats unfolds on the 2.7-mile (4.3km) **Profile Trail** (trail head off Hwy. 105 near Banner Elk). Climbing gradually from streambed forests with dense thickets of rhododendron, the trail passes through hardwood and hemlock forest, on to bald heath, and at last—*voilà!*—the naked rocks where those rare mountaintop flowers have been hiding all along.

ⓘ **Grandfather Mountain,** 2050 Blowing Rock Hwy., Linville, NC (✆ **800/468-7325** or 828/733-4337; www.grandfather.com)

✈ Asheville

🛏 $$ **Holiday Inn Express,** 1943 Blowing Rock Rd., Boone (✆ **888/465-4329** or 828/264-2451; www.hiexpress.com). $$ **Best Western Mountain Lodge,** 1615 Tynecastle Hwy., Banner Elk (✆ **828/898-4571;** www.bestwesternnorthcarolina.com).

220 Alpine Flowers

The Slopes of Mount Haleakala
Aloha High & Wild
Maui, Hawaii

HOME TO MORE THREATENED SPECIES THAN ANY OTHER U.S. NATIONAL PARK, HALEAKALA maintains fences to keep out the feral goats, deer, and pigs that have stripped bare neighboring landscapes. Keeping out a $30-million solar telescope was another question.

Don't let the lush plantings of Hawaii's luxury resorts fool you—most of those poolside frangipani and birds of paradise and other tropical blooms are transplants that have displaced native flowers. In fact, Hawaii lists more endangered native species than any other U.S. state. Especially on Maui, resort development has destroyed habitat at a fearful rate—no wonder tourist leis nowadays are generally made of silk or plastic flowers.

Isolated in the middle of the Pacific Ocean, the Hawaiian Islands had an enormous number of endemic species to start with. But they're now so besieged, even the state flower, the yellow hibiscus *(pua aloalo),* is endangered. Hawaiians see this shrub's blossoms as symbols of

10 Places Where the Bighorns Still Climb

Once there were two million bighorn sheep in North America; by the early 20th century, hunting and diseases contracted from domestic sheep had reduced their numbers to only a few thousand. Since the 1960s, hunting bans, habitat protection, and reintroductions have begun to restore all three subspecies: Rocky Mountain bighorn sheep, desert (or Nelson's) bighorn sheep, and the most endangered of all, Sierra Nevada (or California) bighorns. Bring your binoculars to spot these shy creatures on their hillside ranges in the following parks:

221 Anza-Borrego Desert State Park, California Anza-Borrego was specifically set aside as a habitat for desert bighorn sheep, which have lighter coats, longer legs, and smaller bodies than their Rocky Mountain cousins. Most likely viewing spots: the overlook on Montezuma Valley Road (S22) in summer, the summit of Yaqui Road (S3) in winter and spring, the entrance to Tamarisk Grove campground, and along the Borrego Palm Canyon Nature Trail. *760/767-5311. www.parks.ca.gov.*

Joshua Tree National Park.

222 Joshua Tree National Park, California Considering all the human rock climbers in this stunning Mojave desert park, it's no surprise that four-legged rock climbers like the desert bighorn would thrive. When grass is scarce—as it often is—the herd of about 250 bighorns browse on cactuses. Most sightings occur around the jumbled granite Wonderland of Rocks, though larger herds live in the remote Eagle Mountains to the east and in the Little San Bernardino Mountains. *760/367-5500. www.nps.gov/jotr.*

223 Mount Williamson Preserve, California Part of the John Muir Wilderness, this bighorn sheep preserve protects one of only two native populations of Sierra Nevada bighorn sheep, in a 4-mile-wide (6.4km) strip of preserve that stretches north for miles along the east face of Mount Williamson, California's second-highest mountain. In 2010, the preserve was finally opened year-round to visitors; there are no roads but you can hike up the Shepherd's Pass trail. *www.sierranevadawild. gov/wild/john-muir.*

224 Kofa National Wildlife Refuge, Yuma, Arizona A "save the bighorns" campaign mounted by the Arizona Boy Scouts in 1936 inspired the state to establish this refuge on a rugged stretch of Sonoran Desert backcountry. Today some 1,000 desert bighorns scramble around the Kofa and Castle Dome mountains, low ranges where hikers can explore old mines and hidden waterholes created for the bighorns. Warning: It can be brutally hot in summer. *928/783-7861. www.fws.gov.*

225 Canyonlands National Park, Moab, Utah   One of the country's few native herds of desert bighorn sheep survived on the slopes of this dramatic high desert plateau, carved into intriguing shapes by the Colorado River. Their numbers have grown from barely 100 in the 1960s to some 350 today. Hike into the side canyons to view them, foraging on the scrubby vegetation of the steep, rocky terrain. ✆ **435/719-2313.** www.nps.gov/cany.

226 Georgetown Wildlife Viewing Area, Colorado   Rocky Mountain bighorn sheep are Colorado's state symbol, easy to spot even outside the big parks. Just outside this beautifully preserved silver-mining town, on the shores of Georgetown Lake, an observation platform with spotting scopes homes in on the 300 to 400 sheep that've settled on its rock-strewn hillsides. www.colorado.com/Georgetown.aspx.

227 Whiskey Mountain Habitat Area, Wyoming   The National Bighorn Sheep Center in Dubois, Wyoming, has an interpretive center devoted to the Rocky Mountain bighorns that winter on this windswept range. From November to March, the center offers guided 4WD tours of the preserve; they'll also give you instructions for a 6.6-mile (10.6km) self-guided driving tour. ✆ **888/209-2795** or 307/455-3429. www.bighorn.org.

228 Koo Koo Sint Viewing Area, Montana   On Highway 200 just 6 miles (10km) east of Thompson Falls, a roadside pullout offers ringside seats for Rocky Mountain bighorns' autumn mating rituals. Female sheep coming down from their summer mountain habitat meet roaming males in this mountain meadow; watch the amorous males go head-to-head to win their mates. www.travelmt.com.

229 Banff National Park, Alberta   The Rocky Mountain bighorn sheep population thrives in the wilds of western Canada, where habitat loss is not as significant as in other parks. You can often see them grazing right by the roadside of Highway 93, the Icefields Parkway from Banff to Jasper (keep a watch out when passing through steep rocky road cuts), or the quieter parallel route Highway 1A, the Bow Valley Parkway. ✆ **403/762-1550.** www.pc.gc.ca.

Banff National Park.

230 Vaseux Protected Area, British Columbia   After the last ice age, a few Sierra Madre bighorn sheep migrated north into southeastern British Columbia. The largest surviving herd of them lives here, on the rocky bluffs and subalpine grasslands around mountain-ringed Vaseux Lake. Follow old logging access roads into the protected area, then follow hiking trails to explore along Vaseux Creek and McIntyre Canyon. www.env.gov.bc.ca/bcparks.

the human soul—blooming pale yellow in the morning, they darken in color throughout the day and wither by nightfall. The yellow hibiscus now lives only in three enclosed sites on Maui, where browsing deer can't find them. (Look for cultivated specimens at the upcountry **Kula Botanical Garden,** Hwy. 377; 🕾 **808/878-1715;** www.kulabotanicalgarden.com).

Resort development is one thing, but atop the summit of the world's largest dormant volcano, Mount Haleakala, is an even more jarring development: The University of Hawaii's Science City, a cluster of high-tech observatories taking advantage of Haleakala's altitude and clear skies. In 2010, a 7-year construction project began for yet another, the Advanced Solar Technology Telescope. Native Hawaiians protested this further desecration of their sacred mountain, but the National Science Foundation has modified its plan for least impact on the native flora and fauna; though winding Haleakala Crater Road will be widened for construction, its original width will be restored once the work is done. "Least impact" is a relative term, however, and naturalists remain skeptical.

For the slopes of Haleakala are known as a safe haven for native plants—90% of its flora is endemic to Hawaii. Down near the park entrance, the half-mile **Hosmer Grove Nature Trail** winds through a cool fern-draped cloud forest where you can see rare native silver geraniums—*nohoanu*—with their satiny white petals. Head to the summit along the dramatic switchbacks of **Haleakala Crater Road**

and you see a different landscape entirely, jagged flats of red and black lava rock where it seems nothing could grow. But at the **Kalahaku Overlook** (accessible only on the drive down) you will see, bristling improbably from this cinder desert, the truly bizarre silversword plant. Overcollected almost to extinction, silverswords need time to mature: For up to 50 years, it's a simple sphere of spear-sharp silvery leaves, until at last a spiky stalk shoots up, often taller than a human, with a sunflowerlike head of tiny purple blooms.

Hikers on the **Halemau'u Trail** can turn off on the Silversword Loop, about 10 miles (16km) up the trail, to see even more of these *Star Trek*–ish marvels. When you're on foot, Haleakala's upland shrub lands really reveal their variety—the yellow pea blossoms of the *mamane* shrub, the drooping lavender bellflowers of the blackberrylike *'akala,* or the coffeelike black berries of rambling *kukaenene,* favorite food of the Hawaiian goose. While the telescopes at the top scan the skies, what will happen to these modest creatures on the ground?

ⓘ **Haleakala National Park,** Maui, Hwy. 378 🕾 **808/572-4400;** www.nps.gov/hale)

✈ Kahului

🛏 $$ **Banyan Tree House,** 3265 Baldwin Ave., Makawao (🕾 **808/572-9021;** www.bed-breakfast-maui.com). $$ **Hale Ho'okipa Inn,** 32 Pakani Place, Makawao (🕾 **808/572-6698;** www.maui-bed-and-breakfast.com).

Volcanoes **231**

Mount Rainier National Park
Flood Cascades Through the Cascades
Ashford, Washington

IN THE FALL OF 2006, A MASSIVE FLOOD CLOSED MOUNT RAINIER NP FOR 6 MONTHS, WASHING out several roads, trails, and buildings; streams changed courses so radically, some park features may never reopen.

You can see Mount Rainier from the Puget Sound ferries, a snow-capped peak looming like a backdrop to the Seattle skyline, towering above the rest of the Cascades' range. It's an impressive postcard vista—but just wait until you get to the park itself (an easy day trip from Seattle, little more than an hour away) and start exploring.

Mount Rainier has been hit with a double-whammy: It's a volcano—dormant, but still not extinct—that's also wreathed in glaciers. Between glacial retreat and volcanic rumblings, the landscape is constantly being reshaped. Jagged basaltic lava rocks lie tumbled in the beds of mountain streams pouring crystal-clear waters off of the glaciers; wildflowers spangle new meadows as the glacier line recedes; down along the Ohanapecosh River, a grove of immense ancient Douglas firs and western red cedars awaits the next flood or landslide.

It's a big park, so of course it has a lot of wildlife—mountain goats, black-tailed deer, elk, cougars, black bears, the whole mountain crew. Over the many years since 1899, when Rainier was made a national park, the resident animals have largely lost their fear of humans. Pull out your binoculars to see mountain goats (which are, technically speaking, antelopes, not goats) scamper from rock to rock on Goat Island Mountain, on **Mount Fremont,** and at **Skyscraper Pass,** all reachable on trails leading from Sunrise Point. Hike through a flowered subalpine meadow and you'll see playful marmots—big, shaggy cousins to squirrels—loll on the rocks, catching some rays, seemingly oblivious to human observers. While you're up there, you may even be able to catch a glimpse of the shy pikas, tiny rabbit relatives that inhabit rocky talus slopes. If you don't see them, you may at least hear their strange high-pitched beeping call.

Vulcanologists estimate it'll be another 500 years before Rainier's set to erupt again. But even if there is no lava flow, these precipitous glacier-mantled slopes are prone to flooding and debris flow. At any point during your visit to Mount Rainier, you may notice a sudden rise in river levels, earth tremors, or a rumbling noise from up valley—all signs that a landslide of glacial debris is heading your way. The park even has a siren system to warn visitors; if you hear one blare, hurry immediately to higher ground.

ⓘ **Mount Rainier National Park,** Nisqually-Longmire Rd., Ashford, WA (✆**360/569-2211;** www.nps.gov/mora)

✈Seattle

🛏$$ **Paradise Inn,** near Paradise visitor center inside park (✆ **360/569-2275;** www.mtrainierguestservices.com). $$ **Stone Creek Lodge,** 38624 State Rd. 706 E., Ashford (✆**800/819-3942** or 360/569-2355; www.stonecreeklodge.net).

Mount Rainier National Park.

Mount Taylor
Turquoise Mountain
Northwestern New Mexico

THE 2009 LISTING OF MOUNT TAYLOR AS A TRADITIONAL CULTURAL PROPERTY MAY SAVE Mount Taylor from new uranium mining, which would damage the mountain itself and contaminate the nearby San Jose River.

The quadrathletes come every winter. Beginning in the old logging town of Grants, they hop on road bikes and pedal madly uphill, ditching the bikes when the road turns to gravel. Then they run uphill for a while, jump on cross-country skis for the next leg, and end up with a mile of hectic snowshoeing to the summit of Mount Taylor—where they whip around and reverse the sequence, racing back to the starting line, a 42-mile (68km) round-trip.

In summer, however, things are more relaxed. Hikers drive an hour west from Albuquerque to the trail head for the **Gooseberry Springs Trail,** a 3.5-mile (5.6km) hike that climbs a gentle 2,100 feet (630m) to the summit. Though the lower slopes are cloaked in aspen and the top in ponderosa pine, for much of the ascent open grassy slopes afford lofty views of the vast mesa-studded plateau. An extinct volcano, Mount Taylor stands alone above the high desert plain, its many-peaked crest and scooped upper valley a ghost of its ancient preeruption heights. Yet it's still the highest peak in northwestern New Mexico, and when you get to the top, you'll catch your breath with a stunning panorama, stretching for miles in every direction.

Standing awed by nature is really what Mount Taylor is all about. Though in 1849 it was named to honor then-President Zachary Taylor, to the ancient Acoma people it is revered as Kaweshtima, or "place of snow" (it's still snowcapped much of the year). To the Laguna people, it is "Tsibina," or "mother veiled in clouds"; to the Hopi, "Tsiipiya," or "cloud ancestors"; to the Zuni, "Dwankwi Kyabachu Yalanne," or "home of the rainmaker spirits." To the

Navajos, it is "Tsoodzil," or "turquoise mountain," the southern one of the Four Sacred Mountains. It's a site of pilgrimage for 30 different Native American peoples, with archaeological relics and shrines scattered around its slopes and ritual blessing places on its peak.

In the **Cibola National Forest,** which includes Mount Taylor, restored grassland, piñon-juniper forest, and subalpine conifer forest have covered the scars of 19th- and 20th-century logging and grazing. But Mount Taylor also happens to sit atop one of the country's richest deposits of uranium ore, which sparked mining booms in the 1950s and 1970s. Amid rising demands for nuclear power, new mining applications have been filed to drill and explore the area. Besides ravaging the mountain itself, mining would contaminate the Rio San Jose (which is even more sacred to the Acoma). Five Pueblo tribes have fought back, persuading the state in 2009 to designate Mount Taylor as a Traditional Cultural Property. Lawsuits and countersuits have flown back and forth; now the courts must decide.

(i) **Cibola National Forest,** Mount Taylor Ranger District (C) **505/287-8833;** www.fs.fed.us/r3/cibola)

✈ Albuquerque

🛏 $$ **Cimarron Rose Bed & Breakfast,** 689 Oso Ridge Rd. (Scenic Rte. 53), Grants, NM (C) **800/856-5776** or 505/783-4770; www.cimarronrose.com). $$$ **Los Poblanos Inn,** 4803 Rio Grande NW, Los Ranchos de Albuquerque, NM (C) **505/344-9297;** www.lospoblanos.com).

Hawaii Volcanoes National Park
Where There's Smoke . . .
Volcano, Hawaii

HAWAII VOLCANOES NATIONAL PARK IS A LANDSCAPE IN MOTION—OFTEN QUITE LITERALLY, AS two of the world's most active volcanoes, Kilauea and Mauna Loa, continue to erupt and pour molten lava into the sea.

Dormant volcano? Think again. Since 1983, the Big Island's Kilauea Volcano has been erupting constantly. Generally these are "quiet" eruptions, with slow-moving red lava oozing over the landscape, occasionally even spilling over the park roads. As recently as March 2011, however, molten lava in a remote corner of the park erupted as high as 80 feet (24m) in the air, while a nearby crater floor collapsed with plumes of gray smoke. Though no one was hurt this time, over the past 25 years some $100 million worth of property has been destroyed by Kilauea's eruptions, while the lava flow has also added 560 acres (227 hectares) of new land. It's a landscape in continual, violent flux, as beautiful as it is frightening.

Near the park's visitor center, you can view the **Kilauea Caldera,** a 2½-mile-wide (4km), 500-foot-deep (150m) pit with wisps of steam rising from it. Going counter-clockwise on Crater Rim Road, you'll drive past the Sulphur Banks, which smell like rotten eggs, and the Steam Vents, fissures where trails of smoke, once molten lava, escape like sighs from the inner reaches of the earth. At the **Thomas A. Jaggar**

Lava flow at Hawaii Volcanoes National Park.

Museum there's a viewpoint for Halemaumau Crater, which is half a mile (.8km) across but 1,000 feet (300m) deep; walk right to the rim to gape at this once-fuming old fire pit, which still gives off some fierce heat out of its vents. Near the Kilauea Iki Crater, the .5-mile (.8km) Devastation Trail is a sobering walk across a desolate treeless cinder field, where a volcanic eruption wreaked havoc in 1959. By the Thurston Lava Tube Overlook, however, you'll see a softer side of this volcanic landscape, a misty verdant fern forest springing up on the lip of a crater, around an ancient lava tube cave. At the far end of the Chain of Craters Road lies Puu Loa, an ancient site considered sacred to the volcano goddess Pele, where a .5-mile (.8km) boardwalk loop trail reveals thousands of mysterious Hawaiian petroglyphs.

If the volcano is actively erupting, call the visitor center for directions to the best locations for night viewing—it's quite a sight to see, as brilliant red lava snakes down the side of the mountain and pours into the sea. **Blue Hawaiian Helicopter** (② 800/745-2583 or 808/871-1107; www.bluehawaiian.com) runs several tours right over the bubbling caldera, for a bird's-eye view you'll never forget.

ⓘ **Hawaii Volcanoes National Park,** Hawaii Belt Rd. (Hwy. 11), Volcano, HI (② **808/985-6000;** www.nps.gov/havo)

✈ Hilo

🛏 $$ **Kilauea Lodge,** 19-3948 Old Volcano Rd., Volcano Village (② **808/967-7366;** www.kilauealodge.com). $$ **Naniloa Volcanoes Resort,** 93 Banyan Dr., Hilo (② **808/969-3333;** www.hottours.us).

Volcanoes **234**

Rotorua
Land of Mists
North Island, New Zealand

THOUGH GEYSER ACTIVITY HAS BEEN TAPERING OFF ON THE NORTH ISLAND, SEVERAL GEYSERS continue to play regularly around this geothermal valley, presided over by the active volcano of Mount Tarawera.

There's something unsettling about the landscape around Rotorua—the sulfuric "rotten eggs" aroma, the steam hissing out of fissures in the earth, the volcano peak of Mount Tarawera in the hazy distance. In this case, human actions aren't to blame for the fluctuations in the environment; it's just life as usual in the spa town of Rotorua.

Rotorua has been a spa destination since the 19th century, when the Te Arawa people (the local population is still about one-third Maori) began guiding visitors to the picturesque Pink and White Terraces, spectacular limestone formations—some called them the "Eighth Wonder of the World"—

on the shores of silica-rich Lake Rotomahana. Afterward, tourists "took the waters" at the region's many hot springs. Then came the big event of 1886, when Mount Tarawera erupted, spewing much more lava than Mount St. Helens later would in 1980. The Terraces were annihilated, the local landscape radically reshaped. Tarawera is still visible 24km (15 miles) southeast of town, a massive hump of lava domes cleft down the middle by the force of the 1886 eruption. **Volcanic Air Safaris** (② **64/7/348-9984;** www.volcanicair.co.nz) offers helicopter rides over the crater.

While the spas are still popular, nowadays geothermal attractions are Rotorua's strongest tourism draw. Right in town, there's the **Whakarewarewa Thermal Reserve (Te Puia),** on Hemo Road, a rocky landscape full of mud pools, and the Pohutu Geyser, which shoots upward 16 to 20m (52–66 ft.) 10 to 20 times a day. South of town on Highway 5, you can see the **Buried Village of Te Wairoa,** excavated after the 1886 eruption; **Waimangu Volcanic Valley,** with the world's largest hot-water spring and the mysterious rising and falling turquoise lake in Inferno Crater; and **Waiotapu,** where you can see the Lady Knox Geyser, New Zealand's largest bubbling mud pool, and arsenic-green Devils' Bath. The fiercest of the thermal valleys is northeast of town on Highway 30: the Maori-owned **Hell's Gate,** which has hot-water lakes, sulfur formations, Rotorua's only mud volcano, and the largest boiling whirlpool in New Zealand.

Perhaps the most sobering sight is in the middle of the city: **Kuirau Park,** off Pukuatua and Ranolf streets, dotted with hot bubbling mud pools. There are still active vents smoldering up at Tarawera. As recently as 2000, a spontaneous eruption blasted the park; you can still see the dead trees in a cordoned-off area. Take nothing for granted.

ⓘ **Rotorua visitor center,** 1167 Fenton St. (✆ **64/7/348-5179;** www.rotorua.co.nz)
✈ Rotorua
🛏 $$ **Rydges Rotorua,** 272 Fenton St. (✆ **64/7/349-0900;** www.rydges.com). $$ **Wylie Court Motor Lodge,** 345 Fenton St. (✆ **64/7/347-7879;** http://new.wylie court.co.nz).

---

235 Volcanoes

Mount Kilimanjaro
Snow Today, Not Tomorrow?
Tanzania

THE FAMOUS SNOWS ATOP AFRICA'S MOUNT KILIMANJARO—THE WORLD'S HIGHEST FREE-standing mountain—could disappear as soon as 2025, eradicated by drier climate and higher temperatures.

The Masai tribesmen called it **Oldoinyo Oibor,** or "White Mountain." In Swahili, it's Kilima Njaro, or "Shining Mountain." Ernest Hemingway titled his famous short story "The Snows of Kilimanjaro." Clearly, those majestic snow-capped peaks are what make this extinct volcano the most famous mountain in Africa, beyond the fact that it's the continent's highest peak. That snowy plateau, 4,600m (15,100 ft.) above the Tanzanian plains just south of Kenya, is a mesmerizing sight indeed—here, in equatorial Africa, is a mountaintop with *snow.*

Yet over the past century, Kilimanjaro has lost 85% of its glacial ice cap, which is rapidly getting thinner as well as shrinking in area. Rising temperatures, especially at

this latitude, cause increased surface melt, which decreased snowfall fails to replenish. One once-popular route to the top, the Umbwe (Western Breach) route, is now rarely used because of rock slides caused by receding ice. What will go next?

Nearly 30,000 climbers a year attempt to climb Kilimanjaro, straining quotas set by park management. At least a quarter of those fail to reach the top; every year a few die, from hypothermia, falls, or rock slides. As world-class peaks go, it's relatively straightforward—not a technical climb, but a strenuous, steep multiday hike, made even more physically challenging by the extreme altitude. You'll pass through four different climate zones. First comes the

227

lush, steamy **Kilimanjaro Forest Reserve** surrounding the base; then the grassy moorlands of the shouldering slopes; above 3,900m (12,800 ft.), the mountain suddenly becomes steeper and more barren, with rocky scree underfoot. Last of all, you hit what's left of the glacial ice fields, dazzling in the reflected African sun.

There are several routes to the summit. The 5-day **Marangu Route**—nicknamed the Coca-Cola Trail—is currently most popular; it starts from the Marangu Park Gate. The **Lemosho Trail,** which begins at Londorossi Gate, is easier and more scenic, though it takes 9 days. Whichever route you take, you must obtain park permits and hut reservations in advance (available through a licensed tour operator or local hotels in Moshi); at the park gate you'll hire a guide, and possibly a porter (you won't be allowed on the mountain without a guide). Park fees are substantial, but they include overnight hut accommodation on the mountain; guides and porters ask ridiculously low wages, hoping for generous tips on top. If you book with a tour operator (recommended), your package will include most of this, along with a cook to prepare all meals en route.

ⓘ **Kilimanjaro National Park,** Tanzania (www.tanzaniaparks.com)

✈ Kilimanjaro International

TOUR Destination Africa Tours (✆ **27/ 12/333-7114;** www.climbingkilimanjaro. com). **Roy Safaris** (✆ **255/27/2502115;** www.roysafaris.com). **Tanzania Serengeti Adventure** (✆ **255/73/297-5210;** www.tanzania-adventure.com).

8 Prairie, Plain & Desert

Death Valley.

American Prairie Reserve

Malta, Montana

FOUNDED IN 2004, THIS INNOVATIVE RESERVE SEEKS TO PROVIDE CRITICAL HABITAT FOR ENDANgered prairie species—pronghorn antelopes, long-billed curlews, swift foxes, blackfooted ferrets, and American bison.

Watch them course over the plains, at speeds of up to 60 miles per hour (97kmh): pronghorn antelope, North America's fastest land mammals. Trouble is, these wide-roaming creatures require large areas of intact prairie, which don't exist in modern-day North America. Pronghorn are considered an "indicator species" of healthy prairie habitat, along with species like the endangered long-billed curlew, North America's largest shorebird, which breeds on short or mixed grasslands. Growing numbers of both species prove that good things are happening on the American Prairie Reserve.

It's an interesting conservation model. Since 2004, the privately funded APR has been buying up ranchland in northeast Montana's glaciated hills; fences and creek dams are knocked down and vegetation is replanted to replace alfalfa monocultures. So far APR has acquired more than 123,000 acres (50,000 hectares) adjacent to the existing 1.1 million-acre (445,000-hectare) Charles M. Russell National Wildlife Refuge (containing the Fort Peck Reservoir, the fifth-largest man-made lake in the U.S.). The plan is to expand the reserve to 3-plus million acres (1.2 million hectares), larger than Yellowstone National Park. Although some local ranchers oppose what they see as a "land grab," those same ranchers have been inspired to become more conscientious stewards of their acreage, often partnering with the Nature Conservancy. It's all good news for the habitat.

True, it is a challenge to visit this preserve, miles from any airport along gravel roads that rains turn to a sticky glop nicknamed "gumbo." (Four-wheel drive is essential.) At first glance the landscape seems like a dull flat sweep of scrubby grass, but it's a species-rich ecosystem that rewards closer acquaintance. Visitors can hike, snowshoe, hunt, fish, or camp out on the reserve; trails for horseback riding and mountain biking are being developed, and there are plans to offer sightseeing plane flights and safari expeditions (underscoring the comparison to Africa's Serengeti). It's a fine bird-watching destination, with some 180 species documented, from hawks to songbirds; the reserve is also home to several prairie dog towns and a growing herd of more than 200 American bison, reintroduced to the area. Come here in September or October to watch the drama of rutting elk; on a spring dawn, you may even catch sage grouses at their unique courting ritual, called a lek.

There's evidence of human habitation on the prairie lands as well—petroglyphs at the **Indian Rock Cultural Site;** a traditional Buffalo Jump where Plains Indians herded bison off cliffs to harvest their fur, hides, and meat; and the restored Prairie Union School, a one-room log schoolhouse where grades one through eight were educated from 1943 to 1956. In the nearest town, Malta, some 40 miles (64km) from the reserve's entrance, you can learn about dinosaurs, pioneer farmers, and the native tribes at the **Phillips County Museum** and adjacent **Great Plains Dinosaur Museum.**

ⓘ**American Prairie Reserve,** Holzhey Ranch Rd., near Malta, MT (ℂ **877/273-1123;** www.americanprairie.org)

✈Lewiston

🛏 $ **Fourchette Bay Campground,** Fort Peck Lake, Charles M. Russell Wildlife Refuge (ℂ **406/526-3411**). $$ **Maltana Motel,** 138 S. 1st Ave. W., Malta (ℂ**406/654-2610**).

Kennebunk Plains Preserve
Where Blazing Star Still Blazes
West Kennebunk, Maine

UNDER PRESSURE FROM URBAN SPRAWL, WILDLIFE HABITATS IN SOUTHERN COASTAL MAINE NEED protection—especially a one-of-a-kind eco-niche like the Kennebunk Plains.

Come here in late summer and you can't miss it: a wide expanse of grassland spangled with vivid purple wildflowers. It's known as the northern blazing star, and you won't find it anywhere else in Maine—or hardly anywhere else in the world. This 135-acre (55-hectare) parcel of land holds a virtual monopoly on the northern blazing star, with an estimated 90% of the world's specimens.

Kennebunk Plains is an oddball landscape for New England anyway. Such a classic prairie habitat hardly ever exists so close to the ocean—many of the plants that thrive here, such as little bluestem grass, are common out on the Great Plains but unknown in Maine. And though this parcel is open to the public to walk around in, you'll notice that the protected grasslands extend well beyond the preserve's borders, occupying some 2,000 acres (800 hectares) of coastal plain with their deep deposits of sand, not washed up from the sea but dumped by ancient glaciers.

Working with the Maine Department of Inland Fisheries and Wildlife, the Nature Conservancy deliberately starts small fires—known as "prescribed burns"—on the preserve at periodic intervals, to scale back outlying patches of pitch pine and scrub oak forest. It's an ancient land-management strategy, the same used by Native Americans when they raised blueberries on this plain. By preserving the old ways, the Kennebunk Plains' 21st-century stewards hope to preserve this last remnant of what once was a common ecosystem.

Several rare or endangered bird species have found a haven on these unusual grasslands, including grasshopper sparrows, upland sandpipers, vesper sparrows, and horned larks. Black racer snakes thrive here too, one of only two known populations in the state. That's what happens when you get an oddball landscape—it enables entirely different species to thrive where they otherwise wouldn't. That's what diversity's all about.

ⓘ **Kennebunk Plains Preserve,** Hwy. 99, West Kennebunk, ME

✈Portland

🛏 $$$ **The Colony Hotel,** 140 Ocean Ave., Kennebunkport (ℂ**800/552-2363** or 207/967-3331; www.thecolonyhotel.com/maine). $$ **Yachtsman Lodge,** Ocean Ave., Kennebunkport (ℂ **207/967-2511;** www.yachtsmanlodge.com).

The Agassiz Dunes Preserves
Dances with Prairie Chickens
Fertile, Minnesota

INVASIVE PLANT SPECIES THREATEN THIS RARE GRASSLAND ECOSYSTEM, WHILE HABITAT FRAGMENTATION leaves small isolated populations of prairie chickens without a chance for healthy genetic mixing.

Once upon a time, a great glacial lake shimmered across the upper Midwest, west of today's Great Lakes. When the waters receded, a vast flat prairie land remained, where bison grazed, prairie dogs burrowed, and hawks circled overhead. Then the settlers came to plow it all under. But what could they do with the ridges and "blow-outs" (inland sand dunes) that had once been glacial Lake Agassiz's shoreline? That hilly, dry, infertile terrain wouldn't support much except tough grasses and gnarled bur oaks. Useless.

Ecologists finally noticed the Sand Hills, and realized they had a treasure on their hands. In early spring, pasque flowers run wild over the rippling terrain; in late summer, blazing stars, purple coneflowers, and sunflowers add vibrant color. Even more important, patches of rare habitat inevitably become havens for rare species—like the Poweshiek skipper butterfly, vesper sparrows, upland sandpipers, red-headed woodpeckers, ruffed grouse, or the plains pocket gopher.

And where you've got ancient prairie, you just may get the greater prairie chicken. Nature designed this endangered bird to live in mixed-grass plains, with its intricately barred plumage for camouflage and its ground forager's diet of insects, seeds, and fruits. Prairie chickens shuttle back and forth from the tall, dense grass, where they hide their nests in late spring, to more open short-grass prairie, where hatchlings peck around in summer. The most arresting sight comes in April or May on the short grass, as adult males perform their fascinating courtship dance—drumming their feet, ballooning out their orange neck patches, and letting loose a booming call you can hear a mile away.

The greater prairie chicken is in trouble (though not so bad as its cousins, the now-extinct heath hen and nearly extinct Attwater's prairie hen). With little grassland left, the last prairie chickens live in small isolated populations that inevitably become weakened by inbreeding. That's why ecologists are studying the population that roosts around Fertile, Minnesota: some on the 640-acre (259-hectare) **Agassiz Environmental Learning Center (AELC)** on the edge of town, and others on the 417-acre (169-hectare) **Agassiz Dunes Natural and Scientific Area** a couple miles south of town. The AELC is better geared for visitors, with interpretive displays at its Nature Center, a botanical garden of native plants, and 10 miles (16km) of trails for hiking, horseback riding, or cross-country skiing. It's a little quieter and more undeveloped out at the Agassiz Dunes NSA, where the greater prairie chickens are more in evidence. If you're lucky, you may even catch that spring mating dance.

ⓘ **Agassiz Environmental Learning Center,** 400 Summit Ave. SW, Fertile, MN 📞 **218/945-3129;** http://aelcfertile.org). **Agassiz Dunes Natural and Scientific Area,** off Hwy. 32, Fertile, MN (www.nature.org).

✈ Bemidji

🛏 **$$ AmericInn Lodge & Suites,** 1821 University Ave., Crookston, MN 📞 **800/634-3444** or 218/281-7800; www.americinn.com). $$ **Super 8 Motel,** 108 S. Amber, Fosston, MN 📞 **888/288-5081** or 218/435-1088; www.super8.com).

239 Prairie Wildlife

Badlands National Park
Big News in Prairie Dog Town
Southwest South Dakota

SEVERAL ENDANGERED SPECIES HAVE BEEN REINTRODUCED TO THE BADLANDS—BIGHORN sheep, shaggy bison, the swift fox, black-faced ferrets—but invasive plant species continue to threaten this extreme landscape.

The Badlands aren't so bad, really—just misunderstood. This windswept, treeless plain, carved by erosion into jagged spires and buttes and deep-gouged canyons, must have been hell for the early Sioux Indians and French-Canadian trappers to traverse; no wonder they slapped a disparaging moniker on it. But precisely because the land was impossible to farm, today it's the country's largest surviving stand of mixed-grass prairie, a complex tapestry of nearly 50 different kinds of grasses, from the tall big bluestem to the short buffalo grass, along with a summertime profusion of wildflowers.

Where you've got prairie, you ought to have prairie dogs, of course. For close-up views, follow Sage Creek Rim Road along the northern edge of the park to **Roberts Prairie Dog Town,** a 300-acre (121-hectare) complex of burrows set up for observation. Along with some 6,000 black-tailed prairie dogs, you may see another rare prairie dweller: the black-footed ferret, with its long weasel body and raccoonlike face. Said to be the most endangered mammal in North America, the black-footed ferret was actually ruled extinct in 1979, until a few survivors were discovered

in Wyoming. Biologists bred the last 18 of them in captivity, then reintroduced 36 captive-bred ferrets here in 1995. It's now estimated that there are 250 in the park and surrounding areas. With so little prairie habitat left, this is one of the last places

Badlands National Park.

this native ferret can thrive—especially since its main food is prairie dogs, another rapidly waning species.

Drive the park's 30-mile (48km) **Loop Road** along the Badlands wall, a massed series of spires and ridges that rise abruptly from the prairie floor, where pronghorn antelope, mule deer, and shaggy bison graze; bighorn sheep can be spotted on the rocky slopes. Or venture off the road on foot, along the gently rolling **Medicine Root Loop,** a 4-mile (6.4km) hiking trail where you can distinguish the different grasses of this prairie ecosystem. Unfortunately, park management must constantly fight the spread of non-native plants, such as Canada thistle, exotic grasses, and knapweed, inadvertently brought in by human visitors.

There are a few bad things about the Badlands. You can't drink the water; it's too full of sediment. Those buttes are tricky to climb, with their loose, crumbly rocks. The parkland can be blistering hot in summer, prone to heavy rainstorms and lightning; punishing blizzards roll through in winter. And it is a long drive from almost everywhere. But remoteness has its virtues: So long as there's prairie, we'll still have bison, prairie dogs, and, once more, ferrets.

ⓘ **Badlands National Park,** SD 240 at Cedar Pass (✆ **605/433-5361;** www.nps.gov/badl)

✈ Rapid City

🛏 $$ **Cedar Pass Lodge,** Badlands National Park (✆ **877/386-4383** or 605/433-5460, mid-Mar to mid-Oct; www.cedarpasslodge.com). $ **Badlands Ranch and Resort,** 20910 Craven Rd., Interior, SD (✆ **877/433-5599** or 605/433-5599; www.badlandsranchandresort.com).

Prairie Wildlife 240

Custer State Park & Wind Cave National Park

A Home Where the Buffalo Roam

South Dakota

THREATENED BY DISEASE, CONFINED TO A FEW LIMITED RELICS OF THEIR ORIGINAL GREAT PLAINS habitat, American bison are now also losing genetic purity, as ranchers cross-breed them with domestic cattle.

Once upon a time, herds of American bison were so huge, they filled the Great Plains, shaggy masses grazing as far as the eye could see—the most numerous species of large mammal on earth. But then came years of mass slaughter by Plains Indians; white hunters in the late 1800s finished off the herds. In 1889, only 1,091 bison remained in all of North America.

The population has certainly rebounded since then—but most of the half-million American bison today are raised as livestock on commercial ranches. Only about 30,000 are in conservation herds; fewer than 5,000 are free-ranging and disease free. Two of the most important herds, however, thrive within just a few miles of each other, roaming the unspoiled plains of western South Dakota.

Custer State Park's herd is one of the world's largest: 1,300 strong, thanks to a patient breeding program using reintroduced individuals. Just west of the Wildlife Station visitor center stands a set of corrals where bison are held after an annual September roundup (open to the public)

A buffalo in Custer State Park.

to thin the herd and keep it healthy. Calves are born in the spring; you can spot them easily in the herd, with their lighter tan coats. The 18-mile (29km) **Wildlife Loop Road** circles through the bison's favored habitat of open grasslands and pine-clad hills, where white-tailed deer, pronghorn antelopes, elk, and mule deer roam as well.

The herd at **Wind Cave National Park** is smaller—around 400 to 450 bison—but it is outstandingly pure, one of only four worldwide that have no hybrid individuals (most bison today are the products of crossbreeding with domestic cattle). Even better, it's the only herd that is free from brucellosis, an infection that has ravaged many bison herds. Another bonus: Wind Cave is only about one-third the size of Custer, so you've got a good chance of spotting its bison, elk, and pronghorn antelope as you drive through the mixed-grass prairie of Bison Flats in the southern end of the park. (And by the way, don't miss touring underground Wind Cave, the park's star attraction.)

To complete the Wild West profile, you'll find wild mustangs only a short drive away, at the **Black Hills Wild Horse Sanctuary.** In this spread of canyon, pine forest, and open prairie along the Cheyenne River, some 500 rescued mustangs—America's largest wild horse herd—can live out their lives without ever wearing a saddle or being led into a stall. The sanctuary supports its work by charging for tours, which generally include close-up encounters with friendly mustangs.

ⓘ **Custer State Park,** US 16A, Custer, SD ℂ **605/255-4464;** http://gfp.sd.gov). **Wind Cave National Park,** US Hwy. 385, Hot Springs, SD ℂ **605/745-4600;** www.nps.gov/wica). **Black Hills Wild Horse Sanctuary,** 12163 Highland Rd., Hot Springs ℂ **800/252-6652** or 605/745-5955; www.wildmustangs.com).

✈ Rapid City

🛏 $$ **Alex Johnson Hotel,** 523 6th St., Rapid City ℂ **800/888-2539** or 605/342-1210; www.alexjohnson.com). $$ **Sylvan Lake Lodge,** SD 87 and SD 89 ℂ **888/875-0001** or 605/574-2561; www.custerresorts.com).

Pontotoc Ridge Preserve
Keeping the Cross Timbers Happy
Southeast Oklahoma

As NEARBY RESIDENTIAL DEVELOPMENT SUCKS GROUNDWATER FROM THE SEMI-ARID PONTOTOC Ridge Preserve, preserve managers at Pontotoc Ridge fight Eastern red cedar and other invasive species that crowd out native plants.

To the first white explorers crossing the North American continent, the Cross Timbers seemed like the work of the devil. An impenetrable tangle of mixed oaks and undergrowth, it bristled all over a north-south limestone ridge, blocking the entrance to the Great Plains. The Plains Indians had only made it worse by their crafty custom of burning it down to increase forage land for bison—fire just made the Cross Timbers grow back thicker and wilder than ever. Limestone outcrops hid treacherous caves, and wild beasts lurked in its thickets.

Nowadays Oklahoma is a civilized place—so civilized that there's just about nothing left of the Cross Timbers. Its shallow, rocky soil didn't make good cropland, but over the years farmers hacked it down for pasture, let it be overrun by invaders like red cedar and sericia lespedeza, or—worst of all—kept it from burning down.

Nearly 3,000 acres (1,200 hectares) of the Cross Timbers are left, however, in one place: the Pontotoc Ridge Preserve. It's a vital mosaic of complementary habitats: As you hike along the preserve's trails, you'll notice the landscape change from oak savannas on the uplands, to tallgrass prairie blending into mixed-grass prairie on rocky slopes, leading down to hardwood forest in the deeper soil along Delaware Creek. The abutting edges of different ecosystems always encourage species diversity. Now that controlled burns have thinned out the savanna's mix of post oak and blackjack oak, a rich understory of sun-loving herbaceous plants has flourished, providing food for wild turkey, deer, bobwhite, and quail.

Migratory songbirds—painted buntings, summer tanagers, black-billed cuckoos—visit the woodlands, while Bell's vireos and prairie warblers dart between the oaks and the nearby prairies, where prolific wildflowers attract a dizzying number of butterflies. (With more than 90 documented species to date, it's been identified by the Audubon Society as a regional hot spot of butterfly diversity.) Limestone outcrops support pincushion cactus, shooting star, and nodding ladies' tresses. One of the preserve's abundant springs is one of only four known sites where the Oklahoma cave amphipod lives. The bottomland forests—mostly American elm, slippery elm, sugarberry, and green ash—welcome bald eagles and pileated woodpeckers, both endangered.

Rich as this landscape looks, it's basically a semiarid region. As the growing population of nearby Ada sucks more water from this limestone aquifer, the springs and streams of Pontotoc Ridge are more important than ever. It's not just the endangered flora and fauna that need Pontotoc Ridge; two-legged Oklahomans need it too.

(i) **Pontotoc Ridge Preserve,** Rte. 2, Stonewall, OK ((C) **580/777-2224**)

✈ Oklahoma City

🛏 $$ **Holiday Inn Express,** 1201 Lonnie Abbott Industrial Blvd., Ada ((C) **888/465-4329** or 580/310-9200; www.ichotelsgroup.com). $ **Best Western Raintree Inn,** 1100 N. Mississippi Ave., Ada ((C) **580/332-6262;** www.bestwesternoklahoma.com).

Tallgrass Prairie National Preserve

Strong City, Kansas

ONE OF THE RAREST TYPES OF PRAIRIE HABITAT, A RIPARIAN BOTTOMLAND PRAIRIE, IS SLOWLY being replanted and coaxed back to life in this once-overgrazed Kansas preserve.

From out of a car window, the landscape of the Tallgrass Prairie Preserve looks like a lot of—well, grass. Seen one grass, seen it all, right?

That's why you owe it to yourself to get out of that car and start hiking around. For one thing, you haven't really understood how *tall* the tallgrass is until you stand next to it, feeling it tower over your head, at least by late summer when it has attained its full height. (Prairies farther west are shortgrass or mixed-grass, but this significantly less arid region can support taller grasses.) Another thing you'll discover is that this is not a monoculture, but a biodiverse mosaic of some 40 to 60 species of grass. The prairie is dominated by big bluestem, Indian grass, and switch grass, sprinkled with more than 300 species of forbs and wildflowers (the number of butterflies here is incredible). In bottomlands along the creeks, the grass grows tallest, alongside various woody trees and shrubs; wet seeps favor sedges and prairie cord. Up on the windblown hilltops, the grass changes yet again, to the shorter hairy grama.

All in all, this tallgrass prairie supports more than 500 species of plants, nearly 150 species of birds, 39 species of reptiles and amphibians, and 31 species of mammals. While it's easy to spot the bigger ones, like the prairie pocket gopher, the prairie vole, the white-footed mouse, and the white-tailed deer, many of these residents are tiny and shy. And what you're seeing is just the tip of the iceberg—most of the prairie's biomass is underground, in a tough web of roots that absorbs more carbon from the atmosphere than any other ecosystem in America. (Another powerful argument for preserving prairies.)

Named a preserve in 1996, this 11,000-acre (4,450-hectare) prairie land survived through the years because the Flint Hills are just what the name promises—a landscape so rocky, it wasn't worth plowing under for agriculture, as most other prairie was. But work must still be done to restore the rarest habitat, the bottomland prairie that runs along creeks. The interpretive **Bottomland Trail** explains the features of this riparian prairie along a mile-long loop; to see replanting in progress, hike the 6-mile (9.7km) **Fox Creek Trail.** And in 2009, another important prairie element was reintroduced—a small herd of bison, which will graze the preserve along with domestic cattle. In May 2010, the first bison calf in over a century was born in the Flint Hills. Now there's cause for celebration.

(i) **Tallgrass Prairie National Preserve,** 2480 KS Hwy. 177, Strong City, KS (© **620/ 273-8494;** www.nps.gov/tapr)

✈ Kansas City

🛏 $$$ **Grand Central Hotel,** 215 Broadway, Cottonwood Falls, KS (© **620/ 273-6763;** www.grandcentralhotel.com). $ **Prairie Fire Inn & Spa,** US Hwy. 50, Strong City (© **620/273-6356;** www. prairiefireinn.com).

Willow Creek Preserve
The Butterfly Effect
West Eugene, Oregon

ENCROACHING DEVELOPMENT THREATENS THIS SLIVER OF NORTHWEST PRAIRIE, HOME TO IMPERILED plant species like Bradshaw's lomatium, the Willamette daisy, Kincaid's lupine, and the elsewhere-extinct Fender's blue butterfly.

Until 1989, entomologists had crossed the Fender's blue butterfly off their lists. As far as they could tell, it was gone. Kaput. Finito. Extinct.

And then they found them again, in this surviving sliver of native wet prairie on former farmland remarkably close to downtown Eugene, Oregon. Not surprisingly, the butterflies were found close to where the rare Kincaid's blue lupine grows. That makes perfect sense; the Kincaid's blue lupine is the only place where the Fender's blue will lay its eggs. Its larvae remain there, feeding on the bright purple flower spikes, for nearly a year. In late spring, the larvae hatch into adults, beautiful dark-blue butterflies about an inch long. As adults, they will feed on a wider variety of wildflowers. But that only lasts for 9 days before they lay their eggs—on the lupine, of course—and then die. The new larvae snuggle into the lupines, and the whole cycle begins again.

That's what happens when you preserve the old-time habitats. Spreading over 508 acres (206 hectares), Willow Creek Preserve is an intact remnant of the upland grasslands, ash woods, and perennial streams that used to cover this Northwest river valley. It's estimated that 99.8% of the native wet prairie has been lost to development since the 1940s. But here along Willow Creek, more than 200 native plant, 100 bird, and 25 butterfly species survive in healthy diversity. In late spring you'll find the starlike yellow clusters of the endangered Bradshaw's lomatium, while tall feathery blue camas perfectly complement snug yellow buttercups as they grow side by side in an open meadow. In midsummer, the endangered Willamette Valley daisy arrives, with its fat yellow center and pinkish ray petals. Lacy Oregon white-topped asters come along at the end of the summer.

In adjacent areas, trees and shrubs have taken over the native prairie; at Willow Creek, periodic burning holds them back, as nature intended, and lets the sun-loving flowers maintain their territory. (Bradshaw's lomatium, in fact, has increased by 50% in the areas where fire has been used to manage growth.) Non-native species like Scotch broom and Himalayan blackberry that have driven out the original species are regularly cleared out. Where the waist-high, fine-leaved tufted hairgrass should dominate, volunteers tear out the tough common teasel, an invasive thistle that's trying to take over. Sure, it takes a lot of work—but one glimpse of a Fender's blue butterfly makes it all worthwhile.

(i) **Willow Creek Preserve,** W. 18th Ave. at Willow Creek, West Eugene, OR (*©* **541/ 343-1010**)

✈ Eugene

⊨ $$ **Valley River Inn,** 1000 Valley River Way, Eugene (*©* **800/543-8266** or 541/743-1000; www.valleyriverinn.com). $$ **The Secret Garden,** 1910 University St., Eugene (*©* **888/484-6755** or 541/484-6755; www.secretgardenbbinn.com).

Santa Rosa Plateau
There's Gold in Them Thar Hills
Riverside County, California

POLLUTION, FIRE CONTROL, AND INVASIVE SPECIES HAVE CROWDED OUT MOST OF CALIFORNIA'S unique vernal pools, habitat for a wide range of highly adapted organisms, including 27 species "of special concern" for the U.S. Fish and Wildlife Service.

Halfway between the congested urban sprawl of Los Angeles and the congested urban sprawl of San Diego lies the only slightly less congested urban sprawl of inland Riverside County. And yet, astonishingly enough, in the middle of all this—right off busy Interstate 15—lies an 8,000-acre (3,200-hectare) parcel of open California nature land, a habitat for mountain lions, mule deer, badgers, and bobcats tucked into the green and gold hills of the Santa Ana mountains.

This mosaic of chaparral, sage scrubland, and live-oak woodlands looks so typically Western, you'd almost expect the Lone Ranger to come galloping around the next hill. In fact, it is a former ranch, with historic adobe bunkhouses still standing under the massive twisting branches of very rare Engelmann oaks. The ranch's grazing lands, however, preserved a rare ecological holdout: the largest bunchgrass prairie in Southern California. Several trails lead through tall stands of deep-rooted, fire-resistant purple needlegrass, rippling in the wind. Fire resistance is key; using controlled burning, park rangers stave off invasion by trees and shrubs, leaving the terrain to the hardy grass and to sun-loving spring wildflowers. You'll see everything from delicate little mariposa lilies, checkerblooms, and shooting stars to the vibrant Johnny-jump-ups, lupines, and brilliant yellow California poppies. Look for the brown drooping blossoms of the chocolate lily, one of the world's few brown flowers, but sniff carefully—you'll see why it's also called the skunk lily.

Come in spring or early summer—these huge seasonal pools collect atop the plateau's flat-topped basaltic outcroppings in spring, and vanish entirely by summer's end. When winter storms dump rain on these mesas, their hard surface won't drain the rainfall, so it just sits there in shallow declivities, waiting to evaporate. We're not talking mere puddles, either—the largest pool covers 39 acres (16 hectares) at its fullest. It's enough of a wetland to attract migrating water birds like green-winged teals and Canada geese. As spring warms up, though, the pools slowly begin to shrink, revealing successive rings of moist soil where flowers spring up from May on. Walk the boardwalk **Vernal Pool Trail,** where you can closely observe the tiny blooms of some incredibly rare plants—California Orcutt grass, San Diego button-celery, thread-leaf brodiaea, Orcutt's brodiaea, and Parish's meadow foam—as well as vivid carpets of the more common yellow goldfields and purple downingia. You'll be out of luck by July or August—all that will be left is a naked scoop of dark rock, a ghost of the lake that used to be.

Santa Rosa Plateau.

(i) **Santa Rosa Plateau Ecological Reserve,** 39400 Clinton Keith Rd., Murrieta, CA (✆ **951/677-6951;** www.santarosaplateau.org)

✈ Riverside

⊨ $$ **Comfort Inn & Suites,** 41005 California Oaks Rd., Murrieta (✆ **877/424-6423** or 951/894-7227; www.comfortinn.com). $$ **Hampton Inn,** 28190 Jefferson Ave., Temecula (✆ **800/426-7866** or 951/506-2331; www.hamptoninn.com).

Prairie Wildlife **245**

Wild Horse Sanctuary
Phantom & Friends
Shingletown, California

ALTHOUGH SLAUGHTERING HORSES IS ILLEGAL IN THE UNITED STATES, STRAY AMERICAN HORSES still somehow end up on dining tables in Europe and Asia. This sanctuary is one of the few remaining places where wild horses are safe.

Who says that wild mustangs vanished along with the Wild West? Don't tell that to the Phantom Stallion, who defiantly roamed the hills near Dayton, Nevada, as recently as 2006. When this beautiful, untamable white mustang—made famous by a series of children's books—was finally captured, there was one logical place to send him to spend the rest of his days: The Wild Horse Sanctuary in Shingletown, California.

Calling to public attention the Bureau of Land Management's quiet practice of slaughtering unadoptable wild horses found on public lands, a group of animal advocates founded this California preserve for rescued wild horses in 1978. It's a beautiful site, 5,000 acres (2,023 hectares) of lush pastureland near **Lassen National Park** (which accounts for the volcanic rock cropping out of these mountain meadows). Extensive pine and oak forests provide winter cover for a herd of around 300 horses, as well as a number of tough, ornery little burros that have joined their ranks. Naturally, other animals live here as well—deer, raccoons, badgers, black bears, gray foxes, quails, and wild turkeys, as well as less friendly neighbors such as coyotes, bobcats, and mountain lions. Within the shelter of the herd, the horses are safe from those natural predators, as they never would be if they were maverick mustangs fending for themselves.

Saving wild horses is an expensive business, and the sanctuary sells a few foals every year to raise money, making room for older horses that are less adoptable. Its visitor facilities are still a work in progress, but on Saturdays and Wednesdays they do invite the public to walk around, getting close-up views of the wild horses. Even better are the 2- and 3-day weekend pack trips they offer in spring and summer, and a 4-to-6-day cattle drive in the fall. (Overnights are spent in a set of frontier-style sleeping cabins on the verge of a pristine vernal lake.) Volunteers are also welcome to come help feed the wild horses in winter, when grazing is scarce, and to build visitor facilities. Hey, every bit helps.

ⓘ **Wild Horse Sanctuary,** 5796 Wilson Hill Rd., Shingletown, CA ✆ **530/474-5770;** www.wildhorsesanctuary.org)

✈ Redding

🛏 $$ **The Weston House,** Red Rock Rd., Shingletown ✆ **530/474-3738;** www.westonhouse.com). $ **Hat Creek Resort,** 12533 Hwy. 44h, Old Station, CA ✆ **530/335-7121;** www.hatcreekresortrv.com).

246 Coastal Plains

Chitwan National Park
The Royal Rhinos of Nepal
Nepal

CARVED OUT OF A SETTLED AREA, CHITWAN NATIONAL PARK IS OFTEN AT ODDS WITH THE LOCAL population, whose farms may be raided by marauding tigers or grazing rhinos.

Think of Nepal and you picture Himalayan peaks, right? Well, that's not all there is to Nepal. Along the Indian border in the southwest, Nepal spills into the flat Ganges floodplain. These swampy, malarial lowlands made a supremely effective barrier in the days before DDT. As many as 2,000 one-horned Asian rhinoceroses browsed here in relative peace and quiet.

Then between 1950 and 1960, new insecticides rid the Ganges plains of mosquitoes. The population tripled, the forest was slashed in half, and crops were planted in its place. As if habitat destruction wasn't bad enough, rhinos began to be hunted for their horns, which are believed to have magical properties. Suddenly there were only 100 rhinos left.

That's when the government stepped in, taking 932 sq. km (360 sq. miles) of the former hunting grounds of the Nepali Ranas, expelling 22,000 residents, and turning it into Royal Chitwan National Park. Nobody dared poach rhinos here—not with the Royal Nepalese Army patrolling its borders. Today there are more than 500 Asian rhinos at Chitwan, enough that several individuals are exported every year to other parks.

While the main body of the park is jungle, a dense forest of sal and teak trees, at least one-fifth of the park is elephant grass savanna along the flood plain of the Rapti River. This plain is dotted with several shallow oxbow lakes, where the thick-skinned rhinos hang out with storks and other marsh birds, otters, rare gharial crocodiles, and the even rarer freshwater Gangetic dolphins. The rhinos cool off at water's edge, then wander over to browse on the tall grasses a little farther from the river, where several kinds of deer and the mighty guar antelope also graze. The intersection of jungle and grasslands makes ideal habitat for another endangered species: the Bengal tiger, which has rebounded from 25 individuals to more than 100.

Canoeing on the Rapti gives you a great view of the water birds; you can also observe wildlife through binoculars from observation towers at Machans. Near the visitor center, special breeding centers have been set up for endangered animals such as the gharial crocodile, Asian elephants, and two rare species of vulture. Venture into the jungle to score more wildlife sighting; it's a good idea to go with a guide, not only to identify species and prevent getting lost, but also to deal with any run-ins with rhinos, who can be extremely territorial. Your last option may be touristy but it's irresistible—take an elephant ride into the jungle, perched in a canopied howdah on the elephant's back.

ⓘ **Chitwan National Park visitor center,** Sauraha (www.rhinos-irf.org)

✈ Bharatpur

🛏 $$$ **Tiger Tops Jungle Lodge & Camp,** Chitwan National Park (✆ **977/ 1/436-1500;** www.tigermountain.com). $$ **Machan Wildlife Resort,** Chitwan National Park (✆ **977/1/422-5001** or 977/ 56/20973; www.nepalinformation.com/ machan).

A rhino in Chitwan National Park.

Apalachicola Bluffs & Ravines Preserve
Flooding the Florida Plain
Bristol, Florida

WHILE UPRIVER DAMS ALTER ITS NATURAL SEASONAL LEVELS, THE APALACHICOLA RIVER HAS had its shore habitats smothered by sand and gravel, dredged up by U.S. Army Corps of Engineers navigation improvement projects.

Everybody wants a piece of the Apalachicola River. Fishermen want it to provide them with largemouth bass, striped bass, and catfish. Boaters want it to float their houseboats and river cruisers. The seafood industry wants its fresh water to feed the oyster beds in Apalachicola Bay. Naturalists want it to nurture waterfowl and endangered mussels and sturgeon. Communities along the entire river system—which stretches from northwest Georgia along the Flint and Chattahoochee rivers to the Florida border, where they merge underneath Lake Seminole and become the 106-mile-long (171km) Apalachicola—want it to provide water for drinking, irrigation, and hydropower. Ever since the early 1800s, the U.S. Army Corps of Engineers has been tinkering with this river system, continually dredging navigation channels and, in the 1950s, building four hydroelectric dams. Even in good years, these conflicting needs compete, battled over by the three state governments of Georgia, Alabama, and Florida. In a drought year (like 2007 or 2008), it can be a fight to the death.

Featured in the film *Ulee's Gold,* the lower Apalachicola—Florida's largest floodplain—is an area known not only for bass fishing and quail hunting but also for raising tupelo honey, a precious variety made by bees that feed around the increasingly rare tupelo tree. Today it encompasses several protected areas: Apalachicola National Forest, Torreya State Park, Tates Hell State Forest, the Apalachicola Wildlife and Environmental Area, and the Apalachicola Bluffs and Ravines Preserve, former timberland that has been painstakingly restored by the Nature Conservancy.

At the preserve, a 3.8-mile (6.1km) nature trail—aptly named the **Garden of Eden trail**—winds through a mix of rare habitats. First comes a longleaf pine/wiregrass uplands (look for Florida yew trees, once of the world's rarest evergreens, as well as the magnolias and oak-leaf hydrangea). Then you'll pass through dramatic steephead ravines, a rare geological feature that nurtures unique species such as the Apalachicola dusky salamander. On the sand hills, in spring you'll see wildflowers like trillium, wild ginger, and Gholson's blazing star; in fall you'll spot toothed basil and lopsided Indian grass.

The trail ends on a panoramic bluff 135 feet (41m) above the Apalachicola River, where bald eagles, Mississippi kites, and swallowtail kites swoop overhead. It's a breathtaking view of a landscape that's still in the process of being preserved. A historic 2010 agreement between the army engineers and the Nature Conservancy began to open dams to allow shad, striped bass, and sturgeon to migrate upstream. It's a step toward allaying the impact of all those years of aggressive river management. Let's hope it lays the groundwork for more.

(i) **Apalachicola Bluffs and Ravines Preserve,** 10394 NW Longleaf Dr., Bristol, FL ((C) **850/643-2756**)

✈ Panama City or Tallahassee

$$ **Gibson Inn,** 51 Ave. C, Apalachicola ((C) **850/653-2191;** www.gibson inn.com). $$ **Apalachicola River Inn,** 123 Water St., Apalachicola ((C)**850/653-8139;** www.apalachicolariverinn.com).

The Grand Bay Savanna
Delicate Death Traps
Mississippi & Alabama

RAPID POPULATION GROWTH HAS DISRUPTED THIS SENSITIVE COASTAL WETLAND, HOME TO several rare carnivorous plants. Non-native plants proliferate, and water quality continues to decline.

Insects, beware—you do not want to drink the water cupped so invitingly inside a pitcher plant's beautiful curved blossom. Once you get trapped inside those slippery petals, there's no way out. Sooner or later the deadly enzymes the flower secretes will digest you. It's a killer.

Down on the Gulf Coast, there used to be a lot of wet pine savannas where pitcher plants could lay their murderous traps. Unfortunately, as roads were built and land was cleared for housing and/or industry, that coastal plain was irrevocably altered. Visit the Grand Bay Savanna, a huge swath of nature reserves straddling the border between lower Alabama and lower Mississippi, to see what this land once looked like. Prime sites are the **Grand Bay National Wildlife Refuge** and the **Mississippi Sandhill Crane National Wildlife Refuge,** both on the Mississippi side of the reserve.

When landowners developed this area, they thought they were doing the right thing by preventing forest fires in the pine plantations bordering their bayou-front homes. Wrong. Without fire, the pine woods get too dense and new shrubs invade, sucking moisture out of the boggy ground and turning it to solid land. But pitcher plants prefer sun-dappled bogs—as do sundews, bladderworts, orchids, and

snapdragons, all of which you'll see flourishing on the pine savannas at Grand Bay. These wildflowers are uniquely adapted to live where water is close to the surface, there's a fair amount of sunlight, and the soil is nutrient poor. (Who needs nutrients from the soil when you can eat insects, anyway?) Now that this land has been set aside for conservation purposes, ecologists are doing prescribed burns to keep the ecosystems in balance.

Not only does Grand Bay Savanna have a pitcher plant bog, but it has rare regional varieties of other flowers that love pitcher plant bogs—Texas pipewort, Walter's sedge, myrtle-leaved St. John's wort, coastal plain false-foxglove, thin-stemmed false-foxglove, stalked adders-tongue—plus a host of orchids: spreading pogonias, large white fringed orchids, yellow fringeless orchids, and giant spiral ladies' tresses. While the beautiful, tall crimson pitcher plant is well known, it's accompanied by the much rarer yellow trumpet pitcher plant, the parrot pitcher plant with its odd hooked lips, the side-saddle pitcher plant, and another rare carnivore called Chapman's butterwort. As you walk the refuges' short nature trails—Grand Bay's boardwalked **Escatawpa Trail** or Sandhill Crane's **C.L. Dees Nature Trail**—bring your wildflower field guides to identify what you're seeing. But don't be surprised if some of these plants are so rare, they're not even listed.

(i) **Grand Bay National Wildlife Refuge,** 6005 Bayou Heron Rd., Moss Point, MS (*©* **228/497-6322;** www.fws.gov/grandbay). **Mississippi Sandhill Crane National Wildlife Refuge,** 7200 Crane Lane, Gautier, MS (*©* **228/497-6322;** www.fws.gov/mississippisandhillcrane).

✈ Gulfport

🛏 $$ **Best Western Oak Manor,** 886 Beach Blvd., Biloxi, MS (*©* **800/591-9057** or 228/435-4331; www.bestwesternoakmanor.com). $ **Edgewater Inn,** 1936 Beach Blvd., Biloxi (*©* **800/323-9676** or 228/388-1100; www.edgewaterinnbiloxi.com).

---

249 | Coastal Plains

Green Swamp Preserve
Defending the Venus' Flytrap
Supply, North Carolina

LOCAL ADVOCATES HAVE HAD TO FIGHT MANY PROPOSED PROJECTS—A LANDFILL, A HIGHWAY, a septage waste disposal—that would damage this rare coastal ecosystem. Nearby communities still divert its water to supply golf courses, resorts, and houses.

What do you see when you look at a swamp? Some people see a rich, diverse ecosystem that shelters unusual flora and fauna. But others, apparently, see a perfect site to dump trash.

That's what happened in 2000, when a giant landfill was proposed for the grounds of North Carolina's Green Swamp Preserve. If local residents hadn't mounted a protest, Green Swamp would now be lying underneath a mountain of garbage taller than the Cape Hatteras Lighthouse. And in 2011, the swamp's advocates had to rally again, to oppose a plan to dispose of septage waste on a portion of the Green Swamp.

Though it's called a swamp, it's really a pocosin—so named from an Algonquian term meaning "swamp on a hill"—and it's one of the very last examples of such a coastal bog. The pocosin doesn't look dark and murky like your classic swamp, but if you stepped off the boardwalk trail onto its spongy soil (please don't step off, though!), you'd realize just how waterlogged it is.

Gallberry, titi, and sweetbay are the dominant evergreen shrubs, and American alligators hang out here. Hey, what's a swamp without an alligator or two?

Beside the pocosin, you can also hike through another rare survivor, a longleaf pine savanna—a once common regional habitat that elsewhere has declined into a monoculture of loblolly pine. In contrast, these savannas have a thriving, complex ecosystem. Within the dense undergrowth of wiregrass, growing in tall tawny tufts between slender, ramrod-straight pine trunks, you'll find an incredibly diverse collection of orchids and carnivorous plants—four kinds of pitcher plants, two bladderworts, sundew, and one of the last thriving populations of the endangered Venus' flytrap, with its menacing toothed scarlet leaves.

Many of the plants in the Green Swamp savanna have benefited from periodic burning; not only are they fire tolerant, but they've actually adapted to germinate better under fire conditions. The old-growth trees are often infected with red heart disease—but then, that's the absolute favorite spot for red-cockaded woodpeckers to nest, where they can easily drill a big hole in the softened trunk. (Look for holes surrounded with a shiny ring of sticky pine sap, which conveniently keeps out predators.) Once these woodpeckers have built these solid nests, they return to them year after year, making this woods one of the last strongholds of this highly endangered bird. Red-cockaded woodpeckers and Venus' flytraps—how many one-of-a-kind creatures must be sacrificed in the name of trash?

ⓘ **Green Swamp Preserve,** State Hwy. 211, 5½ miles (9km) north of Supply, NC (© **910/395-5000;** www.swfwmd.state. fl.us/recreation/areas/greenswamp.html)

✈ Wilmington

🛏 $$$ **Graystone Inn,** 100 S. 3rd St., Wilmington (© **888/763-4773** or 910/763-2000; www.graystoneinn.com). $$ **The Wilmingtonian,** 101 S. 2nd St., Wilmington (© **800/525-0909** or 910/343-1800; www.thewilmingtonian.com).

Coastal Plains 250

Roundstone Bog
Magic Under Your Feet
County Galway, Ireland

HEAVY RAINS AND UNSEASONABLY LONG, HOT DRY SPELLS, BOTH CAUSED BY CLIMATE CHANGE, are taking a toll on this fragile coastal bog, already at risk from excessive foot traffic and deforestation. A new airstrip at Clifden may stress the system even further.

Once you pass Oughterard on the N59, all bets are off. The wooded green landscape of Galway suddenly turns into a flat, treeless, plum-colored plain of rippling sedge grasses. Park your car and just try to walk on that terrain—the ground shivers and quakes under your feet, and at any moment you may plunge knee-deep into water.

Find a solid track to walk upon, though, and you'll discover that the harsh rock-strewn land is softened by gorse, lichens, mosses, and wildflowers. The strange reddish color you saw from the car is actually a tapestry of russets, golds, greens, blues, and peaty chocolate brown, a mix of all the heathers of Ireland. This is the famous Roundstone Bog of Connemara, the crown jewel of Ireland's wild west.

Though much of Roundstone Bog falls within **Connemara National Park,** you don't have to go all the way to the park entrance in Letterfrack to explore it. Follow signs off N59 to the charming seaside village of Roundstone and then take minor roads between Roundstone and Clifden, the main town on the west coast. Look for gates that lead to walking tracks.

Connemara is technically a blanket bog, lying flat across miles of terrain and supporting grasses, sedges, and heathers. The bogs began to form 2,500 years ago, as heavy precipitation caused iron to leach down from the acidic soil, forming a hard pan that trapped water. Dying vegetation rotted, sank into the waterlogged soil, and condensed into peat. (Peat is still an important local source of fuel—look for stacks of turf bricks that cottagers have left by the roadside to air-dry.) Extensive deforestation sped the process, as much of the region's trees were hacked down for shipbuilding. Today, two-thirds of Connemara

Horses in Connemara.

is bog. Purple moor grass dominates, but its overall color is variegated with ling heather, cross-leaved heath, Mackays heath, Irish heath, St. Dabeoc's heath, bell heather, and silky white tufts of bog-cotton. As you suddenly come upon ponds and marshy areas, you'll find flowers such as tormentil, sundew, bog asphodel, lousewort, and milkwort, many of them carnivorous insect eaters. Rock basins catch enough rainwater to form small lakes, while hummocks grow into small islands wooded with holly, yew, oak, or willow.

In 1919, British aviators John Alcock and Alvin Whitten Brown completed the first North America–to–Europe airplane flight by crash-landing into the soft, springy surface of Roundstone Bog. In 2011, a controversial airstrip will open in Clifden, after decades of protest and construction challenges. (As it turns out, it's not so easy to build an airport on bog land.) Civilization marches on, but somehow the primeval mysteries of the bog prevail.

ⓘ **Connemara National Park,** N59, Letterfrack, County Galway (✆ **353/95/41054;** www.connemaranationalpark.ie)

✈/🚆 Galway City (80km/50 miles)

🛏 $$ **Lough Inagh Lodge,** Recess (✆ **353/95/34706;** www.loughinaghlodge hotel.ie). $ **Errisbeg Lodge,** R341, Roundstone (✆ **353/95/35807;** www.errisbeg lodge.com).

10 Places to See North American Prairie

Three kinds of prairies once covered an estimated 140 million acres (57 million hectares) of America: tallgrass prairie to the east, dominated by so-called sod grasses (bluestem, Indian grass, switch grass); short-grass prairies closer to the Rocky Mountains, where hardy buffalo grass and grama grass dominated; and a more varied mosaic of mixed-grass prairie in between. Prairie grasslands are perhaps the planet's most efficient ecosystem for removing carbon from the atmosphere—and yet 96% of these tough grasslands have been lost. Against all odds, these parcels have survived:

251 Lynx Prairie Preserve, Lynx, Ohio Part of the Edge of Appalachia Preserve, this National Natural Landmark protects a rare ecosystem: pockets of rare Allegheny short-grass prairie tucked into these Ohio woodlands. Limestone bedrock supports blue-stem grasses and wildflowers. From the East Liberty Church on Tulip Road, a 1.5-mile (2.4km) loop traverses woodlands and these surprising islands of grass, known as cedar barrens—come in late spring or early summer to see the wildflowers at their brilliant peak.

252 Cressmoor Prairie Preserve, Hobart, Indiana This 41-acre (17-hectare) parcel of land is a remarkable hunk of pure black-soil prairie in the northwestern corner of Indiana. Walk its 2-mile (3.2km) mown trail and you'll soon be surrounded by prairie grass as high as 5 feet (1.5m), studded with brilliant flowers like prairie lilies, sunflowers, blazing stars, and a whole range of asters and goldenrods. ℘ *219/879-4725. www.heinzetrust.org/Nature/CressmoorPrairie.aspx*

253 Nachusa Grasslands, Franklin Grove, Illinois This preserve totals 3,000 acres (1,200 hectares), a network of 13 different units, mostly tallgrass prairie and dry prairie. A meticulous seed-gathering and replanting campaign has brought many rare plants, including the threatened prairie bush clover, back to abundance here, along with endangered butterflies and grassland birds like the dickcissel, grasshopper sparrow, and Eastern meadowlark. ℘ *815/456-2340. www.nachusagrasslands.org.*

Oglala National Grasslands.

254 Terre Noire Natural Area, Arkadelphia, Arkansas There used to be 12 million acres (5 million hectares) of blackland prairie, from Alabama to Texas. Less than 1% of this imperiled ecosystem survives, mostly in Arkansas. There are no marked trails at this 490-acre (198-hectare) site along Highway 51 in southwestern Arkansas, but you can hike all over its rolling terrain, where dense thickets of oak and pine alternate with grasslands. A mix of grasses, predominantly little bluestem, is spangled in spring with such rare wildflowers as the blazing star and pale purple coneflower. *www.nature.org.*

255 Neal Smith National Wildlife Refuge, Prairie City, Iowa With some 5,000 acres (2,000 hectares) of restored tallgrass prairie—mostly seeded by plants rescued elsewhere by volunteers—this refuge sustains larger prairie residents such as American bison, white-tailed deer, elk, pocket gophers, badgers, pheasants, red-tailed hawks, and Indiana bats. Excellent exhibits at the Prairie Learning Center provide background; then you can hike the signposted 2-mile (3.2km) Tallgrass Trail or take an auto tour through the reclaimed prairie lands. *② 515/994-3400. http://tallgrass.org.*

256 Tallgrass Prairie Preserve, Foraker, Oklahoma At the southern end of the Flint Hills, some 45,000 acres (18,200 hectares) of former ranchland on the Osage Indian Reservation stand as the largest remnant of North America's once-vast tall-grass prairie. While a handful of oil wells still dot the landscape, a free-roaming herd of 2,500 bison, easily viewed from scenic turnouts along the preserve's roads, has been reintroduced to graze the land. Two short nature trails explore the prairie, near the restored ranch house that serves as preserve headquarters. *② 918/287-4803.*

257 Manitoba Tall Grass Prairie Preserve, Tolstoi, Manitoba Here in the so-called Prairie Provinces, most prairie land was ploughed under for the vast wheat fields of Canada's breadbasket. Yet these 2,000 hectares (5,000 acres) in the Red River Valley were strewn with just enough boulders and swampy sloughs to make them untillable. Among the preserve's endangered flowers are the western prairie fringed orchid and small white lady's slipper. A short self-guided trail loop is off Highway 209; the longer Agassiz Interpretive Trail is off Highway 201. *② 204/942-6156. www.natureconservancy.ca.*

258 Buffalo Gap National Grassland, Kadoka, South Dakota No fewer than 56 different species of grass grow on various parcels of this extensive preserve. Taller grasses thrive in moist seasons, and shorter grasses come into their own in the height of summer. It's rife with prairie dogs, and the rare burrowing owls that take over their empty burrows. There's a 5.5-mile (8.9km) loop trail with great badland vistas near Wall, South Dakota. *② 605/745-4107 or 605/279-2125.*

259 Oglala National Grasslands, Crawford, Nebraska Rock hounds are drawn to this 95,000-acre (38,400-hectare) short-grass prairie preserve in north-western Nebraska, a desolate-seeming badlands where fossils abound, stark rock formations are heaped around the Toadstool Geologic Park, and 10,000-year-old bison skeletons are excavated at the Hudson-Meng Bison Bonebed. Visit the sod house to imagine early prairie settlers' lives. *② 308/432-0300.*

260 Pawnee National Grassland, Briggsdale, Colorado Lying in the rain shadow of the Rockies, this windswept 60-mile-wide (97km) plateau ripples with the distinctive dry green of short-grass prairie. Try the Birdwalk Trail starting out from the Crow Valley Campground to see lark buntings, Western meadowlarks, and mountain plovers; to spot the high-circling hawks and falcons for which the park is famous, hike to the Pawnee Buttes, which thrust momentously upward from the plateau. *② 970/346-5000 or 970/353-5004.*

Pawnee National Grassland.

Eshqua Bog & Chickering Bog
Fantastic Fens
Central Vermont

FED BY GROUNDWATER, THESE FRAGILE HABITATS ARE HIGHLY SUSCEPTIBLE TO UNDERGROUND pollution from septic systems and other contaminants from nearby towns.

Everybody knows about the brilliant colors Vermont puts on in autumn. Tour buses clog Routes 4 and 12 every October, crammed with leaf-peeping tourists, and hotel rates shoot sky high. But fewer tourists know about Vermont's other show—in June, when its wildflowers finally burst into bloom.

Only an hour's drive apart (if you take I-89—much longer if you enjoy yourself on scenic Rte. 12), these two pocket preserves rival each other in the wildflower department. Though we usually think of orchids in terms of big, dramatic tropical rainforest blooms, New England has its own delicate orchids, mostly growing in wetlands like these. The first to show up every June all happen to be pink: dragon's mouth (also sometimes called swamp pink, for obvious reasons), grass pink, rose pogonia, and pink lady's slippers, which are more evident at Chickering Bog. Soon after, the headliner comes onstage: the showy lady's slipper, with its waxy white petals and curling purple underlip, standing up to a yard high. Showy lady's slippers are hard to miss at either Eshqua or Chickering when they erupt; Eshqua also has a few of the smaller and rarer yellow lady's slippers, and in July yet another lovely orchid blooms here, the white bog-candle.

Both preserves also feature the dramatic Northern pitcher plant, a purplish flower with inward-curved petals that collect water. It looks vaguely orchidlike, but it's got a deadly secret: Insects eventually drown inside this "pitcher" and are quietly digested by the plant. There's another insect-devourer in these fens, too: the innocent-looking sundew with its tiny white flowers—and sticky, bug-trapping leaves.

If you want to get technical, neither Eshqua Bog nor Chickering Bog is really a bog—bogs get their water from acidic sources, mostly rainwater, while fens are fed by calcium-rich groundwater. Fens have more nutrients, and thus support more diverse plant communities. A marshy depression at the base of a long hill, Eshqua has everything from blueberries and cranberries to larches, buckthorn, bunchberries, and cinquefoil; Chickering, which is slowly filling in (it's really wet at the north end), displays bog rosemary, rhodora, leatherleaf, red chokeberry, and blue flag iris.

Both preserves have a single short walking trail, about a mile long, much of it elevated on a boardwalk—not to protect your shoes, but to keep this fragile, peaty habitat from damage. After all, you can't grow flowers like this in a flowerbed; you've got to have a bog. Or a fen.

ⓘ**Eshqua Bog Natural Area,** Garvin Hill Rd., Hartland, VT. Chickering Bog Natural Area, Lightening Ridge Rd., Calais, VT. Nature Conservancy of Vermont (✆**802/ 229-4425**).

✈Rutland

🛏$$$ **Kedron Valley Inn,** 10671 South Rd., South Woodstock, VT (✆ **800/836-1193** or 802/457-1473; www.kedronvalley inn.com). $$ **The Inn at Montpelier,** 147 Main St., Montpelier, VT (✆ **802/223-2727;** www.innatmontpelier.com).

Death Valley
Extreme Junction
Furnace Creek, California

HUNDREDS OF SPECIES HAVE ADAPTED TO DEATH VALLEY'S EXTREME CONDITIONS—BUT THE rising temperatures of climate change could push them over the edge. Invasive tamarisk trees and airborne pollution pose more immediate threats.

Harsh, yes. Remote, yes. But there's something compelling about this below-sea-level desert valley, cut off by mountain ranges from the rest of California. A freak of nature, birthed by seismic faults, it is a stark landscape of scalding sand flats, jagged canyons, and glittering outcrops of crystals left behind by withered lakes. Despite scorching temperatures (think 120°F/49°C in summer) and next to no rainfall (1.9 in./4.8cm a year, on average), more than a million tourists come each year to marvel at this extreme landscape.

The name memorializes forty-niners who perished here en route to the California gold fields. Life was hardly easier for the borax miners with their 20-mule wagon teams in the late 1880s. But once it was designated a national monument in 1933, the region's harsh desert beauty became its strongest selling point.

Along Highway 190 lies a string of attractions. **Badwater** is the lowest spot in North America, 282 feet (86m) below sea level; the visual contrast between it and **Telescope Peak,** only 15 miles (24km) away, is stunning. The **Artist's Palette** driving loop displays a wind-chiseled range of hills in a spectrum of mineral hues. For camera-ready panoramas, visitors stop at either **Zabriskie Point** or **Dante's View,** though those vistas are often hazed over as polluted air drifts into the valley from metropolitan areas. Dust thrown up by cars on unpaved park roads, or even people walking on the fragile desert crust, compounds the problem.

The cracked, bleached saltpan at the bottom of the valley is usually devoid of vegetation, but nearly 1,000 species of plants root around here, some 50 of them endemic. Wildflowers such as desert star, blazing star, desert gold, mimulus, encelia, poppies, verbena, evening primrose, and phacelia carpet the valley floor from mid-February to early April (check the park's website for seasonal wildflower predictions). Death Valley also has its own bizarre sand dunes—drifted piles of fine, loose quartz granules eroded from the surrounding rocks.

Most native mammals are small—gophers, mice, rats—and nocturnal, foraging only after the cruel sun has gone down. Believe it or not, Death Valley even has fish—five species of pupfish, including the endangered Devil's Hole pupfish in western Nevada. At **Salt Creek,** just north of Furnace Creek, a boardwalk nature trail allows you to view the tiny Salt Creek pupfish, wriggling in the trickling creek. Even this severe landscape nurtures life, if you know where to look—now there's a message of hope for the planet.

ⓘ **Death Valley National Park,** Greenland Blvd., Furnace Creek, CA (✆ **760/786-3200;** www.nps.gov/deva)

✈ Las Vegas

🛏 $$–$$$ **Furnace Creek Inn & Ranch,** Hwy. 190 (✆ **800/236-7916** or 760/786-2345; www.furnacecreekresort.com). $ **Furnace Creek Campground,** Furnace Creek (✆ **877/444-6777** or 760/786-2441; www.recreation.gov).

Pinnacles National Monument
Life on the Fault Edge
Paicines, California

AN ECCENTRIC MOSAIC OF OVERLAPPING ECOSYSTEMS, PINNACLES NATIONAL MONUMENT IS in danger of being loved to death by hikers and climbers who leave littered landscapes and polluted streams behind them.

It's like a textbook study of the forces of nature. Chapter 1: The Power of Plate Tectonics—just look at these jagged crags, spires, and hoodoos, carried an amazing 195 miles (314km) north from the Mojave Desert by grinding shifts along the San Andreas Fault. Chapter 2: Ecosystem Dynamics—just see how biodiverse this landscape is, with species thriving on the intersections between habitats.

Set among the rolling brown hills of California, only 80 miles (129km) south of San Francisco, it's not surprising that the Pinnacles National Monument is one of the

most popular weekend climbing spots in central California year-round. Some weekends, it seems every spire and monolith has a climber clinging to its surface. But nature lovers have a long history with the Pinnacles—in 1908, its freakish rock formations inspired local advocates to lobby for protection, making Pinnacles one of the first parks in the national system.

Here, where tectonic plates grind against each other, several ecosystems also meet—chaparral, grassland, woodland, riparian, rocky scree—but instead of clashing, they stimulate each other. Besides

Pinnacles National Monument.

the rare big-eared kangaroo rat, Gabilan slender salamander, Pinnacles shield-back katydid, and Pinnacles riffle beetle, the park has the world's highest bee diversity—nearly 400 distinct species buzzing around its high chaparral and grasslands. Talus caves—narrow stream canyons roofed over with tumbled boulders—make the park a haven for bats as well, including the rare Townsend's big-eared bats. And then there are the extremely rare California condors, more than a dozen of which were released to the wild here (an early-morning hike up the strenuous **High Peaks Trail** gives you your best chance of seeing one of these endangered scavengers). Other birds of prey, such as prairie falcons, peregrine falcons, and golden eagles, are nesting again at Pinnacles; hikers should check with rangers to see where their breeding sites have been cordoned off.

With so many visitors, the Pinnacles faces several challenges. Carelessly discarded litter and human waste jeopardize the streams that are vital for survival in this dry microclimate. The condors, which are carrion eaters, have tested for high lead levels after feasting on contaminated carcasses. Exotic species such as the yellow star thistle, carried in as tiny seeds on hiking boots, threaten to overrun native plants. Wind and erosion also continue to exert their force on the pinnacles, which are still moving ¾ to 1¼ inches (2–3cm) a year. A century of protected status has preserved this unique landscape remarkably—but nobody should take it for granted.

ⓘ **Pinnacles National Monument,** 5000 Hwy. 146, Paicines, CA (ℂ**831/389-4485;** www.nps.gov/pinn)

✈ Monterey Peninsula Airport

🛏$$ **Keefer's Inn,** 615 Canal St., King City, CA (ℂ **800/745-9050** or 831/385-4843; www.keefersinn.com). $ **Pinnacles Campground,** off CA 25 near the eastern entrance (ℂ **877/444-6777;** www.recreation.gov).

264 Desert

Cuatro Cienegas Biosphere Reserve
The Cactus Connection
Central Mexico

SEVERELY OVERGRAZED, INVADED BY EXOTIC SPECIES, AND DRAINED TO IRRIGATE LOCAL AGRIculture, North America's largest desert loses more acres of rare habitat every year.

Consider the cactus, North America's iconic desert dweller. Everybody knows the saguaro, but there are so many more—like the rotund Mexican fire-barrel cactus, with its purple needles and flaming orange blossoms; the dark-green tree cholla with its vivid purple blooms; or the tiny cat-claw cactus, a tangle of long gray needles topped by a maroon flower.

Scientists believe that the cactus first evolved in what is now Mexico. More than one-third of all cactus species still live here—mostly in the great Chihuahuan

Desert, sandwiched between the east and west Sierra Madre ranges, from southern New Mexico and west Texas down south to Zacatecas. With its high elevations, the Chihuahuan Desert is surprisingly cool and wet for a desert, and it's still a biodiversity hot spot, though its once-lush grasslands have been perilously overgrazed, and its groundwater pumped out for irrigation. No fewer than 345 different cactus species grow here, some so rare that they appear only on one rocky outcrop. You can see most of those species in a huge greenhouse at the Chihuahuan Desert Research Institute in Fort Davis, Texas. But it's even more thrilling to see them in the wild, blooming alongside sunflowers in the desert scrub, where lizards and scorpions scuttle, roadrunners and cactus wrens flit about, and the drowsy air hums with an astonishing variety of bees.

Cactus Central lies in central Coahuila state, near the town of **Cuatro Cienegas.** *"Cienega"* means a small marshy lake, hundreds of which dot this area, fed by thermal springs in the nearby Sierra San Marco mountains. When early-20th-century droughts dried up the desert's lakes and streams, these marshes became a refuge for rare native fish, snails, and other invertebrate species. (Learn about them at the town's excellent herpetarium, at Morelos Sur 112.) That unique confluence of mountains, desert, marshy oases, and gypsum dunes—their fine white sands formed from evaporated saline lakes—gives this valley more than 70 unique endemic species, more than any other spot in North America.

Much of the area surrounding Cuatro Cienegas is a UNESCO Biosphere Reserve, a stunning desert basin cupped by rugged mountains. Stop by the **Turtle Pond Visitor Center** off Highway 30, where a self-guided nature trail identifies the desert vegetation, so you can tell your lechugilla from your ocotillo, your creosote bush from your saltbush. A short hike leads to a picnic area by the shore of a dazzling blue pond, **Poza Azules,** where the waters are so clear, you can see the tiny fish swimming around.

Swimming isn't allowed here—the biological balance is too fragile—but luckily other ponds nearby have been developed for swimming: **Rio los Mezquites** at the 9km marker on Highway 30, and **Poza La Becerra** at the 18km marker. During guided tours of the dunes (inquire at the visitor center), visitors hike around Las Arenales, a short drive off Highway 30 at marker 25km. As you're hiking, count how many different cactuses you find in the rocks and crevices. But beware: Cactus poachers have driven many of this valley's species to the brink of extinction—don't even *think* of collecting specimens with anything more than a camera.

(i) **Cuatro Cienegas Biosphere Reserve,** Hwy. 30, 7km (4⅓ miles) south of Cuatro Cienegas

✈ Laredo, TX

🛏 $ **Hotel Ibarra,** Zaragoza 200, Cuatro Cienegas (© **52/869/696-0129**). $$ **Hotel Plaza,** Hidalgo 202, Cuatro Cienegas (© **52/869/696-0066**).

Desert 265

The Nazca Lines
Designing the Desert
Nazca, Peru

RUDELY BISECTED BY THE PAN-AMERICAN HIGHWAY, THIS FRAGILE ANCIENT SITE SOMEHOW survived the floods and mudslides of 2007, and escaped damage in 2010's major earthquakes. Its luck may not hold out much longer.

Sure, you can see the Nazca Lines from ground level, but it wasn't until the age of airplanes that observers saw these ancient geoglyphs as they were meant to be seen—from the air. Sprawling over nearly 1,050 sq. km (400 sq. miles) of the San Jose desert in southern Peru, the Nazca Lines may be the most mysterious of

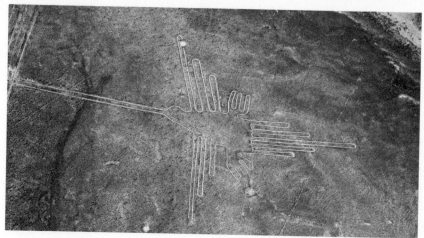

A Nazca Lines' geoglyph.

ancient wonders: at least 10,000 rocky lines forming some 300 gargantuan designs—trapezoids, zigzags, spirals, even plant and animal shapes. But while they cover a lot of ground, the designs are only a few centimeters deep, scratched centuries ago out of a thin crust of reddish rocky scree. The next big flood could wash them away.

No one knows why pre-Inca peoples carved these geoglyphs, probably between 300 B.C. and A.D. 700. There are plenty of theories, though: that they were an astronomical calendar; that they marked underground sources of water; that they were pointers to direct divine spirits to bring rains; even that they were landing strips for alien spacecraft. (The animal shapes do match age-old Andean fertility symbols, particularly those associated with water.) But it's still mind-boggling to imagine these ancient people designing an aerial pattern they'd never be able to view.

In just a few decades, however, this age-old sight has been irreparably damaged. In 1934, the Pan-American Highway was built across the Nazca Valley, rudely bisecting one lizard figure; nowadays drivers cut cross-country to avoid paying tolls, their wheels carelessly jolting across some of the lines. Farms and residences creep closer; new factories blow in pollution; and global climate change and deforestation have recently triggered severe flooding and mudslides. Tomb raiders dig for ancient artifacts, potholing the terrain, and squatters have set up illegal camps dangerously close to the lines. Even tourism is a threat: The more people who walk here, the more damage is caused to this delicate terrain. To view it responsibly, flyovers really are the best way to go; several charter airlines at the Nazca airport offer sightseeing flights.

From the window of an airplane, you can easily identify specific shapes—a parrot, a hummingbird, a spider, a condor, a dog, a llama, a whale, a monkey—and they're huge: the spider is 55m (180 ft.) long, the monkey 100m (328 ft.) wide. The eeriest of all is one humanlike figure with his hand raised in greeting—an ancient astronaut, perhaps?

✈ Lima

🛏$$ **Casa Andina Classic Nasca,** Jr. Bolognesi 367, Nazca (©**866/220-4434** in North America, or 511/213/9739; www. casa-andina.com). $ **Hotel Alegria,** Calle Lima 166, Nazca (©**51/56/522-497;** www. hotelalegria.net).

Desert
266

Dana Biosphere Reserve
Riding the Great Rift
South-Central Jordan

Illegal woodcutting, overgrazing by nomadic herds, and hunting of rare animals like the Nubian ibex still threaten to degrade this biodiverse desert gem. Creating more eco-tourism jobs may shift the paradigm.

Whether you're coming north from Petra 304 or south from the Dead Sea 26, by the time you reach the Great Rift Valley, you'll know beyond a doubt that Jordan is a desert country—80% desert, in fact. But within that term "desert," there are so many variations—and the Dana Biosphere Reserve has all of them. There's the rugged mountain terrain of the **Qadishyah plateau,** 1,500m (4,900 ft.) high, where Nubian ibex clatter on the rocks and lesser kestrels swoop above the cliffs. There are the steeply dropping canyons, or *wadis*, their reddish sandstone walls wind-carved into dramatic shapes, bristling with juniper, oak, and acacia. There's the desert floor, 50m (164 ft.) below sea level, where sand cats prowl and spiny-tailed lizards skitter around rocky rubble and drifting dunes. Those abrupt changes in elevation create such stunning panoramas, even a short hike reveals new views at every turn.

Within a mere 116 square miles (300 sq. km), this reserve encompasses four biozones, in such close proximity that species diversity runs wild. Nowhere else in the world does Mediterranean cypress grow this far south; nowhere else has so many breeding pairs of the plump yellow Syrian Serin finch. Those steep drops in elevation attract an amazing variety of migratory birds, some 1.5 million passing through every year.

Jordan's largest nature reserve, Dana Biosphere was given protected status in 1989—and not a moment too soon. Increasing agriculture in the area—mostly olive orchards and vegetable gardens—had pushed traditional nomadic herders into smaller regions, which were quickly becoming overgrazed. Rather than pit environmental protection against the needs of local residents, however, the DBR's managers, Jordan's Royal Society for the Conservation of Nature, have also focused on improving life for the local Ata'ta people. Engineers have worked with local farmers to develop more efficient irrigation and water management; herders have been allotted defined grazing zones; extensive reconstruction has revived the once-dilapidated ancient stone village of Dana lying just east of the reserve. A stunning new solar-powered ecolodge, set dramatically on the desert floor within the reserve, provides many new jobs.

Among the many archaeological sites scattered about the reserve, hikers can explore 4,000-year-old mine shafts in **Wadi Feynan**—a reminder that centuries ago, this desert community thrived on trade and copper mining. If things work out as planned, eco-tourism can provide the valley with a new economic base, one that will ensure the biodiversity of this desert treasure for future generations.

ⓘ **Dana Biosphere Reserve** (✆ 962/3/227 0498; www.rscn.org.jo)

✈ Amman

🛏 $$ **Dana Guesthouse,** Dana Village (✆ 962/6/461-6523; www.rscn.org.jo). $$$ **Feynan Ecolodge,** inside Dana Biosphere Reserve (✆ 962/6/464-5580; www.feynan.com).

9 Ancient Ruins

Stonehenge

The Caves of Lascaux & Valley of the Vizérè

Rock of Ages

France

After surviving for 15,000 years or more, Lascaux's ancient cave paintings have been seriously damaged by decades of artificial light and carbon dioxide. Although it's no longer possible to visit Lascaux, the caves of the Valley of the Vizérè—which are vulnerable to damage due to pollution, climate change, and tourist traffic—are still open to the public.

Scientists at Lascaux called it the "green sickness"—the atmospheric changes that were destroying the world's most famous cave painting caused by millions of tourists viewing the underground chambers to see artwork such as bulls, wild boars, stags, horses, and deer.

Discovered by four French boys in 1940, these caves in Le Dordogne astonished with their hundreds of figures rendered in vivid colors. Archaeologists dated some of the 600 engravings to the Stone Age. Opened to the public in 1948, the caves became one of France's hottest tourist sites. Unfortunately, the artificial lights, increased air circulation, and carbon dioxide exhaled by visitors had an adverse effect on the walls. A fungus possibly caused by a climate-control system appeared in 2001, and when black spots of mold materialized in 2008, the cave was closed to many of the scholars who had been allowed inside. Today, only a few experts are allowed to work inside for a few days a month. Qualified archaeologists can apply to visit by writing to the **Direction Régionale des Affaires culturelles** (Service Régionale de l'Archéologie, 54 rue Magendie, 33074 Bordeaux; ✆ **33/5/57-95-02-02**).

Visitors can still view a replica at Lascaux 11, an aboveground structure that offers faithful copies of some 200 paintings.

Only 200 visitors are allowed per day. From April to October, you can buy tickets outside the **Montignac tourist office** (place Bertrand-de-Born; ✆ **33/5/53-51-82-60**). Even though the setting is artificial, the images on view are still breathtaking.

Those looking for a more authentic experience can find it at the Valley of the Vizérè, also in Le Dordogne, where three caves are open to visitors. Having learned a lesson from Lascaux, they strictly limit the number of visitors, so call in advance for reservations, up to a year ahead if possible. The **Grotte de Font-de-Gaume** (on D47, 1.5km/1 mile outside Les Eyzies; ✆ **33/5/53-06-86-00**) is decorated with Stone Age paintings of bison, reindeer, horses, and other animals, juxtaposed with graffiti from 18th-century British schoolboys. More recently unearthed, **Grotte des Combarelles** (D47, 17km/11 miles north of Bergerac; ✆ **33/5/53-06-86-00**) has carved figures dating back to the Stone Age, depicting musk oxen, horses, bison, and aurochs (wild oxen) in detail. Perhaps the most impressive of all is the **Cap Blanc cave** (Marquay, Sireuil; ✆ **33/5/53-06-86-00**), which was first discovered in 1909; it's the world's only prehistoric sculpted frieze open to the public, featuring huge figures of bison, horses, and reindeer.

While you're in the area, don't miss the **Musée National de la Préhistoire in Les Eyzies** (✆ **33/5/53-06-45-45**), which displays a hoard of artifacts excavated from many other sites in the area. All provide rare glimpses into the lives of our ancestors.

ⓘ **The Caves of Lascaux:** off D706, 2km (1¼ miles) from Montignac, France (✆ **33/5/53-51-95-03**), closed Jan. **The Valley of the Vizérè:** Les Eyzies tourist office, 19 rue de la Préhistoire (✆ **33/5/53-06-97-05**; www.leseyzies.com).

🚆 Condat-Le-Lardin (The Caves of Lascaux) or Les Eyzies (The Valley of the Vizérè)

🛏 $$ **Hotel Le Relais du Soleil d'Or,** 16 rue du 4-Septembre, Montignac (✆ **33/5/53-51-80-22**; www.le-soleil-dor.com), closed Feb. $$$ **Hotel Les Glycines,** Rte. De Périgueux, Les Eyzies-Tayac-Sireuil (✆ **33/5/53-06-97-07**; www.les-glycines-dordogne.com).

268 Cave Dwellers

Altamira Cave
Picassos of Prehistory
Cantabria, Spain

TOURIST TRAFFIC HAS IRREPARABLY DAMAGED THESE CAVE PAINTINGS THAT DATE BACK TO THE Ice Age. In addition, experts say that the Altamira Cave may collapse sometime in the future.

Michelangelo's painting the ceiling of the Sistine Chapel was nothing new—a bunch of nameless artists did the same thing 15,000 years ago, at the end of the Ice Age. In an S-shaped set of caves at Altamira, Spain, instead of the Creation they depicted bison, boars, and horses, leaping and plunging across the cave ceiling. Whoever these artists were, they created perhaps the most beautiful cave paintings anywhere.

The paintings are almost all in one main room of the cave system, called the Polychrome Chambers. Bison are the star players here, with the most stunning section featuring 21 red bison stampeding across the ceiling—you can practically hear them stamp and snort. Using only three colors—ocher, red, and black—these are large-scale pictures, practically life-size, and executed in meticulous realistic detail, rippling muscles, bristling manes, and all. The paintings were ingeniously positioned to take advantage of natural bulges and furrows in the rock, giving a three-dimensional realism to the animals. Another unusual feature is eight engraved anthropomorphic figures, various handprints, and hand outlines, almost as if the artists were determined to leave their own signatures.

Although the cave was discovered in 1868, it wasn't until 1879 that a little girl—daughter of the nobleman who owned the land—noticed paintings on the ceilings of the dark cave. Because they were so well preserved, archaeologists insisted they were forgeries; not until 1902 were they authenticated. Over the course of the 20th century, the Altamira cave became so popular with visitors that, inevitably, harmful bacteria were tracked in and damaged these masterpieces. Even more damaging were the walls built in the 1950s to prop up the ceiling of this karst cave, which seemed on the verge of natural collapse: The walls

Altamira Cave.

cut off the main chamber, thus irrevocably altering the atmospheric conditions that were responsible for its perfect preservation in the first place. The cave has been repeatedly closed to the public ever since the 1970s; currently no visitors are allowed, but cave officials hope to grant limited access again eventually, so keep checking for updates.

In the 1960s, anticipating such closures— or even total collapse of the cave—a couple of exact replicas were built, one for the Deutsches Museum, another to be displayed in Madrid. In 2001, an even more precise replica was opened a few hundred feet away from the original cave. Called the **National Museum and Research Center of Altamira,** it's much more convincing than Lascaux's replica ❷❻❼ The ceiling paintings were copied using sophisticated computerized digital-transfer technology that captured every crack, stain, and hollow of the original. Who needs to damage the real thing any further, when all of the incredible artistry lives on here?

ⓘ **Cuevas de Altamira,** Santillana del Mar (✆ **34/94/281-8815;** http://museode altamira.mcu.es/index.html)

✈ Santander

🛏 $$ **Casa del Marqués,** Cantón 26, Santillana del Mar (✆ **34/94/281-88-88**). $ **Hotel Siglo XVIII,** Revolgo 38, Santillana del Mar (✆ **34/94/284-02-10**).

Rock Shelters of Bhimbetka
Human Timeline
Madhya Pradesh, India

WITHOUT PROTECTION FROM THE NATIVE TREES THAT USED TO SHELTER THE AREA, THE BHIMBETKA site is battered by scorching heat, hail, and heavy rains, and invasive fig-tree roots are breaking up the rocks.

You can't ignore it; the very name Bhopal is synonymous with environmental disaster. It almost doesn't matter that these ancient caves have sheltered their artworks for 12,000 years—who comes to Bhopal anymore to see them?

It's a pity. Tourism to Bhopal (45km/28 miles away) died abruptly in 1984, after the deadly gas leak at a Union Carbide pesticide plant, but the area has two amazing historical sites: the Buddhist complex at Sanchi ④⑩ and the caves of Bhimbetka, which contain the earliest record of human life in India. Since they were first discovered in 1957, some 700 rock shelters have been identified around here; you can tour 15 of the most spectacular ones, which have been developed with walkways, lighting, and guides.

And what extraordinary art they contain. Unlike the older European caves, where most of the art depicts animals, the figures in Bhimbetka's rock shelters are mostly human—and they're not just hunting but dancing, feasting, worshiping, harvesting, waging war, giving birth, and burying their dead. Studying them, you can see the range of weapons they used, from bows and arrows and swords to barbed spears and pointed sticks. Because they were painted in different eras (the most recent date back only to medieval times), you can trace changes in religious rites, artistic styles, and even fashion, from loincloths to tattooed bodies to tunics. The range of animals portrayed is specifically Indian: alongside bison and horses you'll find rhinoceroses, tigers, lions, elephants, crocodiles, and peacocks. (Check out "Zoo Rock," nicknamed for the number of animals it depicts.) The best paintings are arrestingly dramatic, showing the terror of a hunter cornered by an angry bison, or the panic of a mother elephant whose child is being taken by trappers.

Notice how generations of cave dwellers used and reused their walls as a canvas, covering faded Paleolithic hunting scenes with bolder depictions of a warlike later era. The paints they used were chiefly colored earth, vegetable dyes, and animal fats, which were "fixed" chemically by the oxide in the rocks. That fluke enabled them to survive for centuries, even though they're not in sealed caves, but in open chambers within massive sandstone outcrops. Heaped high on wooded hills where the inhabitants could keep watch on the plains below, they're a stunning feature of the landscape—but just wait until you go inside.

ⓘ **Bhimbetka,** in Ratapani Wildlife Sanctuary, Hwy. 69 southwest of Bhopal (✆**91/ 748/022-4478**)

✈ Bhopal

🛏$ **Jehan Numa Palace,** 157 Shamla Hill, Bhopal (✆ **91/755/266-1100;** www. hoteljehanumapalace.com)

Wonderwerk Cave
Origins of Man
Kuruman, South Africa

INSIDE THE DEPTHS OF WONDERWERK CAVE, ARCHAEOLOGISTS PUZZLE OVER EVIDENCE OF 2 million years of human habitation. Can they solve its riddle before continuing erosion collapses the cave?

Standing outside the Wonderwerk Cave, visitors invariably catch their breath. Here on the plains of northeastern South Africa, you'd never expect a cavern this immense: Its yawning entrance is so big, a wagon and a team of oxen could enter and turn around in it. Eons of erosion have hollowed out the dolomitic limestone, with its beautiful stratified colors, to a depth of about 139m (456 ft.), plunging down for several levels underground. No wonder this cathedral-like cave was named Wonderwerk, which is Afrikaans for "miracle."

Deep as Wonderwerk is, human beings have occupied its many rooms over the years—for 2 million years, in fact, making it possibly the longest documented inhabited cave in existence. Near the entrance, walls are daubed with primitive bushman paintings. From artifacts found here, archaeologists deduce that the earliest levels of the cave were inhabited during hand-axe times. Stone tools and animal remains suggest an early hunter-gatherer society; fire-cracked stones prove that those early cave dwellers used fire in the cave. Other signs of civilization include red ocher fragments, quartz crystals, and colored pebbles that were likely used for adornment.

You'll begin your visit by looking at those artifacts in **The McGregor Museum** in Kimberly, about 43km (27 miles) away. McGregor, which now curates the cave, displays all material excavated from Wonderwerk, including Oldowan stone tools and fossils, animal bones, and dried grass once used for bedding. Contact the museum to book a private tour of the cave, which has been closed to the general public due to concerns about erosion and collapse. A metal fence blocks off the entrance to prevent casual visitors.

Wonderwerk is hardly a pristine site. Back in the 19th century, a former owner lived in the cave and used it for a sheep shelter; in the 1940s its condition was badly compromised when local farmers dug up its bat guano for fertilizer. Privately owned until 1993, its significance began to emerge only when serious excavation began in the mid-1970s.

Touring Wonderwerk, you'll see the signs of archaeologists still at work, trying to puzzle out the cave's evidence about Stone Age culture in this far corner of Africa. Who lived here, and why? What was the religious significance of their rituals? And, intriguingly, why do the flora specimens collected here correlate to a far wetter environment than the current arid Northern Cape? What does that tell us about climate change? Wonderwerk Cave's investigations are still a work in progress. By limiting visitation, the archaeological team hopes to prevent further damage to this fragile site.

ⓘ **McGregor Museum,** Kimberly (✆ **27/ 53-839-2706;** www.museumsnc.co.za)

✈ Kuruman Airport

🛏 $ **Amaziah Guesthouse,** 3 Engelbrecht St., Kuruman, 8460 (✆ **27/82-927-1190**). $ **Casa Linge Guesthouse,** Corner Seodin and Purchase Ave., Kuruman (✆ **27/ 53-712-3051**).

Cueva de las Manos
A Show of Hands
Patagonia, Argentina

CUEVA DE LAS MANOS HAS ESCAPED THE EFFECTS OF RAMPANT TOURISM THAT PLAGUE OTHER cave painting sites. There's no buildup, no state-of-the-art visitor center, no bus-tour hordes straggling through—at least not yet.

At first you'd swear a bunch of first-graders had been let loose in this rock niche in the Rio Pintura canyon: A flurry of stenciled handprints, in red and yellow and white, cover the walls by the hundreds, like a bunch of eager pupils waving to get the teacher's attention.

These handprints are perhaps 600 years old. No one knows why they're there. From the size of the hands, it seems they would have belonged to 13-year-old boys—it's possible that stamping your handprint in this sacred cave was a coming-of-age ritual among the native Tehuelches. You'll also notice that they're nearly all left hands; presumably the boys used their right hands to hold blowpipes for the paint, several of which have been found lying around the cave. And if you look hard, you may be able to find one startling handprint with six fingers—freaky.

Long before the Tehuelches started painting hands here—as long as 8,000 or 9,000 years ago—**Cueva de las Manos** (Cave of the Hands) was already decorated with prehistoric rock art, particularly detailed hunting murals. As befits a site on the Patagonian steppes, of course, the animals in those hunting scenes are guanacos; among the handprints at one spot you can also see the three-toed footprint of a rhea, South America's equivalent of an ostrich. Notice also the big red splotches on the ceiling—anthropologists guess those were made by tossing up a *boleadora,* or leashed hunting ball, that had been dipped in ink.

The **Rio Pinturas canyon** is rugged, scenic, and remote—remote even for Patagonia—which is why the cave wasn't really discovered until the 1970s. As a result, it's still in good shape, even though it's relatively exposed to the elements. The entrance to this *alero,* or rock overhang (it isn't a true cave), is quite large, 15m (49 ft.) wide and 10m (33 ft.) high, but it does slope upward and becomes more protected back by the paintings. Railings have been erected to prevent visitors from touching the paintings, but otherwise it's undeveloped; it's actually on private land, and open to the public only by permission of the owner.

Cueva de los Manos certainly is off the beaten track; it still isn't included on most tour itineraries, being so far from Patagonia's other attractions. But that makes it all the more impressive, wild and lonely and as yet unspoiled.

ⓘ**Cueva de los Manos,** in Francisco P. Moreno National Park, RP 97, south of Baja Caracoles

✈Perito Moreno

🛏$$ **Belgrano,** Av. San Martín, Perito Moreno (✆**54/43/2019**). $ **Cueva de las Manos** (✆**54/11-5237-4043;** cuevadelasmanos@hotmail.com).

TOUR Patagonian Travel Adventures (✆ **831/336-0167;** www.patagonia adventures.com)

10 Places to See Petroglyphs

From the dawn of time, humans have felt compelled to interpret their environment with art—and by carving it in stone, they ensured it would last through the centuries. Etched into the surface of caves, canyon walls, and hillsides, these petroglyphs (as opposed to "pictographs," or paintings on rock) are more than just graffiti from the ancients—anthropologists see them as cultural history and, most often, sites of religious importance to their makers. Most are still considered sacred sites by their descendants, which makes it even more imperative to protect them.

Here are 10 outstanding petroglyph sites that have survived—so far:

272 Nine Mile Canyon, North of Price, Utah Actually 40 miles (64km) long, this eastern Utah canyon is like a drive-through gallery of more than 10,000 petroglyphs, carved into its black rock face around A.D. 1000 to 1200 by the long-vanished Fremont Indians. Hunters, shamans, horses, elk, snakes, turkeys, bighorn sheep, owls, and even centipedes are depicted; the best is a large hunting scene in Cottonwood Canyon. *www.byways.org/explore/byways/15780. www.ninemilecanyoncoalition.org.*

273 Petroglyph National Monument, Albuquerque, New Mexico On the outskirts of Albuquerque, Pueblos and other prehistoric Native Americans carved

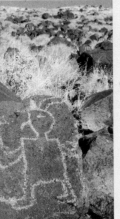

some 25,000 pictures into the dark basaltic boulders of this volcanic escarpment along the Rio Grande. Despite a number of lawsuits, the city is enlarging two highways through the monument close to the Boca Negra Canyon, the most visited section of the park. ✆ *505/899-0205. www.nps.gov/petr.*

274 Tutuveni, Tuba City, Arizona A sacred site of unparalleled cultural importance to the Hopi people and a vital resource for archaeologists, Tutuveni has suffered much damage by vandals and souvenir hunters. Spray-painted graffiti has destroyed approximately 10% of the symbols that are carved into the stones here, which record more than 1,000 years of Hopi history and culture. *Hopi Cultural Preservation Office:* ✆ *928/734-3612.*

275 Valley of Fire, Overton, Nevada Only 55 miles (89km) from Las Vegas, this dramatically eroded Mojave rockscape preserves a set of stunning 3,000-year-old rock carvings by Pueblos and prehistoric basket makers. A mere .5-mile (.8km) loop trail through Petroglyph Canyon reveals panel after panel

Petroglyph National Monument.

of slick dark rock etched with astoundingly expressive figures—big-horned sheep, dancers, birds, and suns. ✆ *702/397-2088.*

276 Puako Petroglyphs, Holoholokai Beach Park, Hawaii On a shelf of pahoehoe lava rock the size of a football field, some 3,000 intricate figures carved by ancient Hawaiian artists make up the largest rock art site in the Pacific, a site full of *mana,* or spiritual power, for the Hawaiian people. *Mauna Lani Resort.* ⓒ **808/885-1064.**

⑦ Cerros Pintados, Tarapaca, Chile   In the barren Atacama Desert of northern Chile, the Cerros Pintados—or "Painted Hills"—displays more than 350 figures of humans, animals (mostly alpacas and llamas), and intricate abstract symbols on some 66 panels carved, sculpted, or painted onto 3.2km (2 miles) of bare hillsides. The scale is often titanic—one human figure is 100m (328 ft.) high. Dated between A.D. 500 and 1450, the geoglyphs have been damaged by illegal mining, erosion, and unsupervised tourism. *www.turismochile.com.*

⑧ Coa Valley, Portugal   The first carvings here were made in Paleolithic times (40,000–10,000 B.C.); the most recent were chiseled at the beginning of the 20th century. In the 1990s, a dam project nearly submerged these long-hidden carved boulders and canyon faces along 17km (11 miles) of the river Coa, in northeast Portugal, but it was prevented by an international protest campaign. Carvings are still being excavated in this little-known archaeological gem. ⓒ **351/279/768 260.**

⑨ Twyfelfontein Uibasen Conservancy, Namibia   In the stark red Namibian desert, these 6,000-year-old rock engravings created by the San bushmen of the Kalihari almost seem to glow under the desert sun. Whereas most bushman art in Africa (at Tsodilo in Botswana, and several sites in South Africa) is painted, here nearly 2,000 figures are carved onto open rock faces, including elephants, rhinoceroses, ostriches, and giraffes. ⓒ **264/67687047.**

⑩ Ku-ring-gai Chase National Park, New South Wales, Australia   Just northeast of Sydney, this park full of gum trees and rainforest also has several panels of Aboriginal rock art carved into the relatively soft Sydney basin sandstone. A 2.5km (1.5-mile) trail to the basin leads you past the best-known ones, featuring kangaroos, emus, and wallabies (note the hunters' boomerangs). ⓒ **61/2-9472-8949.**

⑪ Dampier Rock Art Complex, Murujuga, Western Australia   It's the world's largest collection of petroglyphs—and neighboring industrial developments are killing it. Pollution generated by local petrochemical plants on the Burrup Peninsula is dissolving the natural varnish of the rock faces, into which ancient Aboriginals chiseled some 250,000-plus figures, more than 10,000 years ago. You can find these engravings—many of them extraordinarily beautiful—incised on boulders and rock outcrops all over the peninsula. Go early in the morning, before the rocks get too hot. *www.burrup.org.au.*

The Hill of Tara
Gone with M3
County Meath, Ireland

NOW THAT A NEW HIGHWAY RUNS PAST IT, THE HILL OF TARA WAS RECENTLY PLACED ON THE World Monuments Fund's watch list. The hope is that this will help to preserve the Gabhra Valley, between the Hill of Tara and the Hill of Skryne, from further damage.

Ireland is a nation of storytellers, where seemingly every mossy stone and country crossroads has a tale spun about it. But even so, there's no disputing the legendary significance of the Hill of Tara, traditional seat of the High Kings of Ireland. No wonder plans to run a superhighway past it generated storms of outrage.

On first glance, Tara today doesn't look like much—a 90m-high (300-ft.) hill dotted with grassy mounds, some ancient pillar stones, and depressions that show where the Iron Age ring fort, Ráith na Ríogh, encircled the brow of the hill. But audiovisuals at the visitor center deconstruct just what those mounds represent, as if peeling away the centuries from this time-hallowed ridge. Prominent on the hilltop are the ring barrow called **Teach Chormaic** (Cormac's House) and the **Forradh,** or royal seat, with a granite coronation stone known as the **Lia Fáil** (Stone of Destiny), standing erect at its center. The trenches of three other smaller ring forts are nearby, as well as an excavated passage tomb just to the north, the astronomically aligned **Mound of the Hostages,** which dates to 2000 B.C.

The wood timbers of the old royal halls rotted long ago; the last great *feis*—a triennial banquet of princes, poets, priests, and politicians—was held in A.D. 560, after which the rise of Christianity forced ancient Celtic traditions into hiding. But Tara was always more than just one hill—it was the epicenter of Ireland's foremost kingdom, and several other important prehistoric sites are in the same valley. From the Hill of Tara, in the distance you can spot the great burial mound of Newgrange and the Hill of Slane, where St. Patrick readied himself to take on the Irish pagans—which, of course, he needed to do at Tara, Ireland's symbolic heart.

The N3 highway, heading northeast out of Dublin toward the town of Kells, already ran close enough to Tara to shake its foundations; now a larger limited-access motorway is even closer, 2.2km (1⅓ miles) away, with a major interchange right near the sacred hill. During construction, a number of megalithic souterrains—underground buildings—some dating from the 7th century, were bulldozed, probably the homes of important nobles and courtiers living near the king's fort. When a 2,000-year-old henge named Lismullin with megalithic decorations on its stone was unearthed in March 2007, construction was temporarily halted—but work on the road has been completed, despite vociferous citizen protests. In 2008, the hill was placed on the World Monuments Fund list of 100 most endangered sites. Will it be too little too late?

ⓘ**Hill of Tara,** off the N3, Navan, County Meath (☏**353/46/902-5903**)

✈Dublin

🚌Navan

🛏$$ **Bellinter House,** Naven Naven, Meath (☏**800/238-0767**). $ **Lennoxbrook Country House,** Kells (☏**353/46/45902**).

Dun Aengus
A Ruin & a Riddle
Aran Islands, Ireland

EROSION HAS TAKEN ITS TOLL ON DUN AENGUS, AN IRON AGE FORT SITUATED ON THE HIGH CLIFFS of the Aran Islands. Acid rain and higher winds brought on by climate change are increasingly problematic.

Set broodingly on a 90m-high (300-ft.) western cliff, Dun Aengus looks ready to crash into the sea at any moment. And it's true, geologists tell us; battered by the elements, that limestone karst is already in the process of crumbling. But this mysterious Iron Age fort is hanging tough.

The weathered look of this rough-piled mass of dark gray stones is part of its aura. Walking around Dun Aengus (or to give it its proper Gaelic name, Dún Aonghasa), at times you'll come perilously close to the edge of the cliff, with no guardrail between you and certain death on the rocks below.

Though it's closer to the edge than it used to be, this sea-cliff location was undoubtedly always an important element of its defense, not to mention its vantage point for spotting the ships of any invader.

Who built Dun Aengus? Scholars disagree: It could have been an ancient Celtic tribe called the Fir Bolgs or the work of 8th- or 9th-century Danes. Nor can scholars agree on what the fort was used for. When you walk up the hill (a 20-min. hike from the visitor center), you pass a chevaux-de-frise zone, where sharp stones jut defensively out of the ground, and its walls

Dun Aengus.

are certainly defensive—3m (10 ft.) high in some places, and the thickest 4.3m (14 ft.) thick. Yet the design of the structure—three concentric semicircles opening to the sea—looks more like a theater than a fortress. If it was a fort, why are there no dwellings inside, or any provision for bringing in water in case of siege? And within the centermost horseshoe, what is the purpose of that large table rock, almost like a sacrificial altar?

The Aran Islanders are a hardy lot, living in stone cottages, speaking only Gaelic among themselves, and casting out to sea every day in small round currachs made of tarred canvas. In many ways life here hasn't changed much for centuries—it's a time warp experience to ferry over from modern Galway City to Kilronan, the main town on the island of Inishmore (Inis Mór). At the docks you can rent bikes or hail a minivan or, even better, an old-fashioned jaunting cart to get around the island; it's only 7km (4⅓ miles) west to Dun Aengus.

There are several similar structures nearby: **Dun Dubhchathair,** 2.5km (1½ miles) southwest; **Dun Eochla,** the same distance northwest; and **Dun Eoghanacht,** 7.2km (4½ miles) west-northwest. Though smaller than Dun Aengus, they have the same primitive power, the same sense of mystery. If only these stones could speak!

ⓘ **Dun Aengus** (✆ **353/99/61008**)

✈ Inis Mór; Galway City

🚢 Kilronan

🛏 $$ **Galway Harbour Hotel,** New Dock Rd., Galway (✆ **353/91-894-800;** www. galwayharbourhotel.com). $$ **Kilmurvey House,** coast road, Inis Mór (✆ **353/ 99/61218**).

Fortresses & Ceremonial Sites 284

Stonehenge
Sacred Stones in Peril
Salisbury Plain, England

ONE OF THE WORLD'S MOST MYSTERIOUS SITES, STONEHENGE HAS STOOD IN SILENT MAJESTY FOR centuries upon windswept, grassy Salisbury Plain. No matter how many pictures of it you've seen, standing next to those immense stones still inspires a shiver of awe. The last thing you want is huge lorries trundling past to spoil their mystique.

But that's the scenario that these ancient stones may face. Since 1991, there have been 51 different schemes to reroute or widen the congested A303 Highway, the main road from London to the southwest, which passes close to Stonehenge. Several versions proposed burying the A303 in a tunnel—hiding the road from view, but potentially shaking the stones' foundations, damaging unexcavated relics, and disturbing the chalk grassland habitat. Widening the A303 holds some benefits for Stonehenge—it would eliminate the A344, which currently cuts right north of the stone circle—but various parties involved (the National Trust, English Heritage, an ad hoc group called Save Stonehenge) have different notions of where to reroute the road. While the latest proposal was axed in 2007 for budgetary reasons, advocates continue to fine-tune the scheme, while English Heritage seeks alternative funding for a proper visitor center, relocated farther from the stones than the current tiny ticket office.

It's no small issue, for Stonehenge is the United Kingdom's most important ancient monument. Scholars have determined that it was first laid out around 3100 B.C. as a circle of upright timbers, then rebuilt around 2500 B.C. using 5-ton bluestones floated on rafts from Wales. Two centuries later, the ancient builders replaced the bluestones with 45-ton Sarsen sandstone blocks. Moving rocks this big is quite a feat; you can still see drag marks in the earth. How did ancient workers stand these rocks on end, much less lift the distinctive cross-pieces to place on top? The biggest mystery, though, is why it was built at all. Archaeologists suggest that because the circle is perfectly aligned with the sun on the summer solstice, it was the site for some sun-worship ceremony—a finding that has made the site hugely popular with modern-day Druids and hippies.

That Stonehenge has survived this long is amazing. Over the centuries, many stones fell over or were carted away by farmers, visitors chipped off bits for souvenirs, and wind and weather have done their best to erode their exposed surfaces.

Since 1978, immediate access to the stone circle has been cut off to general tourists, who have to circle around it on a walkway that never gets closer than 15m (50 ft.) to the actual stones. The massive blank stones still cast a mystical aura, even from that distance, but plan ahead and you can join a group tour to enter inside the circle (see the website below for details).Time your visit to coincide with a solstice, equinox, or Druidic holy day—and hope that the traffic holds off.

ⓘwww.stonehenge.co.uk/index.php

✈Heathrow

🛏$$ **Mornington Hotel,** 12 Lancaster Gate, Bayswater (✆ **800/633-6548** in North America, or 44/20/7262-7361; www. bw-morningtonhotel.co.uk). $$ **Sanctuary House Hotel,** 33 Tothill St., Westminster (✆ **44/20/7799-4044;** www.fullershotels. com).

---

285 Fortresses & Ceremonial Sites

Fort St. Elmo
Fortress at Risk
Malta

FORT ST. ELMO HAS STOOD PROUD THROUGH CENTURIES OF SIEGES, AIR RAIDS, AND INVASIONS, only to be left in a deteriorated state due to lack of maintenance and exposure to the elements.

Fort St. Elmo looks exactly like you'd expect a fortress to look—massive, forbidding, encasing the headlands of Valletta, Malta's capital, in impregnable walls of sun-bleached sandstone. That evocative look was put to use in the 1978 film *Midnight Express*, in which Fort St. Elmo stood in for the Turkish jail where a hashish-smuggling American student serves a nightmare sentence. The fort's impressive walls had their beginnings as a watchtower in the early 16th century, on a strategic peninsula overlooking both of Malta's main natural

harbors. Construction began in earnest in 1533, soon after the Knights of Malta—formerly the order of St. John, driven out of the Holy Land after the Crusades—based themselves on this mid-Mediterranean island. By the time of the Ottoman siege of 1565, it was a full-fledged citadel in the classic star fort layout. Bearing the brunt of the siege, the fort was reduced to rubble before falling to the Turks, although the Knights eventually held the island and drove out the invaders.

In the centuries since, Fort St. Elmo was continually expanded and renovated, adopting Italian, French, Spanish, and British influences at different eras, depending on which power ruled Malta at the time. It evolved into a 50,400-sq.-m (543,000-sq.-ft.) structure incorporating defense walls, parade grounds, arsenals, and a chapel, all designed to shelter 100 knights and soldiers. In 2008, however, the World Monuments Fund placed the fort on its 100 Most Endangered Sites watch list, citing significant deterioration due to poor maintenance, aging, and exposure to the elements. The government responded to this wake-up call by dispatching soldiers to evict squatters and deter vandals; in 2009, the Infrastructure Ministry announced plans to rehabilitate the fort, a project still being developed by the local planning authority.

These days, the republic of Malta—which won independence from Britain in 1964—is a neutral country with no need for such massive fortification; instead, portions of the half-abandoned fort house Malta's police academy and **The National War Museum,** which commemorates the harsh conditions of World War II, when German and Italian forces bombed Malta and tried to starve its people into submission. The star exhibit is a Gloster Gladiator bi-plane named *Faith,* which—with its sister planes *Hope* and *Charity*—played a vital role in Malta's air defense. You can explore the fort on a self-guided tour; guided tours are led on Saturdays or Sundays (check for schedules). On Parade Days, full-scale military reenactments are performed, but there's often a unit of the Knights of Malta Military hanging around, their reproduction armor and colorful red-and-yellow medieval uniforms paying tribute to this fort's long, proud history.

ⓘ www.malta-information.com

✈ Malta international Airport

🛏 $ **British Hotel Valletta,** 40 Battery St., VLT 01, Valletta (✆ **356/21/224-730**). $ **Castille Hotel,** Castille Sq., c/w St. Paul's St., Valletta (✆ **356/2122-3677/8;** www.hotelcastillemalta.com).

Kuelap Fort
Fortress of the Cloud People
Chachapoyas, Peru

KUELAP'S ISOLATION HIGH IN THE ANDES HAS KEPT IT WELL PRESERVED THROUGH THE CENTURIES. However, the Peruvian government's plan to attract tourists threatens this ancient city.

If Kuelap had been easy to get to, it might have beaten out Machu Picchu as Peru's most famous archaeological site. After all, this ruined prehistoric fort is at least twice as old as Machu Picchu, and quite a bit bigger—with its massive limestone walls and hundreds of buildings, it's the largest ancient building in the Americas. Some archaeologists estimate that Kuelap, which took 200 years to build, contains three times more stone than the Great Pyramid at Giza.

But it always took grit and persistence to get here: a jolting 12-hour bus ride from Chiclayo, an overnight stay in the provincial town of Chachapoyas, and then another bone-rattling 3-hour journey with a local guide up the mountain to the fortress. (That is, unless you were mad enough to hike or ride a horse up the final climb from the village of Nuevo Tingo.)

Perched high and lonely on this Andes peak, Kuelap was built by the Chachapoya, a warrior race who thrived in Amazonian cloud forests from the 9th to the 15th century A.D., when they finally were conquered by the Incas. Mummies found in the area suggest that the Chachapoyans were unusually tall, light skinned, and fair haired, another reason for their nickname, "cloud people." The Incas occupied the fort themselves several years later, after the Chachapoyans had abandoned it, and then abandoned it themselves when the Spanish destroyed their empire.

Kuelap seems stark and forbidding at first, with its bristling golden walls and tricky narrow entrance passages. Having been so isolated, though, the fort is in a remarkable state of preservation, with hundreds of buildings used for everything from ritual sacrifice to lookout towers to communal kitchens; its decorative carvings are still sharply incised. Yet it doesn't feel all scrubbed up; the lush cloud forest vegetation creeps over the stones, and llamas graze placidly outside the walls. There are still so few visitors, you might be rambling about by yourself, communing with the spirits of these enigmatic pre-Incans.

Though it was discovered in 1843—60 years before Machu Picchu—Kuelap wasn't really opened to tourism until the 1970s. But there's been a lot of interest in this ancient mountain stronghold lately, especially since the 2007 discovery of 80 human skeletons. Kuelap's on the verge of being the next "hot" destination—who knows what that will do to spoil its sense of mystery?

ⓘ **Los Tambos Chachapoyanos** (www.kuelap.org)

Kuelap Fort.

✈ Chiclayo

🛏 $$ **Choctomal Lodge, Choctomal Village** (✆ 800/999-0558)

TOUR Kuoda Tours (✆ 51/84/263-010 in Peru; www.inturkuoda.com). **Peruvian Secrets** (✆ 44/1248-430621; www.peruviansecrets.co.uk). **Chachapoyas Tours** (✆ 866/396-9582 in North America, or 407/583-6786; www.kuelapperu.com).

287 Fortresses & Ceremonial Sites

El Fuerte de Samaipata
The Fort That Wasn't
Bolivia

NEGLECT AND POPULARITY EQUALLY THREATEN EL FUERTE DE SAMAIPATA'S MYSTERIOUS SANDstone ruins. Its fragile state prompted UNESCO to name it a World Heritage Site in 1998.

They may call it El Fuerte, but there's no way this was meant to be a fort. What military purpose could ever have been served by those fanciful animal shapes, the jaguars, snakes, and cats carved into this immense reddish sandstone? And that stone water tank looks utilitarian enough, until you examine the two long parallel stone troughs that run downhill to the town, with zigzag channels radiating away from it. No wonder some folks think this was a landing strip for alien spacecraft.

When the Spanish conquistadors first stumbled on these enigmatic ruins in the mountains of central Bolivia, they were baffled, too. But, being conquistadors, they called it a fort and used it as such. Later, they too abandoned it and let the weeds take it over. Only in modern times have archaeologists tried to solve the riddle of Samaipata. Why, for instance, were those stone seats on this hillside arranged in just that way—a circle of 12 seats facing inward, and another three inside the circle facing out? Was it a religious ceremony, a court of judgment, or what? And even stranger, once you follow the two parallel water troughs, you notice that their lines converge at a certain point in the sky—the point where Venus and Jupiter had a parallel rising at sunrise on August 20, 1066. Or was it the flyover of Halley's Comet in March 1066 that the lines commemorate?

A 2-hour drive from Santa Cruz, Bolivia's largest city, El Fuerte de Samaipata is a popular day outing, and with the spectacular views from this high Andes hilltop, you can see why. But as a set of ruins, it's not developed much—the city downhill from the carvings is only half excavated, and remnants of several temples around the hill are badly overgrown. With its jumbled Inca, pre-Inca, and Spanish elements, the site is a little confusing—hire a guide from Santa Cruz if you really want to get some insight. Locals who come here seem less interested in interpreting the culture than in simply roaming around the carvings. As a result, the inner area has finally been cordoned off—so much foot traffic has damaged these ancient sandstone forms, already seriously eroded by the elements.

It remains to be seen how the authorities will continue to develop this site. Nowhere else in the Americas did any culture develop a huge sculptured rock like this—you get the sense that there must be a great story behind it. But can that story be unlocked before the carvings and buildings crumble irretrievably?

✈ Santa Cruz

⊨ $$$ **Hotel Los Tajibos,** Av. San Martin 455 (*©* **591/3/3421-000;** www. lostajiboshotel.com)

TOUR Rosario Tours (*©* **591/3/369-656;** www.welcomeargentina.com/rosario/outings.html). **Michael Blendinger** (*©* **591/33/9446-816;** mblendinger@cotas.com.bo).

Cradle of Civilization **288**

The Pyramids of Giza
Desert Scandal
Cairo, Egypt

UNRESTRICTED DEVELOPMENT AND AIR POLLUTION FROM NEARBY CAIRO THREATEN THE ANCIENT pyramids and the Great Sphinx, and the government is still in turmoil after Egypt's 2011 revolution.

Of all the original Seven Wonders of the Ancient World, only one is still standing: the Great Pyramid of Cheops. Granted, its pinnacle was lopped off, and the polished white limestone that once faced its sloping sides was scavenged ages ago. But there it is in the Egyptian desert, the largest in a trio of stupendous royal tombs, with a quirky monument called the Sphinx alongside. It's quite a sight to see—if only you could see it.

It used to be that aggressive throngs of souvenir vendors, tour touts, and taxi drivers crowded the entrance to the pyramids, but the revolution has scared away millions of tourists, which are vital to Egypt's survival; in February 2011, tourism was down by 80%. As of June 2011, the military was guarding the pyramids and there were restrictions on tourist access. There were also reports of damage to some antiquities. The haphazard sprawl and pollution of Cairo come right to the edge of the archaeological zone, yet Egyptian officials—still delicately piecing together a government after the 2011 popular uprising—seem unconcerned about protecting the site. Three Egyptian children were even recently injured by an explosive device found by the pyramids.

It's difficult now to get that iconic long-distance view of the three pyramids looming in the desert; you can't really see them until you're so close, you're staggered by their size—an estimated 2,300,000 stones compose the **Great Pyramid** alone, weighing on average 2½ tons apiece (some are even 9 tons). Oriented precisely to the points of the compass, they were built for three Pharaohs of the 4th Dynasty (ca. 27th c. B.C.)—the Great Pyramid of Cheops, the slightly smaller Second Pyramid of Chephren, and the much smaller red-granite Third Pyramid of Mycerinus—and designed to imitate the rays of the sun shining down from its zenith, so that the buried king might ascend to heaven using his pyramid as a ramp. The great mystery is how they were erected at all, given the primitive technology available. Obviously it took a lot of manpower, or rather slave power: The construction of the Great Pyramid was like a gigantic 20-year public works project, giving the workers extra income during the annual flooding of the Nile.

The **Great Sphinx** wasn't part of the original plan, but was improvised to get rid

The Pyramids of Giza.

of a limestone knoll that blocked King Chephren's view of his pyramid—a brilliant bit of serendipity, as it turned out. It's a gargantuan likeness of Chephren himself, dressed up as Harmachis, god of the rising sun. Fragments of orange-red paint still cling to the battered face, which was vandalized by medieval Muslims. Its soft limestone, however, has required continual restoration; in the late 1980s, the paws (and the left shoulder, which fell off in 1989) got a makeover, though there was no way to repair the broken-off royal "artificial beard."

Most tourists expect a visit to the famed pyramids to be a once-in-a-lifetime thrill, not a tawdry letdown. (At least some of the circus atmosphere has been diminished with the pre-revolution ban on camel rides and horseback tours.) It's the only Ancient Wonder we have left—what a pity it's come to this.

ⓘ **Egypt State Information Service** (www.sis.gov.eg)

✈ Cairo International

Cradle of Civilization 289

The Valley of the Kings
Danger Under the Desert Sands
Luxor, Egypt

DECADES OF BAD URBAN WATER DISPOSAL AND FAULTY IRRIGATION SYSTEMS ARE THE MOST serious threats to the ancient underground tombs in the Valley of the Kings. Political unrest is only exacerbating these issues.

This is Egypt—a desert country where 90% of the population crowds onto 5% of the land, along the banks of the Nile. The problem has always been a lack of water. So who'd have expected that this world-famous necropolis may be destroyed by too much water?

But that's what's happening beneath the famed Valley of the Kings, where a critically backed-up natural underground reservoir is beginning to erode the stone foundations. It's a particular problem because the pharaohs of Thebes (now Luxor)—unlike their Lower Nile predecessors at Memphis (now Giza)—built their royal tombs underground, a cunning strategy to foil the sort of tomb robbers who'd pillaged the pyramids. The pharaohs deliberately chose high, dry ground for their tombs—but apparently it wasn't high or dry enough. Since the construction of the Luxor Bridge, 7km (4⅓ miles) north of the Valley of Kings, was completed in 1997, the clay substratum of the ground beneath the monuments had already been compromised; the pooling water was an accident waiting to happen.

More than 60 personages (mostly royalty) in the 18th, 19th, and 20th dynasties built their mazelike subterranean crypts here, brilliantly decorated and stuffed with treasure. In the end, of course, they were no more thief-proof than the pyramids—only Tutankhamun's treasure survived intact up to modern times—but the stunning artistry on their walls makes a visit here well worth the long trip up the Nile from Cairo.

A number of tombs are open to the public on a rotating basis, though the rules for touring them are strict: Photography is forbidden (most paintings are widely reproduced anyway), visitors must be quiet and file in one by one, and nothing must be touched. With thousands of tourists visiting the valley each day, that's still a lot of extra humidity and dirt for the ancient walls to be exposed to. If you're lucky, on the day you visit you may be able to see the burial chamber of the **tomb of Ramesses VI** (12th c. B.C.), where magnificent ceiling paintings depict the stars and other heavenly bodies; or the dazzling quartzite sarcophagus in the **tomb of King Tutankhamun** (though most of Tut's treasures were moved long ago to the Egyptian Museum in Cairo).

North of Luxor, the picturesquely jumbled ruin of the **Temple of Karnak** faces the same underground threat, and its elaborately incised round columns could collapse any day now. Engineers at both sites are hard at work, digging trenches and repairing irrigation systems, trying to solve the problem before it's too late. Will they succeed?

ⓘ **Nile St.,** Luxor (✆ **20/95-382-215**)

✈ Luxor International

🛏 $$ **Steigenberger Nile Palace,** Khaled Ben El Walid St. (✆ **20/95/2366-999**). $$ **Luxor Hilton,** next to the Temple of Karnak (✆ **800/HILTONS** [445-8667] or 20/95/237-4933; www.hilton.com).

290 Cradle of Civilization

Abu Mena
Guided by Camels
Alexandria, Egypt

IRRIGATION TO CROPS IN NEARBY FIELDS HAS CAUSED THE WATER TABLE AT ABU MENA TO RISE. As a result, the water has eroded the soft, clay soil beneath the ancient city and several buildings have collapsed.

If you want to see what Luxor's fate could be, behold what has already happened at Abu Mena. Once the greatest Christian holy city of the east, a bustling pilgrimage site that sparkled with marble and glittered with mosaics, its carefully excavated foundations are now caving in.

Long ago, Abu Mena was a forlorn spot in the Libyan desert, where Menas—a Libyan-born Roman legionary who converted to Christianity and died a martyr's death in Phrygia—was buried when the camel bearing his corpse home stopped in the desert and refused to budge. Ninety springs of water were said to flow miraculously from the grave, creating an oasis of vineyard and olive groves. A few years later, a shepherd who found Menas's grave gained mystical healing powers. After he cured Roman emperor Constantine's daughter, Constantine ordered a church to Menas built on the site.

By the late 4th century the little desert church was so overwhelmed with pilgrims seeking healing miracles from St. Menas that a large basilica was built in its stead, soon joined by an even grander basilica with 56 marble columns and rounded niches of polychrome marble—distinctively Coptic touches found nowhere else

in early Christian architecture. By A.D. 600, Abu Mena had become a substantial city of churches, monasteries, houses, and artisans' workshops, an ancient version of Lourdes with its own thriving culture. Wandering the mazelike streets of the ruined city, you can clearly distinguish the great basilica and the bath complex where pilgrims took the curative waters. Pottery flasks containing the holy water were much-sought-after relics, decorated with an image of St. Menas with two camels.

Conquering Muslims razed the city repeatedly from the mid–7th century onward, until eventually it disappeared beneath the shifting sands. It was rediscovered by German archaeologists in 1905; more recent excavations in the 1990s uncovered such fascinating features as a dormitory for poor pilgrims, an abbot's palace, a cemetery, and a complex of wine presses and cellars.

The main buildings of Abu Mena—the basilica, baths, baptistery, and church—are still intact, but in the northwest precincts of the city you can already see caved-in areas. The crypt under the church—the holy tomb that gave rise to this entire city—has been closed to the public and filled with sand to stave off collapse. Meanwhile, antiquities

10 Places to See Stone Circles

Everybody can picture the world's most famous circle of prehistoric standing stones, England's Stonehenge ㉘. But while Stonehenge is one of the most complete stone circles still standing, many others around the world are equally compelling. It isn't just their age—a spiritual aura lingers around these sites, some confluence of cosmic energy or electromagnetic pull . . . or just plain magic. Here are some of the most impressive remnants:

㉑ **The Stone Circles of Senegambia, Gambia & Senegal**   One of the world's most notable groups of stone circles boasts a staggering 1,000 stones spanning 350km

Avebury.

(217 miles) of the River Gambia. This World Heritage–designated attraction is divided into four groups: the Sine Nygayène, Wanar, Wassu, and Kerbatch—encompassing 93 stone circles, tumuli, and burial grounds, some of which date to between the 3rd century B.C. and the 16th century A.D. The stones were crafted with iron tools into cylindrical pillars. *www.visitthegambia.gm.*

㉒ **Avebury, Wiltshire, England**   The largest megalithic site in England, built from 3000 to 2400 B.C., Avebury could have fit the entire Stonehenge site inside the smallest of its three concentric circles. Despite centuries of depredation, more than 100 pitted and worn stones survive, some of them once nearly 60 tons in size. Gentle grassy slopes mark its once-immense ditch and bank. ✆ **44/1672/539250.** *www.avebury-web.co.uk.*

㉓ **Stanton Drew, Somerset, England**   Only 13km (8 miles) south of Bristol, a peaceful set of open fields outside the village of Stanton Drew holds a well-kept secret: Britain's second-largest stone circle, 113m (371 ft.) in diameter, with 27 of its original 36 stones, though many are broken and/or toppled. Two other smaller circles stand nearby; it's on private land, but open to the public. *www. stone-circles.org.uk.*

㉔ **Boscawen-Un, Near St Buryan, Cornwall, England**   The completeness of this small ellipse, along with its untamed setting, gives it an especially Druidical flavor. Lichened and overgrown with gorse, the 19 neatly spaced granite stones rise toward the west, as if angling the face of the circle; the distinctively slanted center stone points toward the point of midsummer sunrise. *www.intocornwall.com.*

㉕ **The Rollright Stones, Long Compton, Oxfordshire, England**   Cut from the same golden limestone as the colleges at nearby Oxford, the ragged stones known as the King's Men stand shoulder to shoulder in a near-perfect circle, 32m (105 ft.)—or 38 Druid cubits—in diameter. Legend says a king and his followers were turned to stone by witches from Long Compton (known as a center of witchcraft).

A solitary monolith nearby is called the King's Stone; another set of gnarled rocks, called the Whispering Knights, form a gateway to the site. *www.rollrightstones.co.uk.*

296 Ring of Brodgar, Near Stromness, Orkney Islands This sparsely populated archipelago 10km (6¼ miles) north of the Scottish mainland is dotted with Pict and Norse cairns, but the oldest and most impressive monument is the Ring of Brodgar (1560 B.C.), on the island called Mainland. Brodgar still has nearly half of its original 60 stones, surrounded by a deep ditch carved out of solid bedrock. *℗44/1856/872856. www.visitorkney.com.*

The Ring of Brodgar.

297 Callanish, Isle of Lewis, Scotland On this northernmost island of the Hebrides, a remarkably intact Neolithic temple, built around 1800 B.C., is laid out in the unusual shape of a Celtic cross. At its center is a circle of 13 standing stones, hewn from the rugged local gneiss, around a burial cairn. Legend says the stones were an ancient race of giants, turned to stone by St. Kiernan when they refused to convert to Christianity. *℗44/1851-621422. www.isle-of-lewis.com.*

The stones of Callanish.

298 Beltany, Raphoe, County Donegal, Ireland Built around 2000 B.C., this large hilltop circle still has 64 closely set 1.8m-tall (6-ft.) stones (originally there may have been 80), though many stones are broken and tipping. Lumpy turf inside the circle suggests it was a burial site, though one triangular cup-marked stone aligns mysteriously with sunrise on May 1—the pagan holiday known as Beltane. *℗353/74-9121160. www.discover ireland.com.*

299 Carnac, Brittany, France Carnac's Field of Megaliths takes the prize for most megaliths at one site—nearly 3,000 monumental stones, some up to 20m (66 ft.) tall, stand lined up enigmatically in three different groupings, each with a circle at the end. Erected around 4500 to 3300 B.C., these great pre-Celtic megaliths may represent some form of ancestor worship. *℗33/2/97-52-89-99.*

300 Almendres Menhir, Near Evora, Portugal One of Europe's oldest circles (some of it dates to 5000 B.C.), Almendres is actually two overlapping circles on an east-facing hilltop, built at different times and oriented to the two different equinoxes. Don't miss the solitary huge stone *(menhir)* a short walk away, and ponder the riddle of how it's connected to the circle. *www.ancient-wisdom.co.uk.*

officials battle to have old-fashioned irrigation stopped immediately, and replaced with modern methods that don't flood the soil. With no buffer zone established, Abu Mena has crops growing right up to its borders, part of a World Bank–funded land-reclamation project that was the agriculture officials' pride and joy a decade ago. Nowadays, it's more like Egypt's shame.

ⓘ www.stmina-monastery.org

✈ Alexandria

🛏 $ **Union Hotel,** 164 26th July Rd., Alexandria (© **20/3/480-7537**). $$ **El Salamlek Palace,** Montazah Gardens, Alexandria (© **20/3/547-7999**).

Babylon
One Sacrilege After Another
Al Hillah, Iraq

BABYLON, A CITY OF BOTH HISTORY AND LEGEND, HAS BEEN SERIOUSLY DAMAGED BY WAR AND development, and those remain its two major threats. The U.S. war in Iraq continues to endanger the ancient city.

Desperate Iraqi citizens aren't the only ones destroying their country's patrimony. In 2003, American troops committed even greater sacrilege: building a helipad atop a mound of mud-brick debris in the ruins of ancient Babylon. Heavy vehicles rumbled over centuries-old pavements, trenches were dug into artifact-filled soil, and carved figures in the Ishtar Gate were destroyed by soldiers prying out bricks for souvenirs.

The most fabled of ancient cities, Babylon has occupied this prime Mesopotamian site on the Euphrates River since the 3rd millennium B.C. In the 18th century B.C. it was the capital of Hammurabi's empire, where the world's first code of law was written. Under Nebuchadnezzar II (605–562 B.C.), the city was transformed into a brilliant capital, with such landmarks as the Etemenanki ziggurat, the Ishtar Gate, and the Hanging Gardens, named one of the Seven Wonders of the Ancient World (though some historians believe those were actually in Nineveh). Even under Persian rule, Babylon was an administrative capital and center of learning, especially astronomy and mathematics. Twice it was the largest city in the world—from 1770 to 1670 B.C. and from 612 to 320 B.C., with a population that may have topped 200,000. In the ancient world, that would have been huge.

Babylon had lain abandoned for centuries, its sunbaked bricks carted away until only foundations remained. Then in 1985, Saddam Hussein started rebuilding on top of the old ruins, ordering a combination of restoration and new construction to duplicate the city of Nebuchadnezzar—a copy, granted, but with that special Hussein flair. He erected an immense picture of himself and Nebuchadnezzar at the entrance to the ruins, and had his own name inscribed on building bricks, just as that ancient ruler had done, horrifying many archaeologists. The Ishtar Gate was recreated, and the ceremonial stone boulevard leading from it, Processional Way, was restored. Hussein built a ziggurat-style palace for himself over some old ruins, and was just about to string a cable car over Babylon when war broke out (since the downfall of Hussein, the work has ground to a halt).

At first the presence of U.S. troops protected Babylon from looters, but soon the protectors were causing more trouble than they were preventing. U.S. Marines lived in Saddam's palace, and the rest of the city was turned into a military depot, which was transferred to Polish forces in September 2003. World outrage, however, prompted the occupying forces to return the site to Iraq's antiquities officials in January 2005. Although American combat troops have left, nearly 50,000 troops remain and may stay in the area beyond 2011.

Iraqi leaders have spun ideas for continuing Hussein's rebuilding project once the war is over, creating a new cultural center with shopping malls, hotels, and perhaps a theme park—why not? Archaeologists are already shaking their heads.

ⓘ It is not advisable to travel to Iraq at the present time; check with your embassy for updates.

302 Legendary Cities

Urkesh
Sifting Through the Tell
Tell Mozan, Syria

BURIED AND LOST FOR CENTURIES, THE ANCIENT CITY OF URKESH WAS FINALLY UNEARTHED BY archaeologists in the past 2 decades. Built of adobe, the walls and buildings of Urkesh are now vulnerable to wind and rain and must be protected if they are to be preserved.

For years, the legendary city of Urkesh taunted archaeologists like a cruel mirage. Agatha Christie and her husband, archaeologist Max Mallowan, searched for it in the 1920s and 1930s, but they ruled out the Tell Mozan area. When a UCLA team began their dig here in 1984, they had no guarantee that this 150-hectare (370-acre) mound in the middle of a stark flat plain in northeast Syria held anything at all.

As they began to dig, they found the remains of mud-brick city walls and several houses, along with what seemed a royal palace, a monumental temple terrace, and an enigmatic underground pit, buildings that dated from the right period—5000 to 1500 B.C. But not until 1995, when they unearthed several seal impressions in the palace, could they definitively say that, yes, they had finally solved the mystery of Urkesh. For archaeologists, the thrill of discovering a whole new culture would be like an astronomer discovering a new planet.

Around 3000 B.C., the writings of Mesopotamian peoples like the Hittites and Akkadians frequently mentioned Urkesh as the great holy city of the Hurrians, a nation with its own unique language and mythology, and with great wealth based on copper mining in the Anatolian mountains to the north. Still, no trace of the Hurrians themselves existed anywhere—a baffling riddle for archaeologists. This mound didn't look too promising at first, for it had been plowed extensively and quarried for building stone. Generations had built their houses on top of the collapsed ruins of earlier houses, building up the mound century by century, so there was a lot of debris to plumb.

Today, the excavated ruins at Tell Mozan seem sharply gouged out of the flat, windswept top of the tawny mound, which rises 28m (92 ft.) above the surrounding plain. Excavators have reconstructed the foundations of the temple—now known to be a temple to Kumarbi, the Hurrians' chief god.

Despite recent political upheaval in the country, work continues on the royal palace, slowly and meticulously. Cagelike scaffolding covered with weatherproof fabric is used to protect the mud-brick structures once they're uncovered. (The scaffolding also helps visitors imagine what the buildings might have looked like.) It's a fascinating opportunity to watch state-of-the-art excavation in progress.

But adobe is such a vulnerable material, more needs to be done to strengthen the walls now that they are exposed to the elements. There is so much left to do at Tell Mozan—can they peel back all the layers of the past before the present catches up with them?

ⓘ Consult your embassy about travel conditions before visiting.

✈ Al Qamishli

🛏 $$ **Al Qamishli Hotel,** Al Saied Al Reas St., Al Qamishli (𝒞 **96/52/443355**).
$$ **Al Sufara'a Hotel,** Al Saied Al Reas St., Al Qamishli (𝒞 **963/52/432993**).

Legendary Cities **303**

Ancient Byblos
Oil on the Water
Jbeil, Lebanon

IN JULY 2006, AN ISRAELI BOMBING ATTACK ON LEBANON RIPPED OPEN OIL TANKS, UNLEASHING 15,000 gallons of oil along Lebanon's Mediterranean coast. While the cleanup was a success, Jbeil is still at risk from political unrest.

Most historians regard Byblos as the oldest continuously inhabited city in the world; some consider it the first real city ever built. There are so many ruins here, you'll find ancient columns carelessly toppled by the roadside. It has gone by many names: the Phoenicians called it Gebal, the Greeks Byblos, the crusaders Gibelet. Legend says it was founded by the god Chronos himself, and that Thoth invented the linear alphabet here.

Set high on a cliff just above Jbeil's harbor, the archaeological zone is a fascinating juxtaposition of ruins from many eras. You enter through a castle the crusaders built in the 12th century, when it was an important military base for them. Within the zone, several huts and building foundations date back to Neolithic times, around 5000 B.C., when it first began to take on the shape of a town. Byblos's most impressive ruins date from its Phoenician era: the Great Temple of Resheph, the Temple of Baalat Gebal, and the Temple of the Obelisks. Jumping forward in time, there's also a fine historic house from the days when the Ottoman Turks ruled. Near the cliff edge, a beautiful Roman theater offers panoramic sea views that remind you why this city was such a prize to myriad rulers—it was the greatest seaport in the eastern Mediterranean, back when the eastern Mediterranean was the center of the civilized world.

Notice the conglomeration of different architectural styles: As Byblos was absorbed into one empire after another, successive occupiers—Assyrians, Persians, Greeks, Romans, Muslims, Turks—kept rebuilding these temples instead of razing them. The **Temple of Resheph,** for instance, was rebuilt during the Greco-Roman period as a temple of Adonis, the city's patron god in that era; you can also see remains of a Roman colonnade just outside the **Temple of Balaat Gebal.**

Near the archaeological zone, on Rue du Port, check out the **Church of St. John the Baptist,** the crusaders' 12th-century cathedral, which looks as Arab as it does Romanesque, with Byzantine mosaics scattered all around.

With Lebanon in the grips of an Israeli blockade, an international team of rescuers had to be flown in to hand-clean the oil from the foundation stones of the port's two medieval towers. The oil spill may have been cleaned up, but the warfare that caused it rages on. This means it is vital to check conditions here before planning a trip. In fact, very few tourists these days get to Byblos, and the town's economy is drying up. It's the oldest city in the world—who will care for it now?

(i) Check with your embassy about travel conditions before visiting.

✈ Beirut

🛏 $$ **Byblos Sur Mer,** Rue du Port (✆ **961/9/548 000;** www.byblossurmer. com)

304 **Legendary Cities**

Petra
Red Rock Wonder
Southern Jordan

ALTHOUGH AIR POLLUTION, EARTHQUAKES, AND EROSION FROM WIND AND RAIN PUT THIS ANCIENT city carved out of rock at risk, Petra's most serious threat may be from uncontrolled tourism. More damage is done each year as a growing number of tourists scramble over the site looking for souvenirs.

You twist and turn through the Siq, a narrow mile-long sandstone gorge through the Jordanian desert. You come to the last bend—and there before you, just visible in the gap, is a dramatic columned temple cut right out of a cliff face. The fierce desert sun flashes on its columns and pediments and mythological figures; you catch your breath in wonder.

More than 900,000 tourists squeezed through that narrow entrance in 2010, a new record for Petra, Jordan's premier ancient landmark. With no areas railed off, they were free to scale its sheer walls, scrawl on the rocks, break off bits of stone for souvenirs. Already threatened by seismic activity, air pollution, and erosion from the winter rains, how much longer can Petra safely host such crowds?

Petra sprang up between 400 B.C. and A.D. 100, a natural stopping point on important trade routes. Camel caravans paid heavy duties to Petra's tax collectors, whose wealth gave rise to a grand cityscape chiseled out of the rose-colored living rock. Deep in this natural stronghold, this Arab tribe was conquered by no one, though many tried; not until Red Sea shipping bypassed caravan routes did a diminished Petra finally fall under control of Rome. Its ancient buildings have been eroded by desert sand and wind, but because they were gouged out of the cliffs rather than free-standing rocks, they haven't toppled like many buildings of similar eras. Their original plaster and paint have worn off, but the city still glows with the natural color of the rose-red rock.

As you emerge from the Siq, the first wonder you see is the **Khazneh,** a site featured in *Indiana Jones and the Last Crusade.* Legend had it that a wicked pharaoh buried a sumptuous treasure here, and in later centuries Bedouins aimed random bullets at the urnlike round tholos centered in the Khazneh's broken pediment, hoping

The desert fortress of Petra.

it would burst open and spill forth the pharaoh's riches. Beyond lie the spectacular royal tombs, which became more than just burial places—they were 1st-century architectural fantasies, picking up an eclectic mix of elements from cities like Alexandria and Rome, their ornate facades completely out of proportion to the small chambers within.

The citizens of Petra were quite the cultural chameleons: Temples built to Nabataean deities were later adapted to Roman gods, and possibly to Christian saints in the Byzantine era. On a summit behind the yellow-sandstone **Temple of Dushara,** you'll even see the remains of a fort built by 12th-century crusaders. Another climb to the cliff top will take you to the **High Place of Sacrifice,** a circular ceremonial arena set up explicitly for gruesome acts of blood sacrifice—and also killer views of the surrounding desert.

ⓘ www.petranationalfoundation.org

✈ Amman or Aqaba

🏨 $$$ **Marriott Petra,** Queen Raina Al Abdullah St., Wadi Mousa (✆ 962/3/215-6407; www.marriott.com). $$$ **Golden Tulip,** King's Way, Wadi Mousa (✆ 962/3/215-6799; www.goldentulip.com).

TOUR Abercrombie and Kent Jordan (✆ 962-06/566-5465 in Amman; www.abercrombiekent.com); **Desert Eco Tours** (✆ 972-52/276-5753 outside Israel, or 54/276-5753 in Israel; www.deserteco tours.com); and **Petra Moon Tourism** (✆ 962-03/215-6665 in Petra; www.petra moon.com).

Aphrodisias
A Marvel in Marble
Southeastern Turkey

AFTER A CENTURY OF EXCAVATIONS, THE FAMED MARBLE OF APHRODISIAS IS IN SORRY SHAPE. Some of the earlier excavators didn't properly prepare the ancient stones, which are now exposed to the elements. While excavation is still ongoing, many previously revealed areas are already beginning to crumble; some have had to be closed to visitors.

If you want to build a beautiful city, it helps to start out next to a marble quarry. With all that exquisite white and blue-gray marble on hand, it's not surprising that Aphrodisias attracted the finest sculptors of its day. What sculptor wouldn't want to try his hand at depicting the city's patron goddess, Aphrodite, goddess of love?

While Ephesus 320 may be Turkey's best-known archaeological site, the more remote Aphrodisias is just as large and valuable—and much less crowded. It's still easy to picture the town as it was laid out in Greco-Roman times—a temple, agora, council house, baths, theater, and huge stadium. The builders of Aphrodisias filled these buildings with statues, sculpted decorations, and carved inscriptions, taking advantage of the local talent pool. One fine example is the Tetrapylon, a beautifully preserved ornamental gate with fluted Corinthian columns and a triangular lintel full of mythological figures. Several statues around the site have been moved for safekeeping, most of them to the on-site museum.

Later generations were great recyclers—when chunks of stones fell from earlier monuments, they simply used them again, inserting many early inscriptions in walls of later buildings. More than 2,000 inscriptions are visible, mostly from the days of the Roman Empire. Notice, though, that the names Aphrodite and Aphrodisias were often struck out—once this became a Byzantine Christian city, renamed Stavropolis ("City of the Cross"), its leaders wanted to erase its pagan past. These Christians also converted the Temple of Aphrodite into a basilica, another great adaptive reuse project.

Though there was continuous settlement here from the Bronze Age on, Aphrodisias was hard hit by earthquakes in the 4th and 7th centuries A.D., when many of the classical-era buildings were toppled and laid under rubble. What's left of the Sebastion, for example, is nothing but a tumbled collection of huge marble chunks, parts of a unique temple built to worship the emperor Augustus. The modern village of Geyre covered the site until the 20th century, when cottages were moved to allow archaeologists to plumb the classical city beneath.

From a distance, the ruined columns and massive building blocks of Aphrodisias still gleam on their grassy site, surrounded by slim cypress trees. It's only when you get closer that you see what dire condition some sections have fallen into. The damage could still be reversed—will the Turkish government invest in Aphrodisias before it's too late?

ⓘ **Aphrodisias** (✆ **90/256/448-8003**)
✈ Izmir

🛏 **$$ Richmond PAMUKKALE TERMA Hotel,** Karahayit Koyu, Karahayit (✆ **90/258/271-4078**; www.richmondhotels.com.tr). **$ Beyaz Kale Hotel,** Oguzkan Cad. No: 4, Pamukkale (✆ **90/258-272-2064;** http://beyazkalehotel.com).

Mesa Verde National Park
Fire in the Canyon
Southwestern Colorado

WILDFIRES ARE THE MAJOR THREAT TO MESA VERDE NATIONAL PARK AND THE ANCIENT CLIFF dwellings left behind by the Anasazi people.

Wildfires have been a fact of life in the American Southwest since time immemorial—and time immemorial is what Mesa Verde is all about. Over 1,500 years ago, the Ancestral Puebloans (also called the Anasazi) first began to settle in these canyons and mesas, giving up their nomadic hunter-gatherer lifestyle for permanent agricultural settlements. Safe in their cliff-faced dwellings, with a water supply seeping down through the sandstone, they could ride out the inevitable fires.

But in the 20th century, fire suppression was the name of the game. As a result, this Southwest landscape now carries an increased fire load of dense vegetation that turns tinder-dry in droughts—which,

in this era of climate change, are becoming more and more frequent. In the summers of 2000 and 2002, the park was closed for several weeks, with more than half its land blackened by lightning-caused fires. It's the biggest challenge facing park management at Mesa Verde National Park, the largest archaeological preserve in the United States.

With more than 4,000 sites, Mesa Verde is an astounding place to visit. A long drive with many overlook points leads through a stunning canyon to the mesas where the Ancestral Puebloans built their vertical cities. Stop at the Far View Visitor Center to book ranger-led tours of its three most awesome sites—**Cliff Palace, Balcony**

Mesa Verde National Park.

House, and **Long House.** Cliff Palace is just what its name promises—a 151-room, four-story apartment house set under the rim of a cliff, with stepped-back roofs forming penthouse courtyards for the next level up. The 45-room Balcony House hangs above Soda Canyon, with stone stairs, log ladders, and narrow crawl spaces for the agile residents to scramble about from level to level. The Long House stretches across a long alcove in Rock Canyon, with 150 rooms and 21 kivas (subterranean chambers used for ceremonies and meetings) and a large public plaza for community gatherings.

You can't enter those protected ruins on your own, but there's plenty else to see. Behind the **Chapin Mesa Museum,** a paved .25-mile (.4km) trail leads to **Spruce Tree House,** a 130-room dwelling set inside an 89-foot-deep (27m) alcove; another 3-mile (5km) trail from Chapin Mesa runs along a canyon rim to an impressive panel of petroglyph rock art. A 6-mile

(10km) drive along the **Mesa Top Loop Road** alone has 10 stops where you can either overlook dwellings or take a short walk to dwellings. A .5-mile (.8km) hike from Wetherill Mesa allows you to compare 13th-century Step House with three 7th-century pit houses made by earlier Puebloans. It's as if you're watching these ancient people gradually perfect their idea of how to use the land for protection from the elements—wind, rain, and fire.

ⓘ **Mesa Verde National Park,** off US 160, Cortez, CO (✆ **970/529-4465;** www. nps.gov/meve)

✈ Cortez

🛏 $$ **Holiday Inn Express,** 2121 E. Main, Cortez (✆ **800/626-5652** or 970/ 565-6000; www.coloradoholiday.com). $$ **Best Western Turquoise Inn & Suites,** 535 E. Main St., Cortez (✆ **970/565-3778** or 800/547-3376; www.bestwestern.com).

---

307 Birth of the New World

Hovenweep National Monument
The Towers They Left Behind
Southern Utah & Colorado

Erosion and flash floods threaten the unique sandstone towers and other structures built by the ancient Anasazi people at Hovenweep.

At Mesa Verde **306** and Canyon de Chelly **308** you'll see Ancestral Puebloan dwellings—but in this isolated valley, straddling the Colorado-Utah border, it's anybody's guess why they built these 20-foot-high (6m) sandstone towers, pierced with tiny windows. Were they sentry towers? Grain silos? Ceremonial chambers? Town halls? Celestial observatories?

Far fewer visitors find their way here, and yet in some ways it's the most intriguing Ancestral Puebloan site of all. At the visitor center—located by the best preserved of the towers, Square Tower, in the

Utah half of the monument—you can get directions on how to reach five other sections (Cajon, Cutthroat Castle, Goodman Point, Holly, and Hackberry/Horseshoe) spread over a 20-mile (32km) stretch of high desert plateau. They're remote and difficult to find, along poorly maintained dirt roads—but that solitude and isolation make these mysterious ruins even more compelling.

By the late 1200s, as many as 2,500 people lived in this canyon-carved plateau. Instead of hollowing out cliff faces, the Hovenweep builders created multistory free-standing buildings—some square, some round—plastering together large fitted sandstone blocks with a mortar of clay, sand, and ash. These centuries-old shells are surprisingly solid, testament to the extraordinary engineering techniques the Ancestral Puebloans had developed by this late period of their civilization. Set ingeniously on top of great boulders, the towers were built apparently from the inside out, one floor at a time, using no outside scaffolding.

You'll notice that almost all of these settlements were placed at the heads of canyons, usually near springs of water. While some towers have features that suggest a defensive role, as if to guard their canyons, others incorporate features of the ceremonial kivas found at other Anasazi sites—perhaps those springs were considered sacred. Protecting water sources must have been crucially important in this arid terrain; you'll see examples of the small stone dams the resourceful Hovenweep people built on mesa tops to capture

rainfall to irrigate their crops. In the end, it was a 23-year drought that finally drove these people from their exquisitely built towers, to resettle farther south, where their descendants are modern-day Pueblo and Hopi Indians.

Although the Ancestral Puebloans found this area rich farmland, it's only sparsely vegetated today—and without plants to anchor the soil, landslides and flash floods are an ever-present risk. What's more, there's much more seismic activity here—no matter how well those Anasazi built these towers, an earthquake could topple them tomorrow.

ⓘ **Hovenweep National Monument,** McElmo Route, Cortez, CO (✆ **970/562-4282** or 435/719-2100; www.nps.gov/hove)

✈ Cortez

🛏 $$ **Holiday Inn Express,** 2121 E. Main, Cortez (✆ **800/626-5652** or 970/565-6000; www.coloradoholiday.com).

Canyon de Chelly
Hanging Out with the Anasazi
Northeastern Arizona

SCIENTISTS, ARCHAEOLOGISTS, AND SOME ENVIRONMENTALISTS FEAR THAT AGRICULTURAL AND business activities by the Navajo tribe are damaging fragile ecosystems and ancient dwellings and artifacts in Canyon de Chelly.

Though Canyon de Chelly is a national monument, it's on Navajo reservation land—and that's where the problem begins. The National Park Service is anxious to preserve this major archaeological site, with its 5,000-year-old dwellings and rock art from the Ancestral Puebloans (also known as the Anasazi). But for the Navajos, these sandstone canyons are also a place to grow corn, graze their livestock, and lead visitors around on lucrative

horseback and four-wheel-drive tours. What that's doing to the canyon's delicate ecosystem is a source of running debate.

Granted, it's not just the animals. Invasive species, especially tamarisk and Russian olive trees, have gained a foothold and are altering streambeds, causing erosion, and creating a fire hazard. But expensive eradication projects get hung up in negotiations between the land's Navajo owners and the parks system.

When this remote section of northeastern Arizona was made a Navajo reservation, archaeologists hadn't yet discovered the value of its Ancestral Puebloan remains. Ancestral Puebloan civilization reached its zenith between A.D. 1100 and 1300, but evidence suggests that these particular canyons were occupied as long ago as A.D. 300. In the nooks and crannies of the canyons, you'll see more than 100 ancient dwellings hollowed into the rock walls, including several circular sacred rooms, or kivas. The most recent, and most impressive, ruins are the ghostly pale **White House Ruins** in Canyon de Chelly, but visit adjacent **Canyon del Muerto** as well to see its ancient tombs—the Tomb of the Weaver, near the Antelope House ruins, and the Mummy Caves.

Two scenic drives lead you through the park: the 15-mile (24km) **North Rim Drive,** which overlooks Canyon del Muerto, and the 16-mile (26km) **South Rim Drive,** which overlooks Canyon de Chelly (pronounced "duh Shay"). Hiking trails lead down to the Antelope House and White House ruins, but to really explore the canyon floor, you'll have to hire an authorized Navajo guide. Along the way, don't get so hung up on the relics that you forget to notice the scenery—at several spots the canyons open up to breathtaking rugged vistas of glowing red-and-yellow stone.

It's a sacred ground for the Navajos as well; you can see their ancient pictographs, designed in colorful paint on dark patches where seeping water oxidized on the sandstone walls (known as "desert varnish"). In contrast, the Ancestral Puebloans' designs were petroglyphs, created by chipping away the desert varnish to expose lighter-colored rock beneath. Commemorating important tribal events, both kinds of rock pictures are windows into an ancient way of life. The Navajo have been guardians of this land for a long

Canyon de Chelly.

time—can we question the wisdom of how they choose to care for it?

ⓘ**Canyon De Chelly National Monument,** off Rte. 191, Chinle, AZ (✆928/674-5500; www.nps.gov/cach)

✈Flagstaff

🛏$$ **Holiday Inn Canyon de Chelly,** Indian Rte. 7, Chinle (✆800/HOLIDAY [465-4329] or 928/674-5000; www.ichotels group.com). $$ **Thunderbird Lodge,** Chinle (✆800/679-2473 or 928/674-5841; www.tbirdlodge.com).

TOUR De Chelly Tours (✆ 928/674-3772). **Canyon de Chelly Tours** (✆928/674-5433; www.canyondechellytours.com). **Justin's Horse Rental** (✆928/380-4617). **Totsonii Ranch** (✆928/755-6209; www.totsoniiranch.com).

Chan Chan Archaeological Zone
Urban Planning, Chimu-Style
Moche Valley, Peru

GLOBAL CLIMATE CHANGE HAS CAUSED FLOODING AND RAINFALL TO POUR DOWN PERU'S MOCHE Valley, contributing to the erosion of Chan Chan's archaeologically significant adobe ruins.

Excessive tourist traffic? That's the least of Chan Chan's problems. This enormous pre-Incan city in northern Peru is still off the beaten track, and likely to remain so. It's a pity that half the tourists who presently throng Machu Picchu couldn't be diverted to this crumbling adobe metropolis, one of the most important archaeological sites in Peru—and one of the most endangered.

There are nine walled palace complexes here, each with its own tombs and temples and throne rooms and reservoirs, but their riches were ransacked long ago by the Spaniards and subsequent *huaqueros* (grave robbers, or treasure hunters). Excavation began at Chan Chan in the mid-1960s, and the site is still being plundered—on top of that, now that the fragile adobe has been exposed, it's eroding at a fearsome rate.

Until defeated by the Incas in 1470, the capital of the once-vast Chimú Empire was the largest settlement in pre-Columbian America. Begun around 1300, it reached all the way from Huanchaco port to Campana Mountain, an area covering more than 25 sq. km (9⅔ sq. miles) of desert floor, which unfortunately means you may need a taxi to travel between the four main excavated areas (taking a taxi is also a good idea for avoiding the muggers who occasionally lurk around the quiet ruins). Once you get the hang of its urban layout, you'll see how architecture defined social class in this highly stratified society. The

principal complex to visit is the **Tschudi Palace,** which has been partially restored. Note the aquatic-theme friezes in its ceremonial courtyard and the walls of the Sanctuary, which are textured like fishing nets. (The abundance of ocean motifs here is not surprising, considering how close the residents were to the Pacific Ocean.)

The **Museo de Sitio de Chan Chan,** along the road back toward Trujillo, displays ceramics excavated from Chan Chan and explains the layout of the city and its history. Two smaller pyramid temples, **Huaca Esmeralda** and **Huaca Arco Iris,** much closer to Trujillo, are also well worth visiting. Huaca Arco Iris (Rainbow Temple, also called Huaca El Dragón) has some dazzling rainbow-shaped friezes and bas-reliefs with snake, lizard, and dragon motifs. At Huaca Esmeralda you can see some friezes that have not yet been restored, an interesting contrast to the crisply restored ones elsewhere.

ⓘ **Museo de Sitio de Chan Chan,** Jr. Independence cuadra 5, Trujillo (✆ **51/44/807210**)

✈ Trujillo

🛏 $$$ **Hotel Libertado Trujillo,** Jr. Independencia 48 (✆ **51/44/232-741** or 51/1/442-995 for reservations; www.libertador.com.pe. $ **La Casa Suiza,** Los Pinos 451 (✆ **51/044/461-285;** www.casasuiza.com).

310 Birth of the New World

Tikal
Temples of the Jaguar Clan
El Peten, Guatemala

INCREASED TOURISM IS ADDING TO THE DETERIORATION OF THE PYRAMIDS IN TIKAL, WHICH ARE already hammered by the hot, humid climate.

Nestled in lush subtropical jungle, where parrots and toucans and monkeys chatter in the canopy overhead, the Mayan ruins of Tikal are the ace in Guatemala's tourist deck. Once ruled by a dynasty known as the Jaguar Clan lords, this immense temple complex is a fascinating look into the heart of an ancient culture.

Perhaps Guatemala has been too eager to exploit Tikal's popularity, however: Tourist masses are beginning to deteriorate these pre-Hispanic monuments, already eroded by exposure to the humid rainforest climate. With very few guards to monitor them, vandalism and graffiti are common.

Day-trippers leave litter around the site, which has attracted vultures, and formerly wild animals are becoming dependent on being fed by tourists.

Tikal is a huge site, believed to have covered 65 sq. km (25 sq. miles), although only about 5% of the ruins have been excavated so far. It was once the ceremonial heart of a city of 100,000 people, who gathered on its plazas for everything from religious rites (often including human sacrifices) to ball games (where the losers sometimes became human sacrifices). The chief sights are half a dozen rectangular pyramids of gray limestone; notice how precisely cut

One of the many pyramids at Tikal.

and mortared the stones are, even though the Mayans had no iron tools. These pyramids go by intriguing names like the **Temple of the Masks,** the **Temple of the Jaguar Priest,** and the **Temple of the Double-Headed Serpent,** which at 63m (207 ft.) was the tallest building in North America until the late 1800s—it could be called the first skyscraper. It's quite a climb to its top plateau, but as you look out over the rainforest, try to imagine the ancient city as it was during Tikal's heyday, from about 600 B.C. to A.D. 900.

For the Mayans, pyramid building was an act of devotion, to exalt their god/kings by setting them on man-made mountains. The exteriors are huge, with broad, steep ceremonial stairways leading solemnly to their peaks, but inside are only small chambers for ceremonial purposes. At public events, kings and nobles were seated grandly atop the pyramids; the acoustics

are so perfect that you can speak at a normal volume from Temple I and be heard clearly on Temple II, all the way across the Grand Plaza.

Hundreds of standing stones dotting the grounds minutely record historic events and long-dead kings, with either carved pictures or glyph symbols. Jaguars do still prowl the surrounding jungle, though they're too wary to let you spot them. Who knows? Maybe the ghosts of the ancient Mayan kings aren't so far away.

ⓘ **Tikal Parque Nacional,** near Flores, Guatemala

✈ Flores

🛏 $$$ **Jungle Lodge,** Tikal National Park (☏ **800/910-6180;** www.enjoyguatemala. com). $$ **Jaguar Inn,** Tikal National Park (☏ **502/926-0002;** www.jaguartikal.com).

Birth of the New World 311

El Mirador
Mayan Eden
Northern Guatemala

WHILE ARCHAEOLOGISTS ARE STILL EXCAVATING THE LARGEST AND EARLIEST MAYAN RUINS YET discovered at El Mirador, bands of looters steal artifacts, and illegal logging and fires destroy the jungle around them.

Flying over the Guatemalan jungle in the 1930s, famed aviator Charles Lindbergh looked down in surprise. What were those immense, mysterious green mounds looming up in the Mirador basin?

Standing today atop the **La Danta pyramid**—the largest pre-Columbian structure ever discovered in America—you'll still see mysterious green mounds in all directions. Now we know, however, what they are: Jungle-choked ruins of the cradle of Mayan civilization. Archaeologists judge that perhaps 40 various settlements are set around the Mirador basin, a huge virgin rainforest full of howler monkeys, parrots,

and jaguars. Dating back to the 6th century B.C.—much older than better-known Tikal ③⑩—this area includes five major cities: El Mirador, Tintal, Xulnal, Nakbé, and Wakná. At the heart, the great El Mirador, royal city of the Snake King dynasty, was home at its height to 100,000 people, spread over 39 sq. km (15 sq. miles) with some 4,000 temples and an intricate system of raised limestone causeways, like ancient skyways.

Never heard of El Mirador? Few travelers have. The area is too remote for casual tourists—there is no road anywhere close, and even "luxury" helicopter tours require several hours of hiking or horseback riding through the jungle, following tracks laid out by machete-wielding *chiclistas* harvesting *chicle* for chewing gum. You'll see the archaeological team still at work, reclaiming El Mirador from its jungle shroud. They have already unearthed some wonders, however. The gigantic **La Danta (Tapir) pyramid** makes the Great Pyramid in Egypt look puny: Set on a base that could cover 36 football fields, its white stone peak towers 230 feet (70m) over the jungle. Nearby, huge **El Tigre** is almost three-quarters its size, with a similar triadic design, three pyramids set on a larger base. Faced with cut stone, these monuments are decorated with stucco panels depicting Mayan mythology. A huge frieze that was recently uncovered, for example, depicts a dramatic scene from the Mayan epic *Popol Vuh:* twin heroes Hunahpú and Ixbalnqué swimming away from the underworld, holding aloft the rescued head of their father the maize god.

Walking around the partially excavated cities, you'll notice rude trenches dug by looters, intent on valuable artifacts—particularly the fine cream-colored ceramics made by El Mirador's last residents, during a brief reoccupation in Late Mayan times.

It's estimated that as many as 1,000 pottery pieces are smuggled out every month, even before the museum is built to display El Mirador's finds.

Determined to develop El Mirador properly, the Guatemalan government and heritage coalitions are building a visitor center, museum, and lodging in the gateway town of Carmelita and training local people to work as guides and excavation assistants. They hope to construct an eco-friendly railway linking the five main cities, bypassing the need for highway construction. More than the ruins are at stake—the Mirador basin, a declared biosphere reserve, has lost over 75% of rare rainforest habitat in the past 10 years. El Mirador could save this impoverished region—so long as it doesn't lose its soul in the process.

ⓘ www.miradorbasin.com

🛏 $$ **Casona Del Lago,** Calle 1a, Zona 1, Santa Elena (✆ **502/2366-2841** or 502/7952-8700; www.hotelesdepeten.com)

TOUR Ecotourism and Adventure Specialists (✆ **800/297-1880**; www.mirador park.com). **Tikal Connection** (✆ **502/4211-1027**; http://tikalcnx.com).

---

312 Birth of the New World

Teotihuacán
Ghost Town of the Gods
Mexico

TEOTIHUACÁN IS THREATENED BY TWO MODERN URBAN PROBLEMS EMANATING FROM NEARBY Mexico City: smog and suburban sprawl. Air pollution corrodes the pyramids and damages the murals, frescoes, and other irreplaceable features at this historic site.

Once upon a time, some 200,000 people lived here, the absolute epicenter of ancient Mesoamerica society. In A.D. 500, it had more people than Rome and sprawled over 31 sq. km (12 sq. miles). Yet we know precious little about the people of Teotihuacán, least of all why they abandoned

this great metropolis so abruptly around A.D. 750. Were they invaded by enemies? Was there an epidemic? Were there just too many people for the region's food and water supply to support?

While historians ponder these mysteries, Teotihuacán is under siege again

Teotihuacán.

today—from the polluted air of overpopulated Mexico City, from hordes of daytrippers, and from encroaching sprawl.

When the site was discovered early in the 20th century, the temple had disappeared and the pyramid—the third-largest pyramid in the world, after the Great Pyramid of Cholula (near Puebla) and Egypt's Great Pyramid **288**—was an overgrown mass of rubble. As excavation and restoration proceeded, the beauties of this city were rediscovered. One amazing aspect of Teotihuacán is how it was laid out in accordance with celestial observations. Climb 248 steps to the top of the **Pyramid of the Sun** to see its precision: The front wall of the pyramid is exactly perpendicular to the point on the horizon where the sun sets at the equinoxes, and the rest of the grand buildings lie at right angles to it.

Walking up the main north-south street, the Calzada de los Muertos (Avenue of the Dead), look for a bit of wall sheltered by a modern corrugated roof: the fragment of a jaguar painting suggests what this street looked like when all its original paintings were intact. Proceed to the **Pyramid of the Moon;** upon its plaza sits the Palace

of Quetzalpapalotl, where lavish figures of Quetzal-Mariposa (a mythical bird-butterfly) are painted on walls or carved in pillars; behind it, the Palace of the Jaguars has murals and frescoes of jaguars. At the south end of the Avenue of the Dead, in the immense sunken square named the Ciudadela (Citadel), there's the **Feathered Serpent Pyramid** and the **Temple of Quetzalcoatl,** with large serpents' heads jutting out from collars of feathers carved in the stone walls.

Whatever its original name was, the Aztecs named it Teotihuacán when they discovered these ruins, a name meaning "Place Where Gods Were Born." Doesn't a divine birthplace deserve a little more respect?

ⓘ San Juan Teotihuacán, Mexico

✈ Mexico City

🛏 $$$ **Hotel Four Seasons,** Reforma 500, Mexico City (✆ **800/332-3442** in North America, 800/268-6282 in Canada, or 55/5230-1818; www.fourseasons.com). $–$$ **Hotel Imperial,** Paseo de la Reforma 64, Mexico City (✆ **55/5705-4911;** www.hotelimperial.com.mx).

Tiwanaku

Building Blocks in Bolivia

Bolivia

MANY OF TIWANAKU'S ARCHAEOLOGICAL SITES ARE IN POOR CONDITION. DAMAGE FROM LOOTERS continues to be a risk, and the site is also threatened by erosion.

We don't know how the ancient Tiwanaku people built this city, with its massive stone blocks, complex plumbing, ingenious farming methods, and haunting monoliths. For all their technological sophistication, the Tiwanaku had no written language—we can only piece together the riddle, from crumbling evidence.

What we do know is that this site has been plundered ever since the Incas discovered it in the 14th century, a hundred years after the Tiwanaku vanished. The Spanish conquistadors rummaged here for gold; 18th- and 19th-century builders quarried the site for stone; in the early 20th century the military used it for target practice. Then came that botched restoration in the 1960s, where major landmarks were moved and clumsy walls thrown up where they didn't belong.

But perhaps Tiwanaku's advanced state of decay is part of the story this site has to tell visitors—the story of a once-great culture that collapsed after the water levels dropped in nearby Lake Titicaca, which eventually receded many miles away. The Tiwanaku culture lasted 28 centuries, from 1600 B.C. to A.D. 1200, and for 5 of those centuries they dominated South America, ruling a vast region from southern Peru down to northern Argentina and Chile—and then the drought did them in.

This city was founded in approximately 200 B.C., but between A.D. 600 and 800 its population boomed to somewhere between a quarter-million and 1.5 million people. To sustain such a population in this high plateau was nearly impossible, if it hadn't been for their raised-field agriculture, an amazing terraced irrigation system that scientists are still studying with awe. But what really impresses visitors to this Tiwanaku capital is the bold scale of its architecture, based on massive ashlar blocks transported from quarries 40km (25 miles) or more away—even though the Tiwanaku had not developed the wheel.

Highlights of the site, which have been excavated and at least partially restored, include the Kalassaya, the main temple area, dominated by the stone-carved Sun Gate that could accurately gauge the position of the sun; the Semi-Underground Temple, decorated with stones representing different leaders from around the world; and the Akapana pyramid, believed to be an observatory and temple to worship the sky. Take time to appreciate the stylized geometric decorations carved so precisely onto the surviving stones. An on-site museum displays several ceramics, monoliths, and figurines unearthed here—when you think how much was carried away, it's amazing this much was left.

Many plundered pieces ended up in La Paz, at the **Museo Nacional de Arqueologia,** Tiwanaku 93, La Paz (©591/2/2311-621). Who knows where the rest ended up?

ⓘTiwanaku, La Paz-Puno Rd.

✈La Paz

🛏$$ **Hotel Rosario del Lago,** Rigoberto Paredes and Av. Costanera, Copacabana, Bolivia (© 591/102/862-2141; www.hotelrosario.com/lago)

TOUR Diana Tours, in La Paz (©591/2/2350-252; www.diana-tours.com/Index2.html). **Crillon Tours,** in La Paz (©591/2/2337-533; www.titicaca.com).

10 Crumbling Landmarks

Machu Picchu.

The Acropolis
A Frieze in the Air
Athens, Greece

ACID RAIN AND SMOG RISING UP FROM ATHENS ARE EATING AWAY THE MARBLE OF THE ACROPO-lis's structures, including the famous Parthenon. Restoration and a new museum hope to reverse centuries of damage.

For 25 centuries, these marble columns and pediments have floated above the rat race of Athens, glowing beige at dawn, golden at high noon, rose at sunset, ethereal white in the moonlight. Successive waves of invaders took over this sheer rocky outcrop, each inflicting a different damage—Persians razed it to rubble, Romans made it a brothel, Christians converted it to an orthodox church, Turks stored gunpowder here. Earthquakes and explosions did their part as well. Still, nothing could erase the serene, sacred beauty of the Acropolis.

An ambitious restoration project, ongoing since 1975, has slowly been refitting this world-famous architectural complex, trying to reverse the damage caused by nature, history, and clumsy earlier restoration. While most fragments are original, new marble has been added in critical spots; titanium dowels hold together fragile structures. Despite the inevitable scaffolding, the Acropolis is still an awe-inspiring sight. (*Tip:* Come at 5pm, after tour groups leave, to contemplate its beauty in relative peace.) Stunning as its various components are, it's the total ensemble that matters, in a way that posters and postcards could never convey.

Though you enter through the Roman-era Beulé Gate, that's merely an entrance to the real entrance: the monumental Propylaia arch. Just above the Propylaia, to the right, is the beautifully proportioned Temple of Athena Nike; to the left, the Erechtheion, tomb of an Athenian king, its pediments supported by a row of female figures, or caryatids. But the real star of

the show is the Parthenon, the great temple dedicated to Athena. Big as it is, this temple seems ineffably light and graceful, with 46 slender columns ranged along the outsides. A masterful optical illusion, its columns and stairs appear straight, yet all are minutely curved, with each exterior column thicker in the middle. The airy look of the Parthenon is also due to the fact that it has no roof—in 1687, the Venetians, trying to capture Turkish-occupied Athens, blew it to smithereens.

In 2009, the Acropolis Museum was opened at the base of the sacred mount to

The Acropolis.

protect and display an incredible collection of statuary removed from the site, much of it finally brought out of storage after 200 years. (Here you'll see the Erechtheion's original caryatids, for example—those up on the hill are modern replicas.) The modern, climate-controlled museum incorporates as much natural light as possible for viewing the artifacts, arranged in chronological order. The climax is a majestic glass gallery displaying 36 of the original 115 Parthenon friezes—all that the Greeks still possess, displayed alongside white plaster casts of those that were carted off to London by 19th-century British diplomat Lord Elgin. It's an eloquent statement about what's still missing.

ⓘ **The Acropolis,** Dionissiou Areopagitou (✆ **30/210/321-0219;** www.theacropolis museum.gr)

✈ Athens International

🛏 $$$ **Hilton,** 46 Vassilissis Sofias Av. (✆ **800/445-8667** in North America, or 30/ 210/728-1000; www.hilton.com). $$ **Athens Cypria,** 5 Diomias St. (✆ **30/210/323-8034;** www.athenscypria.com).

Classical Relics **315**

The Colosseum
Send in the Lions
Rome, Italy

BEGRIMED BY CAR EXHAUST FROM ITS SURROUNDING TRAFFIC CIRCLE AND SHAKEN BY THE SUBWAY rumbling below, the Colosseum—already a ruin—may face structural stresses as temperatures fluctuate with climate change in southern Europe.

Perhaps no classical Roman ruin evokes the excesses of the late Empire like the Colosseum. In A.D. 80, the opening event was a weeks-long bloody combat between gladiators and wild beasts. Later shows kept upping the ante: Vestal virgins from the temple screamed for blood, ever more exotic animals were shipped in to satisfy jaded curiosities, and the arena floor was flooded for not-so-mock naval battles. (Really big events like chariot races were held at the Circus Maximus, on the other side of the Palatine Hill, today a formless heap of ruins.) As you stand on the walkways, gazing through the arches into the bowl of the arena, the cries of those ancient spectators still seem to echo through the ages.

To modern eyes, however, it's the damaged profile of this time-ravaged elliptical shell that we recognize from pizza boxes and movies—reconstructed models in movies like *Gladiator* seem weirdly off-kilter. As it stands today, only one side still sports the original four-tiered design (each level has a different style of column, like a textbook illustration of Doric, Ionic, and Corinthian). The wooden arena floor itself, where gladiators had their bloody face-offs, has rotted away, revealing honeycombed lower levels where elephants, lions, and other wild animals waited to be hoisted up in cages to the arena floor. The seats that once accommodated 50,000 spectators are gone, leaving only tiered ledges of crumbling stone.

Unlike the Pantheon across town, which was spared demolition because it was converted in the Christian era to a church, the Colosseum moldered for years, its marble stripped away to be used on newer buildings. The adjacent Roman Forum, too, is a jumble of fallen stones, ringed with dusty paths and weeds. The ruined state of these landmarks is picturesque in itself, an integral part of their appeal—who'd stand

The Colosseum.

in line for hours (literally hours in summer, unless you spring for a private guide) to see Disney-esque reconstruction? A major Colosseum restoration that began in 1995 is nearing completion, with nearly 85% of the site now open to visitors. But expect periodic closures and scaffolding as environmental stresses continue to damage these ancient stones, not only in the Colosseum but all over Rome.

ⓘ **Piazzale del Colosseo,** Via dei Fori Imperiali (✆ **39/6/3996 7700**)

✈ Leonardo da Vinci International Airport

🛏 $$$ **Hotel de Russie,** Via del Babuino 9 (✆ **888/667-9477** in North America, or 39/6/328881; www.roccofortehotels.com). $ **Hotel Grifo,** Via del Boschetto 144 (✆ **39/6/4871395;** www.hotelgrifo.com).

316 Classical Relics

Pompeii
Ashes to Ashes . . .
Outside Naples, Italy

IN LATE 2010 AND EARLY 2011, TORRENTIAL RAINS CAUSED SEVERAL WALLS TO COLLAPSE INTO rubble at the ruins of Pompeii, triggering an uproar of criticism over the Italian government's neglect of its fragile antiquities.

At any moment, natural disaster could strike. When Mount Vesuvius erupted in A.D. 79, the town of Pompeii was suddenly buried in volcanic ash and mud, utter havoc wreaked in a few desperate hours. Yet, in a cruel irony, its ruins were preserved by the very same volcanic debris, like a fly caught in amber, just as it was 2,000 years ago.

Mount Etna still rumbles above the town—the last time it erupted was 1944, and it could go again any day. In this seismic area, earthquakes are another ever-present threat (Pompeii was still rebuilding from an A.D. 62 earthquake when the eruption hit). But these days the biggest threat to Pompeii may be its own popularity. It's such a convenient day trip from Naples that 2.5 million tourists a year tramp through these fragile streets, many of them carelessly climbing its walls and rubbing its stones. In 2008, the Italian government appointed a special commissioner to rescue the deteriorating antiquities; further collapses in 2010 and 2011 suggest that much remains to be done.

In other cities, a few major classical buildings survived; in Pompeii it was a whole town, chronicling the daily lives of ancient Roman citizens. Not every artifact remains on-site: Pompeiian survivors briefly returned to grab a few treasures, while several precious items were later moved by 19th-century archaeologists to the **National Archaeological Museum** in Naples (Piazza Museo Nazionale 18–19; ✆ **39/81-440166**). Still, plenty is left to see, including some surprisingly erotic frescoes and mosaics.

A few new buildings have been opened, in hopes that the crowds will spread around. Yet certain highlights prevail: the House of the Vettii's black-and-red dining room with its cupid frescoes; the spectacular frescoes in the House of the Mysteries, outside the city walls; and the imposing House of the Faun, with no fewer than four dining rooms and two spacious peristyle gardens. In the center of town is the forum, the heart of Pompeiian life, surrounded by a basilica, the Temple of Apollo, the Temple of Jupiter, and the Stabian Thermae (baths), where you'll even see some skeletons. The open-air Great Theater could hold 5,000 spectators at its bloodthirsty battles between wild animals and gladiators.

The essential thing is to walk these paved streets—respectfully, of course—and visualize the citizens going about their daily routines on that fateful August day. Pompeii is not just about Pompeii—it's a paradigm of what could happen to any community struck suddenly by natural disaster.

ⓘ Information desk at **Porta Marina entrance,** Via Villa dei Misteri (✆ **39/81/ 857-5347;** www.pompeiisites.org)

✈ Naples

🛏 $$$ **Hotel Excelsior,** Via Partenope 48, Naples (✆ **39/81/7640111;** www. excelsior.it). $$ **Hotel Britannique,** Corso Vittorio Emanuele 133 (✆ **39/81/7614145;** www.hotelbritannique.it).

Classical Relics **317**

Herculaneum

. . . *Dust to Dust*

Outside Naples, Italy

EXPOSURE TO THE ELEMENTS, THEFT, VANDALISM, AND SOUVENIR TAKING HAVE ALL DAMAGED Herculaneum's artifacts and buildings, even more so than neighboring Pompeii.

Though they both were destroyed in that same fateful day in A.D. 79, Herculaneum was always smaller than its celebrated neighbor Pompeii; even today, its archaeological zone is only one-fourth the size of Pompeii's. The good news for serious travelers is that Herculaneum doesn't get nearly the same volume of tourist traffic. Come here in the mornings, when the day-trippers are herding like sheep around Pompeii, and you can have its ghostly precincts nearly to yourself.

But Herculaneum also makes less money to fund conservation work, and its ruins are deteriorating at an even faster rate than Pompeii's, damaged by weather, vandalism, water seepage from the adjacent town, and inappropriate excavation carried out years ago.

Herculaneum was first discovered long before Pompeii, in 1709, sheerly by accident, while workers were digging a well. Its excavations are still a work in progress, partly because conditions were more challenging here: Herculaneum was more heavily buried than Pompeii, under hardened mud and lava flow rather than ash. Whereas the weight of ash collapsed buildings at Pompeii, more large, complex structures survived at Herculaneum, which are harder to unearth. Matters are further complicated by the fact that nearby slums cover sections of the buried town. Excavation work is currently halted, given the need to focus on conserving existing ruins.

Most visitors make Herculaneum a hurried add-on to Pompeii, often dropping it entirely from the itinerary when they decide to linger at Pompeii. But Herculaneum

deserves a visit on its own merits. For one thing, it was an entirely different sort of town from workaday Pompeii—an upper-class resort where aristocrats lived in luxury. For a window into their elite lifestyle, don't miss the **Casa dei Cervi** (House of the Stags), with its wealth of sculptures. Among the other fine houses are **Casa del Bicentario** (House of the Bicentenary), **Casa a Graticcio** (House of the Wooden Cabinet), **Case del Tremezzo di Legno** (House of the Wooden Partition), and the **Casa di Poseidon** (House of Poseidon). With plenty of leisure time to spare, these patricians required facilities like the **Amphitheater** (don't miss the exquisite mosaic here), the **Palestra sports arena,** and lavishly adorned baths (Terme Suburbane). Best of all may be the **Villa of the Papyri,** with its amazing trove of charred ancient scrolls. Herculaneum's fascinations are endless—you'll just have to dig a little deeper to find them.

ⓘ **Entrance on Corso Resina,** Ercolano (𝒞39/81/732-4311; www.pompeiisites.org)

✈ Naples

🛏 $$$ **Hotel Excelsior,** Via Partenope 48, Naples (𝒞 39/81-7640111; www.excelsior.it). $$ **Hotel Britannique,** Corso Vittorio Emanuele 133 (𝒞39/81-7614145; www.hotelbritannique.it).

318 Classical Relics

Paestum
Italy's Piece of Ancient Greece
Campania, Italy

ENCROACHING DEVELOPMENT FROM NEARBY CITIES AND TOWNS THREATENS THE ANCIENT CITY OF Paestum, treated as a tourism afterthought despite boasting three of the best-preserved Greek temples anywhere.

Who would have thought that, so near the luxe resorts of the Amalfi Coast, you could wander around a Greek colony founded in 600 B.C.? Even the ancients wrote about

the roses of Paestum, which bloom twice a year, splashes of scarlet perfectly complementing the salmon-colored stones of its Greek temples.

Abandoned for centuries, the ruins of Paestum began to attract archaeologists in the mid–18th century, shortly after Pompeii was discovered up the coast. The malarial swamps that drove out Paestum's medieval residents were finally drained in the 20th century; grazing water buffaloes were corralled onto farms. It's a much less complete ruin than Pompeii, though. Much of the ancient town lies beneath private property and has not been excavated; farmland and modern houses run right up to the archaeological zone, a major highway borders the site, and nearby beach resorts creep closer every year. A road built through the ruins in the 1700s destroyed half of its Roman amphitheater. And after all these centuries, those crumbling ruins have been thoughtlessly patched with modern concrete.

What's fascinating about Paestum is that it's really two ruined cities atop each other. The first was Poseidonia, the northernmost Greek colony in Italy and a vigorous trading center. Poseidonia was renamed Paestum when the Romans took over in 273 B.C. Though they settled right on top of the Greek town, the Romans could not bring themselves to knock down its three mighty temples, which survive in better condition than the Roman remains. The largest is the 5th-century B.C. **Temple of Neptune** (Neptune being the Roman name for Poseidon), which still preserves six columns in front, crowned by a massive entablature, and 14 columns on each side. The nearby **Temple of Hera,** Italy's oldest Greek temple (6th c. B.C.) is surprisingly intact, with 9 chunky Doric pillars in front and 18 on the sides. Set on higher ground, the **Temple of Athena** has 34 stout Doric columns, along with ragged bits of its triangular pediment and a large altar.

Across from the Temple of Athena, the on-site museum displays some metopes removed from the Temple of Hera and some fine tomb paintings from the 4th and 5th century B.C.; don't miss the beautiful paintings of the **Diver's Tomb.** Hundreds of Greek tombs were recently discovered at Paestum, yielding a trove of paintings and clay figures. There is so much yet to be uncovered here—if only the ruins could get a little respect.

(i) **National Archaeological Museum of Paestum,** Via Magna Grecia 917 (©39/828/811023; www.infopaestum.it)

✈ Naples

🚂 Paestum

🛏 $$ **Hotel Schuhmann,** Via Marittima (©39/828-851151; www.hotelschuhmann.com)

Classical Relics **319**

Masada
After the Flood
Israel

SITTING DIRECTLY ON THE SYRIAN-AFRICAN RIFT, KING HEROD'S MOUNTAINTOP FORTRESS HAS endured at least five major earthquakes. After two heavy rainy seasons weakened its ancient walls, the Israeli government has invested heavily in shoring up this national treasure.

It wasn't 40 days and 40 nights, but it was enough of a deluge—massive cloudbursts right over this normally arid hilltop in 2003, and again in 2004. As the mortar weakened between the huge stone blocks, this great Hebrew stronghold seemed on the brink of falling at last.

But more than half a million visitors a year come here; closing down Masada for structural repairs was simply not feasible.

A man praying at Masada.

Besides, to the Israeli people, Masada is more than a tourist attraction—it is synonymous with Israeli pride. Engineers sprang into action, reconstructing walls with original materials and installing seismic monitors on the mountain slopes, to anticipate earthquake activity that could inflict new damage. Flaking ancient frescoes were removed for preservation and installed in a new museum at the foot of the fortress; replicas were installed in their place.

Although a cable car was installed in 1971, some visitors still choose to hike up to the top, taking either the strenuous Snake Path from the Dead Sea Highway or the easier Roman Ramp from the Ahad parking lot. After all, Masada's inaccessibility, atop a desert plateau, was the whole point when King Herod first built this stout fortress around 30 B.C. After Herod's death, with Israel under Roman control, a small Roman garrison occupied the mount. But during the Jewish revolt in A.D. 66, Masada was seized by a tenacious (and well-armed) band of Jewish zealots. Finally, in A.D. 73, 3 years after

Jerusalem had fallen, the Romans got fed up with this last pocket of resistance. They built a ramp to scale the rock—in itself a remarkable piece of engineering—and attacked Masada with 10,000 troops, pulling out all the stops: siege engines, flaming torches, rock bombardments, battering rams. It seemed only a question of time until the 900 defenders surrendered. After one brutal night attack, the Romans, seeing Masada now defenseless, decided to storm the fort at dawn. Expecting to fight their way in, the Romans were astonished in the morning by the Jews' lack of resistance—then awed when they discovered why: The 900 Jewish men, women, and children inside had committed mass suicide rather than succumb.

Excavations over the years have unearthed the most exciting relics in all of Israel: the original palace, synagogue, casement walls, houses, straw bags, plaits of hair, pottery shards, stone vessels, cosmetics, cooking utensils, and scroll fragments marked with Hebrew names—perhaps the very lots cast by the defenders as they decided who would kill the others rather than let them fall into Roman hands. With that kind of patriotic will as an example, no wonder Israel is intent on preserving Masada.

(i) **Masada National Park,** Dead Sea Hwy. (© **972/8/658-4207;** www.parks.org.il)

✈ Jerusalem

🛏 $$$ **Le Meridien Dead Sea,** Ein Bokek (© **972/8/659-1234;** www.star woodhotels.com). $ **Masada Guesthouse and Youth Hostel,** Masada National Park, Rte. 90 (© **972/8/995-3222;** www.iyha. org.il).

Classical Relics **320**

Ephesus
Re-Creating Rome
Southeastern Turkey

AMBITIOUS PLANS TO RECONSTRUCT THE EPHESIAN RUINS—HOPING TO RE-CREATE THE LOOK and feel of the Roman city that once stood here—threaten the integrity of this historic city.

Ephesus has been great many times in its history. In the Greek era, its Temple of Artemis was one of the Seven Wonders of the Ancient World (though all that's left today is one forlorn column in Selçuk). It was a major Roman colony in Asia Minor, and in the early Christian era, Ephesus was where Jesus' mother Mary settled after the Crucifixion (her house, now a church, is in Meryemana) and where St. Paul preached his most famous sermons. But when the crusaders came through in the 1300s, they found only a small Turkish village, its harbor silted up and its temples toppled by an earthquake. And during the Ottoman era, many of Ephesus's finest artifacts were siphoned off by British and Austrian archaeologists.

Today Ephesus is great again—the largest collection of Roman ruins east of the Mediterranean, it's one of Turkey's mustsee tourist stops. Since 1979, the Austrian archaeology team entrusted with the site has aggressively reconstructed excavated areas (about 10% of the original city), moving statues and friezes indoors to the Ephesus Museum in Selçuk and patching together ancient buildings and colonnades. Considering the centuries of earthquake damage and erosion, excavation

has been like assembling a giant jigsaw puzzle. But at what point will ancient Ephesus no longer feel genuine?

The archaeological zone requires 2 or 3 hours to do it justice. Entering at the top of the hill, walk first through the **Upper Agora,** the official part of town, which is full of temples, monuments, fountains, a town hall, and the **Odeon,** where the government council met. Sloping away from it is **Curettes Way** (curettes were priests dedicated to Artemis, Ephesus's patron goddess)—notice the pockmarks on the pavement made by thousands of horses' hoofs over the centuries. Across from the Gate of Hercules (that's Hercules wearing the skin of the Nemean Lion), you'll see how the Ephesians curried favor with Roman emperors, building the two-story Trajan's Fountain and the **Temple of Hadrian,** with its glorious Corinthian-columned porch. Behind the temple are the grand **Roman Baths of Scholastika.**

Across Curettes Way, follow a colonnaded shopping street to the **Terraced Houses,** where the richest citizens lived. Here you can truly imagine the sophisticated lifestyle of the Roman Empire—running water, heating systems, private inner courtyards, and a rich decor of mosaics and frescoes. The nearby **Library of Celsus** was built to impress, with its outsize two-tiered facade and three levels of niches for storing scrolls or books; the **Marble Way** (paved in real marble) leads from there to the **Great Theatre,** a hillside amphitheater that could seat 44,000. Controversy continues over reconstruction of this theater, which authorities hope to use as a concert venue. Could Ephesus succumb to Disney-fication?

✈İzmir

🛏$ **Hotel Bella,** Ataturk Mah. St. John Sok 7, Selçuk (*©***90/232/892-3944;** www. hotelbella.com). $$ **Hotel Kalehan,** İzmir Cad., Selçuk (*©***90/232/892-6154;** www. kalehan.com).

---

321 Classical Relics

Hadrian's Wall
The End of Civilization
Northern England

BESIDES HARSH NORTHERN WEATHER, THE BIGGEST THREATS TO HADRIAN'S WALL ARE THE MANY tourists who feel compelled to walk atop this 2,000-year-old Roman fortification.

The wild and forbidding Cheviot Hills make an effective buffer between England and Scotland—but surveying the site in A.D. 122, Roman emperor Hadrian wasn't convinced that was enough to protect this farthest-flung frontier of his sprawling empire. He ordered his legionnaires to reinforce the border with a great defensive wall, 117km (73 miles) long, from the North Sea to the Irish Sea. In Romans' eyes, it marked where civilization ended and the barbarian world began.

With great fanfare, a footpath was completed in 2003 along the length of the wall, from Wallsend on the east coast to Bowness-on-Solway on the west, even plunging through urban areas of Carlisle and Newcastle. What a great idea it seemed, and it quickly become one of Great Britain's most popular treks—to the point of endangering these fragile old stones. U.K. heritage officials now urgently warn hikers to stick to the signed path, not to tread on the wall's ramparts (tempting as they may look), and to avoid hiking in winter, when the ground is wet and artifacts underground could be damaged.

First built of turf, the whole wall was soon finished in stone, with three legions working for 6 years. There were fortified "milecastles" every 1.6km (1 mile), sentry turrets in between, and full-fledged forts

Hadrian's Wall.

every 8 or 16km (5–10 miles). The Romans built well; though stones were pilfered from the wall for centuries, many fragments still stand. The 45km (28 miles) of wall between Chollerford and Walton is particularly well-preserved, much of it protected in the high wild moorland of Northumberland National Park. The most intact fort remnant is just east of the park at Chollerford: **Chesters Roman Fort and Museum** (www.english-heritage.org.uk/chesters), which guarded a critical bridge over the River Tyne. Moving west through the park, the **Housesteads Fort and Museum** (www.english-heritage.org.uk/housesteads) displays the Roman fort of Vercovicium, commanding a hill's rise; you can visit ongoing excavations at nearby **Vindolanda** (www.vindolanda.com), which also has several reconstructions. West of the park near Haltwhistle, the **Roman Army Museum** (www.vindolanda.com) has outfitted a barracks room to

depict living conditions in the Roman army; a short walk from here you can scale Wall-town Crags, one of the most imposing and high-standing sections of the wall.

If walking's not your thing, the B6318 road traces the wall, with signposts to major sights along the route. But why drive, when you can take the AD122 bus service, cycle along Hadrian's Cycleway, or take the scenic Hadrian's Wall Country train from Newcastle to Carlisle? Visit indeed—but treat the wall with the respect it deserves.

ⓘ www.hadrians-wall.org

🚂 Hexham or Haltwhistle

🛏 $$ **Battlesteads Hotel,** B6320, Wark Village (✆ **44/1434/230 209;** www.battlesteads.com). $$ **Best Western Beaumont Hotel,** Beaumont St., Hexham (✆ **44/1434/602331;** www.bw-beaumont hotel.co.uk).

Middle Ages **322**

Old Acre
Leading the Crusade
Akko, Israel

FIVE DAYS OF ARAB-JEWISH STREET VIOLENCE DURING YOM KIPPUR IN 2008 UNDERSCORED THE simmering political tensions in this ancient walled Israeli city, hampering restoration of its dilapidated historic core.

Holy wars? They used to be good news for Acre. In its time, Acre has been ruled by the Phoenicians, by King David, by Alexander the Great, by the Ptolemaic kings of Egypt, but the crusades were what really made them famous. Throughout the crusades, armies of Christian knights from Europe, heading east to "free" the Holy Land from Muslim rule, made this ancient seaport their home away from home.

Today, however, Acre lies embroiled in new holy wars. Designated as Arab territory in 1947, it was recaptured by Israelis in 1948, but nearly all the inhabitants of the

old walled city are Palestinian Arabs—and the disrepair of those ancient quarters suggests deliberate governmental neglect.

This is a city with many layers of history—literally. On the heights above industrial modern Acre, the walled Old City has an Arab profile, with romantic minarets and palm trees against the sky. During the Ottoman Empire, the Turks held sway, glory years represented by the green domed **Al-Jazzar Mosque,** with the Turkish Bazaar tucked in behind it, and the nearby **Hamman al-Pasha** (Turkish Bath). But the base of old Acre's walls date from

1104, when the knights of the First Crusade renamed Acre "Saint Jean d'Acre" and built a great sandstone fortress here.

Since the 1950s the knights' city has been gradually excavated from underneath the 38m-high (125-ft.) walls of Acre Citadel, the Turks' prison. (Today the citadel houses the **Museum of Heroism,** ✆ **972/4/991-8264,** honoring Jewish underground fighters imprisoned by the British, whose daring escape in May 1947 is depicted in the movie *Exodus.*) A replica of the crusaders' Enchanted Garden blooms beside the visitor center for the Knights Halls, headquarters of the powerful crusader order the Knights Hospitallers. In the first hall off its central courtyard is a graphic example of the layered architecture—the bottom shows the crusaders' arches, the top the Ottomans'. You can just picture these vaulted Gothic ceremonial halls hung with crusaders' banners and coats of arms. Nearby, you can also peek into barracks

and storerooms—a medieval toilet was even uncovered. The **Templars' Tunnel,** in the southeastern part of the Old City, on Haganah Street, is another crusader relic, a 320m-long (1,050-ft.) tunnel carved out of rock as a secret passage from the fortress to the port.

For tourists, nearly everything worth seeing in Acre is in the old town. Named a World Heritage Site by the United Nations in 2001, Acre is required to maintain its historic sites—but the fabric of the city around them is another matter altogether.

ⓘ 1 Weitzman St., Old City (✆ **972/700/ 70-80-20;** www.akko.org.il)

✈ Haifa

🛏 $$ **Akko Hotel,** Salhuddin St. 1, Akko (✆ **972/4/ 987-7100;** www.akkotel.com). $$$ **Palm Beach Hotel and Country Club,** Acre Beach (✆ **972/4/987-7777;** www.palmbeach.co.il).

323 Middle Ages

Famagusta/Magusa
Curtain Call for Othello's Harbor?
North Cyprus

THE TURKISH GOVERNORS OF DIVIDED CYPRUS HAVE DONE LITTLE TO MAINTAIN THIS WALLED port city's medieval ruins—let alone the eerie modern "ghost town" deserted by Greek Cypriots in 1974.

Every century or so, a new gang of rulers swooped down on this eastern Mediterranean island, occupying its finest harbor town. The name Famagusta was bestowed by French crusader knights and Venetian naval commanders; the Greeks prefer Ammochostas ("hidden in sand"), while the Turks call it Magusa. No wonder the city has an identity problem.

Take **Famagusta's Citadel,** for example. Its soaring medieval hall once thronged with crusaders, fleeing the Holy Land after the fall of Acre in 1291. Yet over the main gate, a sculpted panel depicts the winged

lion of Venice, which took over Cyprus in 1489, reviving the port after a miserable century of Genoese rule. The stout southwest tower is called Othello's Tower, after Shakespeare's tragic Moor, supposedly a Venetian commander in Cyprus—but that nickname dates only to the late 19th century, when Shakespeare's British countrymen occupied Cyprus.

Crammed within its medieval ramparts, the inner city is a haphazard mix of modern buildings and poorly maintained historic relics. The pointed arches of 14th-century Gothic churches rise above rubble, traces of wall paintings fading away on exposed interiors. (The derelict walls of St. George's Latin church even sport a few gargoyles.) The city's main cathedral is now the **Lala Mustafa Paşa Mosque,** but the exquisite stone tracery on its portals betrays its Frankish Gothic origins as St. Nicholas Cathedral. Palm trees sprout over the domes of two Byzantine church ruins, **St. Zoni** and **St. Nikolaus.** The round Cypriot Gothic towers of the **Church of St. George of the Greeks** are studded with cannonballs, relics of Famagusta's darkest hour, a 13-month-long siege (1570–71) by Ottoman Turkish forces. Under Ottoman rule, the city's culture changed again; ruined 16th-century Turkish bathhouses also punctuate the old town's narrow streets.

Under British occupation, from 1878 to 1960, trade flourished and the city quickly modernized, expanding beyond the walls. Turkish Famagustans stayed in the labyrinthine inner city, while Greek-Cypriot residents moved south to **Varosha,** on the southern shoreline. After independence in 1960, Varosha became Cyprus's hottest tourist destination—until 1974, when a new Turkish invasion abruptly turned north Cyprus into the Turkish Republic of Northern Cyprus. (Today you can move between the Greek and Turkish zones only at approved crossing points, such as Agios Nikolaos or Nicosia.) As Greek citizens evacuated, Varosha's beachfront hotels, department stores, and modern apartment buildings stood abandoned. More than 35 years later, barbed wire still surrounds Varosha, and Turkish soldiers drive away gawkers while buildings crumble in weed-choked lots. Medieval ruins *and* modern ruins—Famagusta needs to preserve both.

ⓘ www.magusa.org

✈ Ercan Airport

🚢 Famagusta (ferries from Turkey, Israel, and Syria)

🛏 $$ **The Dee European Hotel,** Mustafa Kemal St. (✆ **90/392/366 1222;** www.thedeeeuropeanhotel.com). $$ **Portofino Hotel,** 9 Fevzi Cakmak St. (✆ **90/392/366 4392;** www.portofinohotel-cyprus.com).

Middle Ages

324

The Ponte Vecchio
Bridging the Centuries
Florence, Italy

DEVASTATING FLOODS HAVE BEEN A WAY OF LIFE IN TUSCANY'S ARNO VALLEY SINCE TIME immemorial, sweeping periodically through the architectural jewel of Florence.

It happened in A.D. 1117, and again in 1333 . . . and 1547, and 1557, 1589, 1844, 1966, and 1992. Torrential flooding is historically inevitable along the River Arno. And yet somehow the triple stone arches of the Ponte Vecchio—the very name means "old bridge"—still straddle its banks in Florence.

Standing at the arched opening halfway over, you can gaze out at this beautiful Italian city and imagine all the history this bridge has seen. The original Roman-era wooden bridge was washed away in 1117 and replaced in 1220 by a more durable stone version, lined with shops in the medieval custom. The Ponte Vecchio became the heart of 13th-century Florence. The crenellated stone Palazzo Vecchio was built by its north end (today housing the famous Uffizi Gallery); Florence's cathedral, the Duomo, was erected nearby, distinctively striped in white, green, and pink marble and topped by a huge red-tiled dome. When the 1333 flood wiped out that bridge, it was immediately replaced by the 1345 version we see today.

In 1540, with the Renaissance in high gear—Michelangelo had sculpted his David, Leonardo had painted the Mona Lisa—the second Cosimo de Medici moved into the Palazzo Vecchio and decided to spiff up the bridge connecting his new digs with the Medicis' Pitti Palace across the Arno. He hired Giorgio Vasari to add a private bypass, a windowed corridor over the shops (today it's the Uffizi's portrait gallery annex). Half a century later, Ferdinand de Medici banned the butchers who'd traditionally conducted their smelly business from the Ponte Vecchio, replacing them with ritzy goldsmiths and jewelers. (Crossing the bridge, look for a bust of Benvenuto Cellini, the most famous goldsmith ever.) A third level of shops was gradually tacked on, which coincidentally made the bridge stronger, able to withstand repeated floods.

Since 1944, however—when retreating Nazi forces blew up Florence's bridges, sparing only the Ponte Vecchio by a merciful last-minute decree (allegedly from Hitler himself)—this medieval landmark is Florence's last remaining historic bridge. After the 1966 flood nearly swept its arches away, car traffic was banned and dams were built upriver to manage flood levels. The causes of the flood—deforestation and sediment mining—were reversed. Yet despite all these measures, in 1992 another flood overwhelmed the banks, caused this time by climate-change conditions that have raised river levels across

The Ponte Vecchio.

Europe. Are the Ponte Vecchio's days numbered?

ⓘ Tourist office: Via Cavour 1r (ⓒ **39/055/290832;** www.firenzeturismo.it)

✈ Florence (Amerigo Vespucci Airport)

🚆 Florence

🛏 $$$ **Hotel Hermitage,** Vicolo Marzia 1, Piazza del Pesce (ⓒ **39/055/287216;** www.hermitagehotel.com). $ **Hotel Abaco,** Via dei Banchi 1 (ⓒ **39/055/282289;** www.abaco-hotel.it).

325   Middle Ages

Leaning Tower of Pisa
Tilting Just So
Pisa, Italy

A DECADE-LONG ENGINEERING PROJECT IN THE 1990S ARRESTED THE TILT OF THIS FAMOUSLY leaning bell tower, restoring it to the same angle it had reached in 1838. Maintaining that trademark list will require careful management.

According to Pisan superstition, the leaning tower will never fall. After all, it has withstood earthquakes, World War II bombing, and the relentless Tuscan sun, which makes the stonework continually expand and contract. Benito Mussolini tried to straighten it in the 1930s, but no luck: The concrete poured into its foundation only made it sink further, thus perpetuating Pisa's claim to tourist fame.

The Tower of Pisa may be the most instantly recognizable building in the Western world, along with the Eiffel Tower. A grayish-white stack of colonnaded marble rings with a neat top hat, it has a certain architectural élan, but what really makes it famous is that rakish tilt, 14 feet (4.3m) off the perpendicular. Begun in 1173, this eight-story free-standing bell tower, or campanile, was designed as an addition to the cathedral at Pisa. But as the third story was completed, in 1198, it became obvious that the tower was leaning. The builders discovered that the site they'd chosen wasn't solid rock, as they'd thought, but water-soaked clay, and the tower's shallow foundation couldn't compensate. The architect, Bonnano Pisano, skipped town. Work was halted for decades while Pisa fought an on-again-off-again war with Florence. When the tower was finally completed in 1319, Pisa was a much less powerful city-state than it had been (in 1392 it was annexed by Florence). The bells were finally installed in the top in 1350, but they are no longer rung, for fear the vibrations might rattle the tower.

In World War II, when it was a Nazi observation post, the Allies considered knocking out the Leaning Tower with an artillery strike. A U.S. Army sergeant canceled the strike, thus saving the tower for generations of tourists (and pizza-box designers). As the century wore on, however, city fathers anxiously measured the tower annually—only to confirm that it was leaning a fraction of an inch farther every year. In the 1990s tons of soil were removed from under the foundation and lead counterweights placed at the monument's base, to stabilize it at a safe angle. It's judged to be good for the next 300 years.

Visitors can once again climb the 294 steps to the top and imagine standing beside Galileo Galilei, the Pisa-born physicist and astronomer. Perhaps the historians are right, and Galileo never actually dropped a feather and a cannonball from the top, to prove his theory of bodies in motion. But when it comes to the Tower of Pisa, superstition has a way of trumping fact.

ⓘ **Piazza del Duomo 17** (www.opapisa.it)

✈ Pisa (Galileo Galilei Airport)

🚆 Pisa

🛏 $$ **Hotel Villa Kinzica,** Piazza Arcivescovado 2 (✆ **39/50/560-419;** www.hotelvillakinzica.it). $$ **Royal Victoria,** Lungarno Pacinotti 12 (✆ **39/50/940111;** www.royalvictoria.it).

Middle Ages **326**

The Great Wall
A Great Fall for the Great Wall?
China

SANDSTORMS SWIRL OUT OF THE ARID LANDSCAPE, SCOURING, CRACKING, AND ERODING SECTIONS of the Great Wall of China. Tourism, neglect, and willful destruction by developers have also taken their toll.

They don't call it the Great Wall of China for nothing—standing 6m (20 ft.) wide at the base and between 6 and 9m (20–30 ft.) high, its prime ramparts were wide enough for five horses to ride abreast. It once spanned some 6,200km (3,900 miles), if you connected all the pieces. Nowadays, perhaps only 2,500km (1,600 miles) still stands.

The part most tourists visit—the part familiar to all of us from TV and tourist posters—is clearly medieval, reconstructed of stout stone and brick during the Ming dynasty (1368–1644). However, the Great Wall really begins east of Beijing at Shānhǎiguān, on the coast of the Bó Hǎi Sea, and runs west all the way to the Gobi Desert. That's a lot of wall, and the older sections are built not of stone but of rammed earth—which is crumbling at a terrible rate. Years of destructive agricultural practices have turned the region surrounding the wall in remote Gansu province into an arid desert, where sandstorms brutally whip its packed-earth surface for miles. Vandalism and pilfering have been epidemic for years; in Shaanxi province in 2003, parts of the wall were still being dismantled for road-building materials.

No emperor ever purposely set out to build a Great Wall—it evolved more gradually, over the years. Back in the Warring States Period (453–221 B.C.), rival kingdoms built defensive walls against their enemies, and subsequent emperors connected various bits, adding more where necessary to keep out Huns and Mongols and other invaders. The most developed section is at **Bādálǐng,** only 70km (43 miles) northwest of Beijing, where you'll find a museum, theater, restaurants, souvenir stands, even a cable car. Restoration has left the pale gray stones of its slotted battlements looking suspiciously crisp and new; tourists huddle on its stout stone watchtowers and snap photos of themselves with the wall visibly zigzagging up the green mountains behind them. Even closer to Beijing is the recently restored

The Great Wall of China.

(and less visited) section at **Jūyōngguān,** 55km (34 miles) northwest of the city.

To see a more authentic patch of wall, take a day trip to **Jīnshānlǐng** (✆ 86/10/ 8402-4628), 130km (81 miles) northeast of Beijing near Gu Bei Kou—reachable by taxi or train from Beijing. Here you can hike for 10km (6¼ miles) along the wall to the Mìyún Reservoir. As the number of fellow hikers dwindles and the stones become more timeworn and dilapidated, at last you can sense the Great Wall's venerable spirit.

ⓘ www.wildwall.com

✈ Beijing

🛏 $$$ **Grand Hyatt,** Dōng Cháng'ān Jiē 1, Dōngchéng District (✆ 86/10/8518-1234; www.beijing.grand.hyatt.com). $$ **Shi Jia House,** Shijia Hutong 42, Dōngchéng District (✆ 86/10/5219 0288; www.shijia house-beijing.com).

Lamu
Dreaming in Swahili
Kenya

As Kenya pursues plans to develop a massive modern port on this coastal island, conservation groups fight to have some input on its environmental and cultural impact.

There are only two cars on the whole island; donkeys provide all necessary transportation, squeezing past each other on often shoulder-width streets. You escape the dazzling equatorial sun by plunging into a labyrinth of arches and narrow lanes, lined with lime-washed stone houses, their Persian-flavored doorways flaunting intricate carved teak and mahogany. A long-ago Arab trading port, Lamu is largely Muslim, with a sprinkling of modest mosques and minarets, yet Portuguese cannons still line the 19th-century waterfront, fronted with a "skyline" of distinctly Swahili thatched roofs. The women wear black veils, the older men long loose-flowing *djellabas;* shops and cafes shut up in the heat of the day.

Kenya's oldest settlement, Lamu is a listed World Heritage Site, yet there are no grand must-see landmarks; it's the whole exotic ensemble that matters. The chunky 19th-century **Lamu Fort** is worth visiting mostly for the view from its walls; the market, tucked off to one side of the fort, is a sampler of local color. Exhibits at the Lamu Museum, formerly the English governor's residence, are only mildly interesting; much more informative is the **Swahili House Museum** (near Juma Mosque), which demonstrates the logic behind these traditional houses—the cool courtyards with their pools of mosquito-eating fish, the breeze-catching shaded verandas on the roof, the coral powder whitewash that insulates against the heat. On your second day here, you'll probably stroll down the coast to the island's second

town, Shela, a favored hideaway for aristocrats and celebrities, who have installed sleek decor inside its medina-style town houses. (Stop for a drink with the "in" crowd at the colonnaded Peponi Hotel.) By the third day, you'll be ready to hire a dhow to sail around the island, admiring its rich marine life of dugongs, turtles, and dolphins.

Lamu sank into genteel decline after the Indian Ocean trade dried up, too obscure to be modernized. A hippie influx in the 1960s changed little; even the creeping gentrification of recent years hasn't altered the island's dusty charm. But an ambitious new project most certainly will. Kenya's government intends to build Africa's largest port in Lamu, linking it to the rest of the continent by airports, bullet trains, and superhighways; an oil pipeline and refinery will follow, and after that, resort hotels and amenities are envisioned for the new Lamu. This is no mere pipe dream: As of 2011, contracts had been awarded, and plans were being drawn. Construction will most likely annihilate the mangroves' spawning grounds—but then, Lamu's residents may no longer have to fish for a living. It's a mixed blessing, indeed.

✈ Manda Island

🛏 $$$ **Lamu House,** Lamu seafront (✆ **254/42/4633 491;** www.lamuhouse. com). $$ **Stone House Hotel,** Lamu Old Town (✆ **254/42/4633-544;** www.stone househotellamu.com).

Chichén Itzá
Marvel of the Ancient Mayan
The Yucatán, Mexico

MAYAN ASTRONOMERS PREDICTED THEIR CALENDAR WOULD END AT WINTER SOLSTICE 2012, with a rare celestial alignment. Did they also foresee how air pollution and acid rain would doom the monuments of Chichén Itzá?

Voted one of the Seven Wonders of the World in a 2007 poll, Chichén Itzá (Chee-chen Eet'-zah) is definitely Mexico's most popular Mayan ruin, trampled every year by hordes of tour groups, often on day trips from Cancún. But the real threat comes from the sky—in the form of acid rain. With so much heavy industry around the Gulf of Mexico, the hot, humid Yucatán peninsula is particularly prone to polluted rainfall. Given the softness of local building materials, this immense 9th-century city is suffering.

Chichén's star attraction is the magnificent **El Caracol** (the Observatory), also known as the Pyramid of Kukulcán, a grand white stepped pyramid where astronomers peered through slits in a circular tower to chart the all-important equinoxes and summer solstice. Even its design reflects the Mayans' celestial obsessions: Four stairways leading up the sides each have 91 steps, making a total of 364; add the central platform and you've got 365, equal to the days of the solar year. On either side of each stairway are 9 terraces, equaling 18 on each pyramid face, the same as the number of months in the Mayan calendar. The pyramid is precisely aligned to cast a moving shadow—said to be the spirit of the feathered serpent—on its northern stairway at sunset on the spring and fall equinox, an awesome twice-a-year event. Even more amazing is the Galactic Alignment, a millennially rare alignment of the sun and the Milky Way that Mayan astronomers accurately predicted for winter solstice 2012 (December 21), marking the end of the Mayan calendar and the dawn of a new era.

Astronomy wasn't the Mayans' only interest, as Chichén's artwork abundantly proves. Unfortunately, acid rain damage is most evident here. In the **Juego de Pelota,** Chichén's main ball court, black mold obscures carved scenes of figures playing a jai alai–like game in heavy protective padding—spot the kneeling headless player, blood spurting from his neck, while another player calmly holds his head (legend has it that losing players paid with their lives). In the **Temple of Jaguars,** a now-flaking mural depicts a battle in a Mayan village. In

Chichén Itzá.

the **Temple of the Skulls,** where sacrificial victims' heads were displayed on poles, you can discern carved images of eagles tearing hearts from human victims; the **Platform of the Eagles'** reliefs show eagles and jaguars clutching human hearts in their talons and claws. In the **Temple of the Warriors**—named for the images of warriors marching along its walls—a seated figure of the god Chaac-Mool is surrounded by columns carved into enormous feathered serpents, which nowadays appear to be molting.

In April 2010, the Yucatán government bought the land under the monuments from private owners, ending years of disputes. Will the government now clean up the site, or exploit it with more hotels and glitzy rock concerts? (Elton John played the ruins in 2010, but after protests, Paul McCartney canceled his 2011 gig.) Chichén Itzá's future hangs in the balance, in more ways than one.

✈ Merida

🛏 $$ **Hotel Mayaland,** Zona Arqueológica (📞 **800/235-4079** in North America, or 52/998/887-2495; www.mayaland.com). $$ **Villas Arqueológicas Chichén Itzá,** Zona Arqueológica (📞 **52/985/856-6000;** www.villasarqueologicas.com.mx).

Machu Picchu
Lost City of the Incas
Near Aguas Caliente, Peru

SOME 3,000 VISITORS A DAY NOW TRAMP THROUGH MACHU PICCHU, STRESSING ITS ANCIENT stones. Tourist traffic, deforestation, and overdevelopment have led to repeated landslides—in 2004, 2005, and 2010—stranding thousands of people each time.

Machu Picchu isn't just Peru's top tourist draw, it's the most popular sight in all of South America. In 2010, when torrential rains and landslides forced a 2-month closure of this landslide-prone mountaintop citadel, Peru lost nearly $200 million in tourism revenues. No wonder there's little political will to limit tourism here.

Guided tours can still hike the traditional **Inca Trail** (either a 4-day trek from Qorihuayrachina or a 2-day version from Wiñay Wayna), but most travelers arrive by excursion train from Cusco, climbing a steep switchbacked roadway (on foot or by bus) to finally reach the citadel's entrance. How different from the 16th century, when Spanish conquistadors hunted in vain for Machu Picchu, rumored to be full of Inca gold. Abandoned by its own citizens, for 4 centuries Machu Picchu lay swallowed by jungle, hidden 2,450m (8,000 ft.) high among the clouds in the Andes.

Scholars can't agree whether this 15th-century city was mainly a fortress, a temple complex, a market town, or an astronomical observatory. What they could tell, however, was how skillfully its stonemasons fitted its unmortared walls together. The Incans sought to build in harmony with nature, as you can appreciate from the sweeping panorama by **Funerary Rock,** just inside the entrance: Steep terraces, gardens, granite and limestone temples, staircases, and aqueducts are set gracefully into hillsides, and forms of buildings seem to echo mountain peaks. Celestial observations were important, too; at the famous **Temple of the Sun,** windows are perfectly aligned to catch the sun's rays at the winter solstice in June. The mysterious **Inntihuatana,** or "hitching post of the sun," is a ritualistic carved rock that may have been some sort of sundial. The religious role Machu Picchu played is evident around the **Sacred Plaza,** with its two masterfully decorated temples.

But the recent boom in tourism is taking its toll. Geologists have spotted fault lines in the granite shelf upon which Machu Picchu was built, and uncontrolled development in the base town of Aguas Calientes is polluting the cloud-forest ecosystem. Under pressure from the international community, Machu Picchu's management has reluctantly adopted some protection measures. Since 2003, the numbers of Inca Trail hikers have been restricted; several tour companies now offer hikes that take alternative, less-trampled routes. Helicopter flights over the ruins have been banned, and a proposed cable car project was shelved. Timed-entry tickets and increased

entrance fees may be the next moves. But many visitors already time their arrival so they can see sunrise over the ruins—and there's no solitude even at dawn's early light.

ⓘ Av. Pachacútec, Aguas Calientes (✆ **51/ 84/211-104**)

✈ Cusco

🛏 $$$ **Inkaterra Machu Picchu Pueblo Hotel,** Av. Imperio de Los Incas, Aguas Calientes (✆ **800/442-5042** or 51/1/610-0400; www.inkaterra.com). $$ **Gringo Bill's,** Calle Colla Raymi 104, Aguas Calientes (✆ **51/84/211-046;** www.gringobills.com).

TOUR Andina Travel (✆ **51/84/251-892;** www.andinatravel.com). **Big Foot Tours** (✆ **51/84/238-568;** www.bigfootcusco.com). **Explorandes** (✆ **51/84/238-380;** www.explorandes.com). **Wilderness Travel** (✆ **800/368-2794;** www.wildernesstravel.com).

---

330 Historic Homes

The Tower of London
Where the Ravens Stand Guard
London, England

THE TOWER OF LONDON HAS STOOD FOR CENTURIES, BUT CLIMATE CHANGE HAS CAUSED THE Thames to rise, putting this landmark at risk.

In the 20th and 21st centuries alone, there were major floods in 1928, 1947, 1953, 1959, 1968, 1993, 1998, 2000, 2003, 2006, and 2007—several of them occurring even after 1984, when the massive flood control gates of the Thames Barrier were supposed to have solved the problem.

And when the Thames does overwhelm its banks, several of Britain's most revered landmarks are at risk. First and foremost is the Tower of London, a sprawling fortified compound begun by William the Conqueror

in 1078 to keep the recently conquered Saxons in check. Originally a royal residence, it was set right on the river, handy in the days when river barges were the speediest means of transport. The section fronting on the river has been furnished to recreate the era of Edward I, with guides in period costume and a copy of Edward's throne.

When James I took over from Elizabeth I in 1608, however, the royal family moved out—understandably, for over the years

10 Battlefields to Fight For

Some of history's most pivotal battles were located by random destiny, wherever two armies came face to face. Decades or even centuries might pass before tourists began to visit, with the landscape already irrevocably altered. Efforts to honor such hallowed grounds can lead to modern-day battles between preservationists and real estate developers, between historians and naturalists. Here are 10 battle sites where those dramas are being played out today:

331 Battle of Hastings, Battle, England After Norman archers defeated Anglo-Saxons at Senlac Hill in 1066, William the Conqueror created his own memorial, leveling the hill and erecting a Benedictine abbey. Confiscated under Henry VIII, Battle Abbey became a private estate and gradually fell into ruins; Battle Abbey school moved in after World War I. Sold to the nation in 1976, the abbey ruins and parkland offer visitors an audio tour to help reconstruct the original lay of the land. *44/1424/775705. www.english-heritage.org.uk.*

332 Minute Man National Historic Park, Lexington & Concord, Massachusetts The first shots of the American Revolution were fired here on April 19, 1775, beginning with a dawn skirmish on Lexington's village green and ending amid the farms of Concord later that day. The battle corridor between the towns, along Route 2A, became a national park in 1959, but it took years to clear forest and remove buildings to restore its 1775 appearance. Boston's suburban sprawl continues to nibble at its borders. *978/369-6993. www.nps.gov/mima.*

333 Valley Forge, Pennsylvania Though not technically a battlefield, Valley Forge—the ramshackle camp where General George Washington nursed the Continental Army through the bitter winter of 1777–78—represents a turning point in the Revolutionary War. Trees that screen the park from the busy Pennsylvania Turnpike will soon be lost as the highway is widened right up to park borders. *610/783-1099. www.nps.gov/vafo.*

334 Waterloo, Belgium The agricultural plain where Napoleon's French army fell to the Duke of Wellington's Anglo-Allied forces looks much as it did in 1815, save for one feature: the Lion Mound, an immense grass-covered cone topped by a majestic iron lion, built in 1826 by the King of the Netherlands. Reportedly Wellington himself was shocked that the ridge of Mont-St-Jean—crucial to his battle plan's success—was removed to create this mound. *32/2/385 19 12. www. waterloo1815.be.*

The Lion Mound at Waterloo.

335 San Jacinto State Park, LaPorte, Texas In 1836, Texans won independence from Mexico on this marshy coast on Galveston Bay, defeating General Santa Anna with the battle cry "Remember the Alamo!" A portion is now a Texas state park with a towering monument, but local activists hope to reclaim more of the actual battle territory, restoring it from an oil-refinery landscape along the Houston Ship Channel. *281/479-2431.* www.tpwd.state.tx.us/park/sanjac.

Harpers Ferry.

336 Harpers Ferry, West Virginia The panoramic confluence of the Shenandoah and Potomac rivers has always been a strategic hot spot. In 1859, abolitionist John Brown led a famous raid on its U.S. Arsenal; during the Civil War, the town changed hands eight times. A national park since 1944, its picturesque village and well-preserved battlescape may be spoiled by a proposed office/hotel development adjacent to the park. *304/535-6029.* www.nps.gov/hafe.

337 Monocacy, Maryland Confederate troops would have captured Washington in July 1864 if an outnumbered force of Union soldiers hadn't delayed them at this patch of farmland just outside Frederick, Maryland. Its rolling stream-laced landscape is vulnerable to erosion and flooding, but a greater threat is the advance of Washington D.C.'s metro sprawl. Already bisected by a commuter highway, Monocacy may soon view the smokestack of a waste-to-energy facility. *301/662-3515.* www.nps.gov/mono.

338 Gallipoli, Turkey On this strategic Dardanelles peninsula, Turkish forces fought off British invaders for 9 months in 1915–16. A national park since 1973, Gallipoli is beloved both by Turks and by Australians and New Zealanders whose Anzac units bore the brunt of British losses. The rugged battlefield is obscured with memorials, cemeteries, and encroaching forest; archaeologists using GPS technology have recently located trenches, dugouts, and tunnels, to reinterpret the site. www.anzac.govt.nz/gallipoliguide.

339 Verdun, France World War I's longest and bloodiest battle raged for most of 1916; some 700,000 soldiers died, many of them unburied, their bodies blown to bits. Its forts, bunkers, and pillboxes have deliberately been left shattered and bullet-riddled, telling a haunting tale of trench warfare at its worst. Conifer forests gradually crept over the landscape; a new plan to restore native deciduous woods may uproot more bodies. www.en.verdun-tourisme.com.

340 Pearl Harbor, Honolulu, Hawaii A date that will live in infamy, FDR called it—December 7, 1941, when Japanese bombers attacked U.S. ships at Pearl Harbor, Honolulu. Located on a still-active Navy base, the USS *Arizona* Memorial invites visitors onto a glass platform to gaze down on the sunken battleship, just 6 feet (1.8m) below the water's surface. Preserving an underwater shrine remains a challenge; drops of oil from the Arizona's tank still surface every day. *808/422-0561.* www.nps. gov/usar.

The Tower of London.

the Tower had come to be the realm's most important prison. On the walls of the Beauchamp Tower, you can read the last messages scratched by despairing prisoners; according to legend, two little princes (the sons and heirs of Edward IV) were murdered by henchmen of Richard III in the so-called **Bloody Tower.** Sir Walter Raleigh languished here for 13 years, and Sir Thomas More spent the last 14 months of his life in a whitewashed prison cell in the **Bell Tower.** Many of these prisoners arrived by boat through the spiked iron portcullis of Traitor's Gate, before being publicly executed in the central courtyard on **Tower Green** (including two of King Henry VIII's wives, Anne Boleyn and Catharine Howard).

As a fortress, the Tower also made a safe place to store weapons and treasures. The **Jewel House** contains the Tower's greatest attraction, the Crown Jewels, some of the world's most precious stones set into robes, swords, scepters, and crowns. Prepare to stand in long lines to catch glittering glimpses of the jewels as you scroll by on moving sidewalks.

Guided tours of the compound are led by the **Yeoman Warders** (aka "beefeaters") in their distinctive red-and-gold uniforms. And don't forget to look for the pack of glossy black ravens fluttering around. According to legend, the Tower of London will stand as long as the ravens remain—so just to be safe, one wing of each raven is clipped.

ⓘ **The Tower of London,** Tower Hill (✆ **0870/756-6060;** www.hrp.org.uk/toweroflondon)

✈ Heathrow International

🛏 $$ **Mornington Hotel,** 12 Lancaster Gate, Bayswater (✆ **800/633-6548** in North America or 44/20/7262-7361; www.bw-morningtonhotel.co.uk). $$ **Sanctuary House Hotel,** 33 Tothill St., Westminster (✆ **44/20/7799-4044;** www.fullershotels.com).

Alhambra
Moorish Pleasure Palace
Granada, Spain

Tourists flock to Calat Alhambra and that has become a pressing concern. Crowd control has become a priority to protect the palace; timed tickets are issued to spread out the crowd evenly throughout the day.

The Calat Alhambra—the name means Red Castle—looks forbiddingly somber, looming on a rocky outcropping above the city of Granada in southern Andalusia. But duck inside and you'll discover a Moorish fantasy, a perfect expression of Spain's Muslim past. While a portion of the original rugged 9th-century fort still exists at the core, the castle was transformed starting in 1238 by the Nasrid princes. (Of course, after the Reconquest, in 1526 Holy Roman Emperor Charles V inserted a new Renaissance palace in the middle of this Moorish stronghold.)

The extravagance and sensuality of the Nasrid lifestyle seems diametrically opposite to the fortresslike exterior. Around the arcaded **Patio de los Leonares** (Court of the Lions), with its immense fountain resting on 12 marble lions, every room tells a story; and now that the press of tourists has been reduced, you can actually view these rooms at leisure. In the **Sala de los Abencerrajes**, with its richly adorned honeycombed ceiling, the last emir, Boabdil, staged a banquet for his most powerful rivals, only to have his guards massacre them mid-dinner. In the **Sala de los Reyes**

The Alhambra.

(Hall of Kings), a great banqueting hall with an exquisitely painted leather ceiling, one sultan beheaded 36 Moorish princes because he suspected one had seduced his favorite wife. The **Hall of the Mexuar** was once the sultan's main council chamber; Spanish rulers converted it into a Catholic chapel in the 1600s.

There's even more outside the Alhambra's walls: The **Generalife,** the sultans' summer retreat, where they used to spend their summers locked away with their harems. Look for the **Escalera del Agua** (Water Staircase); an enclosed Asian garden, **Patio de la Acequia,** with water jets arching over its long central pool; and **Patio de la Sultana,** the secret rendezvous point for Zoraxda, wife of Sultan Abu Hasan, and her lover.

This great Spanish castle has instituted a policy of timed admission tickets to spread out each day's crowd of 7,500-plus visitors more evenly through the day. But even if you have a ticket, you can stay in the Nasrid palaces for only half an hour—proving just how stressed the Alhambra is by tourist traffic. Book your ticket in advance through any branch of **BBVA** (Banca Bilbao & Vizcaya; © **34/90/222-44-60;** www.alhambra-patronato.es). Come here at night, when floodlights bathe the exotic gardens and palaces—it's a sight you'll never forget.

ⓘ **The Alhambra,** Palacio de Carlos V (© **34/95/822-09-12)**

✈ Granada

🛏 $$$ **Parador de Granada,** at the Alhambra (© **34/95/822-14-40;** www.parador.es). $$ **Hotel Palacio Santa Inés,** Cuesta de Santa Inés 9 (© **34/95/822-23-62;** www.palaciosantaines.com).

Historic Homes **342**

Taman Sari Water Castle
The Sultan's Swimming Pool
Yogyakarta, Indonesia

THE RUINS OF THE SULTAN'S POOL HOUSE ARE ONE OF YOGYAKARTA'S CHIEF TOURIST DRAWS. A 2006 earthquake, however, has put the fragile palace at risk.

Indonesia can get pretty steamy in the summertime, so naturally Sultan Hamengku Buwono I—an 18th-century Islamic ruler of Yogyakarta—needed a cool retreat. The design of his Taman Sari water castle (the name means "perfumed garden") was totally up-to-date for 1758, an intricate nest of gleaming stone pavilions, fountains, and bathing pools where he and his family, including concubines, could beat the heat. The sultan had cleverly arranged it so that he could discreetly watch his concubines bathing below—and then invite anyone who caught his eye up to his own more secluded pool.

The original complex includes 59 structures—a mosque, meditation chambers, terraces, swimming pools, and a series of 18 water gardens and pavilions surrounded by ornamental lakes. After the plumbing was damaged by an earthquake in 1867, the lakes and pools stood dry for well over a century; squatters eventually moved in and dwelt among the deserted pavilions. Recent renovation brought back a taste of the pleasure palace's grandeur, with the central bathing complex opened to the public again in 2004. Another earthquake in 2006, however, dealt the site a serious setback; researchers are still investigating how to shore up the palace's aging stone to protect it from future quakes.

The central pool area has been filled with water again and smartened up for tourists, but wandering around the meandering passageways and tunnels of the rest of the complex is also an evocative experience. While its fountains and pools resemble European-style water gardens of the same era, these are heavily ornamented with Javanese motifs and distinctly Asian rooflines. Elaborate bas-reliefs are everywhere, many of them bearing inscriptions in an intricately symbolic script. It was said that some of the tunnels led the sultan to his secret supernatural wife Nyai Roro Kidul (Queen of the South Sea); more likely they were an escape route or hiding place for the royal family in times of enemy attack. Though the outlying lakes and canals are still dry, you can

see where an artificial island was raised in the middle of the lake, shaped like a lotus floating in the middle of the pond. Upon it stands a royal pavilion surrounded by flowering trees, wafting scent upon every breeze up to the sultan's bedroom.

It's fun to explore the maze of back alleys and tiny houses that surround the many gates into the ruins (only the main gate charges admission). The water palace is also convenient to the city's atmospheric Ngasem bird market.

✈ Yogyakarta

🛏 $$$ **Sheraton Mustika,** JL Laksda Adisucipto, Yogyakarta (© **274/488588;** www.sheraton.com). $$ **Manohara Hotel,** Borobudur Archaeological Park, Magelang (©**361/731520;** www.baliwww.com).

Gu Gong (The Forbidden City)
Outliving the Emperors
Beijing, China

NEARLY SEVEN MILLION VISITORS A YEAR CROSS THE THRESHOLD OF THIS 500-YEAR-OLD IMPERIAL palace. Between Beijing's air pollution and foot traffic, the ancient pavements and buildings are wearing down.

It may have been forbidden once, but since the last emperor left in 1923, this vast complex where Chinese emperors lived from 1420 to 1923—beginning long before Columbus sailed to the Americas and ending right before Lindbergh flew across the Atlantic—now belongs to the people. Limiting tourist access would be a ticklish proposition for the Chinese government, since most of the visitors are Chinese citizens, getting in touch with their heritage. Many sections may be closed when you visit, due to a massive renovation lasting through 2020.

Still, there's no one must-see section—it's the scale and harmony of the whole that's so impressive, an irrefutable statement of Chinese imperial might. It's truly the most spectacular palace in China, an immense layout of red-walled buildings topped with glazed vermilion tile and ringed by a wide moat. It was originally built by an army of workers in only 14 years, although after various ransackings and fires, most of what you see today was built in the 17th century under the Qīng dynasty. Notice the blue and green tiles trimming several of the up-curled roofs—the Qīngs

中华人民共和国万岁   世界人民大团结万

The Forbidden City.

were Manchus, and this color reminded them of their native grasslands.

You enter through the Meridian Gate, but before you go farther, check out the largest gate, the **Gate of Heavenly Peace,** where Mao Zedong made his dramatic announcement founding the People's Republic in October 1949. (You can't miss it—look for the giant portrait of Mao hanging above the central door.) The **Gate of Supreme Harmony** leads into the perfectly symmetrical outer court, with its three grand ceremonial halls, where the emperor conducted official business.

Then comes the inner court—the emperor's private residence—which was truly the Forbidden City; only the imperial family (plus a host of concubines and eunuchs) were allowed here. Three elegant palaces face onto the inner court, and at its rear is a marvelous garden of ancient conifers, rockeries, and pavilions.

If you can, venture beyond the central axis, where all the tourists mass, to the quiet maze of pavilions, gardens, courtyards, and

theaters on the eastern side—it's well worth paying this section's extra admission fee. Look for the **Hall of Clocks** (Zhōngbiǎo Guǎn) and the **Well of the Pearl Concubine** (Zhēnfēi Jǐng), a narrow hole covered by a large circle of stone. Here, a 25-year-old favorite was stuffed down the well as the imperial family fled during the Boxer Rebellion; she'd dared to suggest that the emperor stay to face the mobs. Defying the emperor? Not a good idea.

ⓘ **North side of Tiananmen Square,** across Cháng'ān Dàjiē, Běijīng (✆ **86/10/ 6513-2255,** ext. 615)

✈ Capital Airport, Beijing

🛏 $$$ **Grand Hyatt,** Dōng Chāng'ān Jiē 1, Dōngchéng District (✆ **86/10/8518-1234;** www.beijing.grand.hyatt.com). $$ **Shi Jia House,** Shijia Hutong 42, Dōngchéng District (✆ **86/10/5219 0288;** www.shijia house-beijing.com).

Sans-Souci Palace
Grandeur Lost
Milot, Haiti

THE 2010 EARTHQUAKE THAT SHOOK HAITI WAS DEVASTATING IN TERMS OF HUMAN LIVES LOST and dealt a severe blow to the impoverished country's tourism efforts. The ruins of Sans-Souci Palace are a major draw, but the site is facing deterioration due to a lack of proper drainage.

Haiti's disastrous earthquake claimed the lives of some 316,000 people and left about another 300,000 injured. The magnitude 7.0 quake hit about 26km (16 miles) west of Port-au-Prince, Haiti's capital, reducing much in its wake to rubble and leaving 1,000,000 people homeless. The quake also took an awful toll on towns and national landmarks. The world responded with humanitarian aid and sent medical teams and engineers to the blighted area. The chaos was compounded by the fact that communication systems, electrical networks, and hospitals had been hit. Although recovery has begun, many Haitian people are still living in camps, and their circumstances are often grim. It is estimated that it will take a decade or more to restore the country and establish a new, healthy economy.

By a stroke of sad irony, prior to the quake Haiti had been tagged as ripe for development as a new tourism hot spot. No less a celebrity than former President Bill Clinton, the United Nations Special Envoy for Haiti, had declared the previous May that tourism was the key to improving the lives of Haitians, whose country is ranked the poorest in the Western Hemisphere.

It is a blessing, then, that one of Haiti's major attractions was spared: Sans-Souci Palace, the centerpiece of the island's National History Park. Recognized on UNESCO's World Heritage list in 1982, the National History Park encompasses the palace; **Citadel Laferriere,** the largest fortress of the western hemisphere; and the buildings of **Ramiers.** Located in the peaceful north end of Haiti, about an hour's drive south of Cap-Hatien, the National History Park was luckily far from the epicenter of the quake.

Sans-Souci was perhaps the grandest of nine palaces built by King Henri Christophe—himself a former slave who led a successful rebellion against French colonial powers—to prove that a Caribbean ruler could live as grandly as any European monarch. Built by former African slaves, it aped the baroque splendor of a European palace; the very name is French, translated as "without worry." After it was completed in 1813, Sans-Souci Palace was considered to be the Caribbean equivalent of Versailles. Yet King Henri lived there only a few years—he committed suicide on the grounds in October 1820, leaving behind a wife and twin daughters. His nephew, Jacques-Victor Henry, took the throne but was bayoneted by revolutionaries on the palace grounds 10 days later. A final blow was dealt to the palace in 1842 when it was hit by another of the earthquakes to which this island nation is so vulnerable.

Ever since, Sans-Souci has lain in dramatic ruins, testament to King Henri's grand aspirations for his tiny kingdom. The nearby fortress, Citadel Laferriere, completes the haunting story, built on a mountaintop to thwart a French invasion, one of King Henri's recurrent fears. Together, however, the two buildings are now considered to symbolize liberty, since they were constructed by former African slaves who had gained their freedom.

Although Sans-Souci has lain in dramatic ruins since the 1842 earthquake, the Global Heritage Fund recently cited it as in danger of further deterioration, due to a lack of proper drainage. Haiti needs tourism more than ever now, and it doesn't have many landmarks left to attract visitors; it is especially essential that Sans-Souci gets a new drainage system and floor now.

ⓘ Port-au-Prince: Secretary of State for Tourism, 8 Rue Legitime (✆ **509/223-2143-5631-5333-0723**)

✈ Cap Haitien Airport

⊨$ **Hotel du Roi Chistophe,** 24 B Cap-Haitien (✆ **509/262/0349**)

Historic Homes **345**

Shackleton's Hut & Scott's Hut
Outposts in the Polar Night
Antarctica

A CENTURY OF ANTARCTIC BLIZZARDS HAS PUMMELED THESE MODEST WOODEN BUILDINGS, which lie in darkness several months at a time, with constant freezing temperatures and hurricane-force winds.

The race to be the first explorer to reach the South Pole captured public attention at the beginning of the 20th century. Both of the leading British contenders, Sir Robert Scott and Sir Ernest Shackleton, left base huts behind in Antarctica ㉓, and the sight of these lone, fragile dwellings on the Antarctic ice still inspires awe.

Making his second Antarctic expedition, Shackleton anchored his ship, the *Nimrod,* at McMurdo Bay in February 1908. He and his men set up this prefabricated wood hut under a protective ridge of volcanic rock at Cape Royds on Ross Island, where they waited to attempt their trek to the South Pole. In these cramped quarters—10x5.7m (33x19 ft.), with a 2.4m (8-ft.) ceiling—15 men slept, ate, and studied through the cold, dark winter. (They conducted a number of scientific investigations while in Antarctica, mainly to underwrite the race to the pole.) Their clothing, equipment, books, and even their food still lie scattered around the musty hut as if they'd just walked out the door. In fact, when a member of Scott's expedition stopped in 2 years later, he

found tins of butter, jam, and gingerbread biscuits, all perfectly fresh. Of course, he took them.

Shackleton's hut was first restored in 1961, and the extreme cold of its surroundings have helped to preserve it. But in recent years more and more visitors have been allowed in—about 700 a year—and even though only eight people go in at a time, brushing their shoes off first and not touching anything inside, inevitably there's been wear and tear. The condition of the hut became so urgent that in 2008 a team of conservators stayed in Antarctica throughout the astral winter to carry out their work in 24-hour darkness. The urgency of this restoration effort testifies to the enduring appeal of this heroic era of Antarctic exploration.

Captain Scott's hut is located on the north shore of Cape Evans on Ross Island. It dates to the British Antarctic Expedition of 1910–13. Recent conservation efforts have saved the battered structure, which was at risk of collapse. Inside are artifacts from earlier expeditions, which, like Shackleton's, were also preserved by the cold.

Shackleton and his team got within 161km (100 miles) of the South Pole—the farthest south any human had yet gone—but he never made it to the pole itself. Scott did, in 1911, but only days earlier Roald Amundsen had already planted the Norwegian flag there. Tragically, Scott and his men died returning to base. Shackleton returned 3 years later on the *Endurance* and became the first to cross the Antarctic over land. A heroic era

indeed—preserving its last few monuments is the least we can do.

TOUR Polar Cruises (© **888/484-2244** or 541/330-2454; www.polarcruises.com). **Quark Expeditions** (© **800/356-5699** or 203/656-0499; www.quarkexpeditions. com). **Escorted Antarctica Tours** (© **800/ 942-3301;** www.escortedantarcticatours. com).

---

346 Historic Homes

Beauvoir
Jefferson Davis's Last Stand
Biloxi, Mississippi

PRESERVATIONISTS RALLIED TO RESCUE WHAT WAS LEFT OF BEAUVOIR AFTER SUFFERING THE wrath of Hurricane Katrina. But how many hurricanes can this historic structure withstand?

After the tumult of the Civil War, former Confederate President Jefferson Davis seemed like a lost soul—barred from politics, stripped of his beloved Mississippi plantation Brierfield, traveling restlessly around the world. At last he found a haven in this serene white cottage on the Mississippi Sound, where in 1877 he settled down to write his memoirs, raise a few crops (oranges and grapes, mostly), and enjoy his final years with his wife, Varina.

Among the many Gulf Coast sites pummeled by Hurricane Katrina in 2005, Beauvoir seemed one of the most tragic scenes. Submerged under a 24-foot (7.3m) storm surge, its green storm shutters were battered, lacy lattices crumpled, the roof ripped off, and its gracious wraparound verandas torn from the raised foundation. The Jefferson Davis Presidential Library that opened here in 1998 was also badly damaged, losing nearly a third of its collection, and several outlying buildings were leveled. But a determined crew of conservators went to work at once, supported by a combination of FEMA grants and private donations. Considering the general

devastation of the Gulf Coast, hiring workers and getting building materials was often a challenge, but Beauvoir's saviors persevered. Repairs on the main house were completed in 2008, though much work still remains to be done on the 51-acre (21-hectare) site. The Library Pavilion where Davis worked on his books was demolished by the storm and is to be replaced with a replica by late 2011.

Surrounded by cedars, oaks, and magnolia trees—many of them dripping with Spanish moss—with wide Gulf views from the front porch and a quiet little bayou tucked behind the house, Beauvoir's Deep South charm must have been balm to Jefferson Davis's soul. As opposed to the stately formality of the Confederate White House in Richmond, this one-story house had a much more relaxed aura. Working in the book-lined library pavilion across the lawn, he wrote two books in a burst of literary energy—*The Rise and Fall of the Confederate Government* (1881) and *A Short History of the Confederate States of America* (1889).

Sadly, he had only a few years to enjoy it—he died in New Orleans in 1889 (he was eventually reinterred in Richmond's Hollywood Cemetery). After Varina's death, the estate became the site of a retirement home for Confederate veterans; a cemetery on the property contains the graves of several Beauvoir residents, including the Tomb of the Unknown Confederate Soldier.

(i) **Beauvoir,** 2244 Beach Blvd., Biloxi (© **228/388-4400;** www.beauvoir.org)

✈ Gulfport-Biloxi International Airport

🛏 $$ **Best Western Cypress Creek,** 7921 Lamar Poole Rd. (© **800/466-8941** or 228/875-7111; www.bestwestern.com). $$ **Hampton Inn,** 1138 Beach Blvd. (© **800/436-3000;** http://hamptoninn1.hilton.com).

Historic Homes

Taliesin & Taliesin West
The Wright Idea
Wisconsin & Arizona

TALIESIN AND TALIESIN WEST BOTH BEAR THE RAVAGES OF TIME, AND DESIGN FLAWS HAVE caused damage to both historic Frank Lloyd Wright buildings.

Ask most Americans to name a famous architect and they'll probably say Frank Lloyd Wright. More than a third of his buildings are on the National Register of Historic Places; 24 are full-fledged National Historic Landmarks. But if you really want to understand what made Wright tick, visit his Wisconsin home, Taliesin.

Here, on a rolling 600-acre (240-hectare) campus with his students living around him, many ideas Wright later translated into blueprints were tried out and tested. Most of this took place during the Depression, however, when commissions were few and far between, and much of the construction was on a shoestring budget. Now those buildings are falling apart.

Though Wright (1867–1959) grew up in Madison, Wisconsin, he spent his boyhood summers in this Wisconsin River valley on his uncle's farm, exploring the natural world, which would later play a large part in his architecture. Naturally he returned here in 1911 after making his mark as an architect in the Chicago area. There's a juicy story attached: He originally built it as

a refuge for himself and his mistress, Mamah Borthwick Cheney. Tragically, in 1914 Mamah was killed in an arson fire at Taliesin. A grieving Wright rebuilt the house. Ten years later, Wright was living here with his third wife, Olgivanna, when the living quarters burned down again and had to be rebuilt a third time. After Wright's death in 1959, Olgivanna lived here until she died in 1985. Today, Taliesin stands in desperate need of funds for proper upkeep. Crashing branches have caved in roofs, poor drainage has weakened foundations, and the hill bearing Wright's home had to be shored up before it slid into the lake below.

Similar problems plague Taliesin West in Scottsdale, Arizona, where, in one case, the clear canvas Wright chose for a roof for the drafting room had to be replaced when the hot Arizona sun led to its deterioration. The structure served as his winter home and school from 1937 until his death. Today, it's the primary campus of his school of architecture and is home to the **Frank Lloyd Wright Foundation.** As with its

Taliesin West.

Wisconsin counterpart, time has taken its toll on the building, and maintaining it is an expensive undertaking. For more information, consult www.franklloydwright.org.

Tours of the Taliesin campus in Wisconsin are offered May to October. The house itself is quintessential Wright design, with cunningly interlocked horizontal planes of fieldstone, wood, and gray concrete seeming to grow right out of a hillside. Several other buildings are scattered around the property, some of which—the Shingle-style Unity Chapel, the Hillside School, and a residence called Tan-y-deri—were among his first designs. Set in a rich agricultural area, Taliesin was also a working farm, and Wright created a set of low-slung barns—the Midway Barns—for that purpose. In 1932, Wright started up the Taliesin Fellowship, a sort of architectural commune (it has since evolved into the Frank Lloyd Wright School of Architecture) living and working at Taliesin. You can still see residential fellows working in its many nooks, stone terraces, and Japanese-style courtyards every summer. They're keeping Wright's legacy alive in one respect—but keeping the house itself intact is an equally essential task.

ⓘ5607 Co. Hwy. C, Spring Green (✆**877/ 598-7900**; www.taliesinpreservation.org) ✈Madison

🛏$$ **House on the Rock Resort,** 400 Springs Dr. (✆ **800/822-7774** or 608/588-7000; www.thehouseontherock.com). $$ **Silver Star Inn,** 3852 Limmex Hill Rd. (✆**608/935-7297**; www.silverstarinn.com).

11 Cityscapes

One of Venice's canals.

Downtown Detroit
Shrinking Motor City
Detroit, Michigan

THE 2010 CENSUS FIGURES SHOW THAT DETROIT'S POPULATION PLUNGED 25% IN THE PAST decade, just as new mayor David Bing is trying to ramp up urban renaissance. A threatened loss of tax credits for landmark rehabs could be the final blow to the city.

While many American cities reinvigorated their downtown areas at the end of the 20th century, in Detroit the problems seemed insurmountable. Plagued with racial tension since 1967 riots, Detroit experienced not only "white flight" to the suburbs, but middle-class "black flight" as well. The swift decline of the American motor industry crippled the city's longtime economic base. What had once been a jewel of a downtown became a mere shell, with hundreds of architectural gems standing derelict.

Despite discouraging downward population trends, Detroit's long-promised rebirth may have finally turned a corner. One prong of the effort involves sports, with state-of-the-art new stadiums built in 2000 and 2002 for the resurging Detroit Tigers baseball team and the Lions football team. Detroit hosted both the Super Bowl and the World Series in 2006, as well as the 2005 MLB All-Star Game and 2009 NCAA Final Four tournament, all strengthening a hopeful bid for the 2020 Olympics.

Another focus involves development of the Detroit River riverfront, spearheaded by a rehab of the mirrored towers of the 1970s-era Renaissance Center, General Motors' headquarters. A cobblestoned, landscaped section of Riverwalk opened in 2007, connecting downtown with the city's recreational jewel, the island of **Belle Isle,** landscaped in the 19th century by Frederick Law Olmsted. (The island's landmark aquarium, however, closed in 2005 and still hasn't reopened.) A third strategy involves casinos—the MGM Grand at US 10 and Bagley Avenue, the **Motor City** on Grand River Avenue, and the **Greektown Casino** on Lafayette all opened in 1999 and added hotels in 2007–08.

For preservationists, the key has been substantial tax credits to restore historic buildings rather than raze them for new construction. Two vintage buildings were relocated to make room for the new baseball stadium, and both the Motor City and Greektown casinos incorporated existing buildings in their designs. Two classic hotels, the Book Cadillac and the Fort Shelby, reopened after total renovations in 2008, and several restored theaters grace the arts district around Grand Circus Park. Other restorations include the **Wayne County Building,** with its iconic clock tower over downtown, and the iconic **Penobscot Building** and **Guardian Building** skyscrapers. Yet landmarks such as Hudson's department store and the old Tiger Stadium were demolished despite protests, and other gems like the Michigan Central railroad station, the National Theater, and the United Artists Theater stand rotting, their rehab prospects dimming. With Michigan threatening to revoke those tax credits, restoration efforts may stall.

Outside of downtown, it's a different story. The current policy is to knock down decaying houses, leaving green "urban prairies" in their place. (Several urban farms have taken root on that new acreage.) Aerial photos of today's Detroit show more green space than houses in many neighborhoods; efforts to shift residents into the most viable neighborhoods are politically sensitive. With its tax base declining, could Detroit be a model for the "shrinking city" of the future?

(i) **Preservation Wayne** (℗ **313/577-3559;** www.preservationwayne.org)

✈ Detroit Metropolitan Airport

🛏 $$ **Detroit Marriott at the Renaissance Center,** 400 Renaissance Center (℗ **313/568-8000;** www.marriott.com). $$$ **The Inn on Ferry Street,** 84 E. Ferry St. (℗ **313/871-6000;** www.theinnonferry street.com).

Cities in Peril 349

Galveston Island
Victoriana by the Sea
Galveston, Texas

As of early 2011, the owners of many of Galveston's historic cast-iron buildings were still waiting for federal disaster aid funds to repair the rusting and damage from 2008's Hurricane Ike.

In the 19th century, Galveston was the crown jewel of Texas. Sitting on a 32-mile-long (51km) barrier island at the mouth of a fine natural harbor, it was Texas's leading port and biggest city—even, briefly, the capital of the Republic of Texas. Stately

A pier in Galveston.

Victorian mansions lined the streets of the East End (north of Broadway, from 9th to 19th sts.), while the Strand District (19th to 25th sts. between Church St. and the harbor)—once dubbed the "Wall Street of the Southwest"—was a showplace of ornate cast-iron facades.

But on September 8, 1900, Galvestonians learned how quickly life could change. In the middle of the night, 20-foot-high (6m) hurricane waves crashed over the long, low island, smashing houses into matchwood and hurling residents from their beds. By morning more than 6,000 islanders—one out of every six—were drowned, and one-third of its buildings wrecked. It still ranks as the deadliest natural disaster in U.S. history.

Galveston valiantly rebuilt, erecting a stout 10-mile-long (16km) seawall and raising the entire island with landfill. Nevertheless, most businesses relocated inland to Houston, and except for a burst of bootlegging and gambling during Prohibition, 20th-century Galveston languished. The only good thing about Galveston's decline: real estate developers never bothered to knock down those Victorian buildings, leaving several dilapidated gems waiting to be restored in the 1960s and 1970s. Nowadays, Galveston has 60 structures listed on the National Register of Historic Places.

Tourism eventually offered Galveston a second act. While weekending Houstonians frequent its miles of brown beaches and several Caribbean cruise ships dock here, Galveston mainly trades on that Victorian image, with carriage tours and quaint B&Bs. Two magnificent East End houses are open to the public: the castlelike stone **Bishop's Palace,** 1402 Broadway (✆ **409/762-2475**), built in 1892; and the opulent brick-and-limestone 1895 **Moody Mansion,** 2618 Broadway (✆ **409/762-7668;** www.moodymansion.org). Every May, the **Galveston Historical Foundation** (www.galvestonhistory.org) organizes weekend tours of several Victorian mansions.

There's only one problem: Galveston is still Texas's most hurricane-prone city. Deadly storms sweep in every few years—Hurricane Alicia in 1983, Hurricane Jerry in 1989, tropical storm Allison in 2001—the most recent being Hurricane Ike, which surged over the unprotected bay shore in September 2008 and flooded Galveston anew. Several beaches were badly eroded and the seawall wasn't repaired until early 2010, but the historic areas bore the brunt of the damage. Several sites took months to reopen; the severely rusted cast-iron facades of the Strand remain exposed to the humid air, awaiting restoration. The extent of the storm damage kept many tourists away, a further blow to the local economy. Will restoration bring Galveston back in time?

ⓘ Tourist office, 2328 Broadway (✆ **888/425-4753;** www.galveston.com)

✈ Houston

🛏 $$ **Harbor House,** #8 Pier 21 (✆ **800/874-3721** or 409/763-3321; www.harborhousepier21.com). $$$ **Hotel Galvez,** 2024 Seawall Blvd. (✆ **877/999-3223** or 409/765-7721; www.wyndham.com).

---

350 Cities in Peril

Mexico City
On Shaky Ground
Mexico

THE MEXICAN CAPITAL'S TREASURES OF SPANISH COLONIAL ARCHITECTURE SIT ON A DEPLETED aquifer that has sunk at least 10m (33 ft.) in the past century—in an area that's already earthquake-prone.

In hindsight, the 8.1 earthquake that hit Mexico City on September 19, 1985, was a turning point. Thousands were left homeless, water mains burst, disease ran rampant; in the end, some 10,000 were dead and an estimated $5 billion worth of property was damaged.

As renovations ensued, the community became aware of the treasures in their midst. From the ruins of the Hotel Prado, Diego Rivera's famous mural *Dream of a Sunday Afternoon in Alameda Park* was saved and installed in a new museum on Plaza de la Solidaridad. Shattered remnants of the neoclassical Rule Building movie palace were preserved to be converted into a visitor center. Workers making repairs in the 680-block historic core unearthed artifacts from the Aztec era and even earlier. After years in which tourism had shifted out to neighborhoods like Chapultepec Park, Zona Rosa, and Xochimilco, the Centro Histórico began to attract a new groundswell of visitor interest.

First, the government addressed two perennial Mexico City problems—its reputation for violent street crime and the brown mantle of smog that hangs over this mountain-ringed bowl crowded with traffic and industry. Recent public-safety measures have reduced crime, and measures like lead-free fuels and tougher emission controls have lowered ozone levels, but visitors still need to be wary.

When the Spanish conquistadors built their capital, they based it on the ruins of the Aztec capital Tenochtitlan, and those layers of history make restoration complicated. The city's immense Zócalo, or central plaza, sits atop what was once Lake Texcoco, creating dangerously soft foundations for the baroque 17th-century **Catedral Metropolitana,** Latin America's largest church. The 17th-century **Palacio Nacional** (also on the Zócalo) is set atop the former palace of Moctezuma II, and the ruins of five Aztec temples have been unearthed around it (check out the **Museo del Templo Mayor** on the Zócalo). Near Alameda Park, the glorious **Palacio de Bellas Artes** (Calle López Peralta), a marble Art Nouveau theater, is also noticeably sinking. The foundations of this great crowded metropolis are anything but stable.

Enter Mexico City's fairy godfather: Mexican business magnate Carlos Slim, reputedly the world's richest man, whose Fundación Centro Histórico has since 2004 poured money into buying centuries-old buildings for rehabilitation and improving the city's aging drainage system. Several streets have been pedestrianized and repaved, electric cables buried, security cameras installed, decrepit facades refurbished. Upscale restaurants and shops have begun to open up, and chic lofts attract young singles. The historic center is looking better these days, but it's a long climb back.

(i) www.mexicocity.gob.mx

✈ Benito Juárez International Airport

🛏 $$ **Best Western Hotel Majestic,** Av. Madero 73 (©**800/780-7234** or 52/55/ 5521-8600; www.bestwestern.com). $ **Hotel Catedral,** Calle Donceles 95 (©**52/ 55/5518-5232;** www.hotelcatedral.com).

Cities in Peril **351**

Buenos Aires

Perpetual Makeover

Argentina

NEW CONSTRUCTION RATES IN BOOMING BUENOS AIRES ARE NOW SIX TIMES THAT OF 20 YEARS ago, much of it in the historic core. Inconsistent landmark protection leaves heritage buildings even more vulnerable to being razed.

For years, the most important opera house in the Americas stood silent, its ornately columned neoclassical facade covered in scaffolding. Management promised Teatro Colón would be ready for its 100th birthday in May 2008, but that date came and went. In the end, a new government committee was formed to monitor the renovation; Teatro Colón finally reopened in May 2010—most of it, at least.

Buenos Aires has always been better at reinventing itself than at preserving the past. Just look around palm-tree–shaded **Plaza de Mayo,** the traditional heart of the city. The only two Spanish colonial landmarks left are the modest white Cabildo (old city hall)—which was whittled down a century ago to create Avenida de Mayo and Diagonal Sud—and the mid-18th-century Metropolitan Cathedral, which was drastically altered in 1836. The plaza is dominated instead by the startlingly pink **Casa Rosada,** Argentina's presidential office (you'll recognize its north wing balcony from *Evita*), an 1880s reconstruction on the site of an old fort. To get a taste of an older Buenos Aires, walk around the San Telmo district's **Plaza Dorrego,** the city's second-oldest plaza, where a few colonial buildings survive; yet even the decayed grace of this mostly 19th-century neighborhood is vanishing with rapid gentrification.

You'll have to hunt down other 18th-century relics. In the Monserrat neighborhood, the baroque **Iglesia de San Ignacio** is the city's oldest church, built by Jesuits from 1710 to 1734, with wonderful period details like a carved-wood altar and an ingenious 1767 sliding canvas of St. Ignatius; you can tour tunnels beneath the church, which sheltered resistance fighters when the English invaded Buenos Aires in 1806. Other colonial-era churches around the city include Nuestra Señora del Pilar, a lovely Franciscan retreat next to the cemetery in the upscale Recoleta neighborhood, and **Iglesia San Francisco,** which dates to 1730 but was given a new German baroque facade in the early 20th century.

Most of Buenos Aires' landmarks are more recent, built in an explosion of civic

The Casa Rosada in Buenos Aires.

pride between 1880 and 1910. Determined to prove their city equal to any European capital, developers laid new Parisian-style boulevards over the original Spanish colonial grid, and lined them with Beaux Arts and Art Nouveau buildings. Built on a lavish scale, often with imported materials, the finest of these included **Teatro Colón,** the domed **Congreso** building on Avenida de Mayo, and the fantastical terra-cotta–tiled **Water Company Palace,** surely the world's most ornate water pumping station.

Now this dynamic capital is reinventing itself again, with an upswing in tourism. Without firm heritage leadership, can Buenos Aires resist leveling more listed buildings in the name of progress?

ⓘ www.bue.gob.ar

✈ Buenos Aires

🛏 $$ **The Cocker,** Av. Juan de Garay 458, San Telmo (✆ **54/11/4362-8451;** www.thecocker.com). $$ **Castelar Hotel & Spa,** Av. de Mayo 1152, Monserrat (✆ **54/11/4383-5000;** www.castelarhotel.com.ar).

Santa Ana de Coro
The Colors of the Caribbean
Venezuela

HEAVY RAINS IN 2004 AND 2005 INFLICTED TERRIBLE WATER DAMAGE ON THE BEAUTIFUL adobe landmarks of Coro, many of which had lasted 300 years in this usually arid coastal climate.

History always seems to desert Coro. Back in 1527, Santa Ana de Coro was founded as the first capital of Venezuela, Spain's newest province; soon after, South America's first bishop was installed here. Explorers seeking the legendary gold of El Dorado based their expeditions in Coro. But the Spanish governors quickly realized that this Caribbean coast location made them easy prey for pirates; they moved the capital inland to El Tocuyo, then down the coast to Caracas. Less than 50 years after Coro's imposing white cathedral was finished, the bishop decamped to Caracas as well. Raided periodically by pirates, Coro was eventually flattened by a cyclone in 1681.

Then came Coro's second act. In the 18th century, nearby Dutch colonies on Curaçao and Bonaire began to trade with Coro, and wealth poured in. The cyclone-damaged city was rebuilt, with grand tiled-roof houses lining its cobbled streets, their earthen walls painted in bright Caribbean colors. On their ornate facades, Spanish and Dutch decorative styles mingled. (Compare the House of the Iron Windows, with its Sevillean wrought-iron grilles and scallop-shell baroque entrance, to the neat Dutch symmetry of the crimson House of 100 Windows.) Tree-lined promenades and leafy parks were laid out. Adobe was used everywhere, even in public buildings and churches, like the mustard-colored churches of San Francisco and San Clemente. Compare their decorative flourishes to the austerity of the 16th-century cathedral, or the 17th-century monastery next to San Francisco, which today holds a museum of religious objects.

The War of Independence in 1821 hit Coro hard, and this time it didn't rebound. Yet years of decline had one advantage: some 600 historic adobe structures survived intact, far more than in neighboring towns such as Maracaibo or Barquisimeto.

There isn't much to do in modern Coro, it's true. Most visitors are trekkers heading for the undulating golden dunes of **Medanos de Coros National Park,** which lies just outside the city limits. Coro's few small museums are mostly worth visiting because they're located in those old colonial mansions—like the **Coro Museum of Art** and the **Alberto Enrique Art Museum,** both on Paseo Talavera, or the ceramics museum in the **Balcon de los Arcayas** house on Zamora Street. Also on Zamora Street, you can tour **The House of the Iron Windows** or the **Casa del Tesoro.** But take time to stroll along the **Plaza Alameda;** admire how the Caribbean sunlight dazzles off the golds, blues, and pinks of those manor houses. They've survived so much—let's hope they can be restored this time.

ⓘ http://coroweb.com

✈ Coro

🛏 $ **Narhuaca Posada Turistica,** Calle Falcon, Casa #188, Paseo Manaure (② **58/ 268/251 2855;** http://posadanarhuaca. com). $$ **La Casa de los Pájaros,** Calle Monzon 74 (② **58/268/252 8215;** www. casadelospajaros.com.ve).

Lima Centro
Crumbling Colonials
Lima, Peru

NOTORIOUS FOR ITS STREET VIOLENCE IN THE 1980S AND 1990S, LIMA BECAME A PLACE tourists simply bypassed. Today, preservationists are beginning to uncover and restore its architectural treasures, hoping to attract tourists again.

Ah, the glory that was Lima, once the power center of Spain's South American empire. Founded in 1535 by Francisco Pizarro (who killed the Incas' emperor to seal the deal), Lima has good historic bones indeed. Girded by a 17th-century city wall, it was largely rebuilt after a devastating 1746 earthquake, with handsome baroque churches and elegant mansions. From the 1940s on, however, a flood of new residents expanded the city too quickly, turning it into a sprawling metropolis ringed by depressing shantytowns (*pueblos jóvenes*). Tourists rarely ventured beyond the upscale Miraflores suburb or the Bohemian quarter, Barranco. Only in the 1990s, when international organizations like UNESCO and the World Monument Fund began to advocate for its preservation, has Lima's historic core begun to rebound.

Begin exploring in the heart of the city, at the **Plaza de Armas** with its great bronze fountain. The graceful yellow towers of Lima's baroque cathedral dominate the plaza; go inside to see the mosaic-encrusted chapel containing Pizarro's tomb. (On the northeastern corner, the busy baroque facade of the **Archbishop's Palace** is deceiving—it was only built in 1924.) Directly south of **La Catedral**, the Jesuit church of **San Pedro** (Azángaro at Ucayali), is the city's best-preserved early colonial church, austere on the outside but a riot of gilded altars and baroque balconies inside. Behind this powerful yellow-and-white-striped neoclassical facade, the **Convento y Museo de San Francisco** (Plaza de San Francisco) displays fabulous Moorish ceilings, beautiful cloisters, and a bone-crammed set of catacombs.

To the west, you'll find opulent homes built for Lima's ruling elite, but in later years subdivided into warrens of cheap apartments. As you walk around, notice Lima's most distinctive architectural feature: elaborate dark wooden balconies, or *miradores*, overhanging the street. A few restored houses are open to the public—**Casa Riva-Agüero** (Camaná 459), with its beautiful green-and-red courtyard, and **Casa Aliaga** (Jr. de la Unión 224), Lima's oldest surviving house. You can't miss the ornately sculpted entrance of **Palacio Torre Tagle** (Ucayali 363), its decorations an intriguing mix of Spanish *mudejar* details and Chinese flourishes. **Casa de Osambela Oquendo** (Conde de Superunda 298), now a venue for cultural events, was the tallest house in colonial Lima, thanks to the cupolaed tower from which its owner watched his galleons sail into port. As you go from mansion to mansion, though, notice how many other buildings on these streets are still run-down, some even occupied by squatters. Can this neglected jewel of a historic district find its way back?

ⓘ **iPerú**, Pasaje Los Escribanos 145 (✆ **51/1/427-6080**)

✈ Jorge Chávez International

🏨 $$ **Casa Andina Classic,** Av. Petit Thouars 5444, Miraflores, Lima (✆ **51/1/213-9739;** www.casa-andina.com). $ **La Posada del Parque Hostal,** Parque Hernán Velarde 60, Santa Beatriz, Lima (✆ **51/1/433-2412;** www.incacountry.com).

TOUR Lima Tours (✆ **51/1/619-6900;** www.limatours.com.pe)

Toledo
The City on the Hill
Spain

HOUSING DEVELOPMENTS ARE SLATED TO SPROUT ON THE OPEN BUFFER ZONES SURROUNDING Toledo, Spain's former capital in the 16th century and a certified historic monument.

It's one of Europe's most famous panoramas, immortalized in the paintings of El Greco—Toledo's ensemble of medieval buildings, crowning a steep hilltop above the River Tagus, with intensely green valleys carving the summit into even sharper relief. The city's silhouette is elegantly punctuated by the pointed Gothic spire of Toledo's cathedral (the head church in Spain) and the stout four-towered fortress of the **Alcazar.** That's the vista that greets train passengers arriving from Madrid; it's a thrilling approach, rattling across the viaduct to stop at the city's small but exquisite Moorish-styled station. Sightseeing tours circle the city on the scenic Carretera de Circunvalación, showing off the dramatic profile from across the river. Soaring stone bridges span the gorge to enter through the keyhole arches of ancient drawbridge gates.

That glorious setting was cited in Toledo's inscription as a World Heritage Site in 1986, and those green valleys were identified as "undevelopable" land, to be preserved as open space. In 2006, however, that zoning was abruptly reversed, with a new city plan to build housing outside the historic quarter—right on the Vega Alta and Vega Baja, the green meadows running along the river. Some 37,000 housing units were slated to go up in this area between now and 2025, completely changing the prospect from the Madrid highway. As bulldozers began to level the **Vega Baja,** however, the discovery of important archaeological remains—relics of the 6th-century Visigoths who once ruled Hispania—put the project on hold while excavations proceed. Remains of an even older past, when Toledo was known to the Roman Empire as Toletum, lie at the city's northwest corner, bisected by a new access road.

With its narrow winding streets, crenellated walls, arched passageways, wrought-iron street lamps, and cloistered museums, Toledo wears its past gracefully. Walking around the historic core, you'll quickly be impressed by the Muslim-inspired decorative flourishes of Mudejar architecture—rounded horseshoe arches, stone fretwork, stylized metal grilles, decorative tiling, and inlaid brickwork. In this historically multicultural city, every street seems to have a house of worship, from the powerful cathedral to austere monastery chapels, from vaulted mosques to ornate synagogues; it's one of the few European cities that still has a thriving historic Jewish quarter. One sight in the Jewish quarter you shouldn't miss: The **El Greco Museum,** featuring an awesome collection of the Mannerist master's vibrant canvases, as well as a reconstruction of his sitting room and studio. Stand before the copy of his famous *View of Toledo* and ponder how little the city has changed in the 4 centuries since he painted. What a shame it would be if, after all that time, that iconic vista should be lost.

ⓘ Tourist office, Puerta de Bisagra (ⓒ **34/92/522-08-43**)

✈ Madrid

🚆 Toledo

🛏 $$ **Hotel Pintor El Greco,** Alamillos del Tránsito 13 (ⓒ **34/92/528-51-91;** www.hotelpintorelgreco.com). $$$ **Parador de Toledo Conde de Orgaz,** Cerro del Emperador (ⓒ **34/92/522-1850;** www.parador.es).

Venice
The Lagoon's Sinking Jewel
Italy

AS THIS WORLD TREASURE SINKS ABOUT 6.4CM (2½ IN.) PER DECADE, A CONTROVERSIAL system of mobile underwater barriers is being built to combat seasonal flooding—with questionable impact on the lagoon's ecosystems.

Set on 118 separate islands, dredged out of a marshy lagoon and shored up on wooden pylons, Venice floats upon the Adriatic Sea like a mirage. Amsterdam and Bruges and a few other European cities may have a network of canals draining their cityscape, but in Venice the canals are the cityscape—creating land to go with it was an engineering triumph over nature.

Nature, however, has a way of striking back. In the first decade of the 20th century, the city's central piazza, St. Mark's Square, flooded fewer than 10 times a year; by the 1980s it generally was underwater 40 times a year, overwhelmed by the Adriatic Sea's idiosyncratic *acqua alta* high tides. In recent years, as sea levels rise and the lagoon flood subsides, the problem has grown even more acute, with as many as 40 floods between September and March. The MOSE project, an expensive system of underwater flood-control barriers, is under construction and due to be completed in 2012, but critics already doubt its effectiveness against rising sea levels. And when you add in the impact of more than 1,000 large ships visiting Venice every year—including massive cruise liners that can barely squeeze through the Giudecca Canal—this beautiful city's future begins to look waterlogged indeed.

Unlike other canal cities, Venice has no streets at all, only canals (more than 150 of them) and paved walkways. Motor launches and anachronistic black gondolas are the way to get around town—that and walking, which usually means getting lost in a maze of narrow stone lanes and high-arched bridges. That perplexing layout was a matter of necessity—buildings were erected wherever land seemed solid enough, while winding channels between islands became canals, like the sinuous Grand Canal, or the unbridged (cross it by ferry) Giudecca channel.

Most tourists simply mill around the colonnaded **Piazza San Marco**—arguably the loveliest public space in the world—and file through the guidebook must-sees: **St. Mark's Basilica,** a glorious Byzantine church with glittering gold mosaics; the iconic Campanile bell tower; and next to it the exotic **Doge's Palace,** with its *Arabian Nights* facade. But getting beyond San Marco is essential to understand Venice. Cruise the **Grand Canal,** lined with Venetian Gothic *pallazzi;* stroll around the city, popping into obscure churches and browsing street markets. Hop on a *vaporetto* and visit the outlying islands—**Murano,** home of exquisite glass makers; **Burano,** the island of lace makers; or the **Lido,** Venice's local beachfront.

Venice is a city of unique sensory impact—a constant murmur of water lapping against stone, a moist shimmer against your skin, and that faint scent of decay. Somehow it manages to be intensely evocative, even magical. It's the sheer Venice-ness of Venice—and it can never be reproduced.

ⓘ ✆ **39/41/529-8711;** www.turismo venezia.it

10 Last-of-Their-Kind Towns

Lost in the forward-hurtling rush of civilization, by some quirk of fate each of these 10 small towns managed to escape modernization. They're not just architectural stage sets, but intact embodiments of distinct cultures—the way things used to be before our global village got so homogenized.

356 Jimingyi Post Town, Huailai, China   A vital way station on Genghis Khan's post road, where imperial couriers could change horses, the crumbling walled town of Jimingyi (Cock Crow) makes a good day trip, 2 hours from Beijing. Fading frescoes decorate its many temples, including 800-year-old Ningyong Temple; aristocratic courtyard houses and a double-roofed gate tower recall its Ming dynasty heyday. *www.chinaculture.org.*

Civita di Bagnoregio.

357 Civita di Bagnoregio, Lazio, Italy   Founded by ancient Etruscans on a tufa-rock plateau overlooking the Tiber valley, in the late 1600s this walled medieval hill town was severed from the rest of Bagnoregio by erosion and landslides (a single pedestrian bridge connects them today). As more tourists discover this romantic decaying hill town, its steadily crumbling outcrop worries preservationists. *www.civitadibagnoregio.it.*

358 Gammelstads Kyrkstad, Luleå, Sweden   Sweden once had 71 such "towns"—clusters of snug one-room wooden cottages where country parishioners could stay overnight to attend Sunday church services. Only 16 have survived, the largest being this 424-cottage settlement around the whitewashed belfry of Nederluleå church, the largest medieval church in Norrland. Guided tours are available. © *46/920/45 70 10. www.lulea.se/gammelstad.*

359 Vlkolínec, Ružomberok, Slovakia   Straggling up the Carpathian slopes, half of this mountain village's traditional deep-gabled log houses are year-round residences, the other half vacation homes. There's little difference between 16th-century and 19th-century houses—none has running water or sewers, and chickens and goats roam free outside. *www.vlkolinec.sk.*

360 Amana Colonies, Iowa   Settled by a German religious sect in 1855, these seven hamlets along the Iowa River maintained a strict communal lifestyle until 1932. In a landmarked district of some 500 historical buildings, every village has its own store, school, bakery, dairy, and church; assigned homes stand in the middle, ringed by barns, craft workshops, and factories (for Amana refrigerators, for instance). © *800/579-2294. www.amanacolonies.com.*

361 Oak Bluffs, Martha's Vineyard, Massachusetts One of the last surviving 1880s "cottage camps" built for summer religious retreats—very popular in late-19th-century America—the Campground in Oak Bluffs features some 300 doll-like Victorian gingerbread cottages, set closely on narrow lanes surrounding the recently restored Tabernacle, an open-sided pavilion where Methodist preachers still hold services. ℰ *508/693-0525. www.mvcma.org.*

Oak Bluffs.

362 Crespi d'Adda, Lombardy, Italy From 1878 to 1928, this model industrial town was built by the enlightened owners of the Crespi cotton mill—a tidy grid of 50 roomy stucco houses, each allotted to two or three workers' families, set in neat low-walled gardens. The village still looks much the same, with most houses owned by descendants of Crespi workers; the factory closed in 2004. ℰ *39/2/9098 7191. www.villaggiocrespi.it.*

Crespi d'Adda.

363 Letchworth Garden City, Hertfordshire, England Inspired by social reformer Ebenezer Howard, this 1903 urban planning experiment pioneered many features still used today—separate zoning for industry and residences, the preservation of trees and open spaces, affordable housing (the so-called Cheap Cottages), traffic roundabouts, and a surrounding Green Belt. The architecture is still charmingly rural and small scale. ℰ *44/1462/487868. www.letchworthgc.com.*

364 Portmeirion, Wales Constructed from 1925 to 1973, this charming but incongruous Mediterranean-style village on North Wales's rugged coast embodied founder Clough Williams-Ellis's utopian theories on harmonizing architecture with nature. Pastel Palladian villas, Arts and Crafts cottages, and an Art Deco hotel are set amid flower-filled terraces, sloping lawns, and mature woods of yews, oaks, and rhododendrons. ℰ *44/1766/770000. www.portmeirion-village.com.*

365 Arcosanti, Arizona "Arcology"—the marriage of architecture and ecology—is the philosophy of Italian architect Paolo Soleri, who launched this prototype community in the high Arizona desert in 1970. The antithesis of urban sprawl, its futuristic-looking cluster of solar-powered domes, vaults, and greenhouses is compact and sustainable; even the concrete is cast in local desert silt. ℰ *928/632-7135. www.arcosanti.org.*

➤ Venice's Aeroporto Marco Polo

🛏 **$$$ Locanda Ai Santi Apostoli,** Strada Nuova, Cannaregio (✆ **39/41/ 5212612;** www.locandasantiapostoli.com).

$$ Pensione Accademia, Fondamenta Bollani, Dorsoduro (✆ **39/41/5237846;** www.pensioneaccademia.it).

Cities in Peril **366**

Intramuros
Within the Walls
Manila, the Philippines

SURROUNDED BY HEAVILY URBANIZED METROPOLITAN MANILA, THIS HISTORIC FORTIFIED quarter—carefully rebuilt after World War II's devastation—treads a fine line between tourism development and historic preservation.

The Philippines' First Lady Imelda Marcos may have been a controversial figure, but she got one thing right: Manila needed to preserve its historic heart and soul. As the Philippine metropolis mushroomed in the 1980s, Marcos campaigned to restore the massive stone walls, gates, and moats of Intramuros, the last vestige of the Philippines' Spanish colonial past.

When the Spanish arrived in 1571, they found the bamboo palisade of Malay leader Rajah Sulayman situated here on the banks of the Pasig River. Intent on gaining a foothold for the lucrative spice trade, the Spanish set up a new colony, constructing a star fort with impressive ramparts, ornate stone gates, marble residences, and mission churches to Christianize the natives. Intramuros—the name means "within the walls"—endured for centuries, even as Manila changed hands, with the British briefly taking over in 1762–64, then the Americans in 1898. In 1942, however, the Japanese army invaded, and by 1945 Intramuros had become the Japanese soldiers' last holdout. A final barrage of American shelling left very little of Intramuros except the baroque adobe **San Agustin Church,** spared because it was the Red Cross headquarters.

For years after the war, shattered Intramuros lay neglected, a sorry weed-choked zone of warehouses, squatters, and petty criminals. Though Fort Santiago was declared a landmark in 1951, it wasn't until 1979 that an independent agency, the Intramuros Administration, truly began to restore the walled city. In the 1980s, Intramuros became a government priority, as its walls were rebuilt, plazas freshly landscaped, and educational institutions relocated here. First Lady Marcos's pet project was **Casa Manila** (General Luna St., near San Agustin Church), an intriguing reconstruction of a wealthy 19th-century Filipino family home—a rare window into the past in a city that seems intent on hurtling into the future.

Today Intramuros charms tourists, who can stroll around its sooty battlements or take a tour in leisurely horse-drawn carriages, or *calesas*. While a few ruined buildings remain rubble, new buildings in the district fit in with appropriately Spanish-styled architecture. But after escaping the rampant commercialization of the rest of Manila, Intramuros may be an oasis at risk. McDonald's and Starbucks have already slipped in; the surrounding moat, long ago drained, is now a golf course, and a sound-and-light museum delivers a noisy version of Philippines history. Plans announced in 2010 to rebuild the ruined **San Joaquin Church** as a museum may signal a better new direction for Intramuros. The last thing Manila needs is another shopping mall.

ⓘ Visitor information, Fort Santiago; http://intramuros.ph

✈ Aquino International Airport, Manila

🛏 $ **White Knight Hotel Intramuros,** Plaza San Luis (✆ **63/2/526-6539;** www. whiteknighthotelintramuros.com). $ **Malate Pensionne,** 1771 M. Adriatico St., Manila (✆ **63/2/523-8304;** www.mpensionne. com.ph).

St. Petersburg
Venice of the North
Russia

ENVIRONMENTALISTS FEAR THAT NEW DAMS BUILT TO CONTROL FREQUENT BALTIC SEA FLOODING may back up pollution in St. Petersburg's already-compromised water supply.

St. Petersburg was a planned city, conceived by Peter the Great to establish a seaport for mostly landlocked Russia. His glittering new capital was set on Baltic marshes, with a network of canals for drainage. The first flood hit in August 1703, only 3 months after the city was founded.

Since then, nearly 300 storm surges have hit the city; the worst were in 1824 and 1924, but lately, with global warming, they've been getting more severe—and more frequent. (The latest, in 2007, raised the water level of the Neva by 2.2m/7¼ ft., submerging roadways.) To manage the flood threat, a connected series of dams across the Gulf of Finland (bearing a six-lane highway on top) was begun in 1980, halted during the 1990s financial crisis, and resumed in 2003; a majority of the project was completed in 2008.

St. Petersburg didn't develop exactly as Peter planned; today it is centered on the south bank of the Neva River, but he envisioned its center being the Peter and Paul Fortress (Petropavlovskaya Krepost), on Hare's Island (Zaichy Ostrov) across from the Winter Palace. The complex includes the Peter and Paul Cathedral, which holds the tombs of all Russian czars

and their families from Peter's day through the last of the Romanovs (assassinated Czar Nicholas II and his family were reburied here in 1997). Also at the fortress, the Trubetskoi Bastion housed such political prisoners as Fyodor Dostoyevsky, Leon Trotsky, and Vladimir Lenin's brother.

The ghosts of the czars still seem to linger at elegant **Palace Square** (Dvortsovaya Ploshchad). Standing under the Alexander Column—a 600-ton monolith topped by a cross-carrying angel, commemorating the Russian victory over Napoleon—imagine all that this asymmetrical plaza has seen, from royal coaches pulling up to the baroque Winter Palace on one side, to Communist solidarity marches in front of the long, curved General Staff Building. Through the grand courtyard of the Winter Palace today, you enter the state **Hermitage Museum** (www.hermitagemuseum.org), a set of extravagantly decorated salons displaying the peerless art collection of the czars—an incredible catalog of Renaissance Italian art, including two rare da Vinci Madonnas, and loads of Dutch and Flemish masters; it has more French artworks than any museum outside of France.

You may also want to stroll around the formal gardens of the **Summer Palace;** glean literary insights at the Dostoyevsky House and Nabokov House museums; walk along Nevsky Prospect, St. Petersburg's greatest boulevard; and photograph the blindingly bright beveled domes of the **Cathedral of the Saviour on the Spilled Blood,** commemorating the spot where Czar Alexander II (who freed Russia's serfs in 1861) was assassinated in 1881. If the floodgates hold, they may shine a long time.

ⓘ www.petersburg-russia.com

✈ Pulkovo-2 International Airport

🛏 $$$ **Corinthia Nevsky Palace,** 57 Nevsky Prospekt (℃ **7/812/380-2001;** www.corinthia.ru). $$ **Hotel Marshal,** Shpalernaya St. 41 (℃ **7/812/579-9955;** www.marshal-hotel.com).

Cities in Peril 368

Istanbul
Big Boom in the Bosphorus
Turkey

OVERCROWDING AND POLLUTION ARE MAJOR ISSUES FOR TURKEY'S CAPITAL, WITH A POPULATION that recently topped 13 million. Seismologists predict another devastating earthquake before 2025. Will Istanbul be ready to cope?

Population explosion is too mild a term. Ever since the 1970s, enormous numbers of Turks have flooded into Istanbul, lured by jobs in new factories; on the city's fringes, cheap new housing sprang up, much of it substandard. With more factories and more cars choking the roads, air pollution rapidly worsened; the water supply and sewage systems just can't keep up. (Pollution concerns probably cost Istanbul its bid for the 2008 Olympics.) In August 1999, a 7.4-magnitude earthquake hit those crowded jerry-built suburbs, leaving 18,000 dead. The city is now replacing those shantytowns with drab earthquake-proof apartment complexes; smog may be reduced by a new subway system, projected tunnels under the Istanbul Strait, and a proposed third highway bridge over the Bosphorus. But will it be too little, too late?

Istanbul has long teetered between Europe and Asia, between Islam and Christianity, between its historic past and the demands of a modern city. (In 2011 elections, the prime minister even floated a plan to make Istanbul two cities, divided along the Bosphorus Strait between Europe and Asia.) But it is those paradoxes that make it such a fascinating place to visit. Consider **Ayasofya,** which for almost a thousand years was the largest Christian church in the world; converted to a mosque in 1453, when Mehmet II took over the city, it became a museum in 1935 under Atatürk, when its dazzling frescoes and mosaics were restored. Or visit the **Blue Mosque,** built by Ahmet I in 1609, a riot of domes and gold minarets with a glowing interior of blue and green decorative tiles. Don't miss the magnificent mosaics of **St. Savior** in Chora, where a wealth of 14th-century decorative detail was restored in the 1940s

The Ayasofya in Istanbul.

after many years under plaster. And then there's **Topkapı Palace,** an exotic marvel of ceramic tiles, inlaid ivory, and ornate friezes and mosaics, loaded with the loot of 4 centuries of Ottoman rulers. A separate admission ticket gets you into Topkapı's Harem, where up to 800 concubines lived in cramped cubicles—except for the sultan's favorites, who occupied his lavish seaview apartments.

Yet this ancient city also offers trendy shopping along Istiklal Caddesi, cutting-edge art at the Istanbul Museum of Modern Art, and chic nightlife amid the 19th-century mansions of Beyoglu. At dawn the call of muezzins in their minarets mingles with the thump of hip-hop music from all-night clubs. To grasp the paradox of Istanbul, roam through the **Grand Bazaar** (Kapalı Çarşısı), a labyrinth of more than 2,600 shops and several individual marketplaces. The exuberant free-for-all of the bazaar—prices can be insane and haggling over merchandise is an age-old custom—could stand as a metaphor for Istanbul itself.

ⓘ www.tourismturkey.com

✈ Atatürk International, Istanbul

🛏 $$ **Sari Konak,** Mimar Mehmet Aga Cad. 42 (ⓒ **90/212/638-6258;** www. istanbulhotelsarikonak.com). $$$ **Mavi Ev** (Blue House), Dalbastı Sok. 14 (ⓒ **90/212/ 638-9010;** www.bluehouse.com.tr).

Hong Kong
The Big Land Grab
Hong Kong S.A.R., China

WATCHDOG GROUPS LED BY THE SOCIETY FOR THE PROTECTION OF THE HARBOUR HAVE aggressively campaigned against land reclamation projects nibbling away at Hong Kong's centerpiece, Victoria Harbour.

That postcard view of Hong Kong's **Victoria Harbour,** bristling with skyscrapers—what glittering urban romance it promises.

This former Crown Colony once seemed a magic portal into the Far East, one with English spoken everywhere and modern creature comforts at hand. Wooden boats bobbed in the harbor beside ocean liners, crumbling tenements leaned against modern high-rises, and rickshaws trundled past gleaming Rolls-Royces. But with a population of seven-million-plus crowded into an area half the size of Rhode Island, this international finance city—the "Wall Street of Asia"—values commercial interests over the charming and picturesque, and since it became an autonomous region of China in 1997, China's leaders show little interest in reining this in.

Real estate is at such a premium, Hong Kong is currently the world's most expensive place to buy a home. For over a century, Hong Kong solved that problem by reclaiming land, bit by bit, from its surrounding channels and bays, until Victoria Harbour was reduced to less than half of its original size. New construction along the waterfront is almost always high-rise, blocking water views, and the few parks and gardens left around the island—particularly near the waterfront—are increasingly hemmed in by fences, roads, and buildings.

That sweeping vista of the skyscraper-ringed harbor is still available from the decks of the green-and-white Star Ferry, a 7-minute ride between Kowloon and Hong Kong Island's Central District. Otherwise, for city panoramas you'll need to get high—as in the top of **Victoria Peak,** via an 8-minute ride on the Peak tram, the world's steepest funicular railway. The modern Peak Tower has a viewing terrace (as well as restaurants, shops, and attractions like Madame Tussauds), where you can still catch glimpses of the harbor between the skyscrapers; walk along the Peak's cliffside footpaths for a taste of this exclusive enclave's expat British vibe. For more exotic Asian atmosphere, ride the rickety old double-decker trams around the northern end of Hong Kong Island, old-fashioned neighborhoods where you can still see laundry hanging from second-story windows, signs swinging over the street, and markets twisting down side alleys. Jump off at Des Vouex Street and Morrison Road to browse the still-colorful shopping streets of the **Western District**—Hillier Street, Bonham Strand, and Man Wa Lane.

Hong Kong's future may be prefigured by the development of nearby Lantau Island for Hong Kong Disneyland, and the explosive growth of Macau—a former Portuguese colony 64km (40 miles) west of Hong Kong, across the Pearl River estuary—into the Las Vegas of the Far East. Where will the growth end?

ⓘ **Hong Kong Tourism Board,** the Peak Piazza or Kowloon Star Ferry Concourse (✆ **852/2508 1234;** www.discoverhong kong.com)

✈ Hong Kong International

🏠 $$ **BP International House,** 8 Austin Rd., Kowloon (✆ **852/2376 1111;** www.

bpih.com.hk). $$ **The Salisbury YMCA,** 41 Salisbury Rd., Kowloon (✆ **852/2268 7000;** www.ymcahk.org.hk).

---

370 Traditional Ways of Living

Machiya Town Houses
Sliding Doors Behind the Shops
Kyoto, Japan

REAL ESTATE PRESSURES HAVE DONE WHAT WWII BOMBERS DIDN'T, RAZING 2% OF KYOTO'S traditional *machiya* town houses every year to make room for new malls and apartment blocks.

For nearly a thousand years, Kyoto reigned over Japan, from the feudal era of 794 to the cosmopolitan society of 1868. The city is such a treasure box of history that Allied bombers in World War II intentionally spared it from destruction, leaving its historic city center—unlike most of southern Japan—gloriously intact.

Most visitors focus on Kyoto's medieval landmarks, like the 14th-century **Temple of the Golden Pavilion,** covered in gold leaf; the 15th-century **Ryoanji Temple,** with Japan's most famous Zen rock garden; the 17th-century **Nijo Castle,** an exquisitely understated palace of Japanese cypress; and **Kiyomizu Temple,** with its grand wooden veranda suspended over a cliff. But Kyoto was still a great city during the Edo period (1603–1867), when it evolved from shogun culture into a modern city with a thriving merchant and artisan class—perfectly embodied in its handsome *machiya* town houses. Chances are, this is what you picture when you think of traditional Japanese lifestyle. Airy and light, with interior gardens, they combined residences and workspace in one property, creating integrated urban neighborhoods for the rising middle class.

A typical Kyoto *machiya* might be only 6m (20 ft.) wide, although a merchant could flaunt his success by claiming wider street frontage. Latticed wooden shutters

cover the shop front, with specific lattice designs indicating the owner's trade. The *kyoshitsubu,* or living space, stretches behind the shop, its polished timber floors covered with woven tatami mats; sliding doors reconfigure the living space, opening rooms to breezes in summer but shutting up against cold in winter. Farther behind that, the deep plot also contains an earthen-floored kitchen, storehouses, perhaps even an interior courtyard. Second stories rise above with slatted "insect cage" windows cut into their earthen walls, allowing ventilation and yet privacy. It's a design that's as functional as it is elegant. For an inside look, make a reservation to tour the **Nishijin Tondaya town house** (✆ 81/75/432-6701; www.tondaya.co.jp).

Unfortunately, these historic buildings require skilled carpentry to maintain, and they don't suit the denser living conditions of crowded modern Japan. Between 1993 and 2003, some 13% of Kyoto's *machiya* were demolished; there are still 28,000 standing, but as you walk around the city, you'll see many that are badly dilapidated or have been clumsily modernized. Preservation groups such as the Kyoto Center for Community Collaboration, however, have been spearheading a turnaround, arousing public interest and teaching conservation techniques to *machiya* owners. Some tour operators now offer themed *machiya* tours, and restored *machiyas* can be booked as a trendy lodging option. The *machiya* renaissance may take off yet.

ⓘ Tourist information, JR Kyoto Station, 2nd floor (✆ **81/75/343-0548;** www.kyoto.travel)

✈ Kansai International, Osaka

🚄 Kyoto, 2½ hr. from Tokyo by bullet train

🛏 $$ **ANA Hotel Kyoto,** Nijojo-mae, Horikawa Dori, Nakagyo-ku (✆ **877/834-3613** in North America, or 81/75/231-1155; www.ichotelsgroup.com). $$$ **IORI Kyoto Townhouse Stays** (✆ **81/75/352-0211;** www.kyoto-machiya.com).

Hutong Neighborhoods
Hiding Out in the Alley
Beijing, China

To combat Beijing's chronic overcrowding, housing officials have been steadily razing the city's iconic hutong courtyard complexes, as foreign visitors rush to tour the remaining few.

Chinese officials were determined to remake Beijing into a modern showcase city for the 2008 Olympics—the hutongs simply had to go. What did it matter that they'd been the basis of Beijing's urban fabric since the 14th century? Hutongs made Chinese society look backward, and with the world's eyes on China, that simply would not do.

Granted, this wholesale destruction began way back in the 1950s, during Mao Tse-tung's Cultural Revolution. Old hutongs were sacrificed in favor of wide boulevards lined with high-rises; hutong dwellers were resettled in apartment buildings with amenities like central heating and indoor plumbing that were rare in the hutongs. But in the new era of Chinese capitalism—the Second Industrial Revolution, some call it—the Beijing Municipal Construction Committee in 2004 announced that it would demolish more of the old housing, displacing 20,000 households. Given the lack of property rights in China, there wasn't much those citizens could do.

But dissent was boiling to a head. In 2003, suicide attempts by displaced hutong residents highlighted the crisis. In 2002, the government had promised landmark protection to several hutongs, but it wasn't until 2007 that it finally spent 1 billion yuan refurbishing 44 dilapidated hutongs in the Dongcheng, Xicheng, Chongwen, and Xuanwu districts. Gentrification may be another force that could restore hutongs—just look at what's happening around the alley of Nan Luogu Xiang, site of a growing number of hipster cafes, bars, restaurants, and hotels.

Several tour companies now include hutong excursions among their city tours, using cycle rickshaws to navigate the narrow lanes. The hutong lifestyle is a perfect expression of traditional Chinese culture. Within its shady courtyards, communal social networks—especially extended families—became the basic building blocks of Beijing cultural life. While some hutongs were built for aristocrats, humbler merchants and craftsmen and laborers

A hutong in Beijing.

huddled together in much smaller court-yards. The name "hutong" comes from the Mongolian word for "well," reflecting the idea of a community's central meeting point. With their upturned eaves, wooden doors and windows, decorative brick-work, and garden plantings (traditionally, pomegranate trees) or fishponds in the central courtyard, these hutong com-plexes have a distinctly Chinese flavor—presumably, the very thing the Olympics were meant to showcase.

Even with the Olympics over, the destruction continues. The **Qián Mén hutong** at the south end of Tiananmen Square is now gone; the well-preserved upper-class Gulou hutongs around the Drum Tower and Shichahai Lake were slated to be replaced (with a theme com-plex named Beijing Time Cultural City) until preservationists won a reprieve in Sep-tember 2010.

Two months later in Shanghai, a fatal blaze killed 58 people trapped on upper floors of a 28-story apartment building—the same sort of housing that displaced hutong residents have been moved into. It had no fire-sprinkler system, and the city's fire hoses couldn't reach that high. So much for progress.

✈ Capital Airport, Beijing

🛏 $$$ **Grand Hyatt,** Dōng Chāng'ān Jiē 1, Dōngchéng District (ℂ **86/10/8518-1234;** http://beijing.grand.hyatt.com). $$ **Lǔsōng Yuán Bīnguǎn,** Bǎnchǎng Hútòng 22, Dōngchéng District (ℂ **86/10/6404-0436;** www.the-silk-road.com).

TOUR Beijing Hutong Tourist Agency (ℂ **86/10/6615-9097). Cycle China Tours** (ℂ **86/10/6402-5653;** www.cyclechina.com).

The Courtyard Houses of Zabid
Outside, Inside
Southwestern Yemen

WITH YEMEN EMBROILED IN POLITICAL FERMENT, MONEY AND ADMINISTRATION MAY NOT BE available to save this dilapidated Red Sea treasure, which is lacking even the infrastructure to attract tourist income.

Sheep and goats roam freely in a maze of dusty lanes, where young children play, the girls in bright dresses, the boys in little-man sport coats. Electrical wires and the occasional satellite dish are stuck rudely along the tops of blank white stucco walls, which line the streets so closely that in some places you could stretch out your arms and touch both sides at once. It's hard to imagine that this city, Zabid, was once the medieval capital of Yemen, a center of learning renowned throughout the Arab world.

Yet within those walls are near-classic examples of southern Arabian domestic architecture, ideally suited for urban desert life. The heart of such houses is an enclosed courtyard, or *qabal,* with wells and basins in their corners; a gracious reception room, or *muraba'a,* opens onto the *qabal,* lined with sofas for both sitting and sleeping. More sleeping rooms may lead off of this; upstairs terraces provide cooler sleeping space for hot summer nights. Anonymous as the outer walls may look, families poured their wealth into interior decor, with brilliant painted ceilings and decorated plasterwork. The courtyard's bricks were laid in fantastical designs—Egyptian arches, Indian floral patterns, African animals, Islamic geometric figures, reflecting all the cultural forces that converged along the Aden-to-Mecca trade route. Layers of lime wash coat the bricks, dazzling in the desert sun.

Islam came early to Zabid, and it's still a deeply Muslim place, with some 86 mosques. These inward-looking homes were built for scholars, merchants, and artisans who prized the sanctity of home life.

But ever since the Ottoman conquest of the 16th century, Zabid has been in decline. The proud circle of walls that once girded Zabid collapsed long ago, yet the city hasn't grown much beyond those medieval boundaries. You can wander among the ruined walls of the old university, littered with rubble; weavers and blacksmiths ply their trades in an ancient souk, between the Great Mosque and the Asa'ir Mosque.

That lost-in-history atmosphere is part of Zabid's charm. While Zabid has modernized haphazardly, rudely jacking concrete buildings into any open site, it is estimated that nearly three-quarters of the historic housing remains, hidden behind those walls. Cash-poor landlords can't charge high enough rents on their dilapidated properties to pay for restoration, but UNESCO attention has attracted some foreign investment to improve Zabid's crumbling urban fabric. Meanwhile, friendly locals often invite intrepid tourists inside their courtyard homes to show off their interiors. Since most Zabid residents speak only Arabic, hire a local guide to facilitate such interactions—and to help you navigate that maze of lanes.

ⓘ Consult your embassy about travel conditions before your visit; www.yementourism.com.

✈ Al-Hodeidah

🛏 **Zabid Tourist Rest House,** Zabid (℡ **967/3/340 270**)

TOUR Yemen Holiday Tour, Sana'a (℡ **967/1/297 369;** www.yemenholidaytour.com)

The Trulli District of Alberobello
Living in a Beehive
Apulia, Italy

PROTECTED UNDER UNESCO WORLD HERITAGE LAW SINCE 1996, THE DISTINCTIVE APULIAN cottages known as *trulli* can be restored only within strict guidelines. Even in the tourist magnet of Alberobello, their exteriors remain pristine.

Nobody else ever built homes quite like these—beehive-shaped cottages with whitewashed limestone walls and conical fieldstone roofs, like something out of a storybook. If you saw just one cozy little *trullo*, you might think it was some modern architect's fantasy, but drive around the rugged landscape of Apulia's Itria valley and they pop up often, charming relics of a traditional peasant way of life that persists only in little pockets of this rural province. But Trulli Central is the once-sleepy rural town of Alberobello, which has preserved so many that the town now lives on summer hordes of Italian day-trippers rather than on its olive groves.

Apulia, the high heel of Italy's boot, is a land of gritty survivors, invaded over the years by everyone from ancient Greeks to Goths, Byzantines, Saracen pirates, and Turks. *Trulli* were built as early as the 13th century, by peasants scavenging whatever materials came easily to hand. What's amazing, when you take a close look, is the

Trulli in Alberobello.

craftsmanship involved: The stones fit together in such a way that not a speck of mortar was needed. This allowed medieval peasants to dismantle the structures quickly if a king came to inspect the district. For such provisional dwellings, they sure have lasted a long time, and now that the ones in Alberobello are under UNESCO protection, their upkeep is strictly regulated.

Trulli-packed Alberobello is a fantastical sight, verging on kitsch. Tacky souvenirs are on sale everywhere, even in converted *trulli*, and vendors can be aggressive. An obvious first stop is the two-story *trullo sovrano* (sovereign trullo) at **Piazza Sacramento;** period furnishings inside give you a sense of what living in one of these houses must have been like. Then cross the main road to find **Piazza 27 Maggio** (near Piazza del Populo), where several *trulli* have been cobbled together to create the **Museo del Territorio,** which displays traditional *trulli* furnishings, farm tools, and other rural artifacts. Here you'll learn the iconography of the *trulli*'s rooftop spires and lime-washed hex signs.

Follow the tourist track up Largo Martellotta to the main *trulli* neighborhood, a maze of curving cobbled lanes running up a hillside with the round houses on every side, an astonishing ensemble of more than 1,000 *trulli*. In Alberobello, even the churches occupy *trulli*—witness the **Church of Saint Anthony** atop the hill, with its large dome and Greek cross layout. To escape the crowds, wander east to the Aia Piccola neighborhood—it has about half as many *trulli*, but it's more residential and more authentic.

(i) Tourist office, Piazza Ferdinando IV (✆ **39/80/4325171**)

🚆 Alberobello, 1¾ hr. from Bari

🛏 $$$ **Grand Hotel Olimpo,** Via Sette Liberatori della Selva (✆ **39/80/432-1678;** www.grandhotelolimpo.it). $$ **Trullo Casa Rosa,** C. da Staffone 222 (✆ **39/80/438-3059;** www.trullocasarosa.it).

Traditional Ways of Living **374**

Taos Pueblo
The House Mountain
New Mexico

DESPITE TOURIST ENTRANCE FEES AND REVENUE FROM ITS SMALL CASINO, THE TIWA PEOPLE'S pueblo in Taos struggles with poverty. Slipshod repairs to the ancient adobe structures threaten their integrity.

In our consumer-culture society, it's downright inspirational—some 150 Taos Pueblo residents living much as their Tiwa ancestors did 1,000 years ago, without electricity and running water, and *by choice*. They cluster in two main buildings—Hlauuma (north house) and Hlaukwima (south house)—a rambling series of rooms piled on top of each other, built of straw and mud with distinctive flowing rooflines that echo the shape of Taos Mountain to the northeast. A connection to the natural world is expressed in every detail—the adobe exterior blends in with the surrounding desert, bright blue doors echo the blue sky above.

The northernmost of New Mexico's 19 pueblos, Taos Pueblo looks much the same today as it did when a regiment from the Spanish explorer Coronado's expedition

Taos Pueblo.

first came upon it in 1540. Though the Tiwa were essentially a peaceful agrarian people, in 1680 they spearheaded the only successful revolt by Native Americans in history, driving the Spanish from Santa Fe until 1692 and from Taos until 1698—you can still see the old church ruined in that uprising. The main pueblo contains several individual homes, built side by side with common walls. Some 2,000 other Tiwas live in conventional homes on the pueblo's 95,000 acres (38,400 hectares), but most still practice ancestral customs, baking their traditional bread in communal beehive-shaped ovens and drinking water from the sacred Blue Lake nearby. Balancing 21st-century life with ancient customs is inevitably a challenge for the Tiwas, however, with the modern town of Taos only a couple of miles away. The tribe's small casino (www.taosmountaincasino. com) adheres to tribal bans on smoking and alcohol—a plus for some visitors, but not the general gaming audience.

As you explore the historic pueblo complex, respect tribe members' privacy. You can visit residents' studios, the San Geronimo Chapel, and the ruined church and cemetery, but do not trespass into *kivas* (ceremonial rooms), private homes, and other areas marked as restricted. Ask permission from individuals before taking their photos; some will request a small payment. You can buy traditional fried and oven-baked bread, as well as a variety of arts and crafts like moccasins, pottery, and jewelry. To try traditional feast-day meals, stop by the Tiwa Kitchen, near the entrance to the pueblo.

Be aware that the pueblo shuts down for tribal ceremonies, including an 8-week period every spring; on the other hand, on certain feast days you may be lucky enough to watch ceremonial dances. Check the tribe's website for schedules.

ⓘ Veterans Hwy. (𝄞 **505/758-1028;** www.taospueblo.com)

✈ Santa Fe

⊨ $$ **El Rey Inn,** 1862 Cerrillos Rd., Santa Fe (𝄞 **800/521-1349** or 505/982-1931; www.elreyinnsantafe.com). $$ **Old Taos Guesthouse,** 1028 Witt Rd., Taos (𝄞 **800/758-5448** or 575/758-5448; www. oldtaos.com).

The Death of the High Street
Working on the Chain Gang
The United Kingdom

INTERNET SHOPPING, CHAIN STORES, AND AMERICAN-STYLE MALLS HAVE ALL CRIPPLED TRADI-tional U.K. "high street" shopping areas. Will the country's recent economic downturn deal the final blow?

More than 5,000 streets throughout the United Kingdom are named High Street. Each one is expected to have its own character, set by local tradesmen selling regionally made products. But that cherished vision of a nation of shopkeepers is increasingly a fantasy scenario.

First came a boom in American-style shopping malls, which quadrupled in number between 1986 and 1997. Against that competition, chain shops seemed to fare better than small independents; Boots Pharmacies supplanted small chemists, WHSmith drove out independent news agents, Marks & Spencer replaced local clothing boutiques, while Tesco and Sainsbury's supermarkets consolidated food shopping (between 1992 and 2003, Yellow Pages listings for fruit-and-veg shops declined nearly 60%, butchers 40%, and bakers 20%). When a 2004 report by the New Economics Foundation titled "Clone Town Britain" rated towns according to the number of chain stores in their central retail districts, the cathedral town of Exeter ranked worst, with only one independent store in its entire shopping district. A 2010 survey showed that 41% of British municipalities are now "clone towns," with chains composing more than half of their stores. With Internet shopping on the rise—up 18% in 2010—fewer people see any reason to visit shops at all.

After the economic downturn in autumn 2008, even the chains were closing branches, leaving more and more vacant windows in town centers—a 12% vacancy rate nationwide, up to 30% in some towns, especially in the North. Bank consolidation shut down a slew of branches; employment agencies and estate agents also closed in record numbers. (The one segment that grew was betting parlors.) Among the factors blamed in a November 2010 report by the British Retail Consortium: high property taxes, inadequate public transport, costly parking, vandalism, lack of local flavor, and not enough variety in the retail mix. "Gangs of yobs are spoiling our town centres by intimidating shoppers," added a 2010 article in *The Sun*, entitled "Hell on High Street."

So where can one find an authentic high street? Tourist magnets such as Bath, Stratford-upon-Avon, and Chester have carefully preserved shopping streets, often with half-timbered historic buildings. But for a real-life everyday high street, consider **Gloucester Road,** a northern artery (A38) that curves through the Bristol suburb of Bishopston, half a mile north of the city center. There's nothing twee or stage-set perfect about it, just a series of tidy two-story terraces—food shops, news agents, clothing boutiques, coffee bars, pubs, and takeaway shops. Chains have made a few inroads—a Tesco Express, a small Sainsbury's, Pizza Hut, Thresher's spirits shop—but they are still outpaced by small independent shops. In this middle-class, family-oriented neighborhood, Gloucester Road's shops serve residents' day-to-day needs, rather than being a shopping destination in and of itself.

You'd best run down to the shops while you still can.

✈ Bristol

🛏 $$ **Tyndall's Park Hotel,** 4 Tyndall's Park Rd., Clifton (✆ **44/117/973 5407;** www. tyndallsparkhotel.co.uk). $$ **Downlands House,** 33 Henleaze Gardens, Henleaze (✆ **44/117/962 1639;** www.downlands house.co.uk).

---

376 **Neighborhoods in Transition**

Spitalfields
To Market, to Market
London, England

GENTRIFICATION IS RAPIDLY CHANGING THE DYNAMIC OF THIS HISTORIC MARKET AREA IN LONDON'S East End. The market itself moved out in 1991—what's left is merely a trendy mall.

Through centuries of British history, persecuted refugees and racial outcasts found a haven in London's East End. In the 18th century, it was Huguenot silk weavers driven out of France; in the 19th century, it was Irish navvies displaced by the Potato Famine and Jews fleeing pogroms in eastern Europe; in the 20th century, it was Bangladeshi immigrants. Check out the mosque in Brick Lane: Originally a Huguenot church, it became a synagogue in the 19th century, then was converted to a mosque for Bangladeshi Muslims in the mid–20th century. Each group brought its own flavor to the neighborhood; each, in turn, moved out of these crowded, unfashionable streets as soon as they could.

A focal point since the 17th century was the Spitalfields meat and produce market, held at first in an open field, which was replaced by a handsome covered market building in 1875. By then, however, the old merchant dwellings surrounding the market had been sliced up into crowded, dilapidated slums, huddled around narrow lanes and alleys. This was the squalid face of Dickensian London, the den of criminals like Fagin and Bill Sykes; Jack the Ripper met some of his victims at the Ten Bells pub on Commercial Street.

In the 1960s, well-meaning preservationists focused on saving those old merchant terraces from the wrecking ball. As one Georgian relic after another was refurbished, squatters were evacuated and house prices skyrocketed. More recently, large modern office blocks have sprouted on the western edge, spilling over from the City of London. The produce market moved out to Leyton in 1991; landmark status protected the remaining third of the Victorian-era market building, but its glass-roofed central hall now sells crafts, vintage clothing, and organic foods, and similar virtuously chic shops line the adjoining streets.

To some locals, the smartness of the "new" Spitalfields seems a betrayal of the East End's colorful past. Case in point: **Christ Church Spitalfields,** a baroque Nicholas Hawksmoor gem on Fournier Street between Brick Lane and Commercial Street, now a posh concert venue. The red-brick Georgian terrace at **18 Folgate St.** (www.dennissevershouse.co.uk) where avant-garde artist Dennis Severs once lived in an anachronistic "still-life drama," each room reflecting a different historic era, is now on public display. A pair of 18th-century town houses at 56 Artillery Lane, derelict since a 1970s fire, have been reborn as the contemporary art center **Raven Row** (www.ravenrow.org). Even the Ten Bells pub now sells imported microbrews and discourages its Ripper associations. Yes, the buildings have been

The Spitalfields market entrance.

preserved—but if the vitality of the East End lives on anywhere, it's in the kebab shops and curry restaurants along Brick Lane.

ⓘ www.spitalfields.co.uk
✈ Heathrow International

✎ $$ **Mornington Hotel,** 12 Lancaster Gate, Bayswater (ℂ **800/633-6548** in North America, or 44/20/7262-7361; www. bw-morningtonhotel.co.uk). $$ **Sanctuary House Hotel,** 33 Tothill St., Westminster (ℂ **44/20/7799-4044;** www.fullershotels. com).

Neighborhoods in Transition 377

Prenzlauerberg
In Search of a Kiez
Berlin, Germany

GERMAN REUNIFICATION WAS ENOUGH OF A SHOCK TO THE SYSTEM FOR LONG-DIVIDED BERLIN. In Prenzlauerberg, urban evolution is playing out at dizzying speed.

Built as housing for factory workers in the 1860s, the cramped five-story tenements of East Berlin's Prenzlauerberg became a magnet for artists, thinkers, students, and orange-haired punks in the days of the Soviet-controlled German Democratic Republic. It was the sort of radical quarter where you'd expect political activity, like the government resistance that emanated from the Protestant Gethsemane church on

Gethsemanestrasse. For a cheap meal, you could always have a grilled sausage at **Konnopkes Imbiss,** under the U-Bahn tracks between Schönhauser Allee and Danziger Strasse. This northern suburb had a definite character, a real *kiez* (German for a neighborhood you feel connected to).

But with reunification, those historic tenements with their trees and interior yards seemed pretty attractive to young professionals eager to renovate prime real estate. Unlike other districts of East Berlin, Prenzlauerberg hadn't been bombed in World War II; somehow it had also escaped being replaced with the GDR era's typical boxy concrete apartment blocks. A few atmospheric landmarks had survived, like the handsome 19th-century brick water tower that rises over Kollwitzplatz, the **Prater Beer Garden** (Berlin's oldest) on Kastanienallee, and a handful of disused breweries ripe for redevelopment. (One of them, the **Kulturbrauerei** on Sredzkistrasse, now houses a warren of bars, restaurants, and a cinema beneath its brick towers and chimney stacks.) Remnants of the days when this was a Jewish neighborhood persist in an old synagogue on Rykestraße and a Jewish cemetery on Schönhauser Allee. A mound of postwar rubble cleared from other districts grew into a wooded hilltop in leafy Volkspark to the east.

And so in the early 1990s free market forces took hold and the yuppies moved in,

repainting the dull facades in bright colors and designs. Nightlife exploded, particularly around Kollwitzplatz and Kastanienallee, with a fairly active gay scene; a constant rotation of hip boutiques, galleries, and sidewalk cafes attract the leisured classes by day. Weekly street markets at Kollwitzplatz and Helmholtzplatz add to the lively atmosphere. Students and punks—those perennial urban colonizers—were soon priced out of the area.

In the hyperactive post-reunification climate, nothing in Berlin stays the same for long. Already the really hot nightlife has moved elsewhere (to the east), and the first wave of yuppies are starting families—there's a surprising number of baby strollers around. It's anybody's guess what the character of Prenzl'berg will be in the end, but at least those classic old buildings have been refurbished.

ⓘ Tourist information, in the Kulturbrauerei (✆ **49/30/4435 2170;** www.tic-in-prenzlauerberg.de)

✈ Berlin-Tagel

🛏 $$ **Ackselhaus Blue Home,** Belforter Strasse 21 (✆ **49/30/4433-7633;** www.ackselhaus.de). $$ **Myers Hotel Berlin,** Metzer Strasse 26 (✆ **49/30/440140;** www.myershotel.de).

378 Neighborhoods in Transition

Cesky Krumlov Inner Town
Watching the River Flow
Czech Republic

Climate change, deforestation, and melting Alpine glaciers are raising river levels throughout Europe, increasing the risk of seasonal flooding for historic river towns like Bohemia's Cesky Krumlov.

Since the fall of communism in 1989, the Czech government has invested heavily in sprucing up historic Cesky Krumlov, a near-perfect assemblage of medieval and Renaissance-era town houses. Under Communism this area had little money to

Gargoyles on St. Vitus cathedral.

spare for "development," which turned out to be a boon—no glass-and-steel monstrosities to spoil the architectural beauty. Tourism is now a mainstay of the local economy, and the town is jam-packed every summer, especially at the summer solstice for the *Slavnost petilisté ruze* (Festival of the Five-Petaled Rose), when townsfolk dress up in Renaissance costume and the streets are full of living chess games, music, plays, and staged duels.

But in 2002, it all threatened to wash away, as Ceský Krumlov's low-lying Inner Town was inundated by the worst flood since 1890. Downstream in Prague, the surging Vltava River submerged several baroque palaces and synagogues, but its atmospheric Old Town remained above water. Ceský Krumlov wasn't so lucky. Though the river is much smaller here, up by the Austrian border, Krumlov had been founded at a convenient fording place, on low ground within a tight crook of the river; it's nearly surrounded by water, and the mistimed opening of an upstream dam released a catastrophic gush all at once.

The ancestral tapestries and rococo interiors of 16th-century Ceský Krumlov Château remained dry on its rocky mount across the river, but Inner Town's picturesque cobblestoned streets disappeared under the swirling waters.

And this is the area that tourists really fall in love with—the harmony of its red roofs, the stenciled colors on its gabled house fronts, the narrow traffic-free lanes (check out the town model at the **Okresní Muzeum,** Horní ulice 152). Inner Town contains many charming buildings, such as the late-Gothic **St. Vitus Cathedral** (great views from its tower), the Radnice (Town Hall), at námestí Svornosti 1, with Gothic arcades and Renaissance vaulting, and the **Hotel Ruze,** Horní 154, a 16th-century amalgamation of Gothic, Renaissance, and rococo influences. If you've ever seen the 2006 movie *The Illusionist,* you'll recognize the picture-perfect ensemble of this Bohemian jewel.

As you wander along the river, notice high-water marks on some of the quirky bankside houses. Scientists gloomily predict that the Vltava will flood again and again in the future. In 2009, the town embarked on a controversial flood-prevention plan—replacing a weir, razing an entire island, and clearing the riverbanks' willows and alders to erect concrete barriers. This lovely town is already a little less lovely.

ⓘ **Tourist Information Centre** (☏ **420/ 380/704-622;** www.ckrumlov.info)

✈ Prague or Vienna

🛏 $$$ **Hotel Ruze, Horní** 154 (☏ **420/ 380/772-100;** www.hotelruze.cz). $ **Pension Na louzi,** Kájovská 66 (☏ **420/380/ 711-280;** www.nalouzi.cz).

379 Neighborhoods in Transition

Art Nouveau Riga
The Paris of the North
Riga, Latvia

RIGA HAS BECOME NOTORIOUS FOR THE WORST TRAFFIC CONGESTION IN EUROPE AND ALL THE air pollution that goes with it. Will a new bridge and bypass highway save the city center's architectural gems?

It's true that Latvia was a Russian possession from 1710 to 1918, and part of the Soviet Union for another half century after that, but nevertheless, the Latvia capital of Riga always felt more German than Russian. Until 1891, German was still the official language of this bustling Baltic port, Russia's third-largest city after Moscow and St. Petersburg. No wonder Riga's biggest claim to fame is a spectacular flowering of a German architectural style: Jugendstil.

Though it's often called the Paris of the North, Riga's Art Nouveau architecture is much more akin to Vienna's, though it's even more pronounced, characterizing more than a third of the central district's buildings. After the city's medieval walls were demolished in the mid–19th century, sweeping boulevards and stylish suburbs were laid out, paving the way for a turn-of-the-century building boom. Luckily, that boom coincided with the rise of several talented local architects, notably Mikhail Eisenstein (father of Russian film director Sergei Eisenstein); these young designers embraced the exuberance of Jugendstil as an expression of Latvian nationalism.

Walk along Alberta Street, to the east of Kronvalda Park, where a flurry of construction from 1901 to 1908 composed a magnificent ensemble of buildings, many by Eisenstein. You'll want binoculars or a telephoto lens to pick out all the ornamental details, from stone sculptural reliefs to wrought-iron gates and balconies, colorful stencils, and brilliant touches of stained glass. Nearby Elizabetes, Strelnieku, Kr. Barona, A. Caka, and Gertrudes streets are also particularly rich; notice how the clean lines of the architecture sweep your eyes upward to ornate steeples, clocks, cornices, and rooftop decorations. The imaginative detail is incredible—from amazingly expressive human faces to droll pelicans, chubby squirrels, sleek greyhounds, and majestic lions. In **Esplanade Park,** you can see the evolution of the style: In the **Academy of Arts,** Jugendstil elements have been imposed on a Neo-Gothic base, while at the **State Museum of Fine Arts,** the eclectic exterior is graced with classic Jugendstil touches like the entrance staircase and sculptured figures over the front doors.

355

A cafe-lined street in Art Nouveau Riga.

But gaping at those early-20th-century marvels isn't so easy these days, given the explosion of traffic in Riga's city center. Riga has taken steps to address the problem at last: In 2008, the new Southern Bridge across the Daugava began to route traffic past the city center, a wildly expensive (and probably corrupt) project that may not solve congestion at all in the long run. (Access roads are still under construction.) Paris itself has recently made great strides in reducing urban congestion; why not the Paris of the North, too?

ⓘ www.virtualriga.com

✈ Riga

🛏 $$$ **Grand Palace Hotel,** Pils iela 12 (📞 **371/6/704 4000;** http://grandpalace riga.com). $$ **Laine Hotel,** Skolas iela 11 (📞 **371/6/728 8816;** www.laine.lv).

Neighborhoods in Transition **380**

Old Jewish Ghetto
Under the Wrecking Ball
Budapest, Hungary

WITH NO CITY PLANNING TO GUIDE RESTORATION OF THE HISTORIC ERZSÉBETVÁROS NEIGHBOR-hood, grass-roots activists offer alternative visions for commemorating the ghetto's history.

The war is on for the soul of Jewish Budapest, and the battleground is Erzsébetváros, the 19th-century Jewish quarter on the Pest side of the Danube River. The first shots were fired in mid-2004, when more than a dozen abandoned buildings in this run-down neighborhood were snapped up by condo developers. Suddenly, in a blaze of "cowboy capitalism," even landmarked buildings were being torn down and new projects were going up everywhere.

During World War II, Hungary's Jews weren't exterminated to the extent that they were in other countries; many continued to live here after the Soviets "liberated" Budapest. Yet decades of Communist

government weakened their religious identity, even though Hungarian Jews were granted more freedoms than Jews in many Soviet-controlled regimes—Budapest kept its rabbinical school and had the only matzo factory behind the Iron Curtain. Erzsébetváros's **Grand Synagogue** is still an active house of worship—the second-largest synagogue in Europe and one of the city's architectural jewels, a twin-towered 19th-century fantasy of Byzantine and Moorish motifs. (Interestingly, its restoration was funded by actor Tony Curtis, to commemorate his Hungarian forebears.) The **Jewish Museum** sits next to the Synagogue at Dohány 2, with a

Holocaust Memorial in the garden. There are other synagogues close by, on Rumbach Street and on Kazinczy Street. Also on Kazinczy Street is the **Mikveh,** or Jewish ritual bath (Budapest is famous for its thermal baths). But many Jewish residents of this neighborhood are not observant.

Budapest still has about 100,000 Jewish citizens, but in the second half of the 19th century, twice that number were packed into Erzsébetváros. You can get a glimpse of that past in **Gozsdu Court,** a series of seven small courtyards between Kiraly and Dob streets, just north of the Great Synagogue. Back in the late 19th and early 20th centuries, this was a hive of small stores and tradesmen's workshops, a buzzing center of the community. But in 2006, in the backyard of Király 15, construction workers razing an old building knocked down the last fragment of the stone wall the Nazis built in 1944 to enclose the Jews in their ghetto. It was replaced by a memorial wall in 2010, but that contains little of the original.

A 2008 moratorium on new construction may have come too late, with an estimated 40% of the quarter already altered; several dilapidated buildings stand poised in limbo between the restorations and the new construction. Alongside traditional restaurants such as Kádár (Klauzál Ter. 9), Hanna (Dob 35), and Frölich Confectionery (Dob 22), you'll also find trendy open-air pubs and cafes like Siraly (Kiraly 50); Kuplung (Kiraly 46); Szoda (Wesselenyi 18); or Spinoza (Dob 15). They have Jewish roots too, but it's a different generation entirely.

ⓘ Tourist information (✆ **36/1/322-4098;** www.budapestinfo.hu)

✈ Budapest

🛏 $$ **Hotel Erzsébet,** Károlyi Mihály 11–15, Budapest (✆**36/1/889-3746;** www.danubiusgroup.com). $$ **Hotel Papillon,** II. Rózsahegy 3/b (✆**36/1/212-4750;** www.hotelpapillon.hu).

381 Neighborhoods in Transition

The Lower Ninth Ward
The Road Back
New Orleans, Louisiana

IN AUGUST 2005, HURRICANE KATRINA AND ITS AFTERMATH NEARLY WIPED NEW ORLEANS off the face of the earth. Though wealthier pockets have revived, the city's poorer neighborhoods are still in critical condition.

New Orleans has always been a true original among American cities, a quirky town where people dance with parasols at funerals; believe in voodoo and vampires; eat exotic foods like beignets, po' boys, and gator-on-a-stick; and throw plastic beads off Mardi Gras floats. And in some respects, the Katrina disaster was also a special case, a man-made tragedy more than a natural one. Decades of misguided engineering destroyed the delta's wetlands and erected shoddy levees; on top of that came the one-two punch of inadequate

federal disaster aid and corrupt, inefficient local government.

New Orleans's oldest neighborhoods—like the French Quarter, with its Spanish-flavored wrought-iron balconies and flower-filled courtyards—were built above sea level, and suffered less damage. Luckily, those are the city's prime tourist areas, and a few months after Katrina they were back in business, bringing revenue back to a city that desperately needed it. Even the historic black neighborhood of Treme escaped relatively unscathed, thanks to its traditional architecture style, with raised house foundations. Sponsors were solicited to ensure that the city's traditional festivals, Mardi Gras and Jazz Fest, would take place in 2006; the Saints football team, displaced from the Superdome in 2005, returned in 2006 for a championship season.

But venture beyond the French Quarter and the Garden District and the Central Business District and you'll still see signs of the havoc Katrina wrought. The greatest devastation fell on the lower Ninth Ward, a poor but proud bastion of black working-class home ownership. The lower Ninth got flooded from two sides, from the Mississippi River and the Industrial Canal, and was completely submerged. Electricity and water weren't restored for more than a year; even street signs weren't replaced until shortly before Katrina's fifth anniversary.

With most of its shattered houses removed, the Ninth Ward today seems spookily bucolic, full of neat grassy plots (to prevent city seizure, owners must maintain empty lots) with only faint traces of house foundations. Fresh construction looks spick-and-span alongside surviving houses, many of which still wear, like a badge of honor, the grim spray-painted symbols left by National Guard rescuers in 2005. Ninth Ward residents who moved back say it's like living in a ghost town; few businesses have returned, and many schools are still shuttered. Still, there are pockets of hope, like the **Musician's Village** being built in the upper Ninth Ward by Habitat for Humanity, inspired by New Orleans musicians Harry Connick, Jr. and Branford Marsalis. A set of stunning contemporary houses-on-stilts built by actor Brad Pitt has been more controversial, as they bear little architectural reference to the Ninth Ward's traditional shotgun-style housing stock.

Come to New Orleans—the city needs your tourist dollars. But don't just party on Bourbon Street, browse the art galleries, and listen to the jazz at Preservation Hall. Volunteer to go down into the Ninth Ward and help rebuild houses. It'll be the most rewarding vacation of your life.

ⓘ To volunteer, contact www.common groundrelief.org or www.lowernine.org.

✈ Louis Armstrong New Orleans International

🛏 $$$ **Hotel Monteleone,** 214 Royal St. (ⓒ **866/338-4684** or 504/523-3341; www. hotelmonteleone.com). $$ **Hotel Villa Convento,** 616 Ursuline Ave. (ⓒ **504/522-1793;** www.villaconvento.com).

Neighborhoods in Transition · 382

Little Italy

Ghosts of the Godfathers

New York City, New York

HALF A CENTURY AGO, HALF THE NEIGHBORHOOD CLAIMED ITALIAN ANCESTRY; NOW IT'S ONLY about 5%, with all but a 2-block area officially designated as part of Chinatown. Little Italy hangs on, but it's only a shadow of its former self.

From Mulberry Street just north of Canal Street, imagine what Little Italy once was like, when it covered 17 city blocks. In the late 19th century, a wave of Italian immigrants, mostly from Sicily and Naples, moved into this tenement neighborhood as the upwardly mobile Irish vacated. Note the red-brick tenement architecture, narrow but deep, designed to squeeze in as many small rooms as possible; their street faces are hung with a maze of iron fire escapes.

A restaurant in Little Italy.

The Church of the Most Precious Blood, 109 Mulberry St., is still the focus of the traditional **Feast of St. Gennaro,** an 11-day festival with parades and food stalls which has lit up the streets every September since 1926. A few stores remain on Mulberry and intersecting Grand Street: There's **DiPalo's Fine Foods** at 200 Grand St., the **Alleva Dairy cheese shop** at 188 Grand St., and **E. Rossi & Co.** music and gifts store at 193 Grand St. At the intersection of Mulberry and Broome streets, you can stop for cannoli and espresso at the old-fashioned tile-floored **Caffé Roma** pastry shop; **Caffé Ferrara** around the corner at 195 Grand St. is larger and brighter, though a bit less atmospheric. But with their sidewalk touts trawling for tourist business, most of the Italian restaurants that line Mulberry Street offer standard Italian meals at anything but bargain prices.

Above Grand Street, Mulberry gets a little quieter. At Spring Street, leafy little DeSalvio Park still retains some of the old neighborhood's feel; just east on Spring Street, **Lombardi's Pizza** is the resurrection of a 1905 coal oven pizzeria. At the corner of Prince and Mott streets, a red-brick wall surrounds the cemetery of the austere 200-year-old landmark **St. Patrick's church,** which became a regular parish church when the new St. Patrick's was built uptown on Fifth Avenue. (The churchyard figures prominently in Martin Scorsese's classic Little Italy movie *Mean Streets.*)

A smaller Italian-American enclave hangs on in west Greenwich Village—near Father Demo Square, on Bleecker Street west of Sixth Avenue—but as younger generations of Italians improved their economic status, most moved out to the suburbs. Although Manhattan's Little Italy has withered, its spirit lives on up in the Belmont section of the Bronx, where several thriving food stores and restaurants along Arthur Avenue supply Italian specialties to Italian-American suburbanites. Even Umberto's Clam House—the Mulberry Street restaurant where mobster Joey Gallo was famously "offed" in 1972—has moved to Arthur Avenue. Little Italy has truly migrated.

ⓘ **NYC & Company** ℂ **212/484-1222;**
www.nycvisit.com)

✈ John F. Kennedy International, Newark
Liberty International, LaGuardia

🛏 $ **Union Square Hotel,** 209 E. 14th
St. ℂ **212/614-0500;** www.nyinns.com).
$$ **Hotel Belleclaire,** 250 W. 77th St. at
Broadway ℂ **877/468-3522** or 212/362-
7700; www.hotelbelleclaire.com).

Neighborhoods in Transition **383**

Baltimore's Row Houses
Getting the Scoop on the Stoop
Baltimore, Maryland

BALTIMORE'S POPULATION DECLINED BY A FULL THIRD FROM 1950 TO 2000; THE 2010 census shows another 10% drop. That shrinking tax base will impact efforts to restore derelict row house neighborhoods.

Think Baltimore, and what do you picture? Most probably, if you've seen the movies *Tin Men, The Accidental Tourist,* or *Hairspray,* you'll immediately envision a long, straight street lined with a continuous front of matching row houses. It's Baltimore's quintessential urban feature, where famed Baltimoreans from Betsy Ross and Edgar Allan Poe to critic H. L. Mencken have lived. Ever since the 1790s, the vast street grid of this working-class port city has been lined with terraces of small single houses. Wave after wave of new immigrants settled into these tightly packed house fronts, where they could ride streetcars or walk to their jobs and grab a piece of the American dream.

But in the second half of the 20th century, the American dream decamped to the suburbs—and in Baltimore, the defection was particularly severe. The Inner Harbor rejuvenation of the 1980s spurred some gentrification—Mayor William Schaefer jump-started urban homesteading by selling 500 abandoned downtown row houses for $1 apiece, and refurbishment transformed Federal Hill, Fells Point, and Canton—but elsewhere, block after block of row houses stood derelict. From the late 1990s on, the city government's solution was to send out wrecking crews and knock them down, leaving gaping holes in already decrepit inner city neighborhoods.

Granted, the term "row house" covers an extremely wide range of housing stock. The houses can be three or four stories high in some posh areas, simple two-story structures in others. The front doors may open onto small porches, petite front yards, or, more often, a low bare stoop with a railing. (Many of these humble stoops, though, are made from fine local white marble, which housewives traditionally scrubbed to a shine with Bon Ami scouring powder.) While most houses are built of brick, in some neighborhoods each house in a row features its own distinctive stone pediment or cornice; in others, the brick has been covered with a stuccolike protective veneer called Formstone, popular in the 1950s.

Visit the **Patterson Park/Highlandtown Historic District** in East Baltimore to see a still-intact streetscape of middle-class row houses, where various owners added their own touches, from Formstone to picture windows to porch seating. Mount Vernon's and Bolton Hill's landmark 19th-century row houses are more upscale, with brownstone exteriors and iron fences. It's the overall profile, though, that lingers in the eye—the low, orderly, harmonious silhouette of these city blocks, and how they earned Baltimore its nickname, "City of Neighborhoods."

✈ Baltimore-Washington International

🛏 $$$ **Baltimore Marriott Waterfront Hotel,** 700 Aliceanna St., Inner Harbor East (© **410/385-3000**; www.baltimoremarriott waterfront.com). $$ **Brookshire Suites,** 120 E. Lombard St. (© **410/625-1300**; www. harbormagic.com).

384 Neighborhoods in Transition

Lancaster County
Sprawl Meets the Plain Folk
Pennsylvania

IN TRADITIONAL AMISH LANCASTER COUNTY, NON-AMISH NOW OUTNUMBER AMISH 17 TO 1. Suburban sprawl drives up land prices, attracts strip malls, and threatens farming as a local way of life.

Sure, Lancaster County looks bucolic—all those rolling hills, winding creeks, neatly cultivated farms, and covered bridges, not to mention the presence of Amish farmers, dressed in their old-fashioned black clothes and driving buggies at a slow clip-clop along country roads. Two-thirds of the country is farmland, nearly all of it small family-owned farms (the average farm size is only 78 acres/32 hectares).

But in 1998, suburban sprawl was identified as Pennsylvania's number one environmental problem, and Lancaster County—only 50 miles (80km) west of Philadelphia along Route 30—was singled out as the most endangered area in reports by

An Amish family in Lancaster County.

10 Unique Accommodations

Four walls, a sloping roof, a door, square windows—we think we know what a house should look like. But throughout the ages, people have found creative housing solutions to various environmental challenges—from harsh weather to scarce building materials, from clan solidarity to protection from invasion. Here are 10 examples that have survived into modern times:

385 Barumini, Sardinia, Italy Dating back to the Bronze Age, *nuraghe* are dwellings built of rough-cut gray stone, tightly clustered around a central cone-shaped tower set on strategic high ground. Found only in Sardinia, these curious beehive-shaped settlements were apparently deserted and repopulated often during Phoenician, Punic, and Roman invasions. *www.nuraghi.org.*

Sassi dwellings in Matera, Italy.

386 Matera, Italy The word *sassi* literally means stones—as in the steep ravine walls that prehistoric southern Italians burrowed into, carving out tiny windowless homes linked by underground passageways—safe refuges in times of invasion. Abandoned *sassi* have now been renovated into hotels, restaurants, and chic residences, Matera's main tourist draw. © **39/835/334033**. *www.sassiweb.it.*

387 Gjirokastra, Albania The word *gjirokastra* means "silver fortress"—an apt name for this Ottoman town in southern Albania, with its distinctive 17th-century Turkish *kule* tower houses. Piled on the steep hillsides surrounding a 13th-century citadel, these slate-roofed stone houses stacked their rooms vertically. You enter on the top floor via a ladder, which could be swiftly pulled in when enemies arrived. *www.united-albania.com.*

388 Cappadocia, Turkey The original inhabitants of this Turkish hinterland hollowed out dwellings in pink cliffs of soft tufa rock; centuries later, they sheltered early Christians fleeing persecution. Open-air museums in both Goreme and the nearby Zelve Valley preserve frescoed churches and living quarters; eroded pillars known as "fairy chimneys" add to Cappadocia's distinctive landscape. *www.goreme.org.*

389 Matmâta, Southern Tunisia Filmmaker George Lucas discovered a ready-made sci-fi setting for his *Star Wars* in this small Berber village, where prehistoric ancestors dug homes around a large circular pit, two stories deep, leading to each family's private network of cave chambers and connecting passageways. Today's villagers greet floods of tourists; some of these troglodyte homes have even been turned into hotels. © **888/474-5502**. *www.tunisusa.com.*

390 Ksour District, Western Tunisia The traditional Berber mud-and-stone oasis complex—a *ksar*, or plural *ksour*—combined family dwellings with communal granaries, ovens, shops, and mosques. As time passed, villagers walled them up to use as forts during foreign invasions. Crumbling abandoned *ksour* stand as haunting relics in the desert, many clustered around the modern town of Tataouine. *www. ksour-tunisiens.com.*

391 Ulan Bator, Mongolia Round white felt-covered yurts—or in Mongolian, *gers*—are an ancient adaptation by Mongolian nomads to their peripatetic lives on the Central Asia steppes. Hung on a collapsible wood lattice, *gers* could be packed onto a camel or yak for easy transport, yet they are no mere tents, often boasting carved doors and pillars and rich hand-woven fabrics. Day-trip tours to outlying *ger* settlements leave from Ulan Bator. *www.mongoliatourism.gov.mn.*

392 Hukeng, China In rural Fujian province, for centuries ethnic Hakka and Minnan peoples have traditionally lived in clan groups in tile-roofed *tulous*—huge communal complexes of rammed earth, with hundreds of rooms overlooking a central courtyard. Despite the Cultural Revolution's efforts to disperse clans, some 3,000 remain, mostly unmodernized and in disrepair. Several around Hukeng are open to the public; overnight tours run from Xiamen. *www.discoverfujian.com.*

393 Ogimachi, Japan In the Japanese Alps of central Honshu, extended families bunked together in shared *gassho-zukuri*—snowfall-shedding houses with tall A-frame thatched roofs (the name translates to "hands joined in prayer," which is what the roofs resemble). The hamlet of Ogimachi contains many 200- to 300-year-old thatched houses amid its rice paddies and mulberry orchards; the open-air museum Shirakawago Gassho Zukuri Minkaen features several. ✆ *81/5769/6-1231. http://shirakawa-go.org.*

394 Coober Pedy, Australia Early-20th-century opal miners in Australia's rough-and-ready interior found a unique solution to the punishing heat and dust of Outback existence: live in underground "dugouts," in holes left by earlier miners or the sun-bleached mullock heaps of mining waste. Even the hotels and restaurants here are mostly underground. It certainly gives new meaning to the term "down under." *www.opalcapitaloftheworld.com.au.*

The Goreme open-air museum, Cappadocia.

the Sierra Club and the World Monuments Fund. Since then, the county has embarked on an aggressive program to conserve farmland, mostly by locking in easements on existing farms, and has tried to funnel new growth into identified "urban" zones.

In Lancaster County, farmland is valuable not only because it produces food, but because it attracts tourism—which adds $1 billion a year to the county's economy. While locals may appreciate the outlet shopping malls along Route 30, tourists are more drawn to the area's wonderful farmer's markets (try the Central Market in Lancaster, the Bird-in-Hand Market on Route 340 in Bird-in-Hand, or the Green Dragon Farmers Market in Ephrata), as well as outlets for traditional handicrafts like pie baking, quilt making, furniture making, and basketry. Individual farmers cash in on tourism with everything from buggy rides and petting farms to roadside stands and bed-and-breakfasts. The challenge is to strike the right balance between tourist infrastructure (hotels, shops, restaurants) and the pastoral landscape that draws the tourists.

In summer, the main roads around Lancaster can be clogged with traffic, and horse-drawn vehicles cause bottlenecks; get a good area map so you can venture onto quiet back roads, where you have a better chance of seeing Amish farmers in their daily rounds. (Just remember: Photographing them seriously violates their beliefs.) Stop at local farm stands to buy their excellent produce, and you'll have a natural opportunity to exchange a few words. Several Amish farmhouses east of Lancaster have been recast as tourist attractions: the **Amish Farm and House** in Lancaster (www.amishfarmandhouse. com), the **Amish Country Homestead** in Bird-In-Hand (www.amishexperience.com), and **Amish Village** in Ronks (http://the amishvillage.net). Also in Lancaster, the **Landis Valley Museum** (www.landisvalley museum.org) is a 21-building "living arts" complex where costumed interpreters demonstrate Pennsylvania German culture and folk traditions.

ⓘ **Pennsylvania Dutch visitors bureau** (✆ **800/723-8824;** www.padutchcountry. com)

✈ Philadelphia

🛏 **$$ Lancaster County Farm Stays** (www.afarmstay.com). **$$$ Bird-in-Hand Village Inn** (✆ **800/914-2473** or 717/768-1538; www.bird-in-handvillageinn.com).

Neighborhoods in Transition ⬤ **395**

Sweet Auburn
Odd Twist of Civil Rights History
Atlanta, Georgia

DESERTED BY THE BLACK PROFESSIONALS AND ENTREPRENEURS WHO ONCE MADE IT VITAL, Atlanta's historic Sweet Auburn neighborhood is struggling to reinvent itself without losing its character.

Sweet Auburn earned its nickname honestly. From the 1890s to the 1960s, prosperity flowed from the 10-block area around Auburn Avenue, the center of African-American enterprise in racially segregated Atlanta. But after the civil rights struggles of the 1960s, as segregation laws were repealed, blacks moved out of Sweet Auburn, no longer limited to its blacks-only enterprises. Suddenly it was just another inner-city neighborhood, and the construction of a new highway, I-75/85, slashed right through its heart.

West of the highway, you can still see such imposing buildings as the Beaux-Arts headquarters of the Atlanta Life Insurance Company (148 Auburn), founded in 1905 by former slave Alonzo Herndon; the offices of the *Atlanta Daily World* (145 Auburn), the first black-owned daily newspaper; the Royal Peacock Club (186 Auburn), which hosted black musicians such as B. B. King, the Four Tops, the Tams, and Atlanta's own Gladys Knight; and the Odd Fellows Building (228 Auburn), which boasted a rooftop dance hall and the only movie theater where blacks weren't confined to balcony seating. The pioneering Yates & Milton Drugstore is replicated among the historical exhibits at the **APEX Center** (135 Auburn). Unfortunately, other landmarks became derelict and were eventually razed—the city's first black-owned office building, the Rucker Building (160 Auburn), and the Herndon Building (245 Auburn). Vacant lots punctuate this once-bustling strip.

In the 1990s, concerted efforts arose to make Sweet Auburn sweet again. East of the highway, the first project was the restoration of King's birthplace, a modest Queen Anne–style house at 501 Auburn Ave., which can be visited on guided tours. The red-brick Ebenezer Baptist Church at 407 Auburn—where his father and, later, King himself were pastors—was more recently restored. The National Park Service includes these properties in the **Martin Luther King, Jr., National Historic Site** (www.nps.gov/malu), accompanied by the modern **King Center,** 449 Auburn Ave. (www.thekingcenter.org), now directed by King's son. In its exhibition hall, you can see King's Bible and clerical robe and a handwritten sermon, as well the key to his room at the Lorraine Motel in Memphis, Tennessee, where he was assassinated. Dr. King's white marble crypt sits outside in Freedom Plaza, surrounded by a five-tiered reflecting pool.

But urban renewal poses a challenge, especially with the highway dividing the district's commercial and residential areas. Over the past 20 years, the Historic District Development Corporation (HDDC) has built or rehabilitated more than 110 single-family homes and more than 50 affordable rental units, bypassing free-market gentrification that can price low-income residents out of a neighborhood. Taking a different tack, developers replaced an entire block of Auburn Street with Renaissance Walk, a modern condo-and-retail complex that opened in 2007. Its ground-floor "interpretive center" pays homage to Sweet Auburn's history, but the bricks-and-mortar neighborhood keeps slipping away.

ⓘ http://sweetauburn.us or www.sweet auburn.com

✈ Atlanta

🛏 $$ **The Georgian Terrace Hotel,** 659 Peachtree St. (✆ **800/651-2316** or 404/897-1991; www.thegeorgianterrace. com). $$ **Residence Inn Atlanta Midtown/Historic,** 1041 W. Peachtree St. (✆ **404/872-8885;** www.marriott.com).

TOUR Atlanta Preservation Center (✆ **404/688-3350;** www.preserveatlanta. com)

396 Neighborhoods in Transition

Harry S. Truman Historic District
Where the Buck Stops
Independence, Missouri

THE TRUMAN HOME'S NEIGHBORHOOD REPRESENTS A PERFECT TIME CAPSULE OF MID-20TH-century small-town America, but the town that surrounds it seems stalled.

To understand George Washington or Thomas Jefferson, you visit grand manor houses on Tidewater Virginia estates. But to understand Harry S. Truman, you have to go to a tidy little frame house on a side street of a small Missouri town.

Thrust into the presidency by Franklin Roosevelt's death, Harry S. Truman—who'd been vice president for only 10 weeks—was a plain-spoken Missourian, fond of mottoes like "If you can't stand the heat, get out of the kitchen" and "the buck stops here." You can see a desk sign with that saying, along with a host of other Truman memorabilia, at the **Harry S. Truman Library** in Independence (off US 24 at Delaware St.), along with his doughboy uniform from World War I; his trademark walking canes and straw hats; the upright piano that his wife, Bess, played at White House parties; and the safety plug that was pulled to detonate the Nagasaki bomb. Truman's grave lies in the courtyard.

The place that really conveys Truman's common-man qualities, though, is the Truman home at 219 N. Delaware St. Both Harry and Bess were small-town folks, and their summer White House was simply Bess's family home, a gabled white Victorian house with a scrollwork corner porch, where the Trumans lived from 1918 on. (The family farm Harry ran in Grandview, Missouri, is also part of the historic site.) Get tickets early in the day, because they do sell out—tours are limited to eight people because the rooms are small. Inside the house, virtually untouched since Bess Truman died, you'll see the red kitchen table where Harry and Bess ate breakfast, the book-lined study that was Truman's favorite retreat, and the wide back porch where they played cards and ate meals during hot Missouri summers. It's a wonderful slice of history, and surprisingly affecting.

As Kansas City sprawls ever closer, Independence is neither a suburb nor a self-sufficient county seat; its pawnshops and shabby houses reveal a city that prosperity has passed by. In some sections of town, an epidemic of drug use and methamphetamine traffic has taken a toll. By the 1990s the simple frame houses of this neighborhood had significantly lost value; many were subdivided into apartments. A program of home-renovation tax abatements has spruced up the immediate neighborhood, but Truman's 5-block stroll to downtown—past his office in the local courthouse, the barbershop he once frequented, and a soda fountain where he worked as a youth—tells a different story. Main Street Independence looks desperate for business, with more parking lots than buildings. Perhaps it's fitting that the decline of small-town America should be most evident in the hometown of our most ordinary-guy president.

ⓘ **Truman Site visitor center,** 223 N. Main St. (www.nps.gov/hstr)

✈ Kansas City International

🛏 $$$ **Westin Crown Center,** One Pershing Rd., Kansas City, MO (ⓒ **816/474-4400;** www.westin.com/crowncenter). $ **Holiday Inn Kansas City SE Waterpark,** 9103 E. 39th St., Kansas City, MO (ⓒ **816/737-0200;** www.holidayinn.com).

Neighborhoods in Transition **397**

Over-the-Rhine
Reversing the Tide
Cincinnati, Ohio

URBAN NEGLECT AND FLIGHT LEFT THIS HISTORIC 19TH-CENTURY NEIGHBORHOOD, FILLED WITH Italianate row houses, vacant and deteriorating. A new generation of urban pioneers hopes to reverse the trend.

It wasn't really the Rhine that 19th-century German immigrants crossed, trooping home from work in downtown Cincinnati—it was just the Miami and Erie Canal. Still, once they had crossed it they felt at home, in a vibrant German-speaking community with their own churches, shops, and newspaper (and some 50 breweries). They built solid homes in the then-popular architectural styles, especially Italianate row houses. It was one of the most densely populated neighborhoods in the Midwest, and the sort of working-class urban neighborhood that made America great.

The 20th century, however, did not treat Over-the-Rhine kindly. The stagnant canal was replaced by a failed streetcar line, then a failed subway, and eventually became the traffic-choked Central Parkway. As German-Americans moved up the economic ladder and out of the neighborhood, they were replaced by day laborers, mostly black, from the South. The decline of Cincinnati's prominent machine-tool industry hit hard. By the 1970s, Over-the-Rhine had become just another inner-city neighborhood plagued with drugs, crime, and racial unrest. In 1990, nearly a quarter of its apartments sat vacant and uninhabitable.

Still, some 1,200 historic buildings remain, though many stand vacant and deteriorating. To jump-start investment, developers spruced up the area around 12th and Vine streets to attract young professionals looking to live close to downtown. Meanwhile, Over-the-Rhine Community Housing has focused on developing affordable housing so that current residents won't be priced out of the neighborhood. With a population that's now 80% black, 20% white, Over-the-Rhine must steer a careful course between yuppification and urban renewal.

Despite decades of neglect, Over-the-Rhine still has several attractions. Both the Cincinnati Opera and the Cincinnati Symphony perform at the **Cincinnati Music Hall** (1241 Elm St.), a marvel of eclectic red-brick architecture that some have dubbed Sauerbraten Byzantine. **The Ensemble Theater** (1120 Vine St.; www.cincyetc.com) and the more experimental **Know Theatre** (1120 Jackson St.; www.knowtheatre.com) have restored other historic buildings nearby. Ohio's largest indoor market, the 1850s-era **Findlay Street Market** (open Wed–Sat, at Elder and Race sts.) is riding the crest of foodie interest in farmer's markets. Celebrating OTR's history as a brewing district, the popular annual spring Bockfest is centered in the revived Christian Moehlein craft brewery (1619 Moore St.).

But the main thing remains the housing—block after sloping block of neat three- and four-story brick Italianate beauties, most with their ornate cornices, window pediments, and door lintels intact. Many are in a shocking state of neglect; gaping holes in several blocks show what has been lost already. Can Over-the-Rhine cross back over?

ⓘ www.otrchamber.com

✈ Cincinnati/Northern Kentucky International

⊨ $$$ **Millennium Hotel Cincinnati,** 150 W. 5th St. (✆ **513/352-2100;** www.millennium-hotels.com). $$ **Symphony Hotel,** 210 W. 14th St. (✆ **513/721-3353;** www.symphonyhotel.com).

12 Holy Places

La Sagrada Família.

Angkor Wat
Glory in the Jungle
Siem Reep, Cambodia

MORE THAN A MILLION TOURISTS VISIT THE ANCIENT CITY OF ANGKOR WAT EVERY YEAR, PUTTING tremendous stress on the sandstone temples, stairs, and walkways.

In 1861, it was just a mysterious hulk in the Cambodian jungle, a pile of jumbled laterite and sandstone blocks shrouded in roots and vines. Today, however, the ancient city of Angkor Wat—capital of the Khmer kingdom from 802 until 1295—is Cambodia's chief tourism attraction, a breathtaking sprawl of temples and shrines that covers 98 sq. km (38 sq. miles).

Benefiting from a boom in exotic travel since 1993, Angkor Wat's annual visitor totals have shot from 7,500 to more than a million. Foot traffic is wearing ruts on sandstone stairs and walkways, and the faces of poorly conserved sculptural panels are crumbling away. Several of the site's more than 40 temples are sinking into the sandy ground as area hotels and resorts drain underground water sources. It's one of the world's most endangered classical sites, but the Cambodian government is slowly taking steps to sustain it. Entrance fees have been hiked to limit the number of visitors, and the authority that maintains the site claims to have roped off the most fragile structures, employing more than 270 tourist guards, and diverting people away from the most crowded sites.

The resplendent main temple, also called Angkor Wat, is the star attraction—its four-spired profile has virtually become the symbol of Cambodia. Dating from the 12th century, it stands 213m (700 ft.) high from its base to the tip of its highest lotus-shaped tower, the largest religious monument ever built. Scholars believe that this sandstone temple's symmetry mirrors the timeline of the Hindu ages, like a map or calendar of the universe. Approaching from the main road over a *baray*, or reservoir,

you climb up three steep levels to the inner sanctum; you'll be high up for an inspiring view.

Of course, the most famous—some would say clichéd—view is not from Angkor Wat but of Angkor Wat: from the five-tiered Phnom Bakheng, topping a hill just past the entrance to Angkor Wat. Its narrow staircases get packed with up to 3,000 tourists some evenings at sunset, putting incredible wear and tear on the ancient Khmer temple.

A detail of Angkor Wat.

Another large temple complex called Angkor Thom—or "great city" in Khmer—is dotted with many temples; don't miss the bas-reliefs on the **Terrace of the Leper King** and the **Terrace of Elephants.** One of the most imperiled temples here is the centerpiece of this complex, a fantastical Buddhist temple called **Bayon,** with four huge enigmatic stone faces, each cosmologically aligned with a compass point (the same is true of each of its 51 small towers).

One temple—**Ta Prohm**—has been deliberately left overgrown in foliage, the roots of fig, banyan, and kapok trees cleaving its massive stones. It's an intriguing notion—what if Angkor Wat had been left in the jungle forever? Would it be better off today?

✈ Siem Reap

🛏 $$$ **Sofitel Royal Angkor,** Vithei Charles de Gaulle (✆ **855/63/964-6000;** www.accor.com). $ **La Noria,** off Rte. 6 northeast of Siem Reap (✆ **855/63/964-242**).

Ancient Temples **399**

Pulemelei Mound
Lost in the Jungle
Savaii, Western Samoa

WITHOUT EFFORTS TO PROTECT IT, PULEMELEI MOUND COULD FALL VICTIM TO POLLUTION, population growth, mining, logging, and agriculture, which have destroyed nearby native forests and habitats.

Researchers agree on two points: The Pulemelei Mound is important, and it is big. After that, the arguments start to fly.

The biggest ancient structure in Polynesia (65x60m/213x197 ft. at its base, and 12m/39 ft. high), the stepped pyramid of Pulemelei—or Tia Seu, as some call it—may have been a chieftain's residence, a ritual site for pigeon snaring, a sentry tower, a celestial observatory, or a place of worship. Stone pedestals at the corners of its leveled-off top may have been ceremonial thrones for worthies, or receptacles for conch-shell trumpets that were blown every night to call holy spirits back to this resting place. Some Polynesians believe it was built by the great god Togaloa, or that it was the launching point for the great West Polynesian Diaspora—which makes this place equally significant to Tahitians, Hawaiians, and New Zealand Maoris. Some even believe Pulemelei is the gateway to the afterlife, which explains the neatly aligned entryways scooped out of the earthen slopes on its east and west side, a feature found on no other such mound. Sitting silently, overgrown and crumbling, in the middle of the jungle, it still has a curious aura and power.

Pulemelei's island, **Savaii,** is the largest in this volcanic South Sea archipelago, but it's much more rugged than its neighbors. As South Pacific hideaways go, this is it: lush inland jungles and waterfalls, desolate-looking lava fields, a beach-edged lagoon or two, and very few other tourists, though it's only an hour's ferry ride or a 10-minute flight from the Samoan capital of Apia on Upolu Island. Many historians consider Savaii the cradle of Polynesian civilization—it was a major political capital, and any chieftain who lived here would have been powerful indeed. Archaeologists think the mound was built about A.D. 1100 to 1400, but the settlement that surrounds it seems to have been mysteriously abandoned between 1700 and 1800 and was swallowed up by jungle—until anthropologists started poking around in the 1950s.

Left alone, this pile of packed earth and basalt stones will soon be swallowed by jungle again. But that's another thing no one can agree on—what is to be done with Pulemelei. Located on an old copra plantation, it's still privately owned, though the landowners would like to develop the site for tourism. Local villagers have taken them to court to stop excavations, which they believe desecrate the holy site. When a team of archaeologists carrying on the work of Thor Heyerdahl finally began to dig here in 2003, ritual fires were lit to purify the area, in case human remains were disturbed (Heyerdahl's people discovered none), but it's still a politically sensitive issue. Hire a local guide to lead you through the jungle to Pulemelei, and imagine what this site could look like, when—and if—it's ever properly preserved.

(i) **Pulemelei,** Lesolo Plantation
✈ Savaii

🛏 $$$ **The Savaiian Hotel,** Savaii (✆ **685-51296;** www.savaiianhotel.com). $$$ **Vacations Beach Resort,** Manase Village, Savaii (✆ **685/54001** or 685/54024; www.vacationsbeachfales.com).

400 Ancient Temples

The Temples of Khajuraho
The Sacred & the Profane
Madya Pradesh, India

NEW BUSINESSES AND HOMES ARE CROWDING INTO THE BUFFER ZONE AROUND THE TEMPLES of Khajuraho. There is also growing concern that the temple's erotic art could become targets of religious fundamentalists in India.

The naughty frescoes of Pompeii are nothing compared to the X-rated sculptures decorating these 10th- and 11th-century temples, found in 1838 in the jungles of Madya Pradesh. Built by the Chandela kings, a robust clan of Rajput warriors, 25 exuberant many-spired sandstone temples stand in a cluster (there were originally 85), full of artwork frankly celebrating the pleasures of the human body.

Sexy art aside, these temples are astonishingly beautiful, as increasing numbers of tourists can testify. The only real sin here is how the modern world is encroaching on the site, desecrating what really should feel like a spiritual site.

In these richly sculpted temples, you make a ritual clockwise circuit around the inner sanctum past beautifully rendered friezes of gods, nymphs, animals, warfare, and various bodies twined together in hot-blooded passion. The most spectacular—and most erotically charged—temples are within the Western Group, including the large Lakshmana Temple, the elegantly proportioned Kandariya Mahadev Temple with its 872 statues, Devi Jagadambi Temple (devoted to Kali), Chitragupta Temple (devoted to Surya, the sun god), and the Temple of Vishvanatha. Take your time strolling through, for every sculptured panel has a story to tell. Not all are erotic; many narrate the exploits of the Hindu gods, particularly Shiva and Vishnu in various incarnations. It's all part of the parade of life that these temples extol.

The Temples of Khajuraho.

The Eastern Group consists of both Hindu and Jain temples—you can tell them apart because the ascetic Jain philosophy ruled out sculpture that was too graphic (though voluptuous nudity was apparently okay, as you'll see in the Parsvanatha Temple). One of the most fun temples here is the 11th-century Hindu temple honoring Vamana, a plump dwarf incarnation of Vishnu; also check out the sculpted bells on the pillars of the Ghantai Temple. In the Southern Group, notice the dizzying ornamentation of the Duladeo Temple, one of the last temples built before the Sultans of Delhi squeezed out the Chandela kings.

Across the road from the entrance to the Western Group, the **Archaeological Museum** displays a modest selection of sculptures collected from various Khajuraho

sites—it's a good way to see close-up details of carved figures that usually occur high on the temple walls and spires. To get the most out of your temple tour, rent an audio guide or hire an official guide through the Raja Café, the tourist office, or your hotel. Avoid all those unofficial touts and guides, no matter how much they pester you—and they will.

ⓘ ℂ **502/926-0002.** www.jaguartikal.com.
✈ Khajuraho

🛏 $$$ **Radisson Jass,** By-Pass Rd. (ℂ **91/124-422657**). $$ **Ken River Lodge,** Village Madla (ℂ **91/7732/27-5235;** www.kenriverlodge.com).

The Mosques of Timbuktu
Melting into the Desert
Timbuktu, Mali

BUILT OF MUD, LIKE EVERY OTHER BUILDING IN TIMBUKTU, THESE THREE MEDIEVAL MOSQUES are susceptible to damage from nature's most common wrath—rain.

Yes, Timbuktu really does exist, although it was the early 19th century before any white European traveled there and lived to tell the tale. By then, this desert trading city—situated right where the Niger River flows into the southern edge of the Sahara desert—was long past its golden age, when it had a population of 100,000. Today's population is only about 32,000, but Timbuktu's skyline still boasts three towering medieval landmarks—a trio of mosques once renowned throughout the Islamic world.

There's just one catch: Those mosques are built entirely of mud. Every spring when the rains come, citizens pack fresh mud onto their rounded towers and sloping walls to keep them from dissolving back into the desert (even the streets here are nothing but drifting sand—camels and donkeys fare better than the few taxis). The tan walls of the taller sections bristle with the tips of dark wooden struts, but despite those supports, an unexpected thunderstorm could wipe them out at any time. Only recently have they begun desperately needed structural reinforcement.

Dominating the intersection where Arabia's gold and ivory were traded for sub-Saharan Africa's salt and slaves—imagine the Sahara as an ocean, and Timbuktu as its biggest seaport—medieval Timbuktu used its wealth to become Africa's greatest Islamic center of learning. These aren't just any mosques—they were also universities, or *madrassahs,* with celebrated imams teaching in the courtyards, and libraries containing thousands of precious manuscripts. Most studies centered on the Koran, but related fields such as astronomy, history, and logic were also taught.

The first mosque—**Djinguere Ber,** or the Friday Prayers Mosque—was built in 1327 by Emperor Mansa Mussa. (His Egyptian architect designed an even larger mosque in Djenné, still the largest mud-built structure in the world.) With its main tower like a tapering, stunted skyscraper, Djinguere Ber is big enough for 2,000 worshipers, and is still the central mosque of the city. The other two, **Sankore** and **Sidi Yahya,** were built in the 15th century. Pyramid-shaped Sankore developed into the epicenter of Islamic scholarship in all of Africa, and even today functions as a university.

Though non-Muslim visitors are no longer allowed inside, you can still marvel at the mosques' flowing exteriors (said to have inspired Antonin Gaudí in designing La Sagrada Família). Today you'll see television aerials on Timbuktu's huddled mud houses; there's even an Internet cafe on the high street. But it's still remote and desolate, and the heat is relentless (at midday, nobody ventures outdoors). Strolling around its soft sand streets between the uniformly tawny, low adobe buildings is like entering a dream world—don't miss it.

✈ Timbuktu International

🛏 $$ **Hendrina Khan Hotel,** off Route de Korioumé (✆ **223/292-16-81**). $$ **Hotel Colombe,** Blvd. Askia Mohamed (✆ **223/ 292-14-35**).

TOUR World Heritage Tours (✆ **800/ 663-0844** or 604/264-7378; www.world heritagetours.com). **Intrepid Travel** (✆ **800/970-7299;** www.intrepidtravel. com). **Palace Travel** (✆ **800/683-7731** or 215/471-8555; www.palacetravel.com).

Ggantija

Going Back to Mother Earth

Gozo, Malta

VANDALISM, A SEVERE STORM, AND WORK IN NEARBY STONE QUARRIES DAMAGED THIS ANCIENT temple, leading to a renovation that was completed in 2005. Now its biggest threat comes from tourist traffic.

Legend has it that Ggantija was built, like the name suggests, by a giant—not only that, but a female giant, who made the whole thing in 1 night while holding a baby in her other arm. Being a woman, she built this sanctuary in the rounded curves of the female form; worshipers entered and left the temple through the birth canal, as if reliving their own birth experience.

This stupendous fertility goddess relic—one of Malta's best known destinations, along with Fort St. Elmo ❷❽❺—was constructed between 3600 and 3000 B.C., which makes it the world's oldest manmade free-standing building—although these days it isn't entirely free-standing, but propped up with unsightly metal scaffolding. Still, you can't deny the elemental power of these pitted limestone blocks—stern gray on the outer walls, warm yellow for the inner walls—which weigh up to 60 tons and cover an area of 1,000 sq. m (10,760 sq. ft.); there are two adjacent temples, like a mother and daughter. The rear wall alone rises 6m (20 ft.). Delicately incised geometrical designs ornament the stone, lovely curling shapes that seem hardly possible from artists working with just simple flint knives. A faint blush of red here or there reminds us of the bold red ocher paint that once decorated the megaliths. Imagine being inside these oval chambers when they were roofed over and painted a dark, warm red—it must truly have felt like entering a womb.

Older than the Pyramids of Giza, older than Stonehenge, Ggantija has stubbornly weathered the centuries, along with 50 other megalithic temples on the islands of Malta. No one knows why these Mediterranean people went through an explosion of temple building in this period, or why their culture swiftly declined around 2300 B.C.—it may have been famine, deforestation, or overpopulation. Today, however, the temples are one of Malta's chief tourist attractions, and busloads of tourists tramp through ancient sites that were built to admit only a select few worshipers.

Ggantija is the largest and most intact of all these temples, partly because it's off the beaten track on the small island of Gozo (a 20-min. ferry ride from Malta). But it was the first to be dug up, back in the 1820s, when the art of excavation was in its infancy; many carvings and sculptures apparently disappeared, and stones were disturbed and/or damaged.

ⓘ **Ggantija,** Temples St., Xaghra (✆ **356/ 21/553 194**)

✈ Malta

🛏 $$$ **Westin Dragonara,** 5 Dragonara Rd., St. Julian's (✆ **356/21/381 000;** www.starwoodhotels.com). $$ **San Andrea Hotel,** Xlendi Promenade, Gozo (✆ **356/ 21/565 555;** www.hotelsanandrea.com).

San Agustín Archeological Park
Cult of the Dead
San Agustín, Colombia

LOOTING THREATENS SAN AGUSTÍN ARCHEOLOGICAL PARK, WHICH CONTAINS HUNDREDS OF PRE-Columbian stone statues. During the 1980s and 1990s, at least 17 carvings were stolen.

Mysterious, haunting, enigmatic, eerie—all these adjectives and more apply to the San Agustín Archeological Park. It's a vast city of the dead, with 14 separate sites scattered over nearly 650 sq. km (250 sq. miles). More than 500 massive stone statues stand here, perfectly preserved on groomed lawns, set off with awesome mountain views.

Hardy souls are increasingly traveling here—mostly Colombians, anthropologists, and backpackers with a yen for on-the-edge travel. But given the political situation in Colombia—although relative peace has reigned during the last few years, the country's long, vicious civil war and drug trafficking reputation loom large—travelers should be cautious. At the time of writing, the U.S., U.K., Canadian, and Australian governments still issue warnings against travel to Colombia, particularly rural areas. Coastal Cartagena gets a fair amount of tourism, but not San Agustín, which is deep in the tropical Andes—a 10-hour bus ride from Bogota (backpackers do it overnight to save a night's hotel cost) or a 4-hour ride from the regional airport of Neiva.

Apparently created to serve as guardians of the dead, these statues range in size from tiny (20cm/8 in. high) to gargantuan (7m/23 ft.). Carved from dark, craggy volcanic rocks, they depict gods and mythical animals, grouped in ceremonial arrangements, often around burial chambers. The heads are large and the faces bold, expressive, and challenging. The pre-Inca culture that produced them may have ruled this region from as early as the 6th century B.C. to as late as A.D. 1200, but they seem to have vanished without a trace—even the local indigenous people have no legends to explain the death cult that apparently thrived here.

The main collection is at **Parque Arqueologico,** about 3km (2 miles) west of the town of San Agustín; two other outstanding sites are **Chaquira,** just northeast of the town, with its massive figure etched into the face of a cliff overlooking the Magdalena River; and **Alto los Idolos,** 27km (17 miles) northeast of town, a complex necropolis with stark imposing monoliths on a high Andean hillside. Because so many different sites exist, walking around to all of them would require a few days; horseback excursions and jeep tours are better options (hotels in the area can help arrange these). English-speaking guides can be hired at the Parque Arqueologico.

Although it is wise to heed current travel warnings, these shouldn't hamper plans to visit Colombia. The country has increased its military and police presence significantly since former President Uribe took office in 2002, and as a tourist, you are unlikely to encounter any violence. Colombia needs tourism revenues to develop alternatives to the drug trade, and San Agustín should be one of the keys to drawing tourists.

ⓘ www.colombia.travel

✈ Neiva

⌂⊨$ **Finca El Maco,** Maco, San Agustín (✆**57/8/837 34 37;** www.elmaco.ch)

TOUR Nueva Lengua International (✆ **202/470-2555** in North America., 57/1/753 24 51 in Colombia; www.travel sanagustin.com)

Old Jerusalem
Sacrilege in the Holy City
Israel

THE BIGGEST FACE-OFF THESE DAYS IN OLD JERUSALEM MAY BE BETWEEN ARCHAEOLOGISTS, who want to preserve the city's priceless antiquities, and modern developers. How far can they go before the essential character of Jerusalem is destroyed forever?

Everybody wants a piece of Jerusalem. Not only is this "City on the Hill" a holy city to much of the world—Judaism, Islam, and Christianity all have major shrines here—but it's also deeply embroiled in the Israeli-Palestinian conflict, with every new development weighed for its political implications. A major highway system sits just 9m (30 ft.) from the walls of the Old City, so that visitors have to climb a pedestrian overpass in order to enter the Jaffa Gate. Eccentric, small-scale 19th-century neighborhoods in the New City, with their quaint networks of pedestrian streets, courtyards, and Ottoman-era mansions, are being demolished and replaced with office blocks. A new wave of skyscrapers is planned for the previously low-rise center of West Jerusalem, and 10 new projects are on the books.

For centuries this city has been tugged to and fro. King Solomon erected the first great

Old Jerusalem.

Jewish temple here in 957 B.C.; Nebuchadnezzar destroyed it 4 centuries later. In 34 B.C. King Herod built the greatest religious complex in the eastern Roman Empire—which the Romans leveled in A.D. 70. (At Temple Mount's foot, a surviving fragment of Herod's wall is known as the **Wailing Wall** because for centuries Jews have crowded here to mourn the loss of their temple.) After the Muslim conquest of A.D. 638, Temple Mount was rebuilt with Islamic holy places. **El Aksa Mosque** here is the third-holiest Muslim place of prayer after Mecca and Medina, and the dazzling **Dome of the Rock** protects a rock revered by Muslims as the spot where Prophet Muhammad viewed paradise. To Jews, however, it's the rock where Abraham proved his faith by nearly sacrificing his son Isaac.

As a political compromise, the walled Old City was divided into five sections: Temple Mount, the Muslim Quarter, the Jewish Quarter, the Christian Quarter, and the Armenian Quarter. But even there, factions compete: The dour sandstone **Church of the Holy Sepulchre** in the Christian quarter is a site so holy that Roman Catholics, Armenian Orthodox, Greek Orthodox, Egyptian Coptics, Ethiopians, and Syrian Orthodox all claim it. Founded by Constantine, the first Christian emperor of Rome, it enshrines what tradition claims is the tomb of Jesus Christ (it once also held the Cross that Jesus was crucified on, but the Persians stole that centuries ago).

Outside of the Old City, the **Mount of Olives** contains one of the oldest, perhaps the holiest, Jewish cemeteries in the world, as well as the spot where Jesus ascended to heaven, the spot where Jesus taught his disciples the Lord's Prayer, and the courtyard where Jesus supposedly prayed the night before his arrest, each sanctified with its own church. With a legacy this rich, no wonder everybody's fighting over Jerusalem.

✈ Jerusalem

🛏 $$$ **Jerusalem Sheraton Plaza,** 47 King George St. (📞 **800/325-3535** or 02/629-8666; www.sheraton.com). $$$ **King Solomon Hotel,** 32 King David St. (📞 **02/569-5555**).

Seats of Religion

Church of the Holy Nativity
An Unstable Stable Scene
Bethlehem, Palestine

WHILE GUIDED TOURS STILL COME DAILY TO SEE JESUS' BIRTHPLACE, THE LOCALITY IS SO DRAINED by military turmoil that routine maintenance has been ignored in the decaying church guarding where he was born.

Even if you're not a practicing Christian, you probably know where Jesus Christ was born—the story of his birth in a stable in Bethlehem has been told over and over again for 20 centuries now. But Bethlehem today is no simple village of shepherds, camels, and donkeys; it's a busy, modern town in the West Bank, that political tinderbox torn between Israel and Palestine.

Milling around a plaza called Manger Square, you'll notice different priests protecting their sects' claim to this sacred site—Franciscan priests in brown robes, Armenians in purple- and cream-colored robes, bearded Greeks in black robes with

The Church of the Holy Nativity.

from riding their horses inside, others say built by post-crusade Muslims to humble Christian pilgrims.

Inside, the stately Corinthian pillars that line the basilica's naves bear faded paintings of apostles, bishops, saints, and kings; gilded lamps hang from the oak ceiling, and trapdoors in the stone-and-wood floor give mere glimpses of old Byzantine mosaic glories beneath. But the heart of the church lies not with its ornate gold-and-silver main altar, but down narrow staircases beside the altar: a subterranean marble grotto, draped in worn tapestries. According to ancient tradition, this shallow cave is where Mary gave birth to Jesus; altars mark nearby spots where the manger stood and where the Magi bowed to the baby Jesus. Historically accurate or not, after centuries of adoration this hushed grotto is full of spiritual aura.

While you're here, you should also visit the grand Franciscan church just north of the Church of the Holy Nativity, which offers a competing Nativity site: A stairway from the back of its nave leads to an underground maze of rock-hewn chambers that supposedly include the stable where Joseph and Mary stayed the night of Jesus' birth. In the scrum of modern Bethlehem, finding not one but two holy retreats isn't a bad bargain at all.

long hair tied into a bun. After being tussled over for centuries, it's no surprise that the ancient Church of the Holy Nativity looks dilapidated—competing priests may even come to blows over the right to scrub a certain section of the worn floors. (Having armed Palestinian soldiers occupy the church, as has happened recently, only aggravates the situation.) Though it was first built in A.D. 326 by the Roman emperor Constantine, and rebuilt 200 years later by Emperor Justinian, its present fortresslike facade was the work of 12th-century crusaders, aggressively reinforcing their claim to the site. Unlike the grand portals of most churches, this one has an odd low doorway—some say lowered by Christians to prevent Ottomans

(i) **The Church of the Holy Nativity,** Manger Sq., Bethlehem (✆**972/2/647-7050**)
✈ Jerusalem

🛏 $$$ **Jerusalem Sheraton Plaza,** 47 King George St. (✆**800/325-3535** or 972/2/629-8666; www.sheraton.com). $$$ **King Solomon Hotel,** 32 King David St. (✆**972/2/569-5555**).

TOUR **Egged Tours** (✆**972/2/530-4422**). **United Tours** (✆**972/2/625-2187**). **Alternative Tours** (✆ **972/2-6283282;** raed@jrshotel.com).

Little Hagia Sofia
The Model Mosque
Istanbul, Turkey

AS IF SURVIVING CENTURIES OF WAR, EARTHQUAKES, AND HUMID WEATHER WASN'T ENOUGH, when they put a railroad next to Little Hagia Sophia—that was the last straw.

You'd think a holy place this old would get a little more respect. After all, this is the oldest Byzantine monument in Istanbul, built as the Christian church of Sts. Sergios and Bacchos by Emperor Justinian in A.D. 527 to 536. Many architectural historians believe it was a working model for Justinian's later great church, Hagia Sophia (now the Ayasofya Mosque), which is why this one eventually became known as Little Hagia Sophia. Like the bigger Hagia Sophia, this smaller church was converted to a mosque in 1504 after the Muslim takeover of Istanbul, and the gold Byzantine mosaics that once glittered all over its interior were plastered over. Unlike big Hagia Sophia, though, it is still a working mosque, which you can visit (observe the usual etiquette for visiting mosques—remove your shoes, don't take flash photos, don't walk in front of worshipers, and dress modestly). Its lovely octagonal nave is surmounted by a broad dome, accented by slender columns of colored marble with ornately sculpted capitals; don't miss its especially serene and leafy garden outside.

Little Hagia Sophia is one of Istanbul's lesser known gems (for more on Istanbul, see 368, tucked away by the southern city walls near the shore of the Sea of Marmara. The 20th century, however, has not been kind to it. It was once closer to the sea, until the 1950s, when a landfill project made room for a new coastal road routed close to the mosque. The railway came soon afterward, adding more vibrations to shake the

ancient building. When rising damp became a problem, the foundation was raised in the 1970s—but a recently built sea wall nearby raised the water table and caused the damp to return worse than ever.

When the earthquake of 1999 widened existing cracks in the dome, rainwater seeped in and the mosque—which had just been restored in 1996—began to show serious signs of decay. Unless those unsteady foundations were finally shored up, there was every reason to believe that Little Hagia Sophia would collapse. The mosque was closed for major structural work beginning in 2002—but almost immediately, workers discovered ancient tombs under the site, which ground work to a halt. Some international observers began to fear that the landmark mosque would be left to rot.

It's been a long haul, but the project was finally completed in 2007. The mosque, crisply repainted and plastered, looks in fine form again. After all it's gone through, it deserves a visit.

(i) Lower end of Küçük Ayasofya Cad (www.sacred-destinations.com)

✈ Atatürk International, Istanbul

🛏 $$$ **Çiragan Palace Hotel Kempinski Istanbul,** Çiragan Cad. 84 (© **800/426-3135** in North America, or 90/212/258-3377 in Istanbul; www.kempinski.com). $$ **Mavi Ev** (Blue House), Dalbasti Sok. 14 (© **90/212/638-9010;** www.bluehouse.com.tr).

Kathmandu
Shangri-La in Crisis
Nepal

TO THE MOUNTAIN TREKKERS AND HIPPIES WHO FIRST FLOCKED HERE IN THE 1960S, THIS Himalayan capital seemed like an isolated Shangri-La. But Kathmandu is now a city of around 800,000 people, with rapidly worsening pollution—diesel fumes fill the air, and the sacred Bagmati River has become a jet-black stagnant mess.

In this mountain region, earthquakes, landslides, and floods pose a continual threat; to make things worse, a decade of conflict between the government and Maoist rebels drained the resources needed to protect its wildlife and historic monuments. A peace agreement was signed in late 2006, and as of mid-2011, the terms of the agreement were being met—still, the truce is precarious.

And the cultural heritage of the Kathmandu Valley is so worth saving. This compact mountain valley has not one but three historic towns—Patan, Bhaktapur, and Kathmandu itself, each with a beautiful, if crumbling, collection of buildings around a central square. Kathmandu city

gets its modern name from the two-story wooden pagoda on Durbar Square named **Kaasthamandap** (or Maru Sattal), built in 1596, supposedly from the timber of a single tree, without a single nail or external support. The rest of the Durbar Square complex—the seat of the Malla dynasty that built much of the city—includes nearly 50 temples, shrines, and palaces, including the former royal **Hanumandhoka Palace, Kumari Ghar** (Abode of the Living Goddess), and the vermilion-walled **Taleju temple.** But don't stop there; wander around the city's maze of narrow streets, finding smaller temples, open-air markets, and miniature shrines tucked

A temple in Kathmandu.

around the bustling city, a jumbled juxtaposition of the new and the old.

The most ancient site in the valley is the 1,600-year-old Hindu shrine of **Changu Narayan,** devoted to Vishnu, 12km (7½ miles) east of the city; elaborate stone carving, woodwork, and silver crafting are festooned over seemingly every surface of this temple. Set amid jungle only 5km (3 miles) east of the city, the gold-roofed temple of **Pashupatinath,** sacred to Lord Shiva, is one of the holiest of Hindu shrines, drawing pilgrims from all over Asia. Its stair steps ripple down to the Bagmati River, which despite its pollution remains a revered cremation site.

In Nepal, Hinduism intertwines harmoniously with Buddhism, especially at **Syambhunath** and **Bouddhanath,** two famous stupas, or circular monuments built for meditation. Tibetan monks, Brahmin priests, and Newar nuns all worship at the hilltop Syambhunath complex, 3km (2 miles) west of the city; notice the watchful eyes of all-seeing Buddha painted on all sides of the stupa. Tibetan Buddhists predominate at the monastery complex of Bouddhanath, 6km (3¾ miles) west of the city, with its immense 36m-high (118-ft.) stupa decorated with prayer wheels and 108 tiny images of Buddha, as well as another set of those watchful painted eyes.

✈ Tribhuvan International Airport

🛏 $$$ **Dwarikas Hotel,** Battisputali, Kathmandu (© **977/1/447 3725;** www.dwarikas.com). $$–$$$ **Taragaon,** Boudha (© **977/1/449 1234;** http://kathmandu.regency.hyatt.com).

408 Seats of Religion

Uluru–Kata Tjuta National Park
A Sacrilege at the Sacred Red Rocks
Northern Territory, Australia

THE ULURU–KATA TJUTA NATIONAL PARK IS ONE OF THE MOST SIGNIFICANT ARID-LAND ECOsystems in the world. But while increasing tourism helps the economy, it takes a toll on the landscape.

The native Anangu call tourists *minga*— little ants—because that's what they look like, crawling up the red sandstone flanks of Uluru, central Australia's most storied monolith. Despite often-ferocious winds and withering heat, some visitors still feel compelled to spend 2 to 4 hours scrambling up the great rock. Yes, the views from the top are impressive, but the tourists are committing sacrilege: Uluru is a sacred spot in the Tjukurpa/Wapar belief system. Even more sacred is Kata Tjuta ("Many Heads"), 36 momentous red domes bulging out of the earth 50km (31 miles) to the west.

Anangu leaders have reestablished the historic names Uluru (instead of the colonial name Ayers Rock) and Kata Tjuta (instead of the Olgas), but they haven't banned either rock climbers or sightseeing flights over Uluru—they simply request climbers to refrain from violating the sacred site. Focused on scaling the rock, climbers rarely take time to experience the monolith's richness—the wildlife that thrives in the potholes and overhangs of the red rock surface, the little coves hiding water holes and Aboriginal rock art. But you can see all this on a paved 9.7km (6-mile) **Base Walk** around Uluru, or an easy 1km (.6-mile)

Uluru-Kata Tjuta National Park.

round-trip loop from the Mutitjulu parking lot. Even better is the free daily 90-minute **Mala Walk** with a ranger—often an Aborigine—who can explain the significance of the rock art and the Creation narrative related to Uluru. It's no coincidence that this hike is named after the mala, or rufous hare-wallabies; the Anangu consider them important ancestral guardians, and recently an enclosure was built nearby in the park for a group of ranger-bred mala. Extinct in the wild, the species are to be reintroduced to a landscape they haven't inhabited since the mid-1900s.

Though it looks like a giant meteorite, Uluru did not fall from the sky; it is a mass of hardened sediment heaved upward from the floor of an ancient inland sea. The same seismic forces created the domes of Kata Tjuta, but their conglomerate rock yielded far more dramatically to the sculpting power of rain and temperature. At Kata Tjuta, there are two routes winding through the other-worldly domes: the 7.4km (4.6-mile) **Valley of the Winds walk** or an easy 2.4km (1.5-mile) **Gorge walk.**

Just gazing upon Uluru should be enough—there's something undeniably spiritual in its massive shape, heaving powerfully upward from the dunes, changing color dramatically depending on the slant of the sun. The best time to visit is sunset, when gaudy oranges, peaches, pinks, reds, and then indigo and deep violet creep across its face as if it were a giant opal. But there's something to be said, too, for experiencing the rosy spectacle of Uluru gradually unveiled by dawn, hailed by a chorus of twittering bird song.

ⓘ **Uluru-Kata Tjuta Cultural Centre** (℗ **61/8/8956 3138**)

✈ Ayers Rock (Connellan) Airport

⊨ $$$ **Emu Walk Apartments,** Yulara Dr., Ayers Rock Resort (℗ **61/8/8957 7888;** www.voyages.com.au). $$$ **Outback Pioneer Hotel and Lodge,** Yulara Dr., Ayers Rock Resort (℗ **61/8/8957 7888;** www.voyages.com.au).

Lutherstadt Wittenberg
Nailed to the Door
Wittenberg, Germany

WITTENBERG HAS SURVIVED A LOT OF TUMULT, BUT CLIMATE CHANGE PRESENTS A WHOLE NEW challenge. Though repairs and renovations were promptly carried out after 2002's major flood, the probability of another flood looms on the horizon.

There's a reason they call it a flood plain. Swollen by heavy rains and excessive snowmelt in the Czech mountains, in August 2002 the Elbe River raged through Saxony, looking for a place to spread out. When it reached Wittenberg, the Elbe was already 7.5m (25 ft.) higher than usual, ready to burst its banks. While the church spires of the old town center, set on higher ground north of the river, escaped the worst of it, the waters simply gushed into the flatter working-class suburb of Pratau, turning it into one big lagoon.

As the waters rose, the infrastructure of this former East German region was strained to the utmost. Wittenberg's flood defenses were simply overwhelmed; the main road and railway connections were washed out for days. Residents were evacuated, and when they returned, they found their abandoned homes sodden and thick mud slopped everywhere.

Most of the sights of Wittenberg—officially renamed Lutherstadt Wittenberg, to honor its connection with the great religious reformer Martin Luther—are clustered mainly in the historic center, away from the industrial clutter of the modern town. Look for the round, crown-topped tower of the **Schlosskirche at Friedrichstrasse 1A,** where Martin Luther nailed his radical 95 Theses to the door in 1517 (the brass doors there today are a 19th-century addition, engraved with his theses—in church Latin, of course). Luther's

affectingly simple tomb is inside. Luther preached most of his dangerously dissident sermons, however, at the twin-towered Gothic parish church of **Stadtkirche St. Marien,** Judenstr. 35, where he's even depicted in the great altarpiece painted by Lucas Cranach the Elder (you can see Cranach's house on Marksplatz).

After splitting from the Catholic faith, Luther—no longer bound by priestly celibacy—also married his wife, a former nun, in the Stadtkirche. Their family home, **the Lutherhalle, Collegienstr. 54**—a former Augustinian monastery disbanded at the start of the Reformation—has been turned into a museum displaying Luther's desk, his pulpit, first editions of his books, and the wood-paneled lecture hall where he taught students. The towering **Luthereiche** (Luther's Oak) at the end of Collegienstrasse outside the Elster gate commemorates the spot where Luther in 1520 defiantly burned the papal edict that excommunicated him. Statues of Luther and his humanist scholar friend, Philip Melancthon, have been erected in the cobbled central square, in front of the big white City Hall (Rathaus).

✈ Berlin

🚆 Wittenberg

🛏$$ **Grüne Tanne,** Am Teich 1 (✆ **49/ 3491/6290**)

The Great Stupa of Sanchi
In the Shadow of Bhopal
Madhya Pradesh, India

A THOROUGH 20TH-CENTURY RESTORATION BROUGHT THE GREAT STUPA BACK TO TOP condition. But since the 1984 environmental disaster at nearby Bhopal, tourism has dried up. Is the Great Stupa facing a fourth chapter of decline?

Three times in its history, the Great Stupa of Sanchi was nearly destroyed—once by vandals in the 2nd century B.C.; a second time from the 13th to the 18th century, when Buddhism withered in India; and a third time in the late 19th century when amateur archaeologists and treasure hunters ravaged the newly rediscovered ruins.

It's a shame, because there's something innately appealing about this plump domed Buddhist monument, set serenely on a hill with lovely views of the surrounding countryside. India's finest example of ancient Buddhist architecture, it's the centerpiece of a complex founded in the 3rd century B.C. by the Mauryan emperor Ashoka, who converted to Buddhism after massacring thousands in his military campaigns. Excavations to date have unearthed about 55 temples, pillars, stupas, and monasteries in the complex, an amazing continuum of Buddhist architectural styles. Yet it doesn't overwhelm the visitor—it's a low-rise site of gentle domes and spaces for contemplation.

The proportions of the Great Stupa itself are so harmonious, you're surprised when you get up close to see how big it actually is. At 16m (52 ft.) high, nearly eight stories tall, it anchors the center of the complex like a massive beehive, or maybe a flying saucer. The stupa may once have held inside some ashes of the Buddha, who died in 483 B.C. (smaller stupas alongside, like satellites around a mother ship, contain ashes of his disciples).Originally it was a smaller brick hemisphere; in the 2nd century B.C. the brick dome was enlarged considerably with a sandstone casing, and a balustrade was added. Later, around 25 B.C., four intricately carved gateways of finer-grained sandstone were placed around the stupa, facing the four points of the compass. Mounted on these gates are intricately carved story panels depicting episodes from the life of Buddha. (Notice that the Buddha is never pictured as a human—look for him instead as a lotus, a wheel, a bodhi tree, or a pair of feet.) As a classic stupa, it also has circling pathways designed for meditative circumambulations.

Originally the stupa was a much more gaudy affair—its dome and supporting plinth were coated with white-lime concrete, the railways and gateway were painted red, and the surface of the stupa was painted with swags and garlands. The antenna-like spire on top would have been gilded, too. But it wears its present weathered look well—the peace of the centuries seems to settle upon it like the folds of a sari.

(i) **Madhya Pradesh State Tourism Development Corp.** (www.mptourism.com)

✈ Bhopal

🛏 $$ **Jehan Numa Palace,** 157 Shamla Hill, Bhopal (© **91/755/266-1100;** www.hoteljehanumapalace.com)

Ajanta Caves
Worshiping Art
Maharashtra, India

MORE THAN 2,000 YEARS OLD, THE AJANTA CAVES DISPLAY ROCK PAINTINGS THAT HAVE survived for centuries. However, clumsy restoration and the presence of so many admirers are hastening their decay.

It's quite a proposition, getting to the ancient cave temple of Ajanta, in far-flung Maharashtra, India, about 500km (310 miles) east of Mumbai. What makes it worth the trip is not just the beauty of this Buddhist worship site—though it certainly is beautiful, a horseshoe-shaped cliff above a hairpin bend in the Waghora River—it's the fact that it was chiseled patiently out of the cliff face, chip by chip, using nothing but handheld tools.

Remote as it is, thousands of visitors come here every year, particularly in the summer months. The crush inside the caves can be stifling. Visitors are asked to take their shoes off, photography is forbidden, and barriers prevent people from touching the artworks. The rock surfaces need to be treated to protect the art against inevitable water leakage. The painting in some caves survived the centuries better than in others, where only tantalizing fragments of images remain. Some earlier attempts at restoring the paintings have even worsened their condition. The sculptures have survived better—proof of how hard this stone was to carve—though some are pitted with age.

Ajanta is an incredibly old site—begun in the 2nd century B.C. and executed over the next 700 years by Buddhist monks. Some of its 29 caves are *chaityas*—shrines—and others are *viharas*, or monasteries, where the artworks were meant to inspire spiritual contemplation on the life and teachings of Buddha. Cave 1 is perhaps the most famous *vihara*, renowned for the two fantastic murals of bodhisattvas (precursors of Buddha) flanking the doorway of the antechamber—on one side Avalokitesvara with his thunderbolt in hand, on the other Padmapani holding a water lily. The great *mandala*, or sacred meditative design, on the ceiling of Cave 2 is awesome. Cave 16 has a lovely painting of the princess Sundari, wife of the Buddha's half-brother (she's swooning at the news that her husband is becoming a monk); the most brilliantly painted is Cave 17, where maidens float overhead, accompanied by celestial musicians, lotus

Cave 26 at the Ajanta Caves.

385

petals, and scrollwork. Check out the huge sculpture of the reclining Buddha in the richly carved Cave 26.

It has been said that all Indian art stems from Ajanta—and yet, incredibly, for centuries it lay remote and forgotten, rediscovered accidentally by a boar-hunting British soldier in 1819. As you walk through, don't get overwhelmed by the sheer profusion of detail. Focus instead on imagining the anonymous monks long ago, tending to their devotions, and creating immortal art in the process.

✈ Aurangabad

🛏 $$ **The Ambassador Ajanta,** Jalna Rd., Aurangabad (✆ **0240/248-5211;** www.ambassadorindia.com). $$ **Quality Inn The Meadows,** Gat no. 135 and 136, **Village Mitmita,** Aurangabad (✆ **0240/ 267-7412;** meadows@gnbom.global. net.in).

🛏 $$ **Les Terrasses Poulard,** Grande Rue (✆ **33/2/33-60-14-09;** www.mere poulard.fr)

Pilgrimage Sites 412

Borobudur

Ascending to Nirvana

Central Java, Indonesia

WHEN MOUNT MERAPI ERUPTED IN LATE 2010, MORE THAN 300 LIVES WERE LOST AND volcanic ash was spewed on Borobudur, the largest Buddhist temple standing. UNESCO helped to clear away the ash, and the temple is once again open to visitors.

It was built to be walked on—the winding pathway of this stepped pyramid was specifically designed for meditation, and you'll see hosts of saffron-robed Buddhist priests pacing along, chanting as they wind around the 3.2km-long (2-mile) route to the top. Set on a smooth green plain south of Magelang on the gardenlike island of Java, Borobudur is not only the largest Buddhist monument in the world, but quite simply is one of the most stunning architectural creations you'll ever see. Some two million blocks of lava rock completed the original pyramid-like design, though some have been lost over the centuries. Seen from the ground, it looks like a mountain, bristling with odd little spires; seen from above, it looks like an open lotus blossom, the sacred expression of Buddhism.

But the true brilliance of Borobudur can be understood only if you walk around it. The first six levels (plus another one left underground to stabilize the pyramid) are rectangular in shape, decorated with sculpted bas-relief panels, 1,460 in all. Seen in order, the panels are more or less a spiritual textbook, depicting the life and lessons of Buddha. Each ascending level represents a higher stage of man's spiritual journey.

The top three levels, however, are circular terraces with no ornamentation— Buddhism considers simplicity far more virtuous than decoration. Instead, these upper levels hold a series of beehivelike stone stupas, their bricks arranged in perforated checkerboard patterns, with stone Buddhas tucked inside. Each inscrutable Buddha sits cross-legged, making a hand gesture that signifies one of five spiritual attainments. At the top, one large central stupa crowns the pyramid, empty inside— scholars still debate whether it once contained a bigger Buddha, or whether its emptiness symbolizes the blessed state of nirvana.

One of the many mysteries of Borobudur is why it was ever abandoned. When Sir Thomas Stanford Raffles discovered it in 1814, Borobudur was buried under layers of ash from nearby Mount Merapi. Perhaps it was buried Pompeii-style; or maybe a series of eruptions brought famine to the region, causing the population to move away. Either way, Borobudur lay forgotten for centuries. Nowadays, it's Java's most popular tourist destination. Despite the level of visitor traffic, however, a meditative, tenuous peace still holds sway—given the recent volcanic activity, the site proves just how fragile our ancient archaeological treasures can be.

✈ Yogvakarta

🛏 $$$ **Sheraton Mustika,** JL Laksda Adisucipto, Yogyakarta (© **62/274-488588;** www.sheraton.com). $$ **Mano-hara Hotel,** Borobudur Archaeological Park, Magelang (© **361/731520;** www.baliwww.com).

413 Pilgrimage Sites

Santiago de Compostela
A Pilgrim's Progress
Spain & France

THE PILGRIM'S ROUTE ALONG SANTIAGO DE COMPOSTELA IS AT RISK DUE TO HIGHWAY construction that has already claimed 4.8km (3 miles) of the sacred path.

All roads in Spain once led to the northwestern city of Santiago de Compostela, where the Catholic faithful flocked to visit the **tomb of St. James,** hoping thereby to win a spot in heaven. The pilgrimage route ran from Paris over the Pyrenees and along Spain's northern coast—an enormous distance even by car. (Some hardy souls still make the trek on foot.) Even if you drive only the last section, from Pamplona through León to Santiago de Compostela, you can imagine the joy of weary pilgrims arriving at last in front of this glorious Romanesque cathedral.

Unfortunately, these ancient roads are at risk from the construction of a major new highway. Although alternative highway routes have been proposed, construction has started on the A-12 highway between Santo Domingo de la Calzada and Burgos, which will run counter to the path, and a few miles of the route have already been slashed. Which is all the more reason to try to visit Santiago de Compostela *now,* before more pieces of the path are cut off.

Pilgrimages on this sacred path began in A.D. 813, when priests unearthed what were said to be the remains of St. James (Santiago, in Spanish), the patron saint of Spain. In the 11th century, this huge cathedral was built over his tomb, and a trickle of local pilgrims grew into an international flood. From the Praza do Obradoido, admire its three ornate towers and the wrought-iron enclosed staircase; in an arch inside the middle tower is a statue of St. James, dressed in traditional pilgrim garb (wide-brimmed hat and walking staff), because he traveled widely around western Europe spreading the gospel. The west door's **triple-arched front portico** is famous, with sculpted biblical figures representing the Last Judgment. Look for St. James, in the center beneath Christ. The carved column under him bears five grooves worn into the stone by centuries of pilgrims, leaning forward to place their hands on the pillar and knock foreheads with the carved face at the bottom—the likeness of the portico's designer, Maestro Mateo. It's nicknamed—what else?—Santo dos Croques (Saint of the Bumps).

In our age of jet travel, it's amazing to recall that most medieval folks spent their entire lives in one village, without TV or newspapers or the Internet to tell them about the rest of the world. The few who took a pilgrimage played a vital role in disseminating European culture. Inside, notice how wide the barrel-vaulted aisles are, built to accommodate hordes of pilgrims. On the altar is a huge golden mollusk shell that pilgrims traditionally kissed, as well as a great silver incense burner—the *botufumiero*—which purified the air at night while hundreds of pilgrims slept in the cathedral.

The remains of St. James are in a silver urn in the crypt. Hard as it is to believe,

they went missing for almost 300 years, when, in the 16th century, with Sir Francis Drake raiding the coast, the church fathers hid them so well that they weren't found again until 1879. To verify their authenticity, a sliver of the skull of St. James was fetched from Italy—and it fit perfectly into the recently discovered skeleton.

ⓘ **Catedral de Santiago,** Praza do Obradoiro (✆ **34/981/58-35-48;** www.catedral desantiago.es)

✈ Santiago de Compostela

🛏 **$ Hotel Real, Caldereria 49** (✆ **34/ 981/56-92-90;** www.hotelreal.com). **$$ Los Abetos Hotel,** San Lázaro (✆ **34/981/ 55-70-26;** www.hotellosabetos.com).

TOUR www.followthecamino.com/en/ credential

Pilgrimage Sites **414**

The Last Supper
da Vinci's Wall
Santa Maria delle Grazie, Milan, Italy

IT'S A MASTERPIECE OF COMPOSITION, BOTH TECHNICAL AND DRAMATIC, AND NO MATTER HOW often it's parodied (Mel Brooks, Monty Python, and George Carlin have all had a go at it), the original still takes your breath away. Without proper maintenance, however, we could lose this treasure forever.

It's been said that all that's left of the original *Last Supper* is a "few isolated streaks of fading color"—everything else was layered on by later hands. Leonardo da Vinci's masterful picture of Jesus and his disciples at their Passover Seder began to disintegrate almost as soon as Leonardo finished it, for in executing this mural on the wall of a convent in Milan, he experimented with risky new paints and application techniques. But it is so clearly a work of genius that over the centuries artists and restorers felt drawn to save it, repainting it in the 1700s, the 1800s, and

again quite recently; though modern techniques have improved the sensitivity of these repaintings, it's often impossible to tell what was painted by da Vinci and what was painted by later restorers. In 1943, a bomb demolished the roof—luckily that wall wasn't hit—and the painting stood exposed to the elements for 3 years. It just may be the master's greatest painting, but it's a wonder that anything is left of it at all.

Though born in Florence, Leonardo da Vinci spent many years in Milan (1482–99 and 1506–13), under the patronage of the dukes of Milan. The finicky da Vinci produced endless studies and sketches for projects he never finished; one he did complete, however, was this mural that Duke Ludovico commissioned for the convent of Santa Marie delle Grazie church. Set above a doorway in what was once a dining hall, *The Last Supper (Il Cenacolo Vinciano)* is a huge artwork, 8.5m (28 ft.) wide and 4.6m (15 ft.) tall. There's nothing static about this scene: Jesus, hands outspread (as if to display his future wounds), has just announced that one of his followers will betray him, and the disciples all lean away, aghast, each in his own manner protesting his fidelity. (Judas is the one with his face in shadow, already clutching the bag of money he was paid to betray Jesus.) Christ's sorrowful figure is isolated, the curved pediment of a doorway over his head suggesting a halo; light streams in from the windows behind him, while darkness looms behind the disciples.

Only 25 viewers are admitted at a time (be prepared to wait in line), and you must pass through antipollutant chambers before you get your allotted 15 minutes in front of the painting. A lot to go through, but *The Last Supper* is worth it.

ⓘ **Piazza Santa Maria delle Grazie** (off Corso Magenta; ✆ **39/2/4987588**)

✈ Milan's Aeroporto di Linate or Aeroporto Malpensa

🛏 $$$ **Four Seasons Hotel Milano,** Via Gesú 8 (✆ **39/2/77088;** www.four seasons.com). $$ **Antica Locanda Leonardo,** Corso Magenta 78 (✆ **39/02/48014197;** www.leoloc.com).

---

415 Churches

La Sagrada Família
The Flower of Modernismo
Barcelona, Spain

THE UNFINISHED LA SAGRADA FAMÍLIA IS SCHEDULED TO BE FINALLY COMPLETED IN 2026. But will ongoing construction on an underground tunnel for a high-speed train shake its foundations?

Amid the massed Gothic cathedrals of Europe, La Sagrada Família rises like a breath of fresh air—the exuberantly un-Gothic masterpiece of the great 20th-century architect Antonio Gaudí. Begun in 1882, this church is the glorious flowering of Gaudí's signature style: *modernismo*, a romantic, voluptuous Catalonian offshoot of Art Nouveau that flourished in Barcelona from about 1890 to 1910.

But when Gaudí died in 1926, La Sagrada Família (the Church of the Holy Family) was still far from done. Two portals were later completed, in startlingly contrasting styles by two different sculptors—the stark, blocky figures of the Passion facade and the more fanciful, Gaudí-like Nativity facade—but the Glory portal, the transepts, and several of its 18 spiky mosaic-crowned spires are still unfinished. The joyous flowerlike vaulting of the central nave wasn't completed until 2000. With no government or church funding, the project depends on tourism revenues and private donations; its projected 2026 completion date is seriously in doubt. And now, to cap it all off, an underground tunnel for a new high-speed train from Barcelona to Madrid is in the works (scheduled to be completed in 2013), and drilling will happen only 4m (13 ft.) from the cathedral, possibly shaking it to its intricately engineered foundations.

389

As it expanded beyond its historic core in the late 19th century, Barcelona offered a virtual blank slate for a gifted crew of architects eager to express their Catalan identity—and Gaudí stood head and shoulders above them all. (Other examples of his style can be found along the Passeig de Gràcia and out in the northern suburbs at Parc Güell.) Their *modernismo* rejected monumental symmetry and went instead for forms found in nature, with lots of handcrafted decoration. Gaudí in particular loved drooping masses, melting horizontal lines, and giddy spirals. This cathedral erupts skyward with clusters of honeycombed spires, looking more like encrusted stalagmites than like traditional Gothic towers; its arches are neither pointed Gothic nor rounded Romanesque, but tapering curves of a certain Star Trek–ish flair. (Gaudí's versions of flying buttresses are definitely Space Age struts.) Sculpted figures seem to grow organically out of its portals and arches; brightly colored fruits and flowers sprout from the fanciful pinnacles. La Sagrada Família's rose windows really do look like roses, its fluted columns like flower stalks, rising to a vaulted ceiling pattern that looks like nothing more than a field spangled with daisies.

Gaudí's original plans were discovered only in 1950; with those in hand, the directors of the ongoing project hope to execute the cathedral just as he intended it. But unlike Europe's Gothic cathedrals, which took leisurely centuries to complete, La Sagrada Família is in a race against time. Will that high-speed train beat it to the finish line?

ⓘ **Carrer de Sardenya,** Barcelona (ℂ **34/ 93-207-30-31;** www.sagradafamilia.org or www.sossagradafamilia.org)

✈ Barcelona

🛏 $$$ **Hotel Hesperia Sarriá,** Los Vergós 20 (ℂ **34/93-204-55-51**). $$ **Catalonia Plaza Cataluña,** Bergara 11 (ℂ **34/ 934-451-530;** www.hoteles-catalonia.com).

Churches **416**

The Abbey of Mont-St-Michel
Time & Tide
Normandy, France

WHEN YOU THINK OF THE ENGINEERING REQUIRED TO BUILD THIS IMMENSE CHURCH ON THIS tide-scoured outcrop, it's a marvel it has stood this long. Short-sighted renovations that built the causeway and altered natural tidal patterns have exacerbated the silting up of the bay. Can the government reverse this?

Approaching across the coastal flatlands, you see its Gothic splendor erupt toward the sky, usually cloaked in dramatic fog. Set upon a massive rock just off the Normandy coast, the great Gothic abbey church of Mont-St-Michel rises dramatically from its rampart walls to an ethereal spire topped with a gilded statue of the archangel Michael, the abbey's guardian spirit.

Yet in the past couple of centuries, St. Michael seems to have let down his guard.

The narrow land bridge that once connected Mont-St-Michel to the mainland, exposed only at low tide, was beefed up in 1879 into a permanent causeway, accessible at all hours. Meanwhile, the local folks kept on tinkering with the natural tidal processes—polderizing shallow parts of the bay to create pastureland, making a canal out of the Couesnon River—until the bay gradually silted up. Finally, in June 2006, the French government took action, initiating a hydraulic dam project. The dam

Mont-St-Michel.

is now completed, and will gradually remove the sand between Mont-St-Michael and the mainland.

In the Middle Ages, this was a popular pilgrimage site, founded in the 8th century by St. Aubert; medieval pilgrims could get here only at low tide, walking across treacherous tidal sands, a challenge that increased the spiritual value of the journey. Enhanced over the next few centuries, however, as the abbey's monks grew richer and more powerful, the abbey came to look more like a fortress than a holy retreat—a fact that served it well in the Hundred Years' War (1337–1453), when it almost miraculously resisted capture by the English. The rampart walls also made it easy to convert to a prison after the monks were disbanded, in the days of the French Revolution. Since the late 19th century it's been a national monument, not a church, although recently some new monks have settled in as well.

It's a steep walk to the abbey up Grande Rue, lined with half-timbered 15th- and 16th-century houses. Inside the abbey walls are more staircases to climb. But it's worth it to investigate the abbey's stunning Gothic interiors, most notably the **Salle des Chevaliers** (Hall of the Knights) and graceful cloisters with rosy pink granite columns. Crowning the summit is the splendid abbey church—note the round Romanesque arches in the 11th-century nave and transept, transitioning to the pointy flamboyant Gothic arches of the 15th-century choir area. In the summer, if you're staying on the mount, you can visit the church at night—not a bad idea for avoiding hordes of day-trippers.

ⓘ **The Abbey of Mont-St-Michel** (✆ **33/2/33-89-80-00**)

✈ Orly and Charles de Gaulle

🚆 Rennes

🛏 $$ **Les Terrasses Poulard,** Grande Rue (✆ **33/2/33-60-14-09;** www.mere poulard.fr)

St. Mary's Church

Quintessentially English

Stow-in-Lindsey, Lincolnshire, United Kingdom

POET LAUREATE SIR JOHN BETJEMAN ONCE CALLED THIS RUGGED GOLDEN STONE CHURCH THE "finest Norman church in Lincolnshire." And at over 1,000 years old, it still stands. But with crumbling stones and dwindling congregations, how long will it last?

Poet laureate Sir John Betjeman may have gotten the dates wrong—some historians believe that St. Mary's predates the Norman invasion, having been founded in A.D. 678, burned down by Danish invaders in 870, and rebuilt between 1034 and 1050. It's clearly one of the oldest parish churches in England, with a significant number of its early architectural elements intact—timber roof beams, tall rounded Saxon arches, even ancient graffiti depicting a Viking longboat scratched onto a stone wall.

St. Mary's was once the head church of the diocese of Lincolnshire—around town it's referred to as Stow Minster, and townsfolk still blame those upstart Normans for moving the cathedral to the nearby city of Lincoln. But despite its substantial size, today St. Mary's is just a rural parish church, and like many parish churches in the U.K., its dwindling congregation can't afford to keep up with repairs. And when your church is over 1,000 years old, expect a lot of repairs.

In the Victorian era, St. Mary's barely escaped demolition because its rector at the time had a personal fortune to spend on having it restored; today's rector has no such option. St. Mary's vestry estimates that it will take between £2 and £3 million to fix the church's lead roof, replace crumbling masonry, make the building watertight, and then hire skilled craftsmen to restore the historic decorative details inside, a project they hope to complete by 2015. Even with help from English Heritage and the World Monuments Fund—both of them concerned about losing such a quintessentially English treasure—that's a lot of money to raise.

Within the mottled stone walls of St. Mary's, you can trace a continuous tapestry of English history. Two early English saints, St. Hugh and St. Etheldreda, are associated with the church and depicted in its stained-glass windows. One of its earliest benefactors was the 11th-century Earl of Mercia, Leofric, and his wife Lady Godiva, famous for riding naked through the streets of Coventry to protest high taxes. There's a ghostly 13th-century wall painting of the great English martyr St. Thomas à Becket, an ornate 15th-century stone font with pagan symbols like a dragon and a Green Man carved around its base, and a fine Jacobean carved pulpit. Some of the Pilgrims who later colonized America worshiped here in the 16th century. In World War II, its square crenellated stone tower was used as a landmark for bomber pilots. It's more than just a village church—it's England in microcosm, and that's worth saving.

ⓘ **Church St.,** Stow-in-Lindsey (16km/10 miles northwest of Lincoln; www.stow minster.org.uk)

✈ Heathrow

🚂 Lincoln

🛏 $$ **White Hart Hotel,** Bailgate, Lincoln (© **44/1522/526222**). $$ **Hillcrest Hotel,** 15 Lindum Terrace, Lincoln (© **44/1522/510182;** www.hillcrest-hotel.com).

The Painted Churches of Moldavia
Picture-Book Walls
Northern Romania

ONLY ABOUT A DOZEN OF THESE PAINTED CHURCHES REMAIN TODAY, TUCKED AWAY IN SMALL out-of-the-way towns near the Ukrainian border. Often their congregations are too poor to properly restore and preserve these treasures.

In medieval northern Europe, those grand Gothic windows of stained glass had a purpose—to tell Bible stories to an illiterate congregation. In Greece and other Orthodox countries, intricate mosaics did the same job. But only in northern Romania, in a kingdom once known as Moldavia, even the simplest country church might be painted inside and out with vivid, dramatic narrative murals.

Amid the turmoil of Ottoman invasion, from 1522 to 1547 a handful of now-anonymous artists moved around this mountainous countryside painting frescoes on church after church. (Note the churches' distinctive regional architecture, with round towers and apses, octagonal steeples set on a star-shaped base, and wide-eaved roofs like brimmed hats clapped on top.) These itinerant artists used simple paints, easily manufactured from local minerals; if they were lucky, they were able to slip in a touch of gold leaf or precious lapis lazuli blue. Household ingredients like charcoal, egg, vinegar, and honey were thrown in to preserve the color, which evidently worked—they have withstood the rugged Carpathian climate for over 450 years. In fact, the outside frescoes often have fared better than the inside ones, which are darkened by centuries of incense fumes and candle smoke.

If you can see only one, make it **Voroneţ**, with its amazing Last Judgment on one large west wall; for some reason Voroneţ, nicknamed "the Sistine Chapel of the East," had access to plenty of lapis lazuli, and the blues glow richly here. But **Humor** is worth a detour for all the daring political references its artist slipped in—look for turbaned Turkish enemies in many of his murals. Green is the dominant color at charming little **Arbore**, which has a detailed painting of the story of Genesis. **Sucevita** is not just one church but an entire fortified monastery compound, with thousands of pictures—notice the one blank wall, which was left unfinished, the story goes, when the painter fell off his scaffolding to his death. **Moldoviţa** has a particularly panoramic depiction of the Siege of Constantinople, a major event for the Greek Orthodox Church. All five can be visited in a few hours, on a loop of back roads west of Suceava. Catch them before they fade away.

✈ Suceava

🛏 $$ **Best Western Hotel Bucovina,** 4 Bucovina Ave., Gura Humorului (✆ **40/230/207000**; www.bestwestern.com). $$ **Balada Hotel,** Str. Mitropoliei 3, Suceava (✆ **40/230/522146**).

Mission San Miguel Arcángel
Mission Accomplished
San Miguel, California

AFTER INTENSIVE REPAIRS DUE TO THE DAMAGE SUSTAINED FROM A 2003 EARTHQUAKE, THE mission's courtyard and convent building have reopened, and its church welcomes visitors. Some earthquake-proofing has been done, but will it be enough to protect this historic mission?

It was like a lifeline of civilization along the California coast—the string of adobe monasteries built between 1769 and 1823 by a crew of Franciscan friars, determined to convert the native Indians to Christianity. By the time the padres arrived to found Mission San Miguel Arcángel on July 25, 1797 (it was the 16th of 21 missions), the Indians were eagerly awaiting them. They knew they'd find prosperity in the mission's vineyards, fields, and pastures, not to mention learning vital trades: carpentry, masonry, weaving, blacksmithing, leather work.

While many of the other missions have been turned into tourist sights, San Miguel still functions as a parish church—or at least it did until December 22, 2003. That's when the San Simeon earthquake rattled the central California coast, severely damaging the 200-year-old mission, its foundations already weakened by years of vibrations from the nearby Union Pacific Railroad.

Though San Miguel is one of only four missions owned today by the Franciscan order, it wasn't always so holy—during the California Gold Rush, it was a store, saloon, and dance hall, returned to the Franciscans only in 1928. But through all those years, local priests tended the plain, rectangular adobe main church; until the earthquake, it was judged to be the most authentically preserved of the 21 missions. In fact, its interior has never been repainted—especially important because its walls were elaborately decorated by

Indian artisans, guided by a Spanish priest named Esteban Munras. The challenge of preserving those time-worn frescoes while making the necessary structural repairs infinitely complicates the job at Mission San Miguel, though techniques developed here will no doubt come in handy when the other California missions face their own restorations.

Although most of the missions were closer to the coast, the friars doggedly went where the Indians were, choosing this valley despite its poor soil and hot climate. Being relatively out of the way, it got less tourist traffic than the more famous missions in Santa Barbara, San Juan Capistrano, and Carmel, which accounts for its unrenovated, and therefore authentic, condition. The wood-beamed main church with its historic frescoes is lovely, as is the Mission Museum in the convent building. Take the time to stroll along the cool arched cloister, overlooking its fine old cactus garden—like Mission San Miguel, those hardy cactuses are proven survivors.

(i) (C) **805/467-2131**

✈ San Luis Obispo

⌂ $$ **Garden Street Inn,** 1212 Garden St., San Luis Obispo ((C) **800/488-2045** or 805/545-9802; www.gardenstreetinn. com). $$ **Best Western Cavalier Oceanfront Resort,** 9415 Hearst Dr. (Calif. 1), San Simeon ((C) **800/826-8168** or 805/927-4688; www.bestwestern.com).

420 Churches

Unity Temple
The Birth of Modernism
Oak Park, Illinois

FRANK LLOYD WRIGHT CONSIDERED UNITY TEMPLE TO BE HIS CONTRIBUTION TO MODERNISM. Today the building is showing its age with extensive structural damage.

After a fire destroyed its church around 1900, a Unitarian Universalist congregation asked one of its members, Frank Lloyd Wright, to design an affordable replacement. Using poured concrete with metal reinforcements—a necessity due to a small $40,000 budget—Wright created a building that on the outside seems as forbidding as a mausoleum but inside contains all the elements of the Prairie School that has made Wright's name immortal. Wright believed conventional church architecture was overpowering—he complained that he didn't feel a part of the Gothic-style cathedral across the street, for example—and Unity Temple was intended to offer a new model for houses of worship.

Yet his vision in this regard was somewhat confused and contradictory. He wanted Unity Temple to be "democratic," but perhaps Wright was unable to subdue his own personal hubris and hauteur in the creative process, for the ultimate effect of his chapel, and much of the building's interior, is grand and imperial. This is no simple meetinghouse; instead, its principal chapel looks like the chamber of the Roman Senate.

Wright was a true hands-on, can-do person; he knew his materials as intimately as the artisans who carried out his plans. He added pigment to the plaster (rather than the paint) to achieve a pale, natural effect. Since the church was located on a busy street, he eschewed street-level windows to cut down on noise—instead he used stained-glass windows in the upper-floor windows and ceiling, all done in soft earth tones to bring nature into the mix. His use of wood trim and other decorative touches is still exciting to behold—his sensitivity to grain, tone, and placement was akin to that of an exceptionally gifted woodworker. His stunning, almost minimalist use of form is what still sets him apart as a relevant and brilliant artist.

In 2009, the National Trust for Historic Preservation listed Unity Temple as one of the 11 most endangered historic places in America. Like many of Wright's buildings, most of the problems stem from the design itself. Wright did not include expansion joints, so there is a great deal of cracking throughout the building. Instead of gutters, he also opted for an internal drainage system. The result is that when it rains, water overflows the drains and damages the roof. The good news is that a Unity Temple Restoration Foundation is supervising repairs, under the watchful eye of Chicago architect Gunny Harboe. And while Unity Temple has its problems, it is still considered modern more than 100 years after its construction—let's hope repairs will keep it that way for many more years to come.

ⓘ **Unity Temple Restoration Foundation,** 875 Lake St. (✆ **708/383-8873;** www.unitytemple-utrf.org)

✈ Chicago O'Hare International Airport

🛏 $$ **The Write Inn,** 211 N. Oak Park Ave., Oak Park (✆ **708/383-4800;** www. writeinn.com). $$ **The Carelton of Oak Park,** 110 Pleasant St., Oak Park (✆ **708/848-5000;** www.carletonhotel.com).

10 Prehistoric Mounds to Visit

Barrows, tumuli, cairns, dolmens—whatever you call them, symmetrical earthen mounds (often heaped over a stone structure) were independently developed by ancient cultures around the world. Today their gentle rounded shapes bear mute, mysterious witness to the lives of another era. Perhaps because they were usually built as graves—a honor reserved for warriors or rulers and their families—a spooky, spiritual aura often surrounds them.

Here are a few that have been excavated and preserved:

421 Newark Earthworks, Newark, Ohio   These gentle grassy humps, 3 to 14 feet (1–4.3m) high, enclose a space big enough to hold four Roman Colosseums and are aligned for lunar observations twice as accurately as Stonehenge—it's only when seen from the air that their geometric precision becomes evident, a 40-acre (16-hectare) octagon enclosing a 20-acre (8-hectare) circle. The Hopewell Indians built the mounds around A.D. 250, but in 1933, the property's owners built a golf course over them. A truce between the club and anthropologists resulted in a viewing platform near the parking lot. © *800/600-7178 or 740/344-1919. www.archaeology.org/online.*

422 Serpent Mound, Locust Grove, Ohio   Built by the prehistoric Fort Ancient tribe around A.D. 1000, this earthwork in rural southern Ohio isn't a simple circular mound but a sinuous 1,330-foot-long (405m) shape that, seen from the air, perfectly represents a serpent swallowing an egg. Scholars aren't sure whether it was built to tell a myth or to commemorate an astronomical event like an eclipse or a comet; its head is aligned with the summer solstice. © *937/587-2796. www.greatserpentmound.com.*

423 Cahokia Mounds, Collinsville, Illinois   The biggest mound in the Western Hemisphere sits on this 2,200-acre (890-hectare) site across the Mississippi River from St. Louis, in what was once (A.D. 1100–1200) the biggest city north of Mexico. Its builders, the mysterious Mississippian people, erected 120 other immense earthen structures here, evidently for public ceremonies (there are remains of human sacrifice), and religious temples; the big one, 100-foot-high Monk's Mound, was a royal residence. © *618/346-5160. www.cahokiamounds.org.*

424 Ocmulgee Old Fields, Macon, Georgia   Until the 1930s, when archaeologists finally excavated these ceremonial Mississippian mounds, they were encroached upon by farmland. Although it was declared a national monument in 1936, the government acquired only 702 acres (284 hectares); many mounds are still on private property. © *478/752-8257. www.nps.gov/ocmu.*

425 Effigy Mounds, Harpers Ferry, Iowa   Built around A.D. 600 by a tribe of ancient nomads, these are not only mounds but mounds in the shape of tribal totems—bison, deer, turtles, lizards, and especially bears, eagles, and falcons. This 2,500-acre (1,000-hectare) park on the bluffs of the upper Mississippi River has more than 200 of these mounds, some of which bear traces of fire pits, suggesting that their purpose was highly ceremonial. © *563/873-3491. www.nps.gov/efmo.*

426 Manitou Mounds, Stratton, Ontario The Ojibway name is Kay-Nah-Chi-Wah-Nung, "Place of the Long Rapids," and this site on the north bank of the Rainy River has been held sacred by the Ojibway for over 8,000 years. Near the Kay-Nah-Chi-Wah-Nung Historical Centre, the remains of villages, campsites, and as many as 25 burial mounds have been found. The mounds are a 3km (2-mile) hike from the visitor center, through prairie-oak savanna with some stirring panoramic views. ☎ *807/483-1163. www.fortfranceschamber.com.*

427 Newgrange, Slane, Ireland
Older than Stonehenge, older even than the pyramids of Giza, this massive 5,000-year-old burial mound—actually a megalithic passage tomb, 11m (36 ft.) tall and 79m (260 ft.) in diameter—presides serenely atop a hill near the Boyne River, not far from the Hill of Tara **282**. Its white-quartz facade has been rebuilt, but using authentic stones found at the site. The elaborately carved walls of the internal passage are aligned with sunrise at the winter solstice. ☎ *041/988-0300. www.knowth.com/ newgrange.htm.*

Newgrange.

428 Gamla Uppsala, Uppsala, Sweden Three large 6th-century burial mounds of Viking royalty surmount a ridge by a temple grove used for religious sacrifice (both animal and human) in what was once the capital of the Svea kingdom, and traditionally regarded as the residence of Odin, the chief Norse god. There are 250 other surviving grassed-over mounds in the area (there were once 2,000). ☎ *46/18/16-91-00.*

429 Sammallahdenmäki, Kivikylä, Finland Dating from the Bronze Age (1500–500 B.C.), this remote hillside site in an unspoiled forest of gnarled pines in southeast Finland features 33 burial cairns (excavations have found cremated human bones), covered not with soil but with heaped granite rocks, now weathered and mossed over. *www.nba.fi/en/sammallahdenmakieng.*

430 Bin Tepeler, Salihli, Turkey Along the Izmir-Ankara highway, near the ruins of ancient Sardis, you'll pass a dramatic necropolis with hundreds of tumulus graves heaped in the arid landscape, close to Lake Marmara. Named Bin Tepeler—or "thousand hills"—at least 90 of these mounds were the tombs of Lydian aristocracy and royalty; look for the 69m-high (226-ft.) mound of King Alyattes, father of the legendarily rich King Croesus. *www.biblicaltoursturkey.com.*

Metropolitan A.M.E. Church, D.C.
Where Spirituality & Activism Meet
Washington, D.C.

WASHINGTON D.C.'S OLDEST BLACK CHURCH IS SO IDENTIFIED WITH THE AFRICAN-AMERICAN experience, it's tempting to see its current disrepair as a metaphor for 21st-century African Americans' social woes.

Washington, D.C., has one National Cathedral, an elegant white limestone beauty up Massachusetts Avenue on a grand hill named Mount St. Albans. But to many African Americans, the other "national cathedral" down on M Street is just as important—the Metropolitan A.M.E. Church. Over the years it has taken on the status of mother church for the African Methodist Episcopal Church, the first Protestant denomination formed with a specific racial identity.

The African Methodist Episcopal Church was founded in 1816 in Philadelphia, as an offshoot of the Free African Society. Metropolitan wasn't the denomination's first church, but it was an early one, founded as Union Bethel Church in 1838, splitting off from a Washington, D.C., Methodist congregation that refused to allow free blacks to worship equally. The name changed to Metropolitan in 1871 after Union Bethel merged with another D.C. congregation, Israel Bethel, founded in 1821. The new congregation's plan for a new church building—at the then-whopping cost of $70,000—inspired contributions from A.M.E. congregations around the country. With a distinctive red-brick Gothic facade, carved-wood pews, and beautiful stained-glass windows, it was designed to burnish the A.M.E.'s national reputation—and, situated close to the U.S. Capitol and the White House, to influence national policy.

Over the years, Metropolitan A.M.E.'s history has mirrored African-American history. Before the Civil War, it was a stop on the Underground Railroad; after the war, it promoted literacy among newly free blacks. In segregated Washington, it was one of the largest meeting places where integrated audiences could discuss reform. During the civil rights era, it organized voter registration drives; more recently, it spearheads campaigns to reverse black high-school dropout rates, prison recidivism, hunger and homelessness, and AIDS. Among the famous orators who have spoken here are Frederick Douglass, Paul Laurence Dunbar, Booker T. Washington, Mary McLeod Bethune, Jesse L. Jackson, Vernon E. Jordan, Jr., Gwen Ifill, Dorothy I. Height, and Charles J. Ogletree, Jr. Crowds filled the church in 1895 for Frederick Douglass's funeral.

Considering its august history—in 1973, it was listed in the National Register of Historic Places—the church building's current condition is sad indeed. Wedged in among modern office buildings, its structure has been weakened by water seepage and shaken by adjacent construction; after years of patchwork repairs, all its mechanical systems needed to be brought up to code. Simple roof repairs revealed that the steeple was ready to topple; every time a wall was opened, new damage was discovered. It is estimated that it will take about $11 million to restore the church to its original state, far beyond the congregation's financial means. Extensive fundraising is underway, but will it garner enough support? What price tag can be placed on preserving such a vital piece of African-American history?

ⓘ1518 M St. NW (☎**202/331-1426;** www.metropolitaname.org)

✈Ronald Reagan International Airport

🛏 $$ **Embassy Suites Downtown,** 1250 22nd St. NW (☎ **800/362-2779** or 202/857-3388; www.embassysuites.com). $$ **Georgetown Suites,** 1000 29th St. and 1111 30th St., Georgetown (☎ **800/348-7203** or 202/298-7800; www.georgetownsuites.com).

432 Churches

Prairie Churches of North Dakota
Lighthouses of the Prairie
North Dakota

THEIR STEEPLES ARE VISIBLE FOR MILES, RISING ABOVE THE WHEAT FIELDS AND ROLLING pastures of rural North Dakota—beacons of community in the treeless prairie landscape. They're the state's most distinctive architectural heritage—and they're fast disappearing, due to dwindling congregations and aging structures.

Built in the late 19th and early 20th centuries, these austere frontier churches were the focal points of their farming communities, knitting together first-generation immigrants from Norway, Iceland, Germany, and Ukraine. While the farmers themselves may have lived in simple sod houses, they proudly poured communal labor into their houses of worship, mortaring together round gray fieldstones or cutting down scarce trees to provide wood siding.

A century later, those churches serve increasingly small, aging congregations, who can scarcely foot the repair bills for sagging roofs, tipping steeples, broken windows, splintered floors, wheezy pump organs, and coughing furnaces—let alone combat rising dampness in basements that have hosted hundreds of church suppers. Given North Dakota's sweeping winds and blizzards, these buildings have had a hard life—and it shows.

North Dakota still has the nation's highest number of churches per capita, with 2,300 still standing, three-fourths of them in rural areas. In some cases, a parish may rotate services around half a dozen old churches just to keep them all in operation.

In others, churches are converted to museums or community centers. In all too many other cases, they simply stand empty, rotting away.

Just south of I-94, for example, in the town of Belfield, you can see the abandoned, weathered **Sts. Peter and Paul Ukrainian Orthodox Church,** a domed cruciform church built in 1917 and originally located in the aptly named Ukraina, North Dakota (it was moved here in 1950). North of I-94, **Vang Lutheran Church** (12th St. SW, 12 miles/19km east of Manning) has a particularly fine white steeple with German-Hungarian detailing above the doorway. An even more evocative sight lies farther south in Grant County: small, spare **Hope Lutheran Church** (west of ND 49 in Elgin), standing alone among the wheat fields. It hasn't even got a steeple, only a plain white cross tacked onto its cedar-shingled roof. Built in 1903 to 1904 for $595, it hasn't been a church since 1956, but the Grant County Historical Society still opens it for special-occasion services. Or head east to Morton County, where the neat white-frame **Sims Scandinavian Evangelical Church**—the first

Lutheran church west of the Missouri River, built in 1884—is all that's left of the vanished town of Sims (US 10-BL, near Mandan). Services are still held here every other week, and descendants of the town's founders have restored the parsonage, which is now a museum.

ⓘ **Preservation North Dakota** (www.prairieplaces.org)

✈ Bismarck

🛏 $$ **Country Suites by Carlson,** 3205 N. 14th St., Bismarck (✆ **701/258-4200;** www.countryinns.com). $$ **Trapper's Inn Motel and Campground,** I-94 and US 85 N, Belfield (✆ **800/284-1855** or 701/575-4261).

Haunting Memorials **433**

Taj Mahal
A Love Story in Stone
Agra, India

POLLUTION, FLOODING, AND EXCESSIVE TOURISM THREATEN THIS OVER-THE-TOP mausoleum—but for now you can still marvel at this monument to eternal love.

Even a recent rise in admission prices doesn't deter floods of tourists from shuffling through the Taj Mahal—two to four million tourists every year. Between the crowds and the air pollution that's eating away its white stone facade, tourism officials once considered closing this 17th-century landmark to the public, leaving its fabulous domed symmetry—that graceful center onion dome, the four smaller surrounding domes, the slender punctuating minarets, the serene reflecting pool—visible only from afar.

When you pass through the red-sandstone gatehouse, you enter tranquil Persian-style hanging gardens, a welcome respite from the hectic city outside. When you get up close, you can see that what seemed like a sugar-cube white building is in fact marvelously ornate, with exquisite detailing covering the marble inside and out—a technique called *pietra dura*, which came from either Italy or Persia, depending on which scholar you read. Islamic crescent moons, Persian lotus motifs, and Hindu symbols are gracefully combined. Past the central pool rises the arched octagonal

The Taj Mahal.

building containing the tomb of Mumtaz, its white dome ringed by four minidomes. Two red mosques flank the mausoleum on either side, one required by the Muslim faith, the other a "dummy" built for the sheer love of symmetry.

Only when you enter the buildings can you view the interiors' stunning lapidary decoration, inlaid with precious stones—agate, jasper, malachite, turquoise, tiger's-eye, lapis lazuli, coral, and carnelian. Notice how the panels of calligraphy, inlaid with black marble, are designed to get bigger the higher they are placed, so the letters appear the same size to a beholder on the ground level. When Shah Jahan himself died, his tomb was placed beside Mumtaz's, the only asymmetrical note in the mausoleum chamber. The two tombs (oriented, of course, toward Mecca) are surrounded by delicate filigreed screens, ingeniously carved from a single piece of marble.

Shah Jahan placed this memorial beside the Yamuna River, despite the constant risk of flooding, because it was next to the bustling market of the Tajganj, where it is said he first saw Mumtaz selling jewels in a market stall. Work started in 1641, and it took 20,000 laborers (not to mention oxen and elephants) 22 years to complete; its marble came from Rajasthan, the precious stones from all over Asia. In the late 19th century, the badly deteriorated Taj Mahal was extensively restored by British viceroy Lord Curzon; what will today's Indian government do to preserve this treasure?

ⓘ **Tajganj,** Agra (✆ **91/562/233-0496**)

✈ Agra

🛏 $$$ **Welcomgroup Mughal Sheraton,** 194 Fatehabad Rd., Taj Ganj, Agra (✆ **91/562/233-1701;** www.welcomgroup. com). $$ **Jaypee Palace Hotel,** Fatehabad Rd. (✆ **91/562/233-0800;** www.jaypee hotels.com).

---

434 **Haunting Memorials**

Graveyards of Edinburgh
History at Rest
Edinburgh, Scotland

EDINBURGH'S VENERABLE KIRKYARDS OFFER A WEALTH OF HISTORY, BUT ALL HAVE FALLEN PREY to time and vandalism. Currently, all five are on the World Monuments Fund's Watch List.

In the heart of Edinburgh, where centuries of Scottish history lie in jumbled layers, five time-hallowed cemeteries lie behind rusting iron railings, waiting to divulge their stories. Their monuments and headstones, carved out of the local gray stone, are evocatively soot blackened and bordered by vivid green moss. By day they offer peaceful oases in the lively city; by night, the atmosphere is distinctly spooky.

Lying just west of Edinburgh Castle, ancient **St. Cuthbert's Kirkyard** (5 Lothian Rd.) has been a burial site for over 1,000 years. (The church building itself dates

only to the 19th century.) The most famous names found among St. Cuthbert's worn gravestones are Thomas de Quincey (1785–1859), author of *Confessions of an English Opium Eater,* and the artist Alexander Nasmyth (1758–1840). South of Edinburgh Castle, surrounding Greyfriars Kirk—one of Edinburgh's oldest buildings, begun in 1602—the large shady **Greyfriars Kirkyard** is famous in its own right, thanks to Greyfriars Bobby, a Skye terrier who lived loyally beside his master's grave for 14 years. (When Bobby finally died in 1872, he was buried at the churchyard's entrance.) The ghost of 17th- century judge "bloody" George Mackenzie is said to haunt Greyfriars; poet Allan Ramsay (1686–1758) is also buried here, as is architect James Craig (1739–95), who designed Edinburgh's New Town expansion.

At the other end of the Royal Mile, closer to Holyrood Palace, **Canongate Kirkyard** (153 Canongate) is a magnet for poetry lovers, particularly fans of the great Scottish poet Robert Burns: It contains the graves of poet Robert Fergusson, a major influence on Burns, and Burns's mistress, identified only as Clarinda. Political economist Adam Smith (1723–90), author of *The Wealth of Nations*, is also interred here. From the mid–18th century on, Edinburgh's rising middle class sought burial plots on the slopes of Calton Hill, where you'll find **Old Calton and New Calton cemeteries** (divided in 1819 when Waterloo Place was laid out). Philosopher David Hume (1711–76) and Sir William Scott's publisher William Blackwood (1776–1834) lie in Old Calton, while architect David Bryce (1803–76) lies in New Calton, but even the most ordinary citizens' gravestones here often boast elaborate sculptural decoration.

Unfortunately, time, neglect, and vandalism have taken their toll on all five sites. The last straw came in 2009, when vandals damaged headstones and iron tomb railings in Canongate Kirkyard, causing about £25,000 in damage. In 2010, a local task force was organized to restore the graveyards, hoping to capitalize on the popularity of walking tours such as the **City of the Dead tours** (www.blackhart.uk.com). In March of 2011, Edinburgh's city council teamed up with the Edinburgh World Heritage Fund and the World Monuments Fund to design a comprehensive scheme to care for the historic cemeteries. As a record of Edinburgh's—and Scotland's—historic evolution, they are irreplaceable.

(i) **VisitScotland Information Centers** (www.edinburgh.org)

✈ Edinburgh

🛏 $$ **Holiday Inn Express,** Picardy Place (© **44/131-558-2300;** www.hiexpress.com/hotels). $$$ **The Scotsman Hotel,** 20 North Bridge (© **44/131-556-5565;** www.thescotsmanhotel.co.uk).

Haunting Memorials **435**

Cimitero Acattolico per gli Stranieri
A Romantic Resting Place
Rome, Italy

OSCAR WILDE IN 1877 CALLED THIS "THE HOLIEST PLACE IN ROME"; HENRY JAMES BURIED his fictional heroine Daisy Miller here. Today, though, the gravestones are deteriorating from pollution and some areas are sinking so badly that gravestones are collapsing.

The name's a mouthful—the Non-Catholic Cemetery for Foreigners, an outsiders' refuge if there ever was one. There are plenty of places in the Eternal City for Catholic Italians to be buried, but the Church wouldn't allow Protestants to be buried in consecrated ground. This rambling walled garden on the outskirts of

town was the only option for Americans and other Europeans who happened to be living in Rome when they died.

Unsupported by the Church, the graveyard depends on modest voluntary entry fees, charitable donations, and money from plot owners to maintain its landscaping. With so many other sites to see in

Rome—classical ruins, Renaissance palaces, baroque churches, the Vatican, not to mention those La Dolce Vita streetscapes and trendy shopping streets—very few visitors make their way out here. And yet an extraordinary number of famous people are interred in this cypress-shaded spot. For lovers of English literature, the most compelling are the graves of the Romantic poets Keats and Shelley.

John Keats—author of some of English literature's finest odes and sonnets—moved to Italy in 1820, seeking a mild climate to ease his tuberculosis. Living in rented rooms near the Spanish Steps (now operated as the Keats-Shelley House, Piazza di Spagna 26), attended by a friend, the painter Joseph Severn, he declined swiftly and died in February 1821, age 25. His simple gray tombstone says, "Here lies one whose name is writ in water"—though of course Keats's fame after his death grew far beyond the limited success of his lifetime. Severn, who remained in Rome for years afterward, asked to be buried next to him, a testament to Keats's friendship.

Upon Keats's death, the far more successful poet Percy Bysshe Shelley wrote one of the world's great elegies, "Adonais," mourning Keats's tragic early death. By a cruel twist of irony, Shelley himself died a year later, drowned off the coast of Tuscany in a sailing accident—with a volume of Keats's poetry in his coat pocket. Shelley—himself only 29 when he died—was buried here next to the grave of his infant son William, who'd died of fever in Rome 3 years earlier. The writer Edward Trelawny, a friend of Shelley's and Byron's, was buried nearby 30 years later.

Browse around the graves and you'll see inscriptions in more than 15 languages; the various faiths represented include Eastern Orthodox, Islam, Zoroastrianism, Buddhism, and Confucianism, as well as Protestants. Funded by the French government, the similar Père Lachaise cemetery outside Paris draws streams of tourists to the tomb of rock star Jim Morrison; meanwhile, the Protestant Cemetery languishes in neglect and obscurity.

ⓘ **The Non-Catholic Cemetery in Rome,** Via Caio Cestio 6 (✆ **39/6/5741900;** www.protestantcemetery.it)

✈ Leonardo da Vinci International Airport

🛏 $$$ **Hotel de Russie,** Via del Babuino 9 (✆ **800/323-7500** in North America, or 39/6/328881; www.roccofortehotels.com). $ **Hotel Grifo,** Via del Boschetto 144 (✆ **39/6/4871395;** www.hotelgrifo.com).

---

436 Haunting Memorials

Easter Island
Mute Witnesses
Rapa Nui, Chile

CONSERVATIONISTS WARN THAT CONTINUED CLEAR-CUTTING OF FORESTS, WHICH DESTROYS native habitats and contributes to soil erosion, could ultimately turn the remaining fertile lands of Easter Island into barren rock.

Though it may be the most remote inhabited place on earth—4,000km (2,500 miles) off the coast of Chile—Easter Island lives on tourism. And just about every visitor comes here to see the same thing: an enigmatic horde of some 600 immense stone figures hewn from dark volcanic tufa rock.

You can't deny the power of these sculptures. The faces are huge, with jutting

Moai on Easter Island.

or abandoned midroute to their pedestals. When the first Europeans visited the islands in 1722, the moai were upright; 50 years later, the next visitors found them knocked over, whether by desperate islanders or by hostile neighbors we'll never know.

Even more baffling, how were such massive sculptures built by such primitive people? Experts assume that the moai were hauled from the quarry to the coast on a wooden sledge atop log rollers—hence the need for cutting down trees. Apparently the eyes weren't added until they were levered upright onto the platforms. Perhaps the islanders thought the eyes gave the moai spiritual power—when the statues were knocked from their platforms, most were toppled face forward, as if to hide the eyes in shame.

Some statues have been reerected; they stand in an inscrutable row, staring wordlessly over this volcanic blip in the middle of the Pacific. Cruise ships pull up, disgorging 800 to 900 passengers at a time; private island-hopping charter planes pop in, letting privileged travelers tramp around, snap a few shots of the moai, and then jet off somewhere else. In an already damaged environment, the level of tourism in summer (Nov–Mar) is reaching critical levels—and most of it is short-term visitors who contribute little to the local economy. Dependent on tourist dollars, modern-day Easter Islanders are exploiting their last precious resource as carelessly as their ancestors exploited those now-vanished forests. Will they be able to safeguard these mysterious sites before it's too late?

brows and square jaws and startling white coral eyeballs. Every statue is strikingly individual, which suggests that they represented specific ancestors rather than gods. They were designed to be mounted grandly on ceremonial stone platforms, ringed around the edge of the island.

But these big statues are shrouded in mystery. Fossil evidence suggests that Rapa Nui (the native name, which means "Navel of the World") was once covered with palm trees, which the original islanders may have razed during a frenzy of statue building—an act that spelled environmental doom for this isolated population. (Trees are being replanted, but it's still a shadeless place.) Because that first population died out, no oral tradition has been passed down to explain why the statues, or moai, were built; many were found lying half-finished in an inland quarry, tumbled carelessly on their sides,

ⓘ **Easter Island** (Isla de Pascua), 5½ hr. from Santiago (www.netaxs.com/trance/rapanui.html)

✈ Mataveri (on Easter Island)

🛏 $$$ **Hotel Iorana,** Ana Magoro (ⓒ **32/100312**). $$$ **Hotel Hanga Roa,** Av. Pont (ⓒ **32/100299;** www.hotelhangaroa.cl).

13 Neglected Moderns

Bethlehem Steel Works.

Erie Canalway National Heritage Corridor
Clinton's Ditch Redux
Albany to Buffalo, New York

NAMED A NATIONAL HERITAGE CORRIDOR IN 2001, THE ONCE-GREAT ERIE CANAL'S RESURRECtion as a living-history attraction is still spotty at best. New York State's recent budget woes may hamstring further development.

Perhaps it was inevitable—once New York City no longer needed the Erie Canal, the Erie Canal was left to die. Superseded by the St. Lawrence Seaway, interstate highways, and air freight, this monumental artificial waterway withered away. Old towpaths lie deserted, and moss and weeds sprout along its stone walls. Once-prosperous upstate New York—with 80% of its population living along the canal's corridor—continues to falter.

Critics mocked New York Governor DeWitt Clinton for his scheme of linking the Hudson River and the Great Lakes, but "Clinton's Ditch," opened in 1825, transformed New York State into a commercial powerhouse. An engineering marvel of its age, the original Erie Canal was 363 miles (584km) long, 40 feet (12m) wide, and 4 feet (1.2m) deep; flat-bottomed barges were pulled along it by horses and mules plodding on a waterside towpath. Quaint as it

The Erie Canal.

seems, this revolutionary (and nonpolluting) method of transport cost one-tenth the price of hauling goods on land. New York City swiftly became America's most important port, and industrial cities boomed along the canal's course—Albany, Schenectady, Utica, Syracuse, Rochester, Buffalo. In just 9 years, enough tolls were collected to pay off its $10-million construction cost, a whopping sum at the time.

While a trickle of commercial traffic still uses the Canal, historic designation has encouraged the state to resurrect sections for recreational use. Sections of towpath have been connected with existing roads to create 366 miles (589km) of Canalway bike trail (for a map, contact Parks and Trails New York at www.ptny.org). Twelve miles (19km) north of Albany in Waterford, where the Mohawk River flows into the Hudson, you can visit the Erie Canal Historic Corridor visitor center at Peebles Island State Park. From Waterford, take a canal boat tour with the **Erie-Champlain Canal Boat Company** (© **518/577-6363;** www.eccboating. com), riding through a series of five locks around Cohoes Falls that eventually raise boats 169 feet (52m), the highest canal lift in the world.

A handsome 19th-century weighlock building in Syracuse is now the **Erie Canal Museum** (318 Erie Canal Blvd. E.; http://eriecanalmuseum.org), featuring several permanent exhibits on canal history. But you'll get a better sense of the canal just east of Syracuse, in Kirksville, hiking along a peaceful 36-mile (58km) stretch of canal towpath at **Old Erie Canal State Historic Park.** In nearby Chittenango, a striking set of restored canal boats are displayed at the Chittenango Landing Canal Boat Museum. Then head northeast to Rome, where a recreated 1840s townscape at **Erie Canal Village** (www.eriecanalvillage.net) offers a step back in time, with costumed interpreters and narrow-gauge train excursions.

(i) **Erie Canalway National Heritage Corridor Commission** (© **518/237-7000;** www.eriecanalway.org)

✈ Albany, Syracuse, Buffalo

🚃 $$$ **The Morgan State House,** 393 State St., Albany (©**888/427-6063** or 518/427-6063; www.statehouse.com). $$ **Bed and Breakfast Wellington,** 707 Danforth St., Syracuse (© **800/724-5006** or 315/474-3641; www.bbwellington.com).

---

438 | Industrial Age

Rivers of Steel
Heritage Lost
Greater Pittsburgh, Pennsylvania

RAZED IN THE 1970S AND 1980S AS THE AMERICAN STEEL INDUSTRY FLOUNDERED, LITTLE is left of the steel mills that once lined the Allegheny and Monaghela rivers. Preservationists now scramble to resurrect historic vestiges of this era.

Steel town? Not Pittsburgh—not any more. Once upon a time, Pittsburgh steel was used everywhere—in the Brooklyn Bridge, the Panama Canal, the Empire State Building, the Oakland Bay Bridge, the United Nations headquarters. The Pittsburgh football team is still called the Steelers, but high-tech industries and medical centers now support an ever-shrinking population.

With those belching smokestacks gone, Pittsburgh's skyline looks completely different.

Perhaps Pittsburgh was too hasty in erasing the gritty evidence of its former industrial might. Preservationists are now striving to recast what's left into the **Rivers of Steel Heritage Area.** The most substantial element is the U.S. Steel Works in Homestead, south of Pittsburgh, which was the world's largest producer of steel back in World War II. Once covering nearly 400 acres (160 hectares), the works were shut in 1987 and mostly demolished, save for a row of towering brick smokestacks along the Monongahela River. Much of the site has been replaced with a shopping mall, but supporters hope to create an urban national park from the remaining features: the rusted hulk of the Carrie Furnaces; the Pump House, scene of a bloody 1892 face-off between 10,000 striking workers and 300 Pinkerton detectives hired by industrialist Henry Clay Frick; and the Bost Building, a Victorian-era hotel that was union headquarters during the Homestead Strike, now a museum and visitor center. Self-guided walking tours of the area are available, as well as monthly hard-hat tours of the Carrie Furnaces.

In other area towns, some of Big Steel's associated industries escaped the wrecking ball. Across the Monongahela in Braddock, the Edgar Thomson Works, one of Andrew Carnegie's original century-old mills, still produces hot iron to be made into steel; south along the river in Rices Landing, the preserved W.A. Young & Son's Foundry and Machine Shop once turned out factory machinery; northeast in Tarentum, you can explore the Tour-Ed Mine, which produced coal to power those factories. Tiers of abandoned beehive coke ovens still stand amid weeds in Shoaf, a company village near Scottdale.

In Pittsburgh itself, the chief reminder of Big Steel is the cultural institutions founded by the steel barons: the **Carnegie Museum of Art**, 4400 Forbes Ave., Oakland; the **Carnegie Museum of Natural History**, 4400 Forbes Ave., Oakland; the **Carnegie Science Center**, 1 Allegheny Ave.; and the **Frick Art & Historical Center**, 7227 Reynolds St. And the workers who made the steel? They're commemorated by the Nationality Rooms in the Cathedral of Learning at the University of Pittsburgh, 24 classrooms decorated in the architectural styles of Pittsburgh's major immigrant groups.

(i) **Rivers of Steel Heritage Area Visitor Center**, 623 E. Eighth Ave., Homestead (✆ **412/464-4020**; www.riversofsteel.com)

✈ Pittsburgh

🛏 $$ **Holiday Inn Pittsburgh at University Center**, 100 Lytton Ave. (✆ **888/465-4329** or 412/682-6200; www.ichotelsgroup.com). $$ **Courtyard Pittsburgh Waterfront**, 401 W. Waterfront Dr., West Homestead (✆ **412/462-7301**; www.marriott.com).

Industrial Age **439**

Bethlehem Steel Works
Reinventing a Steel Town
Bethlehem, Pennsylvania

THE EPITOME OF A BIG STEEL COMPANY TOWN, BETHLEHEM'S SKYLINE IS STILL HAUNTED BY the skeletons of empty steel mills. Which repurposing will prevail—a museum of industrial history or a glitzy casino resort?

Pittsburgh may deny its Rust Belt roots, but at the other end of the state, Bethlehem, Pennsylvania, has taken a different tack. Founded in 1861 in this quiet Moravian town, the Bethlehem Steel Corporation became the nation's second-largest steel producer, at its peak sustaining a 5-mile-long (8km) steelworks that covered thousands of acres and accounted for one-fifth of the town's revenue. In 1957, some 165,000 workers were on the payroll, many of them immigrants from Eastern and Southern Europe.

Although the Bethlehem Steel Corporation is still in business elsewhere, the hometown works in Bethlehem ground to a halt in November 1995. The great steel mills on the south bank of the Lehigh River stood silent and rusting, their black smokestacks cold. Train tracks that shuttled freight trains continually in and out of the plants lay weed-choked and empty. It was a haunting scene, with a certain decaying majesty.

The nation's largest brownfield site still stands mostly deserted. Some buildings were razed at once, making room for a commerce center called Bethlehem Works, which attracted only a few small firms. The next great hope was the National Museum of Industrial History, an affiliate of the Smithsonian. But as that project stalled, a new savior appeared on the horizon. In December 2006, Pennsylvania awarded a gaming license to Las Vegas Sands Corporation to open a casino on another section of the property, with attached restaurants, shops, a concert hall, and eventually a hotel. The developers soon discovered how well-built those old factories were; they stubbornly resisted demolition, causing significant delays in the project. Finally opened in 2009, the main casino's design honors the legacy of the site, with exposed steel trusses and brick walls, a massive ore crane incorporated into the casino entrance, and lighting that imitates the red nighttime glow of blast furnaces.

With this commercial anchor in place, the industrial history museum moved ahead, with a scaled-down design. Some heavy machinery from the Bethlehem plant was salvaged for the new museum, but exhibits will mostly feature historic artifacts from the Smithsonian's collection, with no specific Bethlehem connection. Located in Bethlehem Steel's red-brick former executive offices, the museum is slated to open in late 2011.

While the Sands development is doing brisk business, many in town wonder whether the flash and glitter of a casino belong in a town founded by a religious sect, whose tidy fieldstone buildings still line the historic district across the river. The poetic desolation of the abandoned mills looks pretty good in contrast.

ⓘ **National Museum of Industrial History,** 530 E. 3rd St. (✆ **610/694-6644;** www.nmih.org)

✈ Lehigh Valley International

🛏 $$$ **Hotel Bethlehem,** 437 Main St. (✆ **800/607-2384** or 610/625-5000; www.hotelbethlehem.com). $$ **Sands Casino Resort Bethlehem,** 77 Sands Blvd. (✆ **877/726-3777;** www.pasands.com).

440 Industrial Age

Cannery Row
Sanitized Steinbeck
Monterey, California

IN THE EARLY 1900S, THE SARDINE-CANNING INDUSTRY TURNED HARBORSIDE MONTEREY INTO a gritty slum. With the sardines fished out of Monterey Bay, however, that colorful scene has mutated into a family-friendly tourist zone.

"Cannery Row in Monterey in California is a poem, a stink, a grating noise, a quality of light, a tone, a habit, a nostalgia, a dream." So wrote John Steinbeck in the opening of his 1945 novel *Cannery Row*—hardly a description of the cheery place you'll find today.

Cannery Row.

A fleet of sardine boats once nosed up to these wharves and unloaded their catch directly onto the conveyor belts of a dozen canneries; rattling machines stuffed the little fish into tins and packed them straight onto Southern Pacific freight trains. During the two World Wars especially, America's appetite for canned sardines seemed limitless, and the canneries boomed. Given the odors and the noise, Ocean View Avenue—a street once known for its seaside resort hotels—was fit only for bordellos and flophouses. No wonder Steinbeck, fresh off the success of his Dust Bowl epic *The Grapes of Wrath,* reveled in such a pungent milieu.

If you come to Cannery Row today expecting to see Steinbeck's "whores, pimps, gamblers, and sons of bitches," you'll be sorely disappointed. The so-called Silver Tide of sardines—funneled into Monterey Bay by an upwelling of cold, nutrient-rich waters through the underwater Monterey Canyon—abruptly gave out in the early 1950s, fished to death by specialized boats called purse-seiners. Ocean View Avenue's name was officially changed to Cannery Row in 1958, but the industry was already dead.

Still, Steinbeck's bestseller had captured the popular imagination, and in the 1960s, restaurants moved into those industrial

buildings. The final stroke came in 1984 when the disused Hovden Cannery was transformed into the **Monterey Bay Aquarium,** a state-of-the-art facility devoted to the ecology of this rich bay. In one respect at least, the Monterey Bay Aquarium is true to Steinbeck's book: Its approach is based on the groundbreaking tide-pool studies of Steinbeck's close friend, marine biologist Ed Ricketts, who worked out of a weather-beaten laboratory at 800 Cannery Row.

Although Monterey's Cannery Row was never razed—as industrial buildings may have been in other seaport towns—today it is packed with family restaurants, mid-priced hotels, and souvenir shops. The corrugated iron walls of old cannery buildings are painted bright, cheery colors—and the stench has disappeared. Probably because of the Steinbeck connection, historic markers around the district remind visitors of its past, but a festival mall atmosphere has taken over. The train tracks behind the canneries have become a paved trail for cyclists, joggers, and in-line skaters. A short distance away, fishing operations continue at a few nondescript piers, but the so-called historic district is distinctly flavorless. Steinbeck would have had nothing but scathing remarks to describe it.

On the other hand, he'd probably love that aquarium.

ⓘ www.canneryrow.com

✈ Monterey Peninsula Airport; San Francisco International

🛏 $$ **Best Western DeAnza Inn,** 2141 N. Fremont St. (✆ **800/858-8775** or 831/ 646-8300; www.bestwestern.com). $$ **El Adobe Inn,** 936 Munras Ave. (✆**831/372-5409;** http://el-adobe-inn.com).

---

441 **Industrial Age**

TWA Terminal at JFK Airport
Come Fly with Me
New York, New York

WHEN TWA AIRLINE CEASED OPERATIONS IN 2001, ITS ICONIC JFK TERMINAL WAS ORPHANED. Despite landmark designation, it was partially demolished to accommodate a JetBlue terminal. Could a new hotel save it?

With its streamlined white concrete parabolas, Eero Saarinen's TWA Flight Center at John F. Kennedy International Airport didn't seem so much a building as a boomerang or a seagull's wing, momentarily arrested in flight. Those aerodynamic curves were repeated inside as well, in a soaring lobby of smoked glass and smooth concrete where there wasn't a straight line in sight.

When Saarinen's landmark was built in 1962, the airport was still called Idlewild and the building, prosaically, Terminal 5. Sadly, Saarinen died in 1961 before he could witness his creation's instant acclaim. In an architectural era dominated by the glass-box skyscrapers of the International Style, Saarinen's sculptural terminal was a breathtaking leap forward. Among its innovative features were the airline industry's first electronic departure boards, closed-circuit television, and baggage carousels. Instead of plodding down ordinary hallways to catch their flights, passengers strolled into exotic red-carpeted tubes. Even the staircases, seating areas, recessed light fixtures, and counters were designed with distinctive sleek ovoid shapes, a look copied so often afterward that it's easy to forget how radical it was when it first appeared. Everything about the place trumpeted Trans World

Airlines' sophistication and preeminence in the world of air travel.

When American Airlines bought out TWA in 2001, however, Terminal 5 ceased operations. The Port Authority of New York and New Jersey, which owns the airport, couldn't decide what to do with the terminal, a National Historic Landmark that couldn't be razed. It stood abandoned for several years before JetBlue Airways agreed to use the front of Terminal 5 as an entry and ticketing area if it could build a huge new terminal expansion behind it. By its 2008 opening, however, JetBlue had chosen a different course, plopping its hulking 26-gate addition down where TWA's satellite gate pods once stood, like a heavy blue tail weighing down TWA's high-flying white kite. While JetBlue's entrance faces Saarinen's masterpiece—and faintly echoes its design with a curved front wall—a rerouted access road takes JetBlue passengers directly to the new space, so they never set foot inside the old terminal.

And so the Port Authority, which spent millions to restore Saarinen's terminal, anticipating JetBlue's tenancy—still has a ghost terminal to occupy. In February 2011, it called for bids on a 150-room boutique hotel to be tucked between the two terminals, using Saarinen's soaring entry hall as its lobby. Done right, it could give new life to that breathtaking interior. But how many appendages can be tacked onto TWA's once-ethereal expression of flight?

✈ John F. Kennedy International

🚆 $ **Union Square Hotel,** 209 E. 14th St. (✆ **212/614-0500;** www.nyinns.com). $$ **Hotel Belleclaire,** 250 W. 77th St. at Broadway (✆ **877/468-3522** or 212/362-7700; www.hotelbelleclaire.com).

Industrial Age **442**

Malmi Airport Terminal
Sinking in Helsinki
Helsinki, Finland

FINLAND'S SECOND-BUSIEST AIRPORT, WITH ITS STUNNING TERMINAL BUILDING, IS SLOWLY sinking into swampland—and the city of Helsinki is negotiating to replace it with housing developments.

When the Malmi airport was first conceived in the 1930s, Finnish authorities consulted aviation hero Charles Lindbergh about their proposed site. Lindbergh vetoed the location—its unstable clay soil wouldn't support heavy aircraft, he said. The Finns went ahead with Malmi anyway. Since you couldn't build houses on a swamp, they reasoned, you might as well put an airport there.

They did dress it up with a striking terminal building, a marvelously clean functionalist design by architects Dag Englund and Vera Rosendahl: a white three-story cylinder with circling bands of windows, topped by a neat control tower and flanked by two low wings. When the 1940 Summer Olympics were suddenly switched from Tokyo to Helsinki, Finland could proudly showcase the capital as an ensemble of such forward-thinking architecture.

The 1940 Olympics were eventually cancelled because of World War II, but they came to Helsinki after the war, in 1952—by which time Lindbergh's prediction had proven all too true. To handle the international passenger planes arriving for the games, a new main airport had to be

built with stronger runways. (Malmi only had one hangar, anyway—there'd never been enough solid land to build a second one.) Malmi was henceforth relegated to light and midsize aircraft, including private planes, pilot training planes, aerial photographers, parachute jumpers, taxi planes, and police and ambulance helicopters. It's still Finland's second-busiest airport, with nearly 42,000 landings in 2010. The airfield also provides a green oasis in Helsinki's metropolitan sprawl, a nesting ground for endangered bird species like the curlew, the corncrake, and the red-backed shrike. A popular jogging/cycling trail rings the airport; model aircrafters and hot-air balloonists gather there on weekends.

Now Helsinki wants that swampland back again—to build houses after all. Despite the fact that Malmi is still a working airfield, and the only backup to Helsinki-Vantaa International, the city is trying to cancel its land agreement with the Finnish government, which should extend until 2034. Environmental impact studies and detailed proposals are still going back and forth. The authorities claim they will preserve the landmark terminal building (which has sunk nearly half a meter/1⅔ ft. into that shifting ground over the decades); they just want to close the runways. But for aviation enthusiasts, the whole point of the terminal is that it's still the heart of a working airfield. What else should a functionalist gem do if not to serve its intended function?

ⓘ**Helsinki-Malmi Airport** (www.pelasta malmi.org)

✈ Helsinki-Vantaa International

▭$$ **Hilton Helsinki Kalastajatorppa,** Kalastajatorpantie 1 (✆ **800/445-8667** in North America, or 358/9/45811; www. hilton.com). $$$ **Sokos Hotel Vaakuna,** Asema-aukio 2 (✆ **358/20/1234-618;** www.sokoshotels.fi).

443 Industrial Age

Battersea Power Station
Power in a Beautiful Package
London, England

PLANS FOR A MASSIVE REDEVELOPMENT OF THE DERELICT BATTERSEA POWER STATION HAVE been tied up for years, awaiting agreements between private investors, local community boards, and Her Majesty's government.

Battersea Power Station has been a London landmark ever since it was built in 1933. Designed by Sir Giles Gilbert Scott—who also designed Britain's beloved red telephone booths—its tapering white concrete chimneys have been featured on a Pink Floyd album cover and in movies from Alfred Hitchcock's *Sabotage* to the Beatles' *Help!* to the Batman movie *The Dark Knight.* It's even been the punch line for a Monty Python comedy sketch.

When the London Power Company first proposed this massive coal-fired plant on the south bank of the Thames, the public was skittish about such a large-scale power grid, much larger than anything existing. To win public support, the company strove to make it aesthetically pleasing as well as functional. Still Europe's largest brick structure, its stately proportions and exterior decorative detail lend it confident majesty. Inside, the Art Deco control room features parquet floors and wrought-iron stairways, not to mention Italian marble in the turbine hall.

New technology eventually made Battersea's pollution-belching turbines obsolete, and in 1975 the older half was shut down. Historic preservationists quickly secured landmark protection before the second half was also shut down in 1983. (It now has a Grade II listing, meaning it can't be demolished or altered without government approval.) In the 1980s, a scheme to convert Battersea into a theme park went so far as to remove the roof and west wall before developers ran out of money. The power station sat empty, exposed to the elements, until 2003, when new owners moved forward with a mixed-use design to turn the plant's soaring halls into a retail mall, with new hotels, offices, and residences nearby.

But when the developers tried to remove the four decaying chimneys in 2005, a wave of protests brought demolition to a screeching halt. In November 2006, new owners took over, hiring architect Rafael Viñoly to create a new master plan, retrofitting the main building to contain offices, event

10 All-American Lighthouses

Throughout the 19th century, expanding America's bustling shipping corridors depended on a network of sturdy, often lonely lighthouses. Superseded by improved navigational technology, only about 600 of these romantic coastal towers are left; many face extinction. Here are 10 that preservationists are working to save:

White Island.

444 White Island, New Hampshire On the Isle of Shoals, 10 miles (16km) off the New Hampshire coast, poet Celia Thaxter lived as a child in this white 1859 brick-and-stone lighthouse on White Island. It's still a working lighthouse (though the light is now automated), but it was badly battered in storms in 1984, 1991, and 2007. However, an enthusiastic group of seventh-graders is working to restore its severely cracked interior. *www.lighthousekids.org.*

445 Sankaty Head, Nantucket, Massachusetts New England's most powerful light shone since 1850 from this white-and-red-striped, brick-and-granite structure overlooking dangerous shoals on the outer end of Nantucket Island. Over the years it became a popular tourist attraction, with particularly breathtaking views from its 70-foot-high (21m) bluff. Erosion of the steep bluff threatened its existence, however, and in 2007 the entire lighthouse was moved 405 feet (123m) inland. *www.sconsettrust.org.*

446 Esopus Lighthouse, Esopus, New York The Esopus Lighthouse—aka the Middle Hudson Lighthouse or "the Maid of the Meadows"—was opened in 1871 to warn Hudson River craft of treacherous mud flats. Growing out of the roof of a substantial white-frame house squeezed onto a granite pier in the middle of the river, it had become seriously dilapidated by 1990. A major restoration saved it from collapse; its light was finally turned back on in 2003. *www.esopuslighthouse.org.*

447 Mispillion River Lighthouse, Delaware First lit in 1873, the Mispillion Lighthouse provided a beacon for sailors headed upriver to Milford, Delaware, its square-towered lantern room rising from a handsome L-shaped Carpenter Gothic house. In 1929, it was replaced by an unglamorous steel skeleton tower, and over decades of private ownership, its condition rapidly deteriorated. Struck by lighting in 2002, it was a mere shell when new owners in 2004 moved its remains, beacon and all, to rebuild it in Shipcarpenter Square in Lewes. *www.lighthousefriends.com.*

448 Bodie Island Lighthouse, Cape Hatteras, North Carolina It's been built and rebuilt three times since 1847—first to correct a Pisa-like tilt, then to replace the tower blown up by Confederate soldiers in the Civil War. The third time was the charm, and now this 150-foot-high (46m), black-and-white banded stone tower can be seen for miles. Though it's not as tall as its famous neighbor, the Cape Hatteras

Lighthouse, Bodie's light still operates, warning ships of the perilous Outer Banks waters. *www.nps.gov/caha/index.htm.*

⑭⑭⑨ Morris Island Lighthouse, Charleston, South Carolina   A beloved landmark guarding the entrance to Charleston harbor, the Morris Island Light dates to 1876 (its predecessor was destroyed in the Civil War); it has survived many hurricanes and an earthquake, but time has taken its toll. The foundation is weakened, the tower leans, and beach erosion swept away its once-grand living quarters, leaving the lighthouse stranded alone 1,600 feet (490m) offshore. Walk over the dunes of Folly Beach to see this faded brown-and-white beauty. *www.savethelight.org.*

⑮⑤⓪ Raspberry Island Lighthouse, Bayfield, Wisconsin   The Great Lakes have their lighthouses too—rough waters made the shipping channel around Lake Superior's Apostle Islands particularly hazardous, creating a need for the Raspberry Island Light to be built in 1863. Touted as the Showplace of the Apostle Islands, the substantial red-roofed white-frame house below the light tower was repeatedly expanded for lightkeepers' families and assistants. But its bluff-top site faces serious erosion from Superior's pounding waves. *www.nps.gov/apis.*

⑮⑤① Nottawasaga Island Lighthouse, Collinwood, Ontario   One of six so-called "Imperial Towers" around Ontario's Georgian Bay, the 26m (85-ft.) limestone Nottawasaga Lighthouse was built in 1858 on an isolated Lake Huron island (today a bird sanctuary) prone to lightning storms—in fact, a lightning strike in 2010 is causing the structure to crumble. The Canadian Coastguard has closed it for safety reasons and local fundraising efforts to save it are underway. *www.visitgeorgianbay.com.*

⑮⑤② Sand Island Lighthouse, Alabama   Standing 125 feet (38m) tall, this slim black tower near the mouth of Mobile Bay was the third built on this Gulf Coast island—once 400 acres (160 hectares), now eroded to a narrow strip of sand. Built of wood on a granite base, it was hit badly by hurricanes in 1906 and 1919. Left to crumble for many years, it now belongs to the nearby town of Dauphin Island. *www.sandislandlighthouse.com.*

⑮⑤③ Isla de Mona Lighthouse, Puerto Rico

Isla Mona, off Puerto Rico's west coast, has had a checkered history as a pirate hideout and smugglers' haven. When Puerto Rico was ceded to the U.S. after the Spanish-American War, a steel lighthouse was promptly erected in 1900—and not just any steel lighthouse, but one designed by Gustave Eiffel (yes, the designer of the Eiffel Tower). It worked steadily until 1976, when it was replaced by an automated light. Now abandoned, the rusting hulk of the original structure remains in disrepair. ✆**787/724-3724.**

Isla de Mona Lighthouse.

Battersea Power Station.

spaces, and a conference center, powered by its own zero-carbon energy plant. Residences, shops, hotels, and even a new Underground station and a new U.S. Embassy would surround the Power Station. By February 2011, approvals had been secured from the local council, the Mayor of London, and the secretary of state, clearing the way for construction to begin in 2012. Considering how often this project has gone off the rails, even the commencement of construction is no guarantee that the Battersea project will come to fruition, however.

Battersea's sister power station, Bankside—also designed by Sir Giles Gilbert Scott—has since found new life as the Tate Modern Gallery. Many believe that Battersea was the more beautiful of the two, but it currently sits as a molding, desolate hulk, waiting for renovation plans to become reality.

ⓘ www.battersea-powerstation.com

✈ Heathrow International

🛏 $$ **Mornington Hotel,** 12 Lancaster Gate, Bayswater (ⓒ **800/633-6548** in the U.S., or 44/20/7262-7361; www.bw-morning tonhotel.co.uk). $$ **Sanctuary House Hotel,** 33 Tothill St., Westminster (ⓒ **44/ 20/7799-4044;** www.fullershotels.com).

Cyclorama Center
Theater in the Round
Gettysburg, Pennsylvania

THOUGH THE CYCLORAMA PAINTING HAS BEEN MOVED, THE SLEEK DRAMATIC BUILDING BUILT to house it still stands empty on the edge of the Gettysburg battlefield. Will the National Park Service let it stay?

Way back before 3-D IMAX movies, this was the ultimate in visual experiences: a 360-degree oil painting surrounding the spectator, putting you right in the middle of the artwork's setting. Cycloramas were all the rage in Europe and America in the late 1800s, set up in special auditoriums with foreground props and landscaping to intensify the realistic impact. Once they fell out of fashion, however—superseded by moving pictures—most cycloramas were destroyed or rotted away in some damp cellar.

Not the Gettysburg Cyclorama, though. Originally painted for an 1883 exhibition in Chicago, this stirring painting by noted French cyclorama artist Paul Philippoteaux soon generated three copies, one of which was exhibited to admiring crowds for 20 years in Boston. Even veterans of the battle praised Philippoteaux's meticulously detailed depiction of Pickett's Charge, that valiant but ultimately hopeless Confederate attack on the Union forces at Gettysburg. After several years of private ownership, Boston's Cyclorama was brought home to Gettysburg in 1913, and eventually acquired by the National Park Service in the 1940s.

In 1963, to commemorate the battle's centennial, the Cyclorama became the centerpiece of a striking new visitor center. Famed Modernist architects Richard Neutra and Robert Alexander designed the building, a round white concrete drum with a long glass-sheathed causeway, tucked snugly into the rolling Pennsylvania farmland overlooking the battlefield. At the time the National Park Service (NPS) praised the Cyclorama Center as the new prototype of national park visitor centers, heralding the future of the national park system.

By the turn of the century, however, this immense painting—359 feet (109m) long, 27 feet (8.2m) high, weighing close to 3 tons—required extensive repairs. At least part of its deterioration, the NPS claimed, was caused by the Center's interior design flaws. The NPS closed the Cyclorama Center and sent the painting off for restoration. When it returned, it was installed in a new state-of-the-art visitor center—leaving the old cyclorama building an empty shell at the north end of Cemetery Ridge.

Neutra himself described the Cyclorama Building as the building closest to his heart—its design was conceived as an expression of global harmony and dedicated to Abraham Lincoln. Yet the NPS has opposed listing it as a National Historic Landmark, insisting that it's more important to preserve a different facet of history—that section of the battlefield that lies beneath it. Court rulings in 2008 and 2010 have prevented demolition, but this new Battle of Gettysburg rages on.

ⓘ **Gettysburg National Military Park Battlefield,** 97 Taneytown Rd. (✆ **717/334-1124;** www.nps.gov/gett). **Mission 66** (www.mission66.com).

✈ Baltimore-Washington International

🛏 $$$ **Best Western Gettysburg Inn,** 1 Lincoln Sq. (✆ **866/378-1797** or 717/337-2000; www.gettysburg-hotel.com). $$ **Quality Inn,** 380 Steinwehr Ave. (✆ **800/228-5151** or 717/334-1103; www.gettysburgqualityinn.com).

Cook County Hospital
The Real ER
Chicago, Illinois

IN 2008, FOUR WINGS WERE KNOCKED DOWN AT CHICAGO'S STATELY COOK COUNTY Hospital, a Beaux Arts landmark built in 1914. It took a public outcry to halt further demolition.

When it comes to hospitals, shiny and new always seems better. Even a venerable institution like Chicago's Cook County Hospital, purposely built to treat the urban poor, eventually began to seem outdated. In 2002, an entirely new Cook County Hospital was opened nearby, equipped to provide the latest in 21st-century healthcare. Its nearly century-old predecessor was slated for demolition, to be replaced with a large park—a welcome amenity in this Near West Side neighborhood with its jumble of medical buildings.

But then the public outcry began.

When Cook County Hospital opened in 1914, it was a product of the Beautiful City movement, which sought to make every public building an impressive monument. Architects Paul Gerhardt and Richard Schmidt created a Beaux Arts showplace, its facade adored with fluted Ionic columns and sculptured pediments, bands of gray granite alternating with yellow brick and glazed terra-cotta tile in gray, yellow, and cream colors. Massive as it was—2 blocks long, eight stories high—it was so superbly proportioned, it seemed elegant rather than heavy. Details were applied lavishly, from baroque cartouches and ornate cornices to delicate heads of lions and cherubs. The poorest patient could feel proud to be treated in such a majestic edifice.

The campaign to save County was only partly about architectural grandeur, however—its historic importance mattered equally. As the nation's largest public hospital, in its early years it admitted so many immigrants, it was nicknamed Chicago's Statue of Liberty. Chicago's shifting demographics brought an entirely black patient base, then more Hispanics and Asians. Yet County maintained its stature as one of the world's great teaching hospitals; it housed the nation's first blood bank (1937), first trauma center (1966), and first AIDS clinic (1983). Its doctors made breakthrough advances in treating sickle cell anemia, and its emergency room was legendary for its excellence (the TV show *ER* was modeled on County).

A flurry of public protests stopped demolition in 2003; redevelopment plans were batted back and forth while politicians battled (this is Chicago, after all) and the building sat empty. In January 2008, bulldozers moved in—but only to demolish four wings jutting from the south side of the building, later additions that weren't architecturally distinguished. Finally, in March 2010, the city council appropriated $108 million to renovate County instead, converting it to health-department offices. Sometimes the good guys *can* win.

ⓘ **Old Cook County Hospital,** 1835 W. Harrison St.

✈ O'Hare International

🛏 $$ **Best Western River North,** 125 Ohio St. (📞 **800/727-0800** or 312/467-0800; www.rivernorthhotel.com). $$ **Homewood Suites,** 40 E. Grand St. (📞 **800/225-5466** or 312/644-2222; www.homewoodsuites chicago.com).

Flushing Meadows
All the World's a Fair
New York, New York

LIKE A COLLECTION OF URBAN FLOTSAM, THIS PARK FULL OF NEGLECTED RELICS FROM TWO World's Fairs could stand as a metaphor for our tarnished faith in the future.

You can spot them from the Grand Central Parkway, wedged between LaGuardia Airport, the Mets' baseball stadium, and the tennis center where the U.S. Open is played: a slightly forlorn ensemble of Space Age structures stranded in the outer borough of Queens. There's a tall trio of concrete observation towers where the Jetsons would feel at home; a circular pavilion that looks like a sci-fi Stonehenge; and, most distinctive of all, the **Unisphere,** a 140-foot-high (43m) globe of

the world, its oceans an airy grid of stainless steel with three gleaming orbit rings.

Here, in a former city ash dump, New York City's powerful parks commissioner Robert Moses created a 1,200-acre (490-hectare) park to host the 1939 World's Fair. Defying the lingering Depression and the looming threat of World War II, it was a brave declaration of faith in the future—and a financial failure. The world was quite a different place by 1964, when a second World's Fair was launched on the

The Unisphere at Flushing Meadows.

same site, this time promoting peace through international cooperation. Not officially sanctioned by the Bureau of International Expositions, the 1964 Fair didn't attract pavilions from the larger nations, but smaller countries and U.S. corporations filled the void. A number of fine-dining restaurants included the famous Le Pavilion, and the Walt Disney company debuted several audio-animatronic displays, such as "It's a Small World" and a talking Abraham Lincoln statue. The Fair was big, bold, and exciting—and it also lost money.

After the Fair, many exhibits were razed or shipped elsewhere ("It's a Small World" flew west to Disneyland), but strolling around the park today, you can glimpse several World's Fair ghosts. What's now the **Queens Museum of Art** had many incarnations—the New York State Building in the 1939 Fair, the United Nations' first home in the late 1940s, and finally the New York City Pavilion in the 1964 Fair. Inside, you'll find the Panorama of New York, a scale model of the entire city that was built in 1964 and is still updated regularly. Next to a weathered sculpture of a supersonic jet and a gleaming pair of actual space rockets, another building has become the **New York Hall of Science** museum. The Unisphere, the 1964 Fair's U.S. Steel exhibit, got a face-lift after it won landmark designation in 1989 (the water jets surrounding it finally began to spout again in 2010). It took until 2009, however, for the nearby **New York State Pavilion**—that now-roofless Stonehenge structure, designed in the Futurist style by Philip Johnson—to be landmarked. Weeds sprout from its plaza and its towers teeter silently overhead, waiting for rehabilitation.

✈ John F. Kennedy International, Newark Liberty International, LaGuardia

🛏 $ **Union Square Hotel,** 209 E. 14th St. (✆ **212/614-0500;** www.nyinns.com). $$ **Hotel Belleclaire,** 250 W. 77th St. at Broadway (✆ **877/468-3522** or 212/362-7700; www.hotelbelleclaire.com).

Historic Spots 457

Martin Luther King, Jr. Library
An Open Book
Washington, D.C.

ONE OF WASHINGTON, D.C.'S FEW MODERNIST BUILDINGS, THE MAIN PUBLIC LIBRARY WON A battle for landmark status in 2007—making much-needed renovations even more complicated.

Washington, D.C., has never been big on modern architecture—fluted white columns and massive neoclassical pediments are more its style. Still, the nation's capital does have one Modernist gem: the Martin Luther King, Jr. Memorial Library, the central building of D.C.'s public library system. Designed by Ludwig Mies van der Rohe, an undisputed master of the International Style, it was Mies's last building; he never lived to see it completed.

One of just two monuments in Washington dedicated to the slain civil rights leader, the library is a minimalist box of black-painted steel and bronze-tinted glass. At street level, a loggia invites pedestrians inside, with the upper floors cantilevered overhead. Only four stories high, the library seems graceful rather than bulky, with the black girders of its exterior grid emphasizing its horizontal sweep. Mies also conceived of it as a

The Martin Luther King, Jr. Library.

see-through library, at least at night, when the dark glass becomes transparent—you can look right through an interior grid of black-girdered bookshelves and overhead light strips, seemingly suspended in mid-air. Many of the interior fittings, too, reflect Mies's Bauhaus sensibility—granite-topped circulation desks, Steelcase tables, chrome-plated hardware.

In the decades since it opened in 1972, however, the library—like many public buildings in this chronically underfunded city—has become considerably run-down. The air-conditioning system and elevators have been a perpetual problem, their designs complicated by that see-through concept. The advent of the digital age has radically redefined the space needs of a public library, as well. On the ground floor you'll notice a shadow on the floor where massive card catalogs once stood; now librarygoers stand in long lines to use the few computers. Wi-Fi has been installed, but laptop users complain that there are never enough electrical outlets—features that weren't essential back in 1972. Ugly security detectors at the entrances add a brutal note. Another persistent problem has nothing to do with the building's design: The downtown location has made

it a prime hangout for the homeless, who sleep at the desks and wash themselves in its restrooms.

Unlike the Watergate apartment complex and the Kennedy Center—Washington's only other notable Modernist structures—the King Library sits on a nondescript downtown corner, not a striking riverside site. Until the library was granted landmark status, in June 2007, the D.C. government considered razing it; proposals for converting Mies's building into a museum have also been floated. But as some skeptics have noted, landmark status is no guarantee of safety—Washington, D.C., has razed certified landmarks before.

ⓘ 901 G Street NW, Washington, DC

✈ Ronald Reagan Washington National, Dulles International, Baltimore-Washington International

🛏 $$ **Hilton Washington,** 1919 Connecticut Ave. NW (© **800/445-8667** or 202/483-3000; www.washington.hilton. com). $$ **One Washington Circle Hotel,** 1 Washington Circle NW (© **800/424-9671** or 202/872-1680; www.thecircle hotel.com).

10 Classic Movie Palaces

Though the first moving pictures were projected onto linen sheets hung on the walls of ordinary rooms, exhibitors soon realized that people came to the movies to escape reality—and they set upon extending the fantasy from the films to the theaters themselves. Many borrowed themes from world architecture, particularly exotic Chinese, Aztec, and Egyptian motifs, but the most popular look was Art Deco, with its streamlined chrome and sinuous curves. But with the rise of the multiplex, these grand palaces were boarded up, used for other purposes, or demolished. Here are 10 that have escaped the wrecking ball:

458 Uptown Theater, Chicago, Illinois   With nearly 4,500 seats, the Uptown Theater was the second-largest movie palace in the United States, after Radio City Music Hall. The design is Spanish Revival; a deliriously ornate five-story entrance lobby rests behind an eight-story facade. Initially built in 1921 for live performances (it had its own orchestra), by the 1940s it was mostly a movie house. A designated Chicago landmark, it's been closed since 1981. In 2011, Alderman Harry Osterman pledged to work with another alderman, the owner of the building, and Friends of the Uptown to renovate the grand old building. *www.uptowntheatre.com.*

459 Gateway Theater, Chicago, Illinois   When it opened in 1930, the Gateway featured the latest rage: "atmospheric-style" decor, with a dark-blue star-spangled ceiling like a sky over the 2,100-seat auditorium, and classical statuary and vines on the side walls. Praised for its acoustics, the Gateway remained an active single-screen cinema through the 1970s. In 1985, a Polish-American community group, the Copernicus Foundation, took over and restored the theater, using it for community gatherings and special events. © **773/777-8898.** *www.copernicusfdn.org.*

460 Loew's Jersey Theater, Jersey City, New Jersey   This astonishing baroque theater opened its doors at 54 Journal Sq. in 1929, with a grand lobby dominated by a chandelier. Its large clock tower, featuring a copper statue of St. George and the dragon, is a local landmark. Slated for demolition in 1987, it was saved by a grass-roots campaign and today shows both vintage and contemporary films and hosts live performances. © **201/798-6055.** *www.loewsjersey.org.*

The Egyptian Theatre.

461 The Egyptian Theatre, Hollywood, California
This grand theater opened in 1922, the same year King Tut's tomb was found, and explorations in Egypt inspired its motif—a columned forecourt, hieroglyphics, murals, and a tiled fountain. Built by Sid Grauman as a palace fit for premieres, it continued to host premieres until 1968. Closed in 1992 and damaged in the 1994 Northridge earthquake, it was restored by the American Cinematheque in the late 1990s and now shows classic and contemporary films. Tours are available. *www.americancinematheque.com.*

462 El Capitan, West Hollywood, California When the El Capitan Theater opened in 1926, it featured a Spanish colonial exterior and an elaborate East Indian interior. Designed for live plays, the El Capitan gradually became a movie house; in 1941, the world premiere of *Citizen Kane* was held here. The declining El Capitan was bought in 1989 by the Walt Disney Company, which restored much of its original decor. © *323/467-7674. http://elcapitan.go.com/index.html.*

463 The Alex Theatre, Glendale, California Built in 1925, The Alex Theatre began as a vaudeville theater and first-run movie house, designed with Greek and Egyptian motifs. The atmospheric decor featured a stage set simulating an ancient garden. In 1940, a 100-foot-tall (30m) Art Deco neon tower topped by a spiked starburst was added. Renovations began in 1992, and it is now a performing arts and entertainment center. © *818/243-7700. www.alextheatre.org.*

464 Tampa Theatre, Tampa, Florida The Tampa Theatre opened in 1926 in downtown Tampa as a breathtaking example of an "atmospheric theater," simulating an immense Mediterranean courtyard with statues, flowers, and gargoyles under a "sky" of twinkling stars and floating clouds. Faced with demolition in 1973, it was rescued through community efforts and reopened in 1978. *711 N. Franklin St.* © *813/274-8981. www. tampatheatre.org.*

The Tampa Theatre.

465 The YAM Movie Palace, Portales, New Mexico This splendid example of geometric Art Deco architecture was Portales's pride when it opened as the Portola Theater in 1926. Like many small-town Art Deco beauties, its future was in question until a combination of private and state funds were raised to restore it and reopen as a performance space. *www.portales.com/visitors/attractions.*

466 Coronet Cinema, London, England Prime among new cinemas converted from existing theaters was the 1898 Coronet Theatre in Notting Hill Gardens, an imposing Palladian theater where, legend has it, Sir John Gielgud saw his first Shakespeare play. Converted to a movie house in 1923, this landmark cinema has shown movies ever since. *www.coronet.org.*

467 Capri Theater, Goodwood, South Australia A sleek Art Deco palace built in this Adelaide suburb in 1941, the Capri's most outstanding feature is its classic Wurlitzer theater organ. The Capri, in fact, has the largest theater organ in the Southern Hemisphere, which is played before film screenings 3 nights a week. *141 Goodwood Rd.* © *61/8/8272 1177. www.capri.org.au.*

Salk Institute
Inspiring Science
La Jolla, California

KNOWN FOR ITS UPLIFTING PACIFIC OCEAN VIEW, THE CAMPUS OF THIS PRESTIGIOUS BIOLOGI-cal research institute offers no room for a much-needed expansion—except right in the middle of that cherished vista.

When Dr. Jonas Salk—world famous for developing the polio vaccine in the 1950s—set out to found an independent research institute for biological science, he shrewdly recognized that a beautiful campus would help attract the best researchers around. He chose a breath-taking cliff-top location on the Torrey Pines Mesa of La Jolla, San Diego's loveli-est suburb, and hired noted modern archi-tect Louis I. Kahn to design the complex.

Even Salk may have underestimated Kahn's stroke of genius. Asked to provide laboratories for 56 faculty fellows to work in, Kahn made the lab areas open and flex-ible, to enhance the give-and-take of scien-tific collaboration—and then gave each scientist an individual study for privacy and reflection. He set them in a mirror-image pair of long two-story buildings, flanked by green lawns and facing each other conge-nially across a wide travertine-paved plaza open to the sky and sea. For the crowning touch, the courtyard is bisected with a sin-gle shimmering channel of water, flowing straight as an arrow toward the Pacific Ocean.

Classically simple and harmonious in design, the campus buildings are neverthe-less anything but stark. Wood-framed win-dows and panels of sun-bleached shingles give texture to their exposed concrete facades. Instead of a regimented straight line, they're a succession of slightly angled modules, so that every fellow's office has an inspiring ocean view. Modern as it is in some respects, in others the complex dem-onstrates Kahn's reverence for the ancient architecture of Italy, Greece, and Egypt—the institute feels like a modern Acropolis.

Over the years, the 27-acre (11-hectare) campus has worn incredibly well, winning landmark status in 1991. When more labo-ratories and administrative offices were built in the 1990s, that serene centerpiece was left untouched. But in 2008, the Salk Institute won approval to shoehorn a new lab building, greenhouses, and a commu-nity center onto the increasingly tight campus. In order to attract top research talent these days, the directors argue, they need to offer more amenities and state-of-the-art lab space—and the only place left to build is at the open end of that centerpiece courtyard.

This is in fact a scaled-down plan, in response to a storm of protests from neigh-bors and preservationists. A glass atrium was added, to preserve the courtyard view from the road. Nevertheless, the harmony of Kahn's oceanview composition may be spoiled forever. Free tours of the grounds are offered throughout the week; call for a reservation, before the construction begins (slated for 2013 or 2014). It may be your last chance to see this modern masterpiece in its uncluttered glory.

ⓘ 10010 N. Torrey Pines Rd., La Jolla
📞 **858/453-4100**)

✈ San Diego

🛏 $$ **Best Western Inn By the Sea,** 7830 Fay Ave., La Jolla 📞 **800/526-4545** or 858/459-4461; www.bestwestern.com/ innbythesea). $$ **Park Manor Suites,** 525 Spruce St. 📞 **619/291-0999;** www.park manorsuites.com).

The Berlin Wall
Shadow Across the City
Berlin, Germany

THROUGHOUT THE CITY OF BERLIN, CRUMBLING CONCRETE, HISTORICAL MARKERS, AND GREEN parks delineate where the Berlin Wall stood 50 years ago. Amid a frenzy of real estate development, how long will they remain?

Like an old dueling scar, the shadow of the Berlin Wall cuts across the heart of Germany's capital. Built in 1961 by Soviet-controlled East Germany, the Berlin Wall was meant to prevent citizens from defecting to the West via West Berlin, the non-Communist sector of this city that the Allies divvied up after World War II. It began as barbed wire and morphed into a double wall of hulking concrete, with searchlights trained on a booby-trapped no man's land between inner and outer walls. Yet East Germans kept risking death to sneak across, using everything from false passports and tunnels to hot-air balloons. Some 5,000 people succeeded, but Soviet guards fatally shot 255 East Germans in midescape. After the Soviet Union dissolved, jubilant Germans on both sides cheered the bulldozers on November 9, 1989, when the Wall collapsed.

As the capital of a reunited Germany, Berlin was transformed in the 1990s by a blitz of new construction, as if trying to erase the memory of those grim years. In 2006, however, the government finally completed the **Berlin Wall Trail** (Berlin Mauerweg), a 160km (99-mile) walking and cycling route tracing former border-patrol roads around West Berlin. Signboards offer historical background, pointing out border crossings, a few remaining watchtowers, and memorials to escapees, as well as green parkland tracing the Wall's former course.

Most memorials to the Wall lie along this route. Start at the **Berlin Wall Memorial,** on Ackerstrasse at Bernauer Strasse, an open-air complex of memorials centered around a weather-stained section of the original double Wall. Along Bernauer Strasse, signboards narrate the **Berlin**

A segment of the Berlin Wall.

Wall History Mile. Near the Bundestag, Germany's parliament, off the Schiffbauer-damm promenade you'll find sections of Wall incorporated into the **Parlament der Bäume** (Parliament of Trees) memorial park and a ground-floor exhibit inside the new Bundestag library (Marie-Elisabeth-Lüders-Haus). Look across the River Spree for seven somber white crosses (the Weisse Kreuze), erected by West Berliners in 1971 to mark where the Wall met the river. South on Friedrichstrasse, the **Museum Haus am Checkpoint Charlie** (Friedrichstrasse 44) tells the story of Checkpoint Charlie, the infamous crossing point into the American sector. A few streets west, another grimy section of Wall is preserved at the **Topography of Terror museum** (Niederkirchnerstrasse 8), where Hitler's Gestapo headquarters once stood. Farther east along the river, the Mühlenstrasse roadway is flanked by

the longest Wall section still standing, a stretch of crumbling white concrete boldly decorated by international artists in 1990, now called the East Side Gallery.

Although the Berlin Wall Trail project met a fair amount of political resistance, it has preserved the last few crumbling fragments of the Wall, shifting many of them from their original sites to make way for new construction. Future generations can now reimagine the looming presence of the Wall—and hope history won't repeat itself.

ⓘwww.berlinwalks.de

✈Berlin-Tagel

🛏$$ **Ackselhaus Blue Home,** Belforter Strasse 21 (✆ **49/30/4433-7633; www.ackselhaus.de**). $$ **Myers Hotel Berlin,** Betzer Strasse 26 (✆ **49/30/ 440140; www.myershotel.de**).

14 Disposable Culture

A wigwam motel in Arizona.

Fenway Park
Granddaddy of All Ballparks
Boston, Massachusetts

MANAGEMENT HAS, AT LEAST TEMPORARILY, STOPPED MAKING NOISES ABOUT REPLACING Fenway Park. Since the old stadium seats so few people and it can't accommodate luxury boxes, however, it might be only a matter of time before the owners change their minds.

"Stadium" is almost too grand a term for Fenway, the oldest baseball park in the major leagues. Built in 1912, it's smaller than modern parks, and full of quirks that only add to its mystique. Seats are narrow, often wood-slatted chairs dating back to 1934; many have poor sightlines and no legroom. The scoreboard is still, incredibly, hand-operated; pitchers warm up in bullpens right on the edge of the diamond, in plain view of the spectators. And then there is the 37-foot-high (11m) left field wall known as the "Green Monster" for its tendency to rob opposing hitters of their home runs. (During pitching changes, left fielders have been known to sneak inside the Green Monster to get relief from the sun.)

From management's perspective, it would be great to have more seats to sell—Fenway can hold only 36,298 spectators, or 34,482 for day games (one bleacher section has to be covered over to keep sun glare from distracting batters). It would be an enormous relief to replace the dingy, cramped locker rooms and have a drainage system that would keep the outfield playable during heavy rains. And so a number of different plans are on the table, everything from piecemeal renovations to building an entirely new stadium.

But current management acquired the Red Sox on a Save Fenway platform, and change isn't popular in Red Sox Nation. The 2005 movie *Fever Pitch* didn't exaggerate anything: Sit among Red Sox fans in the stands and you'll definitely remember that the word "fan" comes from "fanatic." The seats may be uncomfortable but they're gratifyingly close to the field, without the wide swaths of grass other parks have put between the fans and the players. In 2003, a new section of seats—more like bar stools, at nosebleed heights—opened atop the Green Monster; uncomfortable as they are, they're the most sought-after seats in the park.

If you can't get tickets to a game—and in the heat of a pennant race, they're more scarce than *R*s in a Boston accent—take a Fenway Park tour (conducted year-round, though there are no tours on game days or holidays). You actually get to peer inside the cramped space behind the Green Monster and walk out onto the warning track, stop in the press box, and visit the Red Sox

Fenway Park.

Hall of Fame. Best of all, you get a running commentary on all the legends who've played here. Raze Fenway? Sacrilege.

(i) **Fenway Park,** 4 Yawkey Way, Boston, MA ((C) **877/REDSOX-9** [733-7699] tickets, 617/226-6666 tours; www.redsox.com)

✈ Logan International

⊨ $$ **Doubletree Guest Suites,** 400 Soldiers Field Rd. ((C) **800/222-TREE** [7633] or 617/783-0090; www.doubletree.com). $ **The MidTown Hotel,** 220 Huntingdon Ave. ((C) **800/343-1177** or 617/262-1000; www.midtownhotel.com).

Wrigley Field
Cubs Losing Their Den?
Chicago, Illinois

THE CUBS WERE BOUGHT BY NEW OWNERS IN 2009 AND, FOR NOW, THEY ARE STILL PLAYING at their classic ballpark. But question marks still hang over the fate of the team and Wrigley Field. Will the Cubs be sold again? And if so, will they lose their classic ballpark?

Unlike their colleagues in Boston, the Chicago Cubs haven't played in the World Series since 1945 and haven't won the darn thing since 1908. Chicagoans love their Cubbies, champs or not, and they love their home field, one of baseball's classic venues. Built in 1914, Wrigley Field is the second-oldest venue in baseball (after

Wrigley Field.

Fenway Park **470** although the Cubs didn't move in until 1916 (roughly a decade after their last Series victory!). Back in 1988, lights were finally installed for night play, but they're rarely used—the Cubs still prefer to play mostly day games. With its ivy-covered outfield walls, hand-operated scoreboard, a view of Lake Michigan from the upper deck, and the El rattling past, it's old-fashioned baseball all the way.

After years, however, of being owned by the *Chicago Tribune* company, the Cubs were sold in 2007 and again in 2009—and new owner Joe Ricketts hasn't promised not to sell the team separately from its landmarked stadium. Could this mean that the Cubs find a new (larger, more modern) home? If so, what other fate might await Wrigley Field?

Wrigley is small enough that every seat is a decent seat, and the place truly earns its nickname the Friendly Confines—fans are passionate, friendly, well informed, and good-natured (much more so than Red Sox fans). Riding the Red Line El to the Addison Street stop, you can look down into the park from the train, and hear the roar of the crowd as soon as you step onto the platform. During the regular season on nongame days, you can take a 90-minute tour of the vintage stadium, visiting the press box, dugouts, both visitors' and Cubs' clubhouses, and the playing field itself (© **773/404-CUBS** [2827]).

Officially, Wrigley Field can seat 39,600 fans, but the walls are so low that enterprising owners of surrounding houses have built stands on their roofs where they seat their own ticket holders. Other Wrigley quirks: Ground rules declare that if a ball gets stuck in the ivy, it's a double; a pennant is flown after every game with a big W or L to alert passers-by to the outcome of the game (so who needs the Internet?). Best of all, when the opposing team hits a home run out of the park, somebody on the sidewalk outside picks up the offending ball and throws it back in. You've gotta love a ballpark where that happens—and hope against hope it's not lost.

ⓘ **Wrigley Field,** 1060 W. Addison St., Chicago, IL (© **773/404-CUBS** [2827]; www.cubs.mlb.com)

✈ O'Hare International

🛏 $$$ **Hotel Allegro Chicago,** 171 N. Randolph St. (© **800/643-1500** or 312/236-0123; www.allegrochicago.com). $$ **Homewood Suites,** 40 E. Grand St. (© **800/CALL-HOME** [225-5466] or 312/644-2222; www.homewoodsuiteschicago.com).

Sports Shrines 472

Houston Astrodome
Under the Dome
Houston, Texas

STANDING EMPTY, THE ASTRODOME WAS PUT TO SUDDEN USE IN AUGUST 2005 WHEN SOME 25,000 Hurricane Katrina victims were housed there on an emergency basis for 2 weeks. It was a sad chapter in the life of a building once called the Eighth Wonder of the World, but plans to turn it into a movie studio may give the old stadium a new lease on life.

How could Houston possibly have a baseball team? Given the sweltering Texas heat and humidity, summer games would be brutal for spectators, let alone players.

But in the early 1960s, ex-mayor Judge Roy Hofheinz offered a stunning solution: Build an indoor stadium, complete with air-conditioning, enclosed under a giant sky-lit dome. And so major-league baseball came to Houston with a team named the Colt .45s, soon renamed the Astros in recognition of Houston's growing role in the space program. Their $35-million new home opened in 1965, an 18-story-high domed circular stadium covering 9½ acres (3.8 hectares), with a stunning column-free span of 642 feet (196m). It wasn't just for baseball—the Astrodome could host football as well, with ingenious movable seating to accommodate up to 42,000 spectators (the parking lot held 30,000 cars). Not only that, but the Astrodome boasted 53 luxury suites, a revenue-boosting innovation that ballparks across the country immediately coveted.

The Astrodome field was covered with a specially bred type of grass, but soon it became clear that the dome's 4,000-plus Lucite panes focused the sun's rays into a nasty glare. The windowpanes were painted white, the grass died, and the Astros played the rest of the season on green-painted dirt. A new type of green nylon artificial grass was then developed, which quickly earned the name AstroTurf. (It took several seasons for players to realize the toll that AstroTurf play took on their knees.)

Over the years, inevitably the Astrodome began to show its age, especially as the development of retractable roofs made its fixed ceiling seem quaint. In 1997, the Houston Oilers moved to Tennessee after their owner had repeatedly demanded a new stadium; when the Astros also threatened to leave, the city built Enron Field (now Minute Maid Park) downtown in 2000. Then Reliant Stadium went up next door to the Astrodome in 2002 to house a new football team, the Houston Texans. Soon the big rodeos and concerts also moved to Reliant, leaving the Astrodome empty except for high-school football games and business conventions.

But the news is not all bad. Although a scheme to convert the Astrodome into a luxury hotel was rejected, there are now plans to convert it into a motion picture, media, and sound production facility. Could that mean a new chapter lies ahead for this old classic?

✈ George Bush Intercontinental Airport

🛏 $$ **La Quinta Inn Reliant Center,** 9911 Buffalo Speedway (✆ **800/531-5900** or 713/668-8082; www.laquinta.com). $$$ **The Magnolia Hotel,** 1100 Texas Ave. (✆ **888/915-1110** or 713/221-0011; www.magnoliahotels.com).

473 Sports Shrines

Hialeah Park Race Track
By a Nose
Hialeah, Florida

THINGS LOOKED GRIM FOR HIALEAH PARK RACE TRACK AFTER A 2005 HURRICANE, AND THE track is still troubled. Quarter horses are running, but that doesn't bring in much money, and owners are trying to build a slots parlor to attract more tourists.

Hurricane damage in 2005 hastened the deterioration of this Florida track, already caught up in business problems, a long-term decline of horse racing, and competition from nearby Gulfstream Park. Being a listed landmark and bird sanctuary may have hurt more than it helped. In 2006, the track was abandoned, but today it is once again in business as a venue for quarter horse racing.

Though Hialeah was built for greyhound racing and evolved into a top track for thoroughbred horses, it's also known for its flamingos, that dazzling flock of 300-plus stilt-legged pink beauties presiding over the infield's palm-bordered artificial lake. Hialeah's trademark, a distinctively Floridian touch, those flamingos became so famous that the lake was designated an Audubon Society sanctuary. The rest of the park should be so lucky.

Here's Hialeah's history in a nutshell: opened in 1921 (greyhound track, amusement park, horse track), nearly wiped out by the great hurricane of 1926, reopened as a horse-racing track with a spectacular new grandstand and tropical landscaping in 1932. Add nearly 70 years of racing, with horses from Seabiscuit and War Admiral to Citation and Seattle Slew pounding the turf here, and you get what came to be the East Coast's most important winter meet. From there, however, you have to fast-forward to 2001, when the track was closed to the public; to 2005, when the already-empty and neglected facility was damaged by Hurricane Wilma; and to 2007, when its stables were demolished despite landmark eligibility. In a surprising turn of fate, the park reopened again and the horses are running, although quarter horses are exclusively racing at this point.

All of this may only be a temporary reprieve for one of the earliest tourist attractions in south Florida, which helped to define the Sunshine State's charm for visitors from the 1930s on. Frequently described as the most beautiful racetrack ever built, Hialeah gave a touch of class to horse racing, a sport that unfortunately declined in the United States over the second half of the 20th century. Today the park is just a shadow of its former glamorous self.

Although it's been listed on the National Register of Historic Places since the 1970s, and was deemed eligible for National Historic Landmark status in 1988, Hialeah's owner never pursued the landmark process—a common fate for sports facilities, whose owners are afraid that landmark status will prohibit renovations needed to increase profitability. At press time, the park was struggling to get a license for slot machines. If they aren't able to manage this, the park's survival may once again be at stake.

ⓘ www.hialeahparkracing.com

✈ Miami International

🛏 $$$ **Sonesta Beach Resort Key Biscayne,** 350 Ocean Dr., Key Biscayne (ⓒ **800/SONESTA** [766-3782] or 305/361-2021; www.sonesta.com). $$ **Indian Creek Hotel,** 2727 Indian Creek Dr., Miami Beach (ⓒ **800/491-2772** or 305/531-2727; www.indiancreekhotel.com).

Entertainment 474

Coney Island
Last Act on the Brooklyn Boardwalk?
Brooklyn, New York

WHILE MASS-MARKET THEME PARKS LIKE SIX FLAGS AND BUSCH GARDENS PROLIFERATE, THE granddaddy of them all—Coney Island—struggles to survive, a string of small private amusements huddled at the end of New York's D and F subways.

All that's left of its glory days are two iconic rides, the eight-story-high Cyclone wooden roller coaster (built in 1927) and the ingenious double Ferris wheel known as the Wonder Wheel (1920), both protected as historic landmarks. The Parachute Jump, a relic of the 1939 World's Fair, remains as an architectural landmark, but no longer operates as a ride.

The Coney Island Cyclone.

Back in the summers before air-conditioning, families fled New York's tenement neighborhoods to find cool breezes at Coney Island beach, where snazzy amusement parks like Luna Park, Dreamland, and Steeplechase Park packed in the crowds. After World War II, however, rising crime and the spread of car culture sounded Coney Island's death knell. Originally the Cyclone was one of three 1920s-era roller coasters; the Tornado burned down in 1977 and the Thunderbolt went out of business in 1983 and stood rusting for years before a mysterious late-night demolition in 2000. Astroland, which opened in 1962 with a futuristic space-age theme, closed in 2007. The minor parks that remain offer mostly kiddie rides, haunted houses, bumper cars, and cheesy game arcades. A handful of food stands and bars remain in business, most notably the original Nathan's hot dog outlet on Surf Avenue.

Some of the boardwalk's midway glamour was recently restored, however, with a postmodern hipster gloss. Brooklyn artists have painted retro murals on several side walls, and **Coney Island USA** (www. coneyisland.com) operates a museum and sideshow performances at West 12th Street and Surf Avenue every weekend, as well as organizing the kitschy Mermaid Parade every June. The New York City parks department has spruced up the wooden boardwalk itself and installed new facilities along the wide white-sand Atlantic beach. Only a short walk east, where Dreamland once stood, the **New York Aquarium** (Surf Ave. and W. 8th St.; ✆ **718/265-3400;** www.nyaquarium.com) is a first-rate facility featuring dolphins, sea lions, seals, and walruses. Down the beach to the west, on the old Steeplechase Park site, KeySpan Park is home to the Mets' popular farm team, the **Brooklyn Cyclones** (✆ **718/449-8497;** www.brooklyncyclones.com). Plans are afoot to reopen the vintage B&B Carousel in a pavilion near KeySpan Park.

Developers, hungry to capitalize on this prime beachfront, are currently fighting to build hotels and residential high-rises along Surf Avenue. Would this bring prosperity to the neighborhood, or spoil its essential character? Coney Island has survived up to now, a grungy shadow of its former self—but the ball could drop at any moment.

ⓘ **Coney Island,** Surf Ave. between W. 10th and W. 12th sts., Brooklyn, NY (www. coneyisland.com)

✈ John F. Kennedy International, Newark Liberty International, LaGuardia

🛏 $ **Union Square Hotel,** 209 E. 14th St. (✆ **212/614-0500;** www.nyinns.com). $$ **Hotel Belleclaire,** 250 W. 77th St. at Broadway (✆ **877/468-3522** or 212/362-7700; www.hotelbelleclaire.com).

Entertainment
475

Wellfleet Drive-In
Steamy Summer Nights
Wellfleet, Massachusetts

WELLFLEET'S DRIVE-IN IS ONE OF THE LAST SURVIVORS OF VINTAGE OUTDOOR MOVIE THEATERS. But the costs of converting from old celluloid projectors to new digital systems is steep, which may force Wellfleet to call it a wrap.

Sooner or later, it was inevitable that someone would combine Americans' love affair with the automobile to their appetite for movies—and so was born the drive-in movie. The first drive-in opened in 1933 in Camden, New Jersey; in the baby boom years after World War II, their numbers mushroomed, rising to nearly 5,000 nationwide by the late 1950s. The drive-in movie served two audiences: young parents, who wanted to catch a movie while their children slept in the back seat, and high schoolers, who took advantage of the car's privacy for make-out sessions.

But by the late 1960s, drive-ins were on the wane, for several reasons: They lacked air-conditioning; distributors often refused to give them first-run films, forcing managers to rely on slasher movies and X-rated films; and their large lots became increasingly desirable real estate as communities sprawled outward. The rise of home video in the early 1980s killed off many more.

Built in 1957, the Wellfleet Drive-In is open from mid-April or early May to mid-October, showing first-run films after dark on a 100x44-foot (30x13m) outdoor screen. While moviegoers can get the film's soundtrack via old-fashioned monaural speakers you clip to your car window, you

can also tune to a special frequency on your FM radio to pick up the soundtrack in stereo. The lines of sight were designed for 1950s-height vehicles, so SUVs and campers and pickups are restricted to the back of the lot. In keeping with drive-in movie tradition, a double feature is shown every week, with an intermission for trips to the snack bar (vintage ads seduce you with visions of dancing popcorn buckets). Kids can blow off steam at a playground on-site, and a 1961-vintage minigolf course next door makes a great preshow activity.

Part of the reason for the Wellfleet Drive-In's survival (two other Cape drive-ins, in Hyannis and Yarmouth, closed years ago) is that its longtime owner figured out ways to supplement drive-in revenues—a popular flea market occupies the parking lot on weekend days, and there's a year-round indoor movie theater next door. When the owner died in 1998, two longtime employees kept it going.

A recent resurgence of nostalgia for drive-ins has helped some defunct sites reopen, and even a few new drive-ins have been built, though there are still only 400 or so in the United States, half of them in California. But will the costs of converting from old celluloid projectors to new digital systems be too steep for vintage drive-ins? Don't wait to find out how this picture ends; grab a bucket of dancing popcorn and experience one now.

(i) **Wellfleet Drive-In,** Rte. 6, Eastham-Wellfleet ((C) **508/349-7176;** www.well fleetdrivein.com)

✈ Hyannis

🛏 $$ **Viking Shores Motor Lodge,** Rte. 6, Eastham ((C) **800/242-2131;** www. vikingshores.com). $$ **Even'tide,** 650 Rte. 6, South Wellfleet ((C) **800/368-0007** in MA only, or 508/349-3410; www.eventide motel.com).

476 Entertainment

Weeki Wachee Springs
The Mermaids' Tale
Weeki Wachee, Florida

AT 60 YEARS OLD, THIS RUN-DOWN RELIC OF A BYGONE ERA FACED EXTINCTION. HOWEVER, the new owner, the state of Florida, has preserved this park—and its famous mermaids.

Thanks to its quirky geology, the state of Florida has freshwater springs busting out all over, but of them all, Weeki Wachee Springs has to be the prizewinner. This booming natural spring, located just an hour north of St. Petersburg, pumps an incredible 170 million gallons of 72°F (22°C) water every day into the Weeki Wachee River. It's also the deepest naturally formed spring in the United States, with sections of underwater cavern as deep as 407 feet (124m) underwater.

Nowadays, a natural attraction like this would probably have been set aside in its pristine state, featured as the environmental wonder it is. But in 1947, an ex-Navy frogman named Newton Perry saw Weeki Wachee Springs and had one thought: mermaids.

Perry—who had developed an air hose that would allow swimmers to breathe underwater for long stretches of time—correctly read the post-war hunger for entertainment and travel. He built an 18-seat amphitheater into the limestone shelf beside a spring and recruited comely young women to sheathe their legs in a fake tail and put on underwater mermaid ballet performances. By today's standards, the shows were fairly primitive—the shapely

swimmers simply swirled around smiling, waving, drinking bottled soda, and eating—but they did it underwater, an astonishing feat indeed. It also helped that

A mermaid at Weeki Wachee.

Weeki Wachee was situated alongside two-lane Highway 19, a big road in those preinterstate days.

By the 1950s, Weeki Wachee was an extremely popular tourist stop, offering landscaped gardens, a beach, and "jungle cruise" rides as well as the mermaid show. The ABC television network bought it in 1959, expanded it, and promoted it heavily on its television shows. The mermaid shows became glossy extravaganzas, running up to 10 performances a day.

But when Disney World opened in 1971—located at a nexus of new interstate highways—mere mermaids began to seem old hat. A seasonal water park, fed by the springs, was added in 1982, but as the years passed, Weeki Wachee's faded glories attracted fewer and fewer visitors. At the time of its 60th anniversary in 2007, the run-down park faced permanent closure. Rumors were that the land's owner, Southwest Florida Water Management District (nicknamed Swiftmud) was unable to sell the property to new owners and planned instead to turn it into a state park.

In 2008, the announcement came: The state of Florida would take over Weeki Wachee Springs but its historic mermaid shows have been preserved. While mainstream parks like Disney continue to make old-school tourist spots obsolete, it's refreshing that at least Weeki Wachee carries on as a true vestige of an earlier—and more innocent—era of tourism.

ⓘ 6131 Commercial Way, Weeki Wachee (Hwy. 19 at Hwy. 50; ℂ **877/469-3354** or 352/596-2062; www.weekiwachee.com)

✈ Tampa International

⊨ $ **Quality Inn Weeki Wachee Resort,** 6172 Commercial Way (ℂ **352/ 596-2007**)

Entertainment 477

Watts Towers
Folk-Art Fanatic
Los Angeles, California

THE WATTS TOWERS STAND AS A GLORIOUSLY ECCENTRIC WORK OF ART, BUT THEY ARE threatened by earthquakes and their inner-city location.

A gritty inner-city neighborhood threatened to engulf them; earthquakes have shaken their foundations; their own creator abandoned them years ago, leaving them to rack and ruin until art lovers "discovered" them and opened the site to the public in 1960. Something remains indomitable about Watts Towers, the largest piece of folk art ever created by a single person. It's as if the sheer human will that built them imbued these skeletal steel fantasies with their own will to survive. Given all they have working against them, from earthquakes to their blighted neighborhood, it is a wonder how much longer they can last.

Simon Rodia, an immigrant Italian tile setter, began this project—calling it Nuestro Pueblo, or Our Town—sometime in the early 1920s, working on it in his spare time for the next 33 years. Nine intricate cement-and-steel structures gradually rose to the sky, as high as 99 feet (30m), from the tiny yard of his cottage by the streetcar tracks. Though Rodia had no engineering degrees and used the simplest of tools, he was a skilled craftsman with an old-world pride in his handiwork.

The towers are surprisingly strong, though even they sustained some damage in the 1994 Northridge earthquake.

As time passed, the childless recluse became compulsively devoted to the project. Neighborhood punks tried to vandalize it and he built a wall; during World War II, local gossips sought to raze the towers, accusing Rodia of using them to transmit secret information to the Japanese. Rodia persisted—until 1954, when he abruptly quit the project and moved out, offhandedly leaving his property to a neighbor. He claimed to have lost all interest and would not give interviews, except to say, "I had in mind to do something big and I did it." We'll never know what inspired him.

Topped with futuristic-looking spires, these steeples of interlaced steel are encrusted with a zany profusion of brightly colored mosaics, created out of anything that came to hand—seashells, pottery, mirrors, you name it. Look for chips of green glass (which came from old 7UP bottles) and blue glass (from Milk of Magnesia bottles). Rodia's day job was at the legendary Malibu Potteries, so it seems likely that many fragments of valuable Malibu tile are embedded in the towers. Tours are offered every half-hour on a first-come, first-served basis.

The Watts Towers.

ⓘ **Watts Towers,** 1727 E. 107th St., Los Angeles (✆ **213/847-4646;** www.watts towers.us)

✈ Los Angeles International

🛏 $$ **Beverly Garland's Holiday Inn,** 4222 Vineland Ave., North Hollywood (✆ **800/BEVERLY** [238-3759] or 818/980-8000; www.beverlygarland.com). $$ **Roosevelt Hotel,** Hollywood, 7000 Hollywood Blvd. (✆ **800/950-7667** or 323/466-7000; www.hollywoodroosevelt.com).

478 Entertainment

Luna Park
Saving the Face
Sydney, Australia

UNLIKE MODERN THEME PARKS THAT TRY TO SIMULATE FOREIGN COUNTRIES OR MOVIE SETS, Luna Park remains a charming collection of straightforward rides with just enough tawdriness to lend it a spark of nostalgic flavor. It faces ongoing troubles with lawsuits.

Luna Park.

No child who has ever walked into Luna Park, through the grotesque gaping grin of the Face, could fail to be wowed. First opened in 1935 and continually refurbished throughout the 1950s, Luna Park was Sydney's homegrown version of Disneyland, and while it may not have had the Disney imagination going for it, it made up for that with a sturdy Aussie sense of fun. Though its history from the 1970s on has been rocky—numerous redevelopment proposals, shutdowns, safety and noise violations, and the tragic death of 13 people on the Ghost Train in 1979—adults who were hooked as children have continually risen to save the park, through street protests, lawsuits, National Heritage Board actions, and, finally, specific government legislation on its behalf. (Copenhagen's Tivoli Gardens is the world's only other amusement park that's a government-legislated landmark.)

Luna Park's most recent reincarnation opened in April 2004 and so far is thriving, aside from a few lawsuits (almost de rigueur, considering Luna Park's history). The entrance is still through **the Face,** a giant smiling polyurethane mask nearly 9m (30 ft.) wide. Behind the Face, the Midway stretches through the park to **Coney Island,** the original 1930s fun house—a cornucopia of vintage amusements like rotating barrels, moving platforms, and large slides (modified, of course, to meet modern safety standards) plus a bank of arcade games. Along the **Midway,** you'll find major rides like an antique carousel (the Racing Cockerels), a Ferris wheel, a flying saucer ride, and the 1960s-era Wild Mouse. A boardwalk ambles along the park's seaside edge. The Midway's heritage-listed **Crystal Palace** has been retrofitted as a function space, while an event venue called the Luna Circus replaces a beloved ride known as the Big Dipper, which was ruled too noisy to remain in this densely developed neighborhood.

You can ride to Luna Park via the Sydney Harbour ferry (Milsons Point is the stop) and there are even views across the harbor of Sydney's most iconic sight, the Opera House. It's not a perfect restoration, but it's enough to keep the Luna Park spirit alive—and that keeps the Face grinning.

ⓘ 1 Olympic Dr., Milsons Point (✆ **61/ 2/9922 6644;** www.lunaparksydney.com)

✈ Sydney International Airport

🛏 $$$ **North Sydney Harbourview Hotel,** 17 Blue St., North Sydney (✆ **61/2/ 9955 0499** or toll-free in Australia 300/785 453; www.viewhotels.com.au). $$ **Wattle Private Hotel,** 108 Oxford St., Darlinghurst (✆ **61/2/9332 4118;** www.the wattle.com).

Back Beat on the Reeperbahn
Hamburg's Music Clubs
Hamburg, Germany

OF THE FOUR VENUES THE BEATLES PLAYED IN HAMBURG, ONLY THE KAISERKELLER REMAINS, and even that has been vastly altered. What hasn't changed, though, is the raw energy of the Hamburg music scene, thriving alongside the Reeperbahn's X-rated sleaze.

It's an essential pilgrimage for Beatles fans: touring Hamburg's red-light district, where the fledgling English band played several gigs in 1960, 1961, and 1962. The infamous Reeperbahn, main drag of the St. Pauli red-light district, is undeniably rough and sleazy—Hamburg's tourism officials are well aware that its gritty atmosphere attracts tourists. (Amsterdam's equally famous red-light district, in contrast, seems sanitized.) But the music clubs are still there, sandwiched in among sex clubs, brothels, and bars. Whether they're the same clubs where the Beatles played is another question.

The Beatles' first Hamburg gig, starting in July 1960, was at the Indra Club, a shabby girlie lounge with worn red carpeting on a Reeperbahn side street called Große Freiheit. Around the corner at 33 Paul-Roosen Strasse is the former Bambi Kino, a run-down cinema where club owner Bruno Koschmider housed the Beatles in squalid cubicles behind the screen. The Indra Club at Große Freiheit 64 today is a modern renovation, so named to capitalize on the Beatles' fame—the original Indra abruptly closed in October 1960, after which the Beatles were shifted to Koschmider's other club, the Kaiserkeller, at 38 Große Freiheit, much closer to the Reeperbahn action. Here they performed on a makeshift stage, alternating with Rory Storm and the Hurricanes, whose drummer was Ringo Starr (Pete Best was still the Beatles' drummer). Extensively revamped since then, the **Kaiserkeller** is now owned by the next-door venue, Große Freiheit 36 (© **49/40/317778-0**), a prominent live-music venue which opened in 1985.

A month after debuting at the Kaiserkeller, the Beatles were lured to the Top Ten Club, a brassy new nightspot right on the main drag, at Reeperbahn 136, where they played backup to headliner Tony Sheridan. Though legal problems soon sent them home, they returned in March 1961 for a 3-month engagement. The Top Ten Club survived for years, but finally closed; from outside the building, you can see the attic windows where the Beatles lived during that 1961 gig.

Returning to Hamburg in April 1962, the Beatles were popular enough to be booked at the hot new nightclub the Star Club, across from the Kaiserkeller at 39 Große Freiheit (go through the archway into the courtyard). The Star Club closed in 1969, was converted to a sex club, then burned down; the Star Club Hof cafe that's there now is another attempt to cash in on Beatles fame. You can, however, get a cheap meal at the **Gretel & Alfons cafe,** a few doors down from the Star Club, where the Beatles hung out between gigs.

Reeperbahn is all the more significant when you realize that New York's CBGB's is now closed and that other famous clubs that hosted the greats of popular music are vulnerable. London's 100 Club, which hosted acts like the Sex Pistols and the Jam, got a reprieve in 2011, when Converse took on sponsorship. So, while it was saved, like many of the clubs of Reeperbahn, it is one of a vanishing breed.

✈ Hamburg

🛏 $$$ **East,** Simon-von-Utrecht Strasse 31 (✆ **49/40/309930;** www.east-hotel.

de). $ **Fritzhotel,** Schanzenstrasse 101–103 (✆ **49/40/822-22-830;** www.fritz hotel.com).

Route 66
Get Your Kicks
United States

ROUTE 66 HAS TAKEN A BEATING OVER THE YEARS. IN SOME CASES ALL THAT REMAIN OF THE highway's kitschy landmarks are their signs. What is left is threatened by vandalism and decay.

There is possibly nothing more American than the lure of the open road, and for many decades, Route 66 delighted travelers with a chance to see the country and enjoy the many roadside attractions that sprang up to serve them. This iconic

Route 66.

highway has been immortalized in song by singers like Nat King Cole and Bob Dylan, on celluloid by television series like *Route 66,* and in print by Jack Kerouac's *On the Road.* Even after years of being revered, it still has the power to capture the collective imagination.

Route 66 was finished in 1926 and emerged as the main highway from the interior of the country leading to the west coast. The route covered widely varying terrain—originally running through Illinois, Missouri, Kansas, Oklahoma, Texas, New Mexico, and Arizona before ending in Los Angeles, California. It carried Dust Bowl farmers in the '30s and was dubbed "The Mother Road" in John Steinbeck's *The Grapes of Wrath.* During World War II, it was used to transport troops and supplies across the eight states it traverses. The road really came into its own, though, during the car culture of the 1950s when it became the ultimate road trip, with travelers stopping to gas up at vintage Shell stations, eat at diners, and spend the night in hotels shaped like wigwams. Today many of the original buildings flanking it are on the National Register of Historic Places.

The highway's glory days began to fade when President Dwight Eisenhower signed the Interstate Highway Act. The country's new interstates drew travelers who jumped at the chance to get to their destinations sooner. This led drivers to veer past Route 66 and many of its wonderfully kitschy businesses. In some cases the signs remain, but the buildings themselves are just memories. Buildings still standing are vulnerable to vandalism, decay, and abandonment, and some communities along the route have simply disappeared.

Luckily, there is still a lot to love about this historic 2,000-mile (3,200km) highway, and in 2008 it was added to the World Monuments watch list, which is supporting several projects to preserve and restore it. Traveling the road today, you'll go from large cities where signs marking the route are few to small towns and grass prairies. If you have the itch to hit the road, get started by visiting nps.gov (see its website below), where you'll find maps, itineraries, and a list of highlights in each state. There's still time to get your kicks on Route 66!

ⓘ www.nps.gov/history/nr/travel/route66

481 Roadside Relics

The Merritt Parkway
Gateway to New England
Fairfield County, Connecticut

RUNNING THROUGH CONNECTICUT'S MOST POPULOUS COUNTY, THIS NATIONAL SCENIC Byway is losing its distinctive beauty, through bridge decay, degraded landscape, and poor maintenance.

Back in the early 1930s, automobile culture was still new and thrilling. Running 37 miles (60km) from suburban Greenwich to Stratford, Connecticut, the Merritt Parkway followed a new paradigm for highway design, pioneered by New York State's recently built Bronx River, Saw Mill River, and Hutchinson River parkways. Envisioned as a "ribbon park," it would have no roadside billboards. It would be only for passenger cars—no heavy trucks, bicycles, pedestrians, or horse buggies. The four lanes of traffic— two in each direction—would be divided by a parklike strip of greenery; dense bushes and trees would screen the highway from the towns it passed through. Occasional open vistas were showcased, and landscaping would provide seasonal interest—flowering trees in spring, deciduous hardwood for fall color, evergreens for winter cover.

Connecticut residents, worried about an influx of New York traffic, were mollified by on- and off-ramps that limited intersections with local roads. Instead, the Merritt would fly over roads or glide under them, on 69 graceful bridges. It was these bridges that really made the Merritt special. Inspired by the City Beautiful movement, architect George L. Dunkelberger's bridges were all different, individually styled in Art Deco, neoclassical, French Renaissance, Gothic, or rustic designs. Elegant sculptures, bas-reliefs, and fanciful wrought iron decorated their arches and supports.

It was one of the great Depression-era public works projects, providing much-needed jobs for 6 years. And when the first leg opened in 1938, public acclaim confirmed it: A highway *could* be a work of art. (It's one of the few roads listed on the National Register of Historic Places.)

As time passed, however, automobile culture got bigger and cruder. The interstate highways of the 1960s introduced straighter lines, minimal landscaping, and higher speeds. Nowadays, drivers accustomed to those multilane behemoths recklessly navigate the Merritt's narrow lanes, tight shoulders, and short entry ramps, gunning past its stop-sign entrances to merge aggressively into traffic. (The Merritt's lower 55-mile-per-hour speed limit is rarely observed.) Many ramps had to be redesigned; metal guardrails were erected on the median strip or the shoulder, as well as hulking cast-concrete barriers. Newer expressways introduced utilitarian overpasses of blank concrete and steel; three of the original bridges were torn down, and others were redesigned. For driver safety, road crews have widened its shoulders and cleared mature trees. From 1939 to 1988, the Merritt had one tollbooth, but these days it depends for upkeep on the underfunded Connecticut Department of Transportation, and maintenance has been shoddy.

Enter the not-for-profit Merritt Parkway Conservancy, which since 1999 has worked to restore the Merritt: cleaning and repairing bridges, replanting dogwoods and mountain laurels, clearing invasive plants and vines, and opening a small parkway museum in Stratford (6580 Main St.), along with legal and political advocacy. Much remains to be done, but the Merritt's story may have a happy ending after all.

ⓘ www.merrittparkway.org

✈ New York City

🛏 $$ **The Roger Sherman Inn,** 195 Oenoke Ridge, New Canaan (✆ **203/966-4541;** www.rogershermaninn.com). $$ **The Westport Inn,** 1595 Post Road E., Westport (✆ **800/446-8997** or 203/418-2500; www.westportinn.com).

Roadside Relics 482

The Oldest McDonald's
Speeder the Chef's Drive-In
Downey, California

THIS ICONIC RETRO MCDONALD'S NEARLY FELL IN THE 1994 NORTHRIDGE EARTHQUAKE. Preservations sought to save it, and eventually the franchise decided to restore it to its original kitschy glory.

This burger shack in Downey wasn't the McDonald brothers' first restaurant (that was a hot dog stand in Arcadia), the first place where they pioneered their "fast food" assembly-line operation (that would have been their San Bernardino burger bar), or even the first of their restaurants to have golden arches in its design (that was in Phoenix). But when this site—their fourth franchise outlet—opened in 1953, the formula was finally set, and this location has remained in business ever since— the oldest McDonald's still in operation.

There's something weirdly familiar and yet strange about its vintage red-and-white-striped tile exterior and the pair of parabolic golden arches supporting its roof. The employees wear '50s-vintage uniforms with white shirts, paper hats, and bolo ties. Strictly a walk-up restaurant (no PlayPlace here), it has outdoor tables where you can take your burger and milkshake after you've ordered your food at the window. The roadside marquee is hard to miss, with its 60-foot-high (18m) neon-outlined figure of a chipper character named Speedee the Chef, the chain's long-retired early mascot, Ronald McDonald's great-grand-daddy.

A year after this restaurant opened, a milkshake-machine salesman named Ray Kroc saw the potential in the McDonald brothers' formula, bought out their little chain, and the rest is history. The Downey restaurant is our last reminder of the modern megachain's simple beginnings. After it was damaged in the 1994 Northridge earthquake, this outlet—which had been losing money—was nearly closed down. Historic preservationists fought to keep it, and eventually in 1996 the McDonald's corporation woke up to an opportunity to honor its own past. Refurbishment restored the historic features, and a museum and gift shop were added (displays of vintage Happy Meal toys, anyone?). However you feel about the parent chain, there's something undeniably fascinating about seeing its 1950s incarnation, from long before the fast-food concept supersized into something entirely different.

ⓘ **Historic Speedee McDonald's,** 10207 Lakewood Blvd. (✆**562/622-9249**)

✈Los Angeles International

🛏$$ **Beverly Garland's Holiday Inn,** 4222 Vineland Ave., North Hollywood ([tell] **800/BEVERLY** [238-3759] or 818/980-8000; www.beverlygarland.com). $$ **Roosevelt Hotel,** Hollywood, 7000 Hollywood Blvd. (✆**800/950-7667** or 323/466-7000; www.hollywoodroosevelt.com).

---

483 Roadside Relics

Googie Design
Cruising Space-Age Googieland
Orange County, California

FOR YEARS SERIOUS ARCHITECTS LOOKED DOWN ON GOOGIE ARCHITECTURE, WITH ALL ITS pop-culture-styled curves and cantilevers and bold colors. Today preservationists are scrambling to save what's left.

A close cousin of New Jersey's Doo-Wop style, even in its 1950s Southern California heyday Googie architecture was considered way too commercial, a design style fit only for bowling alleys, motels, coffee shops, strip malls, liquor stores, and car washes—surely not anything with substance.

Well, times change, tastes change; Googie design now has picked up a gloss of hipster cachet. Unfortunately, most of it was carelessly razed in the past few decades as road construction and suburban redevelopment spiraled in Orange County.

The name "Googie" was eventually applied to the whole movement, derived from the inventive design of Googie's Coffee Shop at Sunset Boulevard and Crescent Heights in Los Angeles. The hotbed of Googie, though, was here in Orange County, where a late-1950s real estate boom was jump-started by Disneyland's 1955 opening. The futuristic promise of Tomorrowland echoed over and over outside the park

as well, with Sputnik-shaped signs and launchpadlike roofs. Starbursts, boomerangs, and amoebas replaced rectilinear forms; cartoonish lettering replaced formal typefaces on signs. Neon was an essential ingredient; so were chrome details (not surprising, in midcentury car culture) and Formica and fiberglass accents in bold colors. Advances in plate-glass technology allowed vast expanses of windows, too, making the most of California's sunshine in those presmog years. Postwar fascination with South American and South Pacific motifs was thrown in as well, courtesy of the many returning servicemen who settled in sunny Southern California.

The **Anaheim Convention Center** in Anaheim (800 W. Katella) is a big-scale Googie example, its domed white roofline and swoops of glass looking distinctly flying-saucer-like. Take Katella east to State College Boulevard and go south 2 blocks to Angel Stadium, where a tall green roadside sign with a rakish halo sets a Googie

443

keynote for the ballpark. Then retrace your route on Katella west to South Harbor Boulevard, turn right, and cruise northward to Lincoln Avenue; head west on Lincoln to Brookhurst, turn right and go south on Brookhurst to Garden Grove Boulevard, where a left-hand turn will take you east back to Harbor Boulevard. These are all traffic-clogged major thoroughfares—exactly where you can still hope to find a few roadside signs and small businesses that sport the vintage Googie look. They're still there, but every year, you have to look harder and harder.

✈ John Wayne Airport in Santa Ana

🛏 $$$ **Disney's Grand Californian Hotel,** 1600 S. Disneyland Dr. (✆ **714/956-MICKEY** [956-6425] or 714/635-2300; www.disneyland.com). $$ **Candy Cane Inn,** 1747 S. Harbor Blvd. (✆ **800/345-7057** or 714/774-5284; www.candycane inn.net).

Roadside Relics 484

Paul Bunyan Statues
Roadside Giants
Minnesota Lake Country

WHILE ROADSIDE KITSCH SEEMS TO BE DISAPPEARING ACROSS THE COUNTRY, IT'S STILL ALIVE and well along the secondary highways of northern Minnesota. Here is where the legend of Paul Bunyan resides.

It seems that every small Midwestern town has some plaster or fiberglass animal mounted on a pole outside of town—a rainbow trout, a beaver, a moose—to proclaim itself to visitors. But why mess around with a mere animal when you could have the North Woods' most enduring legend—the King of the Lumberjacks, Paul Bunyan, and his big blue ox, Babe?

You really know you've hit the North Woods when you arrive in Brainerd, Minnesota, and see the 11½-foot-tall (3.5m) fiberglass Paul Bunyan statue beside the tourist information stand on Highway 371 just south of town. Brainerd's city fathers apparently aren't too cool for the old Bunyan image, because they commissioned this statue recently, after failing to acquire a much larger seated Paul Bunyan figure from the now-defunct Paul Bunyan Center. That statue wound up at **This Old Farm,** 17553 Hwy. 18, Brainerd (✆ **218/764-2524**), an endearing mishmash of old-style attractions which combines a restored 1940s farm, a corn maze, an arcade (where Paul sits), and a small ho-hum amusement park.

Brainerd, in fact, has established itself as the anchor for a 100-mile (161km) paved **Paul Bunyan Trail** that winds through lake country. And some 70 miles (113km) farther upstate, in the town of Akeley, on Main Street you'll find the next Paul Bunyan statue, a really big one—he'd be 25 feet (7.6m) tall if he stood up. Instead he crouches down kindly, resting his ax beside him, with his hand gently cupped to hold tourists for photo ops. The black beard on this one is seriously impressive.

Forty miles (64km) north of Akeley, you come to Bemidji—purportedly Bunyan's birthplace—where the granddaddy of all Paul Bunyan statues stands downtown, next to the tourist office, on the pine-edged shore of Lake Bemidji (created, so the folklore goes, by one of Paul's footprints). Eastman Kodak once named this America's second-most-photographed roadside icon, a classic piece of Americana erected in 1937. This rather crude Paul Bunyan figure stands 18 feet (5.5m) high and weighs 2½ tons; oddly, instead of

Paul Bunyan and Babe the Blue Ox.

the classic black beard, he has a Snidely-Whiplash-like handlebar mustache. Next to him stands a 5-ton Babe the Blue Ox.

There's also a Paul Bunyan Amusement Park beside the statues, and south of town is the **Paul Bunyan Animal Farm,** 3857 Animal Land Dr. (☏218/759-1533), a small petting zoo. It might as well cash in on the name—everybody else up here does!

ⓘ**Visit Bemidji,** Paul Bunyan Dr., Bemidji, MN (☏218/759-0164; www.visitbemidji.com)

✈ Brainerd Regional Airport, Bemidji Regional Airport

⊨$$ **Hampton Inn,** 1019 Paul Bunyan Dr. S., Bemidji (☏800/426-7866 or 218/751-3600; http://hamptoninn1.hilton.com). $ **AmericInn,** 1200 Paul Bunyan Dr. NW, Bemidji (☏800/634-3444 or 218/751-3000).

485 **Roadside Relics**

The Red Routemaster
Double-Decker Tradition
London, England

For half a century, the red double-decker buses trundling around London were a visible symbol of the city. Accessibility requirements, fuel efficiency, and emission standards rendered the Routemasters obsolete. Now only two heritage routes are still using these wonderful old buses.

True, by the dawn of the 21st century the red Routemasters were inadequate for

new public-transport standards—they couldn't accommodate wheelchairs, and

10 Signs That Go Blink in the Night

The beauty of the neon sign was that you could twist those glass tubes into any shape you wanted. And as America took to the highways in the 1950s and 1960s, advertisers took advantage of that, spangling the nighttime streetscape with colorful whimsies touting everything from bowling alleys to ice-cream stands to Tiki bars.

Good old-fashioned neon lighting has been outmoded by fiber-optic technology. The good news is that preservationists are working to save neon signs for future generations, either on-site or in museums. After all, what would America be without a few giant neon donuts around?

486 Electric City, Scranton, Pennsylvania In 1910, in the pre-neon age, this flashing electric circular sign was erected eight stories high atop the steep-gabled Victorian-era Scranton Electric Building proclaiming Scranton as the electric city. Its purpose: to promote the fact that Scranton was the first U.S. city to install electric streetcars. The sign went dark in 1972, but it was restored and relit in 2004. *© 570/963-5901.*

487 The Stinker Station, Twin Falls, Idaho Opened in 1936, this Idaho gas station chain made the most of its era's penchant for whimsical roadside advertising. Original owner Farris Lind based his success on low prices that undersold the competition, so naturally he developed as his mascot a black-and-white neon skunk. There are still neon skunks adorning a few outlets around the state, but the biggest and best is at 1777 Kimberly Rd. in Twin Falls. *© 208/734-6560.*

488 The East Gate, Los Angeles, California This pagoda-shaped California landmark turns on enough lights to illuminate a small town in China. It opened in 1938 in Los Angeles in an enclave modeled by a Hollywood set designer to serve Chinese Americans displaced by the building of Union Station. The East Gate was the entrance to a mini-mall that housed 18 stores (now known as Old Chinatown Plaza, 1100 N. Broadway). There are other vintage neon buildings on-site, making it a bright destination for travelers stopping in Los Angeles. *www.oldchinatownla.com.*

489 Leon's Frozen Custard, Milwaukee, Wisconsin It's said that this vintage burger and custard stand at 3131 S. 27th St., opened in 1942, was the model for Al's Diner in the TV show *Happy Days*. While other local eateries dispute this fact, this Milwaukee landmark with its radiating strips of neon under the carports and its unmissable roadside marquee is worth visiting just for the signage, though the burgers and malts are a delicious bonus. *© 414/383-1784.*

490 Superdawg Drive-In, Chicago, Illinois With its neon-studded canopies, the Superdawg drive-in—founded in 1948 at 6363 N. Milwaukee Ave.—features more than a delicious snack: It's a local landmark, known for the two tall hot dogs cavorting on its roof. The male hot dog is for some reason wearing a loincloth. Modesty, perhaps? Whatever the reason, this drive-in's an excellent example of mascots gone wild. *www.superdawg.com*.

491 The Seven Dwarfs, Wheaton, Illinois Though several tubes are burned out, the fabulous neon sign at the Seven Dwarfs Restaurant and Fountain, 917 E. Roosevelt Rd., still welcomes customers with a friendly waving pig wearing a chef's hat. As for Snow White and the dwarfs, they show up on murals inside this friendly-family diner. ✆ **630/653-7888**.

492 The Elephant Car Wash, Seattle, Washington With 380 blinking lights, the big pink elephant in the jaunty hat on the Elephant Car Wash sign at 616 Battery St. in downtown Seattle has been a source of delight since the early 1950s. Although the carwash chain now has nine locations in the Seattle area, the downtown branch is the one with that iconic revolving sign. *www.elephantcarwash.com*.

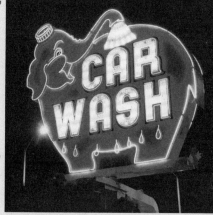
The Elephant Car Wash.

493 Rancho Grande Mexican Restaurant, Tulsa, Oklahoma Along Route 66—a grand thoroughfare of neon signage during its heyday—several fascinating neon relics remain. One of these is at the entrance of the Mexican restaurant at 1629 E. 11th St., Route 66's in-town route through Tulsa. Built in 1953, it features a dapper black-hatted caballero slinging a yellow neon lasso around the name of the restaurant. ✆ **918/584-0816**.

494 Western Hills Motel, Flagstaff, Arizona Neon was the perfect medium for beckoning weary drivers off the road at night into roadside motels. Farther west along Route 66, this low-slung fieldstone motel (with a pool!) is still in operation at 1580 E. Rte. 66 behind its classic roadside marquee featuring a red covered wagon and horses, which apparently were once animated. The name of the motel glows blue above the unmistakably huge word "motel" in yellow. ✆ **928/774-6633**.

495 Crescent Bowl, Bowling Green, Kentucky In a town named Bowling Green, you'd expect a few bowling alleys, right? Well, bowling is by no means as popular a sport as it was in the mid–20th century, and those old lanes are fast disappearing, along with their vintage neon signs. This old-school establishment at 2724 Nashville Rd. may have seen better days inside, but outside a vintage bowling-themed sign glows for all to see. ✆ **270/843-6021**.

they required new engines for fuel effi-ciency and emission controls. Neverthe-less, it seemed unthinkable that they should be withdrawn from service entirely by 2006. On the last day of service, December 9, 2005, so many people lined the final route that traffic was stopped completely, making the usually timely bus 10 minutes late in reaching its garage.

The Routemaster was, in fact, a classic piece of British design, superbly fitted to carry a maximum of passengers and still negotiate London's narrow, winding streets. Built of durable but light aluminum and easy to repair, it featured a rear open platform that made it easy to hop on and off, although that feature also increased labor costs, requiring a ticket-taking con-ductor on the bus as well as a driver. Not all were red, in fact; several green Routemasters were also in operation, mostly on outlying routes.

By the time of its demise, the Route-master had already been replaced on many routes by single-level buses, and some were converted to private sightsee-ing operations with an open top deck (not practical otherwise—England is, after all, a country where it rains frequently). In all, nearly 3,000 Routemasters were built, and

around 1,000 were still running in 2005. They were largely replaced by long, articu-lated buses, slower and heavier than Routemasters and much less adept at steering around the London street maze (but easier for fare skippers to slip onto).

The outcry over the withdrawal of the Routemaster was so great that the former London Mayor Ken Livingstone agreed to keep them on two short versions of regu-lar routes, called Heritage Routes: Route 9, a 5km (3-mile) route which runs from Royal Albert Hall to Aldwych via Hyde Park cor-ner and Piccadilly Circus, and Route 15, between Trafalgar Square and Tower Hill via St. Paul's Church and Charing Cross. Between these two routes, a significant number of tourist destinations will still be served by the red double-deckers.

✈ Heathrow International

🛏 $$ **Mornington Hotel,** 12 Lancaster Gate, Bayswater ℂ **800/633-6548** in North America or 44/20/7262-7361; www.bw-morningtonhotel.co.uk). $$ **Sanctu-ary House Hotel,** 33 Tothill St., Westmin-ster ℂ **44/20/7799-4044;** www.fullers hotels.com).

Milestone Motel
An Overnight Sensation
San Luis Obispo, California

CLOSED IN 1991, NOW EMPTY AND NEGLECTED, THE FIRST MOTOR INN STILL RETAINS THE design that has inspired roadside motels across the United States.

Architecturally, there's nothing distin-guished about this low-slung set of stucco buildings, a vague pastiche of Mission architecture with a three-story tower meant to evoke the Santa Barbara mis-sion's famous bell tower. But back in 1926, motorists traveling between Los Angeles

and San Francisco would have seen it as a rare destination, exactly halfway up the coast and located right on Highway 101 (the same El Camino Real route used by California's early Spanish settlers). It was neither a traditional hotel nor one of the rustic campgrounds that had recently begun to sprout around gas stations in the infancy of America's automotive age. This place even had a new sort of name: a motor hotel—or, to fit better on a roadside sign, a "mo-tel."

As the bronze plaque on its front wall attests, architect Arthur Heineman gets full credit for inventing the motel concept. His location was ideal: at the midway point in San Luis Obispo, right beside Highway 101, the main north-south road in those days. (It was also at the north end of Monterey St., up the road from where San Luis Obispo's own historic Spanish mission was located.) It cost $80,000 to build; guests were charged a stiff $1.25 a night for a two-room bungalow with a kitchenette, an indoor bathroom (with a shower!), and parking conveniently located right outside the room. All the bungalows faced onto a central palm-lined courtyard with a pool and picnic tables. It combined a certain level of swanky comfort (car owners in the 1920s were, after all, among the more affluent citizens) with car-friendly efficiency. A restaurant and dance hall were included in the complex as well. Plans were to erect a whole chain of Milestone Motels up and down the California coast; the Depression, however, put an end to that scheme.

Though it was originally named the Milestone Mo-Tel, the motel was renamed the Motor Inn and had become severely rundown by the time it closed in 1991. Since then it has sat empty, with boarded-up windows and a chain-link fence hung with yellow warning signs surrounding the site. (It can be viewed, though, from The Apple Farm Inn, located next door.) Various owners have proposed plans for a face-lift that never comes to fruition. Parts have already been demolished and others may soon go from sheer dilapidation; bringing the motel up to current building code would most likely be prohibitively expensive by this time. Even from outside the fence, though, you can see that classic design, adapted over the years to thousands of Travel-Lodges and Motel 6s and other roadside lodgings across the country. Heineman's brainstorm was an idea that worked.

ⓘ 2223 Monterey St., San Luis Obispo

✈ San Luis Obispo

🛏 $$$ **Apple Farm Inn,** 2015 Monterey St., San Luis Obispo (✆ **805/544-2040;** www.applefarm.com). $$ **Garden Street Inn,** 1212 Garden St. (✆ **800/488-2045** or 805/545-9802; www.gardenstreetinn. com).

---

497 Vintage Hotels & Motels

Century Plaza Hotel
Saved from the Ball & Chain
Los Angeles, California

JUST A COUPLE OF YEARS AGO THINGS LOOKED BLEAK FOR THE CENTURY PLAZA HOTEL, BUT thanks to the efforts of the Los Angeles Conservancy, this glamorous landmark has been saved from the wrecking ball. Yet changes to its surroundings and the hotel itself have compromised its integrity.

At the heart of Century City in Los Angeles is the Century Plaza Hotel, a breathtaking 19-story curved glass hotel that is the epitome of 1960s modernism. Designed by Minoru Yamasaki, who went on to design the World Trade Center, it was completed in 1964, fronted by spectacular fountains on the Avenue of Stars. Century City itself was designed as a business mecca, and many lawyers and executives

The Century Plaza Hotel.

active in the film industry keep offices there. Soon it became a beloved tourist sight as well as a destination spot for presidents and celebrities.

Once known as the "West Coast White House," Century City Plaza served as a home away from home for Presidents Lyndon Johnson, Richard Nixon, Gerald Ford, and George Bush, who bunked there whenever they visited Los Angeles. President Bill Clinton, who usually liked to stay with friends in the area, would also occasionally check in. Century Plaza played host to many social events and award dinners over the years, attracting Hollywood elite like Cary Grant, Tom Hanks, and Sharon Stone, to name just a few. In 1969, Nixon chose the hotel to host a party for the Apollo 11 astronauts, celebrating their historic trip to the moon.

Until recently, the hotel was directly across from ABC Entertainment Center and the Shubert Theater, both casualties of the wrecking ball. In their place is the 2000 Wilshire project that stands between the Avenue and Century City's twin towers. In 2009, it was feared that a similar

fate might face the Century Plaza Hotel, when owners announced that they would raze the building to make way for two new towers. Luckily, this elicited outrage from local groups and preservationists, and, that same year, the building was named one of America's 11 Most Endangered Historic Places by the National Trust for Historic Preservation. But not all of the news is good for this great landmark: Proposed development includes two 46-story skyscrapers to be built behind the hotel, which will change the landscape dramatically. Worse yet, a large portion of the lobby will be hollowed out to connect the new buildings, shops, and plazas with nearby streets.

The hotel is currently operating as a Hyatt Regency, welcoming guests to this once-endangered architectural treasure. Hey, if you can't be a star, you can live like one. To book a stay, check out the website below.

🛏 $$$ **Hyatt Regency Century Plaza** (✆ **310/228-1234;** www.centuryplaza. hyatt.com)

Doo-Wop Motels
Catch the Kitsch
Wildwood, New Jersey

THE PANORAMA OF THE WILDWOOD STRIP IS LIKE A LOW-RENT VERSION OF EARLY LAS VEGAS. But with many of those classic 1950s hotels already demolished, this corner of the Jersey shore is a last holdout of the Rat Pack signature style.

By the mid–20th century, it wasn't enough for a motel just to have a room with an attached bathroom, a parking space, and a pool; the joint had to have a theme. And along this strip of beach towns on the south Jersey Shore, the wackier the theme, the better. Jazz it up with pulsating neon, accent it with bright paint schemes, throw in zigzag rooflines and balconies, and slap on free-form arches, fins, and boomerangs, and there you'd have it: a Doo-Wop motel.

A pack of these classic Doo-Wop motels still stand, officially recognized by the State of New Jersey as the Wildwoods Shore Resort Historic District. Ocean Avenue in Wildwood Crest is the main drag, lined today with more than 50 vintage motels. But another 50 or so were knocked down quite recently, between 2000 and 2005, victims of the area's real estate boom. Historic preservationists in the area are vigilant about protecting what's left.

The Wildwood resort area really took off in the 1950s as the new Garden State Parkway made this coastal strip easily accessible to vacationers from New York City, Philadelphia, and Baltimore. Though the basic motel layout was the same, each establishment tried to lure motorists with color, light, and snazzy themes tied to pop songs, exotic travel destinations, and '50s movie extravaganzas. (Wildwood also bills itself as the birthplace of rock 'n' roll because Bill Haley's "Rock Around the Clock" was recorded here.)

In Wildwood Crest, the **Caribbean Motel** (5600 Ocean Ave.; www.caribbean motel.com) has a traffic-stopping sign in red neon script, a swooping front ramp, and fake palm trees by the pool. Then there's the **Royal Hawaiian,** which looks like a flying saucer landed atop a massive tiki hut with lava rock walls (500 E. Orchid Rd.; www.royalhawaiianresort.com). A swashbuckling pirate strides over the yellow neon sign above the entrance of the **Jolly Roger** (6805 Atlantic Ave.; www.jolly rogermotel.com), while knights and coats of arms adorn the facade of the **Crusader Motel** (Cardinal Rd. and Beach). Follow Ocean Avenue north into Wildwood to see the **Starlux,** a silver-sheathed Space Age beauty with a soaring, glass-walled lobby (305 E. Rio Grande; www.thestarlux.com), and roll on into North Wildwood to see the futuristic arched carports and cool blue neon signs of the **Chateau Bleu** (911 Surf Ave.) and the classic Candyland-ish sign of the **Lollipop Motel** (23rd and Atlantic aves.).

Though some properties on the Wildwood Strip look a little faded, others have been spruced up, attracting a whole new generation of urban hipsters.

ⓘ **Greater Wildwoods Tourism Improvement and Development Authority** (✆ **800/WW-BY-SEA** [992-9732]; www.wildwoodsnj.com)

✈ Atlantic City or Philadelphia

Gulf Boulevard's Vintage Motels
Retro by the Seaside
Treasure Island, Florida

GULF BOULEVARD'S VINTAGE MOTELS SPORT EYE-CATCHING NEON SIGNS AND SUN-KISSED charm. They were hit in the early 2000s condo boom and the few buildings that survived now share space with modern structures.

Back in the 1950s, trying to cash in on the post-war automotive travel boom, some civic booster for this 3½-mile-long (5.6km) Gulf Coast barrier island dreamed up a corny marketing stunt: Bury a couple chests full of money in the pearly white sand and let some tourists dig them up. Cheesy as the stunt was, it worked—and the island got a new name out of it.

Connected to the St. Petersburg peninsula by three classic Art Moderne causeway bridges, this beachside community developed fast in the 1950s. Two-story stucco motels popped up all along Gulf Boulevard, their rooms overlooking central courtyards dominated by palm-shaded, turquoise swimming pools. Across the street, gulf beaches beckoned with their soft sands and amazing sunset views.

But then development blossomed elsewhere—farther south, in Naples, Sanibel, and Fort Myers, and then in central Florida, around Orlando. Busch Gardens went up in northeast Tampa. For years, all the action seemed to be somewhere else, and Treasure Island got left behind. No developers came along to raze those vintage mom-and-pop motels and replace them with chain lodgings, and they never lost their ocean views and beach access.

So far, so good, until the early 2000s, when property values soared and a wave of condo fever hit Treasure Island. Though local zoning laws permit buildings to be only five stories high—that's a lot higher than these classic motels—many motel owners, faced with the high costs of maintaining aging buildings, allowed their motels to be replaced with boxy five-story condo towers. The first significant loss was the stylishly angular Surf Motel in 2004, but more followed.

These Gulf Boulevard motels may not be as architecturally goofy as their contemporaries on the Jersey Shore—their basic shapes are simpler and sturdier, built to withstand the occasional hurricane—but instead of razzmatazz, each motel offers its own pastel color scheme, neat landscaping, pool, striped beach umbrellas and chaise longues, and in many cases a shuffleboard court. Though most are air-conditioned, they still have casement windows that you can open to catch gulf breezes. Vintage neon signs have been preserved outside a few of the motels, notably the **Sands Beach Resort** and the **Thunderbird.** The palm trees here are real, and brilliant hibiscus spills from the planters.

But walk along the beach and you'll see the beachfront skyline disrupted more and more by condo towers. The essential character of Treasure Island already seems lost, but enough may be left to turn back the clock.

ⓘ www.treasureislandflorida.org

✈ Tampa International

🛏 $ **The Sands Beach Resort,** 11800 Gulf Blvd. (ⓒ **727/367-1969;** www.sandsoftreasureisland.com). $$ **Thunderbird Beach Resort,** 10700 Gulf Blvd. (ⓒ **800/367-2473;** www.thunderbirdflorida.com). $ **Tahitian Resort,** 11320 Gulf Blvd. (ⓒ **888/606-5809** or 727/360-6264; www.tahitianresort.com).

Wigwam Motels
Teepee Time
Kentucky/Arizona/California

IN THE 1930s AND 1940s, SEVEN WIGWAM VILLAGES WERE BUILT ACROSS AMERICA; today only three of these quirky lodgings remain.

Frank Redford was so fascinated with Indians that he decided to build a chain of wigwam-shaped motor courts across America. True, the shape he actually used for his tiny tourist cabins wasn't a wigwam at all, it was a teepee. But as wacky roadside themes went out of style, these curiosities became anachronisms.

Like many other such establishments built in the dawn of the automobile travel age, the 1930s and 1940s, Redford's Wigwam Villages offered overnight guests privacy with tiny separate lodgings, marked by kitschy themes that emphasized the character of the region. In the end, only seven Wigwam Villages were built, but cramped and quirky as they are, they have so much character that three remain perfectly preserved today.

Redford's first village went up in 1934 near Horse City, Kentucky, built to house his collection of Native American relics. Intrigued (obsessed, frankly) with his idea, he patented the design in 1937, closed the small Horse City site, and built a larger Wigwam Village in Cave City, near the popular tourist attraction of Mammoth Cave. Later branches went up in 1940 in New Orleans (closed in 1954) and Bessemer, Alabama (closed in 1964); after the war in the late 1940s, three more went up, in Orlando (the largest of the chain, razed in 1974) and two more which have survived along Route 66 **480** America's main east-west highway in the preinterstate era, known for its wacky themed restaurants, motels, and gas stations.

The concept was fairly standard: 15 to 20 white stucco teepees, 30 feet (9m) tall, decorated with red zigzag stripes. Somehow a tiny bathroom was squeezed into the cone-shaped huts, and diamond-shaped windows were discreetly spaced around the base (real teepees, of course, don't have windows). The original exterior design also featured red swastikas, a traditional Indian motif, but when that symbol became associated with Nazi Germany in the late 1930s, the swastikas were painted over. A 50-foot-tall (15m) teepee contains the motel office/gift shop/restaurant; guest teepees are clustered around a central court (the California one has a kidney-shaped swimming pool). The California and Kentucky motels have been updated with satellite TV and Internet access, but the Arizona branch—run by the same family that's owned it since the late 1940s—doesn't even have phones in the rooms. Both the Kentucky and the Arizona Wigwam Villages still boast the original 1930s-vintage cane-and-hickory lodge-pole-style furnishings.

Be sure to reserve well in advance if you want to stay in these teepee lodgings. The rooms may be tiny and inconvenient, the kitschy Indian theme politically incorrect, but as nostalgic artifacts they can't be beat, and they're very much in demand.

✈ Louisville, KY; Flagstaff, AZ; San Bernardino, CA

🚐 $ **Wigwam Village Motel,** 601 N. Dixie Hwy., Cave City, KY (✆ **270/773-3381;** www.wigwamvillage.com). $ **Wigwam Village Motel,** 811 W. Hopi Dr., Holbrook, AZ (✆ **928/524-3048**). $ **Wigwam Motel,** 2728 W. Foothill Blvd., Rialto, CA (✆ **909/875-3005;** www.wigwam motel.com).

Resource Index
Conservation Resources

IN RESEARCHING THIS BOOK, WE DISCOVERED AN ENCOURAGING NUMBER OF ORGANIZATIONS around the world that are actively working to preserve endangered natural, historical, and cultural treasures. While we've mentioned several in specific write-ups throughout this book, here's a list of important organizations we've come to depend on—invaluable resources to anybody who cares about conservation and the environment.

International

Conservation International
2011 Crystal Dr., Suite 500
Arlington, VA 22202
United States
☏ **703/341-2400**
www.conservation.org

Friends of the Earth International
P.O. Box 19199
1000 GD Amsterdam
The Netherlands
☏ **31 20 622 1369**
www.foei.org

Global Heritage Fund
625 Emerson St., Suite 200
Palo Alto, CA 94301
United States
☏ **650/325-7520**
www.globalheritagefund.org

Greenforce
21 Heathmans Rd.
London SW6 4TJ
United Kingdom
☏ **44/207 384 30288**
www.greenforce.org

Greenpeace International
Ottho Heldringstraat 5
1066 AZ Amsterdam
The Netherlands
☏ **31/20 7182000**
www.greenpeace.org/international

The Nature Conservancy
4245 N. Fairfax Dr., Suite 100
Arlington, VA 22203-1606
United States
☏ **703/841-5300**
www.nature.org

Wetlands International
P.O. Box 471
6700 AL Wageningen
The Netherlands
☏ **31/318 660910**
www.wetlands.org

Wildlife Conservation Society
2300 Southern Blvd.
Bronx, New York 10460
United States
☏ **718/220-5100**
www.wcs.org

**World Wide Fund (WWF) for Nature/
World Wildlife Fund**
Av. du Mont-Blanc 1196
Gland, Switzerland
www.panda.org

WWF United States
1250 24th St. NW
Washington, DC 20037
☏ **202/293-4800**

WWF Canada
245 Eglinton Ave. E., Suite 410
Toronto, Ontario M4P 3J1
☏ **416/489 8800**

WWF United Kingdom
Panda House Weyside Park
Godalming
☎44/1483 426 444

WWF-Australia
Level 13 235 Jones St.
Ultimo, NSW 2007
☎61/2 9281 5515

United States

American Rivers
1101 14th St. NW, Suite 1400
Washington, DC 20005
☎202/347-7550
www.americanrivers.org

National Audubon Society
225 Varick St.
New York, NY 10014
☎212/979-3000
www.audubon.org

Defenders of Wildlife
1130 17th St. NW
Washington, DC 20036
☎800/385-9712
www.defenders.org

National Wildlife Federation
11100 Wildlife Center Dr.
Reston, VA 20190
☎800/822-9919
www.nwf.org

Environment America
44 Winter St., 4th Floor
Boston, MA 02108
☎617/747-4449
www.environmentamerica.org

The Sierra Club
85 Second St., 2nd Floor
San Francisco, CA 94105
☎415/977-5500
www.sierraclub.org

Environmental Defense Fund
257 Park Ave. S.
New York, NY 10010
☎800/684-3322
www.edf.org

The Wilderness Society
1615 M St., NW
Washington, DC 20036
☎800/THE-WILD (843-9453)
www.wilderness.org

Canada

Nature Canada
85 Albert St., Suite 300
Ottawa, OntarioK1P 5E7
☎800/267-4088 or 613/562-3447
www.naturecanada.ca

United Kingdom

The Wildlife Trusts
The Kiln, Waterside, Mather Rd.
Newark, Nottinghamshire NG24 1WT
☎44/1636 677711
www.wildlifetrusts.org

English Heritage
1 Waterhouse Square
138-142 Holborn
London EC1N 2ST
☎44/20 7973 3000
www.english-heritage.org.uk

Natural England
1 E. Parade
Sheffield S1 2ET
☎44/845 600 3078
www.naturalengland.org.uk

Australia

Australian Conservation Foundation
Floor 1, 60 Leicester St.
Carlton, Vic 3053
✆ **61/3/9345 1111**
www.acfonline.org.au

Australian Wildlife Conservancy
P.O. Box 8070
Subiaco East, WA 6008
✆ **61/8/9380 9633**
www.australianwildlife.org

New Zealand

**Royal Forest and Bird
Protection Society**
Level One, 90 Ghuznee St.
P.O. Box 631
Wellington 6140
✆ **64/4/385 7374**
www.forestandbird.org.nz

Indexes

Geographical Index

Alphabetical Index

Photo Credits

Notes